Texas Politics Today, Enhanced Edition

Texas Politics Today, Enhanced 18th Edition

Mark P. Jones • Ernest Crain

with Morhea Lynn Davis • Christopher Wlezien • Elizabeth N. Flores

 **CENGAGE**

Australia • Brazil • Mexico • Singapore • United Kingdom • United States

Texas Politics Today, Enhanced 18th Edition

Mark P. Jones, Ernest Crain, Morhea Lynn Davis, Christopher Wlezien, Elizabeth N. Flores

Product Director: Thais L. Alencar

Product Manager: Richard Lena

Product Assistant: Haley Gaudreau

Marketing Manager: Valerie Hartmann

Content Manager: Dan Saabye

IP Analyst: Nancy Dillon

IP Project Manager: Kelli Besse

Production Service and Compositor: SPi Global

Art Director: Sarah Cole

Text Designer: Reuter Design

Cover Designer: Sarah Cole

Cover Image: joe daniel price/Getty Images

For product information and technology assistance, contact us at **Cengage Customer & Sales Support, 1-800-354-9706** or **support. cengage.com**.

For permission to use material from this text or product, submit all requests online at **www.cengage.com/permissions**.

Library of Congress Control Number: 2018959360

Student Edition:
ISBN: 978-1-337-79984-3

Loose-leaf Edition:
ISBN: 978-0-357-02891-9

Cengage
20 Channel Center Street
Boston, MA 02210
USA

Cengage is a leading provider of customized learning solutions with employees residing in nearly 40 different countries and sales in more than 125 countries around the world. Find your local representative at **www.cengage.com**.

Cengage products are represented in Canada by Nelson Education, Ltd.

To learn more about Cengage platforms and services, register or access your online learning solution, or purchase materials for your course, visit **www.cengage.com**.

Printed at CLDPC, USA, 10-19

Brief Contents

Detailed Contents

State Learning Outcomes

Texas Politics Today helps you meet the State Learning Outcomes for GOVT2306:

1. Explain the origin and development of the Texas constitution.

2. Demonstrate an understanding of state and local political systems and their relationship with the federal government.

3. Describe separation of powers and checks and balances in both theory and practice in Texas.

4. Demonstrate knowledge of the legislative, executive, and judicial branches of Texas government.

5. Evaluate the role of public opinion, interest groups, and political parties in Texas.

6. Analyze the state and local election process.

7. Describe the rights and responsibilities of citizens.

8. Analyze issues, policies, and political culture of Texas.

Chapter		GOVT 2306 State Learning Outcomes (SLO)
1:	Texas Culture and Diversity	**SLO 8** Analyze issues, policies, and political culture of Texas.
		SLO 7 Describe the rights and responsibilities of citizens.
		SLO 5 Evaluate the role of public opinion, interest groups, and political parties in Texas.
2:	Texas in the Federal System	**SLO 2** Demonstrate an understanding of state and local political systems and their relationship with the federal government.
		SLO 7 Describe the rights and responsibilities of citizens.
3:	The Texas Constitution in Perspective	**SLO 1** Explain the origin and development of the Texas constitution.
		SLO 3 Describe separation of powers and checks and balances in both theory and practice in Texas.
		SLO 7 Describe the rights and responsibilities of citizens.
4:	Voting and Elections	**SLO 6** Analyze the state and local election process.
		SLO 7 Describe the rights and responsibilities of citizens.
5:	Political Parties	**SLO 5** Evaluate the role of public opinion, interest groups, and political parties in Texas.
6:	Interest Groups	**SLO 5** Evaluate the role of public opinion, interest groups, and political parties in Texas.
7:	The Legislature	**SLO 4** Demonstrate knowledge of the legislative, executive, and judicial branches of Texas government.
8:	The Executive	**SLO 4** Demonstrate knowledge of the legislative, executive, and judicial branches of Texas government.
9:	The Judiciary	**SLO 4** Demonstrate knowledge of the legislative, executive, and judicial branches of Texas government.
10:	Law and Due Process	**SLO 7** Describe the rights and responsibilities of citizens.
		SLO 4 Demonstrate knowledge of the legislative, executive, and judicial branches of Texas government.
		SLO 8 Analyze issues, policies, and political culture of Texas.
11:	Local Government	**SLO 2** Demonstrate an understanding of state and local political systems and their relationship with the federal government.
		SLO 6 Analyze the state and local election process.
		SLO 8 Analyze issues, policies, and political culture of Texas.
12:	Public Policy	**SLO 8** Analyze issues, policies, and political culture of Texas.

Letter to Instructors

Dear Texas Government Instructors:

You may be familiar with previous editions of *Texas Politics Today*, as it has served as the standard text for the introductory Texas government course for many years. As in the past, we have focused exclusively on **state learning outcomes** and core objectives. Each chapter learning objective is targeted to help students achieve one or more of these learning outcomes, and we have explicitly organized each chapter to help students use higher-order thinking to master these objectives. We link each major chapter heading to one of the chapter objectives and recap how the student should achieve those objectives in both the new chapter summaries and review questions.

We have put together a strategy for meeting **core objectives**—each photo, figure, screenshot, boxed feature, essay, and project-centered Get Active feature prompts students to engage in critical thinking, develop communication skills, evaluate social responsibility, and reflect on their own sense of personal responsibility. Each of these exercises is designated by icons throughout the text:

★ **CTQ**   Critical Thinking Questions

★ **CSQ**   Communications Skills Questions

★ **SRQ**   Social Responsibility Questions

★ **PRQ**   Personal Responsibility Questions

New to This Enhanced Edition

- Chapters about elections, parties, and interest groups focus on the ideals of democracy and challenge students to evaluate whether these ideals are realized in practice.

- Chapter 11 explores the implications of state control over municipal policies, annexation and the unitary nature of state government in Texas.

- We provide the latest coverage of ideology and social policies related to marijuana, abortion, civil rights, gender politics, immigration, health care, crime and firearms, among others.

- We include expanded coverage of tea party politics and Republican Party factionalism, political polarization, changes in the ballot form, as well as the latest 2018 election results throughout.

- Chapters 1, 4, 5, 6, 7, 9, and 11 feature expanded coverage of the effects of the state's demographic changes and the rising importance of Latinos in the future of Texas politics.

- Enhanced visuals include new intuitive graphics to illustrate federalism, ballot organization, political party structures, interest group tactics, the plural executive system, the governor's appointive powers, and the forms of municipal government. New easy-to-follow process-oriented charts take students step by step through the dynamics of the constitutional amendment, legislative, electoral, and criminal justice processes.

- The role of social and digital media in Texas politics is discussed and illustrated in every chapter throughout the text.

- We have called upon our resources among a wide range of officeholders and political activists to write exclusive new **Politics in Practice** features. These features conclude each chapter with a specific and fully developed exercise to close the gap between the theoretical themes and the actual practice of Texas politics; they put a face on the political system and give students a glimpse of how it operates from an insider's viewpoint. Because our essayists are political practitioners who often view their role in the political system from a policy perspective, we have balanced the liberal and conservative viewpoints and developed critical thinking questions to prompt students to probe political and policy alternatives. We have included essays from the governor and his staff, legislators, lobbyists, analysts, campaign consultants, political activists, and local officials.

- Updated and targeted **Texas Insiders** and **How Does Texas Compare** boxes are visually distinct and provide the reader with an uninterrupted flow through the text.

- Each chapter ends with new **Think Critically and Get Active** projects that support purpose-driven activities and introspection to close the gap between theory and practice in the state and local political systems.

- Pedagogy links to targeted objectives throughout the chapter and delivers to students a cohesive learning experience.

MindTap: Your Course Stimulus Package

For the instructor, MindTap is here to simplify your workload, organize and immediately grade your students' assignments, and allow you to customize your course as you see fit. Through deep-seated integration with your Learning Management System, grades are easily exported and analytics are pulled with just the click of a button. MindTap provides you with a platform to easily add in current events videos and RSS feeds from national or local news sources. We hope these compelling features will benefit your students as they experience Texas politics today. Please contact us personally to let us know how this text works for you.

Sincerely,

Mark P. Jones: mpjones@rice.edu
Ernest Crain: ernestcrain@hotmail.com
Morhea Lynn Davis: salas15@epcc.edu
Christopher Wlezien: wlezien@austin.utexas.edu
Elizabeth N. Flores: eflores@delmar.edu

Letter to Our Students

Dear Student:

Americans in general, and perhaps Texans more than most, are apathetic and disillusioned about politics. Government seems so big, so remote, so baffling that many people have a sense of powerlessness. Now you have an opportunity to do something about this. *Texas Politics Today* explores Texas government, its background, the rules of the political game, and the political players who make the most important decisions in Texas. The text plainly explains public policy, why it is made, and who benefits from it. The book shows you how to think about yourself in the political universe, how to explore your own political values and ethics, and how to make a difference.

However, we know that you probably did not enroll in this course to achieve some kind of altruistic or idealistic goal, but to get credit for a course required for your degree plan. And we know that most of you are not political science majors. So we have written this book to be a reader-friendly guide to passing your tests and a hassle-free tool for learning about Texas government and politics.

Here are some tips on how you can exploit student-centered learning aids to help you make the grade:

- Target your focus on the **learning objectives** that open each chapter. Each chapter is organized around them, and your instructor will use them to track your progress in the course. Bulleted **chapter summaries** give you a recap of how the chapter handles these objectives, and **review questions** help you break the larger chapter objectives into manageable themes that you should understand as you prepare for exams.

- Zero in on the **key terms** defined in the margins and listed at the end of each chapter. These are the basic concepts that you need to use to understand Texas politics today.

- Go behind the scenes with the **Texas Insiders** features to see who influences policy making in Texas. These features put a face on the most powerful Texans and help you close the gap between theory and practice in Texas politics.

- Put Texas in perspective with the **How Does Texas Compare?** features. These features invite you to engage in critical thinking and to debate the pros and cons of the distinct political institutions and public policies in force across the 50 states.

- View Texas politics from the inside with the **Politics in Practice** features, and compare the theory and reality of the state political system.

- Link to the websites in the **Think Critically and Get Active!** features to explore current issues, evaluate data, and draw your own conclusions about the Texas political scene.

- Take advantage of carefully written photo, figure, and table captions that point you to major takeaways from the visuals. These visuals provide you with critical analysis questions to help you get started thinking about Texas politics.

- Use the digital media highlights to become an active part of the Texas political scene and help define the state's political future.

The Benefits of Using MindTap as a Student

For the student, the benefits of using MindTap with this book are endless. With automatically graded practice quizzes and activities, an easily navigated learning path, and an interactive ebook, you will be able to test yourself inside and outside of the classroom with ease. The accessibility of current events coupled with interactive media makes the content fun and engaging. On your computer, phone, or tablet, MindTap is there when you need it, giving you easy access to flashcards, quizzes, readings, and assignments.

You are a political animal—human beings are political by their very nature. You and other intelligent, well-meaning Texans may strongly disagree about public policies, and *Texas Politics Today* is your invitation to join the dynamic conversation about politics in the Lone Star State. We hope that this book's fact-based discussion of recent high-profile, and often controversial, issues will engage your interest and that its explanation of the ongoing principles of Texas politics will help you understand the role you can play in the Texas political system.

Sincerely,

Mark P. Jones: mpjones@rice.edu
Ernest Crain: ernestcrain@hotmail.com
Morhea Lynn Davis: lsalas15@epcc.edu
Christopher Wlezien: wlezien@austin.utexas.edu
Elizabeth N. Flores: eflores@delmar.edu

Resources

Cengage Unlimited

Now in bookstores and online, higher ed students can subscribe to Cengage Unlimited to access all Cengage learning materials—across courses and disciplines—for $119.99 per term.

Cengage Unlimited includes:

The first-of-its-kind digital subscription designed specially to lower costs. Students get total access to everything Cengage has to offer on demand—in one place. That's 20,000 eBooks, 2,300 digital learning products, and dozens of study tools across 70 disciplines and over 675 courses. Currently available in select markets. Details at www.cengage.com/unlimited

Students

Access your *Texas Politics Today* resources by visiting

https://www.cengage.com/shop/isbn/9781337799843

If you purchased MindTap access with your book, click on "Register a Product" and then enter your access code.

Instructors

Access your *Texas Politics Today* resources via
www.cengage.com/login.

Log in using your Cengage Learning single sign-on user name and password, or create a new instructor account by clicking on "New Faculty User" and following the instructions.

Texas Politics Today, Enhanced 18th Edition Text Only Edition

ISBN: 9781337799843
This copy of the book does not come bundled with MindTap.

MindTap®

MindTap for *Texas Politics Today*, Enhanced 18th Edition

ISBN for Instant Access Code: 9781305952225 | ISBN for Printed Access Card: 9780357028865
MindTap for *Texas Politics Today, Enhanced 18th Edition* is a highly personalized, fully online learning experience built upon Cengage Learning content and correlating to a core set of learning outcomes. MindTap guides students through the course curriculum via an innovative Learning Path Navigator where they will complete reading assignments, challenge themselves with focus activities, and engage with interactive quizzes. Through a variety of gradable activities, MindTap provides students with opportunities to check themselves for where they need extra help, as well as allowing faculty to measure and assess student progress. Integration with programs like YouTube and Google Drive allows instructors to add and remove content of their

choosing with ease, keeping their course current while tracking local and global events through RSS feeds. The product can be used fully online with its interactive ebook for *Texas Politics Today, Enhanced 18th Edition*, or in conjunction with the printed text.

Course Reader for MindTap is now available for every political science MindTap through the MindTap Instructor's Resource Center. This new feature provides access to Gale's authoritative library reference content to aid in the development of important supplemental readers for political science courses. Gale, a part of Cengage Learning, has been providing research and education resources for libraries for more than 60 years. This new feature capitalizes on Cengage Learning's unique ability to bring Gale's authoritative library content into the classroom. Instructors have the option to choose from thousands of primary and secondary sources, images, and videos to enhance their course. This capability can replace a separate reader and conveniently keeps all course materials in one place within a single MindTap. The selections within Course Reader are curated by experts and designed specifically for introductory courses.

Instructor Companion Website for *Texas Politics Today*

ISBN: 9780357028858

This Instructor Companion Website is an all-in-one multimedia online resource for class preparation, presentation, and testing. Accessible through Cengage.com/login with your faculty account, you will find available for download: book-specific Microsoft® PowerPoint® presentations; a Test Bank compatible with multiple learning management systems; and an Instructor's Manual.

The Test Bank, offered in Blackboard, Moodle, Desire2Learn, Canvas, and Angel formats, contains learning objective–specific multiple-choice and essay questions for each chapter. Import the Test Bank into your LMS to edit and manage questions, and to create tests.

The Instructor's Manual contains chapter-specific learning objectives, an outline, key terms with definitions, and a chapter summary. Additionally, the Instructor's Manual features a critical thinking question, a lecture launching suggestion, and an in-class activity for each learning objective.

The Microsoft® PowerPoint® presentations are ready-to-use, visual outlines of each chapter. These presentations are easily customized for your lectures. Access the Instructor Companion Website at www.cengage.com/login.

Cognero for *Texas Politics Today*, Enhanced 18th Edition

ISBN: 9780357028896

Cengage Learning Testing Powered by Cognero is a flexible, online system that allows you to author, edit, and manage test bank content from multiple Cengage Learning solutions, create multiple test versions in an instant, and deliver tests from your LMS, your classroom, or wherever you want. The Test Bank for *Texas Politics Today* contains learning objective–specific multiple-choice and essay questions for each chapter.

Acknowledgments

We are grateful to our families for their patience and encouragement as we have developed the manuscript for this book, and we especially appreciate our students and colleagues who have given us helpful practical advice about how to make the book a more useful tool in teaching and learning Texas politics. We would like to give special thanks to Denese McArthur of Tarrant County Community College, who has contributed to the Instructor's Manual, and Hoyt DeVries of Lone Star College–Cy-Fair, who authored this edition's Test Bank.

In addition, we thank the Politics in Practice contributors for this edition.

Chapter 1	**The Face of Latino Immigration** *by Ana Hernandez* State Representative, Texas House District 143	
Chapter 2	**Texas in the Federal System** *by Greg Abbott* Governor of Texas	
Chapter 3	**The Constitutional Right to Education** *by Holly McIntush* Attorney & Member of the Fort Bend ISD Group Legal Team	
Chapter 4	**Everything Is Bigger in Texas, with a Twist of Red** *by Luke Macias* Founder of Macias Strategies	
Chapter 5	**One Face of the Texas Tea Party** *by Julie McCarty* President of the NE Tarrant Tea Party	
Chapter 6	**The Practice of Environmental Lobbying** *by Luke Metzger* Executive Director of Environment Texas	
Chapter 7	**On Being a Legislator: A View from the Inside** *by José Rodríguez* State Senator, Texas Senate District 29	
Chapter 8	**The Texas Executive Branch: Does it run you, or do you run it?** *by Drew DeBerry* Former Director of Budget & Policy for Texas Governor Greg Abbott	
Chapter 9	**Choosing Judges: My View from the Inside** *by Wallace B. Jefferson* Former Chief Justice of the Texas Supreme Court	
Chapter 10	**Marijuana Policy Reform in Texas** *by Phillip Martin* Executive Director of the Texas House Democratic Caucus	
Chapter 11	**A View from Inside County Government** *by Veronica Escobar* Former El Paso County Judge and current U.S. Representative, U.S. House District 16	
Chapter 12	**The Practical Politics of Texas's Budget** *by Eva DeLuna Castro* State Budget Analyst & Program Director, Center for Public Policy Priorities	

Reviewers

We would also like to thank the instructors who have contributed their valuable feedback through reviews of this text:

Patrizio Amezcua, *San Jacinto College-North*
Jeff Hubbard, *Victoria College*
Drew Landry, *South Plains College*
Jeremy Loy, *Weatherford College*
Dawna Montanelli, *Texarkana College*
John David Rausch, Jr., *West Texas A&M University*
Geoffrey Shine, *Wharton County Junior College*
Steven Tran, *Houston Community College*
M. Theron Waddell, Jr., *Galveston College*

Previous edition reviewers:
Mary Barnes-Tilley, *Blinn College–Brenham*
Sarah Binion, *Austin Community College*
Larry E. Carter, *The University of Texas at Tyler*
Neil Coates, *Abilene Christian College*
Malcolm L. Cross, *Tarleton State University*
Kevin T. Davis, *North Central Texas College*
Laura De La Cruz, *El Paso Community College*
Brian R. Farmer, *Amarillo College*
Frank J. Garrahan, *Austin Community College*
Glen David Garrison, *Collin County Community College–Spring Creek*
Diane Gibson, *Tarrant County College, Trinity River Campus*
Jack Goodyear, *Dallas Baptist University*
Alexander Hogan, *Lone Star College–CyFair*
Floyd Holder, *Texas A&M University–Kingsville*
Robert Paul Holder, *McLennan Community College*
Timothy Hoye, *Texas Woman's University*
Jeffrey Hubbard, *Victoria College*
Casey Hubble, *McLennan Community College*
Bryan Johnson, *Tarrant County College*
Woojin Kang, *Angelo State University*
Denese McArthur, *Tarrant County College*
Eric Miller, *Blinn College–Bryan*
Patrick Moore, *Richland College*
Dana A. Morales, *Lone Star College–Montgomery*
Lisa Perez-Nichols, *Austin Community College*
Paul Phillips, *Navarro College*
Herman Prager, Ph.D., *Austin Community College*
John David Rausch, Jr., *West Texas A&M University*
David Smith, *Texas A&M University–Corpus Christi*
Robert B. Tritico, *Sam Houston State University*
Jessika Stokley, *Austin Community College*

About the Authors

Mark P. Jones is the James A. Baker III Institute for Public Policy's Fellow in Political Science, the Joseph D. Jamail Chair in Latin American Studies, and a professor in the Department of Political Science at Rice University. His articles have appeared in publications such as the *American Journal of Political Science*, the *Journal of Politics*, *Legislative Studies Quarterly*, *Texas Monthly*, *The Hill*, and the *Texas Tribune*. Jones is among the most quoted commentators on Texas politics in the state and national media, and his research on the Texas Legislature and on public opinion and elections in Texas is widely cited by media outlets and political campaigns. Jones received his B.A. from Tulane University and his Ph.D. from the University of Michigan.

Ernest Crain did his graduate work at the University of Texas at Austin, spent 35 years teaching Texas government at San Antonio College, and now lives in Montgomery County, Texas. Crain has co-authored *Understanding Texas Politics*, *Politics in Texas: An Introduction to Texas Politics*, *The Challenge of Texas Politics: Text with Readings*, *American Government and Politics Today: Texas Edition*, and *Texas Politics Today*. His special areas of interest include party competition, comparative state politics, and Texas public policy.

Morhea Lynn Davis is professor of government at El Paso Community College, where she has served as blackboard trainer and mentor, faculty senator, government discipline coordinator, and a member of numerous faculty committees. Davis has a Master of Arts degree from the University of Texas at El Paso, with a major in both organizational behavior and political science. She is a very active community volunteer and grant writer, and has consulted for and participated in many political campaigns. Her published articles range in topics from the current political environment to the viability of primaries and caucuses in today's election processes.

Christopher Wlezien is Hogg Professor of Government at the University of Texas at Austin. He previously taught at Oxford University, the University of Houston, and Temple University, after receiving his Ph.D. from the University of Iowa in 1989. Over the years, Wlezien has published widely on elections, public opinion, and public policy; his books include *Degrees of Democracy*, *Who Gets Represented?*, and *The Timeline of Presidential Elections*. He has founded a journal, served on numerous editorial boards, established different institutes, advised governments and other organizations, held visiting positions at many universities around the world, received various research grants, and won a number of awards for his research and teaching.

Elizabeth N. Flores is professor of political science at Del Mar College. She teaches courses on national government, Texas government, and Mexican-American politics, and serves as program coordinator for the Mexican-American Studies Program. Flores earned a Master of Arts degree in political science at the University of Michigan and a Bachelor of Arts degree in political science (magna cum laude) at St. Mary's University. Her awards include the 2014 League of United Latin American Citizens (LULAC) Council Educator of the Year Award, the 2013 Del Mar College Dr. Aileen Creighton Award for Teaching Excellence, and a 1998 Excellence Award from the National Institute for Staff and Organizational Development (NISOD).

Prologue: Texas's Political Roots

The English-Scots-Irish culture, as it evolved in its migration through the southern United States, played an essential part in the Texas Revolution. Sam Houston, Davy Crockett, Jim Bowie, and others were of Scotch-Irish descent, and these immigrants led the Anglo-American movement west and had a major impact on the development of modern mid-American culture.

The successful end to the Texas Revolution in 1836 attracted more immigrants from the southern United States. Subsequently, the Anglo-Texan population grew dramatically and became the largest Texas ethnic group. As a result, Anglo Texans controlled the politics and economy and Protestantism became the dominant religion.

The Anglo concept of Manifest Destiny was not kind to Latinos and Native Americans. Native Americans were killed or driven into the Indian Territory (located in present-day Oklahoma), and many Latino families were forced from their property. Even Latino heroes of the Texas Revolution with names like De León, Navarro, Seguín, and Zavala were not spared in the onslaught.[1]

Politics and Government: The Early Years[2]

The Republic of Texas had no political parties. Political conflict revolved around pro-Houston and anti-Houston policies. Sam Houston, the hero of the battle of San Jacinto, advocated peaceful relations with the eastern Native Americans and U.S. statehood for Texas. The anti-Houston forces, led by Mirabeau B. Lamar, believed that Native American and Anglo-American cultures could not coexist. Lamar envisioned Texas as a nation extending from the Sabine River to the Pacific.

JOINING THE UNION

Texas voters approved annexation to the United States in 1836, almost immediately after Texas achieved independence from Mexico. However, because owning human property was legal in the republic and would continue to be legal once it became a state, the annexation of Texas would upset the tenuous balance in the U.S. Senate between proslavery and antislavery senators. This and other political issues, primarily relating to slavery, postponed Texas's annexation until December 29, 1845, when it officially became the 28th state.

Several Texas articles of annexation were unique. Texas retained ownership of its public lands because the U.S. Congress refused to accept their conveyance in exchange for payment of the republic's $10 million debt. Although millions of acres were ultimately given away or sold, those remaining continue to produce hundreds of millions of dollars in state revenue, largely in royalties from the production of oil and natural gas. These royalties and other public land revenue primarily benefit the Permanent University Fund and the Permanent School Fund. The annexation articles also granted Texas the privilege of "creating … new states, of convenient size, not exceeding four in number, in addition to said State of Texas."[3]

EARLY STATEHOOD AND SECESSION: 1846–1864

The politics of early statehood soon replicated the conflict over slavery that dominated politics in the United States. Senator Sam Houston, a strong Unionist alarmed by the support for secession in Texas, resigned his seat in the U.S. Senate in 1857 to run for governor. He was defeated because secessionist forces controlled the dominant Democratic Party. He was, however, elected governor two years later.

The election of Abraham Lincoln as president of the United States in 1860 triggered a Texas backlash. A secessionist convention was called and it voted to secede from the Union. Governor

Houston used his considerable political skills in a vain attempt to keep Texas in the Union. At first, Houston declared the convention illegal, but the Texas Legislature later upheld it as legitimate. Although only about 5 percent of white Texans owned slaves, the electorate ratified the actions of the convention by an overwhelming 76 percent.[4]

Houston continued to fight what he considered Texans' determination to self-destruct. Although he reluctantly accepted the vote to secede, Houston tried to convince secessionist leaders to return to republic status rather than join the newly formed Confederate States of America—a plan that might have spared Texans the tragedy of the Civil War. Texas's secession convention rejected this political maneuver and petitioned for membership in the new Confederacy. Houston refused to accept the actions of the convention, which summarily declared the office of governor vacant and ordered the lieutenant governor to assume the position. Texas was then admitted to the Confederacy.

POST–CIVIL WAR TEXAS: 1865–1885

The defeat of the Confederacy resulted in relative anarchy in Texas until it was occupied by federal troops beginning on June 19, 1865, a date henceforth celebrated as Juneteenth.

Texas and other southern states resisted civil rights and equality for freed slaves, resulting in radical Republicans gaining control of the U.S. Congress. Congress enacted punitive legislation prohibiting former Confederate soldiers and officials from voting and holding public office.

Texas government was controlled by the U.S. Army from 1865 through 1869, but the army's rule ended after the new state constitution was adopted in 1869. African Americans were granted the right to vote, but it was denied to former Confederate officials and military. In the election to reestablish civilian government, Republican E. J. Davis was elected governor and Republicans dominated the new legislature. Texas was then readmitted to the United States, military occupation ended, and civilian authority assumed control of the state. Unlike either previous or subsequent constitutions, the 1869 Constitution centralized political power in the office of the governor. During the Davis administration, Texas began a statewide public school system and created a state police force.

Republican domination of Texas politics was a new and unwelcome world for most Anglo Texans, and trouble intensified when the legislature increased taxes to pay for Governor Davis's reforms. Because Texas's tax base was dependent on property taxes, eliminating human property from the tax rolls and the decline in value of real property placed severe stress on the public coffers. Consequently, state debt increased dramatically. Former Confederates were enfranchised in 1873, precipitating a strong anti-Republican reaction from the electorate, and Democrat Richard Coke was elected governor in 1875.

Texas officials immediately began to remove the vestiges of radical Republicanism. The legislature authorized a convention to write a new constitution. The convention delegates were mostly Democratic, Anglo, and representative of agrarian interests. The new constitution decentralized the state government, limited the flexibility of elected officials, and placed public education under local control. The constitution was ratified by voters in 1876 and an often-amended version is still in use today.

POLITICS AND GOVERNMENT: 1886–1945

Many reform measures were enacted and enforced in Texas in the 1880s, especially laws limiting corporate power. Attorney General James S. Hogg vigorously enforced new laws curtailing abuses by insurance companies, railroads, and other corporate interests.

GOVERNOR HOGG: 1891–1895

Attorney General James Hogg was an important reformer in Texas politics and developed a reputation as the champion of common people. Railroad interests dominated most western states' governments, prompting Hogg to run for governor with the objective of regulating railroads. Although he faced strong opposition from powerful corporate interests that viewed him as a threat, Hogg won the nomination in the 1890 Democratic State Convention.

A commission to regulate railroads was authorized in the subsequent election. The Railroad Commission was eventually given the power to regulate trucks and other vehicles used in Texas commerce and the production and transportation of oil and natural gas.

Politics in the early 1900s distinguished Texas as one of the most progressive states in the nation. Texas pioneered the regulation of monopolies, railroads, insurance companies, and child labor. It reformed its prisons and tax system, and in 1905, replaced political party nominating conventions with direct party primaries.

FARMER JIM: 1914–1918

James E. Ferguson entered the Texas political scene in 1914 and was a controversial and powerful force in Texas politics for the next 20 years. Ferguson owned varied business interests and was the president of the Temple State Bank. Although sensitive to the interests of the business community, Ferguson called himself "Farmer Jim" to emphasize his rural background.

The legislature was unusually receptive to Ferguson's programs, which generally restricted the economic and political power of large corporations and tried to protect the common people. It also enacted legislation designed to assist tenant farmers, improve public education and colleges, and reform state courts.

The legislature also established a highway commission to manage state highway construction. Texas's county governments had been given the responsibility of constructing state roads within their jurisdictions. The result was that road quality and consistency varied widely between counties. The agency's authorization to construct and maintain Texas's intrastate roadways standardized the system and facilitated automobile travel.

Rumors of financial irregularities in Ferguson's administration gained credibility, but his declaring war on The University of Texas would prove fatal. Ferguson vetoed the entire appropriation for the university, apparently because the board of regents refused to remove certain faculty members whom the governor found objectionable. This step alienated politically powerful graduates who demanded that he be removed from office. Farmer Jim was impeached, convicted, removed, and barred from holding public office in Texas.

WORLD WAR I, THE TWENTIES, AND THE RETURN OF FARMER JIM: 1919–1928

Texas saw a boom during World War I. Its favorable climate and the Zimmerman Note, in which Germany allegedly urged Mexico to invade Texas, prompted the national government to station troops in the state. Texas became and continues to be an important training area for the military.

Crime control, education, and the Ku Klux Klan, a white supremacist organization, were the major issues of the period. Progressive measures enacted during this period included free textbooks for public schools and the beginning of the state park system. The 1920 legislature also ratified the Eighteenth Amendment to the U.S. Constitution establishing national Prohibition.

The strongest anti-Klan candidate in 1924 was Miriam A. "Ma" Ferguson, wife of the impeached Farmer Jim. She ran successfully on a platform of "Two Governors for the Price of One," becoming the first female governor of Texas. Detractors alleged that she was only a figurehead and that Farmer Jim was the real governor. Nonetheless, Ma's election indicated that Texas voters had forgiven Farmer Jim for his misbehavior. She was successful in getting legislation passed that prohibited wearing a mask in public, which resulted in the end of the Klan as an effective political force.

National politics became an issue in Texas politics in 1928. Al Smith, the Democratic nominee for president, was a Roman Catholic, a "wet," and a big-city politician. Herbert Hoover, the Republican nominee, was a Protestant, a "dry," and an international humanitarian. Hoover won the electoral votes from Texas—the first Republican ever to do so.

THE GREAT DEPRESSION: 1929–1939

The stock market crashed in 1929 and Texas, along with the entire nation, was economically crushed. Prices dropped, farm products could not be sold, mortgages and taxes went unpaid, jobs evaporated, and businesses and bank accounts were wiped out.

Promising to cut government spending, Ma Ferguson was once again elected governor in 1932 becoming the first Texas governor to serve nonconsecutive terms. The 1933 ratification of the Twenty-first Amendment to the U.S. Constitution brought an end to nationwide Prohibition. Prohibition ended in Texas two years later with the adoption of local-option elections, although selling liquor by the drink was still forbidden statewide.

Politics and Government after World War II: 1948–Today

The 1948 senatorial campaign attracted several qualified candidates. The runoff in the Democratic primary pitted former governor Coke Stevenson against U.S. Congressman Lyndon B. Johnson.

The election was the closest statewide race in Texas history. At first, the election bureau gave the unofficial nomination to Stevenson, but the revised returns favored Johnson. The final official election results gave Johnson the nomination by a plurality of 87 votes. Both candidates charged election fraud.

Box 13 in Jim Wells County, one of several machine-controlled counties dominated by political boss George Parr (the Duke of Duval), was particularly important in the new figures. This box revised Johnson's vote upward by 202 votes and Stevenson's upward by only one. Box 13 was also late in reporting, thereby tainting Johnson's victory. About the election, historian T. R. Fehrenbach wrote, "There was probably no injustice involved. Johnson men had not *defrauded* Stevenson, but successfully *outfrauded* him."[5]

THE 1950s AND 1960s: LBJ, THE SHIVERCRATS, AND THE SEEDS OF A REPUBLICAN TEXAS

Allan Shivers became governor in 1949, and in 1952 the national election captured the interests of Texans. Harry Truman had succeeded to the presidency in 1945 and was reelected in 1948. Conservative Texas Democrats became disillusioned with the New Deal and Fair Deal policies of the Roosevelt–Truman era and wanted change.

Another major concern for Texans was the tidelands issue. With the discovery of oil in the Gulf of Mexico, a jurisdictional conflict arose between the government of the United States and the governments of the coastal states. Texas claimed three leagues (using Spanish units of measure, equal to about 10 miles) as its jurisdictional boundary; the U.S. government claimed Texas had rights to only three miles. At stake were hundreds of millions of dollars in royalty revenue.

Both Governor Shivers and Attorney General Price Daniel, who was campaigning for the U.S. Senate, attacked the Truman administration as being corrupt, soft on communism, eroding the rights of states, and being outright thieves in attempting to steal the tidelands oil from the schoolchildren of Texas. State control of the revenue would direct much of the oil income to the Permanent School Fund and result in a lower tax burden for Texans. The Democratic nominee for president, Adlai Stevenson of Illinois, disagreed with the Texas position.

The Republicans nominated Dwight Eisenhower, a World War II hero who was sympathetic to the Texas position on the tidelands. Eisenhower was born in Texas (but reared in Kansas), and his supporters used the campaign slogan "Texans for a Texan." The presidential campaign solidified a split in the Texas Democratic Party that lasted for 40 years. The conservative faction, led by Shivers and Daniel, advocated splitting the ticket, or voting for Eisenhower for president and Texas Democrats for state offices. Adherents to this maneuver were called Shivercrats. The liberal faction, or Loyalist Democrats of Texas, led by Judge Ralph "Raff" Yarborough, campaigned for a straight Democratic ticket.

Texas voted for Eisenhower, and the tidelands dispute was eventually settled in its favor. Shivers was reelected governor and Daniel won the Senate seat. Shivers, Daniel, and other Democratic candidates for statewide offices had also been nominated by the Texas Republican Party. Running as Democrats, these candidates defeated themselves in the general election.

Lyndon B. Johnson, majority leader of the U.S. Senate and one of the most powerful men in Washington, lost his bid for the Democratic presidential nomination to John F. Kennedy in 1960. He then accepted the nomination for vice president. By the grace of the Texas Legislature, Johnson was on the general election ballot as both the vice-presidential and senatorial nominee. When the Democratic presidential ticket was successful, he was elected to both positions, and a special election was held to fill the vacated Senate seat. In the special election, Republican John Tower was elected and became the first Republican since Reconstruction to serve as a U.S. senator from Texas.

THE 1970s AND 1980s: REPUBLICAN GAINS AND EDUCATION REFORMS

In 1979, William P. Clements became the first Republican governor of Texas since E. J. Davis was defeated in 1874. The election of a Republican governor did not affect legislative-executive relations and had limited impact on public policy because Clements received strong political support from conservative Democrats.

Democratic Attorney General Mark White defeated incumbent governor Bill Clements in 1982. Teachers overwhelmingly supported White, who promised salary increases and expressed support for education. The first comprehensive educational reform since 1949 became law in 1984. House Bill 72 increased teacher salaries, made school district revenue somewhat more equitable, and raised standards for both students and teachers.

In 1986, voter discontent with education reform, a sour economy, and decreased state revenue were enough to return Republican Bill Clements to the governor's office. In 1988, three Republicans were elected to the Texas Supreme Court and one to the Railroad Commission—the first Republicans elected to statewide office (other than governor or U.S. senator) since Reconstruction.

In 1989, the Texas Supreme Court unanimously upheld an Austin district court's ruling in *Edgewood* v. *Kirby*[6] that the state's educational funding system violated the Texas constitutional requirement of "an efficient system" for the "general diffusion of knowledge." After several reform laws were also declared unconstitutional, the legislature enacted a complex law that kept the property tax as the basic source for school funding but required wealthier school districts to share their wealth with poorer districts. Critics called the school finance formula a "Robin Hood" plan.

THE 1990s: TEXAS ELECTS A WOMAN GOVERNOR AND BECOMES A TWO-PARTY STATE

In 1990, Texans elected Ann Richards as their first female governor since Miriam "Ma" Ferguson. Through her appointive powers, she opened the doors of state government to unprecedented numbers of women, Latinos, and African Americans. Dan Morales was the first Latino elected to statewide office in 1990, and Austin voters elected the first openly gay state legislator, Glen Maxey, in 1991. Texas elected Kay Bailey Hutchison as its first female U.S. senator in 1992. She joined fellow Republican Phil Gramm as they became the first two Republicans to hold U.S. Senate seats concurrently since 1874.

When the smoke, mud, and sound bites of the 1994 general election settled, Texas had truly become a two-party state. With the election of Governor George W. Bush, Republicans held the governor's office and both U.S. Senate seats for the first time since Reconstruction. Republicans won a majority in the Texas Senate in 1996, and voters ratified an amendment to the Texas Constitution that allowed them to use their *home equity* (the current market value of a home minus the outstanding mortgage debt) as collateral for a loan.

The 1998 general election bolstered Republican political dominance as the party won every statewide elective office, positioning Governor George W. Bush as the frontrunner for the 2000

Republican nomination for president. Legislators deregulated the electricity market and the state's city annexation law was made more restrictive. Public school teachers received a pay raise but were still paid below the national average. And Texas adopted a program to provide basic health insurance to some of the state's children who lacked health coverage, although more than 20 percent of Texas children remained uninsured.

THE 2000s: TEXAS BECOMES A REPUBLICAN STATE, CONTROVERSY AND CONFLICT

The 2001 legislature enacted a hate crimes law that strengthened penalties for crimes motivated by a victim's race, religion, color, gender, disability, sexual orientation, age, or national origin. The legislature also established partial funding for health insurance for public school employees and made it easier for poor children to apply for health-care coverage under Medicaid.

Republicans swept statewide offices and both chambers of the legislature in the 2002 elections, restoring one-party government in the state, now red instead of blue. A projected $10 billion budget deficit created an uncomfortable environment for Republicans. Politically and ideologically opposed to new taxes and state-provided social services, the legislature and the governor chose to reduce funding for most state programs; expenditures for education, health care, children's health insurance, and social services for the needy were sharply reduced.

Meanwhile, attempts to effectively close tax loopholes failed. For example, businesses and professions of all sizes continued to organize as partnerships to avoid the state corporate franchise tax. The legislature placed limits on pain-and-suffering jury awards for injuries caused by physician malpractice and hospital incompetence and made it more difficult to sue the makers of unsafe, defective products.

The legislature's social agenda was ambitious. It outlawed civil unions for same-sex couples and barred recognition of such unions from other states. It imposed a 24-hour waiting period before a woman could have an abortion.

Although the districts for electing U.S. representatives in Texas had been redrawn by a panel of one Democratic and two Republican federal judges following the 2000 Census, Texas Congressman and U.S. House Majority Leader Tom DeLay was unhappy that more Republicans were not elected to Congress. Governor Rick Perry agreed and called a special session in the summer of 2003 to redraw districts once again to increase Republican representation. Democrats argued that the districts had already been established by the courts and that Perry and DeLay only wanted to increase the number of Republican officeholders. The legislature adopted the Republican proposal and the U.S. Supreme Court affirmed that states could redistrict more than once each decade and rejected the argument that the redistricting was either illegal or partisan.

The Texas government in 2007 waged almost continuous battle with itself. Conflict between the House and the speaker, the Senate and the lieutenant governor, the Senate and the House, and the legislature and the governor marked the session. Legislators did restore eligibility of some needy children for the Children's Health Insurance Program (CHIP).

The 2009 legislature seemed almost placid after the unprecedented House revolt against Speaker Tom Craddick and election of fellow Republican Joe Straus as the new speaker. However, consideration of a contentious voter identification bill caused conflict in the last days of the session and resulted in a parliamentary shutdown. The House adjourned without resolution of the voter identification bill and postponed other important matters to be resolved by a special session.

THE 2010s: CONSERVATIVE POLITICS, POLICIES, AND LITIGATION

In 2010, much of the state's political attention was focused on disputes about Texas's acceptance of federal funds. Texas accepted federal stimulus money to help balance the state's budget but turned down more than $500 million in federal stimulus money for unemployed Texans. The state declined to apply for up to $700 million in federal grant money linked to "Race to the

Top," a program to improve education quality and results. Governor Perry believed the money would result in a federal takeover of Texas schools. Texas also became one of seven states to reject the National Governors Association effort to establish national curriculum standards called the "Common Core."

Governor Perry failed to get the Republican nomination for president in 2012 but continued to make national news arguing for his agenda of low taxes, limited business regulation, and opposition to the Affordable Care Act. Using taxpayer money from the Texas Enterprise Fund, he was able to persuade several businesses to relocate to Texas. Among his most notable successes, the governor helped persuade Toyota to move its headquarters and high-paying jobs from California and Kentucky to the Dallas-Fort Worth Metroplex.

In recent years, the Republican political leadership adopted an ambitious conservative political and social agenda. Outnumbered in the legislative and executive branches, liberal and Democratic strategists turned to the courts to battle against these policies. For example, opponents challenged the state's legislative and congressional districts created in 2011 as being gerrymandered to dilute minority votes and to favor Republican candidates. The courts upheld the legislative districting map with only minor changes.

Meanwhile the state legislature adopted a strict voter photo ID law in 2011 requiring voters to present specific forms of identification as a condition for voting. Opponents charged that these laws were designed to discourage voting by young, minority, and elderly citizens who were less likely to have these forms of identification. Ultimately, federal courts ruled the Voter ID laws was discriminatory and allowed voters to cast their ballots in the 2016 election if they could not reasonably obtain the mandated types of ID and signed an affidavit of citizenship and presented proof of residency.

Although in 2013 the U.S. Supreme Court struck down provisions of the Voting Rights Act (VRA) of 1965 that required states, like Texas, that have a history of racial discrimination to get preclearance of new election laws from the U.S. Department of Justice, challengers can still show that particular elections laws are racially discriminatory and, therefore, a violation of the U.S. Constitution or federal law. Challenges to Texas election laws and redistricting are likely to continue for the foreseeable future.

In 2013 the Texas Legislature also passed regulations that required abortion clinics to meet the hospital-like standards of ambulatory surgical centers. Opponents argued that these regulations compromised a woman's constitutional right to obtain an abortion. Despite the well-publicized filibuster by former state senator Wendy Davis, the law was adopted. Court challenges to the law immediately followed, with the U.S. Supreme Court ruling in 2016 that these (and related) regulations were unconstitutional.

Despite the legal and political turmoil that permeated the political environment, Republicans continued to dominate state politics after the 2014 elections. Former attorney general Greg Abbott defeated Democrat Wendy Davis to become the first practicing Roman Catholic elected as governor, and Texas Republicans firmly embraced tea party politics as the most conservative GOP candidates rolled over "establishment" candidates like Lieutenant Governor David Dewhurst (in his bid for reelection) and several other centrist Republican politicians.

The 2015 legislative session featured a House and Senate where almost two-thirds of the legislators were Republicans and a plural executive, from Governor Abbott to Land Commissioner George P. Bush, that remained 100 percent Republican. While the senate turned to the right with the election of Lieutenant Governor Dan Patrick and the replacement of several veteran centrist conservative senators by freshman movement conservatives, the GOP's establishment wing remained firmly in control of the Texas House under the leadership of Speaker Joe Straus. The result was a legislative session that featured a series of inter-chamber and intra-GOP battles and negotiations, with the more conservative wing of the GOP getting its way on some legislation (such as blocking Medicaid expansion under the Affordable Care Act and passing "Campus Carry" legislation) and the more centrist wing of the party getting its way on some legislation (such as blocking a repeal of the "Texas Dream Act" and passing legislation to increase funding for transportation infrastructure).

The 2016 election did not change the balance of power in Austin. Republicans continued to hold substantial majorities in both the House and Senate and Speaker Straus and Lt. Governor Patrick remain safely ensconced at the helm in their respective chambers.

The tenor and content of the 2017 legislation session laid bare for all to see the internal conflict, or "civil war," that has been taking place within the Texas Republican Party between its movement-conservative wing (represented by leaders such as Lieutenant Governor Patrick) and its more centrist establishment wing (represented by leaders such as Speaker Straus). As the regular and special sessions progressed, Governor Abbott increasingly got behind the movement wing's agenda, with the Straus-controlled House often blocking legislation supported by the governor and lieutenant governor.

An example of movement-conservative backed legislation which the House blocked is a bill that would have prevented cities, counties, and school districts from having ordinances or policies that allow transgender people to use the bathroom or locker room which matches their gender identity instead of that which matches their biological sex (i.e., the "bathroom bill"). At other times, however, the House passed movement conservative backed legislation, in spite of misgivings, due to a fear that blocking it could come back to haunt some centrist Republicans in the 2018 GOP Primary. A prime example of this phenomenon is legislation banning cities and counties from having formal or informal policies that prohibit police officers from inquiring about a person's citizenship status. While in prior sessions the House had successfully killed similar bans on "sanctuary cities," in 2017 the pressure from the movement conservative wing of the Republican Party was too great for the centrist conservatives to resist.

In 2018, Republicans continued their statewide winning streak dating back to 1996, with every statewide Republican candidate victorious, including all of the members of the state's plural executive who were re-elected to their second term in office. Republicans retained their majorities in the Texas Senate and House, but, with Straus's decision to not seek re-election in 2018, the House began the 2019 session with a new speaker, Republican Dennis Bonnen from Angleton (located 40 miles south of Houston), who has served in the House since 1997.

In 2018, Beto O'Rourke came closer to victory in a statewide race than any Texas Democrat in 20 years, but still found himself on the losing side of his epic US Senate battle with Ted Cruz. In spite of Beto's ability to energize young Texans to turn out in record numbers for a midterm, there were still enough older Anglos participating to put Cruz over the top, albeit by a much narrower margin (2.6 percent) than Cruz was hoping for. Cruz's ace in the hole were reliably Republican Anglos over 50 who live in medium-sized metro suburban counties such as Ellis County (south of Dallas) and Montgomery County (north of Houston), and in medium-sized population centers in less populated areas of the state like Lubbock County in West Texas and Smith County (Tyler) in East Texas.

Beto raised more money (in excess of $75 million dollars) than any Texas candidate in history and electrified crowds like no Texas Democrat (or Republican) in recent history. He also breathed new life into a moribund Texas Democratic Party that four years earlier saw Wendy Davis spend close to $50 million dollars only to lose to Republican Governor Greg Abbott by more than 20 percent.

While Beto lost, he had very long coattails and helped Democrats flip two Texas Senate seats and 12 Texas House seats, cutting the Republican majority in the Senate from 21–10 to 19–12 and in the House from 95–55 to 83–67. He also helped lift two Democratic congressional challengers to victory, Colin Allred in the 32nd Congressional District in Dallas and Lizzie Fletcher in the 7th Congressional District in Houston, and was integral to Democratic county-wide sweeps in Dallas and Harris Counties. In addition, two Democrats, Veronica Escobar from El Paso and Sylvia Garcia from Houston, broke through a barrier that had existed for 174 years and became the first Latinas to ever represent Texas in the U.S. Congress.

Texas Political Culture and Diversity

Texas is one of the most diverse states in the country and becomes more diverse with each passing year. In this chapter you will see who we are as Texans, how different groups have struggled to obtain equal rights, and how our culture and diversity affect our state's politics. [JSL]

Fossil Ridge High School

Learning Objectives

LO 1.1 Analyze the relationships among Texas political culture, its politics, and its public policies.

LO 1.2 Differentiate the attributes that describe the major Texas regions.

LO 1.3 Analyze Texans' political struggles over equal rights and evaluate their success in Texas politics today and their impact on the state's political future.

LO 1.4 Apply what you have learned about Texas political culture and diversity.

political culture
The dominant political values and beliefs of a people.

A **political culture** reflects the political values and beliefs of a people. It explains how people feel about their government—their expectations of what powers it should have over their lives, the services it should provide, and their ability to influence its actions. A political culture is developed by historical experience over generations through agents of socialization such as family, religion, peer group, and education. It is characterized by the level of ethnic, social, and religious diversity it tolerates; by the level of citizen participation it allows; by the societal role it assigns to the state; and by citizens' perception of their status within the political system.

A people's political behavior is shaped by the culture that nourished it. The Spanish conquest and settlement of Texas provided the first European influence on Texas culture. Some elements of the ranchero culture and the Catholic religion continue to this day and represent the enduring Spanish influence on our culture. The immigration of Anglo-Saxon southerners in the early 1800s brought Texas the plantation and slave-owning culture. This culture became dominant following the Texas Revolution. Although it was modified to an extent by the Civil War, it remained the dominant Texas culture.

However, ethnic/racial diversification and urbanization have gradually eroded the dominance of the traditional southern Anglo culture over time, with this erosion especially notable over the last 30 years. During the past three decades Texas has not only become one of the most diverse multicultural states in the country, but also it has become one of the most urbanized; two-thirds of the population now resides in one of four major metropolitan regions (Austin, Dallas–Fort Worth, Houston, San Antonio), and Texans living in rural areas today account for only a tenth of the population.

We begin by exploring the state's dominant political culture and ideology, and how they influence partisanship and public policy. Then we look at other aspects of the state's political culture and examine the subtle variations in the state from one region to another. We then review the battles for gender, ethnic/racial, and sexual orientation equality and the impact of these civil rights struggles and their outcomes, along with the state's increasing diversity, on politics and policy.

Political Culture, Partisanship, and Public Policy

LO 1.1   **Analyze the relationships among Texas political culture, its politics, and its public policies.**

Texas's political culture is **conservative**. Many Texans share a belief in a limited role for government in taxation, economic regulation, and providing social services; conservatives support traditional values and lifestyles, and are cautious in response to social change.

Ideology

The Texas brand of conservatism is skeptical of state government involvement in the economy. A majority of Texans favor low taxes, modest state services, and few business regulations. Because they support economic individualism and free-market capitalism, Texans generally value profit as a healthy incentive to promote economic investment and individual effort, while they see social class inequality as the inevitable result of free-market capitalism. For them, an individual's quality of life is largely a matter of personal responsibility rather than an issue of public policy.

Some conservatives accept an active role for the government in promoting business. They are willing to support direct government subsidies and special tax breaks for businesses to encourage economic growth. They may also support state spending for infrastructure, such as transportation and education, that sustains commercial and manufacturing activity.

Social conservatives support energetic government activity to enforce what they view as moral behavior and traditional cultural values. For example, social conservatives, who often

conservative
A political ideology marked by the belief in a limited role for government in taxation, economic regulation, and providing social services; conservatives support traditional values and lifestyles, and are cautious in response to social change.

are evangelical Christians, usually advocate for the use of state power to limit abortion and narcotics or marijuana usage.

A distinct minority in Texas, **liberal** believe in using government to improve the welfare of individuals; they favor government regulation of the economy, actively support the expansion of civil rights, and tolerate social change. Liberals believe state government can be used as a positive tool to benefit the population as a whole. Most Texas liberals accept private enterprise as the state's basic economic system but believe excesses of unregulated capitalism compromise the common good. They endorse state policies to abate pollution, increase government investment in public education and health care, protect workers and consumers, and prevent discrimination against ethnic/racial minorities and members of the LGBT community, among others.

Liberals often believe that a great deal of social inequality results from institutional and economic forces that are often beyond a single individual's control. As a result, they support the use of government power to balance these forces and to promote a better quality of life for middle- and lower-income people. For example, liberals argue that it is fair to tax those with the greatest ability to pay and to provide social services for the community as a whole.

A significant number of Texans have mixed views. On some issues, they take a liberal position, but on others they have a conservative perspective or no opinion at all. Others have moderate views: Figure 1.1 shows that 31 percent of Texans say that they are "in the middle"; that is, their beliefs are between conservative and liberal viewpoints. The "Think Critically and Get Active!" features in this and later chapters will give you the tools to explore Texans' political differences in greater depth and to engage with various ideological groups in Texas.

liberal
A political ideology marked by the advocacy of using government to improve the welfare of individuals, government regulation of the economy, support for civil rights, and tolerance for social change.

Conservatives and Liberals in Texas Today

Figure 1.1 provides information on the ideological self-identification of Texans overall and among subgroups of Texans based on their gender, ethnic/racial identity, and generation. The data are drawn from a series of University of Texas/Texas Tribune statewide polls of Texas registered voters conducted between October 2011 and February 2018.[1] A survey question asked respondents to place themselves on a seven-point ideological scale where 1 was "extremely liberal," 4 "in the middle," and 7 "extremely conservative." Respondents who located themselves as a 5, 6, or 7 are considered to be conservative, as a 1, 2, or 3 to be liberal, and as a 4 to be moderate.

Close to half of Texans (47 percent) identify as conservative, more than double the percentage (22 percent) identifying as liberal. Figure 1.1 highlights, however, that these statewide percentages mask considerable ideological variance among men and women, members of different ethnic/racial groups, and generational cohorts. For example, men as a group are notably more conservative than women (52 percent vs. 42 percent), and Anglos (56 percent) notably more conservative than either Latinos (34 percent) or African Americans (25 percent). At the same time, however, no noteworthy gender or ethnic/racial differences exist in the proportion of liberals, which are fairly equal between men and women and among the three principal ethnic/racial groups in the state with the partial exception of a larger proportion of African Americans than Anglos being liberal. (we lack sufficient data to analyze Asian American ideological self-identification).

Data also are provided for Texans based on their political generation: the Millennial Generation (those born since 1981), Generation X (those born between 1965 and 1980), the Baby Boom Generation (those born between 1946 and 1964), and the Silent Generation (those born between 1928 and 1945).[2] As a group, members of the Millennial Generation tend to be significantly less conservative and more liberal than members of the other generations, with the ideological gulf separating Millennials from their Silent Generation grandparents and great-grandparents far and away the widest. It will remain to be seen if Millennials become more conservative (and less liberal) as they age, or if this more liberal ideological profile will remain a hallmark of the Millennial Generation for years to come.

FIGURE 1.1 Texans' Ideology

Public opinion polling indicates that twice as many Texans self-identify as conservative than as liberal.

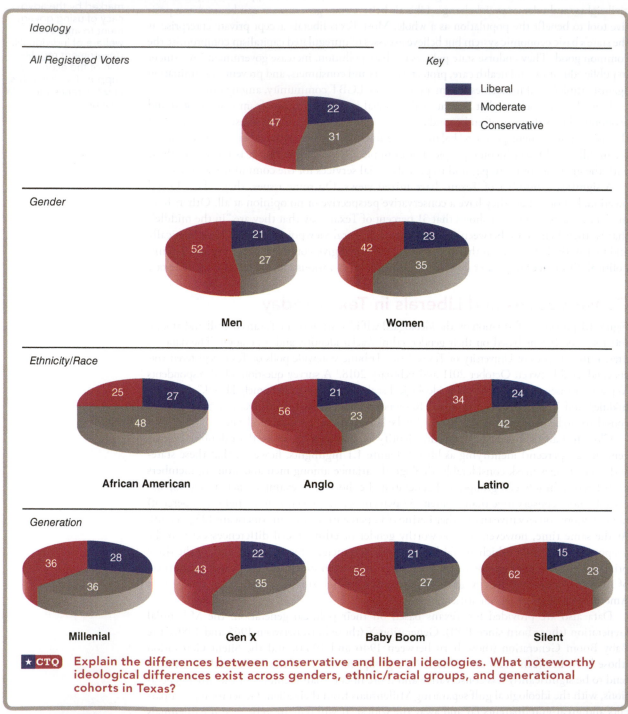

Ideology

All Registered Voters

Key
- Liberal
- Moderate
- Conservative

47 22 31

Gender

Men: 52 21 27

Women: 42 23 35

Ethnicity/Race

African American: 25 27 48

Anglo: 21 56 23

Latino: 34 24 42

Generation

Millenial: 36 28 36

Gen X: 43 22 35

Baby Boom: 52 21 27

Silent: 62 15 23

★ CTQ **Explain the differences between conservative and liberal ideologies. What noteworthy ideological differences exist across genders, ethnic/racial groups, and generational cohorts in Texas?**

Source: University of Texas/Texas Tribune Polls: 2011–2018.

Figure 1.2 highlights the considerable amount of ideological variance across the state's 21 most populous counties, which combined contain almost three-fourths of the Texas population. At the liberal end of the ideological spectrum, by itself, is Travis County (Austin), with an average ideological score of 3.58. The next most liberal counties, Cameron, El Paso, Dallas, and

FIGURE 1.2 Texas Counties from Most Liberal to Most Conservative

The ideological profiles of the largest Texas counties (more than 250,000 residents) vary from liberal Travis County to conservative Brazoria County, with the state's four most populous counties (Harris, Dallas, Tarrant, and Bexar) having similar profiles.

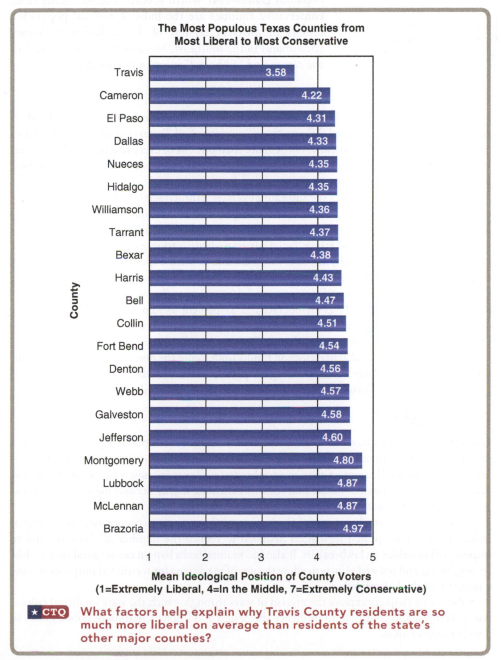

The Most Populous Texas Counties from Most Liberal to Most Conservative

County	Mean Ideological Position
Travis	3.58
Cameron	4.22
El Paso	4.31
Dallas	4.33
Nueces	4.35
Hidalgo	4.35
Williamson	4.36
Tarrant	4.37
Bexar	4.38
Harris	4.43
Bell	4.47
Collin	4.51
Fort Bend	4.54
Denton	4.56
Webb	4.57
Galveston	4.58
Jefferson	4.60
Montgomery	4.80
Lubbock	4.87
McLennan	4.87
Brazoria	4.97

Mean Ideological Position of County Voters
(1=Extremely Liberal, 4=In the Middle, 7=Extremely Conservative)

★ CTQ　What factors help explain why Travis County residents are so much more liberal on average than residents of the state's other major counties?

Source: University of Texas/Texas Tribune Polls: 2011–2018.

Nueces (Corpus Christi), are noticeably more conservative than Travis County. The state's four most populous counties (Harris, Dallas, Tarrant, and Bexar) are grouped closely together, with similar average ideological scores ranging from 4.33 in Dallas County to 4.43 in Harris County.

Eight counties have an average ideological score above the state average of 4.53. These more conservative counties fall into two distinct categories. One group consists of suburban counties adjacent to the state's two dominant metropolises, with Brazoria, Fort Bend, Galveston, and Montgomery counties constituting the principal population centers of the Houston suburbs and Denton County, the second most populous Dallas–Fort Worth suburb. The remaining three conservative counties are the hubs of regional population centers in different regions of Texas: Jefferson County (Beaumont) in the southeast, McLennan County (Waco) in the center, and Lubbock County in the northwest.

★ Did You Know? More than four-fifths (81 percent) of Texans under 30 believes gays and lesbians should have the right to marry compared to less than half (48 percent) of those over 60.3

Partisanship

Texans' conservative political views are reflected in their partisan identification. Figure 1.3 shows that 47 percent of all Texans self-identify as Republicans and 42 percent as Democrats. A little more than one out of every ten Texans (11 percent) is a true independent, someone who does not identify in any way with either the Democratic Party or the Republican Party.

The figure also underscores the substantial gender, ethnic/racial, and generational differences in party identification in Texas. For example, women are significantly more likely to identify as Democrats than men, and men are significantly more likely to identify as Republicans than women. Profound ethnic/racial partisan identification gaps exist, with 83 percent of African Americans identifying as Democrats and a mere 7 percent as Republicans. In contrast 29 percent of Anglos identify as Democrats and 61 percent as Republicans. Among Latinos, 54 percent identify as Democrats and 34 percent as Republicans. One half of Millennials (50 percent) identify as Democrats and 37 percent as Republicans; the proportions are roughly reversed for their Silent Generation elders, who are much more likely to self-identify as Republicans (61 percent) than as Democrats (32 percent).

Public opinion data and actual election results underscore the dominance of the more conservative Republican Party in Texas during the past 20 years. We will examine the ideological and policy differences between the two political parties in greater depth in Chapter 5.

Public Policy

Conservative opinions have been translated into most of Texas's public policies. The state's tax burden is low compared to other states, and the state proportionally devotes fewer financial resources to public services than most other states. Texas is known nationally for its low tax and limited government model that contrasts with the higher tax and more active government model seen in states like California and New York.

Texas also has used the power of the state to enforce certain conservative social values. It has, for instance, passed legislation designed to reduce the number of abortions and to impose stiff penalties on lawbreakers. It also has maintained a ban on casino gambling (unlike its neighbors) and resisted efforts to allow the use of marijuana for medicinal purposes (unlike a majority of the U.S. states).

Subsequent chapters explore the myriad of ways through which the state's political culture has influenced and continues to influence the design and implementation of public policy in a wide range of areas.

FIGURE 1.3 Texans' Partisanship

More Texans self-identify as Republicans than as Democrats, although the Republican advantage is only 5 percent.

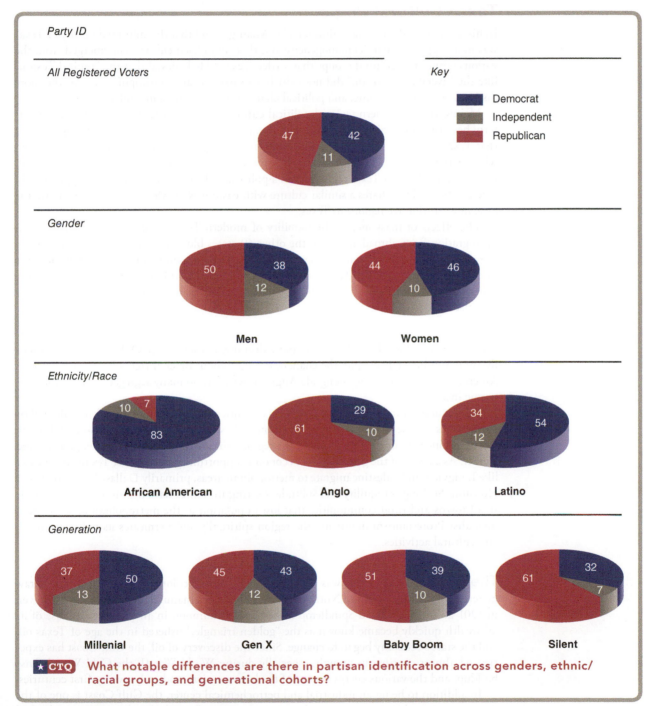

Party ID

All Registered Voters

47 11 42

Key
- Democrat
- Independent
- Republican

Gender

Men: 50 12 38

Women: 44 10 46

Ethnicity/Race

African American: 10 7 83

Anglo: 61 10 29

Latino: 34 12 54

Generation

Millenial: 37 13 50

Gen X: 45 12 43

Baby Boom: 51 10 39

Silent: 61 7 32

★ CTQ   What notable differences are there in partisan identification across genders, ethnic/racial groups, and generational cohorts?

Source: University of Texas/Texas Tribune Polls: 2011–2018.

Texas's Cultural Regions

LO 1.2 Differentiate the attributes that describe the major Texas regions.

Texas Cultural Regions

In his seminal study of Texas culture, D. W. Meinig found that the cultural diversity of Texas was more apparent than its homogeneity and that no unified culture had emerged from the various ethnic and cultural groups that settled Texas.[4] He believed that the "typical Texan," like the "average American," did not exist but rather was an oversimplification of the more distinctive social, economic, and political characteristics of the state's inhabitants.

Meinig viewed modern regional political culture as largely determined by migration patterns because people take their culture with them as they move geographically. Meinig believed that Texas (circa the 1960s) had evolved into nine fairly distinct cultural regions. However, whereas political boundaries are fixed, cultural divisions are often blurred and transitional. For example, the East Texas region shares a political culture with much of the Upper South, whereas West Texas shares a similar culture with eastern New Mexico. Figure 1.4 shows the nine most distinctive regions in Texas.

The effects of mass media, the mobility of modern Texans statewide and beyond, and immigration from abroad and from the other 49 states blur the cultural boundaries within Texas, with its bordering states, and with Mexico. Although limited because it does not take into account these modern-day realities, Meinig's approach still provides a useful guide to a general understanding of Texas political culture, attitudes, and beliefs based on geography and history.

East Texas East Texas is a social and cultural extension of the Old South. It is primarily rural and biracial. Despite the changes brought about by civil rights legislation, African American "towns" still exist alongside Anglo "towns," as do many segregated social and economic institutions.

Politics and commerce in many East Texas counties and cities are frequently dominated by old families, whose wealth is usually based on real estate, banking, construction, and retail. Cotton—once "king" of agriculture in the region—has been replaced by cattle, poultry, and timber. As a result of the general lack of economic opportunity, young East Texans from cities like Longview and Palestine migrate to metropolitan areas, primarily Dallas–Fort Worth and Houston. Seeking tranquility and solitude, retiring urbanites have begun to revitalize some small towns and rural communities that lost population to the metropolitan areas. Fundamentalist Protestantism dominates the region spiritually and permeates its political, social, and cultural activities.

The Gulf Coast Texas was effectively an economic colony before 1900—it sold raw materials to the industrialized North and bought northern manufactured products. However, in 1901 an oil well named Spindletop drilled near Beaumont, in an area that because of its oil wealth quickly became known as the "golden triangle," ushered in the age of Texas oil, and the state's economy began to change. Since the discovery of oil, the Gulf Coast has experienced almost continuous growth, especially during World War II, the Cold War defense buildup, and the various energy booms of the late twentieth and early twenty-first centuries.

In addition to being an industrial and petrochemical center, the Gulf Coast is one of the most important shipping centers in the nation. Investors from the northeastern states backed Spindletop, and its success stimulated more and more out-of-state investment. Local wealth was also generated and largely reinvested in Texas to promote long-term development.

FIGURE 1.4 Cultural Regions of Texas

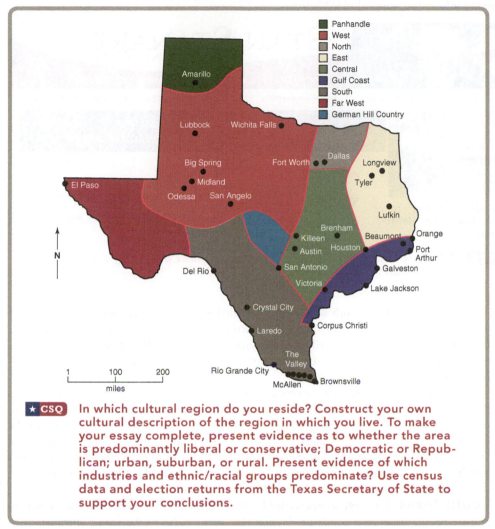

Legend:
- Panhandle
- West
- North
- East
- Central
- Gulf Coast
- South
- Far West
- German Hill Country

★ CSQ **In which cultural region do you reside? Construct your own cultural description of the region in which you live. To make your essay complete, present evidence as to whether the area is predominantly liberal or conservative; Democratic or Republican; urban, suburban, or rural. Present evidence of which industries and ethnic/racial groups predominate? Use census data and election returns from the Texas Secretary of State to support your conclusions.**

Source: Cengage Learning

A Boom Based in Houston Though volatile, the state's petrochemical industry, which is concentrated on the Gulf Coast, has experienced extraordinary growth, creating a boomtown psychology. Rapid growth fed real estate development and speculation throughout the region. The Houston area especially flourished, and Harris County (Houston) grew to become the third-most-populous county in the United States, behind Los Angeles County in California and Cook County (Chicago) in Illinois.

Houston's initial growth after World War II was fueled by a flood of job seekers from East Texas and other rural areas of the state. This influx gave the Gulf Coast the flavor of rural Texas in an urban setting. Houston's social and economic leadership was composed of second- and third-generation elites whose forebears' wealth came from oil, insurance, construction, land development, and/or banking.

Houston's rural flavor diminished over the years as the U.S. economy transformed from industrial to postindustrial. This transformation attracted migrants from the North.

IMAGE 1.1 To comply with federal law Harris County provides election-related information and ballots in English, Spanish, Vietnamese, and Chinese, with this screen-shot showing information provided in Vietnamese.

★ CTQ **What are some arguments in favor and against providing voters with information in languages other than English?**

This migration included both skilled and unskilled workers and brought large numbers of well-educated professionals to Houston from across the country and globe. Today, the Gulf Coast has become a remarkably vibrant and dynamic region, and Houston, the energy capital of the world, boasts many corporate headquarters along with the largest medical complex on earth (the Texas Medical Center).

The Gulf Coast economy also serves as a pole for immigration from the Americas, Asia, Europe, and Africa, which gives modern Houston an international culture comparable to that found in Los Angeles and New York. In fact, voters in Harris County are given the option of casting a ballot in Mandarin Chinese or Vietnamese, in addition to English and Spanish as is the case elsewhere in the state. See Image 1.1 from the Harris County Clerk's website for an example of information on early voting that is provided in Vietnamese.

South Texas The earliest area settled by Europeans, South Texas developed a ranchero culture on the basis of livestock production that was similar to the feudal institutions in distant Spain. The **ranchero culture** is a quasi-feudal system whereby a property's owner, or patrón, gives workers protection and employment in return for their loyalty and service. **Creoles**, who descended from Spanish immigrants, were the economic, social, and political elite, whereas the first Texas cowboys who did the ranch work were Native Americans or **Mestizos** of mixed Spanish and Native American heritage. Anglo Americans first became culturally important in South Texas when they gained title to a large share of the land in the region following the Texas Revolution of 1836. However, modern South Texas still retains elements of the ranchero culture, including some of its feudal aspects. Large ranches, often owned by one family for multiple generations, are prevalent; however, wealthy and corporate ranchers and farmers from outside the area are becoming common.

Because of the semitropical South Texas climate, **The Valley** (of the Rio Grande) and the Winter Garden around Crystal City were developed into (and continue to be) major citrus and vegetable producing regions by migrants from the northern United States in the 1920s. These enterprises required intensive manual labor, which brought about increased immigration from Mexico.

ranchero culture
A quasi-feudal system whereby a property's owner, or patrón, gives workers protection and employment in return for their loyalty and service.

Creole
A descendant of European Spanish immigrants to the Americas.

Mestizo
A person of both Spanish and Native American lineage.

The Valley
An area along the Texas side of the Rio Grande known for its production of citrus fruits.

Far West Texas Far West Texas, also known as the "Trans-Pecos region," exhibits elements of two cultures, possessing many of the same **bicultural** characteristics as South Texas. As is the case in South Texas, its large Mexican American population often maintains strong ties with relatives and friends in Mexico. And the Roman Catholic Church strongly influences social and cultural attitudes on both sides of the border.

Far West Texas is a major commercial and social passageway between Mexico and the United States. El Paso, the "capital" of Far West Texas and the sixth-largest city in the state, is a military, manufacturing, and commercial center. El Paso's primary commercial partners are Mexico and New Mexico. While the rest of Texas is located in the Central Time Zone, El Paso County and adjacent Hudspeth County are in the Mountain Time Zone. The economy of the border cities of Far West Texas, like that of South Texas, is closely linked to Mexico and has benefited from the economic opportunities brought about by the **North American Free Trade Agreement (NAFTA)**, a treaty that has helped remove trade barriers among Canada, Mexico, and the United States. NAFTA has served as an economic stimulus for the Texas Border because it is a conduit for much of the commerce with Mexico. More than three-quarters of U.S.–Mexico land trade crosses the border in Texas. In 2018 NAFTA was modified due in large part to President Donald Trump's belief that the original agreement was a 'bad deal' for the United States, with the new agreement re-branded as the United States-Mexico-Canada Agreement (USMCA).

The Texas Border South and Far West Texas comprise the area known as the "Texas Border." A corresponding "Mexico Border" includes the Mexican states of Chihuahua, Coahuila, Nuevo León, and Tamaulipas. It can be argued that the Texas Border and the Mexico Border are two parts of an economic, social, and cultural region with a substantial degree of similarity that sets it apart from the rest of the United States and of Mexico. The Border region, which is expanding in size both to the north and to the south, has a binational, bicultural, and bilingual subculture in which internationality is commonplace and economies and societies on both sides constantly interact.[5]

South and Far West Texas are "mingling pots" for the Latino and Anglo American cultures. Catholic Latinos often retain strong links with Mexico through extended family and friends in Mexico and through Spanish-language media. Many Latinos continue to speak Spanish; in fact, Spanish is also the commercial and social language of choice for many of the region's Anglos. The Texas Border cities are closely tied to the Mexican economy on which their prosperity depends. Although improving economically, these regions remain among the poorest in the United States.

The economy of the Texas Border benefits economically from **maquiladoras**, which are Mexican factories where U.S. corporations employ lower-cost Mexican labor for assembly and piecework. Unfortunately, lax environmental and safety enforcement in Mexico result in high levels of air, ground, and water pollution in the border region. In fact, the Rio Grande is one of the U.S. most ecologically endangered rivers.

The Texas Border also serves as a major transshipment point for drug cartels as they bring illegal drugs such as marijuana and heroin from Mexico for sale in the thriving U.S. market for illicit narcotics. In addition, a significant share of undocumented immigration into the United States occurs in the Texas Border region.

In recent years the Texas Legislature has boosted funding for additional Department of Public Safety (DPS) officers to be stationed along the border to combat drug and human trafficking and indirectly assist the U.S. Border Patrol. The legislature also extended funding to maintain Texas National Guard troops in the border region temporarily and provided additional funds for local law enforcement in the border counties. A majority of border residents welcomed the

bicultural
Encompassing two cultures.

North American Free Trade Agreement (NAFTA)
A treaty that has helped remove trade barriers among Canada, Mexico, and the United States and is an economic stimulus for the Texas Border because it is a conduit for much of the commerce with Mexico.

maquiladoras
Mexican factories where U.S. corporations employ inexpensive Mexican labor for assembly and piecework.

additional DPS officers and especially the enhanced funding for financially strapped local law enforcement agencies. However, a similarly large majority opposed the presence of the National Guard troops, which they believe unfairly stigmatizes the region, is ineffective because members of the Texas National Guard are not empowered to make arrests, and has more to do with electoral politics than good public policy.

German Hill Country

The Hill Country north and west of San Antonio was settled primarily by immigrants from Germany but also by Czech, Polish, and Norwegian immigrants. Although the immigrants inter-married with Anglo Americans, Central European culture and architecture were dominant well into the twentieth century. Skilled artisans were common in the towns; farms were usually moderate in size, self-sufficient, and family owned and operated. Most settlers were Lutheran or Roman Catholic, and these remain the most common religious affiliations of present-day residents.

The German Hill Country is still a distinct cultural region. Although its inhabitants have become "Americanized," they still retain many of their Central European cultural traditions. Primarily a farming and ranching area, the Hill Country is socially and politically conservative.

Migration into the region is increasing. The most significant encroachment into the Hill Country is residential growth from rapidly expanding urban areas, especially San Antonio and Austin. Resorts and weekend country homes for well-to-do urbanites are beginning to transform the cultural distinctiveness of the German Hill Country.

West Texas

The defeat of the Comanches in the 1870s opened West Texas to Anglo American settlement. Migrating primarily from the southern United States, these settlers passed their social and political attitudes and southern Protestant fundamentalism on to their descendants.

Relatively few African Americans live in modern West Texas, but Latinos have migrated into the region in significant numbers, primarily to the cities and the intensively farmed areas. West Texas is socially and politically conservative, and its religion is Bible Belt fundamentalism.

The southern portion of the area emphasizes sheep, goat, and cattle production. In fact, San Angelo advertises itself as the "Sheep and Wool Capital of the World." Nearby Abilene is home to three private Christian universities (Abilene Christian University, Hardin Simmons University, and McMurry University) and, like San Angelo (Goodfellow AFB), is the site of a United States Air Force Base (Dyess AFB). Southern West Texas, which is below the Cap Rock Escarpment, is the leading oil-producing area (the Permian Basin) of Texas. The cities of Midland and Odessa owe their existence almost entirely to oil and related industries.

Northern West Texas is part of the Great Plains and High Plains and is primarily agricultural, with cotton, grain, and feedlot cattle production predominating. In this part of semi-arid West Texas, outstanding agricultural production is made possible by extensive irrigation from the Ogallala Aquifer. The large amount of water used for irrigation is however gradually depleting the Ogallala. This not only affects the current economy of the region through higher costs to farmers but also serves as a warning signal for its economic future.

The Panhandle

Railroads advancing from Kansas City through the Panhandle brought Midwestern farmers into this region, and wheat production was developed largely by migrants from Kansas. Because the commercial and cultural hub of the region was Kansas City, the early Panhandle was basically Midwestern in both character and institutions. The modern Texas Panhandle however shares few cultural attributes with the American Midwest.

Its religious, cultural, and social institutions function with little discernible difference from those of northern West Texas. The Panhandle economy is also supported by the production of cotton and grains, the cultivation of which depends on extensive irrigation from the Ogallala Aquifer. Feedlots for livestock and livestock production, established because of proximity to the region's grain production, are major economic enterprises in their own right. Effective conservation of the Ogallala Aquifer is critical to the economic future of both northern West Texas and the Panhandle.

North Texas

North Texas is located between East and West Texas and exhibits many characteristics of both regions. Early North Texas benefited from the failed French socialist colony of La Réunion, which included many highly trained professionals in medicine, education, music, and science. (La Réunion was located on the south bank of the Trinity River, across from what is today downtown Dallas.) The colonists and their descendants helped give North Texas a cultural and commercial distinctiveness. North Texas today is dominated by the Dallas–Fort Worth metropolitan area, often referred to as the **Metroplex**. The Metroplex has become a banking and commercial center of national and international importance.

Metroplex
The greater Dallas–Fort Worth metropolitan area.

When railroads came into Texas from the North in the 1870s, Dallas became a rail hub, and people and capital from the North stimulated its growth. Fort Worth became a regional capital that looked primarily to West Texas. The Swift and Armour meatpacking companies, which moved plants to Fort Worth in 1901, were the first national firms to establish facilities close to Texas's natural resources. More businesses followed, and North Texas began its evolution from an economic colony to an industrially developed area.

North Texas experienced extraordinary population growth after World War II, with extensive migration from the rural areas of East, West, and Central Texas. The descendants of these migrants, after several generations, tend to have urban attitudes and behavior. Recent migration from other states, especially from the North, has been significant. Many international corporations have established headquarters in North Texas and their employees contribute to the region's diversity and cosmopolitan environment.

Although North Texas is more economically diverse than most other Texas regions, it does rely heavily on banking, insurance, and the defense and aerospace industries. Electronic equipment, computer products, plastics, and food products are also produced in the region. North Texas's economic diversity has allowed it to avoid or at least attenuate some of the boom–bust cycles experienced by other regions in the state where the economy is more dependent on a single industry or a smaller number of industries.

Central Texas

Central Texas is often called the "core area" of Texas. It is roughly triangular in shape, with its three corners being Houston, Dallas–Fort Worth, and San Antonio. The centerpiece of the region is Austin (Travis County), one of the fastest-growing metropolitan areas in the nation. Already a center of government and higher education, Austin has become the "Silicon Valley" of high-tech industries in Texas as well as an internationally recognized cultural center, whose annual South by Southwest Music, Film and Interactive Festival (SXSW) is now a global event.

Austin's rapid growth is a result of significant migration from the northeastern United States and the West Coast, as well as from other regions in Texas. The influx of well-educated people from outside Texas has added to the already substantial pool of accomplished Austinites. The cultural and economic traits of all the other Texas regions mingle here, with no single trait being dominant. Although the Central Texas region is a microcosm of Texas culture, Austin itself stands out as an island of liberalism in a predominantly conservative state (see Figure 1.2).

Politics and Cultural Diversity

LO 1.3 Analyze Texans' political struggles over equal rights and evaluate their success in Texas politics today and their impact on the state's political future.

The politics of the state's cultural regions have begun to lose their distinctive identities as Texas became more metropolitan and economically and ethnically diverse. With this changing environment, a number of groups and individuals have endeavored to achieve greater cultural, political, social, and economic equality in the state.

Texans' Struggle for Equal Rights

Anglo male Texans initially resided atop the pyramid of status, wealth, and civil rights in organized Texas society. They wrote the rules of the game and used those rules to protect their position against attempts by females, African Americans, and Latinos to share in the fruits of full citizenship. Only after the disenfranchised groups organized and exerted political pressure against their governments did the doors of freedom and equality open enough for them to come inside.

Female Texans
Women in the Republic of Texas could neither serve on juries nor vote, but unmarried women retained many of the rights that they had enjoyed under Spanish law, which included control over their property. Married women retained some Spanish law benefits because, unlike under Anglo-Saxon law, Texas marriage law did not join the married couple into one legal person with the husband as the head. Texas married women could own inherited property, share ownership in community property, and make a legal will. However, the husband had control of all the property, both separate and community (including earned income), and an employer could not hire a married woman without her husband's consent.[6]

Divorce laws were restrictive on both parties, but a husband could win a divorce in the event of a wife's "amorous or lascivious conduct with other men, even short of adultery," or if she had committed adultery only once. He could not gain a divorce for concealed premarital fornication. On the other hand, a wife could gain a divorce only if "the husband had lived in adultery with another woman." Physical violence was not grounds for divorce unless the wife could prove a "serious danger" that might happen again. In practice, physical abuse was tolerated if the wife behaved "indiscreetly" or "provoked" her husband. Minority and poor Anglo wives had little legal protection from beatings because the woman's "station in life" and "standing in society" were also legal considerations.[7]

Governor James "Pa" Ferguson (1915–17) unwittingly aided the women's suffrage movement during the World War I period. Led by Minnie Fisher Cunningham, Texas suffragists organized, spoke out, marched, and lobbied for the right to vote during the Ferguson Administration but were initially unable to gain political traction because of Ferguson's opposition. When he became embroiled in political controversy over funding for the University of Texas, women joined in the groundswell of opposition. Suffragists effectively lobbied state legislators and organized rallies advocating Ferguson's impeachment.[8]

IMAGE 1.2 Texan Minnie Fisher Cunningham was a champion for women's suffrage in the state.

Bettmann/Getty Images

★ SRQ Describe legal restrictions on women before the suffrage movement. What explained the opposition to women having the right to vote?

Texas women continued to participate actively in the political arena although they lacked the right to vote. They supported William P. Hobby, who was considered receptive to women's suffrage, in his campaign for governor as "The Man Whom Good Women Want." The tactic was ultimately successful, and women won the legislative battle and gained the right to vote in the 1918 Texas primary.[9]

National suffrage momentum precipitated a proposed constitutional amendment establishing the right of women to vote throughout the United States. Having endured more than five years of "heavy artillery" from Cunningham and the Texas Equal Suffrage Association, legislative opposition crumbled, and in June of 1919 Texas became one of the first southern states to ratify the Nineteenth Amendment. Texas women received full voting rights in 1920.[10]

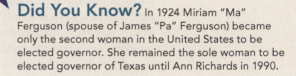

Did You Know? In 1924 Miriam "Ma" Ferguson (spouse of James "Pa" Ferguson) became only the second woman in the United States to be elected governor. She remained the sole woman to be elected governor of Texas until Ann Richards in 1990.

Women were given the right to serve on juries in 1954. Texas's voter ratification of the Equal Rights Amendment in 1972 and the passage of a series of laws titled the Marital Property Act amounted to major steps toward women's equality and heralded the beginning of a more enlightened era in Texas. The Act granted married women equal rights in insurance, banking, real estate, contracts, divorce, child custody, and property rights. This was the first such comprehensive family law in the United States.[11]

Until 1973, as in most states, abortion was illegal in Texas. In that year, Texas attorney Sarah Weddington argued a case before the U.S. Supreme Court that still stands at the center of national abortion debate: *Roe* v. *Wade*. The *Roe* decision overturned Texas statutes that criminalized abortion and in doing so established a limited, national right of privacy for women to terminate a pregnancy. *Roe* followed *Griswold* v. *Connecticut*, a 1965 privacy case that overturned a state law criminalizing the use of birth control.

Most recently, in its 2016 *Whole Woman's Health* v. *Hellerstedt* decision, the U.S. Supreme Court handed down perhaps its most influential abortion-related decision since *Roe*. The Court held key portions of 2013 Texas abortion legislation unconstitutional, including the requirements that abortion clinics comply with the same standards as ambulatory surgical centers (ASCs) and that doctors performing abortions possess admitting privileges at nearby hospitals. Because an indirect effect of these requirements was the closure or pending closure of a large majority of the state's abortion clinics, including all those located outside the state's four largest metro areas, in the opinion of the Supreme Court the law placed an undue burden on women seeking an abortion in Texas, and therefore was unconstitutional.

African American Texans   African Americans from other areas of the United States were brought to Texas as slaves and served in that capacity until the end of the Civil War. They first learned of their freedom on June 19, 1865, a date commemorated annually at Juneteenth celebrations throughout the country, including Texas, where the day has been an official state holiday since 1980. During Reconstruction, African Americans both voted and held elective office, but the end of Reconstruction and Anglo opposition effectively ended African Americans' political participation in the state.

Civil rights were an increasingly elusive concept for ethnic and racial minorities following Reconstruction. African Americans were legally denied the right to vote in the Democratic **white primary**, the practice of excluding African Americans from primary elections in the Texas Democratic Party. Schools and public facilities such as theaters, restaurants, beaches, and hospitals were legally segregated by race. Segregation laws were enforced by official law enforcement agents as well as by Anglo cultural norms and unofficial organizations using terror tactics. Although segregation laws were not usually formally directed at Latinos, who were

white primary
The practice of excluding African Americans from primary elections in the Texas Democratic Party.

Ku Klux Klan (KKK)
A white supremacist organization.

legally white, such laws were effectively enforced against them as well. The white supremacist organization known as the **Ku Klux Klan (KKK)**, members of local law enforcement, and the Texas Rangers actively participated in violence and intimidation of both Latinos and African Americans to keep them "in their segregated place." Lynching was also used against both groups, often after torture.[12]

The KKK was first organized in the late 1860s to intimidate freed African American slaves. A modified, enlarged version was reborn in the 1920s with a somewhat altered mission. The new Klan saw itself as a patriotic, Christian, fraternal organization for native-born white Protestants. Its members perceived a general moral decline in society, precipitated by "modern" young people, and a basic threat to the Protestant white Christian "race." Klansmen sensed a threat to their values from African Americans, Jews, Catholics, Latinos, German Americans, and other "foreigners." The Klan used intimidation, violence, and torture that included hanging, tarring and feathering, branding, beating, and castration as means of coercion. As many as 80,000 Texans (which amounted to almost 10 percent of the adult Anglo male population at the time) may have joined the "invisible empire" in an effort to make the world more to their liking. Many elected officials—federal and state legislators as well as county and city officials—were either avowed Klansmen or friendly neutrals. In fact, the Klan influenced Texas society to such an extent that its power was a major political issue from 1921 through 1925.[13]

In response to this racially charged atmosphere, a number of organizations committed to civil rights were founded or grew larger during the 1920s. These included the National Association for the Advancement of Colored People (NAACP), established in 1909, and the League of United Latin American Citizens (LULAC), which was formed in Corpus Christi in 1929.

When Dr. L. H. Nixon, an African American from El Paso, was denied the right to vote in the Democratic primary, the NAACP instituted legal action, and the U.S. Supreme Court found in *Nixon* v. *Herndon* (1927) that the Texas White Primary law was unconstitutional. However, the Texas Legislature transferred control of the primary from the state to the executive committee of the Texas Democratic Party, and the discrimination continued. Dr. Nixon again sought justice in the courts, and in 1931 the U.S. Supreme Court ruled the new scheme was also unconstitutional. Texas Democrats then completely excluded African Americans from party membership. In *Grovey* v. *Townsend* (1935), the U.S. Supreme Court upheld this ploy, and the Texas Democratic primary remained an all-white organization. Although it had suffered a temporary setback in the episode, the NAACP had proven its potential as a viable instrument for African American Texans to achieve justice.[14]

The Texas branch of the NAACP remained active during the World War II period and served as a useful vehicle for numerous legal actions to protect African American civil rights. African Americans eventually won the right to participate in the Texas Democratic primary when the U.S. Supreme Court ruled in *Smith* v. *Allwright* (1944) that primaries were a part of the election process and that racial discrimination in the election process is unconstitutional. Twenty years later, the first African Americans since Reconstruction were elected to the Texas Legislature.

In 1946, Heman Sweatt applied for admission to the University of Texas Law School, which by Texas law was segregated (see Chapter 2). State laws requiring segregation were constitutional as long as facilities serving African Americans and whites were equal. Because Texas had no law school for African Americans, the legislature hurriedly established a law school for Sweatt and, for his "convenience," located it in his hometown of Houston. Although officially established, the new law school lacked both faculty and a library and, as a result, the NAACP again sued the state. The U.S. Supreme Court ruled that education at Sweatt's new law school, in fact, was not equal to that of the University of Texas Law School and ordered him admitted to that institution. It is worth noting that "separate but equal" facilities remained legal after this case because the Court did not overturn *Plessy* v. *Ferguson*, which granted the constitutional sanction for legal segregation. Instead, the Court simply ruled that the new law school was not equal to that at the University of Texas.[15] The U.S. Supreme Court did not finally outlaw segregation until the *Brown* v. *Board of Education* decision in 1954.

The political and social fallout from the U.S. Supreme Court's *Brown* v. *Board of Education* (1954) public school desegregation decision did not bypass Texas. When the Mansfield Independent School District, just to the southeast of Fort Worth, was ordered to integrate in 1956, angry Anglos surrounded the school and prevented the enrollment of three African American children. Governor Allan Shivers declared the demonstration an "orderly protest" and sent the Texas Rangers to support the protestors. Because the administration of President Dwight D. Eisenhower took no action, the school remained segregated. The Mansfield school desegregation incident "was the first example of failure to enforce a federal court order for the desegregation of a public school."[16] Only in 1965, when facing a loss of federal funding, did the Mansfield ISD finally desegregate.

Federal District Judge William Wayne Justice in *United States* v. *Texas* (1970) ordered the complete desegregation of all Texas public schools. The decision was one of the most extensive desegregation orders in history and included the process for executing the order in detail. The U.S. Fifth Circuit Court of Appeals largely affirmed Justice's decision but refused to extend its provisions to Latino children.[17]

The 1960s are known for the victories of the national civil rights movement. Texan James Farmer was cofounder of the Congress of Racial Equality (CORE) and, along with Dr. Martin Luther King Jr., Whitney Young, and Roy Wilkins, was one of the "Big Four" African American leaders who shaped the civil rights struggle in the 1950s and 1960s. Farmer, who followed the nonviolent principles of Mahatma Gandhi, initiated sit-ins as a means of integrating public facilities and freedom rides as a means of registering African Americans to vote. The first sit-in to protest segregated facilities in Texas was organized with CORE support by students from Wiley and Bishop Colleges. The students occupied the rotunda of the Harrison County courthouse in the East Texas city of Marshall.

Latino Texans Like most African Americans, Latinos were relegated to the lowest-paid jobs as either service workers or farmworkers. The Raymondville Peonage cases in 1929 tested for the first time the legality of forcing vagrants or debtors to work off debts and fines as labor on private farms. The practice violated federal statutes but was commonplace in some Texas counties. The Willacy County sheriff stated in his defense that Latinos often sought arrest to gain shelter and that "peonage was not an unknown way of life for them." The

Did You Know? In 1966 Texas Western (now the University of Texas at El Paso) won the NCAA Division I men's basketball championship, the first championship won by a team where all five starters were African American. They defeated an all-white University of Kentucky team coached by Adolph Rupp.

IMAGE 1.3 Heman Sweatt successfully integrated Texas public law schools after the U.S. Supreme Court began to chip away at the "separate but equal" doctrine in the landmark case of *Sweatt v. Painter* (1950).

Joseph Scherschel/The LIFE Picture Collection/Getty Images

★ SRQ **The Fourteenth Amendment to the U.S. Constitution says that no state shall deny any person the equal protection of the law. Why did the U.S. Supreme Court hold that state laws requiring racial segregation violated this provision?**

trials resulted in the arrest and conviction of several public officials and private individuals. The outcome of the trials was unpopular in the agricultural areas and contrary to the generally accepted belief that farmers should have a means of collecting debts from individual laborers.[18]

World War II Latino veterans, newly returned to the state from fighting to make the world safe for democracy, found discrimination still existed in their homeland. A decorated veteran, Major Hector Garcia, settled in Corpus Christi and became convinced by conditions in South Texas that still another war was yet to be fought on behalf of the region's Latino community. Garcia, a medical doctor, found farm laborers enduring inhuman living conditions; disabled veterans starving, sick, and ignored by the Veterans Administration; and an entrenched, unapologetic Anglo culture that continued to impose public school segregation.

To begin his war, Dr. Garcia needed recruits for his "army." With other World War II veterans, Dr. Garcia organized the American G.I. Forum in a Corpus Christi elementary school classroom in March 1948. This organization spread throughout the United States and played a major role in providing Latinos with full citizenship and civil respect.

One of the incendiary sparks that ignited Latinos in Texas to fight for civil rights was Private Felix Longoria's funeral. Longoria was a decorated soldier who died in combat in the Philippines during World War II. His body was returned in 1949 to the South Texas town of Three Rivers (midway between San Antonio and Corpus Christi) for burial in the "Mexican section" of the cemetery, which was separated from the "white section" by barbed wire. But an obstacle developed: the funeral home's director refused the Longoria family's request to use its chapel because "the whites won't like it." Longoria's widow asked Dr. Garcia for support, but the funeral director also refused his request. Dr. Garcia then sent a flurry of telegrams and letters to Texas congressmen protesting the actions of the director. Then-Senator Lyndon B. Johnson immediately responded and arranged for Private Longoria to be buried at Arlington National Cemetery.[19]

IMAGE 1.4 Texas Southern University students stage a sit-in at a Houston supermarket lunch counter, 1950.

AP Images/ASSOCIATED PRESS

★ PRQ Why did students risk arrest in protests that focused national attention on segregation? Why have ethnic and racial minorities used tactics other than voting to achieve their strategic goals?

The fight to organize labor unions was the primary focus for much of the Latino civil activism in the 1960s and 1970s. In rural areas, large landowners controlled the political and economic systems and were united in their opposition to labor unions. The United Farm Workers (UFW) led a strike against melon growers and packers in Starr County in the 1960s, demanding a minimum wage and the resolution of other grievances. Starr County police officers, the local judiciary, and the Texas Rangers were all accused of brutality as they arrested and prosecuted strikers for minor offenses.

On February 26, 1977, members of the Texas Farm Workers Union (TFWU), strikers, and other supporters began a march to Austin to demand a $1.25 minimum wage and other improvements in working conditions for farmworkers. Press coverage intensified as the marchers slowly made their way north from the U.S.–Mexico border. Politicians, members of the American Federation of Labor–Congress of Industrial Organizations (AFL–CIO), and the Texas Council of Churches accompanied the protestors. Governor John Connally, who had refused to meet them in Austin, traveled to New Braunfels with then-House Speaker Ben Barnes and Attorney General Waggoner Carr to intercept the march and inform strikers that their efforts would have no effect. Ignoring the governor, the marchers continued to Austin and held a 6,500-person protest rally at the state capitol. The rally was broken up by the Texas Rangers and other law enforcement officers. The TFWU took legal action against the Rangers for their part in the repression of the rally. The eventual ruling of the U.S. Supreme Court held that the laws the Rangers had been enforcing were in violation of the U.S. Constitution. The Texas Rangers were subsequently reorganized and became a part of the Texas Department of Public Safety.[20]

One of the first successful legal challenges to segregated schools in Texas was *Delgado* v. *Bastrop ISD* (1948). The suit by Gustavo C. (Gus) Garcia charged that Minerva Delgado and other Latino children were denied the same school facilities and educational instruction available to Anglos. The battle continued until segregated facilities were eventually prohibited in 1957 by the decision in *Hernandez* v. *Driscoll Consolidated ISD*.[21]

Important to Latinos and, ultimately, all others facing discrimination was *Hernandez* v. *State of Texas* (1954). An all-Anglo jury in the small town of Edna had convicted Pete Hernandez of murder in 1950. Attorneys Gus Garcia, Carlos Cadena, John Herrera, and James DeAnda challenged the conviction, arguing that the systematic exclusion of Latinos from jury duty in Texas violated Hernandez's right to equal protection under the law guaranteed by the Fourteenth Amendment of the U.S. Constitution. Texas courts had historically ruled that Latinos were white, so excluding them from all-Anglo (white) juries could not be legal discrimination. To change the system, the Latino team of lawyers would have to change the interpretation of the U.S. Constitution. The stakes were high. If they failed, Latino discrimination throughout the southwestern United States might legally continue for years. Garcia argued before the U.S. Supreme Court that Latinos, although white, were "a class apart" and suffered discrimination on the basis of their "class." The U.S. Supreme Court agreed, overturned the Texas courts, and ruled that Latinos were protected by the Constitution from discrimination by other whites. The *Hernandez* decision established the precedent of constitutional protection by class throughout the United States and was a forerunner of future decisions prohibiting discrimination by gender, disability, and sexual orientation.[22]

IMAGE 1.5 Gus Garcia, legal advisor for the American G.I. Forum, is shown during a visit to the White House. Garcia was the lead attorney in the U.S. Supreme Court decision *Hernandez v. Texas*, 347 U.S. 475 (1954).

Library of Congress Prints and Photographs Division [LC-US262-137627]

★ PRQ Why is it unconstitutional to deny a person the right to serve on a jury because of ethnicity?

Lesbian, Gay, Bisexual, and Transgender Texans

Discrimination against lesbian, gay, bisexual, and transgender Texans has long been commonplace in Texas. Furthermore, state law has criminalized certain intimate sexual conduct by two persons of the same sex.

In 1998 a Harris County sheriff's deputy discovered two men having intimate sexual contact in a private residence, and the men were arrested and convicted for violating a Texas anti-sodomy statute. Their conviction was appealed and eventually reached the U.S. Supreme Court in the case *Lawrence* v. *Texas*. In Justice Anthony Kennedy's majority opinion, he stated that the Texas law violated the due process clause of the Fourteenth Amendment, which does not protect sodomy but does protect personal relationships and the ability to have those relationships without fear of punishment or criminal classification. The Texas statute intended to control the most intimate of all human activity, sexual behavior, in the most private of places, the home. The *Lawrence* decision simultaneously invalidated sodomy laws in thirteen other states, thereby protecting same-sex behavior in every state and territory in the United States.

The right to marry was until recently the frontline of the LGBT battle for equal rights, with this battle complicated by the 1996 federal Defense of Marriage Act (DOMA). DOMA defined marriage as a legal union between a man and a woman and further stipulated that the federal government would not recognize same-sex marriages for purposes of benefits such as social security, veterans' benefits, and income tax filings.[23] In 2013 the U.S. Supreme Court decided the case *United States* v. *Windsor*, in which it held that federal discrimination against same-sex couples violated the Fourteenth Amendment of the U.S. Constitution. And in 2015, in *Obergefell* v. *Hodges*, the U.S. Supreme Court ruled that state bans on same-sex marriage, such as that in force in Texas as the result of a 2005 amendment to the Texas State Constitution, were unconstitutional because, as was the case in *Windsor*, they violated the Fourteenth Amendment.

A current front in the struggle for LGBT equality in Texas is increasingly found at the local level throughout the state, where many cities have adopted nondiscrimination ordinances that among other things provide protections against discrimination for members of the LGBT community. Austin, Dallas, El Paso, Fort Worth, and San Antonio are among the cities that have this type of nondiscrimination ordinance presently on the books. Houston passed a similar ordinance in 2014, but it was overturned by a popular vote (61 percent to 39 percent) in 2015. During the 2017 legislative sessions, a strong (but ultimately unsuccessful) effort was made to pass a law overriding these ordinances as they relate to transgender bathroom access. Table 1.1 summarizes Texas practices that the U.S. Supreme Court has ruled violate the U.S. Constitution.

IMAGE 1.6 Annise Parker became the first openly lesbian mayor of a major U.S. city when she assumed office as Houston's chief executive in 2010.

AP Images/David J. Phillip

★ CTQ   **Why do younger and older Texans have notably different opinions about same-sex marriage?**

Cultural Diversity Today

Demographics
Population characteristics, such as age, gender, ethnicity, employment, and income, that social scientists use to describe groups in society.

Demographics are population characteristics, such as age, gender, ethnicity/race, employment, and income, that social scientists use to describe groups in society, and in Texas these characteristics are rapidly changing. Texas is one of the fastest-growing states in the nation and is becoming more culturally diverse as immigrants from other nations and migrants from other states continue to find it a desirable place to call home.

U.S. Census data and population estimates by the Texas State Demographer underscore how the state has become much more ethnically/racially diverse over the past 35 years (see Figure 1.5). In 1980, 66 percent of Texans were Anglo, 21 percent Latino, 12 percent African American, and less than 1 percent others (see Figure 1.5). During the course of the next 37 years, the share of the Texas population accounted for by Anglos progressively declined and the share accounted for by Latinos and Asian Americans progressively rose, with the

TABLE 1.1 Key U.S. Supreme Court Decisions Protecting Texans' Rights to Equality and Privacy

This table shows important U.S. constitutional decisions that have expanded minority rights in Texas and nationwide.

Unconstitutional Texas Practice	U.S. Constitutional Violation	Landmark Supreme Court Case
Texas laws permitting the Democratic Party to conduct whites-only primaries. Also used in other southern states.	No state shall deny any person the right to vote on account of race—Fifteenth Amendment.	*Smith* v. *Allwright* (1944)
Texas law requiring racially segregated law schools. Professional schools were segregated throughout the South.	No state shall deny any person the equal protection of the laws—Fourteenth Amendment.	*Sweatt* v. *Painter* (1950)
Texas practice of denying Latinos the right to serve on juries.	No state shall deny any person the equal protection of the laws—Fourteenth Amendment.	*Hernandez* v. *State of Texas* (1954)
State laws mandating statewide segregation of public schools and most facilities open to the public. Texas was among the 17 mostly southern states with statewide laws requiring segregation at the time of the decision.	No state shall deny any person the equal protection of the laws—Fourteenth Amendment.	*Brown* v. *Board of Education of Topeka* (1954)
Texas law making abortion illegal; 30 states outlawed abortions for any reason in 1973.	No state shall deny liberty without due process of law—Fourteenth Amendment.	*Roe* v. *Wade* (1973)
Texas law making homosexual conduct a crime; 14 mostly southern states made homosexual conduct a crime at the time of the decision.	No state shall deny liberty without due process of law—Fourteenth Amendment.	*Lawrence* v. *Texas* (2003)
State laws making same-sex marriage illegal; Texas was among 31 states with constitutional provisions that banned same-sex marriage. Most states had statutes defining marriage as between one man and one woman.	No state shall deny liberty without the due process of law; no state shall deny any person the equal protection of the laws—Fourteenth Amendment.	*Obergefell* v. *Hodges* (2015)

▶ How has Texas's southern conservative political culture resisted social change? Why have groups suffering discrimination sought remedy for this discrimination in the U.S. Supreme Court, an institution outside the control of state politics?

proportion of African Americans remaining roughly the same. By 2017, Anglos represented 42 percent of Texans and Latinos 39 percent, with Latinos expected to be the largest single ethnic/racial group in the state when the next U.S. Census is conducted in 2020. Lastly, between 1990 and 2018 the Asian American share of the Texas population more than doubled from 2 to 5 percent.

Voter participation in Texas is comparatively quite low (see Chapter 4). Furthermore, Latino political participation is low even by Texas standards. Given the growing share of

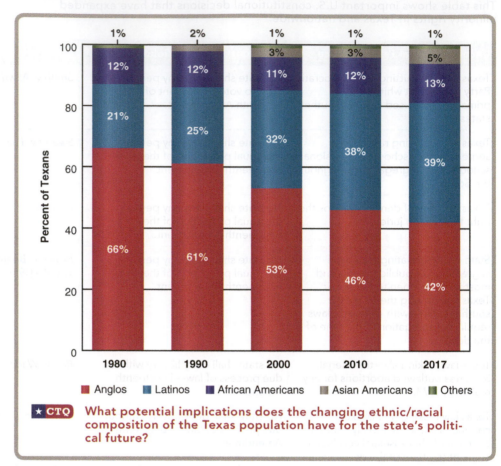

FIGURE 1.5 Texas Ethnic/Racial Populations, Past and Present: 1980–2017
This figure shows the changing ethnic/racial demographics of Texas.

★ CTQ   **What potential implications does the changing ethnic/racial composition of the Texas population have for the state's political future?**

Source: U.S. Census Bureau and Office of the Texas State Demographer.

eligible voters represented by Latinos, if Latinos begin to participate at the same rates as African Americans and Anglos, it could have a dramatic impact on the tenor and substance of politics and public policy in the Lone Star State.

Equally important, changes in the ethnic/racial makeup of the state's population will present decision makers with enormous challenges. Figure 1.7 shows that income inequality parallels ethnic/racial divisions in Texas. Poverty rates are higher and overall incomes are lower among African Americans and Latinos compared to Anglos and Asian Americans. Lower incomes are associated with more limited educational opportunity, inadequate access to health care, and much less robust participation in the state's civic life. Poverty drives up the cost of state social services and is a factor that contributes to crime and familial dysfunction. How Texas adapts to the state's changing demographics is likely to be the focus of political controversy for years to come.

How Does Texas Compare?

Ethnic/Racial Diversity in the United States

Figure 1.6 shows how much diversity is found in each state based on the Herfindahl index, which tells us the probability that two individuals randomly selected in a state will be members of the same ethnic/racial group. The index ranges in potential value from 1.0 (everyone in a state is a member of the same ethnic/racial group) to 0.0 (everyone in a state is a member of a different ethnic racial group). Its actual values in the United States today range from 0.89 in Vermont (the country's least diverse state) to 0.32 in California (the country's most diverse state), with a national Herfindahl Index value of 0.43. Texas ranks fourth among the 50 states and District of Columbia in terms of its level of ethnic/racial diversity, with a value of 0.35.

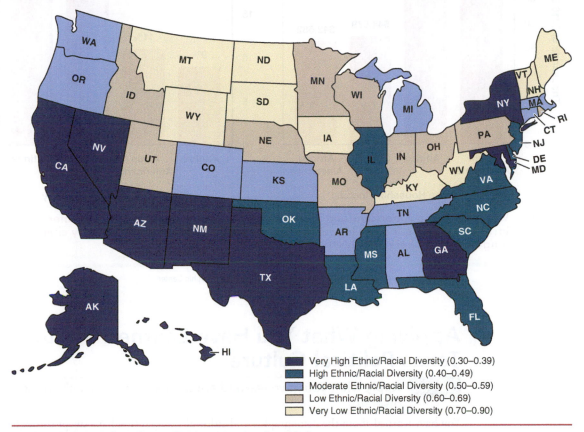

Very High Ethnic/Racial Diversity (0.30–0.39)
High Ethnic/Racial Diversity (0.40–0.49)
Moderate Ethnic/Racial Diversity (0.50–0.59)
Low Ethnic/Racial Diversity (0.60–0.69)
Very Low Ethnic/Racial Diversity (0.70–0.90)

FIGURE 1.6 Ethnic/Racial Diversity in the 50 States

Source: U.S. Census Bureau.

FOR DEBATE

★ CTQ Just as the U.S. states vary in their level of ethnic/racial diversity, so too do Texas's 254 counties. How does your county compare with neighboring counties in regard to its level of ethnic/racial diversity?

★ CTQ How might the level of ethnic/racial diversity affect a state's politics and policies?

FIGURE 1.7 Ethnicity/Race, Income, and Poverty in Texas

Today, inequality among ethnic/racial groups is no longer so much reflected by overt official legal discrimination as by unequal income and unequal access to education and health care.

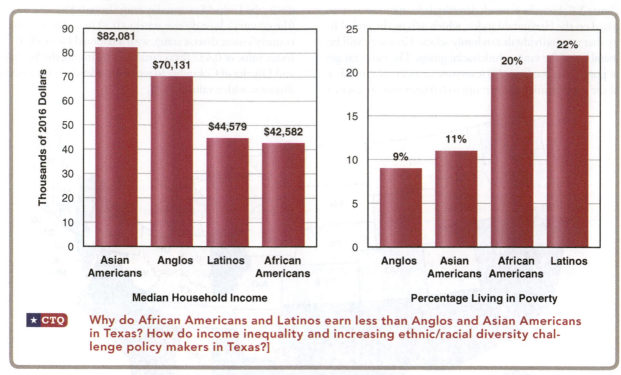

★ CTQ   Why do African Americans and Latinos earn less than Anglos and Asian Americans in Texas? How do income inequality and increasing ethnic/racial diversity challenge policy makers in Texas?]

Source: The Center for Public Policy Priorities and the Texas Demographic Center.

Applying What You Have Learned about Texas Political Culture

LO 1.4   **Apply what you have learned about Texas political culture and diversity.**

You have learned about the demographic and cultural changes that have swept through Texas in recent years. Because this chapter provides an overview of these changes by the numbers, we decided to ask Representative Ana Hernandez to put a face on one of these changes—Latino immigration.

Ana Hernandez was born in Reynosa, Mexico, and raised in the Houston suburb of Pasadena. Hernandez is a practicing attorney and, since first being elected in a 2005 special election at the age of 27, has continuously represented Texas House District 143 on Houston's east side, most recently winning reelection without opposition in November 2018. In 2012 the *Houston Chronicle* listed her as one of the country's "20 Latino Democrats to Watch Over the Next 20 Years."

After you have read Representative Hernandez's essay, we will ask you to reflect on the issue of undocumented immigration, keeping in mind that the estimated 40 percent of immigrants entering the United States legally and overstaying their visa is not committing a crime, even though doing so can result in their deportation. On the other hand, it is a federal crime to cross the border while evading immigration authorities.

We will ask you to evaluate the impact of Latino immigration on the state's political culture. Consider immigrants' contributions to the society and the economy, and identify the economic and social costs of undocumented immigration you may perceive.

POLITICS IN PRACTICE
The Face of Latino Immigration

by Ana Hernandez

STATE REPRESENTATIVE FROM TEXAS HOUSE DISTRICT 143

Like the children of many hardworking families currently in the United States, my early American experience cannot be found in government documentation. I was brought to the United States from Mexico on a visitor's visa when I was an infant. We overstayed our visas and lived for eight years in the U.S. without documentation.

I still remember the constant state of dread in which our family lived. Trips to the store, drop-offs at school and church functions had to be painstakingly choreographed in order to guarantee that at least one of my parents would be able to care for my sister and me in the event that the other was detained and deported.

This remained our normal state of affairs until the passage of the Immigration Reform and Control Act of 1986, a bipartisan measure to address our broken immigration system that was championed by Republican President Ronald Reagan and passed by a Democratic-controlled Congress.

While this attempt at reform was limited in scope and far from perfect, it did provide a means by which my family could obtain legal permanent residency. With the specter of deportation no longer hanging over our heads, my mother and father no longer had to partition their time from one another in order to ensure that I was looked after in the event authorities picked one of them up off the street. Suddenly, we weren't living day to day, moment to moment. We were home to stay.

At age 18, I became a naturalized U.S. citizen. Like so many before me and since, the final citizenship test was a surreal and nerve-racking experience. Though I had attended American public schools all my life, I couldn't help but feel a lead weight in my stomach as the presiding immigration officer administered my examination. One of my first questions was to state the nation's capital. In my nervousness, I answered "Austin, Texas." The officer looked at me for a moment that felt like an eternity … and repeated the question, allowing me to compose myself and state "Washington, DC."

In so many ways, the pathway to citizenship afforded me delivered on one of our nation's most fundamental promises—individual opportunity. Nothing was ever guaranteed in my life—neither success nor happiness. But, by God's grace, I now had the chance to make of my future what I could. I worked hard, earning a scholarship to attend the University of Houston and later graduating from the University of Texas School of Law. I threw myself into every opportunity that came my way, serving overseas in the Peace Corps helping to desegregate the post-Apartheid South African education system, competing for and earning a legislative internship in the Texas Capitol, and finally returning to that same building years later as a State Representative.

My story, that of a young girl from Reynosa, should not be considered remarkable. Rather, it should be only one success spoken about among a chorus of millions. The stories of the countless young men and women whose families currently exist in a state of limbo should make mine appear mundane. Instead, due entirely to a lack of political will to deliver on America's promises, they remain stories unfinished, the authors unfairly denied pen and paper to have a chance to write them.

They are our nation's future and salvation, a generation of talented, educated, passionate Texans—doctors, technicians, engineers. Our next captains of industry, and the policy makers who will grow our economy and carry our country's torch through the next century. Their stories will be told. That is what motivates me. I fight for every dream deferred.

1. Evaluate the costs and benefits of immigration to Texas.
2. What are the costs of deporting undocumented immigrants? Should special consideration be given to individuals, sometimes called "Dreamers," whose parents brought them to the United States as children and whose lives are deeply rooted in the country?
3. What cultural and political changes can the state expect as a result of Latino immigration?

★ Chapter Summary

LO 1.1 Analyze the relationships among Texas political culture, its politics, and its public policies. A political culture reflects people's political values and beliefs. It explains how people feel about their government—their expectations of what powers it should have over their lives and what services it should provide.

The generally conservative ideological position of Texans masks some notable subgroup differences based on gender, ethnicity/race, generational cohort, and geography. For example, men are on average more conservative than women and Anglos more conservative than both Latinos and especially African Americans. At the same time, Millennials are notably more liberal than Texans in other generational cohorts, especially those belonging to the Silent Generation, and residents of Travis County are significantly more liberal than residents of the state's other populous counties.

Texans' predominantly conservative political culture is reflected in voters' greater tendency to identify as Republican than Democratic and in the state's conservative public policies. Republicans control state political institutions and have enacted low tax and spending policies and conservative policies on social issues such as abortion and same-sex marriage.

LO 1.2 Differentiate the attributes that describe the major Texas regions. Texas can be divided into a series of political cultural regions with differing characteristics and traditions: (1) East Texas, (2) the Gulf Coast, (3) South Texas, (4) Far

West Texas, (5) the German Hill Country, (6) West Texas, (7) the Panhandle, (8) North Texas, and (9) Central Texas. Each region is characterized by distinctive historical, ethnic, and economic influences.

LO 1.3 Analyze Texans' political struggles over equal rights and evaluate their success in Texas politics today and their impact on the state's political future. Texas social conservatism inherited from the Old South traditionalistic culture has resulted in resistance to cultural minorities' demands for social and political equality. In several instances, minorities have succeeded in their struggles for equality by appealing to the federal courts outside of the political control of Texas political institutions.

Women were not legally equal to men in early Texas, and their path to equality has been a winding and occasionally hesitant one. Activists finally won the long battle for the right to vote in 1918. It was not until 1972, however, that women won equal rights in real estate, contracts, divorce, child custody, and property rights. The judicial decision in *Roe* v. *Wade* that further clarified the right of women to control their reproductive functions has remained at the center of national controversy with the Supreme Court refining the right to choose as recently as 2016.

African American Texans' struggle for legal equality reflected similar struggles being simultaneously waged in other southern states. The battle to vote in the Democratic primary and the right of admission to public accommodations and public schools were settled only by national courts or congressional intervention.

The Latino struggle in Texas was similar to that of African Americans and was resolved only by national action. Several Latino rights organizations were founded in Texas, and the judicial decision in *Hernandez* v. *Texas* (1954) that established the constitutional concept of a "class apart" became important throughout the United States. The right to form labor unions occupied much of the Latino movement in the 1960s and 1970s.

LGBT Texans are now waging similar battles for legal equality. *Lawrence* v. *Texas* (2003) gained national significance by decriminalizing sexual activity between consenting persons of the same biological sex. A high-profile series of battles for LGBT equality is presently taking place in cities throughout the state over the adoption of ordinances that extend protection against discrimination to members of the LGBT community.

Projections of population growth and immigration predict a shift in Texas's population from an Anglo plurality to a Latino plurality by the end of the current decade. Increased political clout can come with increased population, and Latinos could begin to challenge the political and economic dominance of Anglos. Regardless of the political outcome of population shifts, Texas is becoming more diverse and now has an opportunity to build on its already rich cultural pluralism.

LO 1.4 Apply what you have learned about Texas political culture and diversity. In 1986 President Ronald Reagan signed bipartisan immigration reform legislation into law. It allowed more than 3 million undocumented immigrants to come out of the shadows and legalize their status. Thirty years later, the country's immigration system is once again broken, with 11 million undocumented immigrants presently in the country. A majority of Americans want to find a way for these undocumented immigrants (excluding those with serious criminal records) to legalize their status while simultaneously ensuring that the country gains better control over the immigration process in order to avoid ever again having large numbers of undocumented immigrants residing in the United States.

Key Terms

bicultural, *p. 11*
conservative, *p. 2*
Creole, *p. 10*
demographics, *p. 20*

Ku Klux Klan (KKK), *p. 16*
liberal, *p. 3*
maquiladora, *p. 11*
Mestizo, *p. 10*

Metroplex, *p. 13*
North American Free Trade Agreement (NAFTA), *p. 11*

political culture, *p. 2*
ranchero culture, *p. 10*
The Valley, *p. 10*
white primary, *p. 15*

Review Questions

LO 1.1 Analyze the relationships among Texas political culture, its politics, and its public policies.

- Describe the policy differences between the Texas conservative and liberal ideologies.

- Discuss the most significant differences in ideological self-identification between men and women, across the state's three largest ethnic/racial groups, among the four generational cohorts to which most Texans living today belong, and among the state's largest counties.

- Show how Texans' conservatism is reflected in the state's partisanship and public policies.

LO 1.2 Differentiate the attributes that describe the major Texas regions.

- Briefly describe each of the state's nine major cultural regions. Does the description fit your home area?

- How do the state's major cultural regions differ historically, economically, and ethnically/racially?

LO 1.3 Analyze Texans' political struggles over equal rights and evaluate their success in Texas politics today and their impact on the state's political future.

- Describe the major developments in the struggle of Texas women, African Americans, Latinos, and members of the state's LGBT community to achieve social and political equality. What cultural factors explain the resistance to the social change that their struggles eventually brought about?

- How will Texas's population growth and its changing demographics affect the state's political landscape? What challenges does a more diverse population present for policy makers?

Think Critically and Get Active!

Get involved and learn about your own cultural heritage. Talk to your great-grandparents, grandparents, parents, aunts, and uncles to learn what they know about your culture and family history. Record as much oral history as you can about their personal lives, experiences, and political memories as well as family traditions. You may find this information invaluable in the future when you talk to your own children, grandchildren, and great-grandchildren about their culture.

Research the background and richness of your family culture. Here are a few reliable sources:

- The Church of Jesus Christ of Latter-Day Saints: **www.familysearch.org**

- Institute of Texan Cultures: **www.texancultures.com**

- Texas State Library and Archives Commission: **www.tsl.state.tx.us**

- Texas State Historical Association and Center for Studies in Texas History: **www.tshaonline.org**

The *Handbook of Texas Online* (**www.tshaonline.org/ handbook**) is a great source for information on Texas history, culture, and geography. A project of the Texas State Historical Association, it is an encyclopedia of all things Texan. Use it to sketch the historical changes in the status of one or more of the groups discussed in the civil rights section in this chapter. Then review census data at **www.census.gov** and **www.osd.texas.gov** to evaluate their income, education, and quality of life in today's Texas. Quickly find information on your county or city using the U.S. Census Bureau's QuickFacts resource at **www.census.gov/quickfacts**. Develop a better understanding of support for Democratic and Republican candidates across the state by reviewing electoral returns on the Texas Secretary of State Elections Division website at **www.sos.state.tx.us/elections/**.

Broaden your cultural and political experiences. Study groups that are different from your own to get a perspective on the rich diversity of modern Texas political life at representative websites.

- Engage conservative political views via the Empower Texans website at **www.empowertexans.com**

(@EmpowerTexans) and liberal political perspectives at the *Texas Observer* website at **www.texasobserver.org** (@TexasObserver). The Texas Association of Business at **www.txbiz.org** (@txbiz) advocates for policies to improve the business climate in Texas and keep the economy among the strongest in the world, while the Center for Public Policy Priorities at **www.forabettertexas.org** (@CPPP_TX) advocates for hardworking Texans and their families, especially lower-income Texans.

- Check out two major Latino civil rights organizations, the League of United Latin American Citizens (LULAC) at **www.lulac.org** (@LULAC) and the Mexican American Legal Defense Fund (MALDEF) at **www.maldef.org** (@MALDEF), as well as the leading African American civil rights organization, the National Association for the Advancement of Colored People (NAACP), at **www.naacp.org** (@NAACP), and the leading Asian American civil rights organization, OCA–Asian Pacific American Advocates, at **www.ocanational.org** (@OCANational).

- Explore sites promoting women's rights and the election of women to public office, such as the National Organization of Women (NOW) at **www.now.org** (@NationalNOW) and the National Women's Political Caucus at **www.nwpc.org** (@NWPCNational), and those working to elect more women to public office in Texas, such as Annie's List at **www.annieslist.com** (@AnniesListTX) and the Texas Federation of Republican Women at **www.tfrw.org** (@TFRW).

- Some prominent groups supporting LGBT rights and promoting the election of members of the LGBT community to public office are Equality Texas at **www.equalitytexas.org** (@EqualityTexas) and The Gay and Lesbian Victory Fund at **www.victoryfund.org** (@VictoryFund).

★ **PRQ** **How much respect do you owe people whose political or cultural identity or ethnic/racial or religious background differ from your own? Evaluate the use of labels that members of different groups might find offensive.**

Texas in the Federal System

2

In contrast to the antagonism between Governor Abbott and President Obama, the governor exhibits a newfound cooperative relationship with President Trump on such issues as immigration and the response to Hurricane Harvey flooding (shown here). In this chapter, you will explore the changing relationship between the national government and the state.
AFP Contributor/AFP/Getty Images

Learning Objectives

LO 2.1 Differentiate among unitary, confederal, and federal systems of government.

LO 2.2 Distinguish among the types of powers in our federal system, and explain dual and cooperative federalism within the context of the evolution of federalism in the United States.

LO 2.3 Analyze Texas's relationship with the federal government and the prominent role the state has played in the national debate over coercive federalism.

LO 2.4 Apply what you have learned about Texas in the federal system.

The relationship between the Texas state government and the U.S. federal government has been tense in recent years. The members of the Texas state executive branch, including the governor, lieutenant governor, and attorney general, have increasingly viewed the federal government as encroaching on the state's sovereignty, while the federal government, especially under former President Barack Obama between 2009 and 2017, has attempted to enforce new laws, rules, and regulations in the state. From health care reform to voting rights to environmental policy, Texas and the federal government have disagreed on the proper role of each other in the creation, enactment, and enforcement of public policy. Tension between the federal government and the states is nothing new and has constantly redefined our concepts of federalism. Today's conflicts between the two levels of government may once again change our understanding of the federal system.

We begin by defining federalism and discussing how the concept has evolved over time in the United States. We then turn our attention to Texas and how federalism specifically affects the state's policies, politics, and society.

What Is Federalism?

LO 2.1   Differentiate among unitary, confederal, and federal systems of government.

Governmental systems are often classified into three basic types based on the degree of centralization present in their constitutions: unitary, confederal, and federal. The United States was the first country in the world to employ a federal system of government.

Unitary Systems

unitary system
A system of government in which constitutional authority rests with a national or central government; all regional or local governments are subordinate to the central government.

An overwhelming majority of the world's countries are governed by a **unitary system**, a system of government in which constitutional authority rests with a national or central government; all regional or local governments are subordinate to the central government. Unitary governments may be democratic like those in Chile, France, and Japan or nondemocratic like those in China, Cuba, and Saudi Arabia. They are all considered to be unitary governments simply because the constitution vests the power to govern the entire nation in a single central government.

Unitary governments frequently choose to create regional and local governments for administrative purposes; these regional and local governments are allowed varying latitude in the design and implementation of public policies across the world's unitary systems. However, in the end, these subnational governments remain creations of the national government and have only those powers the national government chooses to give them—powers that the national government is empowered to take away at its discretion.

Confederal Systems

confederal system
A system of government in which member states or regional governments have all authority, and any central government has only the power that state governments choose to delegate to it.

As a consequence of their negative experience with unitary rule under the British, following independence Americans first adopted a confederal system of government, a system that quickly proved to be unworkable. A **confederal system** is one in which member states or regional governments have all authority, and any central government has only the power that state governments choose to delegate to it. This system is also known as a confederation.

Under the Articles of Confederation drafted by the Continental Congress following independence in 1776, all power was placed in the hands of the state governments, and the central government had only the power that the states chose to give it. The best example of a modern-day confederation is the European Union (EU), containing 28 independent nation-states stretching from Ireland in the west to Romania in the east, and from Finland in the north to the Mediterranean island-state of Cyprus in the south, with five more nations on the road to EU membership, and the United Kingdom exiting or seceding under "Brexit."

Federal Systems

The country's failed experiment with a confederal form of government ended with the U.S. Constitutional Convention in 1787. In that year, the Americans meeting in Philadelphia invented an entirely new form of government—a federal system. Federalism represents an attempt to combine the advantages of a unitary government (national unity and uniformity where they are necessary) with the advantages of a confederacy (local control and policy diversity from state to state where possible).

Did You Know? Prior to its short tenure as an independent nation (1836–1845) and current status as a U.S. state (since 1845), Texas belonged to another federal system, the United Mexican States (1824–1835), as the northern half of the state of Coahuila y Texas. Mexico's shift in 1835 from a federal to a unitary system of government under Mexican President Antonio López de Santa Anna sparked a revolt against the Santa Anna dictatorship in Texas, a revolution that culminated in the state's independence in 1836.

Federal states can be either democratic, as in Argentina, Germany, and the United States, or nondemocratic, as in Ethiopia, Pakistan, and Russia. The concept of federalism has flourished in many places throughout the world, especially in nations that encompass a vast territory and/or possess a large or diverse population. Today, in addition to the United States, federal systems are employed by many of the world's largest (in terms of population and/or territory) democracies, including Argentina, Australia, Brazil, Canada, Germany, India, and Mexico.

A **federal system** of government is one in which governmental power is divided and shared between a national or central government and state or regional governments. Although original definitions of federalism considered only two levels of government, the concept can easily be extended to encompass multiple levels of government. In the United States, governmental power is shared among the national government, state governments, and local governments.

federal system
A system of government in which governmental power is divided and shared between a national or central government and state or regional governments.

The U.S. Constitution and Federalism

LO 2.2 **Distinguish among the types of powers in our federal system, and explain dual and cooperative federalism within the context of the evolution of federalism in the United States.**

When the framers of the U.S. Constitution set out to revise the Articles of Confederation in 1787, they opted to give more authority to the central government. One of their critical challenges was the creation of a representative government for a large nation with a diverse population. The Founding Fathers wanted to achieve a balance between parochial interests and broader national concerns. The solution to this challenge was the federal system. James Madison wrote in *Federalist 10*:

> By enlarging too much the number of electors, you render the representatives too little acquainted with all their local circumstances and lesser interests; as by reducing it too much, you render him unduly attached to these, and too little fit to comprehend and pursue great and national objects. The federal Constitution forms a happy combination in this respect; the great and aggregate interests being referred to the national, the local and particular to the State legislatures.[1]

The federal system that James Madison and the other Founding Fathers drafted was designed to create an optimal balance between local and national interests and concerns.

Over the course of our nation's history, the shift in power has been from a form of government in which the states reserved many of their powers to one in which the federal government has become more dominant. For every action, there is a reaction, and this growing power of the federal government has caused an increased level of activism by citizens who believe the pendulum of power in the country has swung too far to the federal government side. These individuals want at the minimum to avoid any further erosion of state autonomy and at the maximum to restore a greater level of power and authority to the 50 state governments. Over the past dozen years, perhaps nowhere in the country has this pushback against the federal government been more visible and vocal than in Texas, where many of the state's most powerful and high-profile politicians have been actively working to shift power away from the federal government and toward the states. (See the "Politics in Practice" feature later in this chapter.)

Types of Powers in Our Federal System

In the U.S. federal system, there are three types of powers—delegated, reserved, and concurrent. **Delegated powers** are those that the Constitution gives to the national government. These include those enumerated powers found in Article I, Section 8 of the U.S. Constitution as well as a few other powers that have evolved over time. Note that there are three types of delegated powers: expressed, implied, and inherent. **Expressed powers** are those powers that are clearly listed in Article I, Section 8 of the U.S. Constitution. **Implied powers** are those delegated powers that are assumed to exist in order for the federal government to perform the functions that are expressly delegated. These powers are granted by the necessary and proper clause in Article I, Section 8 of the U.S. Constitution. **Inherent powers** are those delegated powers that come with an office or position—generally, the executive branch. Although the U.S. Constitution does not clearly specify these powers granted to the executive branch, over time, inherent powers have evolved as powers found to be needed to perform the functions of the executive branch.

A second group of powers in the federal system is known as **reserved powers**. Reserved powers are those powers that belong to the states. The legitimacy of these powers comes from the Tenth Amendment. Finally, there are **concurrent powers**, which are those powers shared by the national government and the states. Examples of these delegated, reserved, and concurrent powers are listed in Figure 2.1.

The U.S. Constitution addresses the sharing of power between the national and state governments in various sections. Article I, Section 8, for instance, lists the enumerated powers "expressly" granted to Congress by the Constitution. Article VI includes the supremacy clause, which provides guidance on how to resolve a conflict arising between a federal law and a state law.

In the event that conflict should arise between federal and state law, the **supremacy clause** states that the U.S. Constitution, as well as laws and treaties created in accordance with the U.S. Constitution, supersedes or preempts state and local laws. That is, when federal law and state law are in direct conflict, the federal law must be followed. The **Tenth Amendment** to the U.S. Constitution also helps define the balance of power in the federal system. The Tenth Amendment is the section of the U.S. Constitution that reserves powers to the states. It reads as follows: "The powers not delegated to the United States by the Constitution, nor prohibited by it to the States, are reserved to the States respectively, or to the people." Some read the Tenth Amendment as limiting the federal government, shifting greater power to the states. The Fourteenth Amendment also affects the balance of power in the federal system. It was adopted following the Civil War and dramatically improved the protection of civil rights and equality for all Americans.

---

delegated powers

Those powers that the Constitution gives to the national government. These include those enumerated powers found in Article I, Section 8 of the U.S. Constitution as well as a few other powers that have evolved over time.

expressed powers

Those powers that are clearly listed in Article I, Section 8 of the U.S. Constitution.

implied powers

Those delegated powers that are assumed to exist in order for the federal government to perform the functions that are expressly delegated. These powers are granted by the necessary and proper clause in Article I, Section 8 of the U.S. Constitution.

inherent powers

Those delegated powers that come with an office or position—generally, the executive branch. Although the U.S. Constitution does not clearly specify powers granted to the executive branch, over time, inherent powers have evolved as part of the powers needed to perform the functions of the executive branch.

reserved powers

Those powers that belong to the states. The legitimacy of these powers comes from the Tenth Amendment.

concurrent powers

Those powers shared by the national government and the states.

FIGURE 2.1 National, State, and Concurrent Powers

This figure shows some examples of delegated national powers, reserved state powers, and those that are shared between the two.

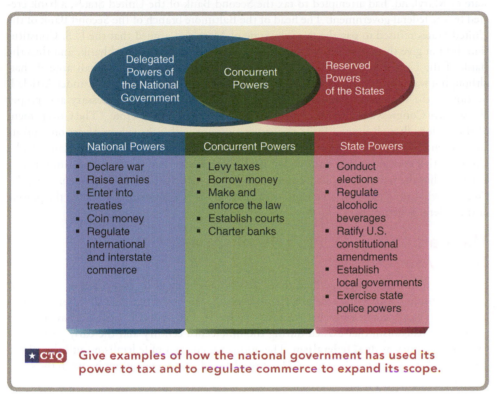

National Powers	Concurrent Powers	State Powers
■ Declare war ■ Raise armies ■ Enter into treaties ■ Coin money ■ Regulate international and interstate commerce	■ Levy taxes ■ Borrow money ■ Make and enforce the law ■ Establish courts ■ Charter banks	■ Conduct elections ■ Regulate alcoholic beverages ■ Ratify U.S. constitutional amendments ■ Establish local governments ■ Exercise state police powers

★ CTQ **Give examples of how the national government has used its power to tax and to regulate commerce to expand its scope.**

Source: Cengage Learning

supremacy clause
States that the U.S. Constitution, as well as laws and treaties created in accordance with the U.S. Constitution, supersedes or preempts state and local laws.

Tenth Amendment
Section of the U.S. Constitution that reserves powers to the states. It reads as follows: "The powers not delegated to the United States by the Constitution, nor prohibited by it to the States, are reserved to the States respectively, or to the people."

The Powers of the National Government

Conflicts between the national government and states have arisen on a number of occasions, in part because of different understandings of two sections of the U.S. Constitution: Article I, Section 8 and the Tenth Amendment. Article I, Section 8 of the U.S. Constitution enumerates the powers granted to Congress, including the power to regulate interstate commerce. It is this **commerce clause** in Article I that has been used to justify several broad national government actions. For example, the U.S. Congress used the commerce clause to criminalize the production and use of medicinal marijuana even in states where the growing and use of homegrown marijuana for medicinal purposes was legal (more about state marijuana laws later in this chapter). The U.S. Supreme Court upheld this use of the commerce clause in its 2005 decision *Gonzales* v. *Raich*. Other major powers granted to Congress under Article I, Section 8 include collecting taxes, providing for the common defense, borrowing money, printing money, declaring war, and regulating immigration and naturalization.

More important for a discussion of federalism, however, is the last clause in the list: "To make all Laws which shall be necessary and proper for carrying into Execution the foregoing Powers, and all other Powers vested by this Constitution in the Government of the United States, or in any Department or Officer thereof."[2] This is known as the **necessary and proper clause**, or the elastic clause, of the U.S. Constitution, which was given a very expansive meaning early in the nation's history.

commerce clause
An enumerated power in Article I, Section 8 of the U.S. Constitution that gives Congress the power to regulate commerce between the states.

necessary and proper clause
The last clause in Article I, Section 8 of the U.S. Constitution; also known as the elastic clause, which was given a very expansive meaning early in the nation's history.

Implied Powers of the National Government

In 1819, the U.S. Supreme Court expanded the power of the U.S. Congress. In *McCulloch* v. *Maryland*, the state of Maryland, seeking to limit competition with banks chartered by the state of Maryland, had attempted to tax the Second Bank of the United States, a bank created by the federal government. The head of the Baltimore branch of the Second Bank of the United States refused to pay the tax. The state of Maryland argued that the U.S. Constitution did not give the national government the power to create a national bank, and thus the Bank of the United States was unconstitutional. Chief Justice John Marshall argued that, although it was true that the creation of a bank was not an enumerated power under Article I, Section 8, the supremacy clause of the Constitution, along with the necessary and proper clause, gave Congress authority to create the bank. Justice Marshall wrote, "The Government of the Union, though limited in its powers, is supreme within its sphere of action, and its laws, when made in pursuance of the Constitution, form the supreme law of the land."[3] The Court further concluded that if the end or goal is legitimate, then the act is constitutional. If Congress has the power to regulate commerce, for instance, then Congress can enact legislation that will help it carry out that end.[4] *McCulloch* v. *Maryland* broadly expanded the powers of the federal government.

The Early View: Dual Federalism and the Tenth Amendment

Even with the broad powers granted to the federal government by *McCulloch* v. *Maryland*, the relationship between the federal government and state governments in its aftermath was one that left clear demarcations between the two levels of government. Scholars have dubbed the type of federalism that existed during the nineteenth century and the early part of the twentieth century as **dual federalism**. The dominant concept of federalism until the 1930s, dual federalism is characterized by four features that indicate demarcations between the states and the federal government:

1. The national government is one of enumerated powers only.
2. The purposes which the national government may constitutionally promote are few.
3. Within their respective spheres, the two centers of government are "sovereign" and hence "equal."
4. The relation of the two centers with each other is one of tension rather than collaboration.[5]

These four characteristics were postulated by Edward S. Corwin in his 1950 eulogy to the concept of dual federalism.[6] Corwin argued that "what was once vaunted as a Constitution of Rights, both State and private, has been replaced by a Constitution of Powers."[7] Although this claim may be debated, it was clear that a new understanding of the relationship between federal and state governments was under way.

The Tenth Amendment was the bulwark for dual federalism. It ensured that states like Texas retained those powers that were not given to the federal government. The Tenth Amendment was written to limit the powers of the national government to those stipulated in Article I, Section 8. But as early as 1789, supporters of the federal system were endeavoring to weaken the Tenth Amendment. In the process of writing the Tenth Amendment, Representative Thomas Tudor Tucker proposed adding the term *expressly* so that the amendment would read, "The powers not *expressly* delegated to the United States."[8] He believed that adding the term would limit the powers of the federal government to those *expressly* stated in the Constitution. James Madison and others argued against the proposal, and it was rejected.

As a result, the Tenth Amendment was left to be interpreted as limiting national powers either a little or a lot. After the replacement of Chief Justice John Marshall with Chief Justice Roger Taney, the Supreme Court began to rein in the national government. When faced with

dual federalism
The understanding that the federal government and state governments are both sovereign within their sphere of influence.

a case that pitted the federal government's power to regulate commerce against the states' internal police power, the Supreme Court would side with the states.[9] This would be the dominant concept of federalism until the 1930s.

The Development of Cooperative Federalism

The exclusion of the term *expressly* made it much easier for the national government to expand its powers, but a new set of national and global challenges served as the trigger that contributed to the shift in power from the state governments to the federal government. Two world wars, the Great Depression, advances in technology, the civil rights movement, and the Cold War with the Soviet Union contributed to a greater need for centralizing power. Edward Corwin summarizes, "The Federal System has shifted base in the direction of a consolidated national power, while within the National Government itself an increased flow of power in the direction of the President has ensued."[10]

Corwin's concept of dual federalism would be replaced by **cooperative federalism**, a relationship in which "the National Government and the States are mutually complementary parts of a *single* government mechanism all of whose powers are intended to realize the current purposes of government according to their applicability to the problem in hand."[11] Cooperative federalism used the power of the national government to encourage the states to pursue certain public policy goals. When the states cooperated, they would receive matching funds or additional assistance from the national government. When the states did not cooperate, funds could be withheld from the states.

The development of the concept of cooperative federalism was largely the result of a vast expansion of federal grants-in-aid. The evolution of federal grants to state and local governments has a long and controversial history. Although some grants from the national government to the states began as early as 1785, the adoption of the federal income tax in 1913 drastically altered the financial relationship between the national and state governments by making possible extensive federal aid to state and local governments.

The Great Depression of the 1930s brought with it a series of financial problems more severe than the state and local governments had previously experienced. Increased demand for state and local services at a time when revenues were rapidly declining stimulated a long series of New Deal grant-in-aid programs, ranging from welfare to public health and unemployment insurance.

Most of these early grant-in-aid programs were **categorical grants**. Under such aid programs, Congress appropriates funds for a specific purpose and sets up a formula for their distribution. Certain conditions are attached to these grant programs:

1. The receiving government agrees to match the federal money with its own, at a ratio fixed by law.
2. The receiving government administers the program. For example, federal funds are made available for Medicaid, but it is the state that actually pays client benefits.
3. The receiving government must meet minimum standards set by federal law. Sometimes additional conditions are attached to categorical grants, such as regional planning and accounting requirements.

Most federal aid, however, now takes the form of **block grants** that specify general purposes such as job training or community development but allow the state or local government to determine precisely how the money should be spent. Conditions may also be established for receipt of block grants, but state and local governments have greater administrative flexibility than with categorical grants. Federal transportation, welfare, and many other grants have been reformed to allow for significant **devolution**—that is, the attempt to enhance the power of state or local governments, especially by replacing relatively restrictive categorical grants-in-aid with more flexible block grants.

cooperative federalism
A relationship where "the National Government and the States are mutually complementary parts of a *single* government mechanism all of whose powers are intended to realize the current purposes of government according to their applicability to the problem in hand."[12]

categorical grants
Federal aid to state or local governments for specific purposes, granted under restrictive conditions and often requiring matching funds from the receiving government.

block grants
Federal grants to state or local governments for more general purposes and with fewer restrictions than categorical grants.

devolution
The attempt to enhance the power of state or local governments, especially by replacing relatively restrictive categorical grants-in-aid with more flexible block grants.

Civil Rights versus States' Rights

Heated civil rights battles developed during the nation's transition from dual federalism to cooperative federalism in the middle of the past century. During this period, states, especially southern states, claimed the federal government was encroaching on states' rights, and no public policy area garnered more opposition from the southern states than civil rights issues.

During the period of dual federalism, the U.S. Supreme Court created the **separate but equal doctrine** in *Plessy* v. *Ferguson* (1896). The Court used a novel interpretation of the Fourteenth Amendment to protect "states' rights" when it held that segregation did not violate the constitutional requirement that no state shall deny any person the equal protection of the laws. It held that state and local governments could pass laws requiring racial segregation because, as long as physical facilities were equal for both races, African Americans were as separate from whites as whites were from African Americans. This interpretation ignored the intent in segregation laws to communicate a sense of social inferiority to African Americans by making it a crime for them to associate with whites. The Court also neglected the fact that the separate African American facilities were either clearly inferior to those enjoyed by whites or simply nonexistent.

The *Plessy* decision allowed continued discrimination against African Americans, and the decision's impact was felt throughout the South. In its aftermath, states enacted **Jim Crow laws**, which mandated racial segregation in almost every aspect of life.

After World War II, the separate but equal doctrine would slowly be weakened, and Texas contributed to this weakening by providing the setting for the Supreme Court case of *Sweatt* v. *Painter* (see Chapter 1). After graduating from Yates High School in Houston and Wiley College in Marshall, Texas, Heman Marion Sweatt, an African American student, hoped to go to law school in Texas. But at the time, the University of Texas at Austin law school did not admit African Americans. African American students from Texas who wanted to attend law school were told to go to schools out of state. The Supreme Court ruled that, in shifting its responsibilities to other states, the State of Texas was not providing separate accommodations—a requirement under the doctrine of separate but equal.

Sweatt v. *Painter* led to the creation of what are now Texas Southern University (TSU) and TSU's Thurgood Marshall School of Law (see Image 2.1). Although graduates of the Thurgood Marshall School of Law represent only 3 percent of the membership of the Texas state bar, they currently account for 14 percent of Texas attorneys who are members of ethnic or racial minorities.[13] Perhaps more significantly, *Sweatt* helped to further weaken the doctrine of separate but equal, paving the way for *Brown* v. *Board of Education* in 1954, which eventually reversed *Plessy* v. *Ferguson*.

Brown v. *Board of Education* would lead to the desegregation of schools as we discussed in Chapter 1. The Twenty-Fourth Amendment (which outlawed poll taxes), the Civil Rights Act of 1964, the Voting Rights Act of 1965, and many other laws that promoted equality would follow. The white political leadership in southern states generally saw such legislation as an encroachment on their sovereignty—or states' rights.

The Voting Rights Act of 1965 and its extensions in 1970, 1975, 1982, and 2006 required, under the law's Section 5, that a small number of states obtain

separate but equal doctrine

Doctrine that resulted from the Supreme Court ruling in *Plessy* v. *Ferguson* that legalized segregation.

Jim Crow laws

State and local laws that mandated racial segregation in almost every aspect of life.

IMAGE 2.1 TSU's Thurgood Marshall School of Law annually awards more JD degrees to members of ethnic/racial groups that are under-represented within the membership of the State Bar of Texas than any other law school in Texas.

Thurgood Marshall School of Law

★ CTQ   How does Texas society benefit from having more African American and Latino lawyers?

approval (referred to as **preclearance**) from either the U.S. Department of Justice or the U.S. District Court for the District of Columbia for any election law changes. Initially, six southern states (Alabama, Georgia, Louisiana, Mississippi, South Carolina, and Virginia) were included, along with selected counties and other local political districts in other states. In 1975, Alaska, Arizona, and Texas were added to this list when the Voting Rights Act (VRA) was expanded to include the protection of linguistic minorities (Asian Americans, Latinos, and Native Americans) in addition to racial minorities (African Americans).

Conservatives have long argued that the VRA violated the Tenth Amendment of the U.S. Constitution by singling out a small number of states, one being Texas, along with selected political subdivisions in other states for additional scrutiny and legal requirements under its Section 5. Furthermore, they objected to the formula used to determine which states and jurisdictions were required to seek preclearance, because the formula was based on electoral results and legislation from the 1960s and early 1970s, which did not reflect present-day conditions.

In 2013, the U.S. Supreme Court agreed with Alabama (where Shelby County is located), Texas, and other states in *Shelby County* v. *Holder* that the criteria (in Section 4 of the VRA) under which states were included in the preclearance group were out of date and needed to be updated in order for Section 5 to be applied. The Supreme Court did not find Section 5 to be unconstitutional, but unless Congress develops a new formula for placing state and local governments under the preclearance requirements, Section 5 is inoperative.

Controversy erupted after the Supreme Court's *Shelby* decision was announced. Some Texans were upset that the decision would allow Texas to implement its 2011 voter photo ID legislation, which a district court had ruled would depress minority voter turnout. The same district court had ruled that the redistricting plans passed by the Republican-controlled Texas Legislature in 2011 discriminated against minorities, and opponents of the *Shelby* decision feared that such practices in the future might go unchallenged. Many Democrats claimed that the passage of these discriminatory laws is evidence that the VRA is still needed in states like Texas. Most Republicans argued that these laws are not discriminatory; they are simply efforts to prevent voter fraud and engage in entirely legal partisan gerrymandering.

Texas's controversial voter ID law, which was denied preclearance in 2012 because it would have a disproportionately negative effect on Latino and African American voters, went into effect in 2013 when the Shelby decision relieved Texas from the preclearance requirement. Opponents continued to challenge the law, and in 2016 the U.S. Fifth Circuit Court of Appeals ruled it had a discriminatory impact. After an interim settlement was in force for the 2016 election, in 2017 the Texas Legislature passed a revised voter ID law that allows voters lacking an ID to still vote if they sign an affidavit and provide one of several non-photo alternatives as proof of residency. Democrats continued to challenge this new law, but it was eventually upheld on appeal in 2018.

While Section 4 remains unconstitutional, many Democrats have looked to Section 3 of the VRA to place Texas and other states back under preclearance. Section 3 provides a vehicle for voting rights advocates to have a state or other political subdivision placed under Section 5 (known as "bailing in") if they can prove in court that the jurisdiction in question has engaged in intentional discrimination against ethnic or racial minority voters. Because this type of overt discrimination is difficult to prove, these efforts represent the legal equivalent of a "Hail Mary pass," but represent one of their few viable options currently available.

preclearance
Any administrative or legislative change to the rules governing elections in covered states must be submitted for preapproval to either the U.S. Department of Justice or the U.S. District Court for the District of Columbia.

Did You Know? Texas was not included among the original six states required to seek preclearance in 1965 because the VRA's architect, President Lyndon Baines Johnson (LBJ), did not want his home state's reputation tarnished by being placed alongside states so strongly associated with racial discrimination and oppression as Alabama and Mississippi.[14]

Texas and the Federal System

LO 2.3 Analyze Texas's relationship with the federal government and the prominent role the state has played in the national debate over coercive federalism.

Some Texans interpret support for states' rights (or state sovereignty) as an effort to thwart civil rights for ethnic and racial minorities. However, other Texans see states' rights as reflecting a genuine concern with a growing federal government that they believe has simply become too large and powerful and now carries out functions that states could perform better—or that individuals can or should do for themselves. They are especially concerned with the coercive power of the federal government over both state governments and individuals.

So far we have been looking at the U.S. Constitution and how the national political and legal climates have affected the relative powers of the national and state governments. Now we will look at federalism from a Lone Star State perspective—at how the national government's powers have affected the state, at the role played by the state in our federal system, and at how Texas political leaders have coped with and reacted to the changing nature of U.S. federalism.

Coercive Federalism and Texas

coercive federalism
A relationship between the national government and states in which the former directs the states on policies they must undertake.

Many Texans would argue that a shift away from cooperative federalism has been under way since the late 1970s. This new form of federalism has been referred to as **coercive federalism**. Coercive federalism is defined as a relationship between the national government and states in which the former directs the states on policies they must undertake. In this shift to coercive federalism, the federal government has centralized more power and has increasingly obstructed the states when they attempt to pursue policies with which the federal government does not agree. Such encroachment on states has not been ideologically one sided. Federalism scholar John Kinkaid writes, "Liberals, lacking revenue for major new programs, and conservatives, lacking public support for major reductions in equity programs, switched from fiscal to regulatory tools."[15] Because neither liberals nor conservatives had the political support to expand or contract programs that promoted equity, lawmakers in Congress and the White House opted to enact new rules.

A classic example of federal encroachment using regulatory mechanisms was the passage of the National Minimum Drinking Age Act of 1984. The law required all states to set their minimum drinking age to at least 21 or run the risk of the federal government's reducing their federal highway construction funding by 10 percent (which today would represent about a half billion dollar cut for Texas), a reduction that would have a dramatic adverse impact on the state's infrastructure. As a result of the passage of this legislation, the approximately two-fifths of the states that were not in compliance raised their minimum drinking age to 21, including Texas, where it was increased from 19 to 21.

During his 14-year tenure in office between 2000 and 2015, former Governor Rick Perry frequently invoked the Tenth Amendment. Perry argued that the federal government has increasingly taken over more activities that were once the purview of state governments. A statement made by Perry during his final gubernatorial campaign nicely summarizes the current philosophy of a majority of Texas Republicans regarding the issue of state sovereignty:

> States are best positioned to deal with state issues, a fact the founding fathers had in mind when they included the 10th Amendment in the Bill of Rights. Over the years, that right has been clouded by ongoing federal encroachments that are reflected in a recent series of attempts by Washington to seize even more control over numerous Texas programs.[16]

Former Governor Perry and his successor, Governor Greg Abbott, both consider the Affordable Care Act of 2010, several Environmental Protection Agency regulations, cap-and-trade legislation efforts, and VRA enforcement as recent examples of the national government placing undue burdens on Texas.

Supporters of federal efforts see the national government as requiring Texas to do what it has been reluctant to do, such as protecting the environment and public health. For instance, environmentalists doubt the Texas Commission on Environmental Quality's (TCEQ) commitment to enforce air and water quality standards, and they believe meaningful state enforcement depends upon the federal threat to withhold transportation funding from states with lax environmental regulation.

Federal Grants-in-Aid in Texas

Grants from the federal government constitute the second largest source of revenue for the state of Texas after state taxes, and the percentage of the state's revenue provided by the federal government has grown in recent decades. In 1978, about a quarter of the state's revenue was supplied by the federal government. During the worst of the Great Recession, the percentage of state revenue accounted for by federal funds briefly exceeded 40 percent, reaching a peak of 42 percent in 2010 as a result of the federal government's stimulus efforts, before dropping back and settling at 33 percent in 2019. Figure 2.2 shows the percentage of Texas revenue coming from the federal government between 1978 and 2019. This growth can be explained in large part by the formulas the federal government uses to calculate need in a state. Texas's rapidly expanding population, a comparatively large low-income population, increasing health care costs, and a rapid rise in the number of senior citizens living in the state have contributed to this growth.

FIGURE 2.2 Percentage of Texas Revenue Coming from the Federal Government (1978–2019)

This figure shows that Texas, like most states, has become increasingly reliant on federal funding to finance state programs in the areas of education, health, and transportation.

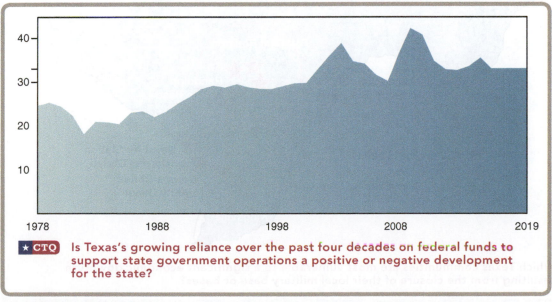

★ CTQ Is Texas's growing reliance over the past four decades on federal funds to support state government operations a positive or negative development for the state?

Source: Cengage Learning.

Indirect Federal Benefits: U.S. Military Bases in Texas

There are more active duty U.S. Air Force, Army, Marine Corps, and Navy personnel and civilian military workers in Texas than in every other state except California and Virginia. (Virginia's second place status is due to its proximity to Washington, D.C.) As of 2017 there were 138,000 active duty military personnel and 55,000 federal civilian defense employees at U.S. military bases in Texas.[17] The state's more than one dozen major and minor installations (see Figure 2.3), with their thousands of active duty troops and civilian workers, provide vital

---

FIGURE 2.3 Major U.S. Military Installations in Texas

This figure shows the location of the principal U.S. Armed Forces installations in the state of Texas. The bases are spread across the state from the Red River Army Depot in Texarkana near the Texas–Arkansas border to Fort Bliss in El Paso near the Texas–New Mexico border.

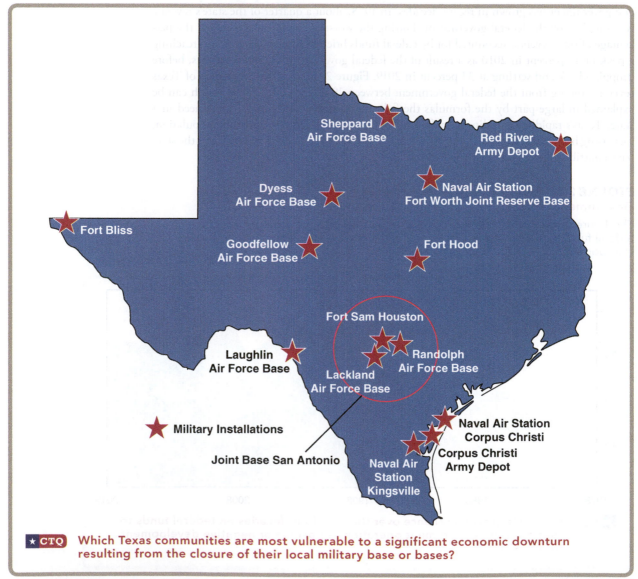

★ CTQ **Which Texas communities are most vulnerable to a significant economic downturn resulting from the closure of their local military base or bases?**

Source: Cengage Learning.

jobs and economic benefits to their communities. They represent an indirect way that the federal government, through its decisions on military staffing and spending, affects the economic health of Texas, annually contributing close to $140 billion to the state's economy.18

The largest three concentrations of soldiers and government civilian defense employees in Texas are in the San Antonio, Killeen–Temple, and El Paso metro areas. Joint Base San Antonio, comprising the Army's Fort Sam Houston, Lackland Air Force Base, and Randolph Air Force Base, leads the pack among the Texas installations. Combined, these three San Antonio installations have 47,000 active duty and 23,000 federal civilian personnel. Joint Base San Antonio is followed in numbers by the Army's Fort Hood in Killeen, with 39,000 active duty troops and 8,000 civilian employees. Among the units stationed at Fort Hood is the legendary 1st Cavalry Division. Third in size is the Army's Fort Bliss in El Paso, with 32,000 active duty troops and 9,000 civilian workers, which counts among its many units the 1st Armored Division. The impact of Fort Hood and Fort Bliss on the economic prosperity of their communities is more substantial than that of Joint Base San Antonio (which is still quite powerful), because the Killeen–Temple and El Paso metro areas where they are located have 470,000 and 910,000 residents, respectively, compared to the 2.5 million resident of the San Antonio metro area.

IMAGE 2.2 Texas's Army, Air Force, and Navy bases directly and indirectly create jobs that benefit communities throughout the state.

Mark P. Jones

Military bases and the economic benefits they generate are tightly linked to the level of prosperity of El Paso, Killeen–Temple, and San Antonio, as well as a half dozen other communities across the state: Abilene (Dyess Air Force Base), Corpus Christi–Kingsville (Corpus Christi Army Depot, Naval Air Station Corpus Christi, Naval Air Station Kingsville), Del Rio (Laughlin Air Force Base), San Angelo (Goodfellow Air Force Base), Texarkana (Red River Army Depot), and Wichita Falls (Sheppard Air Force Base). At the same time, two of the state's four largest metro areas, Austin and Houston, have no major military installation, and Dallas–Fort Worth (DFW) has only the relatively small (especially in the context of the 7.4 million person DFW Metroplex) Naval Air Station–Joint Reserve Base Fort Worth, with a combined active duty and civilian personnel total of only 4,000.

Since 1988, the U.S. federal government has carried out five rounds of its Base Realignment and Closure (BRAC) process. In the most recent round (2005), two Texas military bases—Naval Air Station Ingleside across the bay from Corpus Christi and Brooks Air Force Base in San Antonio—were BRAC casualties; the Red River Army Depot was also slated for closure, only to be rescued by then–U.S. Senator Kay Bailey Hutchison, who had previously come to the depot's rescue during the 1995 BRAC round. Another BRAC round is possible before the end of the decade, at which time several Texas bases could find themselves vulnerable to closure.

Unfunded Mandates

Unfunded mandates are obligations the federal government imposes on state governments while providing little or no funding to pay for the mandated activities. Even after enactment of the Unfunded Mandates Reform Act of 1995 during the administration of President Bill Clinton, the federal government has found ways of getting around the law. Loopholes and exemptions have made it possible for Congress to obligate Texas and other states to

unfunded mandates
Obligations the federal government imposes on state governments while providing little or no funds to pay for the mandated activities.

implement and pay for certain policies or risk losing federal funds. Former Governor Perry was especially critical of unfunded mandates, even criticizing President George W. Bush's No Child Left Behind Act for forcing the states to make changes to their educational systems without providing the federal funds needed to implement the program. Unfunded mandates allow elected officials to take credit for passing legislation while avoiding the hard and generally unpopular work of raising the revenue to fund the program created by the legislation.

The federal government is not the only level of government that adopts legislation containing unfunded mandates. The State of Texas also has created a fair number of unfunded mandates, requiring local governments and other public institutions, such as community colleges and universities, to take certain actions without providing these entities with adequate funds to implement the requirements.

One example of an unfunded mandate is the Hazlewood Legacy Act. In 2009, the Texas Legislature significantly expanded the 1929 Hazlewood Act. The Hazlewood Act exempted qualified veterans and dependent children of disabled or deceased veterans from paying tuition and fees at Texas public colleges and universities up to a maximum of 150 credit hours.

The 2009 Hazlewood Legacy Act allowed veterans to transfer their credit hours to their dependent children (under the age of 26),[19] which substantially increased the number of students benefiting from this measure. As a result of the expansion, the cost of the program increased from $25 million to as much as $379 million by 2019, with much of the cost to public colleges and universities passed on to tuition-paying students.

Although higher education leaders widely agreed with the spirit of the expansion, they complained that it represented an unfunded mandate, in which the Texas Legislature significantly expanded the number of students attending the schools (for free) without appropriating funds to cover the increased cost the schools would bear as a result of the arrival of these non-revenue-producing students on campus. The legislators were able to claim credit for the legislation without paying the costs associated with financing it.

Another example of an unfunded state mandate is a law passed by the Texas Legislature in 2015 (that went into effect in the fall of 2017), under which school districts can be required to install cameras in special education classrooms to prevent the mistreatment of special needs students. The law did not provide any state funds to support this mandate, meaning the school districts have to pay the full cost of the purchase, installation, maintenance, and monitoring of the cameras from their existing resources, with estimated costs in the larger districts ranging from $5 to $10 million.

The Affordable Care Act: A Challenging Case in Federalism

Probably no current controversy better illustrates the competing visions of our federal system than the ongoing debate over national health care reform. Shortly after the passage of the Patient Protection and Affordable Care Act (ACA or, as it is often popularly referred to, Obamacare), former Texas Attorney General Greg Abbott joined 25 other state attorneys general in opposing the new health care law. At issue, among other things, were the law's mandate that individuals purchase health insurance and the requirement that the states expand Medicaid coverage.

The ACA's Medicaid expansion required the states to expand Medicaid coverage to people under 65 (those 65 and older have access to Medicare) earning up to 138 percent of the federal poverty level (see Chapter 12). Under the legislation signed into law by President Obama in 2010, the federal government covers the entire cost of this expansion for the first three years before gradually reducing the federal contribution to 90 percent of the cost in 2020 and beyond. In the original law, states that did not opt in to the Medicaid expansion could face the loss of all of their Medicaid funds. A total of 26 states formally challenged the constitutionality of the Medicaid expansion, 13 filed *amicus* briefs with the U.S. Supreme Court in

IMAGE 2.3 The Affordable Care Act is a recent example of the expansion of the national government that has met with resistance. Texas was one of many states that challenged the constitutionality of the program. Ultimately, the U.S. Supreme Court upheld the ACA under the national government's power to tax and spend.

Chip Somodevilla/Getty Images News/Getty Images

★ CTQ   Why has resistance to the ACA been so intense in Texas?

support of the expansion, and in two states the governor and attorney general took opposing sides on this issue.

The limits on what Congress can do are stipulated in Article I, Section 8 of the U.S. Constitution. Among Congress's powers is the power to regulate commerce. It is this authority that Congress used to justify the ACA. Congress argued that because it has the power to regulate commerce, and the buying of health insurance is a commercial activity, Congress has the power to regulate health care coverage.

Some disagreed that the ACA regulated commerce and concluded that it infringed on states' rights. Although it is the case that some powers are shared between the states and the federal government, others are exclusive to either one or the other. For example, the power to regulate commerce is granted to Congress. The power to provide for the public health and safety is a power reserved to the states by the Tenth Amendment.

Former Attorney General Abbott argued in his *amicus* brief that the ACA did not regulate commerce, but rather that it created policing authority that is generally the purview of the states. In June 2012, in the case of the *National Federation of Independent Business* v. *Sebelius*, the U.S. Supreme Court, led by Chief Justice John Roberts, rejected the federal government's claim that the commerce clause allowed Congress to create the individual mandate. But, Roberts argued, the "penalty" that the law required be paid to the Internal Revenue Service (IRS), is in actuality a "tax," which Congress has the power to levy. As a result, the most controversial aspect of the law—the individual mandate—was deemed constitutional.

At the same time, however, the Supreme Court found that the ACA's requirement that the states expand access to Medicaid or suffer the potential penalty of losing all Medicaid funding was excessively coercive and, therefore, unconstitutional. This ruling removed a major pillar of the ACA and has left a little more than four million Americans without health insurance in those states that have opted not to expand their Medicaid coverage in line with the ACA.

Nowhere was the impact of this ruling more strongly felt than in Texas. Because Texas has, at least for the time being, opted out of the Medicaid expansion, 1.2 million Texans are not eligible to for health coverage under Medicaid; if Texas had opted in (as was the case in California, New York, and other states), these Texans would be eligible for health coverage through Medicaid.[20] And, because the ACA provides health care subsidies only to individuals with incomes more than 138 percent of the federal poverty level, 638,000 of these 1.2 million Texans are ineligible for federal government subsidies to purchase health care coverage through the federally operated health care exchange in Texas. As a consequence, more than 600,000 Texans find themselves today in a health care purgatory known as the "coverage gap"—too wealthy to qualify for Medicaid and too poor to qualify for federal health insurance subsidies.[21]

Figure 2.4 shows that Texas is one of 15 primarily southern and Great Plains states that decided not to expand their Medicaid coverage under the ACA.[22] In contrast, 35 states and Washington, D.C., had decided to move forward with the expansion. The 15 states that have

---

FIGURE 2.4 The Status of State Medicaid Expansion under the ACA

This figure highlights that Texas is among the minority of U.S. states that at the present time have opted not to participate in the ACA-linked expansion of Medicaid.

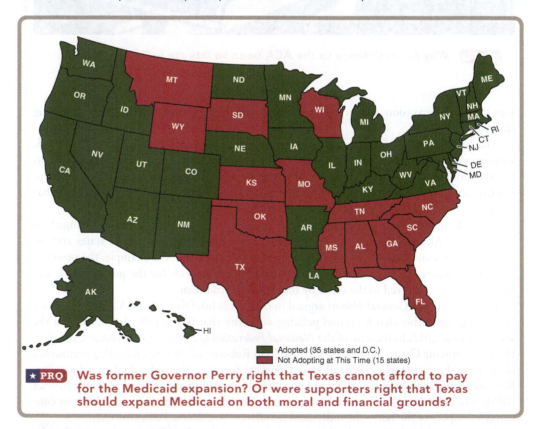

Adopted (35 states and D.C.)
Not Adopting at This Time (15 states)

★ PRQ   **Was former Governor Perry right that Texas cannot afford to pay for the Medicaid expansion? Or were supporters right that Texas should expand Medicaid on both moral and financial grounds?**

Source: Cengage Learning.

not expanded Medicaid contain 4.1 million people, more than one-quarter of them Texans, who would have been insured if their state had opted into the ACA Medicaid expansion.

Former Governor Perry, current Governor Abbott, and other Texas opponents of Medicaid expansion argue the state cannot afford to pay 10 percent of the cost of this expansion in 2020 and beyond. They also believe the current Medicaid system is broken and expanding it is "like putting 1,000 more people on the *Titanic* when you knew what was going to happen."[23] Finally, they also highlight that fewer and fewer doctors are accepting Medicaid patients in Texas and question the wisdom of adding 1.2 million patients to a system in which Medicaid patients already find it very difficult to schedule appointments with doctors.

Supporters of Medicaid expansion argue that not expanding adversely affects the health of over a million Texans who lack insurance as a result of the decision not to expand Medicaid. Of course, many of these 1.2 million people when ill or injured will seek care in the state's hospitals, hospitals that will send them bills that most will never be able to pay. But these debts will not be fully absorbed by the hospitals, and in the end the bills will be paid indirectly by homeowners in the form of taxes to their local hospital districts and by Texans with private health insurance and Texas employers in the form of higher insurance premiums, instead of by the federal government in the form of additional Medicaid payments. Had Texas expanded Medicaid, it would have seen in 2016 alone an increase in federal expenditures to support the expansion in the amount of $7 billion, along with $3 billion more for Texas hospitals in the form of reimbursement for care that is currently uncompensated.[24]

The controversy surrounding the ACA is an excellent example of the friction that can arise between the federal government and the states. This friction is generated by differences in opinions revolving around the proper balance of power between the federal and state governments. This balance is in turn determined by a combination of the rules laid out in the Constitution, in statute, and in the interpretation of these rules by our elected officials and especially our appointed federal judges. We can see that Texas has played an active role in the constant redefining of the concept of federalism, a topic we explore in greater detail in the following pages.

Texas and the U.S. Abortion Debate: From *Roe* to *Whole Woman's Health*

Not only has the U.S. Congress acted to expand the power of the federal government, the federal courts have done so as well. As the federal courts have expanded the scope of rights guaranteed under the Fourteenth Amendment, state action has come under increasing court scrutiny. For example, in 1973, the U.S. Supreme Court ruled in *Roe* v. *Wade* that women have the right to an abortion.

In 2016, 43 years after the *Roe* decision, the Supreme Court, in arguably its most significant abortion-related ruling since *Roe*, used a Texas case to place a limit on efforts by state legislatures in more than a dozen states to restrict women's access to abortion with the goal of reducing the number of abortions that take place in their respective state. The *Whole Woman's Health* v. *Hellerstedt* case placed Texas once again in the national spotlight, highlighting both the ongoing tension between the federal courts and the states and Texas's continued prominent role in this high-profile federal–state dispute.

Prior to 1973, every state enforced its own legislation on abortion, with abortion being legal in a relatively small number of states (and even there only during the latter half of the 1960s), such as New York and Washington, and illegal in an overwhelming majority of the states, including Texas. In 1973, the U.S. Supreme Court, in *Roe* v. *Wade*, declared that Texas's legislation making abortion illegal (except when the mother's life was in danger) was unconstitutional. This landmark ruling, which was based in large part on the Supreme Court justices' belief that the Texas legislation violated a woman's constitutional right to privacy, effectively made abortion through the second trimester of pregnancy legal throughout the country. Pro-choice activists had filed the suit on behalf of a pregnant Texas woman named Norma McCorvey. McCorvey used the pseudonym Norma Roe and the case was filed in Dallas, making the Dallas County district attorney at the time, Henry Wade, the defendant in the suit.

During the 2013 legislative session, Texas once again vaulted to the national stage as the result of the debate over legislation that would place some of the strictest restrictions in the nation on the practice of abortion. In June 2013, this legislation was scuttled on the final night of the 30-day special session by then–State Senator Wendy Davis's 12½-hour filibuster, which brought national attention, including tweets by President Obama and Vice President Joe Biden supporting Davis, to the Texas abortion debate, and to Davis herself. Davis's victory, however, was only temporary; former Governor Perry quickly called a second special legislative session, where with ample time the Republican Party's legislative majorities guaranteed passage of the bill (HB2).

Among other things, the new law prohibited abortions after 20 post-fertilization weeks (unless needed to avoid the mother's death or serious physical injury), required abortion clinic physicians to have admitting privileges at a hospital located within 30 miles of the clinic, placed greater restrictions on the use of abortion-inducing drugs, and mandated that all abortion clinics meet the same standards as ambulatory surgical centers (ASCs).

When HB2 passed, in July 2013, Texas had 40 abortion clinics located in cities throughout the state, including three cities in South Texas (Corpus Christi, Harlingen, and McAllen) and four in West Texas (El Paso, Lubbock, Midland, and San Angelo). One year later, in July 2014, that number had been reduced to 21, and by March 2016 it dropped to 19.

HB2 had been designed to go fully into force in September 2014, which was the final date by which clinics had to remodel or move to meet ASC standards. However, a lawsuit filed by Whole Woman's Health, a major Texas abortion provider with clinics in Fort Worth, McAllen, and San Antonio (its clinics in Austin and Beaumont were closed after the passage of HB2), delayed full implementation of the law.

Opponents of HB2 argued it was designed to make it much more difficult for women to obtain abortions by significantly reducing the number of clinics in Texas and requiring many women to travel long distances, often at a substantial cost. Proponents of HB2 countered that the goal of the law was solely to protect women's health. They further stated that the reduction in the number of clinics and cities with clinics did not significantly hinder a woman's ability to obtain an abortion in Texas.

In 1992 the U.S. Supreme Court, in what is widely referred to as the *Casey* case, concluded that although states had a right to regulate abortion, they could not use these regulations to place an "undue burden" on a woman's access to abortion. In June 2016 the U.S. Supreme Court issued perhaps its most significant abortion-related ruling since *Roe*, a status that until that time had been occupied by *Casey*. In *Whole Woman's Health* v. *Hellerstedt* (Dr. John Hellerstedt is the commissioner of the Texas Department of State Health Services), the court ruled that the HB2 requirements that Texas clinics meet ASC standards and that doctors performing abortions have admitting privileges at local hospitals were unconstitutional. The majority of the justices agreed with the plaintiff that the law placed an undue burden on women, and the Court overturned the ASC and admitting privilege requirements. As a result, instead of having only 10 abortion clinics located solely in Austin, Dallas–Fort Worth, Houston, and San Antonio (which would have been the case had HB2 been ruled constitutional), Texas has 17 clinics in these four major metro areas as well as two in El Paso and one each in McAllen and Waco. The legislature, however, partially succeeded in reducing abortion access because the overwhelming majority of the clinics that closed following the passage of HB2 have not reopened.

States as Laboratories: Marijuana Legalization

Despite the growth in national government power, states remain a vital part of our federal system. States continue to take the initiative in several areas of public policy. And as they do so, states can adopt innovative new policies without committing the whole nation to them. Thus states serve as public policy laboratories, providing insights on how well different policies actually work when taken from theory to practice. Successful policies are likely to be adopted by other states; failures are likely to be shelved or revised significantly by states that were contemplating adoption of the same policy.

One example of recent state innovation and experimentation has been in the area of drug policy. In November 2012, voters in Colorado and Washington decided to make an audacious move to change state drug policy by legalizing the sale of recreational marijuana to those 21 years of age and older and regulating and taxing the production and sale of marijuana. In both states, citizens obtained signatures to place the reforms on the ballot, an option that does not exist in Texas. Although national laws continue to forbid them, retail sales began in both states and, so far, the federal government has acquiesced. Similar referendums were later passed by Alaska, Oregon, California, Maine, Massachusetts, Michigan, and Nevada. The Vermont Legislature also legalized possession of marijuana for recreational use but does not allow its commercial sale, a policy also followed in Washington, D.C.

These cases will provide crucial evidence on the economic, legal, and social consequences of marijuana legalization. They will help answer questions that today are mostly a matter of conjecture, such as the impact of legalization and associated taxes and regulation on the market for illegal marijuana, on the use of marijuana by adolescents, on the abuse of marijuana, on the number of people driving under the influence of marijuana, on the number of individuals penalized and incarcerated for possession, and on the amount of tax revenue generated from marijuana production and sales. Other states can use this information to decide whether or not to proceed with legalization efforts and how best to design legislation if they do move forward.

Although these ten states are in the vanguard of marijuana legalization efforts, depending on the outcomes of their experiments, they may not be alone for long. In 1996, California became the first state to

IMAGE 2.4 Several states have legalized recreational marijuana, with commercial stores such as this one openly selling the product to adults.

David Ryder/Getty Images News/Getty Images

legalize the medical use of marijuana to treat a wide range of illnesses. Since then, due in part to the success of the California experiment, 32 other states have adopted similar medical marijuana legislation, but Texas has not. Its compassionate use law applies only to rare epilepsy cases.

In contrast to California, where the possession of up to an ounce of marijuana for personal use is now legal, in Texas the possession of a similar quantity of marijuana is a Class B misdemeanor, punishable by up to 180 days in prison and a fine of up to $2,000. However, there is presently some movement in Texas at the county level toward de facto decriminalization but not full legalization. For instance, Harris County's First Chance Intervention Program allows first-time offenders accused of possessing 2 ounces or less of marijuana to avoid any criminal charges by completing eight hours of community service or taking an eight-hour cognitive class.

How Does Texas Compare?

Marijuana Legalization and Decriminalization: How Does Texas Compare?

Ten states and the District of Columbia have legalized the recreational use of marijuana (Figure 2.5). An additional 14 states have decriminalized the possession of small amounts of marijuana, with those found in possession of marijuana generally subject to a small civil penalty, similar to that received when a person commits a minor traffic violation. In contrast, in the remaining 26 states, recreational users of marijuana run the risk of arrest and jail time, with the prospects for jail time especially high for repeat offenders.

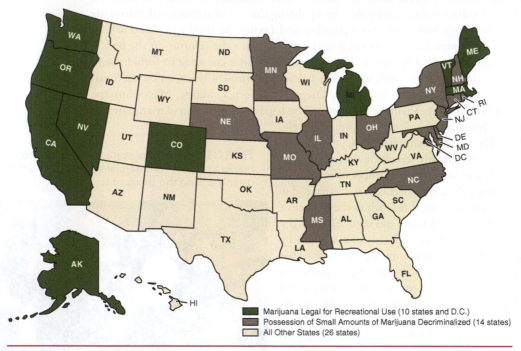

■ Marijuana Legal for Recreational Use (10 states and D.C.)
■ Possession of Small Amounts of Marijuana Decriminalized (14 states)
☐ All Other States (26 states)

FIGURE 2.5 Marijuana Legalization and Decriminalization in the States

Source: National Organization for the Reform of Marijuana Laws (NORML).

FOR DEBATE

★ PRQ Is it a problem that Americans in some states can legally purchase marijuana for recreational use while other Americans purchasing and using the same amount of marijuana can be jailed and/or have a misdemeanor or felony charge on their record for life? Or is this simply an example of how a federal system works in practice, with individual states having a say on which policies they embrace and which policies they reject?

★ PRQ What should be Texas's position on recreational marijuana use: legalize, decriminalize, or continue the status quo in which the recreational use of marijuana remains illegal and subject to criminal prosecution?

Federalism and Casino Gambling

Our federal system allows the nation's 50 states to adopt different laws in a wide range of policy areas—legislation that often reflects the distinct preferences and values of the state's residents. As a result, even states that share borders (see Figure 2.6) can have policies that differ noticeably regarding the same activity. One such example can be seen today when crossing the Texas border into Louisiana, Oklahoma, or New Mexico: the presence of casinos clustered along the Texas border, especially in those parts of Oklahoma and Louisiana nearest the heavily populated Texas metro areas of Dallas–Fort Worth (DFW) and Houston. This clustering is easy to explain: Although neighboring Louisiana, Oklahoma, and New Mexico have over the past 30 years passed legislation allowing casino gambling to flourish, Texas continues to maintain a ban on casino gambling.

Unlike in neighboring Louisiana, New Mexico, and Oklahoma, Class III gambling (generally referred to as casino gambling), principally blackjack, roulette, and slot machines, is constitutionally prohibited throughout the Lone Star State. At present, Texas has only three small Tribal Class II gaming facilities. They are operated by the Kickapoo outside of Eagle Pass, by the Alabama-Coushatta near Livingston, and by the Tigua in El Paso on tribal land under the authority of the federal Indian Gaming Regulatory Act. Class II facilities are restricted to poker, bingo, and bingo-related pull-tab machines designed to look like slot

---

FIGURE 2.6 Casinos Proximate to the Texas Border in Neighboring States

This map highlights the large number of Louisiana, New Mexico, and Oklahoma casinos clustered on their border with Texas along major interstate highways. These locations allow the casinos to attract gamblers from major population centers in Texas.

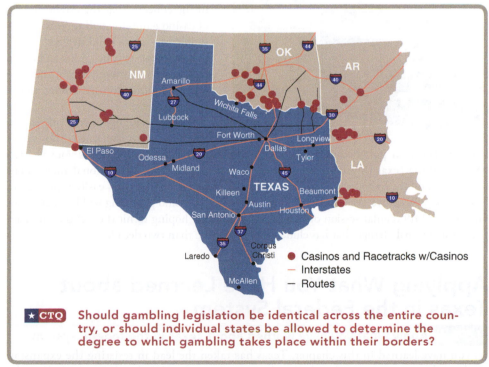

★ CTQ Should gambling legislation be identical across the entire country, or should individual states be allowed to determine the degree to which gambling takes place within their borders?

Sources: Let Texans Decide and Casino City.

machines. The Alabama-Coushatta and the Tigua (Ysleta del Sur Pueblo) gained federal recognition after the Kickapoo, when different federal rules relating to gambling were in force. Both tribes had been seeking the right to operate a Class II gaming facility like the Kickapoo for more than a dozen years, and in the fall of 2015 the federal National Indian Gaming Commission issued a decision allowing both tribes to operate Class II facilities like the Kickapoo. As a result, Class II gaming facilities are presently in operation on Alabama-Coushatta and Tigua tribal land: the Naskila and Speaking Rock casinos, respectively.

Proponents of casino gambling in Louisiana, New Mexico, and Oklahoma point to the economic benefits of casinos, ranging from job creation and tourism to tax revenue. In Texas, advocates for casinos highlight the flow of wealth out of Texas to neighboring states, wealth that would mostly remain in Texas if the state allowed casinos to be built. One study (by a pro-casino group) found that vehicles with Texas license plates accounted for approximately 40 percent to 90 percent of the cars in casino parking lots located within 50 miles of the Texas border.[25]

IMAGE 2.5 The WinStar World Casino and Resort, one of the country's largest casinos, is located in rural Oklahoma, just three miles north of the Texas–Oklahoma border along I-35, a short 60- to 90-minute drive from the DFW Metroplex.

Ian Dagnall/Alamy Stock Photo

The maintenance of the Texas ban on casino gambling is due in large part to two principal sources of opposition, combined with internal disputes among the pro-gambling forces. The first is opposition based on moral principles, with a significant minority of Texans viewing gambling as a vice and believing it to be morally wrong for the state to sanction casino gambling. A second form of opposition is grounded in the concern that the establishment of casino gambling will increase social problems such as child neglect, crime, domestic violence, evictions and home foreclosures, job absenteeism, and poverty stemming from gambling addiction and abuse.

Until now, opponents of casino gambling have retained the upper hand in Texas, in part because of the relatively steep hurdle—a two-thirds vote in each chamber of the Texas Legislature—needed to place the necessary constitutional amendment referendum on the ballot, a referendum opinion polls suggest would pass easily if put before Texas voters. What we can be sure of is that advocates of casino gambling will be back again during the 2019 regular session of the Texas Legislature, hoping to hit the jackpot and pass the constitutional change that has eluded them for more than two decades.

Applying What You Have Learned about Texas in the Federal System

LO 2.4   **Apply what you have learned about Texas in the federal system.**

As you have learned in this chapter, Texas has taken the lead in resisting the expansion of the federal government by challenging a variety of national policies, including the Affordable Care Act and several environmental regulations, in court. So, we invited

Governor Greg Abbott to explain his energetic opposition to these federal programs both as the state's attorney general and now as governor. After you have read the governor's essay, we will ask you to apply what you have learned about the principles of federalism to Abbott's views and to evaluate the real-world operation of American federalism in practice.

As you read Governor Abbott's essay, you will find that, like many Texans, he holds a conservative view of the role of the federal government. Contrary to the governor's view, liberals generally believe that the national government has grown to fulfill basic public needs that states have been unwilling or unable to meet and that the U.S. Constitution gives the federal government broad power to regulate the economy through its power to regulate interstate commerce and to fund a broad range of public services through its power to tax and spend to promote the general welfare.

Greg Abbott is the 48th governor of Texas. Prior to assuming office as governor in 2015, he was the longest serving attorney general in Texas history (2002–2015), a justice on the Texas Supreme Court (1996–2001), and a state district court judge in Harris County (1993–1995). During his tenure in public office Abbott has been a vocal defender of what he sees as the constitutional principles on which Texas and the United States were founded. His wife of 37 years, Cecilia Abbott, is the first Hispanic First Lady of Texas.

POLITICS IN PRACTICE
Texas in the Federal System

by Greg Abbott
GOVERNOR OF TEXAS

As opposed to some nations that were created by conquerors, the United States was established by defenders of liberty. Our Founders fought against a distant government that dictated too much of their lives and taxed them too much. After winning the Revolutionary War, our Founders wanted to ensure an enduring nation that secured freedom for its people. That freedom is the crux of the U.S. Constitution.

Our Founders knew then what we still realize today: if government is not controlled and limited it will sap your freedom. The Founders instilled that control through the balance of powers between the legislative, executive and judicial branches of government. Importantly, essential checks on the federal government were enshrined in the Bill of Rights to protect the people and States from an overreaching federal government.

The Bill of Rights includes the Tenth Amendment, which states: "The powers not delegated to the United States by the Constitution, nor prohibited by it to the States, are reserved to the States respectively, or to the people." The people of the United States created a government by giving it limited authority over their lives and retaining most of the authority to themselves and the states where they live.

As James Madison explained, "powers delegated by the proposed Constitution to the federal government, are few and defined. Those which are to remain in the State governments are numerous and indefinite." The framers believed that States could be trusted with "numerous and indefinite" powers because they were closer (and hence more accountable) to the people. By contrast, Great Britain had illustrated all too well the perils of investing sweeping powers in the less-accountable central government.

The framers knew there could come a time when the federal government they created would overstep its bounds, and it would fall to the States to fight back against federal encroachments. Madison, one of the Constitution's lead architects, warned: "I believe there are more instances of the abridgement of freedom of the people by gradual and silent encroachments by those in power than by violent and sudden usurpations."

He was right. By gradual encroachments, all three branches of the federal government have exceeded the powers granted them by the Constitution. In doing so, they have abridged your freedom. For example, Congress has abandoned the limitations on its enumerated powers and instead is regulating every aspect of your life. The President uses unilateral lawmaking—like executive orders and administrative regulations—to circumvent the engines of democracy altogether. The Supreme Court often ignores the plain text of the Constitution and sometimes makes up provisions that appear nowhere in that document.

As Texas Attorney General, I brought more than 30 lawsuits to challenge such federal overreach. Even courtroom victories, however, are inadequate to achieve permanent solutions to the federal government's systematic expansion of its powers far beyond what the framers intended.

The consequences were predictable. With each passing year upward mobility is becoming more challenging because our independence is being sapped by a centralized government that erodes our freedom and limits the aspiration that elevated this great nation.

Our broken federal system today stems from our collective indifference to the limits the Constitution places on the federal government, and our collective submission to unaccountable bureaucrats and judges who make and enforce today's federal laws. We have effectively submitted ourselves to the rule of men and abandoned the rule of law on which our nation was built.

We face constitutional problems that call for a constitutional solution. The Founders gave us a tool to deal with these challenges. It is in Article V of the Constitution that empowers the States to amend the Constitution to rein in an overreaching federal government.

America was born as a nation in search of one thing: freedom to chart our own pathway. For America to remain the freest nation in history, it is essential to remember that *you*—not some distant government—are the architect of your future. Never relinquish that principle. Use the tool the Founders gave you in Article V to secure your freedom. Using the Article V amendment process, we can reaffirm the framers' faith in strong States as the primary protectors of the people and their liberties.

1. Which of these categories best describes the governor's view of federalism: dual federalism, cooperative federalism, or coercive federalism? Explain why his views fit into this category.
2. What explains the growing scope of the federal government? Do you agree or disagree with Governor Abbott that this encroachment is a serious problem that is best remedied via an amendment to the U.S. Constitution to limit the national government's power?

★ Chapter Summary

LO 2.1 Differentiate among unitary, confederal, and federal systems of government. Federalism is a system of government in which power is constitutionally divided between a national government and state or regional governments. It differs from unitary systems of government, in which power is centralized in the hands of the national government, and confederal systems of government, in which the national government exercises only those powers delegated to it by the confederation's member states.

LO 2.2 Distinguish among the types of powers in our federal system, and explain dual and cooperative federalism within the context of the evolution of federalism in the United States. The view of how much power should be granted to each level of government has changed considerably over our nation's history. During the earliest constitutional period, U.S. Supreme Court Chief Justice John Marshall took a broad view of national powers. By the 1830s, a concept of dual federalism developed in which the national government was limited and distinctly separate from the states, but that view changed in the 1930s when the New Deal began to offer extensive grants-in-aid to the states to help finance common national programs—the basis for cooperative federalism. Since the 1970s, some states, especially conservative ones, have come to resent national government mandates and conditions for receiving federal grants; they view today's federal–state relationship as coercive federalism.

LO 2.3 Analyze Texas's relationship with the federal government and the prominent role the state has played in the national debate over coercive federalism. Texas has contributed to shaping this concept of federalism not only by bringing key Supreme Court cases to the debate, but also because the state's current political leadership has actively participated in the debate. Many Republican leaders in Texas, from former Governor Perry to Governor Abbott, have raised concerns about the impact that the federal government may have on Texas, basing their position for greater state sovereignty on the Tenth Amendment and those other powers reserved to the states in the Constitution. The current debate over health care reform fits into the broader debate over states' rights that has taken place throughout our country's history.

LO 2.4 Apply what you have learned about Texas in the federal system. You used your critical thinking skills to evaluate the views of one of the most important practitioners of Texas politics, Governor Abbott. His essay concludes that, over time, the federal government has gradually encroached more and more in policy areas that he believes the U.S. Constitution reserved for the states. In order to rein in what he views as an overreaching national government, Abbott proposes that the states join together to use the Article V amendment process to modify the Constitution with the goal of reasserting the equality if not primacy of the states in our system of government.

Key Terms

block grants, *p. 35*
categorical grants, *p. 35*
coercive federalism, *p. 38*
commerce clause, *p. 33*
concurrent powers, *p. 32*
confederal system, *p. 30*
cooperative federalism, *p. 35*

delegated powers, *p. 32*
devolution, *p. 35*
dual federalism, *p. 34*
expressed powers, *p. 32*
federal system, *p. 31*
implied powers, *p. 32*
inherent powers, *p. 32*
Jim Crow laws, *p. 36*

necessary and proper clause, *p. 33*
preclearance, *p. 37*
reserved powers, *p. 32*
separate but equal doctrine, *p. 36*
supremacy clause, *p. 32*
Tenth Amendment, *p. 32*

unfunded mandates, *p. 41*
unitary system, *p. 30*

Review Questions

LO 2.1 Differentiate among unitary, confederal, and federal systems of government.

- What distinguishes a federal system of government from both a unitary system of government and a confederal system of government?

- What are the advantages and disadvantages of each type of system of government?

- What would be the pros and cons of replacing our country's current federal system with a unitary system? What would be the pros and cons of replacing it with a confederal system?

LO 2.2 Distinguish among the types of powers in our federal system, and explain dual and cooperative federalism within the context of the evolution of federalism in the United States.

- Explain the difference between delegated and reserved powers, and give examples of each. What is the importance of Article I, Section 8 and the Tenth Amendment in the U.S. Constitution? Define and give examples of exclusive and concurrent powers.

- What is the significance of the implied powers clause and of the necessary and proper clause?

- Explain how the national government has used the necessary and proper clause and the commerce clause to expand the scope of its power. Explain how the dominant concepts of federalism in the United States have changed as the political and legal climate has changed.

- Describe the differences between the concepts of dual federalism and cooperative federalism. What historical developments led to the expansion of national government power?

- Explore the role the national government has played in the advancement of civil rights, environmental protection, and public health. Should the federal government be allowed to use Section 5 of the VRA to provide extra oversight of changes in Texas election laws?

LO 2.3 Analyze Texas's relationship with the federal government and the prominent role the state has played in the national debate over coercive federalism.

- Explain the concept of coercive federalism.

- How does the current debate over the ACA health care reform legislation reflect growing tension in the era of coercive federalism between the federal government on one hand and the state governments on the other, particularly in those instances when the federal political leadership and the political leadership in a specific state or group of states do not see eye to eye on a policy issue?

- Evaluate the arguments for states' rights and the argument that has become increasingly common during the current era of coercive federalism that the national government's powers should be limited. What role has Texas played in recent efforts to limit national government power?

- Assess the claims that states serve as policy laboratories in a federal system and that federalism allows public policy to best reflect the unique and diverse interests of citizens across the 50 states.

Think Critically and Get Active!

Learn more about the debates over federalism. Consider joining the American Constitution Society for Law and Policy or the Federalist Society. Student membership rates are affordable. You may consider attending meetings and, if possible, presenting student research papers at those meetings. Joining may also give your résumé a little more cachet. Be aware that the American Constitution Society is a progressive organization, and the Federalist Society is a conservative and libertarian organization. To learn more and join, explore the following:

- Visit the American Constitution Society at **www.acslaw.org** and read more about them. Membership for students is $10.

- View the Federalist Society at **www.fedsoc.org** and read more about them. Membership for students is $5.

- Watch videos from the American Constitution Society (**www.acslaw.org/multimedia**) and the Federalist Society (**www.fedsoc.org/commentary**), and follow them on Twitter (@acslaw; @FedSoc). These videos

and Twitter feeds will provide you with different perspectives on a host of current issues that feature prominently in the ongoing debate over the functioning of federalism in the United States.

Find out how federalism affects the right to vote. Discover more about voting rights and electoral transparency in Texas. Check out the liberal-leaning Brennan Center for Justice website (**www.brennancenter.org**) and the conservative-leaning Texas-based True the Vote website (**www.truethevote.org**). Follow each organization on Twitter (@BrennanCenter; @TrueTheVote).

Learn more about Texas military bases and their economic impact. Go to the Texas Comptroller's **www .comptroller.texas.gov/economy/economic-data/ military/** as well as the sites of specific U.S. military bases, such as Fort Hood (**www.hood.army.mil**), Fort Bliss (**www.bliss.army.mil**), and Joint Base San Antonio (**www.jbsa.mil**).

Explore the social issues facing federalism. Get more information about marijuana legalization efforts nationwide at **www.norml.org**, a website run by advocates of marijuana legalization, and in Texas at **www.texasnorml.org**. Learn more about efforts to permit casino gambling in Texas at the pro-gambling **www.lettexansdecide.com** as well as about efforts to prevent the expansion of gambling at the anti-gambling **www.stoppredatorygambling/org**.

Follow them on Twitter (@NORML; @TexasNORML; @LetTexansDecide; @SPGambling), and search for websites of organizations opposing marijuana legalization in the Lone Star State.

★ **PRQ**   Texans spent close to $3 billion in 2016 gambling in neighboring states. Should Texas legalize casino gambling to keep as many of these gambling dollars in the state as possible and to draw gamblers from beyond the state's borders? Or are the negative social consequences and moral issues associated with gambling so profound that Texans are best served by the state's not climbing aboard the "casino gambling train"?

3

The Texas Constitution in Perspective

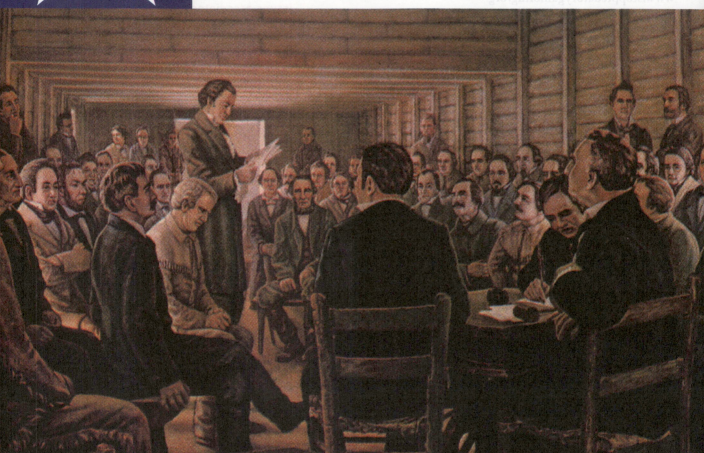

Since the Convention of 1836 met at Washington-on-the-Brazos (as depicted here), Texas has had six constitutions. In this chapter, we will explore how Texas's constitutions have evolved and how its current constitution affects us today.
The Star of the Republic Museum

Learning Objectives

LO 3.1 Explain the origins of the Texas Constitution and the Constitutional Convention of 1875.

LO 3.2 Describe the major constitutional structures, functions, and limits of Texas's legislative, executive, and judicial branches.

LO 3.3 Explain the process of amending and revising the Texas Constitution and the reasons that amendments are frequently necessary.

LO 3.4 Apply what you have learned about the Texas Constitution.

The real character of a government is determined less by the provisions of its constitution than by the hearts and minds of its citizens. Government is a process of decision-making conditioned by its history, its people, and pressures exerted by citizens, interest groups, and political parties.

Still, our national, state, and local governments would be vastly different were it not for their constitutions. Although the exact meaning of constitutional provisions may be disputed, there is general agreement that constitutions should be respected as the legal basis controlling the fundamentals of government decision-making. Constitutions serve as a rationalization for the actions of legislatures, executives, and courts—and of the people themselves. Indeed, the very idea of having a written constitution has become part of the political culture—the basic system of political beliefs in the United States.

Constitutions establish major governing institutions, assign them power, and place both implicit and explicit limits on the power they have assigned. They give governments a legal basis for existing and, because Americans respect constitutions, they promote **legitimacy**—the general public acceptance of government's "right to govern."

legitimacy
General public acceptance of government's "right to govern."

Texas Constitutions in History

LO 3.1 **Explain the origins of the Texas Constitution and the Constitutional Convention of 1875.**

Like all constitutions, the first Texas constitutions reflected the interests and concerns of the people who wrote and amended them. Many of their elements paralleled those of existing state constitutions; others were at the time unique to the Lone Star State.

Early Texas Constitutions

The constitution of the Texas Republic and the first state constitution of Texas were products of the plantation culture of Anglo Protestant slaveholders. These early constitutions adopted some institutions from Texans' experiences during Spanish and Mexican rule and forthrightly rejected others.

Republic of Texas Constitution The first Texas Constitution after independence from Mexico was written in 1836 for the Republic of Texas. In reaction to the prominent influence of the Catholic Church during Mexican rule, the largely Protestant Texans wrote a constitution with careful separation of church and state, forbidding clergymen of any faith from holding office. Opposing Mexico's antislavery policies, Texans made it illegal for masters to free their own slaves without the consent of the Republic's congress and denied citizenship to descendants of Africans and Native Americans. Remembering the abuses of the dictatorial Mexican military and political leader Antonio López de Santa Anna, Texans limited the terms of their presidents to three years and prohibited them from being elected to consecutive terms.

The Republic of Texas Constitution did adopt some provisions from Spanish and Mexican laws. It recognized **homesteads**, owner-occupied properties protected from forced sale under most circumstances. It also enshrined the concept of **community property**, which means that property acquired during marriage is owned equally by both spouses. These elements of Mexican law would later be absorbed into American political culture as other states adopted similar provisions.

Still, the Republic's constitution was mostly a product of the political culture of the Anglo American southern planters. It incorporated English **common law**, developed from judicial rulings and customs over time. The Texas Constitution also lifted many provisions almost word for word from the U.S. Constitution and from the constitutions of southern states like

homesteads
Owner-occupied properties protected from forced sale under most circumstances.

community property
Property acquired during marriage and owned equally by both spouses.

common law
Law developed from judicial rulings and customs over time.

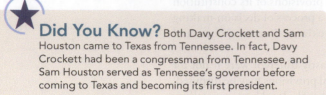

Tennessee from which many Texas settlers had migrated. Acting in haste because of the fear of attack from the Mexican cavalry, the Republic's constitutional convention wrote a concise document establishing a *unitary* form of government, free of many of the detailed restrictions that would later come to limit Texas government.

Constitution of 1845

Texans wrote a new constitution in 1845 in preparation for the state's admission to the United States. Although the 1845 Constitution contained many provisions similar to the Republic's constitution, it also introduced features recognizable in today's state constitution. For example, it was almost twice as long as the Republic of Texas Constitution and restricted the power of the legislature, which was allowed to meet in regular session only once every two years. The statehood constitution reflected the anti-corporate sentiment of the Old South as it required a two-thirds vote in the Texas House of Representatives to establish any corporation and made bank corporations illegal altogether. It limited state debt to $100,000 except in cases of war, insurrection, or invasion, and it established the Permanent School Fund.

The only amendment to the 1845 Constitution was adopted to limit the power of the governor by providing for the election of some of the officers that governors previously were allowed to appoint. Before adoption of the amendment, Texas had a short ballot because the governor had the power to appoint most executive and judicial officers. The amendment produced a **long ballot**, which results from the independent election of a large number of state officials.

long ballot
A ballot that results from the independent election of a large number of executive and judicial officers; in contrast, giving the chief executive the power to appoint most of them results in a short ballot.

Constitution of 1861

The 1861 Constitution was basically the same as that of 1845. The principal exception was that unlike its immediate predecessor, the 1861 Constitution reflected the poignant reality that Texas had become one of the Confederate states at war with the Union—it increased the debt ceiling and absolutely prohibited the emancipation of slaves.

Reconstruction Constitutions and Their Aftermath

Although earlier constitutions contained a number of elements still found in today's Texas Constitution, it was the aftermath of the Civil War—the political reaction to Reconstruction—that affirmed Texans' fear of government and set the stage for the writing of today's state constitution.

Constitution of 1866

After the Civil War, Texans wrote the 1866 Constitution, which they thought would satisfy the Unionists and permit the readmission of Texas under President Andrew Johnson's mild Reconstruction program. This document nullified secession, abolished slavery, and renounced Confederate war debts. Under its terms, a civilian government was elected and operated for several months despite some interference from the federal government's Freedmen's Bureau.

The 1866 Constitution soon became void after the Radical Republicans in Congress passed the Reconstruction Act of 1867, which required the Confederate states to adopt constitutions that met with the approval of the U.S. Congress. As a result of this act, and operating under congressional authority, the military deposed Texas's civilian elected officials and effectively restored military rule.

Constitution of 1869

With most whites either barred from participating in the election or boycotting it, voters elected members to a constitutional convention in 1868.

The convention produced a document that centralized state power in the hands of the governor, lengthened the chief executive's term to four years, and allowed the governor to appoint all major state officers, including judges. It provided annual legislative sessions, weakened planter-controlled local government, and centralized the public school system. The convention in 1868 reflected little of the fear of centralized government power that was later to become the hallmark of Texas government. The proposed constitution was ratified in 1869.

The 1869 Constitution served as the instrument of government for an era that most Texans and traditional historians would regard as the most corrupt and abusive in the state's history. Under Republican Governor E. J. Davis, large gifts of public funds were made to interests such as railroads; tax rates skyrocketed to fund ambitious and wasteful public programs. Many Texans simply refused to pay these exorbitant taxes, and the state government accumulated what was for that time a massive public debt. Law and order collapsed, and much of the state's population fell prey to attacks by Native Americans and outlaws. Instead of using the state police and militia to maintain the peace, Governor Davis made them a part of his powerful political machine and a symbol of tyranny. He took control of voter registration, intimidated unsupportive newspapers, and arrested several political opponents.

In 1874, Davis's handpicked supreme court used the location of a semicolon in the state constitution as a pretext for invalidating the election of Democrat Richard Coke, with Davis going so far as to wire President Ulysses S. Grant to send federal troops to prevent Democrats from taking power. Grant refused, and Democrats slipped past guards at the capitol and gathered in the legislative chambers to form the new government.

According to legend, Davis, determined not to give up his office, surrounded himself with armed state police in the capitol. Only when a well-armed group of Coke supporters marched toward the capitol singing "The Yellow Rose of Texas" did Davis finally vacate his office. For most Texans, Reconstruction left a bitter memory of a humiliating, corrupt, extravagant, and even tyrannical government.

Revisionist historians argue that Governor Davis was not personally corrupt and that Reconstruction brought progressive policies and built roads, railroads, and schools while protecting the civil and political rights of former slaves. They see this period as one in which an activist government attempted to play a positive role in people's lives and the period that followed as a conservative Anglo reaction to these policies.

The Constitutional Convention of 1875

Whichever historical view is more accurate, it is clear that most Texans of the day were determined to write a new constitution to strip power away from the state government. The Texas Grange, whose members were called Grangers, organized in 1873. Campaigning on a platform of "retrenchment and reform," it managed to elect at least 40 of its members to the constitutional convention of 1875. Like most of the 90 delegates, they were Democrats who were determined to strike at the heart of the big government associated with the Reconstruction era.

To save money, the convention did not publish a journal—reflecting the frugal tone of the final constitution. The convention cut salaries for governing officials, placed strict limits on property taxes, and restricted state borrowing; it also was miserly with the power it granted government officials. It stripped most of the governor's powers, reduced the term of office

IMAGE 3.1 E. J. Davis remained loyal to the United States, and his service in the Union army was a bitter reminder of Texas's defeat in the Civil War.

Texas State Library and Archives Commission

★ CTQ How did resentment against Governor Davis lead to the writing of the current Texas Constitution?

IMAGE 3.2 Delegates to the constitutional convention of 1875 substantially limited the power of state government.

★ CTQ   **What did delegates consider abuses of state power that needed to be prevented in the future?**

from four to two years, and required that the attorney general and state judges be elected by voters rather than being appointed by the governor.

Nor did the legislature escape pruning by the convention. Regular legislative sessions were to be held only once every two years. Legislative procedure was detailed in the constitution, with severe restrictions placed on the kinds of policies the legislature might enact. In fact, a number of public policies were written into the constitution itself.

Local government was strengthened, and counties were given many of the administrative and judicial functions of the state. Although the Grangers had opposed the idea of public education, they were persuaded to permit it with the condition that local governments would establish segregated schools.

The 1875 convention largely reacted to Reconstruction abuses by constraining state power. When the convention ended, some of the money appropriated for its expenses remained unspent. Despite opposition from African Americans, Republicans, most cities, and railroad interests, voters ratified the current state constitution of 1876.

The Texas Constitution Today

LO 3.2 **Describe the major constitutional structures, functions, and limits of Texas's legislative, executive, and judicial branches.**

Many students begin their examination of state constitutions with some kind of ideal or model constitution in mind. Comparisons with this ideal then leave them with the feeling that if only this or that provision were changed, state government would somehow find its way to honesty, efficiency, and effectiveness. In truth, there is no ideal constitution that would serve well in each of the uniquely diverse 50 U.S. states, nor is it possible to write a state constitution that could permanently meet the dynamically changing needs and concerns of citizens. Further, because a government is much more than its constitution, honest and effective government must be commanded by the political environment—leaders, citizens, parties, interest groups, and so forth; constitutions cannot guarantee it. Scoundrels will be corrupt and unconcerned citizens apathetic under even the best constitution.

However, this pragmatic view of the role of state constitutions should not lead to the conclusion that they are only incidental to good government. A workable constitution is necessary for effective government even if it is not sufficient to guarantee it. Low salaries may discourage independent and high-caliber leaders from seeking office or lead to potential conflicts of interest if public officials are forced to supplement their incomes from outside sources. Constitutional restrictions may make it virtually impossible for government to meet the changing needs of its citizens, and institutions may be set up in such a way that they will operate inefficiently and irresponsibly.

The events preceding the adoption of the 1876 Texas Constitution did not provide the background for developing a constitution capable of serving well under the pressures and changes that would take place in the century to follow. The decade of the 1870s was an era of paranoia and reaction, and the constitution it produced was directed more toward solving the problems arising from Reconstruction than toward meeting the challenges of generations to follow—it was literally a reactionary document.

The current Texas Constitution is also an expansive document, approximately 88,500 words in length. Eleven times longer than the U.S. Constitution, the Texas constitution is the second longest in the 50 states, bested only by the gargantuan Alabama Constitution.

Bill of Rights and Fundamental Liberty

Although the Texas Constitution has been the target of much criticism, it contains a Bill of Rights (Article 1) that is often held in high regard because it reflects basic American political culture and contains provisions that are similar to those found in other state charters and the U.S. Constitution.

The Fourteenth Amendment to the U.S. Constitution provides that no state shall deny any person life, liberty, or property without due process of law. As the U.S. Supreme Court has interpreted this Amendment, it has ruled that states must respect most of the U.S. Bill of Rights because its provisions are essential to "liberty" and "due process." As a result, many individual rights are protected by both the state and federal courts. If the state courts fail to protect an individual's rights, that person can also then seek a remedy in the federal courts. Table 3.1 shows important basic rights protected by both the U.S. and Texas constitutions.

State constitutional guarantees are not redundant, however, because the U.S. Constitution establishes only *minimum* standards for the states. Texas's courts have interpreted some state constitutional provisions to broaden basic rights beyond these minimums. Although the U.S. Supreme Court refused to interpret the Fourteenth Amendment as guaranteeing equal public school funding,[1] the Texas Supreme Court interpreted the efficiency clause of the Texas Constitution (Article 7, Section 1) as requiring greater equity in public schools.[2] By using Texas's constitutional and **statutory law** (law passed by legislatures and written into books of code), Texas courts have struck down polygraph tests for public employees, required workers' compensation for farmworkers, expanded free speech rights of private employees, and affirmed free speech rights at privately owned shopping malls.

statutory law
Law passed by legislatures and written into books of code.

TABLE 3.1 Basic Rights in the Texas and U.S. Constitutions
These rights are guaranteed by both the U.S. and Texas constitutions.

Basic Right	Texas Constitution	U.S. Constitution
Religious liberty	Article 1, Sections 4–7	First and Fourteenth Amendments
Freedom of expression	Article 1, Sections 8 and 27	First and Fourteenth Amendments
Right to keep and bear arms	Article 1, Section 23	Second and Fourteenth Amendments
Against quartering troops	Article 1, Section 25	Third Amendment
Against unreasonable search and seizure	Article 1, Section 9	Fourth and Fourteenth Amendments
Right to grand jury indictment for felonies	Article 1, Section 10	Fifth Amendment
Right to just compensation for taking property for public use	Article 1, Section 17	Fifth and Fourteenth Amendments
Right to due process of law	Article 1, Section 19	Fifth and Fourteenth Amendments
Right against double jeopardy	Article 1, Section 14	Fifth and Fourteenth Amendments
Right against forced self-incrimination	Article 1, Section 10	Fifth and Fourteenth Amendments
Right to fair trial by jury	Article 1, Section 10	Sixth and Fourteenth Amendments
Rights against excessive bail or cruel and unusual punishment	Article 1, Sections 11 and 13	Eighth and Fourteenth Amendments

▶ Explain how states can set higher standards than the national government does for applying these provisions. What rights does the Texas Constitution protect that the U.S. Constitution does not?

The Texas Bill of Rights guarantees additional rights not specifically mentioned in the U.S. Constitution. Notably, Texas has adopted an amendment to prohibit discrimination based on sex. A similar guarantee was proposed as the Equal Rights Amendment to the U.S. Constitution, but it was not ratified by the states. The Texas Constitution also guarantees victims' rights and access to public beaches. It forbids imprisonment for debt or committing the mentally ill for an extended period without a jury trial. It also prohibits monopolies and absolutely forbids suspending the **writ of habeas corpus**, which is a court order to present a person and show the legal cause for confining the individual; it may result in a prisoner's release from unlawful detention. Article 16 protects homesteads and prohibits the garnishment of wages except for court-ordered child support. The Texas Bill of Rights and other provisions guarantee the average citizen a greater variety of protections than most other state constitutions. We will discuss Texans' basic rights extensively in Chapter 10.

Separation of Powers

Like the state bill of rights, Article 2 of the Texas Constitution limits government. To prevent the concentration of power in the hands of any single institution, the national government and all states at the minimum have provided for a **separation of powers** among three branches of government—legislative, executive, and judicial. The function of the legislative branch is to make laws, and it is by law that governments define crime, establish the basis of civil suits, determine what will be taxed and who will pay how much in taxes, and set up government programs and the agencies that administer them. The function of the executive branch is to carry out the law, to arrest criminals, to collect taxes, to provide public services, to hire government employees, and to supervise their day-to-day conduct. The function of the judicial branch is to interpret the law as it applies to individuals and institutions.

Despite the separation of powers, there is still the potential for any of these three branches to abuse whatever powers they have been given. The Texas Constitution also follows American tradition in subsequent constitutional articles: it sets up a system of **checks and balances**, the concept that each branch of government is assigned power to limit abuses by the others. Table 3.2 illustrates that, under certain circumstances, a function normally assigned to one branch of government can be influenced by another. For example, the veto power that deals with lawmaking (a legislative function) is given to the governor (an executive). Impeachment and conviction, which deal with determining guilt (a judicial function), are given to the legislature. The state senate (a house of the legislature) confirms appointments the governor makes in the executive branch. Although there is a separation of powers, the checks-and-balances system requires that each branch have the opportunity to influence the others. The three branches specialize in separate functions, but there is some sharing of powers as well. In Chapters 7, 8 and 9, you will see how extensively these three branches of government interact in practice.

Legislative Branch

The legislative article (Article 3) is by far the longest in the Texas Constitution. As is the case at the federal level and in 49 states, the Texas Constitution provides for a **bicameral**, two-house legislative body made up of the 31-member Senate and the 150-member House of Representatives. Among the states, only Nebraska has a unicameral, one-house legislature.

The 1876 Constitution raised the number of senators to 31 and representatives to 93, with the provision that the size of the House could increase as the state's population grew, but only up to a maximum of 150 representatives. Following the drafting of the 1876 Constitution and the 1880 census, each senator represented an average of 51,000 people and each representative an average of 17,000. Today, the average is about 11 times more people (189,000) per representative and 17 times more (913,000) per senator than when the constitution was written.

writ of habeas corpus
A court order to present a person and show the legal cause for confining the individual; it may result in a prisoner's release from unlawful detention.

separation of powers
The principle behind the concept of a government in which power is distributed among three different branches—legislative, executive, and judicial.

checks and balances
The concept that each branch of government is assigned power to limit abuses by the others.

bicameral
Consisting of two houses or chambers, such as a senate and a house of representatives.

TABLE 3.2 Texas's Constitutional Checks and Balances

This table shows the major checks and balances in the Texas Constitution. In practice, the political environment determines how effectively they limit each branch of government.

Checks on the Legislature	Checks on the Executive Branch	Checks on the Judicial Branch
• The governor may veto bills passed by the legislature subject to a two-thirds vote to override.	• Texas's House of Representatives may impeach an executive by a majority vote.	• The governor appoints judges to fill vacancies in district and higher courts until the next election.
• The governor may use the line-item veto on appropriations bills.	• Texas's Senate may convict and remove an executive by a two-thirds vote.	• The House may impeach and the Senate may remove state judges.
• The governor may call special legislative sessions and set their agenda.	• The Senate confirms official appointments of the governor by a two-thirds vote.	• The legislature sets judicial salaries.
• The governor may address the legislature and designate emergency legislation that can be considered in the first 30 days of the session.	• The legislature, by statute, creates many executive agencies, assigns them their powers, and appropriates their funds.	• The legislature establishes many lower courts by statute.
		• The legislature may pass new laws if it disagrees with court interpretation of existing ones.
• The courts use *judicial review* to declare legislative acts unconstitutional.	• The courts may declare actions of the governor or state agencies unconstitutional or illegal.	• Two-thirds of the legislature may propose constitutional amendments to overturn court decisions.

▶ How effective are these checks when, as in Texas today, all three branches of government are controlled by the same political party? Do these checks lead to gridlock when control of the three branches is divided between two parties?

Senators are elected for a four-year term (with one-half of the body elected in one general election and the other half in the next, except immediately after redistricting, when all senators stand for election at the same time) from single-member districts. Each senator must be at least 26 years old, be a citizen, and be a resident of the state for at least five years and of the district for one year. Representatives are elected for a two-year term with the entire house elected every two years. Each representative must be at least 21 years old, a citizen, and a resident of the state for two years and of the district for one year.

As in most states, Texas legislators may serve as many times as voters choose to elect them; the longest-serving member of the Texas legislature, Representative Tom Craddick of Midland, has served in the legislature continuously since 1969. In contrast, some 15 states limit the number of consecutive terms legislators may serve or the total number of terms they may serve during their lifetime.

The Texas Constitution sets the salary of a state legislator at $7,200 per year, and it can be changed only by voter approval of a recommendation for an increase made by the Texas Ethics Commission. The Ethics Commission has made no such recommendation but has exercised its power to increase the per diem (daily) allowance for legislators, currently $190, while the legislature is in session. This meager salary is noticeably lower than in other major states; for instance, California legislators receive a salary of $104,118 per year and New York legislators earn $79,500.[3] As a result, most Texas legislators hold jobs outside the legislature, jobs that can create a potential conflict between legislators' personal financial interests and their mandate to represent the public's interest.

In Texas, regular legislative sessions are scheduled by the constitution. They are held once every two years and are consequently referred to as **biennial regular sessions**. These biennial regular sessions last for 140 days between January and May or June of odd-numbered years. In contrast, other major states such as California, Illinois, Michigan, and New York do not limit the length of legislative sessions.

As a result of the relatively short sessions, important legislation may be rushed through the legislative process with insufficient analysis and debate. Other important legislation may never reach the floor or even be discussed in a legislative committee because of time limitations. In fact, legislative leaders often strategically delay action on bills they oppose, knowing that they will die when the legislature adjourns.

Except to deal with extremely rare instances of impeachment, Texas's legislature may not call itself into **special sessions** or determine the issues to be considered during a special session. Governors may convene special sessions lasting no more than 30 days and limited to considering only the legislative matters they present. Governors can call as many special sessions as they wish, providing them with a powerful legislative advantage. For example, after former State Senator Wendy Davis successfully blocked legislation to regulate and limit abortions in a 2013 special session, former Governor Rick Perry announced the next day that he was calling a second special session. The same legislation was reintroduced and, given the additional time, easily passed in just 11 days.

Other constitutional features also limit the legislature. The Texas Constitution establishes more specific procedural requirements than most other state constitutions. Although the provision is often suspended, the constitution requires that a bill must be read on three separate days unless four-fifths of the legislature votes to set aside the requirement. It stipulates when bills may be introduced and how they will be reported out of committee, signed, and entered in the legislative journal once enacted. It even specifies how the enacting clause will read.

Although most states legally require a balanced budget, Texas's constitutional restriction would appear to be more effective than most. Article 3, Section 49 strictly limits the legislature in authorizing state debt except under rare conditions. The comptroller of public accounts is required to certify that funds are available for each appropriations measure adopted. Although specific constitutional amendments have authorized the sale of bonds for student loans, parks and water development, and prison construction, Texas's per capita state debt remains among the lowest in the nation.

Constitutional detail further constrains the legislature by making policies on subjects that normally would be handled by legislative statute. Much of the length of Article 3 results from its in-depth description of state policies such as the Veterans' Land Program, Texas park and water development funds, student loans, welfare programs, a grain warehouse self-insurance fund, and the municipal donation of outdated firefighting equipment. The constitution establishes the design of the great seal of Texas, authorizes the legislature to pass fence laws, and even explains how the state must purchase stationery! Article 16 authorizes the legislature to regulate cattle brands; Article 11 permits the building of sea walls. By including such statute-like details in the Texas Constitution, its drafters guaranteed that

biennial regular sessions
In Texas, regular legislative sessions are scheduled by the constitution. They are held once every two years and are consequently referred to as biennial regular sessions.

special sessions
Legislative sessions called by the Texas governor, who also sets their agenda.

IMAGE 3.3 In 2015, Texans amended the state constitution to make hunting a constitutional right. Here Governor Greg Abbott is shown exercising that right.

Texans for Greg Abbott, a Texas corporation

★ CTQ Is this a matter important enough to be included in the constitution? Or is it a detail that the legislature can be trusted to protect as it adopts hunting regulations?

even relatively unimportant decisions that could easily be handled by the legislature can be changed only by constitutional amendment.

Events may outstrip detailed constitutional provisions, leaving **deadwood**, inoperable constitutional provisions that have been either voided by a conflicting U.S. constitutional or statutory law or made irrelevant by changing circumstances and contexts. For example, the state constitutional provision forbidding same-sex marriages has become inoperative because of a ruling by the U.S. Supreme Court. To remove this or any other unnecessary detail, voters would have to approve a constitutional amendment. The basic distrust of the legislature, however much it may have been deserved in 1876, put a straitjacket on the state's ability to cope with the challenges of the twenty-first century.

deadwood
Inoperable constitutional provisions that have been either voided by a conflicting U.S. constitutional or statutory law or made irrelevant by changing circumstances and contexts.

Executive Branch

Article 4 establishes the executive branch, with the governor as its head. The governor must be a citizen, at least 30 years of age, and a resident of the state for five years immediately preceding his or her election to a four-year term. The constitution no longer limits the governor's salary, and, according to statute, it is presently $153,750.

Although Texas is one of only 14 states that place no term limits of any type on the governor's reelection, Texas governors have historically served very short tenures. In fact, governors served a term of only two years until the constitution was amended in 1972 to lengthen the term to four years. Before former Governor Perry served 14 consecutive years between December 2000 and January 2015, Allan Shivers had the record with just under eight consecutive years served between 1949 and 1957. Bill Clements served eight full years, but his two terms (1979–1983 and 1987–1991) were not consecutive.

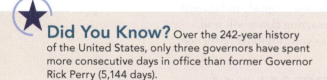

Did You Know? Over the 242-year history of the United States, only three governors have spent more consecutive days in office than former Governor Rick Perry (5,144 days).

Although the constitution provides that the governor shall be the chief executive, it actually establishes a **plural executive**, which is an executive branch in which power is divided among several independently elected officials—the governor, lieutenant governor, attorney general, comptroller of public accounts, commissioner of the general land office, and three railroad commissioners—thereby weakening the governor's power to act as the chief executive. All of these officials are elected for four-year terms with the exception of the railroad commissioners, who are elected for six-year terms on a staggered cycle with alternating positions being filled every two years. There are also provisions for a state board of education to be either elected or appointed. The constitution does allow the governor to appoint one major state officer—the secretary of state—but Texas remains one of only six states lacking a formal cabinet.

plural executive
An executive branch in which power is divided among several independently elected officials, thereby weakening the governor's power to act as the chief executive.

In the tradition of the constitutional plural executive, the legislature by statute has also established an elected commissioner of agriculture and has exercised its option to make the state board of education elected independently of the governor. The result of electing so many state executive officers is a long ballot that many voters find confusing because it is difficult for them to assign responsibility in a complex system of diffused power.

indirect appointive powers
Texas governor's authority to appoint supervisory boards but not the operational directors for most state agencies.

Most of the remaining agencies that the legislature has established to administer state programs are run by appointed multimember boards with substantial formal independence from the governor. The governor has **indirect appointive powers** to appoint supervisory boards but not the operational directors for most state agencies. The governor is empowered to name the members of supervisory boards to six-year staggered terms with the approval of two-thirds of the state senate. Each board, in turn, appoints its agency's director. The governor usually does not appoint the agency administrator directly—the board does.

removal power
The authority to fire appointed officials.

The Texas governor has limited **removal power**, a limited authority to fire appointed officials. The governor may fire his or her own staff and advisors at will, but removal of state officers is more difficult. The governor may fire appointed officers only if two-thirds of the senators agree that there is just cause for removal, making firing almost as difficult as impeachment and conviction. Furthermore, the governor may not remove anyone appointed by a preceding governor. **Directive power** (to issue binding orders to state agencies) is still quite restricted, and **budgetary power** (to recommend to the legislature how much it should appropriate for various executive agencies) is limited by the competing influences of the Legislative Budget Board.

The statutes and the constitution combine to make the governor a relatively weak executive, but the veto power provides the governor with a profound amount of influence over the legislative process. Since 1942, Texas governors have vetoed almost 1,300 bills, and only once during that entire time period did the Texas legislature muster the necessary two-thirds vote to override a governor's veto. In 1979, the legislature narrowly overrode Governor Bill Clements' veto of legislation granting the Comal County Commissioners Court the power to regulate hunting and fishing in the county.

In practice, the Texas legislature often lacks the opportunity to override a veto because major legislation may be adopted during the last days of the session. The Texas Constitution allows the governor 10 days (excluding Sundays) to act during the session and 20 days after it adjourns. For legislation passed during the final days of the legislative session, the governor may avoid the threat of an override by simply waiting until the legislature adjourns before vetoing the bill.

Texas is among 44 states that give the governor **line-item veto** power to strike out particular sections of an appropriations bill without vetoing the entire bill. Several states also allow their governors to item veto matters other than appropriations, but Texas does not, only permitting line-item vetoes of appropriations legislation. The governor of Texas lacks both the **reduction veto** (the power to reduce amounts in an appropriations bill without striking them out altogether) and the **pocket veto** (the power to kill legislation by simply ignoring it after the end of the legislative session).

Judicial Branch

Just as the constitution divides power in the executive branch, Article 5 also fragments the judicial branch. Texas is the only state other than Oklahoma that has two courts of final appeal. The highest court for civil matters is the nine-member Texas Supreme Court; the other, for criminal matters, is the nine-member Texas Court of Criminal Appeals. Leaving some flexibility as to number and jurisdiction, the constitution also creates courts of appeals, as well as district, county, and justice of the peace courts. The same article describes the selection of grand and trial juries and such county administrative officers as sheriff, county clerk, county attorney, and district attorney.

The number and variety of courts are confusing to the average citizen, and coordination and supervision are minimal. State courts have also come under attack because of the lack of qualified judges. The constitution specifies only general qualifications for county judges and justices of the peace, who do not need to be lawyers. There were very likely good reasons for people without legal training to serve as judges during the latter part of the nineteenth century, but today many Texans regard them as an anachronism.

Another factor that affects their qualifications is the way judges are selected. In Texas, judges are chosen in **partisan elections**, general elections in which the candidates are nominated by political parties and their respective party labels appear on the ballot. Trial judges are elected to serve for four years and appeals court judges for six, but judges often leave office before the end of their last term. The governor has the power to fill most judicial vacancies until the next election—a power that gives the governor considerable influence over the makeup of the courts; once in office, the governor's appointees have the advantages

directive power
The power to issue binding orders to state agencies.

budgetary power
The power to recommend to the legislature how much it should appropriate for various executive agencies.

line-item veto
The power to strike out sections of a bill without vetoing the entire bill.

reduction veto
The power to reduce amounts in an appropriations bill without striking them out altogether; this power is not available to Texas's governor.

pocket veto
The power to kill legislation by simply ignoring it after the end of the legislative session; this power is not available to Texas's governor.

partisan elections
General elections in which political parties nominate candidates whose party labels appear on the ballot.

of incumbency and often are returned to office without facing a serious challenge in the next election.

Voting Rights

A major function of state and local governments in the United States is to determine the character of democracy, as they administer elections and set requirements for **suffrage** (the legal right to vote). Article 6 of the Texas Constitution, which deals with suffrage requirements, denies the right to vote to persons under age 18, certain convicted felons, and individuals found mentally incompetent by a court of law. We will discuss the evolution of Texans' suffrage rights extensively in Chapter 4.

Although constitutional restrictions on voter qualifications are now as minimal as any in the nation, Texans still lack certain opportunities to participate directly in state government. Unlike many states, the Texas Constitution does not allow statewide **initiative**, a process that empowers citizens to place a proposal on the ballot for voter approval. Neither does the constitution permit statewide **referendums**, elections that permit voters to determine whether a statute will go into effect.

Likewise, the Texas Constitution does not allow for **popular recalls**, special elections initiated by citizen petitions to remove state officials before the end of their term. Initiatives, referendums, and popular recall are permitted in many other states and even in some Texas cities, but not at the state level in Texas.

Texas permits voters to decide directly on only three statewide matters: ratifying constitutional amendments, establishing a state income tax, and setting legislative salaries. Texas political parties sometimes place propositions on their primary ballots, but the results are purely symbolic and are not legally binding.

Public Education

Article 7 of the Texas Constitution states that a "general diffusion of knowledge being essential to the preservation of the liberties and rights of the people, it shall be the duty of the Legislature of the State to establish and make suitable provision for the support and maintenance of an efficient system of public free schools." In the seminal case of *Edgewood Independent School District* v. *Kirby* in 1989, the Texas Supreme Court found that the existing method of financing the state's public schools violated the Texas Constitution because of dramatic differences in per-student spending levels among the state's school districts. *Edgewood* eventually led to school finance reforms that made funding more equitable across districts, but the case also spawned an ongoing legal debate over the funding of public education in Texas, with judges serving as the arbiters in a continuing series of disputes over what constitutes a suitable and efficient education system. In our Politics in Practice feature, Holly McIntush, an attorney for numerous school districts, including the Fort Bend Independent School District (ISD), describes her frustrating and unsuccessful lawsuit against state school funding formulas that was decided by the Texas Supreme Court in 2016.

Local Government

The Texas Constitution subordinates local governments to the state, and it decentralizes government power by assigning many state responsibilities to local governments, especially counties. As a result, the constitution describes a rigid organizational structure for counties in Articles 9 and 16, and voters of the entire state were once required to approve amendments so individual counties could abolish obsolete county offices like hide inspector, superintendent of schools, and weigher. The constitution now authorizes county voters to abolish certain offices, but there is no provision for county home rule. As in state government, the constitution divides and diffuses county powers through a plural executive system.

---

suffrage
The legal right to vote.

initiative
A process that empowers citizens to place a proposal on the ballot for voter approval. If the measure passes, it becomes law (permitted in some Texas cities but not at the state level).

referendums
An election that permits voters to determine if an ordinance or statute will go into effect (permitted in some Texas cities but not at the state level).

popular recalls
A special election to remove an official before the end of his or her term, initiated by citizen petition (permitted in some Texas cities but not at the state level).

How Does Texas Compare?

Methods of Direct Democracy

Figure 3.1 shows that more than half of the states allow citizens to play some direct role in making or repealing laws through initiative or referendum.

In states with constitutions that permit initiatives, voters may submit petitions proposing changes to statutes or the state constitution. Initiative proposals in most states are placed directly on the ballot if a required minimum number of registered voters have signed the petition. Other states have indirect initiative, in which a successful petition requires the legislature to consider a proposal, which is then placed on the ballot only if the legislature fails to pass it. For example, citizens in California and Colorado have successfully used the direct initiative process, and in Maine and Massachusetts the indirect initiative, to put measures on the ballot legalizing the sale and consumption of marijuana for recreational use.

A second form of direct democracy is the popular referendum, which allows voters effectively to repeal a new law passed by the state legislature. Voters may organize a petition to place the objectionable legislation on the ballot. If the petition contains the minimum number of valid signatures, the law's implementation is delayed until a referendum can be held, and the law is voided if voters reject it.

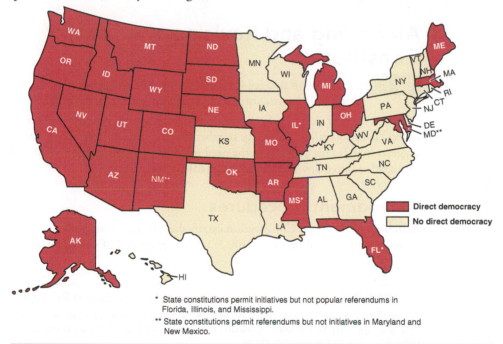

* State constitutions permit initiatives but not popular referendums in Florida, Illinois, and Mississippi.

** State constitutions permit referendums but not initiatives in Maryland and New Mexico.

FIGURE 3.1 States with Constitutional Provisions for Direct Democracy

This figure shows that 26 states have some sort of mechanism for direct democracy, including initiative, popular referendum, or both. The Texas Constitution, however, does not empower Texans to place any type of legislation on the ballot.

National Conference of State Legislatures.

FOR DEBATE

★ **SRQ** Should the Texas Constitution be reformed to allow for initiative and referendum? Or is legislation too complex to be understood by ordinary voters? Would voters be too easily swayed by special interests that could organize expensive campaigns for or against initiatives?

★ **CTQ** Give examples of proposals that you think voters would approve if they had these tools of popular democracy. Given what you know about the Texas political culture, do you think Texans would vote to legalize marijuana?

The legislature has the power to set up structures for city governments and offers municipalities several standard alternative *general-law charters*. Cities with populations of more than 5,000 may adopt *home-rule charters* that establish any organizational structure or program that does not conflict with state law or the constitution.

Generally, the legislature has the power to provide for the establishment of limited-purpose local governments known as *special districts*. Numerous special districts are also established by the constitution itself, and to eliminate one of these requires a constitutional amendment. Many of them have been created to perform functions that general-purpose local governments, such as counties and cities, cannot afford because of constitutional tax and debt limits. Arising out of constitutional restrictions, special districts have multiplied taxing and spending authorities and, except for school districts, operate largely outside of the public's view. In Chapter 11, we will discuss how constitutional provisions for local governments are implemented in practice.

Did You Know? Although at the end of World War II almost two-thirds of the state's 254 counties had a county superintendent of schools, the evolution of public education eventually rendered the position obsolete, and today it continues to exist only in Harris County after Dallas County voters abolished the post in 2017.

Amending and Revising the Texas Constitution

LO 3.3 **Explain the process of amending and revising the Texas Constitution and the reasons that amendments are frequently necessary.**

Given the level of detail in the Texas Constitution, it is frequently necessary to amend it to reflect changing realities. The large number of constitutional amendments ratified since 1876 suggests that Texans understand the need to amend the constitution, even though they have steadfastly resisted any attempts to systematically revise it.

Amendment Procedures

Article 17 of the Texas Constitution establishes the constitutional amendment process as a two-step process, shown in Figure 3.2. First, **proposal of constitutional amendments**

proposal of constitutional amendments
In Texas, the proposal of a constitutional amendment must be supported by two-thirds of the total membership of each house of the legislature—at least 21 senators and 100 representatives.

FIGURE 3.2 The Two-Step Constitutional Amendment Process
Amending the Texas Constitution requires proposal and ratification. Even though the process appears to be fairly difficult, the Texas constitution has been amended more than 46 other state constitutions.

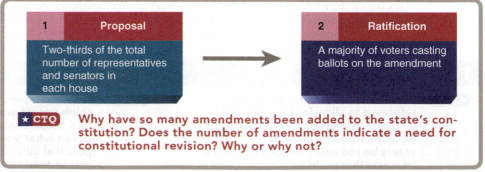

1 Proposal	2 Ratification
Two-thirds of the total number of representatives and senators in each house	A majority of voters casting ballots on the amendment

★ CTQ **Why have so many amendments been added to the state's constitution? Does the number of amendments indicate a need for constitutional revision? Why or why not?**

Source: Cengage Learning.

must be supported by two-thirds of the total membership of each house of the Texas legislature—at least 21 senators and 100 representatives. Second, **ratification of constitutional amendments**, which actually puts them into effect, requires approval by a majority of those persons voting on the amendment in either a regular or a special election. Because such an extraordinary majority of legislators must agree merely to propose constitutional amendments, a number of them are relatively uncontroversial. Since 1876 voters have approved almost three-quarters of all proposed constitutional amendments, and during the past 20 years voters have approved more than 90 percent of proposed amendments.

ratification of constitutional amendments
To actually put a constitutional amendment into effect requires approval by a majority of those persons voting on the amendment in either a regular or a special election.

Recent Constitutional Amendments

Every legislative session over the last half century has proposed at least one constitutional amendment, and most have proposed several. Recent constitutional amendments have sometimes been minor, such as the one in 2017 permitting credit unions and other financial institutions to award prizes by random drawing to promote savings; some have been of mostly symbolic importance, such as the right to hunt amendment in 2015. Still others have been of major substantive importance, such as the 2014 amendment to boost highway spending significantly with up to $2.5 billion per year from general sales tax revenue and up to 35 percent of the motor fuels and car rental taxes.

Since 1997, the legislature has voted to present a total of 1145 proposed constitutional amendments to Texas voters. With few exceptions, voters cast their ballots on these amendments in November of odd-numbered years, when few other issues are being decided and voter participation is extremely low. Since 1997, voter turnout in off-year constitutional amendment elections has ranged from a low of 4 percent to a high of 14 percent and has averaged only 7 percent of the state's voting age population.

In contrast, turnout in state general elections has averaged 36 percent in even-numbered years, when federal, state, and county officials are on the ballot. Table 3.3 shows that average turnout in general elections is more than five times greater than in the odd-year constitutional amendment elections.

Table 3.3 shows that most constitutional amendments presented to voters since 1997 have been approved. Only about one out of every 10 amendments failed to be ratified by voters during this period. Three amendment proposals were rejected in 2011—perhaps not coincidentally, all three of the rejected amendments were portrayed by opponents as backdoor attempts to increase taxes.

Criticisms of the Texas Constitution

The Texas Constitution is one of the longest, most detailed, and most frequently amended state constitutions in the nation. With approximately 88,500 words, it is the nation's second longest after Alabama's; with 498 amendments, it is the fourth most amended state constitution, because Texans have often responded to emerging challenges by further amending their constitution. The constitution, reformers charge, is poorly organized and confusing to most of the state's citizens.

Every state constitution is longer than the U.S. Constitution, but few are as restrictive as the Texas Constitution. The continuing need to amend a detailed and restrictive state constitution means that citizens are frequently called on to pass judgment on proposed amendments. Some of the constitution's defenders maintain that giving Texas voters the opportunity to express themselves on constitutional amendments reaffirms popular control of government. In reality, faced with trivial, confusing, or technical proposals, voters display little interest in amendment elections.

TABLE 3.3 Amending the Texas Constitution in Off-Year Elections: 1997–2017

This table shows that voters ratify most constitutional amendments that the legislature proposes. Notice how few Texans actually participate in the ratification process in off-year elections compared to those who vote in general elections when federal, state, and county offices are on the ballot.

Election Year (month)	Number of Amendments Proposed	Number of Amendments Passed	Voter Turnout (percent of voting age population)	Voter Turnout in Subsequent Even-Year General Election (percent of voting age population)
2017 (Nov)	7	7	5	39
2015 (Nov)	7	7	8	43
2013 (Nov)	9	9	6	25
2011 (Nov)	10	7	4	44
2009 (Nov)	11	11	6	27
2007 (Nov)	16	16	6	46
2007 (May)	1	1	5	46
2005 (Nov)	9	7	14	26
2003 (Sept)	22	22	9	46
2001 (Nov)	19	19	6	29
1999 (Nov)	17	13	7	44
1997 (Nov)	14	12	9	27
1997 (Aug)	1	1	5	27
Average Turnout			7	36

Source: Texas Secretary of State.

▶ Does the low level of voter turnout in these off-year elections undermine the legitimacy of the constitutional amendment process in Texas? Should the constitution be reformed to require that voting on constitutional amendments only take place in general elections in even-numbered years?

Attempts to Revise the Texas Constitution

Attempts to substantially revise the constitution have met with successive failures. Ironically, in 1972, Texas voters had to amend the constitution to provide for its revision. Under the provisions of that amendment, the legislature established a constitutional revision commission of 37 members appointed by the governor, lieutenant governor, speaker of the house, attorney general, chief justice of the supreme court, and presiding judge of the court of criminal appeals. The commission made several proposals. Meeting in 1974, the legislature acted as a constitutional convention and agreed to many of these recommendations. However, the convention divided over the issue of a right-to-work provision, and the final document could not muster the two-thirds vote needed to submit the proposal to the electorate.

In the 1975 regular session, the legislature proposed eight constitutional amendments to the voters. Together, the proposed amendments were substantially the same as the proposals the legislature had previously defeated. If they had been adopted, the amendments would have shortened the constitution by 75 percent through reorganization and by eliminating statute-like detail and deadwood.

The legislature would have been strengthened by annual sessions, and a salary commission would have set the legislators' salary. Although limited to two terms, the governor would have been designated as the chief planning officer and given removal powers and certain powers of fiscal control. The court system would have been unified and its administrative procedure simplified. Local governments would have operated under broader home-rule provisions, and counties would have been authorized to pass general ordinances and to abolish unneeded offices.

Opponents' chief arguments were against more power for the legislature, greater government costs, and the possibility of an income tax—all of which were serious concerns for many Texans. Because the legislature had written the proposals, it was easy for the Texas voter to see such things as annual sessions and flexibility concerning their salaries as a "grab for power" that would substantially increase government expenditures. Despite an emotional campaign, only 15 percent of voting age Texans cast ballots in the election, and they overwhelmingly rejected all of the proposed amendments.

A more recent attempt to revise the state constitution did not get so far as the 1972–1975 efforts. In 1999, Representative Bob Junell and Senator Bill Ratliff supported a revision that would have raised legislative pay, lengthened legislative terms, given the governor more appointive powers, and provided for a merit system for state judges. Their proposals died in legislative committee.

Applying What You Have Learned About the Texas Constitution

LO 3.4 Apply what you have learned about the Texas Constitution.

You learned that the Texas constitution guarantees a constitutional right to free public schools and imposes a duty on the legislature to provide a suitable and efficient system of public schools. Houston Public Media (HPM) has done in-depth reporting on the continuing inequity in Texas public school funding despite this constitutional requirement as is shown in Image 3.4, which highlights the wide variance in spending per student across the state's more than one thousand independent school districts. We asked Holly McIntush to give you further insight as to why her group sued the state to obtain enforcement of this constitutional provision.

Holly McIntush was one of the three members of the Thompson & Horton LLP lead legal team for the Fort Bend

IMAGE 3.4 This HPM graphic shows the inequity in Texas public school funding from district to district and compares the amount of spending in each district to the national norm. Notice that school districts in West Texas tend to spend far more than the national average in sharp contrast to the districts around larger cities such as Houston, Dallas, San Antonio, Fort Worth, and El Paso. Suburban districts in these metro areas are about as underfunded as their urban district neighbors.

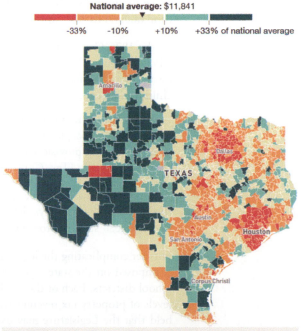

SPENDING PER STUDENT, BY SCHOOL DISTRICT

Adjusted for regional differences, for primary and unified school districts

National average: $11,841

-33%   -10%   +10%   +33% of national average

★ CTQ **Why are urban and suburban school districts underfunded compared to more rural districts? Would spending more money on education result in improved educational outcomes?**

ISD group that represented 81 school districts (Fort Bend ISD et al.) in their school finance lawsuit against the State of Texas. She previously held positions in the Texas House of Representatives and in the Texas Attorney General's Office.

Despite McIntush's efforts, the Texas Supreme Court upheld the constitutionality of the state's system of school finance and declined to get involved in making school finance policy. The court called the system undeniably imperfect and said the state's 5 million school children deserve better, but "we decline to usurp legislative authority by issuing reform diktats from on high, supplanting lawmakers' policy wisdom with our own."[4]

After you have read her essay, we will ask you to consider the difficulty the courts have in closing the gap between theory and practice as they apply such general constitutional language as "suitable" and "efficient." We will ask you to reflect on why the legislature has failed in the eyes of many, including a majority of the state's school districts, to provide adequate funding for public schools and why school districts felt they had no recourse but the legal system through which to seek meaningful implementation of their residents' constitutional rights.

POLITICS IN PRACTICE
The Constitutional Right to Education

by Holly McIntush
Attorney & Member of the Fort Bend ISD Group Legal Team

Since its inception, Texas has recognized that an "educated and enlightened" populace is fundamental to "the continuance of civil liberty, or the capacity for self-government."

At the 1875 Constitutional Convention, the chairman of the education committee told his fellow delegates, "It is for the general welfare of all, rich and poor, male and female, that the means of a common school education should, if possible, be placed within the reach of every child in the State." The Constitution adopted the following year puts it this way:

> A general diffusion of knowledge being essential to the preservation of liberties and rights of the people, it shall be the duty of the Legislature of the State to establish and make suitable provision for the support and maintenance of an efficient system of public free schools. (Tex. Const. art. VII, § 1)

This provision has been the subject of seven Texas Supreme Court decisions over the past three decades as attorneys debate the concrete meaning of the terms "general diffusion of knowledge," "suitable provision," and "efficient system."

Further complicating the legal debate is that the constitutional duty to meet these standards is imposed on the state—yet responsibility for actually doing so has fallen on 1,026 local school districts. Each of those school districts have varying student populations and varying levels of property tax revenue available to fund their efforts. The Texas Supreme Court has held that the Legislature may use local districts to meet its constitutional obligation if and *only if* the legislature provides all districts with sufficient resources to enable them to provide "a general diffusion of knowledge" at similar property tax rates.

The Texas Supreme Court has also said that the legislature must ensure that the public education system adapts to meet "changing times, needs, and public expectations." Neither the student population nor the needs of the state are the same today as they were in 1876, or 1976, or even 2006. The number of students living in poverty has skyrocketed—growing by more than 773,000 students between 2006 and 2016. Texas students speak a dizzying array of home languages—93 in Richardson, 82 in Alief, 64 in Austin, more than 40 in Amarillo, and 35 in Abilene. The types of jobs available to students upon graduation, and the skills and knowledge needed to perform those jobs, are changing just as quickly.

The Texas legislature has responded by demanding that schools produce graduates that are college or career-ready and demanding that students pass more and harder tests in order to move to the next grade level. However, the legislature has refused to determine how much it actually costs school districts to enable their changing student population to meet those demands. In fact, the Texas Education Code has required the Legislative Budget Board to regularly calculate the cost of meeting the rising standards and advise the legislature on how to adjust its formulas; but it has not done so in more than a decade. Instead, the legislature continues to distribute money through antiquated formulas that have not been updated since before the fall of the Berlin Wall.

Thirty years of school finance litigation have taught us that school finance formulas cannot remain static as the state's population, economy, and academic needs change. Yet the legislature has done just that time and again. Every major school finance reform of the past three decades has come after the Texas Supreme Court has stepped in to enforce the constitutional requirements.

In May 2016, after McIntush had written her essay, the Texas Supreme Court issued its opinion in the this controversial case that took four years to wind its way through the state legal system. The Supreme Court concluded that while the state's public school funding system is flawed, it is nonetheless constitutional. And, at the same time the court signaled that it was reluctant to wade too deep into the complex policy area of school finance. As then-Justice Don Willett concluded in the court's opinion, "Our Byzantine school funding 'system' is undeniably imperfect, with immense room for improvement. But if satisfies minimal constitutional requirements."[5]

1. How can the courts determine the meaning of general constitutional language such as "suitable" and "efficient"? Should the courts be making decisions with such a sweeping impact as the system of financing public education, or should public policy in such a broad and critical area like this be determined by the state legislature?
2. Why has the state legislature failed to provide adequate and equitable funding for Texas public schools? Why were the state's school districts forced to turn to the courts in their quest for constitutionally adequate and equitable school funding?

★ Chapter Summary

LO 3.1 Explain the origins of the Texas Constitution and the Constitutional Convention of 1875. The first Texas Constitution combined elements drawn from the U.S. Constitution and the constitutions of the states from which the Anglo settlers had migrated, but it also included unique elements based on the state's experiences as a Spanish colony and Mexican state. The current constitution was written in the period following Reconstruction. Most Anglo Texans viewed the Reconstruction state government

as abusive and tyrannical. In 1875, a state constitutional convention reacted to the Reconstruction regime by limiting state government in almost every imaginable way.

LO 3.2 Describe the major constitutional structures, functions, and limits of Texas's legislative, executive, and judicial branches. The Texas Constitution includes a bill of rights that is more expansive than those in most state constitutions. It follows the national pattern by establishing a separation of powers between legislative, executive, and judicial branches and establishes a system of checks and balances that allows each branch to check or limit the powers of the others.

In addition to the limits that are common to the U.S. Constitution and all state constitutions, the Texas constitution also strictly limits the legislature with short, infrequent sessions, low salaries, and statute-like details that the legislature cannot change without amending the constitution. The governor is limited in his or her role as chief executive because Texas has a plural executive system that includes many independently elected executives over whom the governor has no control. Texas has divided power between two final courts of appeals, and judges are elected in partisan elections.

LO 3.3 Explain the process of amending and revising the Texas Constitution and the reasons that amendments are frequently necessary. Constitutional amendments are proposed by two-thirds of each chamber of the state legislature and must be ratified by a majority of voters before going into effect. The Texas Constitution has been amended more than most, but efforts to systematically revise the state constitution have failed.

The constitution's critics argue that a constitution should establish essential governing principles and structures, but some state constitutions, like that of Texas, also go beyond those essentials to establish many details of routine government and, as a consequence, require frequent amendment to reflect new realities.

LO 3.4 Apply what you have learned about the Texas Constitution. You looked at the Texas constitutional right to education through the eyes of one of the lead attorneys in the latest of a series of lawsuits brought to force reform of the state's system of public school finance. You considered the practical implications of applying general constitutional language to the realities of today's public schools, and you evaluated the role of the courts in implementing broad changes in public policy.

Key Terms

bicameral, *p. 63*

biennial regular sessions, *p. 65*

budgetary power, *p. 67*

checks and balances, *p. 63*

common law, *p. 57*

community property, *p. 57*

deadwood, *p. 66*

directive power, *p. 67*

homestead, *p. 57*

indirect appointive powers, *p. 66*

initiative, *p. 68*

legitimacy, *p. 57*

line-item veto, *p. 67*

long ballot, *p. 58*

partisan elections, *p. 67*

plural executive, *p. 66*

pocket veto, *p. 67*

popular recall, *p. 68*

proposal of constitutional amendments, *p. 70*

ratification of constitutional amendments, *p. 71*

reduction veto, *p. 67*

referendum, *p. 68*

removal powers, *p. 66*

separation of powers, *p. 63*

special session, *p. 65*

statutory law, *p. 62*

suffrage, *p. 68*

writ of habeas corpus, *p. 63*

Review Questions

LO 3.1 Explain the origins of the Texas Constitution and the Constitutional Convention of 1875.

- How did Texas's origins as a Spanish colonial possession and a Mexican state influence the drafting of the state's first constitutions?

- Evaluate the evolution of the state's constitutions from independence through the 1875 Constitutional Convention.

- What are the historical reasons for the restrictive nature of the Texas Constitution? What benefits did the state constitution's writers hope to achieve by limiting state government?

LO 3.2 Describe the major constitutional structures, functions, and limits of Texas's legislative, executive, and judicial branches.

- How does the Texas Constitution differ from the constitutions of other states and the U.S. Constitution?

- Describe the constitutional organization of each of the three branches of Texas government.

- Discuss the major constitutional provisions that restrain each branch of state government. What are the consequences of these restraints?

LO 3.3 Explain the process of amending and revising the Texas Constitution and the reasons that amendments are frequently necessary.

- How is the state's constitution amended?

- Why does Texas amend its constitution so frequently?

- How vibrant is voter participation in the constitutional amendment ratification process?

- What are the strengths and weaknesses of the Texas Constitution? Should the Texas Constitution be substantially revised? Why or why not?

Think Critically and Get Active!

Explore different views of constitutional rights and liberties.

Conservative Groups

- The National Rifle Association at **www.nra.org** (@nra) supports the right to keep and bear arms.

- Students for Concealed Carry on Campus at **concealedcampus.org** (@concealedcampus) has fought to reduce restrictions on carrying firearms on college campuses.

- Texas Right to Life at **www.texasrighttolife.com** (@TXRightToLife) is a pro-life group.

- Texans for Fiscal Responsibility at **www.empowertexans.com** (@EmpowerTexans) is a prominent conservative activist organization in the state.

- Texas Public Policy Foundation at **www.texaspolicy .com** (@TPPF) is a leading conservative Texas think tank.

Liberal Groups

- The Brady Campaign at **www.bradycampaign.org** (@bradybuzz) advocates for gun control.

- NARAL Pro-Choice Texas at **www.prochoicetexas .org** (@naraltx) supports abortion rights.

- Texas Coalition to Abolish the Death Penalty at **www.tcadp.org** (@TCADPdotORG) fights capital punishment.

- The American Civil Liberties Union of Texas at **www.aclutx.org** (@ACLUTx) advocates for the protection of civil liberties.

- The Center for Public Policy Priorities at **forabettertexas.org** (@CPPP_TX) is a leading liberal Texas think tank.

Sample the Texas Constitution. The complete text of the Texas Constitution is at **www.constitution.legis .state.tx.us**. In the index, click on *Article 3, "Legislative Department."* Click on *Section 29* and notice that even the enacting clause for legislation is included in the constitution. Click on *Article 16, Section 6* and notice the level of detail. Read the deadwood provision in Article 9, Section 14. Contrast the legislative and executive articles (Articles 3 and 4) of Texas's Constitution with those of Illinois (Articles 4 and 5) at **www.ilga.gov/commission/ lrb/conmain.htm**.

Evaluate how well Texas limits borrowing. Article 3, Section 59 of Texas's Constitution severely limits state debt. Research how effective these restrictions have been by comparing per capita debt among the 50 states at **www.taxfoundation.org/blog/annual-release-facts-figures-how-does-your-state-compare**.

Play a role in the continual rewriting of the state's fundamental law. Vote in Texas elections to ratify or reject state constitutional amendments. Note that proposals are sometimes detailed and confusing, and beware of biased special-interest group television and Internet ads describing them. Good amendment summaries and analyses written by the nonpartisan Texas Legislative Council can be found among the publications at **www.tlc.state.tx.us**.

Read constitutional amendments that have been proposed by the Texas Legislature, their legislative history, and the level of popular support for them at **www.tlc .state.tx.us/docs/amendments/Constamend1876.pdf**.

★ **PRQ** Are the proposed constitutional amendments that Texans voted on too complex for the average voter to decide? Should you and other voters be called upon to make these sorts of decisions, or should you leave these matters to the legislature?

4

Voting and Elections

Voters sometimes wait in long lines to cast their ballots. In this chapter, you will explore who votes in which elections and how campaigns affect their votes.

John Davenport/ZUMA Press/Newscom

Learning Objectives

LO 4.1 Explain why voter turnout is low in Texas.

LO 4.2 Describe the types of Texas elections.

LO 4.3 Understand how elections are administered in Texas.

LO 4.4 Identify the factors that advantage (or disadvantage) candidates in Texas elections.

LO 4.5 Apply what you have learned about voting and elections in Texas.

Texas has a republican form of government, which means that it is a representative democracy. A representative democracy is based on popular sovereignty, which gives ultimate governing authority to the people who elect officials to act on their behalf. It took many centuries of human struggle to achieve this enviable form of government in Texas and in the United States, but many of the world's people unfortunately still lack the opportunity for meaningful input in their political systems.

Texas government is structured on the principles of Jacksonian democracy. During the period when genuine democracy began to take root in the United States, between the 1820s and 1840s, those who believed in rule by the people held to the notion that the more officials who are elected, the more democratic the system is.

Thus, Texas has a very long ballot, and voters must inform themselves about the qualifications of the large number of candidates who compete for nomination in the party primaries in the spring of even-numbered years. Then, in November, between 4,000 and 5,000 of these party nominees ask the voters to elect them in the general election to numerous county, state, and national offices. At other times during the year, many thousands more are elected in nonpartisan municipal and special district elections as well.

Texans have many opportunities to assert control over their government, and most Texans claim allegiance to democratic ideals, even if those principles have not been perfectly realized in practice. Historical voting restrictions have now been removed, but voter turnout in Texas still remains quite low compared to other states and other nations. Texans' traditional political culture does not put a premium on active citizen participation, and citizens are less likely to vote when one party's candidates are almost guaranteed to win all major state offices. Citizens on the margins of society rarely participate in political activities, just as they are less involved in other organized activities.

Our political system only represents those who actually participate—the rest of the people forfeit their influence. Meanwhile, low-information voters look to the media, activists, and political elites for cues to make their voting decisions. The Texas political system, therefore, gives disproportionate influence to those who do actively participate.

Political Participation

LO 4.1 **Explain why voter turnout is low in Texas.**

Voting in elections is the most basic and common form of political participation. Many people take part in other ways, such as discussing political issues with friends and co-workers, writing letters to local representatives or to newspapers, distributing campaign literature, contributing money to a campaign, placing bumper stickers on cars, or via their activity on Facebook, Instagram, and Twitter. Some people are members of interest groups, whether neighborhood or trade associations, serve on political party committees, or act as delegates to conventions. Yet others participate in demonstrations and sit-ins.

The Participation Paradox and Why People Vote

Elections, of course, are the defining characteristic of representative democracies. It is through our votes that we hold elected officials accountable. After all, votes are what matter to politicians, at least those interested in winning and holding office. If we vote—and reward and punish elected officials for what they do while in office—politicians have an incentive to do what we want. If we do not vote, elected officials are largely free to do what they want. Clearly, voting is important in a representative democracy.

The problem is that a single individual's vote is rarely decisive because few elections are decided by a single vote. This may leave you wondering: Why do people vote? Among political scientists, this is known as the **participation paradox**. The point of this paradox

participation paradox
The fact that citizens vote even though a single vote rarely decides an election.

is not to suggest that people should not vote but rather to highlight that they vote for other reasons.

Who Votes?

Over the years, political scientists have learned quite a lot about why people go to the polls. It is now clear that a relatively small number of demographic and political variables are especially important.[1] The most important demographic variables are education, income, and age. The more education a person has, the more likely the person is to vote. Income is also a factor in voting; even among people with the same levels of education, those with higher incomes are more likely to vote. Age also matters. As people grow older, they are more likely to vote, at least until serious age-related health problems begin to set in. Why do these factors matter? The answer is straightforward: People who are educated, have high incomes, and are older are more likely to care about and pay attention to politics. Thus, they are more likely to vote.

In addition to demographic factors, certain political factors influence the likelihood of voting, especially one's expressed interest in politics and intensity of identification with a political party. The more a person is interested in politics, the more likely the person is to vote. The effect is fairly obvious but nevertheless quite important. Consider that a person who does not have a lot of education or income is still very likely to vote if he or she has a strong interest in politics.

Identification with either of the major political parties also makes a person more likely to vote. This pattern reflects the fact that strong party identifiers, on average, care a lot more about who wins than people who do not identify with a party. It also reflects the mobilization of identifiers by the political parties—that is, the more one identifies with a party, the more likely it is that the person will be contacted by the party and its candidates during election campaigns.

Did You Know? According to the U.S. Census Bureau, the top five reasons given by registered voters for why they did not vote in the 2016 presidential election were: They did not like the candidates or campaign issues (25 percent), they were not interested in voting (15 percent), they were too busy or had schedule conflicts (14 percent), they were ill or had a disability (12 percent), and they were out of town (8 percent).

In one sense, deciding to vote is much like deciding to attend a sporting event, such as an MLS, NBA, NFL, or WNBA game. We do not go to a game to affect the outcome. We go for other reasons, because we like soccer, basketball, or football and care about it. The same is true for voting; education, income, age, interest, and party identification are important indicators of our desire to participate.

Of course, other factors are also important for explaining electoral participation, but the small set of demographic and political variables tells us quite a lot. With this information, we can pretty much determine whether a person will or will not vote in a particular election. We also can account for most of the differences in turnout among different groups, such as African Americans, Anglos, Asian Americans, and Latinos. This issue is picked up later in the chapter.

The Practice of Voting

The legal qualifications for voting in Texas are surprisingly few and simple. Anyone who is a citizen of the United States, at least 18 years of age, and a resident of the state is eligible to register and vote in Texas. The only citizens prohibited from voting are those who have been declared "mentally incompetent" in formal court proceedings and those currently serving a sentence, parole, or probation for a felony conviction.

Did You Know? Up until the 1920s, some states allowed noncitizens to vote. Even today, major cities such as Chicago and San Francisco allow noncitizens to vote in local school board elections.

Establishing residence for voting is no longer a matter of living at a place for a specified time. Residence is defined primarily in terms of intent; that is, people's homes are where they intend them to be. Meeting age, citizenship, and residency qualifications does not mean that a person can simply walk into the voting booth on election day. Citizens must register in order to vote, but states may no longer require long waiting periods between registering and becoming eligible to vote. U.S. Supreme Court rulings allow only a short period of time (30 days maximum) in which the application is processed and the registrant's name is entered on the rolls.

Texas law allows a citizen to register in person or by mail any time of the year up to 30 days before an election in which they wish to vote. Since the passage of federal "motor voter" legislation, a person can also register when obtaining or renewing a driver's license; indeed, every person renewing a driver's license is asked whether he or she wants to register to vote. The secretary of state also makes registration applications available through voter registrar's offices and online. However, Texas is one of only 12 states that do not permit online registration; the online application must be printed, signed and mailed to the county voter registrar.

Once they register, voters are automatically sent renewals at their address of record, but these renewals cannot be forwarded to new addresses. Thus, voters are permanently registered unless the post office returns their non-forwardable certificate to the voter registrar. Names on returned certificates are stricken from the list of eligible voters. Coroners' reports, lists of felony convictions, and adjudications of mental incompetence are also used to purge the voter registration list.

Occasionally, voter registrars may have failed to remove all deceased voters from the list and this failure may have given rise to rumors of dead people voting, though there is little recent evidence of ghosts actually casting ballots. Perhaps the greater controversy surrounding voter registration lists is that anyone can purchase the computer-generated voter list for each county in the state. Political parties and candidates make extensive use of voter lists when trying to identify likely voters during election campaigns, but some voters have raised concerns that this practice compromises their right to privacy and the right to a secret ballot.

Texas does not make it as easy to register as some states that have gone so far as to allow for "same-day registration" in which voters can register at the polls on election day. Several states such as California and Oregon automatically register eligible citizens who have a driver's license unless they object. North Dakota has no registration at all. There, one just walks in, shows identification, and votes.[2]

Once registered, voting in Texas has been fairly easy. Texas was one of the first states to institute early voting, which allows people to vote at a number of different sites before election day. And, those who are disabled, 65 and older, or out of state during the voting period can vote by mail. In every Texas county ballots and election materials must be printed in English and Spanish. In counties where either 10,000 or 5 percent of voting age citizens do not speak English well, ballots and election materials are also provided in their native language.

However, Texas has recently added a controversial new condition for voting. In 2011, the legislature enacted one of the strictest voter photo identification (ID) laws in the nation requiring voters to show one of seven forms of photo identification. In order to vote, citizens had to show a Texas driver's license, Texas ID card, Texas concealed handgun license, U.S. military ID, U.S. passport, U.S. citizenship certificate containing a photograph, or a Texas election identification certificate that the state provides for free.

Its defenders argued that the Texas voter ID law was intended to prevent voter impersonation and assure integrity in the voting process. Opponents argued that there had been very few documented cases of voter impersonation before the Texas voter photo ID law was adopted while approximately 600,000 eligible Texas voters lacked these forms of identification. Some suspected that the Republican-controlled legislature passed the law as a politically motivated effort to suppress minority voting in the state. Regardless of the political motivation for the law, most observers believed it would dampen turnout, particularly among students and

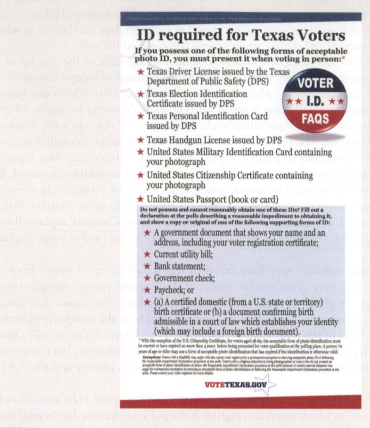

IMAGE 4.1 The Texas Secretary of State used this poster during the 2018 election cycle to educate voters about the state's voter ID requirements.

CTQ Was the voter ID law a reasonable effort to prevent voter fraud? Or was the law's underlying intent to discourage minorities from voting, given that there had been extremely few documented cases of voter impersonation before its passage?

ethnic or racial minorities who are more likely to support Democrats. It thus was more likely to hurt Democratic candidates, and there is some evidence that this was in fact the case during the 2016 election in Texas Congressional District 23.[3]

Opponents brought suit in federal court arguing the ID law had a racially discriminatory intent and effect under the federal Voting Rights Act. The courts struck down the ID law and ordered an interim solution for the 2016 election. The Texas Legislature then responded with a new law in 2017 that softened the ID requirements; people may now vote if they sign an affidavit, under strict penalty of law, swearing that they had a reasonable impediment to obtaining a standard ID and present certain alternatives such as a voter registration card, original birth certificate, paycheck, or utility bill as shown in Image 4.1. This new law was upheld by the US Fifth Circuit Court of Appeals as non-discrminatory.

voter turnout
The proportion of eligible Americans who actually vote.

Voter Turnout in the United States and in Texas

Making registration and voting easier was expected to result in increased **voter turnout**—the proportion of eligible Americans who actually vote. Such has not been the case; indeed,

FIGURE 4.1 How Many People Vote in the United States? Presidential Election Turnout, 1932–2016

Here we see that turnout declined in the early 1970s and has not changed much since. A little more than half of the voting-age population (VAP) now vote in presidential elections.

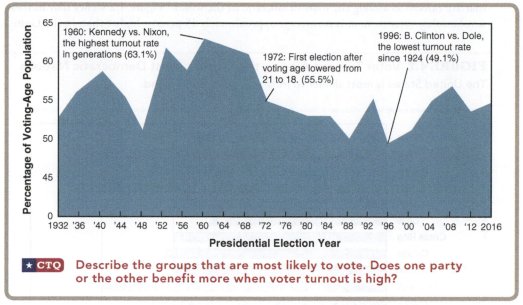

CTQ Describe the groups that are most likely to vote. Does one party or the other benefit more when voter turnout is high?

Source: Cengage Learning

the reverse has been true. Since 1960, turnout has actually declined. This is not to suggest that the actual number of voters has diminished. In fact, the number has steadily increased, from 70.6 million votes for president in 1964 to an estimated 137.1 million votes in 2016—an increase of 94 percent. However, the number of voting-age Americans increased from 114 million to 250 million during the same period—an increase of more than 100 percent. Thus, the **voting-age population (VAP)**, the total number of persons in the United States who are 18 years of age or older, has grown at a much faster rate than the actual voting population.[4]

Figure 4.1 shows voter turnout in presidential elections from 1932 to 2016. Voter turnout peaked in 1960 and has not reached that all-time high since. In 2016, turnout among the VAP was 54.7 percent.[5]

There are two main reasons for the decrease in voter turnout in the United States after the 1960s. The first reason can be traced to the Twenty-Sixth Amendment, which lowered the voting age from 21 to 18 in 1972. The amendment was passed at the height of the Vietnam War, with proponents arguing that a person who could be drafted and sent off to war should be able to vote. By extending the vote to 18- to 20-year-old citizens, the amendment expanded the eligible voting population. As we have already seen, however, these young people are less likely to vote than are older persons—since they were given the right to vote, citizens in the 18- to 20-year-old age group have rarely posted turnout rates as high as 40 percent, even in presidential elections. Thus, adding the age group to the lists of eligible voters in 1972 slightly reduced the overall turnout rate.

Second, identification with the two major political parties dropped after the 1960s, and more than one-third of all Americans now consider themselves *independents*—that is, unattached to either of the parties.[6] (The proportion is greater for younger voters.) As noted

voting-age population (VAP)
The total number of persons in the United States who are 18 years of age or older.

earlier, these voters are less likely to vote than are partisans.[7] A lot of independents do lean toward one of the parties, but in 2016 about 10 percent of U.S. adults were "pure" independents, not leaning toward either major party. This is important because leaners behave a lot like partisans in the voting booth, whereas pure independents are considered more persuadable and so potentially more critical in close elections.

Turnout in American general elections is significantly lower than it is in other countries that are ranked as among the most democratic in the world.[8] Figure 4.2 shows that in these democracies, voter turnout is on average approximately 15 percent higher than in the United

FIGURE 4.2 Voter Turnout Among the World's Most Democratic Nations
The United States is most similar to Ireland, Japan, and Poland.

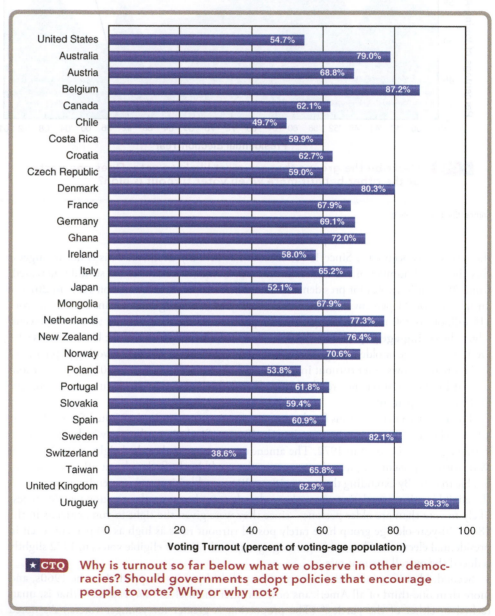

Country	Voting Turnout (percent of voting-age population)
United States	54.7%
Australia	79.0%
Austria	68.8%
Belgium	87.2%
Canada	62.1%
Chile	49.7%
Costa Rica	59.9%
Croatia	62.7%
Czech Republic	59.0%
Denmark	80.3%
France	67.9%
Germany	69.1%
Ghana	72.0%
Ireland	58.0%
Italy	65.2%
Japan	52.1%
Mongolia	67.9%
Netherlands	77.3%
New Zealand	76.4%
Norway	70.6%
Poland	53.8%
Portugal	61.8%
Slovakia	59.4%
Spain	60.9%
Sweden	82.1%
Switzerland	38.6%
Taiwan	65.8%
United Kingdom	62.9%
Uruguay	98.3%

★ CTQ **Why is turnout so far below what we observe in other democracies? Should governments adopt policies that encourage people to vote? Why or why not?**

Source: International Institute for Democracy and Electoral Assistance; Freedom House.

States. Interestingly, American political attitudes seem more conducive to voting than those in countries with far higher turnouts. Low voter turnout in the United States is caused by other factors, including institutional structures (primarily the strength of political parties) and the fact that most states require voters to register—in some nations, citizens are automatically registered to vote when they meet age requirements.

Reasons for Low Voter Turnout in Texas

Most Texans probably think that Texas is in the mainstream of American society. Why, then, is there such a difference between Texas and other urbanized and industrialized states in its political behavior? Why does Texas compare more closely with states of the Deep South in voter turnout? The answer may lie in its laws, socioeconomic characteristics, political structure, party competition, and political culture.

Legal Constraints Traditionally, scholars interested in the variation in turnout across the American states have focused on laws regulating registration and voting. Clearly, the most important of these laws were the restrictions on who may vote, such as the poll tax, property ownership requirements, or the outright exclusion of African Americans and women.

Although these restrictions disappeared some time ago, other barriers to registration and voting persisted, and some remain in effect today.[9] One can ask: Does a state promote political participation by setting the minimum necessary limitations and making it as convenient as possible for the citizen to vote? Or does a state repeatedly place barriers on the way to the polls, making the act of voting physically, financially, and psychologically as difficult as the local sense of propriety will allow? There is no doubt into which category Texas once fell— the application has been uneven, but historically Texas was among the most restrictive states in its voting laws.

IMAGE 4.2 When former Dallas Sheriff Lupe Valdez (right) challenged Governor Greg Abbott (left) in the 2018 general election, 39 percent of the voting-age population turned out to vote.

★ CTQ **Why do so few voters turn out in nonpresidential elections in Texas? Would a larger number of Texans cast their ballots for governor if the election were held at the same time as the presidential election?**

How Does Texas Compare?

Voter Turnout in the State and Nation

Table 4.1 shows that voter turnout in Texas (as in most of the South) has remained fairly stable at levels far below the national average. In the presidential election of 2016, for example, Texas turnout was 43.4 percent, about 11 percent below the rest of the nation. Texas had the second lowest turnout rate of any state in the nation, only above Hawaii.

In midterm elections, Texas's turnout has bounced around from election to election but is consistently lower than in most other states (see Table 4.2). Its turnout rate typically has been between 20 and 30 percent; Louisiana has often vied with Texas for the dubious honor of the lowest turnout in the nation.[10] In 2018, voter participation rose to 39 percent, but still only outpaced Arkansas, New York, and Hawaii. The low turnout in midterm elections heightens the influence of those politically active people in Texas who consistently turn out to vote. Recall our earlier discussion of "who votes" and consider why Texas ranks lower than most states.

TABLE 4.1   Percentage of the Voting-Age Population Voting: Presidential General Elections, 1996–2016

	1996	2000	2004	2008	2012	2016
United States	49.1	51.3	55.4	56.9	53.6	54.7
Texas	41.3	43.1	45.5	45.6	41.7	43.4
Difference (Texas vs. United States)	7.8	8.2	9.9	11.3	11.9	11.3
Rank of Texas among the 50 states	48th	48th	49th	49th	49th	49th

Source: United States Elections Project and the Texas Secretary of State.

TABLE 4.2   Percentage of the Voting-Age Population Voting: Nonpresidential General Elections, 1998–2018

	1998	2002	2006	2010	2014	2018
United States	36.4	36.2	37.1	37.8	33.9	45.4
Texas	26.1	28.8	25.8	26.7	23.9	39.1
Difference (Texas vs. United States)	10.3	7.4	11.3	11.1	10.0	6.3
Rank of Texas among the 50 states	47th	49th	50th	50th	50th	47th

Source: United States Elections Project and the Texas Secretary of State.

FOR DEBATE

★ CTQ **What factors explain why Texas has such low voter turnout compared to other states?**

★ CTQ **Should the government take steps to encourage more people to vote? Why or why not?**

★ CTQ **How would a higher voter turnout affect election results in Texas?**

However, nearly all of these restrictions have been changed by amendments to the U.S. Constitution, state and national laws, rulings by the U.S. Department of Justice, and judicial decisions. Even a cursory examination of these restrictions and the conditions under which they were removed makes one appreciate the extent to which Texas's elections were at one time closed. Consider these changes in Texas voting policies:

1. *Poll tax.* The payment of a poll tax as a prerequisite for voting was adopted in 1902. The cost was $1.75 ($1.50 plus $0.25 optional for the county) and represented more than a typical day's wages for some time. Many poor Texans were kept from voting. When the Twenty-Fourth Amendment was ratified in 1964, it voided the poll tax in national elections. Texas and only one other state kept it for state elections until it was held unconstitutional in 1966 (*United States* v. *Texas*, 384 U.S. 155).

2. *Women's suffrage.* An attempt was made to end the denial of the ballot to women in 1917, but the effort failed by four votes in the Texas legislature. Women were allowed to vote in the primaries of 1918, but not until ratification of the Nineteenth Amendment in 1920 did full suffrage come to women in Texas.

3. *White primary.* African Americans were barred from participating when the first party primary was held in 1906. When movement toward increased participation seemed likely, Texas made several moves to avoid U.S. Supreme Court rulings allowing African Americans to vote. Not until 1944 were the legislature's efforts to deny African Americans access to the primaries finally overturned (*Smith* v. *Allwright*, 321 U.S. 649).

4. *Military vote.* Until 1931, members of the National Guard were not permitted to vote. Members of the military began to enjoy the full rights of suffrage in Texas in 1965, when the U.S. Supreme Court voided the Texas constitutional exclusion (*Carrington* v. *Rash*, 380 U.S. 89).

5. *Long residence requirement.* The Texas residence requirement of one year in the state and six months in the county was modified slightly by the legislature to allow new residents to vote in the presidential part of the ballot, but not until a 1972 ruling of the U.S. Supreme Court were such requirements abolished (*Dunn* v. *Blumstein*, 405 U.S. 330).

6. *Property ownership as a requirement for voting in bond elections.* Texas held to this requirement until the U.S. Supreme Court made property ownership unnecessary for revenue bond elections in 1969 (*Kramer* v. *Union Free District No. 15*, 395 U.S. 621), and for tax elections in 1969 (*Cipriano* v. *City of Houma*, 395 U.S. 701) and in 1975 (*Hill* v. *Stone*, 421 U.S. 289).

7. *Annual registration.* Even after the poll tax was voided, Texas continued to require voters to register every year until annual registration was prohibited by the federal courts in 1971 (*Beare* v. *Smith*, 321 F. Supp. 1100).

8. *Early registration.* Texas voters were required to meet registration requirements by January 31, earlier than the cutoff date for candidates' filings and more than nine months before the general election. This restriction was voided in 1971 (*Beare* v. *Smith*, 321 F. Supp. 1100).

9. *Jury duty.* Texas law provided that the names of prospective jurors must be drawn from the voting rolls. Some Texans did not like to serve on juries, and not registering to vote ensured against a jury summons. (Counties now use driver's licenses for jury lists.)

Texas employed almost every technique available except the literacy test and the grandfather clause[11] to deny the vote or to make it expensive in terms of time, money, and aggravation. This is not the case today. Most serious barriers to voting in Texas were removed long ago, and the legislature has instituted a few provisions that actually make voting easier. As noted earlier however, some new barriers have also been added, most notably, the voter ID law, but the impact of its strict requirements has been somewhat softened recently, and while the new voter ID law surely does not boost turnout, it is unclear how much it depresses it. Putting aside voter ID, restrictive laws in Texas mostly explain why turnout was low in the past and why, with the relaxing of restrictions, it increased somewhat in the 1960s. But legal factors alone do not explain why turnout in Texas remains so much lower than in most other states today. For this, we need to look elsewhere.

Demographic Factors Texas is known as the land of the "big rich" cattle barons and oil tycoons. What is not so well known is that Texas is also the land of the "big poor" and that over 4 million people live in poverty here. Although nationally the proportion of people living below the poverty level in 2016 was 12.7 percent, in Texas the proportion was 15.6 percent. Among African American and Latino Texans, 21 percent have incomes below this level. Of those individuals in Texas living in poverty, more than one-third are children. Understandably, formal educational achievement is also low. Of Texans older than 25 years of age, one in four has not graduated from high school. Among African Americans, the ratio is just less than one of three, and among Latinos, it is almost one out of two.[12]

Given that income and education are such important determinants of electoral participation, low voter turnout is exactly what we should expect in Texas. Because income and education levels are particularly low among African Americans and, especially, Latinos, turnout is particularly low for these groups. Voting by Texas minorities is on the rise, however, and this has led to much greater representation of both groups in elected offices, as we will see. These trends should continue as income and education levels among minorities increase.

Political Structure Another deterrent to voting in Texas is the length of the ballot and the number of elections. Texas uses a long ballot that provides for the popular election of numerous public officers (including many that some critics believe should be appointed). In an urban county, the ballot may call for the voter to choose from as many as 100 to 200 candidates vying for 50 or more offices. The frequency of referendums on constitutional amendments contributes to the length of the ballot in Texas. Voters are also asked to go to the polls for various municipal, school board, bond, and special-district elections. Government is far more fragmented in Texas than in other states, and the election of so many minor officials may be confusing and frustrating for voters.

Party Competition The competitiveness of elections is important to voters. The closer the race, the greater the interest, attention, and participation during the campaign and on election day itself. The problem for Texas and other southern states is that general elections between the two parties are not competitive, and this has been true for a long time even when the party in power changed. In the past, Texas was a one-party Democratic state, and this held until the late 1980s. Since the late 1990s, the Republicans have dominated statewide races. With rare exceptions, then, these races between candidates of the two parties in November elections in Texas have not been competitive. This dampens voter interest and turnout.

Political Culture Insights into voter participation levels have been derived from the concept of political culture, which, as defined in Chapter 1, describes the set of political values and beliefs that are dominant in a society. Borrowed from social anthropologists, this concept has been found to be applicable to all political systems, from those of developing countries to modern industrial democracies. It has been especially useful in the study of American politics, where federalism has emphasized the diversity among regions, states, and communities—a diversity that cries out for some approach that can effectively explain it.

The American political culture is actually a mix of three subcultures, each prevalent in at least one area of the United States.[13] The *moralistic culture* is a product of the Puritan era and is strongest in New England. The *traditionalistic culture* comes to us via the plantation society of the Deep South. The *individualistic culture* was born in the commercial centers of Middle Atlantic states, moving west and south along the Ohio River and its tributaries. It is the mix as well as the isolation of these cultures that gives American politics its flavor.

Important to students of electoral politics is that "the degree of political participation (i.e., voter turnout and suffrage regulations) is the most consistent indicator of political culture."[14] The moralistic culture perceives the discussion of public issues and voting as not only a right but also an opportunity that is beneficial to the citizen and society alike. In contrast, the traditionalistic culture views politics as the special preserve of the social and economic elite and a process of maintaining the existing order. Highly personal, it views political participation as a privilege and uses social pressure as well as restrictive election laws to limit voting. The individualistic culture blurs the distinction between economic and political life. Here, business and politics are both viewed as appropriate avenues by which an individual can advance his or her interests, and conflicts of interest are fairly common. In this culture, business interests can play a very strong role, and running for office is difficult without their support.

Low voter turnout in Texas may be due in part to the state's *political culture*, which is a mix of the traditionalistic and the individualistic. The traditionalistic aspect is especially characteristic of East Texas, settled primarily by immigrants from the Deep South in the years prior

IMAGE 4.3 Signing petitions and attending rallies are important forms of political participation. Although people are less likely to vote in the United States and especially in Texas, by comparison with people in other countries, they are more likely to take part in other ways.

(a)

Marjorie Kamys Cotera / PhotoEdit

(b)

ZUMA Press, Inc./Alamy Stock Photo

★ CTQ **Identify forms of participation other than voting. Which forms of participation give you the greatest influence in Texas politics?**

to the Civil War. The individualistic aspect predominates throughout the rest of the state. As a result, participation in politics is not as highly regarded as it is in states with a moralistic culture; politics in Texas is largely the domain of business interests and traditionalists. People may be less likely to vote in Texas because they do not value political participation itself and because they tend to think that they play only a little role in politics.

Types of Elections in Texas

LO 4.2 **Describe the types of Texas elections.**

Winning an office is typically a two-stage process. First, the candidate must win the Democratic or Republican Party nomination in the primary election. Second, the candidate must win the general election against the other party's nominee. It is possible for a candidate to get on the general election ballot without winning a primary election (as will be discussed shortly), but this is rare. As in most other states, elections in Texas are dominated by the Democratic and Republican parties.

Primary Elections

Three successive devices for selecting political party nominees have been used in the history of this country, each perceived as a cure for the ills of a previously corrupt, inefficient, or inadequate system. The first was the caucus, consisting of the elected political party members serving in the legislature. The "insider" politics of the caucus room motivated the reformers of the Jacksonian era to throw out "King Caucus" and to institute the party convention system by 1828. In this system, ordinary party members select delegates to a party convention, and these delegates then nominate the party's candidates for office and write a party platform. The convention system was hailed as a surefire method of ending party nominations by the legislative bosses. By 1890, the backroom politics of the convention halls again moved reformers to action, and the result was the direct primary, adopted by most states between 1890 and 1920. Texas's first direct primary was held in 1906, under the Terrell Election Law passed in 1903. The **direct primary** enables party members to participate directly in the selection of a candidate to represent them in the general election.

direct primary
A method of selecting party nominees in which party members participate directly in the selection of a candidate to represent them in the general election.

Traditionally regarded as private activities, primaries were at one time largely beyond the concern of legislatures and courts. Costs of party activities, including primaries, were covered by donations and by assessing each candidate who sought a party's nomination. Judges attempted to avoid suits between warring factions of the parties as much as they did those involving church squabbles over the division of church property. This was the basis on which the U.S. Supreme Court in 1935 upheld the Texas Democratic Party convention's decision barring African Americans from participating in the party primary.[15] Because political party activities were increasingly circumscribed by law, the Court reversed itself in 1944 and recognized the primary as an integral part of the election process.[16]

The Court noted that in a one-party state, which Texas was at the time, the party primary may be the only election in which any meaningful choice is possible. Because the Democratic Party seldom had any real opposition in the general election, winning the nomination was, for all practical purposes, winning the office. The party balance in Texas has changed quite a lot in recent years, however. The Republicans have overtaken the Democrats and the GOP primary winner has not lost a statewide election since 1994.

Who Must Hold a Primary?

Any party receiving 20 percent of the gubernatorial vote in the prior election must hold a primary, and all other parties must use the convention system.[17] New parties must meet additional requirements if their nominees are to be on the general election ballot. In addition to holding a convention, these parties must file with the secretary of state a list of supporters equal to 1 percent of the total vote for governor in the last general election. The list may consist of the names of those who participated in the party's convention, a nominating petition, or a combination of the two. Persons named as supporters must be registered voters who have not participated in the activities (primaries or conventions) of any other party. Each page (although not each name) on the nominating petition must be notarized. Such a requirement is, as intended, difficult to meet and therefore inhibits the creation of new political parties.[18]

Financing Primaries

Party primaries are funded partly by modest candidate filing fees, but most of the primaries' costs come from the state treasury. The parties' state and county executive committees initially make the expenditures, but the secretary of state reimburses each committee for the difference between the filing fees collected and the actual cost of the primary. To get on the party primary ballot, a candidate needs only to file an application with the state or county party chair and pay the prescribed fee. The categories of fees, applicable also for special elections, are summarized in Table 4.3.

So that no person is forced to bear an unreasonable expense when running for political office, the legislature provided that a petition may be submitted as an alternative to the filing fee. Such petition must bear the names of at least 5,000 voters for candidates seeking nomination to statewide office. For district and lesser offices, the petition must bear the signatures of voters equal to 2 percent of the vote for the party's candidate for governor in the last election, up to a maximum of 500 required signatures.

Administering Primaries In the county primaries, the chair and county executive committee of each party receive applications and filing fees and hold drawings to determine the order of names on the ballot for both party and government offices. They then certify the

TABLE 4.3 Fees for Listing on the Party Primary Ballot in Texas, Selected Offices

Office	Fee
U.S. Senator	$5,000
U.S. Representative	$3,125
Texas Statewide Officers	$3,750
State Senator	$1,250
State Representative	$750
State Board of Education Member	$300
County Commissioner	$750–$1,250
District Judge	$1,500–$2,500
Justice of the Peace, Constable	$375–$1,000

▶ How much do filing fees limit candidates' access to the state ballot? Should election laws attempt to discourage frivolous candidates?

ballot, choose an election judge for each voting precinct (usually the precinct chair), select the voting devices (paper ballots or voting machines), and arrange for polling places and printing. After the primary, the county chair and executive committee canvass the votes and certify the results to their respective state executive committees.

In the state primary, the state party chair and the state executive committee of each political party receive applications of candidates for state offices, conduct drawings to determine the order of names, certify the ballot to the county-level officials, and canvass the election returns after the primary.

The Majority Rule

The Majority Rule In Texas, as in other southern states (except for Tennessee and Virginia) that were once predominantly Democratic, nominations are by a majority (50% plus 1) of the popular vote. When several candidates seek their party's nomination, one candidate can come in first without necessarily getting more than half. If no candidate receives a majority of votes cast for a particular office in the first primary, a **runoff primary** is required in which the two candidates receiving the greatest number of votes are pitted against each other. Outside the South, where the balance between the two major parties has historically been more equal, only a plurality of the votes (more votes than for anyone else) is required, and consequently no runoff is necessary. The election rule used may influence the number of candidates that run in primaries, as there is more reason to enter the race where the majority rule is used. That is, one does not need to expect to win the first primary, but just finish in the top two and get to the runoff (if the first place candidate does not win more than 50 percent of the vote).

runoff primary
A second primary election that pits the two top vote-getters from the first primary against each other when the winner of the first primary did not receive a majority.

Primary elections in Texas are held on the first Tuesday in March of even-numbered years. The runoff primary is scheduled for the fourth Tuesday in May, or more than two months after the initial party primary election. Although there are earlier presidential primaries, no other state schedules primaries to nominate candidates for state offices so far in advance of the general election in November.

Turnout in Texas primaries is much lower than in general elections. Take 2018, for example: only 2.6 million Texans voted, approximately 13 percent of the almost 20 million people who were 18 years of age or older. The people who do vote in primary elections are hardly representative of the population—they tend to be older, better educated, more affluent, and more ideologically extreme.

Open Primary

Open Primary Party primaries are defined as either *open* or *closed*. These terms relate to whether or not participation is limited to party members. Because the purpose of a primary is to choose the party's nominee, it may seem logical to exclude anyone who is not a party member. However, not every state recognizes the strength of that logic. Texas and 14 other states have an **open primary**, in which voters decide at the polls (on election day) in which primary they will participate. Of course, voters are forbidden to vote in more than one primary on election day, and once they have voted in the first primary, they cannot switch parties and participate in the runoff election or convention of any other party. Voters who did not vote in the first primary are still free to vote in either party's runoff primary, but because of the restriction against switching parties after voting in the first primary, some consider the runoff to be semi-open.

open primary
A type of party primary in which a voter can choose on election day in which primary to participate.

closed primary
A type of primary in which a voter is required to specify a party preference when registering to vote.

In contrast, the typical **closed primary** requires that a person specify a party preference when registering to vote. The party's name is then stamped on the registration card at the time of issuance. Each voter may generally change party affiliation at any time up to 30 days before participating in a primary or a convention. Voters are limited, however, to the activities of the party they have formally declared as their preference. If the individual registers as an independent (no party preference), that person is excluded from the primaries and conventions of *all* parties in nine states. In nine others, unaffiliated voters are allowed to choose the primary in which they would like to participate.

Seven states have partially closed systems that give parties the option of letting voters not affiliated with the party vote in the party's primary. Six states have partially open systems that allow voters to vote in any primary, but in doing so they often are registering as members of that party. Another three states use a top-two primary, in which candidates from different parties compete in a single primary and the top two vote-getters proceed to the general election. Nebraska employs a non-partisan top-two primary for state legislative elections and a partially closed primary for other elections. Primary elections clearly differ quite a lot across states, but those differences have little bearing on the general election. Whether voters participate in a party primary or not, they are completely free to vote for any party candidate in the general election in November.

Crossover Voting   The opportunity always exists in Texas for members of one political party to invade the other party's primary. This is called **crossover voting**. It is designed to increase the chances that the nominee from the other party will be someone whose philosophy is like that of the invader's own party. For example, Democrats might cross over to vote for the more moderate candidate in the Republican primary, or Republicans might cross over into the Democratic primary to support the candidate who is least objectionable from their viewpoint.

crossover voting
When members of one political party vote in the other party's primary to influence the selection of the nominee.

General Elections

The purpose of party primaries is to nominate the party's candidates from the competing intra-party factions. General elections, in contrast, are held to allow the voters to choose the people who will actually serve in national, state, and county offices from among the competing political party nominees and write-in candidates. General elections differ from primaries in at least two other important ways. First, because general elections are the official public elections to determine who will take office, they are administered completely by public (as opposed to party) officials of state and county governments.[19] Second, unlike Texas's primaries, in which a majority (50% plus 1) of the vote is required, the general election is decided by a **plurality vote**, in which a winning candidate needs only to win the most votes, even if that number is less than 50 percent. Figure 4.3 shows the requirements for major party candidates to win office.

plurality vote
An election rule in which the candidate with the most votes wins even if that candidate get less than 50 percent.

General elections in Texas are held every other year on the same day as national elections—the first Tuesday after the first Monday in November of even-numbered years. In years divisible by four, we elect the president, vice president, all U.S. representatives, and one-third of the U.S. senators. In Texas, we elect all 150 members of the state house and roughly half (15 or 16) of the 31 senators. We also elect some board and court positions at the state level as well as about half of the county positions.

However, most major state executive positions (governor, lieutenant governor, attorney general, and so forth) are not filled until the middle of the president's term. In the midterm elections, the U.S. representatives and one-third of U.S. senators (but not the president) again face the voters. All state representatives and half of the senators also are elected in these years, as are some board members, judges, and county officers.

Holding simultaneous national and state elections has important political ramifications. During the administration of Andrew Jackson, parties first began to tie the states and the national government together politically. A strong presidential candidate and an effective candidate for state office can benefit significantly by cooperating and campaigning under the party label. This usually works best, of course, if the candidates are in substantial agreement with respect to political philosophy and the issues.

In Texas, which is more politically conservative than the average American state, fundamental agreement is often lacking. This has been especially true for Democratic candidates.

FIGURE 4.3 Primaries and General Election Cycle in Texas

This figure shows the steps major party candidates must take to win office in Texas. In March and May of even-numbered years, major parties hold primaries among their members to determine who will be their nominees. General elections are public elections held in November so voters can determine who will actually win office among various party nominees and independent candidates.

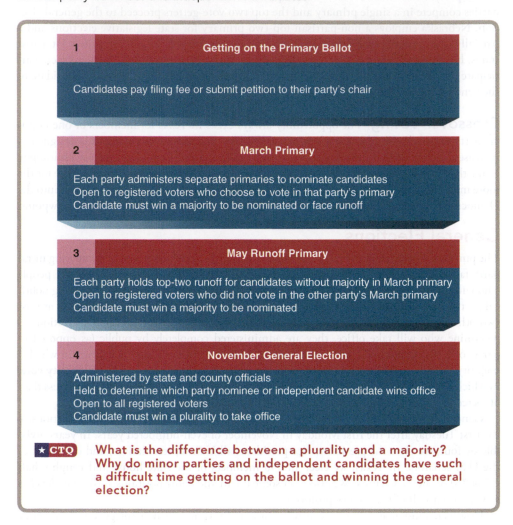

1   **Getting on the Primary Ballot**

Candidates pay filing fee or submit petition to their party's chair

2   **March Primary**

Each party administers separate primaries to nominate candidates
Open to registered voters who choose to vote in that party's primary
Candidate must win a majority to be nominated or face runoff

3   **May Runoff Primary**

Each party holds top-two runoff for candidates without majority in March primary
Open to registered voters who did not vote in the other party's March primary
Candidate must win a majority to be nominated

4   **November General Election**

Administered by state and county officials
Held to determine which party nominee or independent candidate wins office
Open to all registered voters
Candidate must win a plurality to take office

★ CTQ   **What is the difference between a plurality and a majority? Why do minor parties and independent candidates have such a difficult time getting on the ballot and winning the general election?**

Popular Democrats in the state, at times, disassociated themselves from the more liberal presidential nominees of the party. As Democratic candidate for governor in 2010, Bill White played down his connections to former Democratic President Bill Clinton and rarely mentioned the sitting Democratic President Barack Obama.

When the Texas Constitution was amended in 1972 to extend the terms (from two to four years) for the governor and other major administrative officials, the elections for these offices were set for November of midterm election years. This change had two main effects. First, although candidates are also running for Congress in midterm elections, separation of presidential and state campaigns insulates public officials from the ebb and flow of presidential politics and allow them to further disassociate themselves from the national political parties. Elections for statewide office now largely reflect Texas issues and interests. Second, the separation reduces voting turnout in statewide elections and makes the outcomes much more predictable.

As was shown earlier, turnout in midterm elections is usually much lower than in presidential election years, when many people are lured to the polls by the importance of the office and the visibility of the campaign. The independent and the marginal voters are active, and election results for congressional and state-level offices are less predictable. In midterm election years, however, less partisan and less predictable voters are more likely to stay home, and the contest is largely confined to political party regulars. Many incumbent politicians were caught off guard, however, when a highly competitive 2018 midterm political environment drew a turnout rivaling that of presidential election years. Figure 4.4 shows the low levels of participation in the 2016 and 2018 state elections.

FIGURE 4.4 Proportion of Texans Voting in Midterm and Presidential Elections

This chart shows that only a small percentage of all Texans voted in the 2018 midterm primary and general elections that selected the governor and most major state executive officers. About half of the population was registered to vote, and far less actually voted. Voter interest had been only slightly higher in the 2016 presidential primaries and general election. Voter turnout in the 2016 presidential election represented 32 percent of the total population, but 30 percent in 2018.

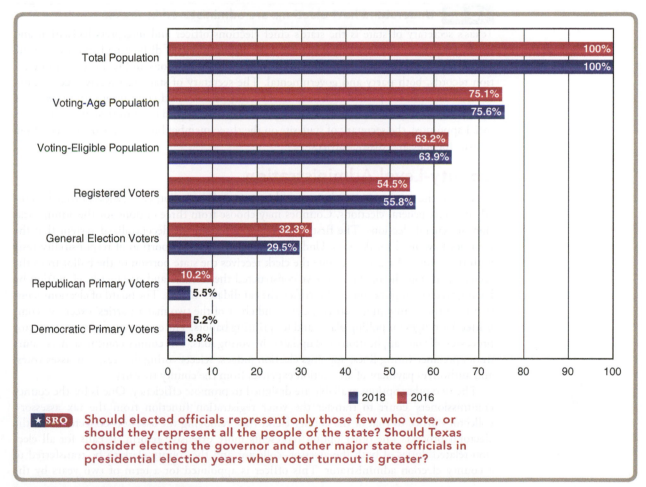

★SRO **Should elected officials represent only those few who vote, or should they represent all the people of the state? Should Texas consider electing the governor and other major state officials in presidential election years when voter turnout is greater?**

Source: U.S. Census and Texas Secretary of State.

Special Elections

As the name implies, special elections are designed to meet special or emergency needs, such as ratification of constitutional amendments or filling vacant offices. Special elections are held to fill vacancies only in legislative bodies that have general (rather than limited) law-making power. Typical legislative bodies with general power are the U.S. Senate and U.S. House of Representatives, state legislatures, and city councils in home-rule cities. (All other vacancies, including judgeships and county commissioners, are filled by appointment.) Runoffs are held when necessary. The elections provide for the filling of a vacancy only until the end of the regular term or until the next general election, whichever comes first.

Because special elections are not partisan, the process of getting on the ballot is relatively easy and does not involve a primary.[20] All that is required is filing the application form in a timely and appropriate manner and paying the designated filing fee. Unlike in general elections, the winner of a special election must receive a majority of the votes.

Did You Know? The conservative legislature adopted the majority rule for special elections after liberal Ralph Yarborough won a U.S. Senate seat in 1957 with a mere plurality of 38 percent in a special election that featured 23 candidates. Those in control of the legislature can and do change the rules of the game to benefit those who share their political views.

The Conduct and Administration of Elections

LO 4.3 **Understand how elections are administered in Texas.**

Texas's secretary of state is the state's chief elections officer and interprets legislation and issues guidelines. The secretary of state has the responsibility of disbursing funds to the state and county executive committees to pay for the primary elections and is the keeper of election records, both party and governmental. The secretary of state also receives certificates of nomination from parties that have conducted primaries and conventions and uses these certificates to prepare the ballot for statewide offices. Along with the governor and a gubernatorial appointee, the secretary of state sits on the three-member board that canvasses election returns for state and district offices.

County-Level Administration

Except for the preparation of the statewide portion of the ballot, county-level officials actually conduct general elections. Counties may choose from three options for the administration of general elections. The first option is to maintain the decentralized system that the counties have used for decades. Under this system, the major portion of responsibility rests with the county clerk. By the time the clerk receives the state portion of the ballot from the secretary of state, he or she will have constructed the county- and precinct-level portion by having received applications and certified the candidates' names. The board of elections (consisting of the county judge, sheriff, clerk, and chair of the two major parties' executive committees) arranges for polling places and for printing ballots. The county tax assessor–collector processes all voter applications and updates the voting rolls. The county commissioners' court draws precinct voting lines, appoints election judges, selects voting devices, canvasses votes, and authorizes payment of all election expenses from the county treasury.

The two other options available are designed to promote efficiency. One is for the county commissioners' court to transfer the voter registration function from the tax assessor–collector's office to that of the county clerk, thus removing the assessor–collector from the electoral process. The other option represents more extensive reform. It calls for all election-related duties of both the assessor–collector and the county clerk to be transferred to a county election administrator. This officer is appointed for a term of two years by the

County Elections Commission, which, in those counties that choose the election administrator option, replaces the board of elections. (Membership is the same, except that in the use of the commission, the county clerk serves instead of the sheriff.)

Ballot Construction

Texas once used the classic **party column ballot**, on which offices were listed in descending order of importance and candidates were listed in columns under the party label. And to vote for all of the candidates of one party, the voter needed only mark the box for the party of his or her choice. Clearly, the party column ballot facilitates **straight ticket voting**, which is selecting all of the candidates of one particular party. But to pick and choose between the parties, a voter had to mark a separate box by each of the many candidates on the ballot.

Like so many other features of an election system, ballot construction reflects both practical and political considerations. Texas began to move away from the strict party column ballot to accommodate the requirements of electronic voting machines and, today most voters will see a ballot on which candidates are listed underneath each office instead of in party columns (see Figure 4.5). Believing that Democrats were benefiting from the single-punch option, the Texas Legislature moved further away from the party-column ballot when it eliminated the option that allows a vote for all of a party's candidates by marking a single box. Of course, voters may still cast a straight-ticket vote, but beginning with the 2020 election, they will need to make a separate mark for each candidate they wish to choose but can still readily find their party's candidates because Republican candidates are consistently listed in the first row under each office; Democrats come next, followed by other candidates.

In contrast, some states use the **office block ballot**, also known as the "Massachusetts ballot" because it originated there. On this type of ballot, the parties' candidates are listed randomly rather than in a readily identifiable pattern. Office block ballots do not offer voters the option of using a single mark to vote for all of the candidates of a single party. To vote a straight party ticket, voters must search for their party's candidates in each of the office blocks. Clearly, this type of ballot facilitates **split ticket voting**, selecting candidates from one party for some offices and candidates from another party for other offices. Minor parties and independent voters usually advocate the use of this ballot type because it makes straight ticket voting for the major parties more difficult and encourages voters to shop around among parties and candidates.

The Politics of Ballot Construction
Understandably, supporters of the major Texas political parties strongly support the use of the party column ballot. It enables lesser-known candidates to ride on the coattails of the party label or a popular candidate running for a major office. There may also be an extra payoff in the use of this type of ballot when a party is listed first. For each office, the parties are slated from top to bottom on the ballot (see Figure 2.5) according to the proportion of votes that each party's candidate for governor received in the most recent gubernatorial election. Thus, candidates of the majority party (Republicans) benefit by occupying the coveted first line (or column) on the ballot. Democrats come second; next come third-party candidates and candidates of parties that were not on the ballot in the last election; and last come the independents.

Getting on the Ballot
For a name to be placed on the general election ballot, the candidate must be either a party nominee or an independent. For any party that received at least 5 percent of the vote for any statewide office in the previous general election, or 2 percent in the prior gubernatorial election, the full slate of candidates is placed on the ballot automatically. Thus, the Democratic and Republican parties have no problem getting their candidates on the ballot, and certification of primary winners is a mere formality.

party column ballot
A type of ballot used in a general election in which all of the candidates from each party are listed in parallel columns under the party label.

straight ticket voting
Selecting all of the candidates of one particular party.

office block ballot
A type of ballot used in a general election in which the names of the parties' candidates are listed randomly under each office.

split ticket voting
A voter selecting candidates from one party for some offices and candidates from the other party for other offices.

FIGURE 4.5 A Typical Texas Ballot from Tarrant County

Recall that Republican candidates are listed first in 2018 because their candidate received the most votes in the last election for governor. Notice that voters were able to vote for all of the candidates of a single party—that is, to vote a straight ticket—by making a single mark on the ballot, an option that was eliminated for elections after 2018.

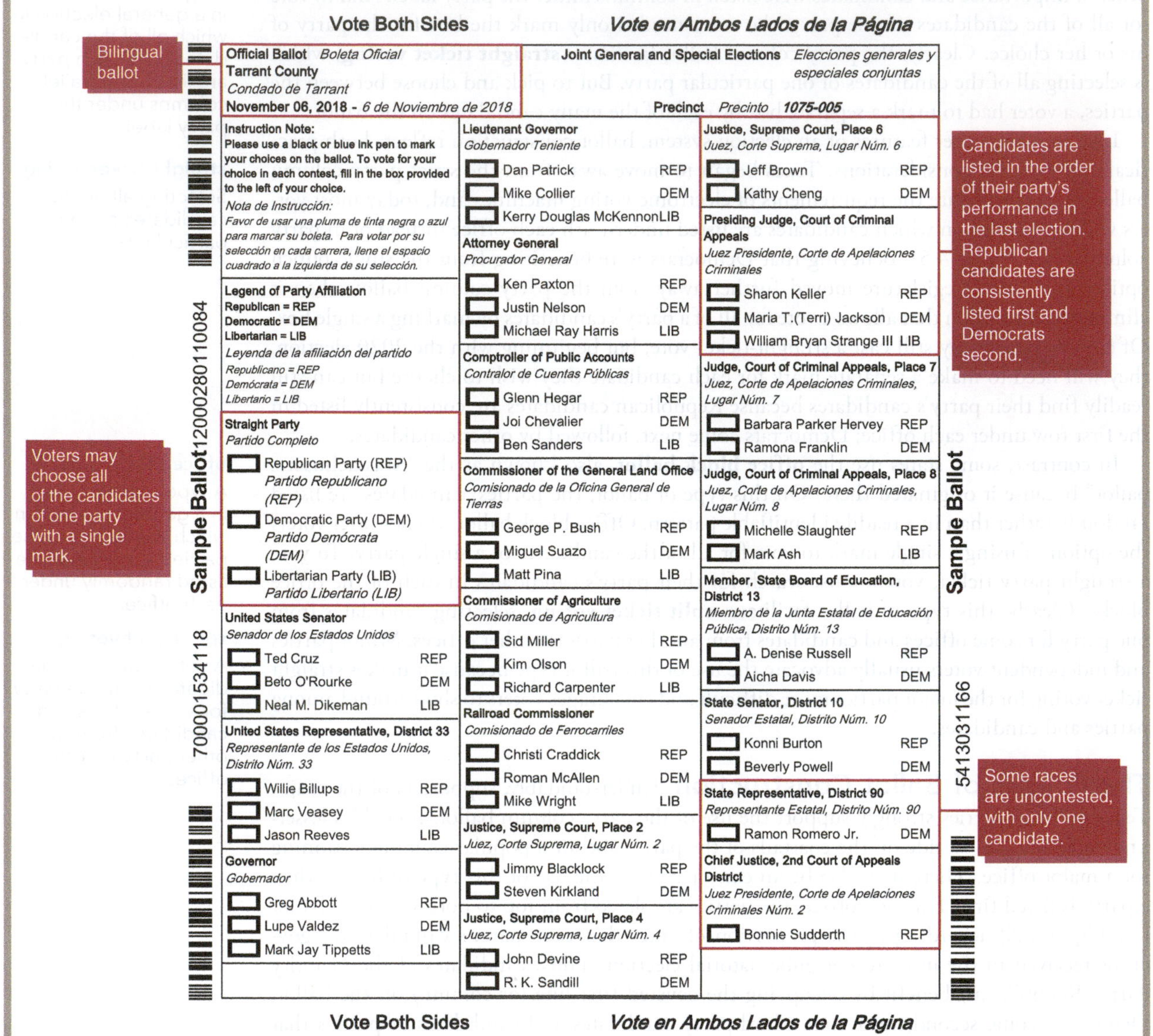

Bilingual ballot

Voters may choose all of the candidates of one party with a single mark.

Candidates are listed in the order of their party's performance in the last election. Republican candidates are consistently listed first and Democrats second.

Some races are uncontested, with only one candidate.

Vote Both Sides — Vote en Ambos Lados de la Página

Official Ballot *Boleta Oficial*
Tarrant County
Condado de Tarrant
November 06, 2018 - *6 de Noviembre de 2018*

Joint General and Special Elections *Elecciones generales y especiales conjuntas*

Precinct *Precinto* **1075-005**

Instruction Note:
Please use a black or blue ink pen to mark your choices on the ballot. To vote for your choice in each contest, fill in the box provided to the left of your choice.
Nota de Instrucción:
Favor de usar una pluma de tinta negra o azul para marcar su boleta. Para votar por su selección en cada carrera, llene el espacio cuadrado a la izquierda de su selección.

Legend of Party Affiliation
Republican = REP
Democratic = DEM
Libertarian = LIB
Leyenda de la afiliación del partido
Republicano = REP
Demócrata = DEM
Libertario = LIB

Straight Party
Partido Completo
- Republican Party (REP) *Partido Republicano (REP)*
- Democratic Party (DEM) *Partido Demócrata (DEM)*
- Libertarian Party (LIB) *Partido Libertario (LIB)*

United States Senator
Senador de los Estados Unidos
- Ted Cruz — REP
- Beto O'Rourke — DEM
- Neal M. Dikeman — LIB

United States Representative, District 33
Representante de los Estados Unidos, Distrito Núm. 33
- Willie Billups — REP
- Marc Veasey — DEM
- Jason Reeves — LIB

Governor
Gobernador
- Greg Abbott — REP
- Lupe Valdez — DEM
- Mark Jay Tippetts — LIB

Lieutenant Governor
Gobernador Teniente
- Dan Patrick — REP
- Mike Collier — DEM
- Kerry Douglas McKennon — LIB

Attorney General
Procurador General
- Ken Paxton — REP
- Justin Nelson — DEM
- Michael Ray Harris — LIB

Comptroller of Public Accounts
Contralor de Cuentas Públicas
- Glenn Hegar — REP
- Joi Chevalier — DEM
- Ben Sanders — LIB

Commissioner of the General Land Office
Comisionado de la Oficina General de Tierras
- George P. Bush — REP
- Miguel Suazo — DEM
- Matt Pina — LIB

Commissioner of Agriculture
Comisionado de Agricultura
- Sid Miller — REP
- Kim Olson — DEM
- Richard Carpenter — LIB

Railroad Commissioner
Comisionado de Ferrocarriles
- Christi Craddick — REP
- Roman McAllen — DEM
- Mike Wright — LIB

Justice, Supreme Court, Place 2
Juez, Corte Suprema, Lugar Núm. 2
- Jimmy Blacklock — REP
- Steven Kirkland — DEM

Justice, Supreme Court, Place 4
Juez, Corte Suprema, Lugar Núm. 4
- John Devine — REP
- R. K. Sandill — DEM

Justice, Supreme Court, Place 6
Juez, Corte Suprema, Lugar Núm. 6
- Jeff Brown — REP
- Kathy Cheng — DEM

Presiding Judge, Court of Criminal Appeals
Juez Presidente, Corte de Apelaciones Criminales
- Sharon Keller — REP
- Maria T.(Terri) Jackson — DEM
- William Bryan Strange III — LIB

Judge, Court of Criminal Appeals, Place 7
Juez, Corte de Apelaciones Criminales, Lugar Núm. 7
- Barbara Parker Hervey — REP
- Ramona Franklin — DEM

Judge, Court of Criminal Appeals, Place 8
Juez, Corte de Apelaciones Criminales, Lugar Núm. 8
- Michelle Slaughter — REP
- Mark Ash — LIB

Member, State Board of Education, District 13
Miembro de la Junta Estatal de Educación Pública, Distrito Núm. 13
- A. Denise Russell — REP
- Aicha Davis — DEM

State Senator, District 10
Senador Estatal, Distrito Núm. 10
- Konni Burton — REP
- Beverly Powell — DEM

State Representative, District 90
Representante Estatal, Distrito Núm. 90
- Ramon Romero Jr. — DEM

Chief Justice, 2nd Court of Appeals District
Juez Presidente, Corte de Apelaciones Criminales Núm. 2
- Bonnie Sudderth — REP

Sample Ballot 1200028011 0084

700001534118

Sample Ballot

5413031166

Vote Both Sides — Vote en Ambos Lados de la Página

★ CTQ **Why would party leaders prefer a ballot arrangement that facilitates straight ticket voting? What are the arguments for and against bilingual ballots such as the one shown here?**

Minor parties have a more difficult time. Although both the Libertarian and Green parties managed to break the 5 percent barrier to get a place on the ballot for the general elections between 2010 and 2016, the Green Party did not receive enough votes for an automatic place on the 2018 ballot. Minor parties without automatic ballot access must earn a place on the ballot by petition. In 2018 not one of the five parties that attempted to obtain access to the ballot via petition was successful.

Except for independent candidates running for president, independents and third party candidates may get a place on the ballot by submitting a petition containing signatures of a number of registered voters who did not vote in that year's Democratic or Republican primaries equal to a particular share of the total vote in the most recent election for governor. For statewide office, signatures equaling 1 percent of the total gubernatorial vote are needed, which meant that in 2016 and 2018 the number of valid signatures needed was 47,183. For district and local offices the number of signatures required is much less daunting: 5 percent of the preceding gubernatorial vote or 500, whichever is lower.[21]

★ **Did You Know?** Getting off a ballot can be as difficult as getting on. Take the case of Tom DeLay, a former member of the U.S. House of Representatives. After he resigned from Congress in June 2006, the Republican Party tried to have him replaced on the general election ballot. U.S. District Judge Sam Sparks ruled that he must remain on the ballot, and the Fifth Circuit Court of Appeals upheld the decision.

Write-In Candidates

Write-in candidates are not listed on the ballot—voters must write them on the ballot. A write-in candidate must file a declaration of candidacy with the secretary of state 70 days before election day. With the declaration the candidate must include either the filing fee or a nominating petition with the required number of signatures. The names of write-in candidates must be posted at the election site. A candidate not properly registered cannot win, regardless of the votes he or she receives. Even when registered, write-in candidates are seldom successful.

The Secret Ballot and the Integrity of Elections

The essence of the right to vote is generally viewed as the right to cast a ballot in secret, have the election conducted fairly, and have the ballots counted correctly. The **Australian ballot**, adopted by Texas in 1892, allowed people to vote in secret. It includes names of the candidates of all political parties on a single ballot printed at the public's expense and available only at the voting place.[22] Given a reasonably private area in which to mark the ballot, the voter was offered a secret ballot for the first time.

Australian ballot
A ballot printed by the government (as opposed to the political parties) that allows people to vote in secret.

Although there are legal remedies, such as the issuance of injunctions and the threat of criminal penalties, Texas has looked primarily to "political" remedies in its effort to protect the integrity of the electoral process. Minority parties have reason to be concerned that irregularities in elections administered by members of the majority party may not be observed or, if observed, may not be reported. Even in the absence of wrongdoing, the testimony of the correctness of an election by individuals with opposing interests helps ensure public faith in the process.

Traditional practice has been that in general and special elections, the county board of elections routinely appoints as election judges the precinct chair of the political party whose members constitute a majority on the elections board. Each election judge is required to select at least one election clerk from a list submitted by the county chair of each political party. Moreover, law now recognizes the status of poll watchers, and both primary candidates and county chairs are authorized to appoint them.

Candidates can ask for a recount of the ballots. The candidate who requests a recount must put up a deposit—$60 per precinct where paper ballots were used and $100 per precinct using electronic voting—and is liable for the entire cost unless he or she wins or ties in the recount. In a large county, a recount can be quite costly. Consider Dallas County, which has more than 800 precincts. Despite this drawback, the current practice marks a real improvement over the days when often ineffective judicial remedies were the only recourse.

Multilingualism   Ballots in all Texas counties are in English and Spanish. In 2002 and 2016 respectively, the U.S. Department of Justice ordered Harris County, which includes Houston, and Tarrant County, which includes Fort Worth, to provide ballots (and voting material) in Vietnamese as well. In 2012, Harris County added Mandarin Chinese to the ballot. In some parts of the country, other languages are required, including Choctaw, Japanese, and Korean. In Los Angeles County alone, ballots are printed in nine different languages (Armenian, Chinese (Mandarin), Cambodian/Khmer, English, Farsi, Korean, Spanish, Tagalog/Filipino, Vietnamese). This all is due to the Voting Rights Act of 1965 and its subsequent amendment in 1992. According to Section 203 of the act, a political subdivision (typically, a county) must provide language assistance to voters if significant numbers of voting-age citizens are members of a single language minority group and do not speak or understand English "well enough to participate in the electoral process." Specifically, the legal requirement is triggered when more than 5 percent of voting-age citizens or 10,000 of these citizens meet the criteria. The 2010 Census showed that more than 40,000 people living in Harris County identify themselves as Chinese, and the U.S. Census Bureau determined that at least 10,000 of them are eligible to vote but are not sufficiently proficient in English, thereby triggering the requirement that ballots and other electoral and voting information be provided in Mandarin Chinese.

Early Voting   All Texas voters can now vote before election day.[23] Some voters can vote by mail—specifically, those who plan to be away from the county on election day, those who are sick or disabled, anyone who is 65 years or older, and people who are in jail but are otherwise eligible to vote. The rest can only vote early in person. Generally, **early voting** begins the 17th day before election day and ends the fourth day before election day. In addition to traditional election day voting sites, such as schools and fire stations, there are several other more familiar places to vote early, including grocery and convenience stores. This innovation has clearly made voting easier in Texas, and people are using it. In the 2018 election, for example, 72 percent of voters cast their ballot early or by mail. Although people are voting earlier, they are not voting in greater numbers, as we noted earlier in the chapter. The growing tendency toward early voting may still have important implications for when and how politicians campaign.

early voting
The practice of voting before election day at traditional voting locations, such as schools, and other locations, such as grocery and convenience stores.

Counting and Recounting Ballots

We take for granted that when we vote, our votes count. As we learned in Florida in the 2000 presidential election, this is not true. The first machine count of ballots in Florida showed George W. Bush with a 1,725-vote lead. In a mandatory machine recount of the same ballots, the same machines cut his lead to 327. We were also told that some 2 to 3 percent of the ballots were not counted at all. How could this happen? What does this mean? The answer is simple: Machines make mistakes. Some ballots are not counted. Some may even be counted for the wrong candidate. This shocked most Americans.

Experts have known for a long time that vote counting potentially contains some error. It is typically of little consequence for election outcomes, however. Counting errors tend to cancel out, meaning that no candidate gains a much greater number of votes. Thus, the errors are important only when elections are very close, within a half percentage point, which is not very common, but it does happen. Control of the lower house in the Virginia legislature came down to one race in 2017, and after several recounts, the results were tied; the election, and with it control of the house, was settled by a coin flip.

IMAGE 4.4 Many voters use touch screens to cast their ballots.

★ CTQ Does touch screen voting solve the problems with paper ballots? How can we tell?

Texas has fairly specific laws about recounts. A candidate can request a recount if he or she loses by less than 10 percent. This is a fairly generous rule compared to other states. The candidate who requests the recount does have to pay for it, however, which means that most candidates do not request a recount unless the margin is much closer—say, one percentage point or less. As for the recount itself, the Texas Election Code states that "only one method may be used in the recount" and "a manual recount shall be conducted in preference to an electronic recount." The procedures are fairly detailed.

Electronic Voting

Partly in response to the events in Florida—and the seeming potential for similar problems in Texas—a number of counties introduced **electronic voting** in the 2002 midterm elections to allow voting by using touch screens. Instead of punching holes in ballots or filling in bubbles on scannable paper ballots, most voters today cast ballots by touching screens. The technology, similar to what is used in automated teller machines (ATMs) and electronic ticket check-ins at many airports, promises an exact count of votes. It is now used for voting throughout much of Texas and the United States. As with the introduction of any new technology, however, problems have occurred.

electronic voting
Voting on a touch screen.

Election Campaigns in Texas: Strategies, Resources, and Results

LO 4.4 **Identify the factors that advantage (or disadvantage) candidates in Texas elections.**

The ultimate aim of party activity is to nominate candidates in the party primary or convention and get them elected in the general election. The campaign for the party's nomination is often more critical in one-party areas of the state—Democrats in South Texas and in some large urban areas and Republicans in many rural and suburban areas. For local and district offices in these areas, the key electoral decision is made in the primaries because the dominant party's nominee is almost certain to win the general election. In statewide elections, the crucial electoral decision is generally made in the Republican primary, where the party's nominee is chosen. The Republican candidate then has a relatively clear path to winning office.

Candidates seeking their party's nomination in a primary pursue a different sort of campaign strategy than they do when they later run in the general election. The primary electorate is usually much smaller and made up of more committed partisans. As a result, primary candidates are likely to strike a more ideological or even strident approach that appeals to activists. Once they have won their primary, candidates will often moderate their views to win over swing voters and independents in the general election. For little-known candidates, money and the endorsement of party elites are more crucial in the primary than in the general election. Little-known candidates can frequently count on the party label to sweep them into office in general elections.

The General Election Campaign

To a large extent, general election outcomes are predictable. Despite all the media attention paid to the conventions, the debates, the advertising, and everything else involved in election campaigns, certain things powerfully structure the vote in national and state elections.[24] In state elections, two factors dominate: party identification and incumbency.

First, where more people in a state identify with one political party than with the other, the candidates of the preferred party have an advantage in general elections. For instance, when most Texans identified with the Democratic Party, Democratic candidates dominated elected offices throughout the state. As Texans have become more Republican in their identification, Republican candidates have done very well; indeed, as was mentioned earlier, Republicans now hold every statewide elected office. Identification with the political parties varies a lot within Texas, however, and this has implications for state legislative elections. In some parts of the state, particularly in the major cities, more people identify with the Democratic Party, and Democratic candidates typically represent those areas in the state house and senate (see Chapter 7). Thus, party identification in the state and in districts tells us a great deal about which candidates win general elections.

Second, incumbent candidates—those already in office who are up for reelection—are more likely to win in general elections. This is particularly true in state legislative elections, where the districts are fairly homogeneous and the campaigns are not very visible, but incumbency is also important in elections for statewide office. Incumbents have a number of advantages over challengers, the most important of which is that they have won in the past. To become an incumbent, a candidate has had to beat an incumbent or else win in an open election, which usually involves a contest among a number of strong candidates. By definition, therefore, incumbents are effective candidates. In addition, incumbents have the advantage of office. They are in a position to do things for their constituents and thus increase their support among voters and among prospective campaign donors.

Although party identification and incumbency are important in Texas elections, they are not the whole story. What they really tell us is the degree to which candidates are advantaged or disadvantaged as they embark on their campaigns. Other factors ultimately matter on election day.

Mobilizing Groups
Groups play an important role in elections for any office. A fundamental part of campaigns is getting out the vote among groups that strongly support the candidate. To a large extent, candidates focus on groups aligned with the political parties.[25]

At the state level, business interests and teachers are particularly important. Republican candidates tend to focus their efforts on the former and Democratic candidates on the latter. Candidates also mobilize other groups, including African Americans and Latinos. Traditionally, Democratic candidates have emphasized mobilizing these minority groups. Mobilizing groups does not necessarily involve taking strong public stands on their behalf, especially those that are less mainstream. The mobilization of such groups is typically conducted very quietly, "under the radar," often through targeted mailings, digital ads, and phone calls.

Choosing Issues Issues are important in any campaign. In campaigns for state offices, taxes, education, immigration, and cultural issues are salient. Just as they target social groups, candidates focus on issues that reflect their party affiliations, but they avoid unpopular positions like higher taxes or budget cuts for education or law enforcement. Where candidates do differ is in their emphasis on particular issues and their policy proposals. These choices depend heavily on carefully crafted opinion polls. Through polls, candidates attempt to identify the issues that the public considers to be important and then craft policy positions to address those issues. The process is ongoing, and candidates pay close attention to changes in opinion and, perhaps most important, to the public's response to the candidates' own positions. Public opinion polling is fundamental in modern election campaigns in America, and campaign messages are often presented in advance to focus groups—test groups of selected citizens—to help campaign strategists tailor their messages in a way that will appeal to particular audiences.

The Campaign Trail Deciding where and how to campaign are critical in planning a campaign strategy. Candidates spend countless hours "on the stump," traveling around the state or district to speak before diverse groups. In a state as large as Texas, candidates for statewide office must pick and choose areas so as to maximize their exposure. Unfortunately for rural voters, this means that statewide candidates spend most of their time in urban and suburban areas, where they can get the attention of a large audience through the local media.

Nowadays, no candidate gets elected by stumping alone. The most direct route to the voters is through the Internet and Texas's 20 mass media markets. Texas has approximately 200 local and cable television stations and 1500 radio stations. In addition, around 80 daily newspapers and many more non-daily newspapers are dispersed throughout the state's 254 counties. Candidates hire public relations firms and media consultants, and advertising plays a big role. These days, a successful campaign often relies on **negative campaigning**, in which candidates attack opponents' issue positions or character. As one campaign consultant said, "Campaigns are about definition. Either you define yourself and your opponent or [the other candidates do]....Victory goes to the aggressor."[26] Although often considered an unfortunate development in American politics, it is important to keep in mind that negative campaigning can serve to provide voters with information about the candidates and their issue positions.

negative campaigning
A strategy used in election campaigns in which candidates attack their opponents' issue positions or character.

Timing The timing of the campaign effort can be very important. Unlike presidential elections, campaigns for state offices, including the governorship, begin fairly late in the election cycle. Indeed, it is common to hear little from gubernatorial candidates until after Labor Day and from candidates for the legislature not until a month before the election.

In the past, candidates often reserved a large proportion of their campaign advertising budget for a last-minute media "blitz." However, early voting has caused candidates to modify this strategy. Recall that in 2018, the vast majority of votes in Texas were cast early, during the weeks leading up to the election, which means that the final campaign blitz came too late to have any effect on most voters. As a result, political campaigns often begin their media blitz in the two weeks preceding election day when early voting is taking place.

Money in Election Campaigns

Election campaigns are expensive, which means that candidates need to raise a lot of money to be competitive. Indeed, the amount of money a candidate raises can be a deciding factor in the campaign. Just how much a candidate needs depends on the level of the campaign and the competitiveness of the race. High-level campaigns for statewide office are usually multimillion-dollar affairs.

In recent years, the race for governor has become especially expensive, and campaign spending has trended upward from one election to the next. In 2006, the four candidates spent about $46 million in total, with then-Governor Rick Perry leading the way at $23 million. In 2010, Perry spent $40 million to Bill White's $25 million and won yet again. In 2014, Governor Greg Abbott spent $50 million and easily beat former state senator Wendy Davis, who spent $47 million, a whopping $97 million in total.

Although lower-level races in Texas are not usually million-dollar affairs, they can be expensive as well. This is certainly true if a contested office is an open seat, where the incumbent is not running for reelection, or if an incumbent is from a marginal district—one in which the incumbent won office with less than 55 percent of the vote. Some candidates in competitive house races have spent more than $1 million and candidates in competitive senate races often spend more than $2 million. In the March 2018 GOP primary in Senate District 8 (Collin and Dallas counties), the two candidates, Phillip Huffines ($8.2m) and Angela Paxton ($3.7m), combined to spend $11.9 million dollars.

Where does this money come from? Candidates often try to solicit small individual contributions online and through direct mail campaigns. However, to raise the millions required for a high-level state race, they must solicit "big money" from wealthy friends or business and professional interests that have a stake in the outcome of the campaign; see some examples in the Texas Insiders feature. Another source of big money is loans—candidates often borrow heavily from banks, wealthy friends, or even themselves.[27]

Banks, corporations, law firms, and professional associations, such as those representing doctors, real estate agents, or teachers, organize and register their **political action committees (PACs)** with the secretary of state's office. PACs serve as the vehicle through which interest groups collect money and then use it to support political campaigns.

> **★ Did You Know?** A small sampling of the PACs includes TXBIZ PAC (set up by the Texas Association of Business), BEEF-PAC (Texas Cattle Feeders Association), BIZPAC (Texas Association of Business PAC), SKYPAC (Satellite Broadcasting & Communications Association of America, Inc., PAC), and TxMPA PAC (Texas Motion Picture Alliance PAC).

political action committees (PACs)
Organizations that raise and then contribute money to political candidates.

Where Does the Money Go?

In today's election campaigns, there are many ways to spend money. Digital advertising, direct mail, newspaper ads, billboards, radio spots, yard signs, and phone banks are all campaign staples. Candidates for statewide and urban races must rely on media advertising, particularly television, to get the maximum exposure they need in the three- or four-month campaign period. Campaigns are professionalized, with candidates likely to hire consulting firms to manage their campaigns. Consultants contract with public opinion pollsters, arrange advertising, and organize direct mail and digital media campaigns that can target certain areas of the state.

We can get some idea about spending in campaigns from what candidates pay for advertising and political consultants in a large, high-cost metropolitan area such as Houston:[28]

- A 30-second TV "spot" costs about $1,500 for a local daytime ad, $2,000 to $5,000 for an ad during the evening news, and $5,000 to $20,000 during prime time (8:00 p.m. to 11:00 p.m.), depending on the show's popularity rating; during some popular programs, such as the Super Bowl, the cost of a local ad is as much as $50,000.

- Prime time for most radio broadcasting is "drive time" (5:00 to 10 A.M. and 3:00 to 8:00 P.M.), when most people are driving to or from work. Drive-time rates range from $250 to $2,000 per 60-second spot.
- Billboards can run from $600 to $15,000 a month, depending on the location (billboards on busy highways are the most expensive).
- Newspaper ads cost around $250 per column inch ($300 to $500 on Sunday). Newspaper ads have, however, become less important than digital media. Today, many campaigns spend less on newspaper advertising than on breakfast tacos.
- Hiring a professional polling organization to conduct a poll in Harris County costs $15,000 to $30,000.
- Hiring a political consulting firm to manage a campaign in Harris County runs up to $50,000, plus a percentage of media buys. (Technically, the percentage is paid by the television and radio stations.) Most firms also get a bonus ranging from $5,000 to $25,000 if the candidate wins.

Clearly, money is important in election campaigns. Although the candidate who spends the most money does not always win, a certain amount of money is necessary for a candidate to be competitive. Speaking with his tongue partly in his cheek, one prominent politician noted, in regard to statewide races in Texas, that even if "you don't have to raise $10 million, you have to raise $8 million."

Control over Money in Campaigns
Prompted by the increasing use of television in campaigns and the increasing amount of money needed to buy it, the federal government and most state governments passed laws regulating the use of money in the early 1970s. The Federal Elections Campaign Act of 1972 established regulations that apply only to federal elections: president, vice president, and members of Congress. It provided for public financing of presidential campaigns with tax dollars, limited the amount of money that individuals and PACs could contribute to campaigns, and required disclosure of campaign donations. In 1976, the Supreme Court declared that it was unconstitutional to set spending limits for campaigns that were not publicly funded; this means there are no spending limits for congressional races nor for presidential races if a candidate does not accept public funds.[29] No Texas campaigns are publicly funded and no limits apply.

Not surprisingly, expenditures in election campaigns continue to increase. The Federal Election Commission reported that $60.9 million was spent in the elections of the 435 House members, an average of only $140,000 per seat. Today, the average is over $1.7 million per U.S. House seat and substantially larger for U.S. Senate elections—at least $28 million. The level of campaign spending is likely to continue to rise.

Later amendments to the Federal Elections Campaign Act made it legal for national political parties to raise and spend unlimited amounts of **soft money**, funds spent by political parties on behalf of political candidates. Party funds could be used to help candidates in a variety of ways, especially through voter registration and get-out-the-vote drives. The U.S. Supreme Court further opened up spending in 1985 by deciding that **independent expenditures** could not be limited.[30] As a result, individuals and organizations could spend as much as they wanted to promote a candidate as long as they were not working or communicating directly with the candidate's campaign organization. The 2002 Campaign Reform Act limited independent expenditures by corporations and labor unions, but this was overturned by the Supreme Court in its 2010 decision in *Citizens United* v. *Federal Election Commission*. This may have implications for state and local bans on corporate spending, including in Texas. The 2002 Act also deprived the parties of their soft money resources, but activists

soft money
Money spent by political parties on behalf of political candidates, especially for the purposes of increasing voter registration and turnout.

independent expenditures
Money individuals and organizations spend to promote a candidate without working or communicating directly with the candidate's campaign organization.

Texas Insiders

Profiles of Texas Campaign Megadonors

Contributions to Texas political campaigns in 2016 totaled $179 million. Table 4.4 lists the 10 largest campaign donors, indicating who contributed, how much they contributed, and in which kinds of public policy decisions they had an interest.

Thinking about the Role of Elites in Texas Politics

Because of the enormous amounts of money spent by just a few campaign contributors, some critics have worried that large contributions buy outsized political influence for their donors. Most observers agree that campaign contributions open doors, giving contributors access to public officials to argue the case for their interests; some critics argue that candidates' reliance on large campaign contributions corrupts state politics and skews public policy toward the interests of wealthier individuals and groups.

Others argue that the influence of large contributions is balanced by other influences, such as small contributions, public opinion, and alert media. They defend the donors' right to give money to candidates who share their viewpoints as a form of expression essential to a free society.

★ PRQ   **Texas campaign finance regulations are designed to hold public officials and campaign contributors accountable by shining the light of publicity on them. Think of other ways to limit potential corrupting influences that do not interfere with freedom of expression.**

TABLE 4.4 Profiles of Texas Campaign Megadonors

Donor	Total Contributions	Donor's Special Interest
Texas Association of Realtors	$9,132,640	Real estate industry; supporting property rights; low property taxes
National Association of Realtors	$4,145,366	Real estate industry; supporting property rights; low property taxes
Texans for Lawsuit Reform	$3,936,560	Limiting lawsuits against businesses and professionals
Farris & Jo Ann Wilks	$3,259,734	Limited government, conservative social values, free enterprise
Associated General Contractors of TX	$2,116,675	Highway and heavy-utility construction contracts
Charles C. Butt (HEB Grocery)	$2,030,000	Supporting public education
Texas Medical Association	$2,007,834	Health care industry
AT&T	$1,950,972	Utility and cable regulation
Empower Texans	$1,855,479	Supporting low taxes; small government; conservative politics
Energy Future Holdings	$1,808,624	Electric utilities

Source: Texans for Public Justice and Texas Ethics Commission.

simply set up nonparty organizations to collect and disperse such funds. Understandably, it has been difficult to effectively control money in election campaigns.

FEC regulations apply only to candidates for national office. For candidates running for state offices, the most important provisions of Texas law regarding money in campaigns are as follows:

- Candidates may not raise or spend money until an official campaign treasurer is appointed.
- Candidates and PACs may not accept cash contributions for more than an aggregate of $100, but checks and in-kind donations in unlimited amounts are permitted.
- Direct contributions from corporations and labor unions are prohibited.
- Candidates and treasurers of campaign committees are periodically required to file sworn statements listing all contributions and expenditures.
- Both criminal and civil penalties are imposed on anyone who violates the law's provisions.
- The Texas Ethics Commission enforces campaign finance regulations by imposing fines, but it rarely refers violators for criminal prosecution and is seen as largely toothless by many politicans.

Raising and spending money on Texas campaigns still is pretty much wide open. For example, corporations and labor unions may not give directly to a candidate, but they may give via their PACs. Note also that there are no limits on the amount a candidate may spend. Probably the most important effect of the campaign finance law in Texas comes from the requirement of disclosure. How much money a candidate raises, who makes contributions, and how campaign funds are spent are matters of public record. This information may be newsworthy to reporters or other individuals motivated to inform the public.

Who Gets Elected

It is useful to think of elected offices in Texas as a pyramid. At the bottom of the pyramid are most local offices; at the top is the governor. Moving from bottom to top, the importance of the office increases and the number of officeholders decreases. It thus gets more and more difficult for politicians to ascend the pyramid, and only the most effective politicians rise to the top. This tells us a lot about candidates and elections in Texas and elsewhere.

In local elections, the pool of candidates is diverse in many ways, including educational background, income, and profession. As we move up the pyramid, however, candidates become much more homogeneous. For statewide office, the typical candidate is middle or upper class, from an urban area, and has strong ties to business and professional interests in the state. Most elected state officers in Texas, including the governor, lieutenant governor, and attorney general, must be acceptable to the state's major financial and corporate interests and to its top law firms. These interests help statewide candidates raise the large amounts of money that are critical to a successful race.

Successful candidates for statewide office in Texas have traditionally been Anglo males. Prior to 1986, when Raul Gonzalez was elected to the state supreme court, no Latino or African American had been elected to statewide office. In 1982, Ann Richards was elected state treasurer, becoming the second woman ever to be elected to statewide office in Texas. She had been preceded by Miriam "Ma" Ferguson who was elected governor in 1924, and then again in 1932, as a surrogate for her husband, Jim "Pa" Ferguson, who had been impeached and was prohibited from holding public office in Texas.

Since then, women and minorities have made some gains in statewide offices. Ann Richards became the first woman elected governor in her own right in 1990. Kay Bailey Hutchison captured the state treasurer's office and in 1993 won a special election to become the first woman from Texas elected to the U.S. Senate. Dan Morales was the first Latino to win a state executive office when he captured the attorney general's office in 1990. More history was made when Morris Overstreet of Amarillo won a seat on the Texas Court of Criminal Appeals in 1990 and became the first African American elected to a statewide office.

Women and ethnic/racial minorities are starting to make inroads in other elected offices in Texas. Women held 24 percent of the seats in the 86th Legislature (2019–2020), and women have at least once held the post of mayor in the state's six largest cities: Houston, Dallas, San Antonio, Austin, Fort Worth, and El Paso. Latinos held 23 percent of the seats in the state legislature, African Americans occupied 11 percent and Asian Americans held 2 percent. Clearly, Texas politics has changed a lot over time. These changes are beginning to reflect the changing composition of the Texas electorate, though with a noticeable lag.

Applying What You Have Learned about Voting and Elections in Texas

LO 4.5   **Apply what you have learned about voting and elections in Texas.**

You learned in this chapter that campaign donors are a huge force driving election campaigns in Texas. However, ideology is becoming a growing force, especially among Texas tea party, or movement conservative, activists, who are frequently at odds with big money interests in the state. So we invited Luke Macias to explain what motivates him as a political consultant for some of the state's most ardent conservative candidates.

Luke Macias founded Macias Strategies in 2011 at the age of 21. In 2012 he served as consultant for five movement conservative Texas House candidates, three of whom (Giovanni Capriglione, Matt Krause, and Jonathan Stickland) were victorious. In 2014 his client base expanded to include additional House and Senate candidates, including Senators Konni Burton and Bob Hall, and *Capitol Inside* named Macias the 2014 primary election cycle's individual "Most Valuable Consultant." Today, Macias remains one of the Texas GOP's most sought after consultants.

After you have read Macias's essay, we will ask you to evaluate the role of money and ideology in Texas politics, to identify how the author reveals his political goals, and to draw conclusions about how the author would view the role of compromise in the political system.

POLITICS IN PRACTICE
Everything's Bigger in Texas, with a Twist of Red

by Luke Macias
Founder of Macias Strategies

Several years ago Erica Grieder, a senior editor at *Texas Monthly*, wrote a book titled *Big, Hot, Cheap, and Right: What America Can Learn from the Strange Genius of Texas*. The book is a great read, but the title alone makes you proud to be a Texan. As an Air Force brat, I lived in two countries and seven different states in the first 13 years of my life. But whenever someone asked me, "Where are you from?" I proudly answered, "Texas." This pride and honor to be Texan is the lens by which I evaluate Texas political campaigns, focusing on Republican politics. In Texas we have higher stakes, more voters, and more passionate battles than you will ever see.

Why do we have higher stakes? One reason could be that our state has a larger GDP than Mexico, Australia, and Spain. Texas will spend over $100 billion dollars this year in our annual state budget, while Oklahoma will spend a little over $7 billion. The stakes are higher, therefore the battles are more expensive and definitely more entertaining.

We also have a lot more voters per legislator than in other states, which requires significantly more effort from our campaigns. New Hampshire has 400 State Representatives each representing around 3,300 voters. Texas Representatives represent an average of 180,000 constituents per district. Seven State Representatives in Texas would cover all of New Hampshire. In March of 2016, Senate District 1 (in which I was professionally involved) had 133,000 voters in the Republican Primary. Let me put that in perspective. The front runner in that race, Bryan Hughes, received nearly double the number of votes that Bernie Sanders received to win the nomination to the U.S. Senate in 2006 in Vermont. So one could say that it requires more effort to get elected to the State Senate in Texas, than to be a U.S. Senator in Vermont and then a top contender for the Presidency of the United States.

All that being said, what makes Texas unique, even compared to states like California and New York who are somewhat comparable in population and budget size, is the fact that we are a majority Republican state for now, and have been for some time. The rightward leaning policies have definitely led to more job opportunities for college graduates and stronger protections for the most vulnerable in society (the unborn). But many conservatives believe that their Republican elected officials' rhetoric doesn't match their record. They run on conservative principles but then kill legislation enacting those principles through the legislative process. As a result, it has required a significant amount of pressure to get these policies enacted. We have seen incredibly fierce primary battles over the last ten years, in some cases leading to over $2 million dollars spent for a single state house seat. Since the vast number of legislative seats are in either safely Republican or Democratic districts and the majority party candidate's certain to win the general election, most important political ideas are decided in both the Democratic and Republican primaries as the parties choose their nominees.

Regardless of how you govern, every Republican runs as the second coming of Ronald Reagan. This doesn't give as many opportunities as I would like to actually discuss policy differences but it definitely reveals that, regardless of a politician's personal views, he will at minimum speak the words that his constituents desire to hear. The good news is that over the last eight years we have seen more incumbents lose their primary, even when they outspend their opponents 5 to 1. The hope is that this results in a closer alignment of rhetoric and record. The less money determines political outcomes the better the constituents will be served and the more important ideas become.

The hope is that Texas voters recognize how fortunate we are to live in this strange genius called Texas and that we continue the policies that give us the opportunities we enjoy today. I'm proud to work in a state that has higher stakes, more voters, and more passionate battles than you will ever see anywhere else.

1. What evidence does the author present that conservative passion can succeed against incumbent Republicans who are able to outspend their more conservative challengers? Why does the author focus his political campaign services on the Republican party primary?
2. Why does the author specialize in supporting more conservative candidates? What policies does he hope these conservatives will enact?

★ Chapter Summary

LO 4.1 Explain why voter turnout is low in Texas. Before you can vote in Texas, you must first register. Once registered, voting in Texas is easy, though the recent passage of voter identification legislation had the potential to make things harder for some people, particularly ethnic/racial minorities.

National turnout has fluctuated between 50 and 55 percent in presidential elections and hovered around 40 percent in midterm elections, much lower rates than we find in most other advanced democracies. Voter turnout in Texas is usually about 10 percent below the national average.

Low voter turnout in Texas may be due in part to the state's socioeconomic characteristics. A comparatively large percentage of Texans live below the poverty level, and many have not graduated from high school; these people are not very likely to vote. The large numbers of ethnic minorities and lack of party competition also account for low turnout in the state.

LO 4.2 Describe the types of Texas elections. In Texas, as in most American states, winning elected office usually requires candidates to win both a primary and general election. Party primaries are used to select the parties' nominees. In Texas, candidates must win the primary by a majority vote or face a runoff primary between the two highest vote-getters.

The election that officially determines who will take office is the general election, in which all party nominees and independent candidates face off against each other. Whichever candidate gets the most votes, the plurality, wins. Except for special elections, the candidate does not need a majority to be victorious.

LO 4.3 Understand how elections are administered in Texas. Getting on the ballot in Texas general elections is difficult. The easiest way is to win the Democratic or Republican primary, and that is not easy. Third-party and independent candidates also find it difficult to get on the ballot.

Ballot design is an important factor in elections. Texas traditionally has used the party column ballot, in which the names of all the candidates of each party are listed in parallel columns. The main alternative is the office block ballot, in which the names of candidates are listed underneath each office. Many Texas counties have now adopted electronic voting systems, which combine features of the two designs.

Another innovation has been the adoption of an early voting option, which allows voting before election day at a variety of locations. In 2016, the majority of all votes in Texas were cast early. This has fairly obvious implications for the timing and effects of election campaigns.

LO 4.4 Identify the factors that advantage (or disadvantage) candidates in Texas elections. In Texas, as in other states, voters' choices on election day are driven to a large extent by party affiliation, and Republican candidates usually win statewide office. Democrats, though, have large pockets of supporters in some areas, particularly the big cities—Austin, Dallas, Houston, and San Antonio—as well as the Rio Grande Valley.

Aside from the partisan balance, incumbency is also important, and candidates need to be able to campaign effectively by mobilizing groups and choosing attractive issue positions. Candidates must raise an increasing amount of funding to be competitive.

LO 4.5 Apply what you have learned about voting and elections in Texas. You looked at election politics in Texas through the eyes of a practicing campaign consultant for tea party candidates. You evaluated the role of money and ideology in Texas politics and explored how some of the state's more conservative candidates have been able to capitalize on some voters' rising conservative passions to win Republican primary elections against better-funded opponents. You considered how these candidates view the role of compromise within our political system.

Key Terms

Australian ballot, *p. 99*	independent expenditures, *p. 105*	participation paradox, *p. 79*	soft money, *p. 105*
closed primary, *p. 92*		party column ballot, *p. 97*	split ticket voting, *p. 97*
crossover voting, *p. 93*	negative campaigning, *p. 103*	plurality vote, *p. 93*	straight ticket voting, *p. 97*
direct primary, *p. 90*		political action committees (PACs), *p. 104*	voter turnout, *p. 82*
early voting, *p. 100*	office block ballot, *p. 97*		voting-age population (VAP), *p. 83*
electronic voting, *p. 101*	open primary, *p. 92*	runoff primary, *p. 92*	

Review Questions

LO 4.1 Explain why voter turnout is low in Texas.

- What explains why some people are more likely to vote than others?

- Why does the number of elections in Texas lead to lower turnout?

- How does Republican dominance of statewide office affect turnout in Texas?

LO 4.2 Describe the types of Texas elections.

- What is the majority vote rule, and why is it used in Texas primaries?

- What is the plurality vote rule, where is it used, and what difference does it make in elections?

LO 4.3 Understand how elections are administered in Texas.

- Why is it hard for candidates to get on the ballot in Texas?

- Ballot design seems a technical issue but is seriously contested by parties and candidates. Why?

LO 4.4 Identify the factors that advantage (or disadvantage) candidates in Texas elections.

- Why are some candidates more likely than others to win elections in Texas? Do candidates have much control over the things that matter?

- Have the efforts of elected officials in the United States and Texas to control money in election campaigns been effective?

- What explains the growing diversity of elected officials in Texas? Is it likely to continue? Why or why not?

Think Critically and Get Active!

Become politically active. Register to vote by following the instructions on the Texas Secretary of State's website: **www.sos.state.tx.us/elections/voter/reqvr.shtml**. Act out, get involved, and register to vote at the Rock the Vote and Mi Familia Vota websites, **www.rockthevote.com** and **www.mifamiliavota.org**, and follow them on Twitter @RockTheVote and @MiFamiliaVota.

Choose your candidates based on the issues. Project Vote Smart provides information about candidates at **www.votesmart.org**. There you can search by zip code to find the elections—federal, state, and local—in which you can vote. The site shows the candidates' positions and has a feature to help you pick the right candidate based on your positions and how important you think each is. Project Vote Smart also lets you see which interest groups support which candidates.

See where candidates get their money. Money is important in election campaigns and may tell you something about candidates too. You can follow contributions in Texas elections at the Texas Ethics Commission website: **www.ethics.state.tx.us**. You can follow contributions in federal elections at the Center for Responsive Politics website: **www.opensecrets.org.**

Keep up with elected officials. You can monitor the "roll call" votes of Texas legislators at Texas Legislature Online at **www.capitol.state.tx.us**. The *Texas Tribune* provides good, politically neutral coverage of the legislative votes and gubernatorial proposals and vetoes; it can be found online at **www.texastribune.org** and followed on Twitter @TexasTribune.

★ PRQ In deciding how you will cast your vote, should you consider candidates' actual positions on public policy, or is it enough for you to cast your vote based on advertising-based images and personalities? How important is your assessment of a candidate's character?

5

Political Parties

Here you see some of the excitement that party politics generates at the Texas Republican Party state convention. In this chapter, you will learn what motivates parties, how they are organized, and the important role they play in the Texas political system.

Rodger Mallison/Fort Worth Star-Telegram/MCT/Getty Images

Learning Objectives

LO 5.1 Identify the characteristics of American political parties.

LO 5.2 Understand the evolution of the party system in Texas.

LO 5.3 Evaluate the importance of party organization.

LO 5.4 Assess the functions of political parties in American and Texas politics.

LO 5.5 Apply what you have learned about Texas political parties.

The Founders created our complicated system of federal government and provided for the election of a president and Congress. However, the U.S. Constitution makes no mention of political parties. The Founders actually held negative attitudes toward parties. George Washington warned of the "baneful effects of the spirit of party" in his farewell address. James Madison, in *Federalist Paper* 10, criticized parties or "factions" as divisive but admitted that they were inevitable. Madison and others thought that parties would encourage conflict and undermine consensus on public policy. Yet despite their condemnation of parties, these early American politicians engaged in partisan politics and initiated a competitive two-party system.

Parties, then, are apparently something we should live neither with nor without. They have been with us from the start of this country and will be with us for the foreseeable future, influencing our government and public policy. It is important, therefore, to gain an understanding of what they are all about.

What is a political party? This question conjures up various stereotypes: smoke-filled rooms of the past where party leaders or bosses make important behind-the-scenes decisions; activists or regulars who give time, money, and enthusiastic support to their candidates; or voters who proudly identify themselves as Democrats or Republicans. Essentially, though, a political party is a broad-based coalition of people whose primary purpose is to win elections. Gaining control of government through popular elections is the most important goal for political parties, and most of the activities parties pursue are directed toward this purpose. Parties recruit and nominate their members for public office. They form coalitions of different groups and interests to build majorities so that they can elect their candidates.

Political parties are vital to democracy in that they provide a link between the people and the government. Parties provide an avenue for the ordinary citizen to participate in the political system; they provide the means for organizing support for particular candidates. In organizing this support, parties unify various groups and interests and mobilize them behind the candidates who support their preferred positions.

Characteristics of American Political Parties

LO 5.1 **Identify the characteristics of American political parties.**

The American political party system has three distinct characteristics not always found in parties elsewhere in the world: (1) two-party system, (2) pragmatism, and (3) decentralization.

Two-Party System

In Texas and the other U.S. states, political competition is usually between the two major parties—the Democrats and the Republicans. Such a system is called a **two-party system** because only two dominant parties compete for political office and minor or third parties have little chance of winning.

The two-party system partly results from our electoral system, which relies on single-member districts—election districts in which one candidate is elected to a legislative body. If only one representative can be elected in a district, voters tend to cast their ballots for the major party candidates that have the best chance of winning and not "waste" their vote on a third party destined to lose. Employing a plurality voting rule in general elections, as we noted in Chapter 4, only reinforces the dominance of a two-party system because there is no electoral reason to run as a third-party candidate or support one unless the party actually has a realistic chance to win. By contrast, under a majority voting rule, which is used in Texas primary elections, there may be a benefit to finishing second because it can lead to a runoff election between the top two candidates if the plurality winner in the first election does not get a majority of the votes.[1]

two-party system
A political system characterized by two dominant parties competing for political offices. In such systems, minor or third parties have little chance of winning.

In addition to the electoral system, laws put in place by the Democratic and Republican parties make it hard for third parties to form. As mentioned in Chapter 4, third parties such as the Libertarian Party or Green Party must surpass a statewide vote threshold in the prior election to obtain automatic ballot status in Texas. Failure to gain this vote share (2 percent in the gubernatorial election or 5 percent in any other statewide contest) means third parties can get on the ballot only by launching petition drives that gather the signatures of registered voters who did not vote in either major party primary. Independent candidates must also meet this standard. For example, the Green Party lost its automatic ballot access in 2016 and was required to collect 47,183 valid signatures from eligible voters to compete in the next statewide election, but its petition drive failed and no Green Party candidates were allowed on the November 2018 ballot. In contrast, the Democratic and Republican candidates just had to win their primaries.

Despite the electoral system and election laws, there have been third parties in the United States and in Texas. Most have come and gone, partly because of the difficulties of competing but also because of the major parties' efforts to absorb third parties by adopting their issues. One notable example is the Populist Party of the 1890s, which was absorbed by the Democratic Party. Only rarely have new parties survived, and only once did a new party replace a preexisting party; during the 1850s the Republican Party emerged after the collapse of the Whig Party. Since then there have been many attempts to form third parties, yet the Democratic and Republican parties remain dominant and the two-party system largely unchallenged.

Pragmatism

Pragmatism
The philosophy that ideas should be judged on the basis of their practical results rather than the purity of their principles.

Pragmatism in politics means that ideas should be judged on the basis of their practical results rather than the purity of their principles.[2] In other words, a pragmatist is interested in what works. American parties are sometimes willing to compromise principles to appeal successfully to a majority of voters and gain public office. They willingly bargain with a fairly wide range of organized groups and take stands that appeal to a large number of interests to build a winning coalition in a two-party system. American parties thus are less programmatic than those in many European countries that have multi-party systems, where parties are more likely to be committed to a particular narrow ideology and their supporters committed to specific programmatic goals.

valence issues
Issues on which virtually all of the public agrees, such as peace and prosperity.

Pragmatism often means taking clear-cut positions only on those issues on which virtually all of the public agrees, what political scientists often refer to as **valence issues**. Leading examples are peace and prosperity, which feature prominently in American elections, especially the economy. This may have been made clearest by former President Bill Clinton's political strategist James Carville, who famously focused Bill Clinton's successful 1992 campaign on the phrase "It's the Economy, Stupid." Almost every campaign consultant has repeated the same advice again and again in state and local campaigns because economic growth is, after all, one of the few policies which almost every voter supports. By contrast, taking clear stands on controversial issues may alienate potential supporters in a general election, especially voters who are not strong partisans. Political parties and their candidates, including those in Texas, thus often prefer to deemphasize **position issues**, on which the public is divided, and instead focus on valence issues. They may also stress leadership potential and statesmanship, as well as family life and personality. All of this said, position issues can be important and prominent in primary elections, which in turn can affect—and complicate—the general election campaign against the candidate of the other party.

position issues
Issues on which the public is divided.

Growing Polarization?   Although the broad electoral coalitions that comprise American parties make it difficult for them to achieve ideological consistency, it would be a mistake to assume that parties in America do not differ from one another. Indeed, most observers think

that American parties have become more programmatic and more polarized in recent years.[3] To succeed, they must satisfy their traditional supporters: voters, public opinion leaders, interest groups, and campaign contributors. The candidates are not blank slates but have their own beliefs, prejudices, biases, and opinions. In most elections, broad ideological differences are apparent. Voters who participated in the presidential election of 2016 could relatively easily differentiate between the populist conservatism of Donald Trump and the more liberal philosophy of his opponent, Hillary Clinton. Similar philosophical differences also were evident between the parties' candidates for Texas state offices in the 2018 election.

Decentralization

At first glance, American party organizations may appear to be neatly ordered and hierarchical, with power flowing from the national to state to local parties. In reality, however, American parties are not nearly so hierarchical. They reflect the American federal system, with its **decentralization** of power to the state and local levels of government. Political party organizations operate at the precinct, or neighborhood, level; the local government level (city, county, or legislative district); the state level (especially in elections for governor); and the national level (especially in elections for president).

State and local party organizations are semi-independent actors that exercise considerable discretion on most party matters. The practices that state and local parties follow, the candidates they recruit, the campaign money they raise, the innovations they introduce, the organized interests to which they respond, the campaign strategies they create, and most important, the policy orientations of the candidates who run under their label are all influenced by local and state political cultures, leaders, traditions, and interests.[4]

Although the American party system is quite decentralized, power has shifted to the national party organizations in recent years. Both the Democratic and Republican national parties have become stronger and more involved in state and local party activities through various service functions. By using new campaign technologies—computer-based mailing lists, direct mail solicitations, and the Internet—the national parties have raised hundreds of millions of dollars. Accordingly, the national party organizations have assumed a greater role by providing unprecedented levels of assistance to state parties and candidates. This assistance includes a variety of services—candidate recruitment, research, public opinion polling, computer networking, production of digital, radio, and television commercials, direct mailing, consultation on redistricting issues, and the transfer of millions of dollars' worth of campaign funding. Not surprisingly, as national parties provide more money and services to state and local parties, they exercise more influence over state and local organizations, issues, and candidates.[5]

decentralization
Exercise of power at the state and local levels of government in addition to the national level.

The Development of the Texas Party System

LO 5.2 Understand the evolution of the party system in Texas.

Although for most of its existence the United States has had a two-party system, many states and localities—including Texas—have been dominated by just one party at various times in history. Texas formerly was a one-party Democratic state but is no longer. To understand political parties in Texas, it is necessary to examine the historical predominance of the Democratic Party, the emergence of two-party competition in the state, and the reality of Republican Party dominance at present.

The One-Party Tradition in Texas

Under the Republic of Texas, there was little party activity. Political divisions were primarily oriented around support of, or opposition to, Sam Houston, a leading founder of the

Republic. After Texas became a state, however, the Democratic Party dominated Texas politics until the 1980s. This legacy of dominance was firmly established by the Civil War and the era of Reconstruction, when Yankee troops, under the direction of a Republican Congress, occupied the South. From the time that the Republican and former Union soldier Edmund J. Davis's single term as governor ended in 1873 until the surprising victory of the Republican gubernatorial candidate Bill Clements in 1978, the Democrats exercised almost complete control over Texas politics.

The Democratic Party was at times challenged by the emergence of more liberal third parties. The most serious of these challenges came in the late nineteenth century with the Populist revolt. The Populist Party grew out of the dissatisfaction of small farmers who demanded government regulation of rates charged by banks and railroads. These farmers—joined by sharecroppers, laborers, and African Americans—mounted a serious election bid in 1896, taking 44 percent of the vote for governor. Eventually, however, the Democratic Party defused the threat of the Populists by co-opting many of the issues of the new party. The Democrats also effectively disenfranchised African Americans and poor whites in 1902 with the passage of a poll tax.

Two events in the early twentieth century solidified the position of the Democrats in Texas politics. The first was the institution of party primary "reforms" in 1906. For the first time, voters could choose the party's nominees by a direct vote in the party primary. Hence, the Democratic primary became the substitute for the two-party contest, the general election. In the absence of Republican competition, the Democratic primary was the only game in town, and it provided a competitive arena for distinct political interests within the state.

The second event to help the Democrats was the Depression. Although the Republican presidential candidate, Herbert Hoover, carried Texas in 1928, Republicans came to be closely associated with the Great Depression of the 1930s. The cumulative effect of this association, the Civil War, and Reconstruction ensured Democratic dominance in state government until the late 1980s.

Ideological Factions in America and Texas

Although members of a political party may be similar in their views, factions, or divisions within the party inevitably develop. These conflicts may involve a variety of personalities and issues, but the most important basis for division is ideology.

Conservatives The meaning of conservatism changes over time and it means different things to different people; some people are economic conservatives while others are social conservatives. As we saw in Chapter 1, economic conservatives believe that individuals should be left alone to compete in a free market unfettered by government control; they prefer that government regulation of the economy be kept to a minimum. They extol the virtues of individualism, independence, and personal initiative. However, conservatives often support government involvement and funding to promote business, including construction of highways, tax incentives for investment, and other government assistance to business. The theory is that this assistance will encourage economic development and hence prosperity for the whole society; critics call this the "trickle-down theory." On the other hand, conservatives are likely to oppose government programs that involve a large-scale redistribution of income or wealth, such as welfare, universal health care coverage, or unemployment compensation.

Some social conservatives view change suspiciously; they tend to favor the status quo—things as they are now and as they have been. They emphasize traditional values associated with the family and close communities, and they often favor government action to preserve what they see as the proper moral values of society. Because conservatives hold a more skeptical view of cultural change than liberals do, they are more likely to perceive immigration, LGBTQ rights, or marijuana legalization as threats to traditional or religious values. Conservatives are also more likely to favor stiffer penalties for criminals, including capital punishment. Conservatives may combine support for the free market with support for traditional values, or they may adopt only one of these views.

Like conservatism, libertarianism is based on a limited government philosophy that rejects government involvement in the economy and is hence conservative on economic issues. However, it also rejects government intrusion into personal choices in such matters as marijuana use and is hence liberal on social issues. In recent years, the Libertarian Party has become an active, if not always influential, force in Texas politics. The Libertarian Party has a hands-off philosophy of government

IMAGE 5.1 Ted Cruz is a conservative Texas Republican who has been supported by both Christian conservatives and tea party activists.

★ **CTQ**   **How do conservatives and liberals differ on public policy?**

Bill O'Leary/The Washington Post/Getty Images

that appeals to many Texas conservatives. The party's general philosophy is one of individual liberty and personal responsibility. Applying their doctrine to the issues, libertarians would oppose Social Security, campaign finance reform, gun control, and many foreign policies. They consider programs like Social Security to be "state-provided welfare" and believe that regulating campaigns promotes too much government involvement. They also oppose U.S. intervention in world affairs. The Libertarian Party faces the same hurdles as other third parties: poor financing, a lack of media coverage, and in some states, getting access to the ballot.

Liberals Liberals believe that it is often necessary for government to regulate the economy and to promote greater social equality. They point to great concentrations of wealth and power that have threatened to control government, destroy economic competition, and weaken individual freedom. Government power, they believe, should be used to protect the disadvantaged and to promote equality. Consequently, liberals are generally supportive of the social welfare programs that conservatives oppose. Liberals champion the right to form unions, unemployment benefits, universal health care, subsidized housing, and improved educational opportunities. They are also more likely to favor progressive taxes, such as the federal income tax, which increase as incomes increase.

Liberals want government to protect the civil rights and liberties of individuals and are critical of interference with any exercise of the constitutional rights of free speech, press, religion, assembly, association, and privacy. They are often suspicious of conservatives' attempts to "legislate morality" because of the potential for interference with individual rights.

Conservatives, Liberals, and Texas Democrats

For many years, factions within the Texas Democratic Party resembled a two-party system, and the election to select the Democratic Party's nominees—the primary—was the most important election in Texas. Until the 1990s, conservative Democrats were much more successful than their liberal counterparts in these primaries, in part because Republican voters, facing no significant primary race of their own, regularly crossed over and supported conservative Democratic candidates. Voters in the general elections, facing a choice between a conservative Democrat and a conservative Republican, usually went with the traditional party—the Democrats. These Republican crossover votes enabled conservative Democrats, with few exceptions, to control the party and state government until the late 1970s.

Conservative Democrats in Texas provided a very good example of the semi-independent relationship of national, state, and local party organizations. Texas conservatives traditionally voted Democratic in state and local races but often refused to support the national Democratic candidates for president. Indeed, the development of the conservative Democratic faction in Texas was an outgrowth of conservative dissatisfaction with many New Deal proposals of Franklin D. Roosevelt in the 1930s and Fair Deal proposals of Harry Truman in the 1940s.

Conservative Democrats in Texas continued their cool relationship with the national party as many of them supported Republican presidential candidates, such as Dwight Eisenhower in 1952, even as they supported conservative Democrats running for state and local offices. Many of these conservative Texans would later begin to support Republicans for state and local offices as well. No Democratic presidential candidate has carried Texas since Jimmy Carter in 1976, no Democrat has won the governorship since Ann Richards in 1990, and no Democrat has won a statewide election since 1994.

> ★ **Did You Know?** When the U.S. House voted on the Civil Rights Act of 1964, 17 of the 21 Texas Democrats and both Texas Republicans voted against the Act. Only 4 Texas Democrats voted in favor of the Act.

Several factors accounted for the historical success of conservative Democrats, but the most important were the power and resources of the conservative constituency. Conservatives have traditionally made up the state's power elite, representing such interests as the oil and gas industry, other large corporations, large farms and ranches (agribusiness), owners and publishers of many of the state's major daily newspapers, and veterans. In other words, the most affluent people in the state are able and willing to contribute their considerable resources to the campaigns of like-minded politicians. These segments of the population are also the most likely to turn out and vote in elections. This was a significant advantage to conservative Democrats competing in the party primary.

Liberals in the Texas Democratic Party have consisted of groups that have supported the national party ticket and civil rights. These groups include the following:

- Organized labor, in particular the American Federation of Labor–Congress of Industrial Organizations (AFL-CIO)
- African American groups, such as the National Association for the Advancement of Colored People (NAACP)
- Latino groups, such as the American G.I. Forum, League of Latin American Citizens (LULAC), Mexican American Democrats (MAD), and Mexican American Legal Defense and Educational Fund (MALDEF)
- Various professionals, teachers, and intellectuals
- Voters in the central cores of the state's largest cities
- Environmental groups, such as the Sierra Club
- Abortion rights groups, such as NARAL Pro-Choice Texas
- Trial lawyers—that is, lawyers who represent plaintiffs in civil suits and defendants in criminal cases

Before the 1990s, liberal Democrats rarely won their party's nomination or held statewide office for more than a few years. In recent decades, liberal Texas Democrats have captured their party's nomination, largely because conservatives are voting in the Republican primary.

Liberal or moderate Democrats may have been routinely nominated for almost all of the state-wide races, but here is the irony for the liberal Democrats in Texas: Although they have gained control of the Democratic Party as conservatives have defected from their ranks, these defections have left the Democrats in the minority and made the Republicans dominant in Texas.

The Rise of the Republican Party

Before the presidential election of November 1988, only three post-Reconstruction Republicans had won non-presidential statewide races in Texas: Senator John Tower (1961–1985), Governor Bill Clements (1979–1983 and 1987–1991), and Senator Phil Gramm (1985–2003). Why had the Republican Party failed to compete in Texas in the past? The most important reason is Texas's experience in the Civil War and during Reconstruction. The Republican administration of Governor E. J. Davis was considered the most corrupt and abusive period of Texas history. We will see how the Republican Party was able to shake its image as the party Reconstruction to become Texas's dominant political force.

The Republicans Become Competitive
The revival of the Republican Party was foreshadowed in the 1950s by the development of the so-called presidential Republicans (people who vote Republican for national office but Democratic for state and local office).

IMAGE 5.2 This 1961 campaign flyer presents U.S. Senate candidate John Tower's positions on some of the most high profile issues of the day, many of which (though not all) remain salient almost 60 years later.

Screen Shot

★ **CTQ** What role did John Tower play in the Republican Party's rise to dominant party status in Texas?

As discussed earlier, conservative Democrats objected to the obvious policy differences of the state and national Democratic parties and often voted for Republican presidential candidates.

The first major step in the rejuvenation of the Republican Party in Texas came in 1961, when John Tower, a Republican, was elected to the U.S. Senate. Tower won a special non-partisan election held when Lyndon Johnson gave up his Senate seat to assume the vice presidency. In his campaign, Tower highlighted his conservative positions on many of the highest profile issues of the early 1960s, including states' rights, right to work, and overcoming socialism (see Image 5.2). Tower was reelected three times (1966, 1972, 1978), leaving office in 1985 after opting not to run for a fifth term. His seat was retained by the Republicans with the election to the Senate of former Representative Phil Gramm over his liberal Democratic opponent Lloyd Doggett in 1984. In November 2002, John Cornyn, a Republican and the state's former attorney general, was elected to replace Gramm.

In November 1978, the Republicans achieved their most stunning breakthrough when Bill Clements defeated John Hill in the race for governor. After losing the governor's seat to a moderately conservative Democrat, Mark White, in 1982, Republicans regained their momentum in 1986, when Clements turned the tables on White and recaptured the governorship. Developments in the 1990s and early 2000s transformed Texas into "Republican country." With the election in 1992 of U.S. Senator Kay Bailey Hutchison, Republicans held both U.S. Senate seats for the first time since Reconstruction. In 1994, Republican George W. Bush defeated incumbent Democratic Governor Ann Richards.

By far the most impressive gains for the GOP came in the November 1998 elections, when incumbent Governor George W. Bush led a sweep of Republicans to victory in every statewide election. For the first time in more than a hundred years, no Democrats occupied any statewide executive or judicial office. Republicans have continued to maintain their monopoly in statewide elections. In 2004, after a successful second effort at congressional redistricting, the GOP captured a majority in Texas's congressional delegation.

The Republican Party is now dominant in lower-level offices in much of the state, where Democrats were once most firmly entrenched. In 1974, the GOP held only 53 offices at the county level; they now hold a majority in county courthouses representing two-thirds of the state's population. The GOP gained a majority of seats in the Texas Senate in 1996 and a majority in the Texas House of Representatives in 2002. Table 5.1 shows the dramatic increases by Republicans in the Texas Legislature and the Texas delegation to the U.S. House of Representatives.

TABLE 5.1 Changes in the Number of Republican and Democratic Officeholders in Texas

Body	1973		2019	
	Democrats	Republicans	Democrats	Republicans
Texas House of Representatives	132	17	67	83
Texas Senate	28	3	12	19
U.S. House of Representatives	20	4	13	23
U.S. Senate	1	1	0	2

▶ What explains the Republican dominance of the Texas political scene today? To what extent will demographic changes affect the future success of the party?

The Era of Republican Dominance?

The Republican Party continues to dominate Texas state politics. Most observers now agree that Texas has experienced a **party realignment**, the long-term transition from a system in which one party is consistently dominant to one in which another party is consistently dominant After more than a century of Democratic Party domination after the Civil War, the pendulum has swung to the Republican Party. Realignment involves more than just casting a vote for a Republican Party candidate; it refers to a shift in attachment to political parties, which is called **partisan identification**. Evidence that Texas is becoming a Republican-dominated state comes from public opinion polls that show that many more Texans are identifying with the Republican Party than in the past. As Table 5.2 indicates, in 1952, an overwhelming percentage of Texans who identified with a political party were Democrats; indeed, only 6 percent considered themselves Republicans, compared with 66 percent for the Democrats. (The remaining 28 percent considered themselves "independents.")

In 2002, exactly 50 years later, polls showed that identification among Texans with the Republican Party exceeded that for the Democratic Party. From Table 5.2, we also can see that the total percentage of partisans decreased during the period, which suggests a period of **dealignment**, in which increasing numbers of voters choose not to identify with either of the two parties and consider themselves to be independents. This is not surprising in transition from the one-party Democratic control to Republican dominance, as many Republican-voting Democrats do not completely switch parties, but consider themselves independents, at least for a while.

The partisan balance evened out between 2002 and 2016, the year Hillary Clinton battled Donald Trump in the presidential election, though the split at the time is deceiving, as a significantly larger portion of independents said they "leaned" toward the Republican Party. (These leaners tend to vote very much like partisans on election day.) By 2016, the

party realignment
The long-term transition from a system in which one party is consistently dominant to one in which another party is consistently dominant.

partisan identification
A person's attachment to one political party or the other.

dealignment
When increasing numbers of voters choose not to identify with either of the two parties and consider themselves to be independents.

TABLE 5.2 Percentage of Voters Indicating a Major Party Identification

This table shows that Texas voters were once heavily identified with the Democratic Party, but now are split between the two parties. Notice, however, that the share of voters who identify with either party has declined slightly.

Year	Democrats	Republicans	Total Party Identifiers
1952	66	6	72
1972	57	14	71
1990	34	30	64
2002	25	37	62
2008	35	36	71
2016	33	35	68
2018	31	34	65

Polls conducted by Belden and Associates (1952 and 1972), Harte-Hanks Communications (1990), American National Election Studies (2002), and the University of Texas/Texas Tribune polls (2008, 2016, and 2018).

▶ Explain why Republican candidates are so heavily favored in elections when just over one-third of Texas voters consider themselves Republicans.

IMAGE 5.3 Republicans have taken great pride in gaining dominance in Texas. This statue was prominently displayed at the party's state convention to symbolize the Republicanization of the state.

AP Images/LM Otero

★ **CTQ**   Can the Republican Party be confident of its continuing control of the state? What changes brought Republicans to power, and what changes will the future bring to the state?

Republicans maintained a small lead among party identifiers, but held a decided 48–41 advantage when leaning independents were included. The partisan balance has changed dramatically in Texas, though it didn't happen overnight.

To a large extent the rise of the Republican Party in Texas reflected the "sorting" of voters' identification to match their conservative ideological orientations.[6] This takes time, as partisan identification in the electorate changes slowly. Political scientists have shown that people's dispositions toward the parties begin to develop at an early age, and that our parents are particularly influential.[7] As these dispositions are reinforced, say, by interactions with friends and neighbors, identifications harden and become resistant to change. This does not mean that they do not change, of course. Part of the big gains for the Republicans in Texas reflected a shift among conservative middle- and upper-class Anglo Democrats. After years of voting Republican in presidential elections but identifying as Democrats, they began thinking of themselves as Republicans.

What stimulated the change was the behavior of the parties and their candidates. Of special importance was the liberal shift in policies under Democratic presidents during the 1960s. Most notable was the expansion of civil rights, because it seems to have led many Anglo voters to defect to the Republican Party (and many African American voters to align with the Democratic Party).[8] Ironically, the main proponent of these policies was Texas's own President Lyndon B. Johnson (1963–1969). He pushed through a lot of other liberal legislation during the period, and there is reason to think that this also influenced voters' perceptions and alignments with the parties. From Table 5.2, it is clear that even these effects were not felt immediately in Texas, as the Democratic lead over the Republicans remained a sizable 43 percent even in 1972.

The performance of Republican presidents also mattered. The election of Ronald Reagan may have been of particular consequence. His victory over the unpopular Democrat Jimmy Carter in 1980 began a 12-year run of Republican control of the White House. Under Reagan the economy boomed, as did his approval ratings, and the Cold War came to an end. During this short time, the Republicans virtually closed the massive gap on the Democrats in Texas. The election of George W. Bush to the presidency in 2000 and then again in 2004 helped solidify the Republican realignment in Texas, as he had been a very popular governor and president in the state.

Party switching by native Texans is only part of the story of realignment. Another factor involves newcomers to the state, who came in large numbers during the 1970s and 1980s. These migrants to Texas were less Democratic in their affiliations, and this helped break down traditional partisan patterns. Perhaps the most important newcomers of all have been those from within Texas—the offspring of Texas residents. As Texans switched affiliations and newcomers from other states further diluted the Democratic advantage, young people reflected their parents' more balanced partisanship. Moreover, the short-term forces that swayed their parents tended to have an even greater impact on them, both as children and as young adults going off to vote for the first or second time.

Sources of Republican Strengths and Weaknesses

Republican support is strong in a broad swath of rural counties and in most small and medium-sized cities, (see Figure 5.1) and is concentrated in these areas:

- The outermost suburban ring around the major metro areas
- Fort Worth and its suburbs
- West Texas north of Interstate 10.
- East Texas
- Hill Country–Edwards Plateau

FIGURE 5.1 Results of the 2016 Presidential Election

This map shows that Hillary Clinton carried only 27 of Texas's 254 counties, but she did carry suburban Fort Bend county along with five of the six most populous counties (Tarrant was the exception). Donald Trump dominated in all of the less populous counties outside the U.S.–Mexico border region.

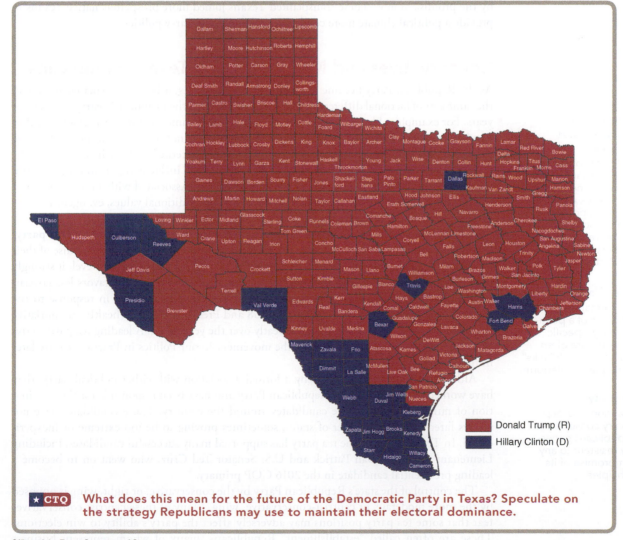

★ CTQ **What does this mean for the future of the Democratic Party in Texas? Speculate on the strategy Republicans may use to maintain their electoral dominance.**

Office of the Texas Secretary of State.

Republican Party support is weaker in the following areas:

- South Central Texas
- Central cities of Austin, Dallas, Houston, and San Antonio
- The Border region from the Rio Grande Valley to El Paso

Public opinion research shows that the Republican Party appeals more to Anglo voters, those who attend church regularly, businesspeople, and families with higher incomes. Not all people in these categories identify with and vote for Republicans, of course, but they are more likely to do so. Not surprisingly, Republican support is strongest in suburban communities and rural and small towns, and this is true around the country. Texas also has a fairly large number of active and retired military officers, who tend to be Republicans.

The party has benefited from the economic growth and prosperity that occurred in Texas from the end of World War II to the early 1980s. During this period, newcomers from more Republican parts of the country were lured to the state by a sympathetic business climate or by the promise of jobs. These transplanted Texans joined more prosperous native Texans to provide a political climate more conducive to Republican Party politics.

Conservatives and Moderates and Texas Republicans

As the Republican Party became dominant in Texas politics, it began to experience some of the same sort of factional differences that had characterized the Democratic Party in Texas for years. For example, a bloc of conservative Christians, sometimes referred to as **evangelical** or **fundamentalist Christians**, began in the 1980s to play an increasingly prominent role in the Texas Republican Party. These social conservatives are concerned with such issues as family, religion, and community morals, and it has been effective in influencing the **party platform**, whose "planks" contain the party's formal issue positions. Associated with a broad spectrum of Protestant Christianity that emphasizes salvation and traditional values, evangelical voters are likely to support culturally conservative politics.

Another group that has grown in influence within the Republican Party is the **tea party**, a faction or group of very conservative Republicans generally resistant to compromise of their principles. A passionate conservative movement that began at the grassroots level, it strongly strongly opposes taxation and the social services it finances; it generally favors less government power over individuals' economic choices. The movement began in response to the federal bailout of financial institutions in 2008 and President Obama's health care initiative the following year, but it has expanded greatly over the years since. A leading tea party activist further explores the motivations of the movement in our Politics in Practice feature later in this chapter.

Although tea party members deny a formal association with either political party, they have worked mostly within the Republican Party and have been responsible for the nomination of numerous conservative candidates around the country. These candidates have not always fared well in a number of states, sometimes proving to be too extreme or inexperienced. In Texas, however, the tea party has supported many successful candidates, including Lieutenant Governor Dan Patrick and U.S. Senator Ted Cruz, who went on to become a leading presidential candidate in the 2016 GOP primary.

The control of the state's Republican Party by the conservative, or right, wing is opposed by the more moderate, or centrist-conservative, wing. Many of these centrist conservatives fear that some tea party positions may adversely affect the party's ability to win elections. These are often called "establishment" Republicans, many of whom represent business

evangelical or **fundamentalist Christians**
A bloc of conservative Christians who are concerned with such issues as family, religion, abortion, gay rights, and community morals, and often support the Republican Party.

party platform
The formal issue positions of a political party; specific elements are often referred to as "planks" in the party's platform.

tea party
A faction or group of very conservative Republicans generally resistant to any compromise of its principles.

interests. They are generally fiscal conservatives, who want to keep taxes low and limit the government's interference in the market, but differ from the tea party faction because they frequently support public spending on infrastructure and education. They also are more tolerant of immigration and civil rights for ethnic and sexual minorities. The establishment Republicans differ from Christian conservatives by placing less of a premium on moral issues. The ideological and policy direction of the party thus remains unclear, both in Texas and in other states.

Can the Democrats Still Compete?

Some observers believe that Texas will emerge as a competitive two-party state in the near future. They note that Democrats still have considerable resources in many local governments, especially in several major cities and in South and Far West Texas.

The Republican Party has failed to generate much support among the state's minority voters. African American support for GOP statewide candidates consistently ranges between approximately 5 and 10 percent. The Republican Party has had greater success among Latinos than African Americans; for example, Governor Abbott won 44 percent of the Latino vote in 2014 and President Trump garnered 34 percent in 2016. Still, a substantial majority of Latinos consistently vote for Democratic candidates in Texas.

Democratic strategists are encouraged by the state's growing Latino population. Ethnic and racial minorities now make up a majority of the state's population, and projections are that the Latino population in Texas will surpass non-Hispanic whites (Anglos) in 2020.[9] In many counties, particularly along the U.S.–Mexico border, Latinos already are in the majority. This is clear from Figure 5.2, which depicts the Latino percentage of the population in each of Texas's 254 counties. Given that they tend on average to support Democratic candidates, the growing number of Latinos could cause the phenomenon of **tipping**—that is, when a group grows large enough to change the political balance in the electorate. Low voter turnout has limited Latinos' impact on past statewide elections, but recent trends offer Democrats reason to hope for a resurgence. The Latino population is growing and younger Latinos have been increasingly trending toward the Democrats as they begin to participate in politics.

IMAGE 5.4 Republican candidates like Governor Greg Abbott have been able to appeal to Texans' conservatism by emphasizing religious themes such as opposition to abortion and same-sex marriage.

AP Images/Tony Gutierrez

★ CSQ **Write a well-composed essay or form a team to create a well-illustrated presentation identifying the differences between Democrats and Republicans on major social and economic issues. You should be able to easily identify at least a dozen differences. How do policy differences affect the electoral coalitions that determine a party's success? Explain the demographic differences between the two parties.**

Republican party strategists hope that many Latino voters will support the GOP because they believe their party is more in tune with some Latino voters' identification with conservative social positions on issues such as abortion and family values. Democrats, on the other hand, still believe that Latinos will be attracted to their party because of its traditional support for civil rights and spending on public services, and because many Latinos have come to regard Republicans' more strident anti-immigrant positions as an affront to their heritage and identity. Some observers have suggested that a substantial number of Latino voters are persuadable

tipping
A phenomenon that occurs when a group grows large enough to change the political balance in the electorate.

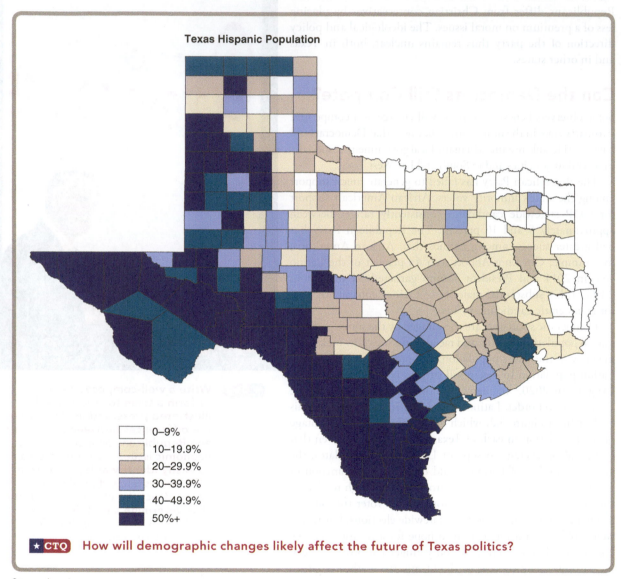

FIGURE 5.2 Texas Latino Population by County

Democrats pin their hopes for the future on demographic changes such as the fast growing Latino population. Latinos already constitute about 40 percent of the Texas population, but many are not yet eligible to vote because they are too young or are not citizens. Among those who are eligible, Latino turnout rates have been lower than for other ethnic or racial groups.

Texas Hispanic Population

- 0–9%
- 10–19.9%
- 20–29.9%
- 30–39.9%
- 40–49.9%
- 50%+

★CTQ **How will demographic changes likely affect the future of Texas politics?**

Cengage Learning

swing voters

Voters who are not bound by party identification and who support candidates of different parties in different election years.

and that they are potentially **swing voters**, those who are not bound by party identification and who support candidates of different parties in different election years.

The GOP cannot assume that Latino party identification will trend its way as the Republican party is shifting its policy on immigration. While some of its candidates, such as Governor Abbott, have been welcoming toward Latinos, others have used harsh rhetoric that many Latinos find offensive. Overall, the Democratic Party seems to have the upper hand among Latinos, but whether Democrats can capitalize on their apparent advantage depends on their ability to register and turn out their supporters in the Latino community. One Democratic strategist described Texas as a nonvoting blue state. How things will play out in the years to come remains to be seen.

The Organization of Texas Political Parties

LO 5.3 **Evaluate the importance of party organization.**

To better understand how political parties are organized in Texas, we can divide the party machinery into two parts: the temporary, consisting of a series of conventions at various levels that happen in each election year, and the permanent, consisting of people elected to leadership positions in the party and who continue in those positions between elections (see Figure 5.3).

FIGURE 5.3 Texas Political Party Organization
This figure shows the three levels of state party organization in Texas. Party primary voters elect precinct and county chairs who serve as the county executive committee. Primary voters may also attend neighborhood precinct conventions that elect delegates to higher conventions that fill out the rest of the state's party structure.

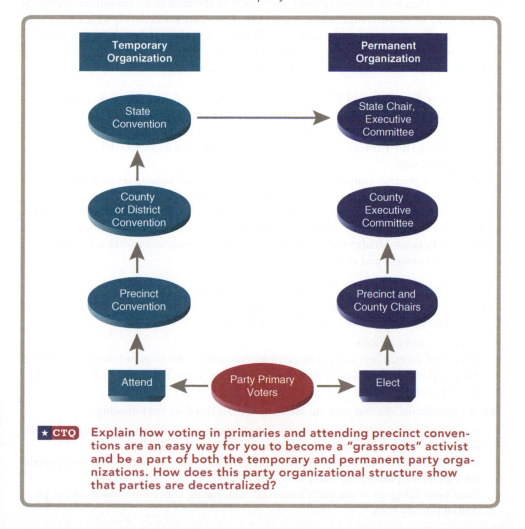

★ CTQ **Explain how voting in primaries and attending precinct conventions are an easy way for you to become a "grassroots" activist and be a part of both the temporary and permanent party organizations. How does this party organizational structure show that parties are decentralized?**

Temporary Party Organization

Consisting of precinct, county or district, and state conventions, the temporary party organizations select delegates to higher conventions that ultimately write party rules, approve the state party platforms, and select the permanent party structures that manage party affairs between conventions.

Precinct Convention

precinct convention
A gathering of party members who voted in the party's primary for the purpose of electing delegates to the county or district convention.

Precinct Convention   The starting point of party activity and a key to getting involved in politics is the **precinct convention**, a gathering of the party faithful that is open to primary voters. After the March primary in even-numbered years, the Democratic and Republican parties each hold precinct conventions at times and places published on party websites. The agenda of these conventions includes adoption of resolutions to be passed on to the county or senatorial district convention and selection of delegates to the county or senatorial district convention.

Although eligibility for participation in this grassroots level of democracy is open to all who vote in the first primary election, attendance is minimal—usually only 2 to 3 percent of those who vote. This low attendance makes it possible for a small, determined minority of the electorate to assume control of the precinct convention and dominate its affairs. Sometimes contending factions or supporters of different presidential candidates are bitterly divided, and some of the attendees will walk out and conduct their own convention, called a "rump convention." Then both precinct groups will appeal to the credentials committee appointed by the county executive committee. The credentials committee will decide which set of rival delegates is officially seated at the county or district convention. Although fairness and justice may occasionally be considered, the decision on which group to seat usually depends on which faction is in the majority on the credentials committee.

County or Senatorial District Conventions

County or Senatorial District Conventions   In the weeks after the primary and the precinct conventions, delegates selected at precinct conventions attend countywide conventions except in the most populous counties, where they attend separate conventions in each senatorial district instead. Delegates vote on resolutions and select delegates to attend the state convention.

As with the precinct conventions, ideological factions and supporters of different presidential candidates compete to dominate the delegate selection process. In Texas, bitter intra-party conflict once divided the Democratic Party more than the Republicans, but as the Republican Party became the dominant party and won control of state politics, it divided into various factions—traditionalists, social and tea party conservatives—that began to fight to control its primaries and conventions as well.

State Conventions

State Conventions   Both the Democratic and Republican parties in Texas hold state conventions in late spring or early summer in even-numbered years. The major functions of these biennial state conventions are to do the following:

- Elect state party officers.
- Elect 62 of the members to the state executive committee, two from each senatorial district.
- Adopt a party platform (see Table 5.3 for examples of recent Texas party platform planks).
- Modify state party rules.

If it is a presidential election year, the state convention also does the following:

- Select the party's nominees to serve as Texas's members of the national party executive committee.
- Select nominees for the state's 38 presidential electors, who will serve if the party carries the state in the presidential election.
- Elect most delegates to the party's national nominating convention based on the presidential primary vote.

TABLE 5.3 Excerpts from Recent Texas Democratic and Republican Party Platforms

This table shows some selected planks in recent Democratic and Republican platforms.

Texas Democratic Party	Texas Republican Party
Believe a democratic government exists to help us achieve as a community, state, and nation what we cannot achieve as individuals, and that it must serve all people	Believe that economic success depends upon free market principles, that it is our duty to protect innocent life, develop responsible citizens founded on the traditional family, and protect our national sovereignty
Believe government should "provide multi-language instruction, beginning in elementary school, to make all students fluent in English and at least one other language . . ."	Support "strengthening our common American identity . . . and assimilation of. . . ethnic groups" and "encourage non-English-speaking students . . . to transition to English within one year"
"Support... legislation to legalize possession and use of cannabis and its derivatives and to regulate its use, production and sale as is successfully done in Colorado, Washington and other states."	"[S]upport a change in the law to make it a civil, and not a criminal, offense for legal adults only to possess one ounce or less of marijuana for personal use, punishable by a fine of up to $100, but without jail time."
[P]roudly and vigorously support a woman's right to choose how to use her body" and oppose "any and all attempts to overturn Roe v. Wade"	Oppose abortion because "all innocent human life must be respected and safeguarded from fertilization to natural death . . . . We are resolute in our support of the reversal of Roe v. Wade."
Would abolish the death penalty in Texas and replace it with the punishment of life imprisonment without parole	Believe that "properly applied capital punishment is legitimate, is an effective deterrent, and should be reasonably swift and unencumbered"
Believe "the state should establish a 100% equitable school finance system with sufficient state revenue to allow every district to offer an exemplary program"	"[S]upport the right to choose public, private, charter, or home education." Support "the teaching of biology of reproduction and abstinence until marriage. . . . [and] school subjects with emphasis on the Judeo-Christian principles upon which America was founded"
"Support comprehensive immigration reform, including an attainable path to citizenship" and the 14th Amendment "which makes all persons born in this country citizens"	Oppose "any form of amnesty . . . including the granting of legal status to persons in the country illegally," and citizenship should be granted at birth only to children born to citizens.
Support "a minimum wage that is at least $15-an-hour that is indexed to keep it from eroding	Believe "the Minimum Wage Law should be repealed"

Source: Texas Democratic Party and the Republican Party of Texas.

▶ How does each of these platform positions reflect the ideological differences between conservative and liberal positions on public policy?

Historically, Texas parties used the convention system to express their preference for candidates for their party's presidential nomination. Voters who wanted a role in choosing their party's presidential candidate had to attend precinct conventions to choose delegates to the county or district conventions and ultimately to the state conventions. The state party conventions then had a free hand in choosing delegates to the national convention, which selects the party's nominee for president.

Over the years, each party has moved toward using a **presidential preference primary** system to allow its party's voters to express their preference among candidates seeking their party's nomination for president. Today, most of the delegates that the state party conventions select to attend national nominating conventions must be pledged to presidential candidates

presidential preference primary
A primary election that allows voters to express their preference among the candidates seeking to become their party's presidential nominee.

based on the outcome of the presidential primary. However, the state convention does sometimes send stealth delegates to the national convention who have pledged to one presidential candidate, but whose loyalties are with another.

Permanent Party Organization

The permanent structure of the party machinery consists of people selected to lead the party organization and provide continuity between election campaigns.

Precinct-Level Organization

At the lowest, or grassroots, level of the party structure is the precinct chair, who is chosen by the precinct's voters in the primary for a two-year term. Often the position is uncontested, and in some precincts, the person can be elected by write-in vote. The chair serves as party organizer in the precinct, contacting known and potential party members. The chair may help organize party activities in the neighborhood, such as voter registration drives. The precinct chair is also responsible for arranging and presiding over the precinct convention and serving as a member of the county executive committee.

County-Level Organization

A much more active and important role is that of county chair. The voters choose who will hold this office for a two-year term in the party primary. The chair presides over the county executive committee, which is composed of all precinct chairs. The county chair determines where the voting places will be for the primary and appoints all primary election judges subject to approval of the county commissioners court. Accepting candidates for places on the primary ballot, the printing of paper ballots, and the renting of voting machines are also the chair's responsibilities. Finally, the chair, along with the county executive committee, must certify the names of official nominees of the party to the secretary of state's office.

The county executive committee has three major functions: assembling the temporary roll of delegates to the county convention; canvassing the returns from the primary for local offices; and helping the county chair prepare the primary ballot, accept filing fees, and conduct a drawing to determine the order of candidates' names on the primary ballot. This is an important consideration since low-information voters may opt for the first name they come across on the ballot.

State-Level Organization

Delegates to the state convention choose the state chair—the titular head of the party—at the state convention for a two-year term. The duties of the chair are to preside over the state executive committee's meetings, call the state convention to order, handle the requests of statewide candidates on the ballot, and certify the primary winners to the secretary of state.

The state executive committee includes a chair and a vice chair of the opposite sex. In addition, the Democratic and Republican state convention delegates choose one man and one woman from each of the 31 state senate districts. Unlike the Republicans, the Democrats also include several members from various special caucuses on their state executive committee. The main legal duties of the state executive committee are to determine the site of the next state convention—sometimes a crucial factor in determining whose loyal supporters can attend because the party does not pay delegates' expenses—to canvass statewide primary returns, and to certify the nomination of party candidates.

The state executive committee also has some political duties, including producing and disseminating press releases and other publicity, encouraging organizational work in precincts and counties, raising money, and coordinating special projects. The state committee may work closely with the national party. These political chores are so numerous that the executive committees of both parties now employ full-time executive directors and staff assistants.

The Functions of Political Parties

LO 5.4 **Assess the functions of political parties in American and Texas politics.**

Political parties developed and survived because they perform important functions. In his conceptualization of parties, political scientist V. O. Key identified three main "faces": the party in the electorate, the party as organization, and the party in government.[10]

The Party in the Electorate

The party in the electorate refers to the identification of citizens with the parties, which we discussed earlier in this chapter. The nature and degree of this party attachment is important, whether they are strong or weak partisans or leaning independents. Party ID affects not only what voters do, but also how they view the political world. These views, in turn, influence what the party organization and party in government do.

The Party as Organization

The party as organization is the formal structure of the party itself, which we have discussed in detail as well. This is what first comes to mind for most people when they think about what a political party is: the precinct, district, and state (and national) conventions that parties hold in election years, and the officers at the various levels who actually set up and run party activities, including the primaries themselves.

Party organizations do more than this, however. They actively recruit candidates for office, and though they do not control how voters cast their ballots, they can try to influence who wins the primary election. Party organizations also work to help their nominees win in the general election. This involves raising money, providing services (campaign organization and advice), and getting out the vote. Getting out the vote includes interactions with the party in the electorate by telephone, social media, and even door-to-door canvassing. The more organized the party, the more effective it is in getting out the vote for its candidates.

Party organizations not only mobilize their supporters to vote, but they also represent their views on public policy as they support the candidates that party members have nominated in the primaries; they shape the party platforms and help organize political campaigns that focus on particular themes that reflect the values and aspirations of their voters. Of course, leaders in the party organization do not simply reflect the views of ordinary party voters; they have their own perspectives and often take the lead on issues that reflect the views of donors and interest groups as well.

The Party in Government

The party in government consists of the elected officials in government and what they do while there. This is something we haven't addressed much at all in this chapter, although future chapters will. For now, consider that the party in government in Texas includes the governor and other statewide officials and also the members of the Texas Legislature. Co-partisans work together in ways that can determine how government institutions work and which policy outputs they produce. Elected officials of the same party have similar preferences on many issues, and they have a shared interest in pushing forward their positions.

The parties in government also serve other functions. They are the parties' most visible faces. Elected officials are on the political front lines, so to speak, driving the policy agenda and the policy-making process. They are at the center of political advocacy and debate.

How Does Texas Compare?

Party Control of Government in the 50 States

Research in political science has shown that states with higher levels of party competition for control of government have higher levels of voter turnout and also tend to spend more on social programs. Although there is some competition between the two parties in all states, some states are much more competitive than others. Figure 5.4 shows the states in which one party controls the executive and both chambers of the legislature (blue for Democratic, red for Republican) and states in which control is divided, depicted in tan. (Nebraska, shown in white, has a nonpartisan legislature, so it is not possible to code party control of both branches.) Keep in mind that the map shows party control in the states and does not necessarily match familiar electoral college maps for presidential elections.

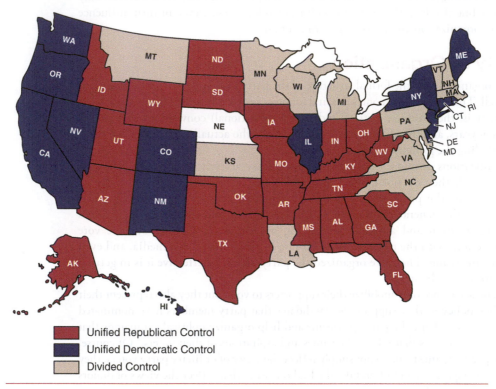

Unified Republican Control
Unified Democratic Control
Divided Control

FIGURE 5.4 Party Control in the 50 States: How Texas Compares
The map illustrates party control of government in the American states in 2019.

Source: National Council of State Legislatures. The figure depicts whether Republicans control both the executive and legislative branches (red), Democrats control both (blue), or control is divided (purple).

FOR DEBATE

★ **SRQ** How would party competition make a state's political system more responsive to residents' needs and preferences?

★ **CTQ** Based on demographic changes in Texas, is the state likely to become more or less competitive in the future?

★ **CTQ** How would you expect public policies to differ in states controlled by Republicans and those controlled by Democrats? Would you expect states with divided control to develop moderate compromises or gridlock?

Not surprisingly, they occupy the attention of the mass media. The parties' leading politicians use the media to frame the political debate for voters, especially their partisans. The goal, of course, is to communicate their positions to the public and mobilize support. In the process, the parties in government help voters make sense of the issues, if only imperfectly. Providing a basic understanding of the parties' positions on the issues of the day allows voters to make a more informed choice between the parties in the voting booth. This is critical to representative democracy.

Applying What You Have Learned about Texas Political Parties

LO 5.5   **Apply what you have learned about Texas political parties.**

You have learned how Democrats and Republicans often differ on ideology and the role they see for government, and how factions have developed with ideological differences even within the same party. We invited a passionate Texas political practitioner, Julie McCarty, to put a face on the ideology of the tea party movement and to give you an insight into its motivation as it strives to reshape the Texas Republican Party.

Julie McCarty is the founding president of the NE Tarrant Tea Party (NETTP). In less than six years, McCarty and her colleagues built the NETTP into the most visible and influential local tea party group in Texas, and into what is widely considered to be the single most powerful force in Tarrant County Republican politics. Over the past few primary election cycles the NETTP's influence has stretched beyond Tarrant County to affect GOP primaries statewide.

After you have read her essay, we will ask you to use your critical thinking skills to distinguish between the rival factions of the Republican Party and apply what you have learned about the differences between liberals, moderates, and conservatives. And, regardless of your political disposition, we will ask you to reflect on how political activity can enrich your personal, social, and emotional life.

POLITICS IN PRACTICE
One Face of the Texas Tea Party

by Julie McCarty
PRESIDENT OF THE NE TARRANT TEA PARTY

September 12, 2009, is a day I will never forget. It's the day I joined nearly 2 million Americans in a march on Washington. We were protesting our out-of-control government and the national debt in the first-ever tea party. My husband and two-year-old daughter were with me, and it changed our lives. To have that many people in agreement with a unified message—and not only that but also willing to apply funds and effort to share that message—well, that meant we were *not alone*.

The discovery that one is not alone is what fuels tea party organizations. Many of them sprang up around the country in 2009—just local gatherings of Americans who have had enough of being ignored by the politicians who are supposed to be representing them. People wanted to be heard and wanted to find community. Many groups took the opportunity to blow off steam and have disbanded since that initial flash, but there are still many strong and active groups fighting to make a difference, and nowhere is the tea party stronger than in Texas. I'll even go so far as to say that nowhere is the tea party stronger than in Tarrant County, Texas. And if you'll allow me, I can take it a step further, and tell you the real strength is in NE Tarrant County.

Tarrant County is the last red metropolitan area in our state. If Tarrant turns blue, Texas turns blue. And if Texas turns blue, the country will not see another Republican president for a very long time. Fort Worth is the biggest city in Tarrant County, and Fort Worth is blue. It is the very solidly red NE corner of Tarrant County that keeps Texas red and maintains hope for the rest of America!

And this is where the NE Tarrant Tea Party fits in. In 2009 I was given a list of conservative-minded patriots in my zip code and agreed to start the Grapevine Tea Party. Before we could even launch our group, I was asked to incorporate Southlake as well. We had two dozen folks show up at our first meeting and determined that going forward, we wanted guest speakers to educate us on the Constitution, the political process, historical lessons, and fiscal concerns. Soon after, Colleyville asked if they could join up, and there was talk of Euless wanting to be involved as well. Rather than take on cities one by one, we changed our name from the Grapevine/Southlake Tea Party to NE Tarrant Tea Party, incorporating patriots in fourteen cities—all determined to keep Tarrant County red by educating voters. Now our meetings draw 150 to 200 people, and double that depending on the guest speaker. Our board members are widely sought for candidate endorsements, and voters know to turn to us for trusted voting recommendations. NE Tarrant was the first area in Texas to flip their State Reps to tea party–backed candidates, and that has triggered a ripple effect into countywide offices as well. Today, if someone wants to run for office in Tarrant County, we are their first stop.

But when I say we want to keep Tarrant red, I don't want to leave the impression that the tea party is just another branch of the Republican Party. Not at all! In fact, we focus the large majority of our efforts in *fighting* the Republican Party. Remember, the tea party rose out of the frustration of We The People being ignored by our representatives … and in Texas those representatives by and large are Republican.

Some Republican office holders like to say the tea party is too far right … too fringe. But if you look at the five principles we espouse, you'll see they fall directly in line with what the Republican Party is *supposed* to stand for:

- Fiscal Responsibility
- Rule of Law
- Personal Responsibility
- National Sovereignty
- Limited Government

When you dig right into it, there are few who could actually successfully argue any of those points, but our representatives certainly try. And as long as they try, the tea party will have its place. We must. Our freedom requires it!

Going forward, the tea party will continue to educate voters, as always. That's what empowers people to make wise decisions at the polls. But as a key part of that, I see us making great progress in learning to work with other groups. Not only are we starting to communicate better with tea parties across the state, but we are also making a stronger effort to help smaller groups get started and grow. When tea party groups statewide broadcast a unified and cohesive message, our voice is louder and our message is stronger. It's hard to label such a large group as fringe or conspiracy theorists. We are not extreme … we are just right.

1. How do members of the tea party differ from other Republicans? Why does the author say that she and her fellow tea party members spend a majority of their time fighting other Republicans?
2. Explain why the tea party is considered conservative. Compare tea party positions with those taken by moderates and liberals.
3. What motivates tea party activists? How do shared values form the basis for a sense of belonging and social interaction within all political groups?

★ Chapter Summary

LO 5.1 Identify the characteristics of American political parties. There are three fundamental characteristics of political parties in the United States: (1) the two-party system, (2) pragmatism, and (3) decentralization.

We have two major parties in the United States and Texas partly because the electoral system—specifically, single-member districts and plurality elections—makes it hard for third parties to succeed. Election laws put in place by the two major parties make it hard for third parties to emerge in the first place.

Parties in the United States and Texas traditionally have been pragmatic, focused on performance more than policy positions. This is largely the result of there being two parties, which makes it necessary to build majority coalitions to compete and to appeal to voters who are moderate and focused on performance. Recently, however, parties in the United States and Texas have become more programmatic, and Democrats and Republicans have become easier to distinguish.

Parties in the United States and Texas are decentralized, with much of the control of the nominating process (the primary) and party machinery in the hands of state and local leaders and voters.

LO 5.2 Understand the evolution of the party system in Texas. For much of its history, Texas was a one-party Democratic state. Until recently, one-party dominance meant that the election to select the Democratic Party's nominees—the Democratic primary—was the most important election in Texas. Moderate and conservative factions within the Democratic Party became the key political players.

After years of domination by the Democratic Party, Texas began to experience strong two-party competition in the 1980s, and in the late 1990s the Republicans became the dominant party in Texas. By the turn of the century, political realignment was fairly complete. By 2003, the GOP controlled the governor's office, all other statewide offices, and both chambers of the state legislature; in 2004, Republicans captured a majority in the state's congressional delegation. The Republicans will no doubt remain dominant in the near future; what will happen in the long run is less clear, particularly as the state's Latino population grows and becomes more involved in politics.

LO 5.3 Evaluate the importance of party organization. Political parties consist of permanent organizations that manage operations in between elections and the temporary structures which are the conventions that convene only in election years. Party primary voters attend precinct conventions that select delegates to county or district conventions which, in turn, choose delegates to the state convention to write the party platform and the rules that govern the party's ongoing operations.

LO 5.4 Assess the functions of political parties in American and Texas politics. Despite the hostility of the Founders to political parties, they have become an important part of American political life. Parties perform critical functions in a democracy. They nominate and elect their candidates to public office, educate and mobilize voters, and run the government at the different levels (local, state, or national).

LO 5.5 Apply what you have learned about Texas political parties. You learned about the policy goals of the tea party movement, which has become a major faction within today's Republican Party, and reflected on the motivations that drive political activists in general. You were given the opportunity to explore the practical differences within the state's majority party and how these differences are expressed in the intra-party politics of the Republican primary.

Key Terms

Review Questions

LO 5.1 Identify the characteristics of American political parties.

- Explain why there are two major parties in the United States and Texas.

- Why have parties in the United States and Texas traditionally been so pragmatic?

LO 5.2 Understand the evolution of the party system in Texas.

- Define realignment, and discuss to what extent it has occurred in Texas politics.

- Discuss the reasons for and describe the events that led to the rise of the Republican Party in Texas.

- Has Texas become a one-party Republican state? Or is there reason to expect increased competition between the parties in the future? Why or why not?

LO 5.3 Evaluate the importance of party organization.

- What are party platforms, and how do political parties in Texas produce them?

LO 5.4 Assess the functions of political parties in American and Texas politics.

- Differentiate between the party in the electorate, the party as organization, and the party in government.

- How do parties help represent the public in government? Are parties always good agents of the public? Why or why not?

Think Critically and Get Active!

Team up with a political party. If you already identify with one, this is easy; if you don't, choose a party. To help you find your way, the state party organizations can be found at the following sites: **www.txdemocrats.org** (@texasdemocrats), **www.texasgop.org** (@TexasGOP), **www.lptexas.org** (@LPTexas), and **www.txgreens.org** (@TXGreens). On-campus organizations include the Young Democrats at **www.texasyds.com** (@TexasYDs) and Young Republicans at **www.texasyr.gop** (@TexasYRs).

Help select your party's nominee. Register and vote in the party's primary election. To vote in the primary, you must be registered at least 30 days in advance. In Texas, you simply decide which party you prefer and vote to select that party's nominee. The only real

restriction is that you must choose one party or the other. Go to your party's precinct convention or caucus. If you vote in your party's primary, you are eligible to attend your party's precinct convention. Contact your party chair, go to your party county executive committee website, or ask the party officials at your primary polling site to find out when and where you should attend. Attendance is often sparse, which means you have a good chance of being heard and even being elected as a delegate.

Attend your party's county- or district-level convention. Delegates selected at the precinct level go on to attend their party's county or district convention. Delegates to these conventions pass resolutions and elect delegates to the state convention, which is held every two years in June. If you are selected as a delegate to the state convention, you have become a serious party activist.

Determine whether you are a liberal or conservative. Sample some liberal and conservative websites to determine whether you are a liberal or conservative. Link up with the liberal *Texas Observer* at **www.texasobserver.org** (@TexasObserver) and the CPPP Blog of the left-leaning Center for Public Policy Priorities at **bettertexasblog.org** (@CPPP_TX); plug into **www.offthekuff.com**.

For the conservative viewpoint, visit the websites of the *Texas Monitor* at **texasmonitor.org** (@thetexasmonitor) and Empower Texans at **www.empowertexans.com** (@EmpowerTexans) and take a look at *Breitbart Texas* at **www.breitbart.com/texas** (@BreitbartTexas).

★ **PRQ** If you are going to be politically active, why is it important to know who shares your viewpoints? Why is it important to understand the viewpoints of people who differ with you?

6

Interest Groups

Pro-life and pro-choice interest groups rally in the Texas Capitol dome as state Senator Wendy Davis filibusters a bill limiting abortions. In this chapter, you will explore the wide variety of tactics that interest groups use to influence public policy in the state.

Tina Phan/MCT/Newscom

Learning Objectives

LO 6.1 Define interest groups and identify their major types.

LO 6.2 Describe how interest groups influence public policies in Texas.

LO 6.3 Analyze the political balance of power among interest groups in Texas.

LO 6.4 Evaluate the role of interest groups in Texas politics and policy formulation.

LO 6.5 Apply what you have learned about interest groups.

Citizens may act alone to influence government, and millions do. But when citizens join together in a voluntary organization that strives to influence public policy, they act as an **interest group**, sometimes known as a pressure group. Interest groups often play a high-stakes political game that determines who gets what from state government and who pays for it. As Congresswoman Barbara Jordan famously said, "The stakes are too high for government to be a spectator sport."

Interest groups compete with each other as they strive to benefit from the state's $217 billion biennial budget. Such groups often depend on government outlays, and they solicit policy makers for a piece of government spending. Construction companies ask the governor to support increased spending on infrastructure projects. Public schoolteachers pressure the legislature for more resources for public education. Advocates for low-income Texans ask lawmakers to increase Medicaid spending and expand Medicaid coverage. Many interest groups press the government to spend more, but usually advocate for less taxation—especially on their own members.

Business and professional groups plead for state regulations friendly to their interests. Because Texas's $1.9 trillion state economy represents a significant share of the national market, out-of-state producers wanting to sell in Texas modify their goods and services to comply with Texas regulations. As a result, Texas regulations can ripple out to other states, and they can determine what entire industries produce and how they produce it.

For some interest groups, their fundamental values or their very way of life is at stake in public policy making. Some ethnic/racial identity–based groups seek government protection for their civil and political rights. Certain faith-based groups try to use government to support their religious values by banning abortion, contraception, or same-sex marriage while gun rights groups urge passage of laws to expand the right to carry firearms. Environmental groups fight for government restrictions on pollution; some agricultural groups fight to preserve the state's agricultural tax exemption.

So many groups, perhaps thousands of them, have their interests at play in the political game that we cannot describe every group and its goals individually. Instead, you should understand the broad types of interest groups that pursue influence in Texas government and policy making.

interest group
A voluntary organization that strives to influence public policy; sometimes known as a pressure group.

Types of Interest Groups

LO 6.1 **Define interest groups and identify their major types.**

Interest groups can be classified in a multitude of ways, but the simplest is to categorize them according to their primary purpose—economic, noneconomic, or mixed. Table 6.1 gives some examples of Texas interest groups in all three categories.

Economic Groups

Economic interest groups seek financial advantages for their members. Business and agricultural groups are interested in keeping their taxes low, securing subsidies, limiting regulation, and receiving government contracts to increase profits. Professional groups want to limit entry into their professions to reduce competition; public education groups fight against school privatization and for increased salaries and benefits for teachers. Labor unions seek generous workers' compensation, better workplace safety regulations, and laws to make it easier for workers to organize unions.

Noneconomic Groups

Noneconomic groups seek the betterment of society as a whole or the reform of the political, social, or economic systems in ways that do not directly affect their members' pocketbooks. Personal (or civil) liberties and environmental groups maintain that the beneficiaries of their

TABLE 6.1 Interest Group Classifications and Selected Examples

Table 6.1 shows the three types of interest groups and examples of each.

Classification	Sector	Examples
Economic	Agriculture	Texas Farm Bureau
	Business	Texas Association of Business
	Energy	Texas Oil and Gas Association
	Labor	Texas AFL-CIO
	Occupations & Professions	Texas Association of Realtors, Texas Automobile Dealers Association, Texas Medical Association
	Tort Reform	Texans for Lawsuit Reform
Noneconomic	Abortion	NARAL Pro-Choice Texas, Texas Right to Life
	Environment	Environment Texas, Texas League of Conservation Voters
	Personal Liberties	American Civil Liberties Union of Texas, Texas State Rifle Association
	Public Interest	Public Citizen Texas, Texans for Public Justice
	Public Policy	Center for Public Policy Priorities, Texas Public Policy Foundation
Mixed	Education	Texas State Teachers Association
	Group Rights	Equality Texas, League of United Latin American Citizens, Mexican American Legal Defense and Education Fund, National Association for the Advancement of Colored People, OCA-Asian Pacific American Advocates

▶ Visit these groups' websites, find out which public policies they advocate, and then use their policy agendas to show the difference between economic and noneconomic interest groups.

efforts are the members of society—things like personal freedom or clean air and water that cannot be directly measured entirely by self-interest. Political reform groups, such as Public Citizen, think of themselves as "public interest" groups because they believe that they are literally acting on behalf of the public. Many individuals who join noneconomic interest groups are motivated by personal values and intense passion like members of the Texas Right to Life movement, who have strong beliefs about conception and when life begins.

Mixed Groups

Many groups do not fit neatly into either the economic or noneconomic classification because they pursue social goals that also have clear economic effects. Groups fighting discrimination on the basis of age, disability, ethnicity/race, gender, or sexual orientation argue that such practices are not only a form of social injustice but also an economic problem that affects wages and promotions in the workplace. Groups pursuing both social equality and economic goals are classified as mixed or hybrid organizations. Few, if any, demands on the political system affect all classes of citizens equally. Any public policy comes with both costs and benefits; some will gain while others will bear an economic burden from almost any government decision.

Interest Groups' Targets and Tactics

LO 6.2 **Describe how interest groups influence public policies in Texas.**

Interest groups are collections of citizens with shared interests that pursue public policy goals on behalf of their members. Their interests are narrower than those of political parties. Unlike political parties, they do not nominate candidates for public office and may work with officials of both parties to secure their goals. Although interest groups sometimes endorse and support candidates for office, their primary purpose is to influence government policy makers.

Interest groups use a variety of tools to influence state decision makers, and they adapt their tactics to target specific officials. They make face-to-face appeals to legislative and executive officials, and they file suit in the courts. Interest groups use electioneering and public relations to sway elected officials by affecting public opinion. Figure 6.1 shows the major tools interest groups use to influence decision makers.

FIGURE 6.1 Interest Groups' Tools of Influence

Interest groups adapt their tactics and the tools of influence they use depending on the part of the political system they are trying to influence. Ultimately their source of power is the ability to persuade.

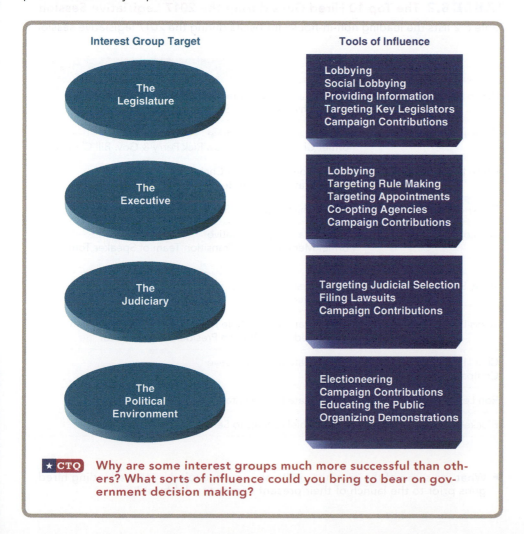

Interest Group Target	Tools of Influence
The Legislature	Lobbying Social Lobbying Providing Information Targeting Key Legislators Campaign Contributions
The Executive	Lobbying Targeting Rule Making Targeting Appointments Co-opting Agencies Campaign Contributions
The Judiciary	Targeting Judicial Selection Filing Lawsuits Campaign Contributions
The Political Environment	Electioneering Campaign Contributions Educating the Public Organizing Demonstrations

★ **CTQ** **Why are some interest groups much more successful than others? What sorts of influence could you bring to bear on government decision making?**

Lobbying the Legislature

lobbying
Directly contacting public officials to advocate for a public policy.

Interest groups' most straightforward tool for influencing public officials is contacting them directly to advocate for a particular public policy—a practice known as **lobbying**. Some interest groups hire individual freelance lobbyists or large lobbying firms to advocate for them on a single issue, while other interest groups employ full-time, in-house lobbyists to work exclusively for them. Table 6.2 provides a list of the top 10 freelance lobbyists during the 2017 legislative session according to the widely respected *Capitol Inside*, which has been ranking lobbyists after each session for a dozen years. All 10 individuals are principals in large lobbying firms that have multiple clients. They include Neal T. "Buddy" Jones of HillCo Partners (see the Texas Insiders feature later in the chapter); Mike Toomey, Bill Messer and Lara Keel of the Texas Lobby Group; Robert Miller, head of the Public Law practice of Locke Lord LLP; and Rusty Kelley, who leads Blackridge. Of the 10, five are former state representatives and all of the others have close past or present ties to the state legislature and executive branch as advisors or friends/relatives of influential legislative actors.

★ **Did You Know?** In 2017 there were 1,928 lobbyists registered with the Texas Ethics Commission.

TABLE 6.2 The Top 10 Hired Guns during the 2017 Legislative Session
Table 6.2 lists the leading non-in-house lobbyists during the 2017 legislative session.

Name	Lobby Firm	Political Posts/Ties
Neal T. "Buddy" Jones	HillCo Partners	Former State Representative Former Chief of Staff to Speaker Gib Lewis
Mike Toomey	Texas Lobby Group	Former State Representative Former Chief of Staff to Gov. Rick Perry & Gov. Bill Clements
Robert Miller	Locke Lord	Former Houston METRO Chair Former State Senate Aide
Rusty Kelley	Blackridge	Former Chief of Staff to Speaker Billy Clayton
Bill Messer	The Lobby Group	Former State Representative Former Member of the Transition Team of Speaker Tom Craddick
John Pitts	Texas Star Alliance	Former General Counsel to Lt. Gov. Bob Bullock Twin Brother of Former House Appropriations Chair
Lara Keel	Texas Lobby Group	Former State Senate Aide President, Red State Women Former Red State Women President State auditor
Clint Hackney	Clint Hackney & Company	Former State Representative
Ron Lewis	Ron Lewis & Associates	Former State Representative
Trey Blocker	Blocker Group	Former Chief of Staff to Senator Craig Estes

Capitol Inside.

▶ What are some of the common political posts occupied by these leading hired guns prior to the launch of their present career as a lobbyist?

Whether lobbyists work for a single client or have a massive client list to serve, they use a variety of strategies to influence different branches of government. We will go inside lobbying operations to explore some of their most effective techniques to win legislators over to their positions. Then we will show how they are also able to bring members of the executive branch and bureaucrats around to their views on public policy.

Preparing to Lobby Before a legislative session begins, a lobbyist must have successfully completed several tasks: (1) learn who is predisposed to support the cause, who is on the other side, and which members can be swayed; (2) memorize the faces of the members, their non-legislative occupations, the communities they represent, and a little about their families; (3) establish rapport through contact with the members of the legislature; (4) get to know the staffs of legislators because members can be influenced through them; and (5) know the legislative issues, including the arguments of opponents.

Lobbyists must plan a strategy for approaching legislators. How do lobbyists approach members of the legislature or the Texas House and Senate leadership? How do they get in the door, and what do they say once they get in? How much influence does a legislator's staff have on the member's decisions? Is it necessary to see all 181 members of the legislature, the lieutenant governor, and the governor?

Because a session lasts only 140 days, interest groups' best lobbyists know that lobbying should begin before the legislative session officially begins. The 19-month period between regular sessions provides lobbyists with ample time to work on relationships, learn what proposals have a chance of passing, draft legislative proposals, and line up sponsors to introduce bills in the Texas House and Senate during the next session.

Socializing Personality can be a valuable asset to a successful lobbyist. Anyone who directly contacts public officials to influence their behavior should be extroverted and enjoy socializing, because the lobbyist's first job is to become known and trusted by legislators and any executive branch officials who have jurisdiction over the interest he or she represents.

Lobbyists organize social functions with legislators to allow them to interact in comfortable settings. A lobbyist may invite legislators to lunch or to a party to begin building a personal relationship of mutual trust. Attending an occasional social event with legislators, however, is not in itself enough to win their trust. Most successful lobbyists spend years cultivating long-standing relationships with decision makers.

Using Tools of Persuasion Socializing does not obligate legislators to support lobbyists' proposals, but it does open the door for lobbyists to gain access to legislators, which at least gives them the chance to make their case. Once in the door, lobbyists find their most effective tool is providing information useful to a legislator—the facts are often persuasive. But to maintain a relationship, the lobbyist must build the legislator's trust, which means providing sound, accurate information about the legislation the lobbyist is supporting or opposing. This includes "off-the-record" admission of the pluses and minuses of the legislation. Honesty is, in fact, the best policy for a lobbyist when dealing with a public official. Lobbyists find that framing the issues in terms of the public interest affects how legislators react, and they try to define their positions before their opponents have a chance to cast them in a negative light.

Lobbyists appeal to legislators' emotions and to their ideologies, or basic philosophies of government. Lobbyists may gently remind legislators of their interest group's support in the

IMAGE 6.1 This image shows lobbyists crowding outside the Texas House of Representatives. Lobbying occurs when agents of interest groups make direct face-to-face contact with public officials in an effort to affect public policy.

AP Images/Harry Cabluck

★ CTQ   **What are the tools of persuasion that lobbyists use to convince government officials to adopt the policies they support? What makes them effective?**

★ **Did You Know?** AT&T consistently spends more money on lobbying than any other single business, more than $4 million in 2016 alone. Other utilities, American Electric Power and CenterPoint Energy ranked second and third.

legislators' past election campaigns or delicately imply the potential for future support. Although lobbyists may not legally offer legislators financial support in exchange for their vote on a bill, it is often simply understood that groups use their resources to help elect legislative candidates who support their interests. Our Texas Insiders feature puts a face on one of the most successful lobby operations in Texas; HillCo has numerous clients and primarily represents business interests.

Targeting Key Legislators Not all members of the legislature are equal, and lobbyists target those with the greatest impact on bills critical to the lobbyist's agenda. Establishing rapport and obtaining feedback from the very powerful presiding officers—the speaker of the house and lieutenant governor—are especially useful. No endorsement is more important to an interest group than that of the presiding officers. If an endorsement for the group's legislative proposal is not forthcoming, the lobbyist must persuade the presiding officers to at least remain neutral in the legislative struggle.

Getting the endorsement of the chair of each committee through which the legislation must pass before it can go to the floor for a vote is an advantage second only to that of winning the support of the presiding officers. Most of the "experts" who testify at legislative committee hearings represent interest groups; lobbyists know that committee hearings are an ideal forum in which to make their case to key legislators.

Influencing the Executive Branch

Interest groups try to influence the Texas Legislature because it creates, finances, and defines government programs, but they also target the executive branch, where enormous sums of money, privilege, and prestige are also at stake. The governor affects policy by appointing officers to head state agencies, and state agencies themselves wield a great deal of power as they award contracts and develop regulations.

Targeting the Rule-Making Process The legislature gives the executive branch and its administrative agencies responsibility for **implementation**, or carrying out broad public policies, enforcing state laws, providing public services, and managing day-to-day government activities. The legislature allows executive agencies a great deal of flexibility as to how to enforce the law; they have administrative **discretion**, which is wide latitude to make decisions within the broad requirements set out in the law. The legislative branch authorizes administrative agencies to establish detailed rules or regulations that determine how the law shall be applied to actual situations.

implementation
Administrative agencies carrying out broad public policies, enforcing state laws, providing public services, and managing day-to-day government activities.

discretion
Wide latitude to make decisions within the broad requirements set out in the law.

Texas Insiders

HillCo: Texas's Premier Lobbying Outfit and Its Influence in Texas

In some years, lobbyists registered with the Texas Ethics Commission outnumber legislators ten to one. Many lobbyists represent only one or two clients, but a few of them conduct sufficient lobby business to qualify as true Texas insiders. Among them is the powerful HillCo.

Founded in 1998 by Neal T. "Buddy" Jones and Bill Miller, HillCo has been involved in almost every big legislative fight over the past 19 years. When Bob Perry and Charles C. Butt saw their business interests threatened, they hired HillCo to help block a high-profile 2011 bill banning "sanctuary cities." One of the most popular and gregarious figures in the Capitol, HillCo partner Bill Miller helped manage Tom Craddick's races for the speakership in the House of Representatives and later helped finance former Lieutenant Governor David Dewhurst's expensive, but ill-fated, campaign for the U.S. Senate in 2012. By 2017, HillCo had contributed $5,795,367 to 495 candidates for office in the previous 20 years according to the National Institute on Money in State Politics.

Among its notable clients, HillCo partners have represented the following:

- Alcoa
- AT&T
- BBVA Compass Bank
- Blue Cross & Blue Shield of Texas
- Dallas Cowboys
- Farmers Insurance
- H-E-B Grocery
- Koch Industries
- Microsoft
- Perry Homes
- Pharmaceutical Research and Manufacturers of America (known as "big PhRMA")
- Tesla Motors

As its website boasts, "HillCo Partners is a full-service public and government affairs consulting firm, providing services in the lobbying, public policy, communications and regulatory arenas. We focus on positively impacting our clients' agendas relating to local and state legislative, tax, and regulatory matters. HillCo's client list includes some of the most respected corporations, businesses, municipalities, associations, franchises and individuals in America." HillCo lists its services as lobbying, policy analysis, regulatory consulting, communications, public and media relations, procurement, advisory boards, and grassroots organization.

★ CSQ   Thinking about the role of elites in Texas politics

Write a carefully constructed essay to describe the techniques that lobby firms such as HillCo use to convince legislators and other policy makers to support their clients' positions. To make your essay thorough, be sure to include each of the services listed on the HillCo website and explain how lobbyists' personal relationships, developed through years of contacts with policy makers, affect the decision-making process.

Sources: HillCo and the Texas Ethics Commission.

Agencies publish proposed rules for public comment in the *Texas Register*, the official publication of the state that gives the public notice of proposed actions and adopted policies of executive branch agencies. All citizens have the right to comment in the rule-making process, but only those aware of and interested in a proposed rule participate. Ordinary citizens do not subscribe to the *Texas Register*, but corporations, labor unions, law firms, and interest groups do. Organized interest groups have a real stake in shaping these regulations that control how they do business and directly affect their profits. Hence, they know when to send their lobbyists and paid experts to give testimony at public hearings, and they are able to mobilize their members to call or write agencies about proposed rules.

IMAGE 6.2 Complaining of foul odors coming from the Southwaste Disposal facility near his property in Houston, Norman Adams requested a hearing before the Texas Commission on Environmental Quality to contest the company's application to expand its operations. Meanwhile, Southwaste, other industry groups, and the Texas Association of Business persuaded the legislature to pass legislation to limit property owners' right to demand public hearings before the agency.

Gary Coronado/Houston Chronicle

★ **CTQ** **How can individual citizens balance the influence of organized interest groups on state agency decisions?**

Agency administrators actively seek input about the impact of their rules and policies from the groups they regulate. The Texas Department of Insurance needs to know how its proposed rules will affect the insurance industry; the Texas Railroad Commission will want to know how new hydraulic fracturing rules will affect the drilling industry's use of "fracking" to extract oil and gas, and the Texas Real Estate Commission consults with the Texas Association of Realtors before adopting new licensing requirements.

Targeting the Appointment Process Lobbyists are actively involved in the appointment process, and they are often able to convince the governor to select agency heads who are friendly to their interests. Most state agencies are headed by boards and commissions recruited from the industry, profession, or group they regulate—they share the same interests. In fact, Texas law requires that many regulatory boards must include members of the business or profession that they regulate. For example, 12 of the 19 members of the Texas Medical Board must be physicians.

Upon retirement from government service, many agency officers go to work for the very industries that they once regulated. Critics doubt that administrative officers can regulate their own business or profession and, at the same time, serve the public interest, especially when they intend to return to the same profession. At least one observer has concluded that "the state's business and political elites are hopelessly intertwined."[1]

clientele groups
The groups most affected by a government agency's regulations and programs; frequently these interest groups form close alliances with the agency based on mutual support and accommodation.

co-optation
Development of such a close alliance between state regulatory agencies and their clientele group that the regulated have, in effect, become the regulators; the interest group has captured such complete control of their regulatory agency that they are essentially self-regulated.

Co-opting State Agencies Such a close working relationship develops between interest groups and state agencies that agencies often view the interest groups that they regulate as their clients and such interest groups are often called **clientele groups**. These are the groups most affected by a government agency's regulations and programs, and they frequently form close alliances with the agency based on mutual support and accommodation.

Lobbyists for clientele groups often defend "their" state agency as well as its funding and legal powers. This blurring of the line between the state agencies and a special interest group is called **co-optation** (also known as agency capture) when such a close alliance develops between state regulatory agencies and their clientele group that the regulated have, in effect, become the regulators. The interest group has captured such complete control of their regulatory agency that they are essentially self-regulated.

A classic example of co-optation, or agency capture, is seen in a recent effort by the Texas Racing Commission (TRC) to unilaterally authorize horse racing and dog racing tracks to operate slot machines. The Texas racing industry was in the midst of a significant financial crisis, with the last of the state's dog racing tracks closing at the end of 2015 and its three major horse racing tracks—Lone Star Park in Grand Prairie (DFW), Retama Park in San Antonio, and Sam Houston Park in Houston—in dire straits. The racing industry saw "historical racing" machines, which are the functional equivalent of slot machines, as a partial way out of their financial dilemma.

At the behest of "their" industry, the co-opted or captured TRC in August 2014 authorized the operation of "historical racing" machines at racetracks, a move that was immediately challenged on very solid grounds as unconstitutional (see Chapter 2) by citizens and state legislators alike. The result was a more than two-year legal and budgetary standoff between the TRC and the Texas Legislature, a standoff that was eventually resolved in February 2016 when the TRC in a narrow 5–4 vote backed down and repealed the rule allowing historical racing, without any machines ever being installed at tracks. This repeal however took place only after Governor Abbott had the opportunity to replace several TRC members as their terms expired.

The Texas Commission on Environmental Quality (TCEQ) provides another example of a clientele group's influence on a state agency. When the TCEQ ruled that Waste Control Specialists (owned by Texas billionaire Harold Simmons, a now-deceased longtime political insider, could not import radioactive waste from other states, the company did it anyway. Waste Control Specialists planned to bury the waste at its waste dump in Andrews County, a rural county north of Odessa along the Texas–New Mexico border. This site sits in close proximity to two water tables, including sections of the Ogallala Aquifer—an important source of water for the High Plains region. The TCEQ warned: "groundwater is likely to intrude into the proposed disposal units and contact the waste from either or both of two water tables near the proposed facility."[2]

After permission to bring in the waste was initially rejected, the company put its lobbyists to work. The team included the former executive director of TCEQ, Jeff Saitas. The company lobbied TCEQ's executive director, Glenn Shankle, who overruled the technical team and gave Waste Control Specialists permission for the site. A few months later, Shankle left TCEQ to become a lobbyist for Waste Control Specialists.

Targeting the Courts

Lobbying is one extremely important interest group tool, but interest groups employ a wide variety of other tactics to influence government policy making as well. For example, interest groups do not directly lobby judges, but they actively campaign for judicial candidates who share their viewpoints, they prevail upon the governor to fill court vacancies with friendly judicial appointees, and they file suit in court to win legal rulings that benefit their interests.

Influencing the Judicial Selection Process
Texas is one of a handful of states that elect their trial and appeals court judges in partisan elections, as you will see in Chapter 9. Candidates must first win the party's nomination in the primary and then prevail in the general election. Voters who elect judges do not usually have a clear understanding of the law or how it should be applied; instead, they depend on party labels and political campaigns to give them voting cues.

Business groups and law firms, many of them having legal business before the courts, contribute large amounts to judicial campaigns. In 2016, the candidates in races for three positions on the Texas Supreme Court raised a combined $4.2 million.

Critics argue that large contributions from pro-business interest groups and corporate law firms have influenced judicial decisions, shifting legal precedent in favor of corporations and putting procedural hurdles in the way of consumers and workers who might sue them. Even the U.S. Supreme Court recognizes that very large contributions to judicial candidates creates a risk that judges will be biased in deciding cases in which megadonors are involved.

Between elections, some judges resign or retire, and the governor is charged with filling the resulting vacancy until the next election. Because such temporary judicial appointees usually seek and win election to full terms, interest groups set up massive lobbying efforts to persuade the governor to appoint judges favorable to their interests. Many Texas judges were first recruited in this way by interest groups that have much to gain or lose from court rulings.

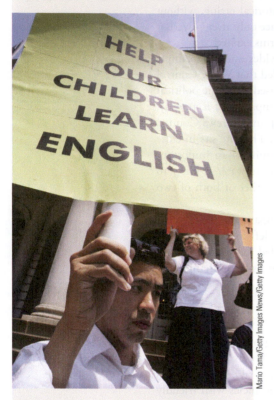

IMAGE 6.3 The League of United Latin American Citizens (LULAC) sued the State of Texas in federal court over inadequate instruction for English language learners.

★ **CTQ** Why would ethnic and political minorities press their interests in the courts rather than the legislative or executive branches?

Filing Suit in Court Major corporations, insurance companies, and powerful professional groups employ attorneys on their staffs or have law firms on retainer to defend their interests when workers and consumers sue them. Influential interests also bring lawsuits to challenge government policies that harm their interests. They may win court rulings that declare hostile legislation is unconstitutional or that inconvenient executive decisions are illegal. Courts might interpret a law or administrative rule in such a way that it works to a group's advantage.

In the past, smaller and less powerful organizations turned to the courts as a last resort after they had lost policy battles in the legislative or executive branches. In recent years, however, changes in the state's political climate, passage of lawsuit reforms, and decisions by the state supreme court have made Texas courts less responsive to groups representing environmentalists, consumers, and ethnic/racial minorities. Some of these groups now simply view filing lawsuits in state courts as a tactic to attract public attention and media coverage of their cause.

Some of these groups have turned instead to the federal courts to enforce environmental and consumer protection policies. Chapters 1 and 4 show that various groups have won federal court decisions that protect voting rights and civil rights. The Mexican American Legal Defense and Education Fund (MALDEF) and allied interest groups won a federal court ruling in 2011 requiring adjustments to discriminatory legislative and congressional districts.

Shaping the Political Environment

Besides working to influence state policy makers directly, interest groups strive to shape the political environment in which policy decisions are made. Interest groups are most effective when they have the support of the public as well as of industry and community leaders, and they engage in political campaigns and other public relations efforts to create a political climate favorable to their agendas.

Electioneering Interest groups use their resources to support candidates disposed toward their interests. They endorse and recommend that their members vote for the candidate most aligned with their values; the organizations' newsletters and websites carry messages of support for their chosen candidates. Endorsements from organizations with a large and committed following, like the National Rifle Association or Texas Right to Life, have the greatest impact. Teachers' organizations, organized labor, and tea party activists sometimes help their favorite candidates by providing campaign workers who go door to door, operate phone banks, engage with potential voters on social media, and hand out literature and yard signs.

Officeholders are responsive to interest groups' potential voting power, the value of their endorsements, and the number of their members who may volunteer in the next election campaign. As a result, interest groups are most influential when they represent members on what political strategists call "voting issues"—that is, single issues, such as opposition to gun control or abortion, about which members feel so passionately as to be decisive for them in determining how they will cast their ballots. Other groups may represent members who by and large favor gun control or protecting the environment, but most of their members rarely decide how to vote based on these single issues alone.

Contributing to Campaigns Interest groups may also be influential because they provide money—a key resource in campaigns. Executives of banks, insurance companies, the petrochemical industry, and utility companies make large individual contributions and also contribute through political action committees (PACs, discussed in Chapter 4). Professional groups such as physicians, trial lawyers, real estate agents, and teachers also form PACs that aggregate contributions into large sums, which they funnel to their favorite candidates.

Most campaign contributions for the state legislature and the statewide offices come from large donors. These campaign contributors give large amounts because the state legislature, the governor, and other elected officials make decisions that affect these donors' economic well-being and their other interests. Donors contribute to gain **access** to public officials, meaning their lobbyists are able to "get in the door" to sit down and talk to them about their needs. Substantial contributions seem to create an obligation on the part of an elected official to listen when a contributor calls. Ordinary citizens find access much more difficult to obtain. During the 2016 electoral cycle in Texas, a total of $116 million dollars were raised by state-level candidates, much of it from PACs. Table 6.3 lists the top 15 PACs in terms of contributions during the 2016 cycle.

access
The ability to "get in the door" to sit down and talk to public officials. Campaign contributions are often used to gain access.

TABLE 6.3 Texas's Biggest PACs

Table 6.3 lists the 15 PACs receiving the largest contributions other than candidates or parties during the 2016 election cycle.

PAC Name	2016 Contributions	Interest Category
Texas Assn. of Realtors	$4,819,480	Real Estate
Texans for Lawsuit Reform	4,332,905	Tort Reform
BANSF Railpac	1,761,517	Transportation
USAA Employee PAC	1,679,956	Insurance
Union Pacific	1,662,188	Transportation
Texas Organizing Project	1,514,831	Labor
Texas Safety and Justice	1,472,980	Electing Progressive District Attorneys
Texas Assn. of Realtors—Issues	1,381,629	Real Estate
Texas Right to Life PAC	1,353,411	Abortion
Annie's List	1,197,869	Electing Progressive Women
Texas Medical Assn. PAC	1,176,625	Health Care
Exelon Corp. PAC	1,129,986	Electric utilities
Border Health PAC	1,066,752	Hospitals/Nursing Homes
AT&T PAC	861,237	Telecommunications utilities
Texas Trial Lawyers PAC	837,711	Opposition to tort reform

Texas Ethics Commission

▶ Why are Texas Realtors so actively involved in trying to influence members of the Texas Legislature and executive branch officials?

Did You Know? Speaker of the House Joe Straus received over $10 million during his 2016 campaign, but announced the following year that he would not seek reelection.

Money in politics is the hot topic of the day because of how the startling amount of money candidates raise and spend in campaigns for elective office at all levels has skyrocketed. Legislative candidates raised $99 million in the 2016 election cycle. The 350 candidates vying for seats in the Texas House raised $76 million, and 68 candidates for the Texas Senate raised $23 million. The candidates who ran for governor raised $100 million in the previous election cycle. Even when candidates face little or no opposition, they often raise large amounts of money; the most powerful legislators are able to put together huge campaign war chests because megadonors want clout with the legislative leadership.

IMAGE 6.4 Public employees such as these teachers become an economic interest group when they demonstrate in support of their job benefits.

AP Images/Deborah Cannon

★ **CTQ**   What is the goal of organizing public demonstrations? What precautions must interest groups take if they are to use public protests as an effective tactic?

Educating the Public
Interest groups shape the political climate by providing the general public with messages designed to build a positive image and to promote their viewpoints. Well-funded interest groups employ the services of public relations firms to promote policy agendas even as they burnish their reputations for honesty, good citizenship, and concern for the well-being of others.

Interest groups may use their organizations' magazines, annual reports, press releases and social media campaigns as vehicles for building their own reputation and educating the public about the wisdom of policy proposals their organizations support. They may purchase print, broadcast, and digital advertising to shape and mobilize public opinion, and many interest groups now sponsor local "grassroots" organizations and political blogs that share their policy views.

Organizing Public Demonstrations
Some interest groups organize marches and demonstrations to generate publicity for their cause. Press and social media coverage is all but guaranteed because demonstrations create a sort of "theater" that is especially well suited for television news and online videos on media sites, YouTube and other venues. When the legislature is in session, demonstrations are plentiful. Public school teachers, immigrants' rights groups, tea party members, and countless others rally in Austin to express their opinion on a whole host of bills.

Using this kind of tactic is a challenge for interest groups that must enlist enough members to be impressive and at the same time keep control of the demonstration. Violating the law, forging signatures on letters sent to lawmakers, blocking traffic, damaging property, and using obscenities do not win support from fellow citizens or public officials. Although some groups have used these tactics, most have found that civil and sincere protests are more effective.

astroturf lobbying
Special interest groups orchestrating demonstrations to give the impression of widespread and spontaneous public support.

Interest groups have a clear advantage if they are well organized at the grassroots level and if they can mobilize large numbers of supporters to contact officials. Some special interest groups have used their financial advantages to orchestrate public demonstrations and social media campaigns designed to give the impression of widespread and spontaneous "grassroots" support for their positions. Such public demonstrations have been dubbed **astroturf lobbying** after the artificial grass used in many sports stadiums.

The Balance of Political Power

LO 6.3 **Analyze the political balance of power among interest groups in Texas.**

Business and professional groups continue to be the most powerful interests in the state, and they are frequently aligned with the majority Republican Party. Generally speaking, the most successful noneconomic interest groups are socially conservative and tea party groups with agendas usually consistent with business interests except on some cultural issues. Environmental groups, organized labor, civil rights organizations, and groups advocating for low-income Texans often support policies at odds with business and usually ally themselves with the minority Democratic Party. Such groups have comparatively less influence over the public policy process in Texas than business and conservative ideological groups.

Texas's Most Powerful Interest Groups

One way of gauging which groups have the greatest sway in state government is by looking at the amount of money they spend to lobby state officials. Figure 6.2 shows that the energy and natural resources business accounted for 15 percent (or at least $29 million) of all lobbying contracts as compiled from official reports in 2016. The health, finance, and communications industries were also among the biggest spenders on lobbying. Among the top individual businesses spending the most on lobbying were energy and utility companies including AT&T, American Electric Power, NextEra Energy, Centerpoint Energy, Oncor Electric Delivery Company, and Entergy Corporation. Obviously, such companies have an intense interest in state utility regulation.

Many smaller interests join together into **umbrella organizations**, in which industries, wholesalers, producers, retailers, and professionals form associations to promote common policy goals by making campaign contributions and hiring lobbyists to represent their interests. For example, the Texas Medical Association, the Texas Trial Lawyers Association, the Texas Association of Electric Companies, the Texas Association of Realtors, and the Texas Association of Builders altogether reported spending more than $4.5 million lobbying on behalf of their members in 2016. The Texas Municipal League spent more than $500,000 representing Texas cities in the initial skirmish that would become an intense battle to defend municipal powers and policies in the following legislative session, as we will later see in Chapter 11.

The Texas Association of Business, Texans for Lawsuit Reform, Texas Medical Association, Texas Realtors' Association, and the Texas Oil and Gas Association have been traditionally regarded as being among the most powerful organizations because they have the money to maintain permanent headquarters in Austin and employ clerical and research staffs as well as lobbyists to make their prominence known. Such special interests have full-time staff, multiple lobbyists, and the ability to disburse sizable campaign contributions. They often achieve more than resource-poor groups, but other factors also tend to affect which interest groups win the influence game.

Most registered lobbyists represent business, but business is a huge category, encompassing both the powerful and the weak. Not everyone in business shares the same viewpoint. Independent and small businesses frequently seek policy outcomes opposed by larger enterprises. Trucking interests are often at odds with railroad freight businesses; oil and gas companies have a different perspective from clean energy companies. Business should not be thought of as monolithic. Powerful business groups may win more than they lose, but they do not own the government and are not guaranteed success.

umbrella organizations
Associations formed by smaller interests joining together to promote common policy goals by making campaign contributions and hiring lobbyists to represent their interests.

FIGURE 6.2 Lobby Spending in Texas

This figure shows which interests spent the most on lobbying in Texas. Various industries spent about $195 million for lobbying in 2017 according to tallies by the National Institute on Money in State Politics. Interest groups had spent only $155 million in the previous year when the legislature was not in session.

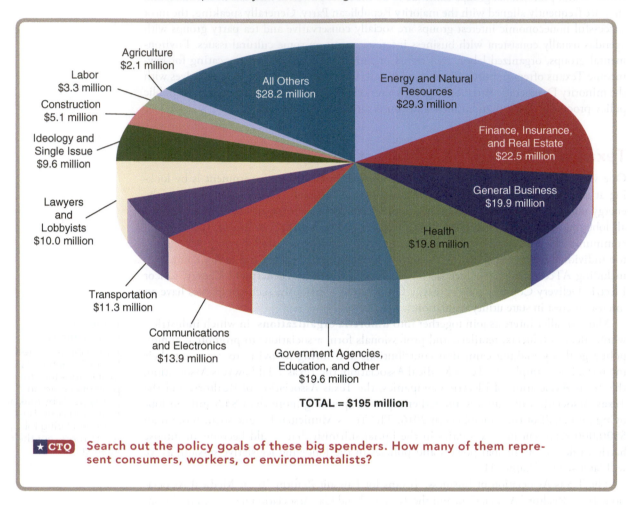

Agriculture
$2.1 million

Labor
$3.3 million

Construction
$5.1 million

Ideology and
Single Issue
$9.6 million

Lawyers
and
Lobbyists
$10.0 million

Transportation
$11.3 million

Communications
and Electronics
$13.9 million

All Others
$28.2 million

Energy and Natural
Resources
$29.3 million

Finance, Insurance,
and Real Estate
$22.5 million

General Business
$19.9 million

Health
$19.8 million

Government Agencies,
Education, and Other
$19.6 million

TOTAL = $195 million

★ CTQ **Search out the policy goals of these big spenders. How many of them represent consumers, workers, or environmentalists?**

National Institute on Money in State Politics and the Texas Ethics Commission.

A Tale of Two Lobbying Efforts: Tesla vs. TADA

Just because interest groups belong to the same general industry does not mean that they are working toward the same common goal. In fact, their goals may be diametrically opposed and the source of considerable conflict (and spending) during the legislative session. A case in point is the battle between Tesla Motors and the Texas Automobile Dealers Association (TADA) during the 2015 legislative session.

Tesla does not employ a traditional dealer-oriented model in which it sends its electric cars to dealers who in turn sell the cars to the public. Instead, it avoids the middlemen dealers and sells its cars directly to consumers. That practice, however, is against the law in Texas, meaning the only way Texans can buy one of Tesla's Model S (pictured in Image 6.5), Model X, or Model 3 cars is to order it online.

After testing the waters during the 2013 legislative session, Tesla CEO Elon Musk went all out during the 2015 legislative session in a bid to obtain the passage of legislation (House Bill 1653 and Senate Bill 639) that would have allowed Tesla to operate 12 stores in Texas. In pursuit of this goal, Tesla spent more than $1 million dollars on almost two dozen lobbyists, including top-tier hired guns such as Neal "Buddy" Jones and Mike Toomey (see Table 6.2).

Opposing Tesla's efforts, however, was one of the most powerful interest groups in Texas, the Texas Automobile Dealers Association (TADA). The TADA has its own in-house lobbyists who were in turn aided by several hired guns this past session. However, the most important lobbyists working on behalf of the TADA goal of killing the Tesla-sponsored legislation were its 1,257 dealerships spread across 284 Texas communities, as is visually displayed in Image 6.6. This image, taken from the TADA website (it also served as the TADA Twitter background), underscores a point the TADA tirelessly makes to every state legislator: that their members are present in every Texas Senate district and almost every Texas House district. The TADA never ceases to remind legislators that TADA dealers are active and valued members of their respective communities, providing vital jobs, sponsoring charity events, supporting Little League teams, and providing a host of other benefits that would all be threatened if automobile manufacturers

IMAGE 6.5 Tesla Motors waged an aggressive but ultimately unsuccessful battle during the 2015 legislative session to allow it to sell its cars, like the Tesla S pictured here, directly to Texans at a dozen stores in the state.

Darren Brode/Shutterstock.com

★ CTQ Tesla CEO Elon Musk calls the current Texas rules governing auto sales, which require auto manufacturers to sell their cars through dealers instead of directly to consumers, as extremely un-Texan. Do you agree or disagree with him?

were allowed to sell directly to the public as Tesla wishes to do. Although most dealers are not all that worried about losing sales to Tesla, they are very worried that the passage of the legislation Tesla is seeking would open the door to adoption of a similar model by other auto manufacturers such as Ford, General Motors, or Toyota—a move which would be devastating for their business.

IMAGE 6.6 Texas auto dealerships are spread across Texas in cities both large and small, with the dealers themselves normally very active and influential members of their communities.

★ CTQ Why are automobile dealers considered to be one of the most formidable interest groups in Texas?

In the end, the TADA's dual effort lobbying strategy was successful. Its in-house and hired gun lobbyists matched efforts with Tesla's Austin hired guns (and corporate in-house lobbyists) while the state's 1,237 dealers directly pressured the specific representative and senator in whose district their dealership was located as well as, in many cases, senators and representatives from nearby districts. The result was that HB 1653 never even made it to a committee vote in the House and SB 639 never made it to a committee vote in the Senate. Elon Musk may be a billionaire ranked by Forbes as the 30th richest person in the United States and the 21st most powerful person in the world, but he was no match for the Texas Automobile Dealers Association.

Interest Group Alliances and the Dynamics of Power

On issues that are narrow in scope, a single group may find itself unopposed. In the legislature, the interest group must persuade only a few key people, such as legislative committee chairs and presiding officers, to win a floor vote. Administrative agency decisions are even more likely to be controlled by a few interest groups because their decisions usually have a concentrated impact on a single occupation or business sector. For example, real estate brokers are very directly affected by the Real Estate Board's licensing requirements and are extremely active in trying to influence board decisions; the public is affected by the standards the board sets, but few are interested enough to become involved in the process.

iron triangles
Long-standing alliances among interest groups, legislators, and bureaucrats held together by mutual self-interest that act as subsystems in the legislative and administrative decision-making process.

Iron Triangles
On such narrow issues, interest groups, legislators, and bureaucrats can develop such a long-standing relationship held together by mutual self-interest that they act as a subsystem in the legislative and administrative decision-making process. Called **iron triangles**, these alliances operate largely outside public view because they dominate a narrow range of routine decisions that are of marginal interest to the general public but are of critical importance to the interest groups and bureaucrats involved. The clientele group uses its resources, size, lobbying skills, and access to state officials to determine policy outcomes.

For example, oil and gas interests have formed a close association with the Texas Railroad Commission, whose members their campaign contributions help elect. The agriculture industry forms a similar symbiotic relationship with the commissioner of the Texas Department of Agriculture as well as the members of the house and senate agriculture committees. Highway contractors form an alliance with the Texas Department of Transportation and interested legislators; privately owned utility companies work closely with the Public Utilities Commission. We will illustrate these alliances more extensively in Chapter 8 as we discuss the state's bureaucracy.

issue networks
Dynamic alliances among a wide range of individuals and groups activated by broad public policy questions.

Issue Networks
Iron triangles may dominate policies of a narrow scope, but broader public policy questions like taxes, education, health care, environmental protection, and abortion have the potential to activate wider-ranging coalitions. Alliances among interest groups, career bureaucrats, academics, think tanks, political bloggers, social media commentators, traditional media editors, neighborhood leaders, radio talk show hosts, and other community activists may form **issue networks**. These broad alliances are dynamic—different activists and interest groups organize around different public issues.

political movement
A mass alliance of like-minded groups and individuals seeking broad changes in the direction of government policies.

Political Movements
Issue networks have the potential to blossom into a larger **political movement**, a mass alliance of like-minded groups and individuals seeking broad changes in the direction of government policies. When the web of opinion leaders in issue networks taps into a large set of issues important to masses of people, they may develop a large following with a fairly stable membership. One example is the tea party, which is not a political party at all, but a very successful political movement.

Beginning among a relatively small network of activists opposing the federal bailouts of the financial industry, the tea party movement gained strength with the passage of the American

Recovery and Reinvestment Act of 2009 (popularly referred to as "The Stimulus") and finally evolved into a full-fledged antigovernment movement by the time the Affordable Care Act of 2010 (popularly referred to as Obamacare) was passed. A small alliance of interested groups had transformed into a mass national political movement. In Texas, the movement's support helped lead to a strong Republican showing in the last five statewide elections, resulting in overwhelming Republican majorities in the Texas Legislature and the adoption of many policies popular with tea party groups. See the Politics in Practice feature in Chapter 5 for a brief history of the founding and development of Texas's most influential local tea party group (the NE Tarrant Tea Party), written by its founding president, Julie McCarty.

Sizing Up Interest Groups and Their Influence

LO 6.4 **Evaluate the role of interest groups in Texas politics and policy formulation.**

Interest groups are formed by people who are exercising their fundamental constitutional rights in a free society. Both the national and Texas constitutions protect freedom of expression and freedom of association, and they specifically guarantee citizens the right to assemble to petition their government "for redress of grievances." The Texas Constitution (Article 1, Section 27) says that "citizens shall have the right ... to ... apply to those invested with the powers of government for redress of grievances or other purposes, by petition, address or remonstrance."

The First Amendment to the U.S. Constitution says, "Congress shall make no law ... abridging the freedom of speech, or of the press; or the right of the people peaceably to assemble, and to petition government for redress of grievances." These constitutional provisions guarantee citizens the right to join together in political parties and interest groups. The rights to form political organizations, along with the right to vote, are essential to the very existence of a democracy.

The Positive Role of Interest Groups

Supporters believe that interest groups provide an essential linkage between members and public officials that makes it possible for the political system to function in a free society. They also believe that our pluralistic society, our governing structures, and our open society protect us from domination by a single narrow elite.

Representation and Mobilization
Interest groups provide members a vehicle to present their values and views in ways that elections cannot. Texas elections are held every two years, but many interest groups operate continuously and offer their members the opportunity to influence day-to-day decision making. At best, elections offer voters the chance to set the general direction of government as they choose one candidate or party over the other, while interest groups develop specialized tactics to give members the chance to affect the details of policy making. Elections are held in geographic districts and statewide, but interest groups represent people according to their specialized occupational, cultural, and professional groupings, allowing them to articulate their members' unique perspectives on public policies.

Democracy calls for politically attentive and active citizens, but many voters are minimally informed, and they cast their ballots based on broad impressions created during political campaigns. Interest groups draw the most interested and informed citizens into the political process, educate their members about issues, and mobilize them to participate in ways that advance their own interests. Interest groups report on the activities of government officials and sometimes keep vote tallies to report to their members on how legislators voted on key issues.

Interest groups inform and educate public officials; they provide policy makers with valuable information both as they lobby individual government officials and as they testify before legislative committees. Because state law makes it a crime to knowingly share false information with state lawmakers, most special interest groups are careful to provide truthful, albeit often one-sided, information. Decision makers need to know how a proposed policy will affect various segments of society and how the affected groups feel about it. Interest groups enthusiastically provide this information to public officials free of cost to taxpayers.

pluralist theory
The view that, in a free society, public policy should be made by a multitude of competing interest groups, ensuring that policies will not benefit a single elite at the expense of the many.

The Benefits of Pluralism
Those who subscribe to the **pluralist theory** take the view that, in a free society, public policy should be made by a multitude of competing interest groups, assuring that policies will not benefit a single elite at the expense of the many. Agricultural, educational, energy, environmental, ethnic/racial, medical, and religious interest groups are just some of the organized interests in Texas, and all compete with one another for the attention and favor of decision makers. Matters involving large amounts of money or important changes in existing policy invite crowds. In such situations, for anything to happen, some compromise among competing interests must occur, resulting in a mix of values incorporated into the policy decision.

Interest groups' defenders argue that the structure of government is designed to make it hard for any group to dominate the state. The structure of government is characterized by:

- The separation of powers
- Checks and balances
- Elected officials responsible to different constituencies at the ballot box at different times
- Appointed officials with fixed terms
- Career bureaucrats

These structures make the political system difficult for any one interest to capture. The house and senate and the governor must agree to create law. The implementation of law is placed in the hands of elected and appointed executive officers and the unelected bureaucrats below them.

The media, especially in the digital age, give citizens access to an unprecedented amount of information and offer a political tool for new and underrepresented voices that otherwise lack financial and other resources to have a significant impact on policy making. Furthermore, interest groups are limited because they operate in an environment where the general public is critical, if not cynical, of the political process.

Media exposure, public opinion, and the competing power of rival interest groups can also have their effect on state policies, especially on policies of sweeping public significance. More far-reaching public policy decisions involve more participants, and the general public is more likely to take an interest. Public officials become quite sensitive to public opinion when voters, especially primary voters, take an active interest in policy decisions—they must get reelected, after all. No amount of interest group influence or campaign contributions can cause public officials to sacrifice their political futures to one group's special needs. The scope of a public policy determines who will control the decision-making process and shape the dynamics of power.

Criticisms and Reforms

Critics are not so optimistic about the role of interest groups in the Texas political system. They believe that interest groups are very selective in mobilizing and informing citizens and that the resources of political influence are concentrated in the hands of a very few. They believe that narrow interests are able to commandeer the machinery of government for their own self-interest, and in the process they employ tactics that taint the integrity of the political system itself.

Elitism and the Culture of Nonparticipation
Many Texans come from a traditionalistic political culture that discourages political participation and defers to the power of governing elites. Many Texans are not members of any interest groups at all, and

many of those who have joined groups are passive, inattentive members, who leave the leadership role to a few activists.

Wealth, political contacts, access to information, and well-managed lobby operations are controlled by a few powerful interest groups that often use these resources to dominate the political process. For example, Texas has no patients' rights association that has political power comparable to that of the Texas Medical Association; organized labor's power in Texas is modest compared to that of employers' organizations like the Texas Association of Business. Consumer organizations do not rival the influence of the numerous organizations of manufacturers and retailers in the state.

Some critics believe an **elitist theory** of interest groups best describes Texas politics; they take the view that that the state is ruled by a small number of participants who exercise power to further their own self-interest. They contend that insurance companies, oil and gas companies, and certain utilities usually have their way with the state because they are able to pour enormous resources into campaign contributions or lobbying. They believe the average citizen cannot compete; highly organized and active groups can threaten the well-being of the unorganized majority.

elitist theory
The view that the state is ruled by a small number of participants who exercise power to further their own self-interest.

Exploitation of Weak State Institutions

Skeptical of government, Texans have tried to limit and divide the power of state institutions. As a result, interest groups have been able to capitalize on numerous structural weaknesses, and they have been able to take advantage of numerous points of access to assert their influence.

For example, the state legislature meets in regular session only once every other year. Legislators cannot keep up with what is happening in state government while they are not in session. They come to Austin in January of odd-numbered years and depend on full-time professional lobbyists to fill them in. Texas legislators have limited staffs or other sources of independent information, and they must often go to lobbyists for the facts. Interest groups are often the behind-the-scenes source of many bills legislators introduce.

Executive agencies often lack independent data sources and, in effect, outsource a great deal of information gathering to the interests they regulate. The Texas Department of Insurance depends on the insurance industry to provide claims information necessary to write regulations and set rates. The Public Utilities Commission, the Texas Railroad Commission, the Texas Commission on Environmental Quality, and many other agencies rely heavily on data reported by the industries they regulate.

Reformers advocate strengthening legislative and executive institutions by providing them adequate resources and professional full-time staffs. Ideally, professional staffs should be competent, well-paid state employees hired based on merit and having sufficient job security to protect them against political interference. Reformers believe that only such professional staffs can provide decision makers with enough balanced and objective information to enable them to make policy in the public interest.

Besides limited staffing, low pay is also an institutional weakness that can be exploited. Paid below the poverty level, legislators must depend on outside sources of income to earn a living, making them vulnerable to the temptations of special interest groups. Many lawmakers are attorneys who, as sitting legislators, have been known to represent special interests before state agencies and courts. Many work for clients who have interests in pending legislation, and no law requires legislators to recuse themselves even when they stand to benefit personally from legislation under consideration.

State representative Gary Elkins—himself the owner of a chain of payday loan stores—has taken to the floor to make a personal plea against saddling his payday loan industry with consumer protection legislation. State representative Carol Alvarado and state senator Royce West have been paid for legal work on behalf of independent school districts that had interests before the legislature. Former state senator John Carona, the CEO of one of the largest homeowners association management company in the country (Accenture), authored a major bill affecting homeowners associations (HOAs), benefiting HOAs and HOA management companies to the detriment of individual HOA residents. And former state representative John Otto served as vice-chair of the house committee that was responsible for tax-related legislation while simultaneously being employed by one of the state's largest accounting firms (Ryan & Co.). Reformers argue for stricter ethics laws to prohibit apparent conflicts of interest such as these.

The Revolving Door The public interest may be compromised by the interchange of employees between government agencies and the private businesses with which they have dealings—a peculiar practice referred to as the **revolving door**. Although 39 other states have some ban on legislators becoming lobbyists immediately after leaving office, Texas has no such restrictions. The federal government and a number of states also require "cooling off" periods before bureaucrats leaving the executive branch can become lobbyists, but Texas does not.

revolving door
The interchange of employees between government agencies and the private businesses with which they have dealings.

In Texas, as ambitious legislators and executive officials retire and move on to other occupations, many become lobbyists for the very interest groups they once regulated. To be certain, few people would be better suited to serve as lobbyists than ex-lawmakers. Former legislators are intricately familiar with the legislative process, many are policy experts, and they often have friendships with lawmakers who are still in office. Interest groups also seek to hire retiring state agency officials as lobbyists because of their familiarity with the policy-making process, their policy expertise, and their connections inside state government.

IMAGE 6.7 Jim Pitts, the former chair of the powerful House Appropriations Committee, is now a lobbyist.

AP Images/Eric Gay

★ **SRQ** Explain the potential conflict of interest when retired legislators lobby their former colleagues.

Former state representative Jim Pitts of Waxahachie served in the house from 1993 to 2015, rising to become the ultra-influential chair of the House Appropriations Committee during his final six years in office. In 2014 he chose not to seek reelection, and in January 2015 he left his $7,200-a-year post as a state legislator for the much more lucrative position of lobbyist. In 2015 alone, Pitt's lobbying contracts combined amounted to approximately $250,000, with major clients including the Texas Hospital Association and Beacon Health Solutions. He also represented the Texas Entertainment Association, the trade association for the state's strip clubs which is lobbying for repeal of a $5 admission fee imposed by the legislature in 2007, popularly referred to as the "pole tax."

The revolving door may create opportunities for retiring public officials, but it also creates the potential for **conflict of interest**, a situation in which public officers stand to benefit personally from their official decisions. Lawmakers and bureaucrats, planning their next career move, might be tempted to make decisions that will benefit prospective employers. For example, former state representative Jamie Capelo co-authored a bill that capped medical liability lawsuits; shortly after leaving office, he became a lobbyist for the interest groups that benefited financially from his bill. It is fairly common for interest groups to hire public officials as lobbyists after they have made policy decisions in their favor.

conflict of interest
A situation in which public officers stand to benefit personally from their official decisions.

Critics wonder how many unscrupulous officials are using public service as a training school or stepping-stone to a more lucrative career as a lobbyist. "People rightfully wonder when did they stop being a lawmaker and when did they start to become a special interest lobbyist."[3]

Suspect Interest Group Practices

Do campaign contributions buy sponsorship of bills and special favors? The public and the press think they do. Public officials and lobbyists say they do not. Anecdotal evidence that contributions buy public policy is mixed, but enough cases have been identified to leave the casual observer with the perception that conflicts of interest do arise.

A practice that seems to be more than merely coincidental is the biennial ritual in Austin after each election when special interest groups hold fundraising events to honor selected legislators. State law forbids giving and accepting campaign contributions 30 days before the start of a legislative session and throughout the session, causing a rush of fundraising activity in the month after election day. Because these lobbyist-sponsored fund raising parties occur after the election, not before, they are not simply an effort to help elect candidates who support their group's cause—they have already been elected. The reason, as one lobbyist said, is to "pay the price of admission" or to obtain good access to legislators. These so-called **late-train contributions** are commonly given to the winning candidates in the executive branch as well. Losers are rarely the beneficiaries of such largess.

The Regulation of Lobbying

Fearing the influence of powerful organizations behind the scenes, reformers supported the creation of the Texas Ethics Commission with the power to enforce lobby and campaign finance reporting laws. Reformers believed that reporting requirements respect basic rights to freedom of expression while requiring that lobbyists' efforts be made public. The rationale for these laws is that the public should at least know who backs which policies and who stands to gain from them.

Lobbyist Reports

Lobbyists for private interest groups, with few exceptions, must file reports with the Texas Ethics Commission if they are paid $1,000 salary per calendar year or if they spend more than $500 per quarter to communicate directly with any members of the legislative or executive branch to influence legislation or administrative action. Lobbyists must report:

- Their actual clients
- The general areas of their policy concerns
- The range within which their compensation falls
- Their expenditures for advertisements, mass mailings, and other communications designed to support or oppose legislation or administrative actions
- Their expenditures on members of the state legislature or state employees in excess of $114 (60% of the legislative per diem) a day on food, drink, transportation, or lodging and $50 on gifts, which must be reported by name, date, place, and purpose

Campaign contributions are reported as we described in Chapter 4, but they are not classified as lobbying expenses.

Evaluating Reporting Requirements

Critics of the lobby reporting law maintain that some provisions

Did You Know? Five house members went straight from the legislature to become lobbyists in 2017: Jimmie Don Aycock Jim Keffer, Marisa Márquez, John Otto, and Wayne Smith.

late-train contributions
Campaign funds given to the winning candidate after the election up to 30 days before the legislature comes into session. Such contributions are designed to curry favor with winning candidates.

Did You Know? A trick Texas lobbyists use to avoid reporting who they took to dinner, a concert, or a sporting event is to split the bill with other lobbyists to keep it below the reporting threshold.

How Does Texas Compare?

Government Accountability and Transparency Among the States

The Pulitzer Prize–winning Center for Public Integrity carries out its *State Integrity Investigation*, in which it assesses the strengths and weaknesses of institutional safeguards against corruption across the 50 states. The result is a scorecard in which every state is given a letter grade (A to F) and ranked (from a high of 1 to a low of 50). The Center for Public Integrity is a tough grader, and the highest-scoring state, Alaska, only received an overall grade of C. The table provides Texas's overall grade (a D–), as well as its grade and rank in each of the

13 separate categories evaluated. Similar information is provided for the country's three other mega-states: California, New York, and Florida.

According to a 2015 report, Texas ranked near the bottom in the nation in several categories, including Public Access to Information (48th), Electoral Oversight (45th), and Lobbying Disclosure (45th). In contrast, Texas institutions do a comparatively good job of providing for transparency and accountability and protecting against corruption in the areas of State Budget Processes (4th), Internal Auditing (4th), Procurement (9th), and State Pension Fund Management (9th).

Public Integrity Report Categories, Grades (and National Rankings)

Category	Texas	California	New York	Florida
Overall Grade	D– (39)	C– (2)	D– (31)	D– (30)
Public Access to Information	F (48)	F (28)	F (11)	F (17)
Political Financing	F (41)	C– (10)	D– (24)	F (28)
Electoral Oversight	F (45)	C– (17)	F (49)	F (46)
Executive Accountability	F (44)	C– (5)	D+ (15)	D+ (16)
Legislative Accountability	F (36)	C– (11)	D– (26)	C+ (2)
Judicial Accountability	F (41)	F (20)	F (48)	F (38)
State Budget Processes	A (4)	A (6)	F (50)	F (48)
State Civil Service Management	F (41)	D+ (10)	C– (1)	F (50)
Procurement	C+ (9)	C– (21)	F (48)	D+ (25)
Internal Auditing	B+ (4)	B– (25)	B+ (1)	B (10)
Lobbying Disclosure	F (45)	B+ (2)	C+ (5)	F (38)
Ethics Enforcement Agencies	D– (19)	C– (4)	F (38)	D– (17)
State Pension Fund Management	C+ (9)	A (2)	C+ (10)	D (22)

The Center for Public Integrity.

FOR DEBATE

 SRQ To enhance accountability and transparency, in which areas would Texas benefit from adopting the institutional models employed in California, New York, and/or Florida, and in which areas would some or all of those states benefit from becoming more like Texas?

leave the public ill-informed because lobbyists' compensation and expenditures are reported in broad categories rather than in specific amounts. In 2015, according to official lobby reports, AT&T paid 101 lobbyists between $4 and $8 million, but the public is left to guess the exact amount.

Reporting which policy a lobbyist seeks to influence similarly requires only checking the appropriate box on a form. For example, AT&T lobbyists may report contacting public officials about "communications." Reformers charge that these requirements provide very little information that the public can use. To be meaningful, lobby reports would need to list the specific bill numbers on which lobbyists worked or the agency rule-making hearings at which they testified.

Although critics fault the Texas Ethics Commission for not vigorously enforcing reporting requirements except in high-profile cases, it serves as a comprehensive repository of campaign financial statements, lists of registered lobbyists, campaign contributions, and campaign expenditures. One critic admitted the Texas Ethics Commission is "a pretty darn good library", noting however that it was at the same time "a pretty poor cop."[4]

The members of the Texas Legislature are provided a list of registered lobbyists and their clients by February 1 of each legislative session, and the public may obtain copies of registration and activity reports from the Texas Ethics Commission website. By tabulating and publicizing these reports, organizations like Texans for Public Justice, the National Institute on Money in State Politics, and the Center for Public Integrity promote transparency in government and help keep the public informed about interest group influence in Texas.

Recent Ethics and Lobbying Reform Efforts

In his 2015 inaugural State of the State address, Governor Greg Abbott declared ethics reform to be one of five high-priority emergency items (see Chapter 8) along with border security, pre-K education, higher education research, and transportation. Abbott achieved the passage of legislation addressing four of these five emergency items, but was largely unsuccessful in obtaining the passage of legislation that would have tightened up the state's notoriously loose rules governing the behavior of lobbyists and public officials. Bills that would have prevented former legislators from lobbying (as Jim Pitts did) for two years after leaving office and would have blocked legislators from profiting from government-related bond work went nowhere.

Amidst the failure of these powerful reforms, the house and senate did manage to pass two fairly consequential bills that would have increased transparency and reduced conflicts of interest, particularly related to state boards and commissions and elected state officials. However, it was later revealed that a loophole had been added that would have allowed a prominent legislator to conceal her spouse's income, and Governor Abbott felt obligated to veto both bills.

In the 2017 legislative session, the Texas House turned the focus of ethics reform to the governor's office itself by passing HB 3305, which would have limited the governor's traditional practice of appointing his campaign contributors to important government positions. Critics argue this practice creates the appearance of conflict of interest in the form of "pay to play" politics. However, the governor was unreceptive to this reform measure and it died in the Texas Senate.

Applying What You Have Learned about Interest Groups

LO 6.5 **Apply what you have learned about interest groups.**

You have learned that among the many self-interested groups influencing Texas public policy, business and economic groups such as the energy industry have considerable influence in Texas. You also learned that less powerful advocacy groups deploy the same sorts of tools attempting to counterbalance the dominance of these industries. We persuaded Luke Metzger, a lobbyist for a leading Texas environmental group, to explain to you the tactics he deploys and the practical obstacles he faces in fighting to protect the Texas environment.

Luke Metzger is the founding director of Environment Texas, a statewide advocacy organization bringing people together for a cleaner, greener, healthier future. He has played a key role in dozens of successful environmental campaigns throughout the state. He regularly testifies before the Texas Legislature and appears frequently in the state and national media. *Capitol Inside* has named him as one of the top 10 "Lobbyists for Causes."

After reading Metzger's essay, we will ask you to evaluate the importance of advocacy groups in challenging some of the most powerful interest groups in the Texas political system and to explore how their tactics affect Texas public policy in practice.

POLITICS IN PRACTICE
The Practice of Environmental Lobbying

by Luke Metzger
Executive Director of Environment Texas

There's something special about Texas—something worth protecting and preserving for future generations. Whether it's swimming at Barton Springs on a hot day, paddling down the Trinity River or hiking through Big Bend National Park, Texas' natural wonders enrich our lives in countless ways.

Yet the places we love and the environmental values so many of us share are too often threatened by powerful industries, shortsighted politicians and more. According to our research, Texas ranks second in the nation for toxic discharges to our water and first in exceeding lead standards for safe drinking water. And Texas has the highest rates of "High Priority Violators" of clean air laws in the nation.

These problems have solutions, but despite strong public support for action, all too often powerful interests stand in the way, spending millions in campaign contributions and lobbyists to maintain the status quo.

Take the example of "fracking" and the Texas Legislature. The combination of two technologies—hydraulic fracturing and horizontal drilling—has enabled the oil and gas industry to engage in an effort to unlock oil and gas in underground rock formations across the United States. "Fracking," however, has also led to tremendous environmental harm and put the health and safety of communities across the country at risk. In response, over 300 Texas cities have adopted ordinances to protect their citizens from harm, adopting measures to keep drilling out of neighborhoods and away from schools. In November 2014, voters in Denton approved a measure on the ballot to keep drilling out of their city altogether.

Texans from across the political spectrum believe local governments should have the right to adopt these kinds of ordinances. For example, a 2015 poll by the University of Texas and the *Texas Tribune* found that Texas voters who strongly identify as Republicans support local control of "fracking" by a margin of 50 percent to 35 percent. But with the Denton vote, the oil and gas industry sensed an opportunity to roll back municipal protections, and they didn't stop with outright bans. The Texas Oil and Gas Association called even sensible setbacks from homes "extreme" and wrote HB 40—legislation to preempt local control.

Having donated $5.5 million to the campaigns of legislators in the 2014 elections, and spent even more on lobbyists, oil and gas interests prevailed over public will and HB 40 became law in the 2015 legislative session. Denton was forced to repeal its ban, and other cities' setback requirements are being challenged by the oil and gas industry.

Unfortunately, this is all too often how Texas politics works. Industries wealthy enough to buy elections and wine and dine lawmakers routinely push for and win agendas at odds with what most Texans believe. But with hard work and strategic campaigns, organized people can beat this organized money.

Defending our environment requires independent research, tough-minded advocacy and spirited grassroots action. That's the idea behind Environment Texas. Together with thousands of supporters from all walks of life, we take the kind of action that wins tangible results for our environment.

For the last ten years, Environment Texas has played a leading role in cleaning up air and water pollution in the Lone Star State. Our lawsuits against Shell and Chevron Phillips reduced air pollution in Houston by one million pounds per year. We helped restore Clean Water Act protections to 143,000 miles of Texas streams. We won voter approval of $50 million to purchase and protect land in the environmentally sensitive Barton Springs watershed. And we helped win a major investment in water conservation by the state water board to help combat a historic drought.

We lose as often as we win, but we are in this fight for the long haul. With the people of Texas standing and working with us, we will ultimately prevail and win the kind of change our environment desperately needs.

1. What are the challenges the author sees facing the Texas environment?
2. Describe the interest group tactics the author uses to try to change the state's environmental policies. How does the author hope to compete in a practical way against some of the most powerful interest groups in Texas?

★ Chapter Summary

LO 6.1 Define *interest groups* and identify their major types. Interest groups are organizations of private citizens exercising their constitutional right to organize in an attempt to influence public policy. Economic interest groups seek to influence public policies that affect their pocketbooks, while noneconomic interest groups strive to realize their religious, political, or personal values. Some groups, like civil rights groups, work for the ideal of equality and financial self-interest as well.

LO 6.2 Describe how interest groups influence public policies in Texas. Interest groups adjust their strategies to maximize their potential influence on each major type of policy maker in Texas government. Their major tactics include lobbying, making campaign contributions, organizing public relations campaigns, and filing suit in the courts.

Interest groups have refined lobbying to an art form as they try to sway members of the legislative and executive branches to their policy positions. Like salespeople for their groups' ideas, lobbyists socialize with decision makers to build personal relationships, making them receptive to emotional appeals, ideological appeals, and persuasive information. Lobbyists conduct research and draft proposed bills for the legislative branch even as they monitor and shape the rule-making process in the executive branch.

Interest groups have also developed electioneering and public relations into a fine art. Campaign contributions give lobbyists access to elected officeholders, and organizing public demonstrations, letter-writing campaigns, and advertising campaigns can help create a political environment that makes public officials receptive to interest groups' appeals.

LO 6.3 Analyze the political balance of power among interest groups in Texas. Business interest groups, such as the Texas Association of Business, the energy and natural resources industries, utilities, and health-related businesses, are dominant in Texas. Socially conservative groups closely aligned with state Republicans have considerable influence as well.

Iron triangles dominate narrow public policy decisions, but once in a while public policy battles over broad issues, such as taxation, abortion, education, or the environment, involve broader interest group alliances as more interest groups and individuals become active on a wider political battlefield.

LO 6.4 Evaluate the role of interest groups in Texas politics and policy formulation. The constitutions of the United States and Texas promote political expression and the right to organize to petition public officials. These rights recognize that representatives can represent their constituents' wishes only when citizens are able to communicate their policy positions effectively.

Interest groups play a positive role in the political system as they mobilize citizens and present their policy viewpoints to public officials. In a diverse, pluralistic state like Texas, no single group is able to dominate completely in a state that has divided and dispersed its institutional powers.

Critics charge that too few Texans have joined any interest groups, and because effective use of interest group tools requires money, the most powerful interest groups are those that represent narrow elites. Interest groups create conflicts of interest by opening the revolving door, tempting officials with campaign contributions, and exploiting weak state institutions.

Public interest groups and the media publicize reports on interest group activity, but lobby reports to the Texas Ethics Commission do not reveal the specific policies on which lobbyists work or the implied understandings that come with campaign contributions.

LO 6.5 Apply what you have learned about interest groups. You heard from a leader of one the state's most influential environmental groups about Environment Texas's policy goals and lobbying strategies, and evaluated the role of interest groups in the Texas political system.

Key Terms

access, *p. 149*
astroturf lobbying, *p. 150*
clientele groups, *p. 146*
conflict of interest, *p. 158*
co-optation, *p. 146*

discretion, *p. 144*
elitist theory, *p. 157*
implementation, *p. 144*
interest group, *p. 139*
iron triangles, *p. 154*

issue networks, *p. 154*
late-train contributions, *p. 159*
lobbying, *p. 142*
pluralist theory, *p. 156*

political movement, *p. 154*
revolving door, *p. 158*
umbrella organization, *p. 151*

Review Questions

LO 6.1 Define *interest groups* and identify their major types.

• What are interest groups? What do they do?

• What are the major types of interest groups? Identify an interest group in each subcategory.

LO 6.2 Describe how interest groups influence public policies in Texas.

- How do interest groups use different approaches to influence each of the three branches of government?

- Do campaign contributions affect public policy making in Texas? How?

- What is lobbying? What does a lobbyist do? What techniques do lobbyists use to influence state officials?

LO 6.3 Analyze the political balance of power among interest groups in Texas.

- Which interests are the most powerful in Texas? Why?

- How does the scope of a proposed policy affect the number of interests that attempt to bring their influence to bear in the decision-making process?

LO 6.4 Evaluate the role of interest groups in Texas politics and policy formulation.

- How is interest group formation a constitutional right? What positive services do interest groups perform for the political system?

- What are the criticisms of interest groups? Define conflicts of interest. Describe regulations that would minimize them.

- Describe the differences between elitist and pluralist theories. Which theory best describes Texas politics? Why?

Think Critically and Get Active!

Find out who is lobbying state government. Go to the Texas Ethics Commission's website at **www.ethics. state.tx.us** to discover which people, corporations, labor unions, and nonprofit organizations are lobbying Texas state government. Use this site to sample interest group reports about lobbying and campaign contributions.

Learn how to lobby at the Texas State Teachers Association website at **www.tsta.org/issues-action.** Click on "Guide to Lobbying" under Take Action at the State Level!

Follow some of the most active and influential interest groups in the Lone Star State on Twitter: Empower Texans (@EmpowerTexans), Environment Texas (@EnvironmentTex), NARAL Pro-Choice Texas (@naraltx), Public Citizen Texas (@PublicCitizenTX), Texans for Public Justice (@TxPublicJustice), Texas Association of Business (@txbiz), Texas Association of Realtors (@TXRealtors), Texas Automobile Dealers Association (@autodealerstx), Texas Farm Bureau (@TexasFarmBureau), Texans for Lawsuit Reform (@lawsuitreform), Texas League of Conservation Voters (@TLCV), Texas Medical Association (@texmed), Texas Oil and Gas Association (@TXOGA), Texas Right to Life (@TXRightToLife), and Texas State Rifle Association (@TSRA_outreach).

★ CSQ Identify the state or local interest group related to your career, professional ambitions, or personal interests. Also search for at least one of each of the following types of organizations: a major corporation, a labor union, a professional organization, a trade organization, a nonprofit organization, and a public interest group. From the groups' websites, make a list of the public policy issues each is promoting, and write a paragraph explaining why the groups take these positions. Briefly describe the organizations' dues, membership, type and frequency of any publications, and social media presence.

★ PRQ How do you distinguish the "public interest" from your own personal self-interest? Do you identify a concept of social justice beyond your own personal needs?

★ PRQ Create a list of at least a half dozen potential conflicts of interest involving public officials using the *Texas Tribune's* Ethics Explorer (A Guide to the Financial Interests of Elected Officials) at www.texastribune.org/bidness/explore. Explain why each of your examples represents an ethical conflict.

7

The Legislature

This chapter will shed light on the inner workings at the Capitol and you will see who our legislators are and how they operate to pass the state's laws.

Jo Ann Snover/Shutterstock.com

Learning Objectives

LO 7.1 Describe the limits on the Texas Legislature and evaluate the concept of the "citizen legislature."

LO 7.2 Analyze the selection of Texas legislators, their qualifications, and the impact of campaign financing and redistricting on elections.

LO 7.3 Analyze the powers of the legislature and its presiding officers.

LO 7.4 Analyze legislative processes, the committee structure, and how a bill becomes a law.

LO 7.5 Apply what you have learned about the Texas Legislature.

The legislative branch is responsible for making law. It is through law that the state makes public policy and basically determines what the state agencies will do. The legislative function is to determine what is a crime, to establish the basis for a civil suit, to establish what services the state will provide, and to provide the funding to carry out the state's priorities.

In Texas, the legislature is bicameral—it consists of two houses, the 31-member Texas Senate and the 150-member Texas House of Representatives. On most matters, the two houses share equal powers and both of them must agree on a proposed bill for it to become law. The Senate does have the special power to confirm or approve the governor's appointments of state officers. By establishing a bicameral legislature, framers of the Texas Constitution followed the pattern set for the national Congress and used in every state other than Nebraska, which has a unicameral, or one-house, legislature.

The chief argument for the use of bicameral legislative bodies is that one house can serve as a check on the other so that legislation will not be passed hastily without adequate reflection, and both chambers must consider every bill before it becomes a law. Bicameralism can also slow the law-making process or can keep laws from passing through one chamber while passing in the other.

Texas has a "citizen legislature," with members who do not hold a full-time professionally paid position. The Texas Legislature is a highly centralized institution dominated by its presiding officers—the lieutenant governor in the Texas Senate and the speaker in the Texas House of Representatives—who use standing committees and a variety of other committees to control the law-making process in the state.

The Limited Legislature

LO 7.1 **Describe the limits on the Texas Legislature and evaluate the concept of the "citizen legislature."**

The Texas Legislature has often been referred to as a "citizen legislature," whose members meet for only 140 days every other year and receive only a small income for the work they do. It has been said that the Texas Legislature is "full-time only part of the time." The limited sessions, heavy workloads, low salaries, and limited staffing keep the legislature in this "citizen" status.

Legislative Terms and Sessions

Texas representatives are elected for two-year terms, but senators are elected for longer four-year terms that are staggered or overlapping. That means that the entire House and half the Senate (15 or 16 senators) are elected every two years. All senators are elected in the first election following redistricting (every 10 years). At the beginning of the post-redistricting session, the senators draw lots to determine which senators will serve a two-year term. One-half of the senators are up for reelection again in two years, whereas the other half will not be up for reelection campaign for four years. All senators will then serve overlapping four-year terms until the districts are again redrawn.

Texas legislators may serve as many terms as voters choose to reelect them. Unlike Texas, some states have adopted **term limits**, which are legal restrictions on the number of times that a politician can be reelected to a particular office or the number of years that a person may hold that office. The adoption of term limits in some states reflects an increasing frustration with government, especially the legislative branch, which seems to be more responsive to organized special interests than to the residents and businesses located within a legislator's home district.

Most supporters of term limits assume that electing new legislators could and should disrupt long-established working relationships between legislators and interest groups.

term limits
Legally mandated restrictions on the number of times that a politician can be reelected to an office or the number of years that a person may hold a particular office.

IMAGE 7.1 When you visit the Texas Senate, you will usually see an empty chamber because the Texas Legislature has short, infrequent sessions.

amadeustx/Shutterstock.com

★ **CTQ**   **What are the advantages and disadvantages of short sessions?**

Unfortunately, it is not clear whether term limits increase or reduce the influence of interest groups. Opponents of term limits argue that limiting legislators' time in office may actually be counterproductive because they result in higher turnover and the election of many inexperienced lawmakers who, lacking expertise of their own, become even more dependent on lobbyists and career bureaucrats for advice, information, and expertise.

Short and infrequent sessions contribute to the "citizen" status of the legislature. The Texas Legislature begins its session on the second Tuesday in January of odd-numbered years and meets for a period of just 140 days. Forty-six states have annual legislative sessions; Texas's is the only legislature among the 10 most populous states to meet on a biennial schedule, once every other year. The limited *biennial sessions* tend to work against professional and deliberative legislative practice and ultimately may work against the public interest. Texas legislators cannot possibly acquaint themselves in only 140 days with the immense volume of proposed legislation presented to them, which usually amounts to thousands of proposed bills and resolutions. Because most of the legislative work must be performed during the short regular session, time becomes critical; many pieces of legislation are never considered.

★ **Did You Know?** In the hustle and bustle of the short legislative session, on April Fools' Day 1971, the Texan House unanimously passed a congratulatory recognition of Albert De Salvo for his "noted activities and unconventional techniques involving population control and applied psychology." The House later withdrew this recognition when it discovered that De Salvo was in fact the "Boston Strangler," an infamous serial killer.

When work cannot be accomplished or a bill favored by the governor did not pass during a regular session, a 30-day *special session*, which can be called only by the governor, may take place after a regular session. Because special sessions interrupt the normal lives of the "citizen legislators" and can cost as much as a million dollars when one is called, they are not very popular with either the legislators or the general public. The governor sets the agenda for the special session; however, legislators can and often do introduce new bills for consideration during the short session. The legislature adjourns once it has voted on the items in the governor's agenda or when it reaches the 30-day limit.

Governors, however, may call the legislature into as many special sessions as they wish, and some have called several back-to-back sessions when the legislature has failed to pass their agendas. When a 2013 special session failed to pass his proposed limits on abortions, former governor Rick Perry called a second special session to begin the very next day.

Although the governor is empowered to call special sessions, the House and Senate can call an "impeachment session" for the sole purpose of deciding the impeachment and removal of state officers from their position. Texas has impeached and removed one governor from office—Jim Ferguson. After impeachment in the House, the Senate may remove an official by a two-thirds vote.

Legislative Salaries and Compensation

Legislators receive an annual salary of $7,200 plus $190 **per diem**, an amount paid for each day a legislator is working, during both regular and special sessions and during the interim when committees meet. They also have a travel allowance on a reimbursement basis when the legislature is in session. The Texas Ethics Commission is constitutionally empowered to establish the per diem allowance, which is increased regularly, but voters must approve any salary increase. Texas lawmakers are among the worst paid large-state legislators in the country and have not received a salary increase since 1975; they have, however, found ways to offset their living expenses through very lax rules governing how a legislator earns money while in office.

Legislators who are lawyers can accept **retainer fees** from a variety of clients, which may include those who do business with state agencies or may have lawsuits against state agencies. Lawyers and non-lawyers alike can receive **consulting fees** from business clients and can act for their clients based on information that they obtain from lobbyists and other information that they gain from their own specialized knowledge of pending legislation, thereby helping their clients benefit from legislation being considered.

Some reformers believe that legislators' pay should be increased to a professional-level salary and their income from sources outside their government paycheck strictly limited. In the current system, the potential for conflict between the public interest and the interests of lawmakers' private businesses or their employers can be construed to be unethical. Although higher pay would not guarantee honest legislators, it would enable the conscientious ones to perform their legislative duties without turning to sources of outside income that could potentially compromise their ability to represent the constituents who elected them.

Legislative Staff

The Texas Legislature has over 2,000 full-time and part-time staff, which is comparable to staffs in other populous states.[2] The Legislative Budget Board, the Legislative Council, and the Legislative Reference Library provide some professional research, and individual legislators also employ their own office staffs from their allotments for office expenses.

Usually, senators and representatives maintain staff in Austin as well as in their home districts. These allotments must pay for staff, equipment, and supplies for both offices, as well as rent and utilities for their home district office. House members generally have about three or four staff people; in the Senate, the average staff size is slightly more than seven. Some senators have as many as 14 staff members, while others have as few as four.

Powerful special interests and administrative agencies, however, have a distinct advantage when it comes to staffing. The need for research data, advice, expertise, and other services obtained from interest groups and administrative agencies makes legislators dependent on these groups for information and advice.[3]

per diem
The amount paid each day that a legislator is working, both in regular and special sessions, and when committees meet during the interim between sessions.

retainer fees
Fees charged by lawyer-legislators for services to clients, including those who have business with state agencies or may have lawsuits against state agencies.

consulting fees
Fees charged by legislators who may contract with business clients to consult on matters pending in the legislature, thereby helping their clients to benefit from legislation being considered.

How Does Texas Compare?

Limits on Legislative Terms, Salaries, and Sessions

Terms Like 34 other states, Texas does not limit the number of terms legislators may serve. Voters are left to decide whether to retain experienced incumbents or replace them with fresh legislators.

Salaries Figure 7.1 shows that the Texas Constitution is much more restrictive than most states with respect to legislative salaries and sessions. Although New Hampshire pays its legislators only $200, no other populous state sets legislative pay as low as Texas. Most large states pay their legislators in the salary range of middle-class employees, and many allow legislators to set their own salary by statute.

Sessions Most states provide annual regular legislative sessions, and 14 states place no limit on their length. Texas is among only five states with biennial legislative sessions. Unlike most legislatures, the Texas Legislature may not call itself into a special session or determine its agenda. Low salaries and limited sessions make it difficult for the Texas Legislature to function as a professional institution and may make members more dependent on interest groups for income and research on public policy. Recent research indicates that more professional legislatures—those with higher salaries, longer sessions, and better staffs—are significantly more responsive to public opinion and enact policies that are more congruent with public preferences.[1]

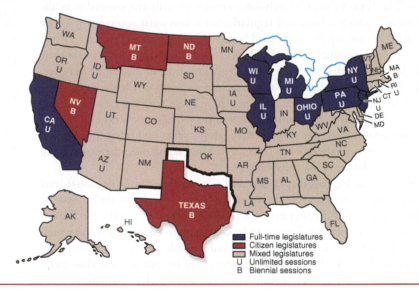

Full-time legislatures
Citizen legislatures
Mixed legislatures
U Unlimited sessions
B Biennial sessions

FIGURE 7.1 Full-Time and "Citizen" Legislature
Note that most large states have full-time legislatures with unlimited annual sessions and yearly salaries over $45,000. In contrast, Texas is among the states that have a "citizen" legislature with limited, biennial sessions and salaries set below $10,000. Many state legislatures have elements of both types.

★SRQ **Explain the advantages of a professional full-time legislature like the ones used by most other large populous states. Why do Texans prefer a part-time citizen legislature?**

Source: Based on data from The Book of the States, 2017 (Lexington, KY: Council of State Governments, 2017), Tables 3.2 and 3.9.

FOR DEBATE

★SRQ **Should Texas limit the number of terms legislators serve? Or would term limits also restrict legislators' experience and, therefore, make them more vulnerable to the influence of lobbyists?**

★SRQ **Should Texas consider increasing legislators' salaries and the length of their sessions? Or would doing this give legislators too much power?**

To counteract the dominance of the special interests' informational influence, both legislative houses have established nonpartisan institutions to provide information to legislators. The House Research Organization provides bill analyses, floor reports, issue focus reports, and interim news to legislators and the public.[4] The Senate Research Center provides research and bill analysis to the Texas Senate and the lieutenant governor's office. The center's staff also attends meetings and conferences of other governmental entities and report to the senators on their content. This kind of help to the legislative staff reduces legislators' dependence on special interests and administrative agencies for information.

Electing Legislators

LO 7.2 **Analyze the selection of Texas legislators, their qualifications, and the impact of campaign financing and redistricting on elections.**

Certain legal, or formal, qualifications, including age, citizenship, and residency status, must be met before anyone can serve in the state legislature. However, the "informal" qualifications, including partisanship, socioeconomic status, gender, and especially access to campaign funding, usually determine who will run for and be successfully elected to the legislature.

Qualifications

To be a Texas state senator, one must be a U.S. citizen, a qualified voter, and at least 26 years of age and must have lived in the state for the previous five years and in the district for one year prior to election. Qualifications for House membership are even more easily met. A candidate must be a U.S. citizen, a qualified voter of the state, and at least 21 years of age and must have lived in Texas for the two previous years and in the district for one year prior to being elected.

On the surface, becoming a senator or representative in the state would seem relatively easy, but a successful candidate for the legislature must have certain qualities to be elected to the state legislature. These qualities, which include party affiliation, demographic identity, occupation, educational level, and economic status, can almost be considered "informal" or unofficial requirements to win election to the legislature. Perhaps the most important quality of a successful legislative candidate is the ability to raise money and to appeal to those who are willing and able to contribute to campaigns.

Party Party affiliation in Texas often determines whether a candidate will win an election or not. Until the late 1980s, the Democratic Party was the dominant party in Texas. Since then, however, the resurgence of the Republican Party has made Texas a strongly Republican state. By the end of 2004, Republicans had established dominance over all three branches of state government and representation in the U.S. Congress, with two Republican U.S. senators and a Republican majority in the Texas delegation to the U.S. House of Representatives.

Campaign Funding Many competent, motivated citizens who want to serve are excluded because they are unable to raise the money necessary to finance an adequate campaign. Thus, the pool of potential candidates is initially reduced by the special interests that make most campaign contributions. Securing office space, creating and maintaining a campaign website and social media presence, printing and mailing campaign literature, building a campaign organization, and purchasing advertisements are all among the necessary ingredients for a successful campaign. A legislator may also use political contributions for such personal expenses as "reasonable household expenses in Austin," which has been interpreted to include the lease on their car, and even NBA and NFL season tickets.

In 2016, the National Institute on Money in State Politics found that the 350 candidates who ran for the Texas House raised an average of $217,144 for their campaigns. The 39 Texas Senate candidates raised an average of $583,368 for their campaigns.[5] The 389 candidates

Texas Insiders

Campaign Contributions in Texas Legislative Elections: Following the Money

Campaign contributors gave $76 million to candidates running for the Texas House of Representatives and $23 million to candidates for the Texas Senate in 2016. Most of the contributions went to incumbents running for reelection and most of them won their races. Along with candidates' incumbency and their party affiliation, campaign funding is an outstanding predictor of general election victory—the legislative candidates who outspent their opponents won most of the time.

Table 7.1 shows the ten legislative races that generated the largest campaign contributions in the 2016 election cycle. All but one incumbent (Doug Miller) in Table 7.1 was victorious and all but one (Juan "Chuy" Hinojosa) was a Republican.

Thinking about the role of elites in Texas politics

Large contributors pursue several strategies: In closely contested races, some contributors may be trying to help elect candidates who best represent their interests and viewpoints. In other instances, their pattern of giving does not seem to be directed at affecting election outcomes but, instead, seems to be an attempt to influence the legislative process itself. For example, Table 7.1 shows that contributors may target their giving toward races involving those who hold powerful legislative positions such as committee chairs and the speakership even when those candidates are from safe districts or unopposed for reelection. Occasionally, a single contributor will give to both candidates in the same closely contested race. Contributors frequently give money to the winner even after election day—so-called "late train" contributions.

Whatever their motivations, large donors usually have considerable success with their legislative agendas. In Chapter 10, we will discuss the stunning legislative successes of Texans for Lawsuit Reform, the largest single funder of Texas legislative campaigns. Other major campaign contributors such as the Texas Association of Realtors and Empower Texas have also seen much of their legislative agenda enacted.

TABLE 7.1 Top Five Contribution Totals in 2016 House and Senate Campaigns

House		Senate	
Representative (and position in 2016)	Total Contributions (all candidates)	Senator (and position in 2016)	Total Contributions (all candidates)
Joe Straus, Speaker	$9,334,728	Brandon Creighton, Chair Select Committee on Texas Ports	$2,231,499
Charlie Geren, Chair, House Administration Committee	$2,461,783	Juan "Chuy" Hinojosa, Vice Chair Finance Committee	$2,115,508
Todd Hunter, Chair Calendars Committee	$1,962,422	Jane Nelson, Chair Finance Committee	$1,962,422
Doug Miller, Chair Special Purposes Districts Committee	$1,386,028	Dawn Buckingham, Not in office in 2016	$1,831,462
Sarah Davis, Chair Appropriations Subcommittee on Budget Transparency & Reform	$1,046,588	Bryan Hughes, Not in office in 2016	$1,744,950

National Institute on Money in State Politics.

▶ What indicates when a campaign contribution might be intended to influence how a legislator votes?

▶ How can voters, small contributors, and less well-organized groups balance the political influence of large contributors?

raised a total of almost $99 million for their campaigns in the House and Senate races.[6] The amount of money needed to win an election is growing and becoming increasingly out of reach for many would-be candidates. Our Texas Insiders feature puts a face on the organizations and individuals who dominate the funding of legislative campaigns.

Demographic Identity The state of Texas has one of the most diverse populations in the United States. It is one of the few states with a majority minority population, meaning that the majority of the population are members of an ethnic or racial minority group.[7] Currently, 42 percent of the population is non-Hispanic white (Anglo), 39 percent is Hispanic,[8] 13 percent is African American, and 5 percent is Asian American.[9] Texas legislators are fairly diverse, but they do not fully mirror the population. **Descriptive representation** is the idea that elected bodies should accurately represent not only constituents' political views but also the ethnic and social characteristics that affect their political perspectives. There is some diversity in the legislature, but the legislature does not fully reflect the state's population as a whole.

As Figure 7.2 indicates, the members of the Texas Legislature are primarily Anglo and male. While African Americans have achieved descriptive representational parity with the state's overall African American population, the representation of women, Latinos, and Asian Americans continues to lag behind the overall population of those groups in Texas.

descriptive representation
The idea that elected bodies should accurately represent not only constituents' political views but also the ethnic and social characteristics that affect their political perspectives.

Occupation Descriptive representation is far less apparent in the occupations of most Texas legislators. In the Texas Legislature, 57 members are business owners or executives, slightly outnumbering the 56 members who are lawyers. Together, these two professions account for more than 60 percent of the legislators. Real estate, consulting, ranching, and medical fields account for most of the professions other than lawyers and business owners.[10] Occupations can and do limit a person's ability to serve in the Texas Legislature. Legislators must have enough flexibility in their occupations to take time away from their jobs to serve in the legislature 140 days every other year and to attend to constituents and other state business when the legislature is not in session.

Education Texas has one of the best educated legislative bodies in the United States, which means that it is unlikely that Texas legislators will ever achieve educational descriptive representation with the general population of the state. Although only 25 percent of Texans age 25 and older hold college degrees, the Texas Legislature ranks fifth in the nation in the percentage of lawmakers with a college degree. According to the National Council on State Legislatures, about 73, percent of lawmakers in the nation hold college degrees; more than 91 percent of Texas lawmakers hold at least a bachelor's degree, and 52 percent have earned higher degrees. Only 4 percent of Texas lawmakers have not attended college.[11]

Texas ranks first in the percentage of lawmakers who are lawyers, with 30 percent of Texas lawmakers holding law degrees. As an informal qualification to become a legislator in the state, educational attainment seems to resonate with voters as being a very important aspect of being electable.

Economic Status Texas lawmakers are required to report their sources of income, real estate assets, and stocks. However, when it comes to reporting the actual financial worth of the lawmakers' income and stock values, the reporting requirements are less precise. Income is reported in ranges, the highest range being $25,000 and above, and stock ownership is reported in ranges from greater than $500 to $10,000 and above as the highest.[12] Given these parameters, it is difficult to determine the actual net worth of Texas legislators, but they appear to have enough income to be able to serve in a "citizen legislature" that pays a salary of $7,200 a year. Both the wealthy legislators and those less well-off are allowed to solicit retainers and consulting fees to supplement their incomes, making it unlikely that their average incomes reflect the economic status of the average Texan.[13]

FIGURE 7.2 Gender, Ethnicity, and Race of Texans and Their Legislators

This figure shows how the ethnic, racial, and gender makeup of the Texas Legislature differed from the population as a whole in 2017. Women are by far the largest underrepresented group.

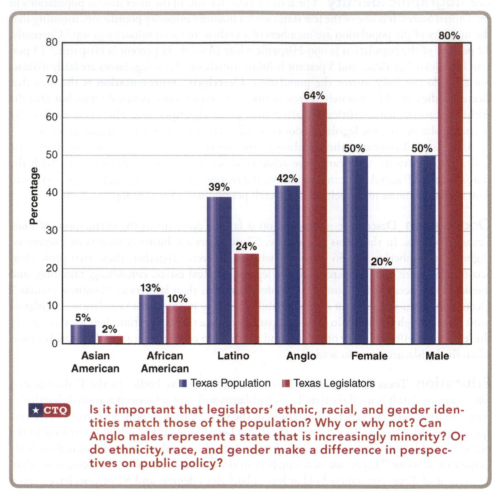

★ CTQ   **Is it important that legislators' ethnic, racial, and gender identities match those of the population? Why or why not? Can Anglo males represent a state that is increasingly minority? Or do ethnicity, race, and gender make a difference in perspectives on public policy?**

U.S. Census Bureau, Office of the Texas State Demographer, and *The Texas Tribune*.

Geographic Districting

single-member district
A district that elects one senator or one representative; districts should be equal in population.

Each legislator is elected from a **single-member district**, with the state representative districts being quite a bit smaller than the senate districts. The 150 House districts should be equal in population, as should the 31 Senate districts. After the 10-year census has been completed, districts must be redrawn to reflect population changes in the state and to equalize the population in each district.

After the 2010 elections, Republicans controlled both the House and Senate with large majorities and were easily able to agree on district maps that were favorable to the Republican Party, as reflected in Figures 7.3 and 7.4.

FIGURE 7.3 Texas House of Representatives Districts, 86th Legislature, 2019–2020

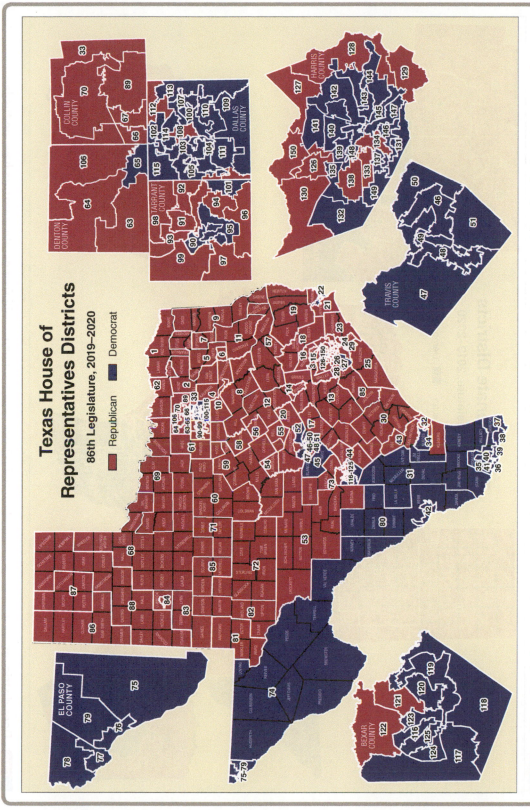

Texas House of Representatives Districts

86th Legislature, 2019–2020

- ▇ Republican
- ▇ Democrat

★ **CTQ** What districting practices were used to create these House districts? Can you explain why the legislature may have drawn District 128 in Harris County the way it is?

Source: Texas Legislative Council Plan H309.

FIGURE 7.4 Texas Senate Districts, 86th Legislature, 2019–2020

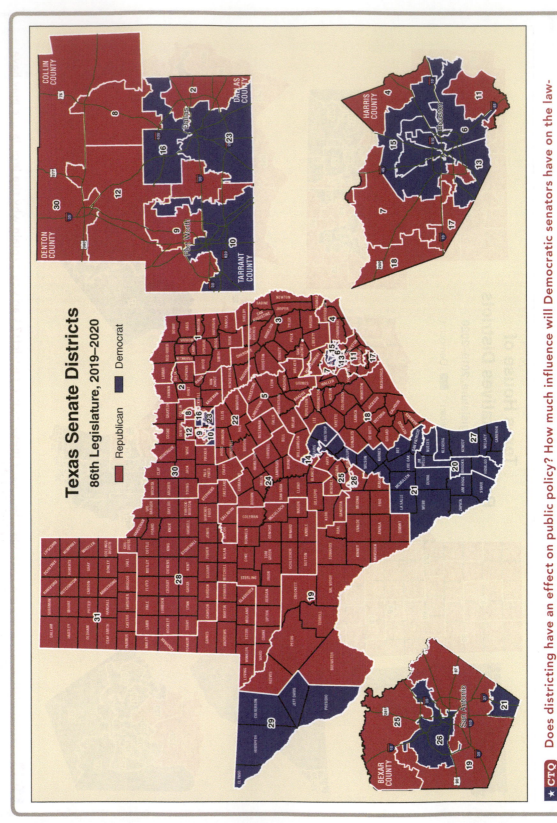

Texas Senate Districts
86th Legislature, 2019–2020

■ Republican
■ Democrat

⭐ **CTQ** Does districting have an effect on public policy? How much influence will Democratic senators have on the law-making process in Texas?

Source: Texas Legislative Council, Plan S172.

Figures 7.3 and 7.4 show how the Texas Senate and House of Representatives district lines are currently drawn. The state legislature is responsible for drawing the districts from which they, themselves, will be elected. Legislators, therefore, have a considerable personal political stake in the districting process, and it is not surprising that they have sometimes found it impossible to agree on where district lines should be drawn.

If the legislature fails to redistrict, the state constitution requires the Legislative Redistricting Board to redraw the lines. This board is **ex officio**, which means that its members hold offices or positions automatically because they also hold some other office. It is made up of the lieutenant governor, the speaker of the house, the attorney general, the comptroller, and the commissioner of the General Land Office. In practice, even this board has sometimes found itself at a stalemate and the courts have been forced to step into the state's redistricting processes.

After the 2010 census, the average population of an electoral district for the Texas House of Representatives was 167,637; House members represented 29,000 more people than they did a decade earlier. Texas senators represented an average of 811,129 residents, an estimated 138,000 more people than they did after the 2000 census.

Malapportionment

Geographic districting uses census data to divide the population into approximately equal districts for every elected position, but this has not always been the case. Historically, as state populations began to shift from rural areas to the cities in the early twentieth century, rurally dominated legislatures simply ignored urban growth as they drew new district lines. The result was sparsely populated rural districts and densely populated urban districts, which maintained rural control over newly urban states like Texas.

However, in the 1960s, U.S. Supreme Court decisions in several cases, including *Reynolds v. Sims*, outlawed **malapportionment**, the drawing of district lines so that one district's population is substantially larger or smaller than another's. The Supreme Court ruled, "Simply stated, an individual's right to vote for state legislators is unconstitutionally impaired when its weight is in a substantial fashion diluted when compared with votes of citizens living in other parts of the State."[14]

Based on the principle of "one person, one vote," this decision mandated **reapportionment**—a redistricting, or redrawing of district lines, after every census to reflect the actual population changes over the previous decade; it required that district lines be drawn so that the population of all districts is approximately equal. In practice, the population of state legislative districts can deviate plus or minus 5 percent from the average, but not more.

Gerrymandering

Gerrymandering is the practice of drawing district lines in such a way as to give an advantage to candidates from a certain party, ethnic group, or faction at the expense of other groups. It should not be confused with malapportionment because gerrymandering is possible even when the population of every district is equal; it is more a matter of which people are drawn into each district rather than how many.

Where district lines are drawn has an enormous impact on the political, ideological, racial, and ethnic makeup of a legislative body and the policies that it produces. During the redistricting process, political careers may be made or broken, public policy determined for at least a decade, and the power of ethnic or political minorities neutralized.

Partisan gerrymandering is the drawing of district lines to maximize the majority party's representation. District lines are drawn so that the majority party's voters are able to elect as many legislators as possible. The U.S. Supreme Court has reviewed several cases of partisan gerrymandering, but has

ex officio
Holding a position automatically because one also holds some other office.

malapportionment
The drawing of district lines so that one district's population is substantially larger or smaller than another's.

reapportionment
The redistricting, or redrawing of district lines, after every census to reflect the population changes over the previous decade.

gerrymandering
The practice of drawing district lines in such a way as to give candidates from a certain party, ethnic group, or faction an advantage.

Did You Know? Drawing district lines for partisan political advantage got the name *gerrymandering* in 1812, when the Massachusetts legislature and Governor Elbridge Gerry, wishing to preserve a Federalist majority, redrew a district in such a convoluted shape that a political cartoonist portrayed it as a salamander and dubbed it the "Gerrymander." The shapes of several current Texas congressional districts exceed the oddity of those originally gerrymandered districts in Massachusetts.

not yet found a constitutional standard that would restrict it. Another look at Figures 7.3 and 7.4 shows that the 2012 redistricting plans relied heavily on partisan gerrymandering, which allowed the Republican voting bloc to maintain large majorities in both houses of the Texas Legislature.

cracking
A gerrymandering technique of dividing up a minority party's voters into so many geographical districts that their voting power in any one district is negligible.

packing
Gerrymandering technique in which members of a party are concentrated into one district, thereby ensuring that the group will influence only one district's election rather than several.

Gerrymandering Techniques
Three basic gerrymander techniques are generally used to draw district lines to benefit the majority party. **Cracking** is the technique of dividing up a minority party's voters into so many geographical districts that their voting power in any one district is negligible; areas that would otherwise support the minority party are split into several districts that the majority party controls. To get a better idea of how cracking a population works, look at Figure 7.5.

Another technique of gerrymandering involves concentrating, or **packing**, the minority party into as few districts as possible to minimize the number of legislators it can elect. The majority party uses this technique when there may be so many votes for the minority party candidate that, if left in non-gerrymandered districts, they could affect the outcome of elections in many districts. Figure 7.5 shows how the packing technique might benefit the majority party.

FIGURE 7.5 A Schematic to Illustrate the Process of Gerrymandering
In the schematic on the left, the blue dots represent eight Democrats and the red dots represent the same number of Republicans in four equally competitive districts, each electing one legislator. The figure on the right shows how the same population can be gerrymandered to guarantee a three-to-one advantage for Democrats. Try your hand at drawing districts with a three-to-one advantage for the Republicans.

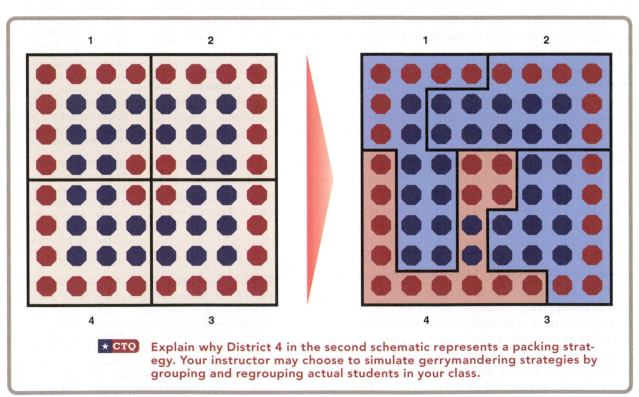

★ CTQ   **Explain why District 4 in the second schematic represents a packing strategy. Your instructor may choose to simulate gerrymandering strategies by grouping and regrouping actual students in your class.**

A third form of gerrymandering is a practice called **pairing**. Pairing is a redistricting technique that combines two or more **incumbent** (currently elected) legislators' residences and parts of their political bases into the same elective district. At election time, the voters are then given the choice between the two current legislators but only allowed to vote for one, thereby ensuring that one will be defeated. The idea behind this type of redistricting is to create a district that will ensure that one incumbent will win over the other—usually for the majority party's incumbent to be able to represent the new district. By cracking or packing the remaining parts of the paired district into neighboring districts, the majority party can control a larger share of the legislative body.

pairing
Placing two current officeholders and parts of their political bases in the same elective district through redistricting.

incumbent
Currently elected officials.

Alternatives to Gerrymandering Several states have recognized the conflict of interest inherent in allowing legislators to draw their own election districts. A number of them have reduced the role of the legislature in redistricting and have instead turned much of the process over to an independent bipartisan or nonpartisan commission. Many Texans would like to see their state follow this lead.

Did You Know? Legislators are often quoted as saying during redistricting that "rather than the voters choosing us, we choose the voters." Redistricting is the process in which politicians choose their voters rather than the other way around.

During the heat of the redistricting controversy in the winter of 2012, Texans were asked what they felt were the state's most pressing problems. Although the expected issues of the economy, unemployment, and border security were at the top of the list, surprisingly, 5 percent of Texans polled pointed to legislative redistricting as one of the state's most important problems.[15] It ranked in seventh place, ahead of gas prices and water supply.[16] A sizable number of Texans—42 percent—supported the creation of an independent redistricting commission to redraw legislative district lines. Twenty-nine percent of Republicans, 43 percent of independents, and 70 percent of Democrats supported the creation of an independent, nonpartisan redistricting commission to reduce political considerations in the drawing of legislative district boundaries.

Democrats and members of minority groups may support creating a redistricting commission in Texas because they believe gerrymandering unfairly costs them political representation as Republican legislators have drawn districts to their party's advantage. Others may support an independent redistricting commission because they believe it is a conflict of interest for legislators themselves to draw the lines from which they are elected. Furthermore, gerrymandering reduces party competition in elections as legislators draw district lines to make sure a member from one party is elected over the other.

Racial Gerrymandering Unlike partisan gerrymandering, which the Supreme Court considers a political matter, racial or ethnic gerrymandering is a special legal issue because the U.S. Constitution forbids government discrimination based on race. In two cases,[17] the Court ruled that drawing district lines to limit racial minority influence violates the Fourteenth Amendment. Not only did the Court rule in both of these cases that racial gerrymandering is unconstitutional, but in one districting case, the Court went so far as to say that the racial intent was obvious because district lines were so "irregular and bizarre in shape that they could not be understood to be anything other than to segregate voters."[18]

The federal Voting Rights Act of 1965 also prohibits policies intended to dilute minority voting strength, which presented a special problem for Texas legislative districting after the 2010 census.[19] Several groups sued the state before the newly drawn maps could be put in place. Because of the Voting Rights Act, Texas and eight other states with histories of racial discrimination were required to submit their district maps to the U.S. Department of Justice (DOJ) or to the U.S. District Court for the District of Columbia for review (preclearance).

In 2013, however, the U.S. Supreme Court (*in Shelby* v. *Holder*) concluded that the formula used to determine which states were required to seek preclearance was unconstitutional (see Chapter 2). This decision resulted in Texas and the eight other states no longer having to obtain preclearance. Texas was thus able to keep using the Republican-dominated district maps drawn by a federal district court in San Antonio, maps which were based heavily on the maps initially created by the Republican majority in the Texas Legislature in 2011.[20]

As a result, the Texas Legislature continues to be dominated by Republicans at the expense of Democrats and the large portion of ethnic and racial minorities who identify with them. Partisan and ethnic gerrymandering partially explains why the legislature does not reflect the political and demographic make up of the state's 28 million residents.

Powers of the Legislature and Its Leaders

LO 7.3 **Analyze the powers of the legislature and its presiding officers.**

The presiding officer of the Texas House of Representatives is the speaker of the house and the lieutenant governor acts as president of the senate. The presiding officers have extensive appointment power over boards, commissions, and legislative committees.

Both legislative chambers have broad powers that allow them to pass laws making public policy and to monitor state agencies, control the budgeting process, and engage in self-policing. As it exercises these powers, the legislature has the assistance of several boards, councils, and commissions that provide leadership and advice to both the House and the Senate.

Powers of the Presiding Officers

The two most powerful individuals in the Texas Legislature are the lieutenant governor and the speaker of the house. The rules of each house, formal and informal, give the presiding officers the procedural power to appoint most committee members and committee chairpersons, assign bills to committees, schedule legislation for floor action, recognize members on the floor for amendments and points of order, interpret the procedural rules when conflict arises, and appoint the chairpersons and members of joint and conference committees. Furthermore, statutes grant the presiding officers institutional powers to appoint the members and serve as joint chairs of the Legislative Budget Board and Legislative Council and determine the members of the Legislative Audit Committee and the Sunset Advisory Commission.

Lieutenant Governor The presiding officer in the Texas Senate is the lieutenant governor, who serves as the president of the senate. The lieutenant governor is elected independently from the governor for a four-year term in a statewide, partisan election, and is paid a $7,200 annual salary.

The lieutenant governor is in the unique position of having important roles in both the legislative and executive branches. As part of the executive branch, the lieutenant governor becomes governor if that office becomes vacant through death, disability, or resignation. In that event, the Senate elects one of its members to serve as lieutenant governor until the next regular election.

As part of the legislative branch, the lieutenant governor also serves as the presiding officer over the state Senate and has a great deal of power as a result (see Figure 7.6).

The Texas Constitution allows for the Senate to write its own rules at the beginning of each 140-day legislative session, and these rules give the lieutenant governor extensive legislative powers as well as organizational, procedural, administrative, and planning authority.

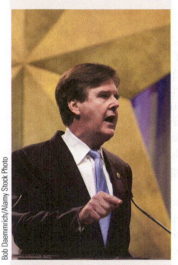

IMAGE 7.2 Lieutenant Governor Dan Patrick holds an office with power that rivals the governor's.

Bob Daemmrich/Alamy Stock Photo

★ CSQ

Write a carefully constructed essay that explains both the lieutenant governor's executive and legislative powers. Specifically, describe how the lieutenant governor is able to control the Texas Senate. Why do you suppose the Senate has written rules that give so much power to its presiding officer when most other states make their lieutenant governor a mere figurehead, like the vice president in the U.S. Senate?

Although not actually a senator, the lieutenant governor can break tie votes on bills, and the Senate rules allow for the entire Senate to convene as a committee of the whole, which allows the lieutenant governor to debate and vote on any bill as long as the Senate is designated as a committee.

Speaker of the House

The presiding officer of the 150-member House of Representatives is the speaker of the house. Unlike the senate, the entire House elects one of its own members to serve as the presiding officer for two-year terms.

In the past, candidates for the speakership have campaigned extensively among fellow representatives from both Democratic and Republican parties. After having put together a successful bipartisan coalition, they were often reelected by using their enormous powers to reward their supporters in both political parties. However, Republicans have recently begun a new practice of endorsing a candidate in their majority party caucus, whom they could potentially elect without needing Democratic votes.

During the session, the speaker maintains order during floor debate, recognizes legislators who wish to speak on the House floor, and decides on procedural matters as the need arises. Unlike the lieutenant governor, as a member of the House of Representatives, the speaker may debate bills and is allowed to vote on all bills and resolutions that pass through the House, although by custom the speaker rarely casts a roll call vote.

Some of the speaker's most important duties and responsibilities are determined by the House Rules of Procedure, which are adopted by a majority vote of the members at the beginning of each regular session of the legislature. The rules give the speaker the authority to appoint members of each standing committee, to designate the chairperson and vice chair for each committee, and to refer all proposed legislation to the appropriate committee. The speaker also appoints members to conference and joint committees, creates select committees, and authorizes committees to conduct business during the interim when the legislature is not in session.

Powers of the Legislature

The powers of the legislature include passing bills and resolutions, representing constituencies, and conducting bureaucratic oversight and investigations. The Texas Senate has the power to approve or disapprove gubernatorial appointments. Some extraordinary powers, like initiating a legislative redress action or impeachment, are only rarely used.

Passing Bills

The primary responsibility of the legislature is to pass bills, which are proposals to pass new laws, change existing ones, or adopt the state budget. A bill may be introduced in either chamber of the legislature; it is designated by the abbreviations HB (House Bill) or SB (Senate Bill) according to where it was first introduced and carries the same designation throughout the legislative process. A bill must be passed by both houses by a majority vote and be presented to the governor to be signed into law. We will explore the major steps in the legislative process later in the chapter.

Bills fall into three categories: special, general, and local. Special bills create exceptions to laws already enacted; general bills apply to everyone in the state; local bills usually apply to a single unit of local government and usually pass at the request of legislators representing the area. Bills normally take effect 90

FIGURE 7.6 Powers of the Presiding Officers

The lieutenant governor and speaker have powerful tools to control the legislative process.

Presiding Officers

Refer bills to committee

Appoint most committees

Appoint committee chairs

Preside over floor action

Appoint conference committees

★ CTQ **How can the presiding officers use these powers to reward their allies and punish their opponents?**

days after they pass unless a two-thirds majority of each house votes to have the bill take effect as soon as the governor signs it.

Because the legislature is required to read and decide upon hundreds of bills during a legislative session, they have several legislative organizations that help with the process, including the Legislative Council and the Legislative Budget Board.

The Legislative Council

The 14-member Legislative Council is a joint legislative committee that supervises a staff that provides research support, information, and bill-drafting assistance to legislators. It is dominated by the speaker and lieutenant governor and includes six members from each chamber appointed by the presiding officers. The Legislative Council staff is specialized in document production, information systems, legal services, and research; it also plays a key role in the redistricting process.[21]

The Legislative Budget Board

The most important of the bills to pass through the legislature is the state's budget, or appropriations bill. The state's budget must be approved for a full two-year cycle and includes items such as transportation, education, health benefits, law enforcement, and state park maintenance. To expedite the process of creating the state's multi-billion-dollar budget, the legislature has the help of the Legislative Budget Board.

Most states, the U.S. government, and most countries have only one budget, but Texas has two. Each agency in state government presents its budget request to both the governor's office and the powerful Legislative Budget Board (LBB). The LBB is a 10-member board whose major function is to provide the governor and the legislature with a draft of the appropriations (budget) bill. The LBB also has broad authority for strategic long-range planning, bill analyses, and policy impact analyses, and it makes recommendations to improve the efficiency and performance of state and local operations.[22]

The 10 members of the board include the lieutenant governor and the speaker of the house, who serve as joint chairs and who appoint an equal number of legislators from each house. The LBB operates continuously, even when the legislature is not in session, under the management of an administrative director appointed by the board; its staff assists the senate and house appropriations committees and their chairs and serves as an oversight committee on how expenditures are managed by the state executive agencies and departments.

Passing Resolutions

Another responsibility of the legislature is to pass resolutions. A **resolution** is a formal expression of legislative sentiment, such as recognizing people, memorializing events, or making decisions that do not involve passing statutes. Resolutions can be passed by only one legislative chamber or passed by both, with or without gubernatorial action. Resolutions can be simple, concurrent, or joint, each with a specific purpose.

A **simple resolution** may be passed by a single house of the legislature; it affects only that house and needs no action by the governor. The House or the Senate can use a simple resolution to change its rules and procedures, to invite a nonmember to address the entire chamber, or to honor someone in the state.

A **concurrent resolution** needs both the House and the Senate to agree by simple majority and is sent to the governor, who then has the option to either sign it or use the veto. Examples of concurrent resolutions include making legislative requests for action by the U.S. Congress, requiring information from state agencies, establishing joint study committees made up of members of both houses, or allowing someone to sue the state.

A **joint resolution** requires approval of both houses but does not require action by the governor. Examples of joint resolutions include proposals of state constitutional amendments, which require a two-thirds vote of both houses before being presented to voters for

resolution
A formal expression of legislative sentiment, such as recognizing people, memorializing events, or making decisions that do not involve passing statutes.

simple resolution
A resolution passed by a single house of the legislature affecting only that house and needing no action by the governor.

concurrent resolution
A resolution requiring the House and the Senate to agree by simple majority and usually requiring approval by the governor.

joint resolution
A resolution, such as one dealing with constitutional amendments, that requires approval of both houses but not the governor.

ratification. The legislature also uses joint resolutions to ratify proposed amendments to the U.S. Constitution.

Representing their Constituents Legislators are elected by voters who have expectations of their representatives. Each senator and representative must decide how to approach the job to meet those expectations. Some legislators see themselves as delegates of those who elected them while others see their role as being trustees of the public interest. As **delegate-type representatives**, members may interpret their role as being in the legislature to represent a majority of voters' interests. Delegates may rely more heavily on the use of polls and other collective information to make decisions. As **trustee–type representatives**, members see themselves as being elected to use their judgment in making decisions in the best interest of the state as a whole regardless of public opinion. Which role representatives use in their approach to the legislative job largely depends on how issues affect their district and the need to strike a balance between the demands of their district and the broader needs of the state.

Conducting Bureaucratic Oversight and Investigations The legislature monitors state agencies to see that these agencies are carrying out public policies as intended—a process known as **bureaucratic oversight**. The legislature requires agencies to submit periodic reports to the legislature concerning how they spend their money and conduct their operations. The legislature has investigative power and has given committees the power to require individuals to testify under oath and to require agencies being investigated to provide documents and records of their operations. Legislative committees commonly use these powers to look into problems in the bureaucracy in order to determine if new or modified legislation is required. Two legislative organizations assist in the oversight and evaluation of state agencies—the Legislative Audit Committee and the Sunset Advisory Commission.

The Legislative Audit Committee The Legislative Audit Committee appoints and supervises the state auditor who, with the consent of the Senate, heads the State Auditor's Office. The six-member Legislative Audit Committee is composed of the lieutenant governor, the chair of the Senate Finance Committee, one senator chosen by the lieutenant governor, the house speaker, and the chairs of the House Appropriations Committee and Ways and Means Committee.

The authority of the office of the state auditor is both broad and deep. Under the direction of the committee, state agencies and departments, including colleges and universities, as well as any entity receiving funds from the state, can be audited. The auditor's office may conduct financial, compliance, efficiency, effectiveness, and special audits as well.

The Sunset Advisory Commission The Texas Sunset Act was enacted in response to the perception by the public that federal and state government spending was escalating beyond control. To enforce the Act, Texas created the 12-member Sunset Advisory Commission, which recommends keeping, abolishing, reorganizing, or giving new scope and authority to state agencies.

The lieutenant governor appoints five senators and one public member, and the speaker appoints five representatives and one public member to the commission. Public members are appointed for two-year terms and legislators for four-year staggered terms. The presiding officers appoint the commission chair. The chair position alternates between Senate and House members. The commission employs a director and a staff that conduct the reviews and present their findings to the commission.

delegate–type representatives
Legislators who interpret their role as being elected to represent a majority of voters' interests in their districts.

trustee–type representatives
Legislators who interpret their role as being elected to use their judgment in making decisions in the best interest of the state as a whole.

bureaucratic oversight
The legislature monitoring state agencies to see that these agencies are carrying out public policies as intended.

The commission reevaluates the need for more than 130 statutory state agencies on a 12-year cycle to determine the need for their continuance. When an agency is created, its particular "sunset" date is included in its charter. About 20 to 30 agencies undergo the sunset review process every biennium.

In the Sunset Advisory Commission's almost 40-year history, the commission has abolished or restructured more than 83 state agencies, including 37 that were completely abolished. The Sunset Advisory Commission estimates that it has saved the state of Texas approximately $980 million during its existence.[23]

Impeachment and Removal from Power The Texas Legislature can call an impeachment session in which the House of Representatives may charge an official with wrongdoing. Executive officers of the state, including the governor, lieutenant governor, the attorney general, the commissioner of the Land Office, and the comptroller of public accounts, may all be impeached by the House. Elected district judges, appellate judges, and the judges of the Supreme Court of Texas and the Texas Court of Criminal Appeals may also be impeached by the House.

Once the House votes to impeach an official, the senate holds a court-like hearing and may, by a two-thirds vote, remove the official from an elected position. The legislature cannot take any other action except for exposing the charges by impeachment and removing the person from office. If impeached officials have committed illegal acts, they may later be prosecuted in regular criminal proceedings. An impeachment session may be called by the legislature without the governor's approval.

Legislative Redress The legislature has the power to monitor and police itself by using a form of **legislative redress**. When wrongdoing by a member of the House or Senate is reported to the leadership, the chamber may create a committee to investigate and determine the fate of the individual who has committed the offense. However, in 2007, House members were caught voting for absentee members using the automated voting machines at each desk.[24] Although this practice was a clear violation of the Rules of the Texas House, no one was disciplined for this behavior.

legislative redress
The power of the legislature to monitor and police itself.

Senate Confirmation Power The Texas Senate must approve of all appointments made by the governor with a two-thirds vote of the senators present. Senatorial courtesy is an unofficial means by which a senator from the home district of an appointee has the right to agree or disagree with an appointment. If the senator objects to a prospective appointee, then the entire Senate will not approve the appointment. It is thus in the governor's best interest to consult with the Senate during the nomination process; knowing in advance that the local senator agrees with the nominee makes confirmation more likely.

The Legislative Process

LO 7.4　Analyze legislative processes, the committee structure, and how a bill becomes a law.

Although many of these functions are important, the major function of a legislative institution is to pass laws. Although the House and Senate use slightly different procedures, the power of the presiding officers is apparent at each step and directly affects whether or not a bill becomes law.

To understand how a bill becomes a law, you must understand the legislative processes that begin with the introduction of the bill into the House or Senate. Although only members of the legislature may introduce a bill or propose a law, many bills originate outside the legislature as ideas of interest groups or the executive branch. Once a bill is introduced, the next steps include referral to committee, committee action, scheduling, floor action, conference committee action, and final passage.

The Legislative Committees

Because of the volume of legislative proposals offered each session, legislators cannot possibly become familiar with all the bills and resolutions—not even all the major ones. As a result, the legislature is organized into committees for the division of labor necessary to ensure that every member participates in the debate and discussion on proposed legislation. Committees are often referred to as "little legislatures," because of the amount of work they do and the power they wield over the law-making process. Once committees make a decision on proposed legislation, it is highly likely that the House or Senate will follow its committees' recommendations.

Legislative committees are organized by subject matter and function. The various types of committees include standing committees, subcommittees, joint committees, ad hoc committees, select committees, conference committees, and interim committees.

Standing Committees
The most common committees are **standing committees**, which are permanent committees that function throughout the legislative session. There are two types, substantive and procedural, which do much of the legislative work in both chambers of the Texas Legislature and are part of the permanent structure of the legislature. Some of the more important substantive standing committees in the Senate include the State Affairs Committee, the Finance Committee, and committees on education, transportation, and criminal justice. Important examples in the house are the State Affairs Committee, the Ways and Means Committee, the committees on higher education, criminal jurisprudence, redistricting, and of course the Appropriations Committee, which operates with several subcommittees.

Substantive committees consider the content of bills that have been introduced; they specialize in various types of public policy, such as taxation, education, or agriculture. They hold hearings and debates; they can **mark up** bills, rewriting or changing them by adding or deleting provisions before reporting them out for consideration by the whole House or Senate. They may also allow bills to be **pigeonholed**, meaning they are set aside and no action is taken on them for the entire legislative session. Many bills are pigeonholed for lack of political support or for lack of time during the short sessions.

Procedural committees deal with the legislative process. For example, the House Rules and Resolutions Committee proposes the rules adopted at the beginning of each regular session to govern legislative procedure throughout the session. The house calendars committees regulate the flow of legislation determining when a bill will be taken up for consideration. Other procedural committees deal with rules and ethics, administration, and investigations.

Standing committees are made up of a chairperson, a vice chair, and members selected by the presiding officers, who must give some preference to the most senior legislators. Most senators and representatives serve on several

standing committees
Permanent committees that function throughout the legislative session. There are two types: substantive and procedural.

mark up
To rewrite or change a bill by adding or deleting provisions before it is considered for passage.

pigeonhole
To set a bill aside and not take any action on it throughout the entire legislative session; many bills are pigeonholed.

IMAGE 7.3 Standing committees do much of the legislative work, gathering information in public hearings and rewriting, or marking up, legislation to make essential political compromises that make a bill's passage possible. Here the Senate State Affairs Committee works on SB 4, the "sanctuary cities" bill.

Marjorie Kamys Cotera

★ CTQ **Explain how the presiding officers influence the work of standing committees.**

committees, and attending committee meetings takes up most of the legislator's time during the one 140-day regular session.

Because several thousand bills are introduced during each legislative session, a division of labor is necessary. Every bill is referred to a standing committee, which conducts public hearings in which witnesses—both for and against—may be heard, debates held, and bills marked up. Because standing committees do the basic legislative work, most legislators rely heavily on them for guidance in deciding how to vote on a bill once it reaches the floor.

subcommittees
Subdivisions of standing committees that consider specialized areas and categories of proposed legislation.

Subcommittees
Some of the standing committees have been further divided into **subcommittees**, which specialize in particular categories of legislation. The subcommittees are usually the first to become familiar with a bill. Made up of a smaller number of standing committee members, subcommittees hold initial hearings, mark up legislation, and then report their work to the full standing committee.

joint committee
A committee that includes both senators and representatives.

Joint Committees
The membership of any **joint committee** is made up of both senators and representatives. Sometimes referred to as boards, these committees can be either temporary or permanent and usually serve a specific function, like the Legislative Budget Board (LBB) or the Legislative Education Board (LEB). The presiding officers appoint the members of these committees, and they either serve as the chair and vice chair or appoint those who do. The purpose of a joint committee is to evaluate state policy proposals that may be considered by both chambers, making the passage of the bill easier and faster in the short session.

ad hoc committees
A committee designed to address one specific task in the legislative process. Its function is temporary, and the committee is disbanded when the function is complete.

Ad Hoc and Select Committees
Ad hoc and select committees are temporary committees as opposed to permanent committees. **Ad hoc committees** are designed to address one specific task in the legislative process, such as conference committees that have the task of ironing out differences between the House and Senate versions of a bill; they are temporary and are disbanded once they have completed their assignment. As with other committees, they are made up of legislators appointed by the presiding officers.

select committees
A temporary committee that is created for one specific purpose and usually serves in an advisory capacity.

Select committees are also temporary committees, usually created to study a particular issue or problem and give advice to the legislature. For example, the speaker appointed a House select committee on opioids and substance abuse in 2017 to take a comprehensive look at the issue and report back to the legislature in 2019. A select committee may include members from one or both chambers, and sometimes includes ordinary citizens with special interest or knowledge about the issue.

interim committees
A committee that meets between legislative sessions.

Interim Committees
Committees that meet between legislative sessions are called **interim committees**; they play a crucial role in the Texas Legislature and help to sustain the biennial legislative cycle. During the 17 to 19 months that the legislature is not in regular or special session, the state is faced with new challenges and needs, so members who are assigned to these committees are directed to consider proposed legislation for the next session or to address new issues that may be facing the state.

Most of the preliminary work on larger, sometimes controversial, bills is done in the interim, which allows the membership to spend less time on those bills during the legislative session. Interim committee recommendations on major issues are often critical when they later get to the floor during the regular session.

The committee structure of the legislature is integral to the consideration of legislation. The presiding officers select committee members and also decide which committee will be assigned a particular bill.

Scheduling

Once it gets out of committee, a bill must be placed on a calendar so that it can be debated, amended, and voted on by each house.

House Calendars Committees

The House of Representatives has two calendars committees that handle the schedules of all bills that come out of their standing committees: the House Committee on Calendars and the House Committee on Local and Consent Calendars. These two committees place a bill on any one of the house calendars:

- Emergency Calendar
- Major State Calendar
- Constitutional Amendments Calendar
- General State Calendar
- Local and Consent Calendar
- Resolutions Calendar
- Congratulatory and Memorial Resolutions Calendar

The calendar schedule includes the time for floor debate and for when the vote on the bill will occur. Members of the House must cast their vote for a bill during the time allotted for the vote, so they must pay special attention to the calendars. Resolutions and bills that pertain to local or noncontroversial matters are placed on the resolutions or local and consent calendars and are usually adopted unanimously as a group without debate for each individual item. The process is not so automatic for major or controversial legislation; when or whether the legislation will be scheduled on a calendar is a decision largely determined by the speaker and the House Calendars Committee chair. If the bill is important or urgent, it may be scheduled on the Emergency Calendar or Major State Calendar, with debate and a preliminary vote scheduled early in the session.

Senate Calendar

Officially the senate has a calendar system that advances bills systematically. A senate rule requires that bills be placed on the calendar and then considered on the senate floor in the same chronological order in which they were reported from the committees. In practice, bills are taken off the calendar for senate floor consideration by a **suspension of the rule**, setting aside the rule that puts bills in chronological order so that other bills can be considered. This requires a three-fifths majority vote of the senate. The process goes something like this: The first bill placed on the senate calendar each session is called a **blocking bill**; it is usually a bill that will never be considered by the full senate. The blocking bill is never taken up on the senate floor; its only purpose is to stop floor consideration of any other bills except by the three-fifths vote to suspend the rule requiring chronological consideration of bills.

suspension of the rule
Setting aside the rule that puts bills in chronological order so that other bills can be considered.

blocking bill
The first bill placed on the senate calendar in each session, which is usually a bill that will never be considered by the full senate.

Three-Fifths Rule

This practice affects the senate's entire legislative process because it allows just 13 senators to block a bill. The irony is that although only a simple majority is necessary for final passage of a bill in the senate, a three-fifths majority is needed to get the bill to the floor for consideration. The senate can let a bill die without having a floor vote for or against—it just fails to reach the floor because it is never taken up for consideration.

For 70 years, the senate required a two-thirds vote to take up a bill for consideration. But in 2011, realizing that enough Democrats opposed the proposed voter identification bill to ensure its defeat, the Republican majority adopted a rule specifically to waive the two-thirds requirement for a bill to require citizens to show state-issued picture identification in order to vote.

Then during the 2015 session, the Republican majority reduced from two-thirds to three-fifths the requirement to take up all bills. Now Democrats cannot thwart Republican leaders on any bill unless they can muster at least 13 senators against taking it up.

Floor Action

Floor action refers to action by the entire House or the entire Senate to debate, amend, and vote on legislation. To take official action, each house requires a **quorum** of two-thirds of its membership to be present. On several occasions, a determined minority opposed to a scheduled action has used quorum-busting tactics by deliberately absenting themselves to deny their chamber the quorum necessary to proceed on any legislation.

During floor action, the Texas Constitution requires that bills must be "read on three consecutive days in each house." The purpose of the requirement was to ensure that laws would not be passed without adequate opportunity for debate and understanding. Bills are read once upon being introduced and prior to being assigned to a committee by the presiding officer. In practice, though, the entire bill is seldom read at this time. Instead, a caption or a brief summary is read to acquaint legislators with the subject of the bill.

The bill is read the second time in each house; if an entire bill is to be read, it is usually on this second reading. At this stage, the bill is debated and amendments may be added by a simple majority. On the third reading, at least one day after approval on the second reading, a two-thirds majority is required to add further amendments, but only a simple majority is required for final passage of the completed bill.

The constitution allows bills that are "cases of imperative public necessity," as so stated in the bill, to be read for the third time on the same day as floor passage, as long as four-fifths of the membership agrees. All bills now routinely contain this provision and usually pass the third reading immediately following floor passage.

House Floor Action The speaker of the house presides over all floor action. The **floor leaders** are the legislators who are responsible for getting legislation passed or defeated. They stand at the front of the chamber, answer questions, and lead debate on the bill; their job is to negotiate, bargain, and compromise to either pass or defeat a bill. Microphones located in the house chamber are available for other lawmakers who wish to speak or ask questions. Each representative is allotted 10 minutes to speak; few of them utilize this limited privilege because most representatives have decided how they are going to vote on bills before they reach the floor.

Floor action usually follows a routine, but it can become quite dramatic and debate can become intense when major legislation is brought up for a vote. Representatives opposing legislation may bring up points of order requiring rulings by the speaker. A **point of order** is a representative's formal objection that the rules of procedure are not being followed on the house floor. If the speaker sustains the point of order late in the session, there may not be time to correct the error, and the bill dies. In 1997, one legislator raised points of order that killed some 80 bills at the end of the session.

Late in the session, opponents may attempt to delay action on a bill in an effort to run out the clock on the session. Unlike state senators, representatives do not have the privilege of unlimited debate, but they have developed other strategies to stop legislative action on a bill that they do not want to come up for a vote. For example, knowing that a bill they oppose

---

floor action
Action by the entire House or the entire Senate to debate, amend, and vote on legislation.

quorum
To take official action, both houses require two-thirds of the total membership to be present.

★ Did You Know?
Frustrated by the failure of a number of bills favored by conservatives, a dozen house members known as the Texas Freedom Caucus objected to bills included on the local and consent calendar that usually pass without objection. As a result, more than 100 bills were killed, among them was a bill to continue essential state agencies that had expired under the sunset review process, and a special session became necessary to salvage these agencies. Because the maneuver happened on Friday before Mother's Day in 2017, it was dubbed the "Mother's Day Massacre."

★ Did You Know?
Floor action can become intense. During the 2017 session, Rep. Matt Rinaldi angered several Latino legislators when he said he had called the US Immigration and Customs Enforcement (ICE) to take some SB 4 protesters into custody. Each side accused the other of threatening violence, and video showed the legislators shoving each other.

floor leaders
The legislators who are responsible for getting legislation passed or defeated.

point of order
A formal objection that rules of procedure are not being followed on the house floor.

is scheduled to come up for debate, opponents may engage in **chubbing**, which slows down the whole legislative process (see Image 7.4). Chubbing includes debating earlier bills for the maximum allotted time, asking the bill's sponsor trivial questions, and proposing so many amendments and raising so many points of order that the house does not get around to the bill to which they object—the ultimate goal being that the session ends before the bill can reach the floor for a vote.

chubbing
Slowing the legislative process by debating earlier bills for the maximum allotted time, asking the bill's sponsor trivial questions, and proposing so many amendments and raising so many points of order that the house does not get around to the bill to which they ultimately object.

IMAGE 7.4 Representative Terry Canales tweets from the House floor in the midst of chubbing during the penultimate day of the 2015 session for the second reading of a bill to take place. Democrats had been chubbing on bills like HB 1798 in order to kill a bill that was further down the calendar (HB 4105) that would have forbidden the state government or local governments from using public funds to issue same-sex marriage licenses. Opponents of HB 4105 were successful as the clock struck midnight on May 14 before it could be voted upon, but their chubbing resulted in dozens of other bills that were a high priority for many legislators also dying along with it, hence the smell of dead bills and desperation among legislators to which Canales refers.

Terry Canales
@TerryCanales40

⚙   👤+ Follow

As HB1798 proceeds, the smell of dead bills and legislative desperation fills the chamber. #chub #txlege

RETWEETS   LIKES
12   12

5:52 PM - 13 May 2015

↩   ♻ 12   ♥ 12   •••

Screen Shot

★ CTQ **How does the short legislative session empower legislators willing to employ delaying tactics such as chubbing?**

voice vote
An oral vote that is not put in the official record.

To vote, house members insert ID cards that allow them to push buttons to record an "yea," "nay," or "present" vote on a large electronic scoreboard. The vote each representative makes is visible as green, red, and white lights next to each legislator's name. In the past, lawmakers decided many bills by **voice vote** only, casting an oral vote that was not recorded in the official record. Casting oral votes did not provide constituents with a way to know how lawmakers voted on bills because their votes were not recorded. A state constitutional amendment finally ended this practice by requiring **recorded votes** at least on a bill's final passage; members' votes must now be entered into the official record of each house.

recorded votes
On final bill passage, votes and the names of those casting them are recorded in each house's journal.

Senate Floor Action   In the Texas Senate, all floor action is presided over by the lieutenant governor. Because most bills that come up for a vote in the senate are voted

★ **Did You Know?** Legislators sometimes allow other legislators to vote for them, although the process is illegal. Sometimes it even appears that ghosts can come back and vote on bills. On August 7, 1991, three votes were cast on Representative Larry Evans's electronic voting machine on the House floor after his death!

filibuster

A prolonged debate by a senator to delay passage of a bill.

off of the calendar by a three-fifths vote, it usually means that the bill has already been considered and very little debate is needed. Only rarely does a senator opposing a bill resort to a **filibuster**—a prolonged debate to delay passage of a bill—on the senate floor. Senators may use a filibuster either to attract public attention to a bill that is sure to pass without the filibuster or to delay legislation in the closing days of the session. In fact, just the threat of a filibuster late in the session may be enough to force a bill's supporters to change the content of the bill to reach a compromise with the dissatisfied senator.

If a filibuster does occur, it means it was impossible to reach a compromise or that the bill's supporters refused to be intimidated by the threat of a filibuster. Wendy Davis, at the time a Democratic senator from Fort Worth, used the filibuster to protest the billions of dollars in spending cuts to public education that resulted from the 82nd Legislative Session. The filibuster forced then-Governor Rick Perry to call a special session to address education spending. Known for filibusters, Senator Davis later conducted a filibuster of legislation to restrict abortions and again forced a special session that gained nationwide attention.

IMAGE 7.5 Representatives urge a yes floor vote on an "annexation reform" bill in 2017. The electronic tote board in the background is used to tally votes. Floor debate rarely determines how legislators will vote on a major bill—they usually decide how they will vote long before the bill reaches the floor.

★ **CTQ** **What political factors affect legislators' decisions to support or oppose legislation?**

committee of the whole

The entire 31-member senate acting as a committee.

conference committee

A temporary committee that meets to resolve differences between Senate and House versions of a bill; a separate conference committee is appointed for each bill with differences between the House and Senate versions.

The entire 31-member senate may act as a committee called a **committee of the whole**, which helps to speed up the process for bills to be considered or voted on. The lieutenant governor appoints a senator to preside over the 31-member committee, and only a simple majority rather than the usual three-fifths is necessary to consider legislation. The lieutenant governor may debate and vote on all questions, but otherwise the senate rules are observed. No journal is kept of the proceedings.

Usually after a modest amount of debate, the Texas Senate takes a vote without the benefit of an electronic scoreboard. Senators hold up a single finger to vote "yea" and two fingers to vote "nay." A clerk records the vote, and only a simple majority is necessary for passage.

Conference Committees

Often the House and Senate pass differing versions of the same bill and a temporary **conference committee** must be appointed to resolve differences between the two versions. Conference committees are made up of five senators and five representatives, and a separate conference committee is appointed for every piece of legislation that passes both houses in differing form.

★ **Did You Know?** Former Texas Senator Bill Meier set the world record for a filibuster in May 1977 by talking for 43 hours, breaking Senator Mike McKool's old record of 42 hours and 33 minutes.

Ap Images /Tamir Kalifa/Austin American-Statesman

To reach the floor for a final vote, a compromise proposal must receive a favorable vote of a majority of the committee members from each house to be reported out of the committee and back to the floor as the **conference committee report**. If a conference committee cannot resolve conflicts between the House and Senate versions of a bill, it is not likely to go back to the floor for a final vote nor to reach the governor for signature.

After a bill has been reported from the conference committee, it may not be amended by either house but must be accepted or rejected as it is written or sent back to the conference committee for further work. In practice, because of the volume of legislation that must be considered in the limited time available, the Texas Legislature tends to accept the conference committee compromise between the House and Senate versions of a bill, and final passage is by a simple majority of both houses.

conference committee report

A compromise between the House and Senate versions of a bill reached by a conference committee and then delivered to each house.

How a Bill Becomes a Law

Figure 7.7 shows the basic steps the Texas Legislature uses to pass legislation. This illustration follows a bill that is first introduced in the House, such as the state appropriations bill,

FIGURE 7.7 How a Bill Becomes a Law

The basic legislative steps are introduction, standing committee consideration, scheduling, and floor debate in each house. This diagram takes the appropriations bill (HB 1) through the legislature from introduction in the Texas House to signing by the governor. Other bills may originate in the Texas Senate and follow similar steps to passage.

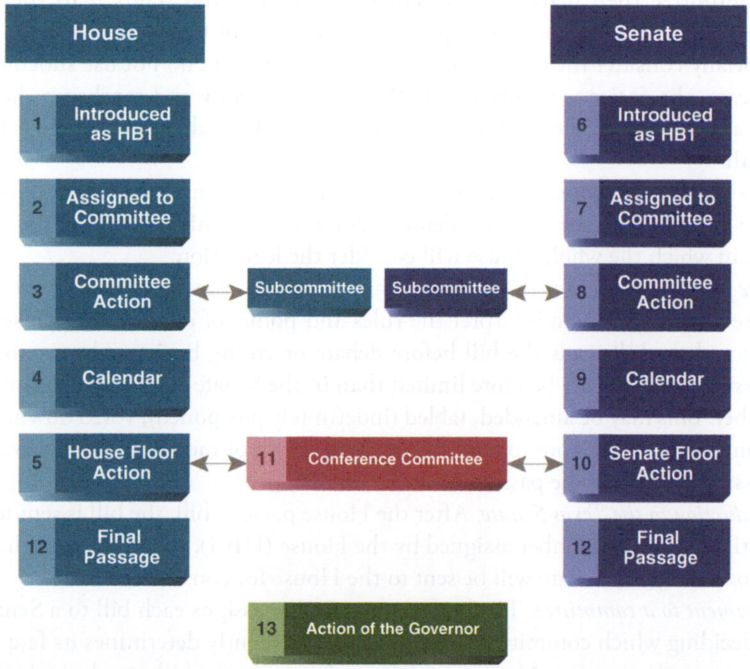

★ CTQ Explain the role of the presiding officers as a bill works its way through the legislative process.

but remember that many bills also originate in the Senate. The numbers in Figure 7.7 correspond to the numbers in the discussion.

1. *Introduction to the Texas House.* Only a representative may introduce a bill in the House, and only a senator may do so in the Senate. Sometimes a senator and a representative agree to introduce the same bill in each of their respective chambers to speed the process. Introduction is followed by a simple reading of the title or synopsis of the bill so that it can be entered into the record; this is considered the first reading of the bill. The first bill introduced in the House of Representatives is the state appropriations bill, designated HB 1. As discussed previously, any bill introduced in the Senate would be given a number reflecting its origin in the Senate (e.g., Senate Bill 13, or SB 13).

2. *Assignment to a committee.* The speaker assigns bills to committees in the House based on their content. Naturally, the appropriations bill is assigned to the House Appropriations Committee. The speaker sometimes has flexibility as to which committee will initially review a bill because several committees have overlapping jurisdiction. In that case, the speaker can frequently determine the fate of the bill by sending it to a committee that will handle the bill the way he wants. If he supports the bill, the speaker will refer it to a committee that will send a favorable report to the floor; if the speaker opposes the bill, he will send it to a committee that will pigeonhole the bill, and it will not reach the floor for a vote.

3. *House committee action.* As noted earlier, committees are often called "little legislatures" because of the power they have over bills. In both the committee and the subcommittee, witnesses who support or oppose the bill may be allowed to testify. Witnesses may be lobbyists, concerned citizens, or bureaucrats who may be affected by the bill. The subcommittee then marks up the bill with changes and sends it to the committee, where it may be further marked up. The Appropriations Committee has subcommittees to initially consider the bill, but most House committees do not use subcommittees; in that case, the entire committee initially hears testimony and marks up the bill. Committees may then report on the bill favorably or unfavorably or may refuse to report on it at all.

4. *House calendars.* A bill that is reported favorably by the committee is placed on one of the house calendars by one of the calendars committees. This establishes the approximate order in which the whole House will consider the legislation.

5. *House floor.* The speaker of the house has the power to recognize representatives on the House floor and also to interpret the rules and points of order. The representative who sponsored the bill reads the bill before debate or voting begins. The size of the House necessitates that debate be more limited than in the Senate—usually 10 minutes for each member. Bills may be amended, tabled (indefinitely postponed), voted down, or sent back to committee. "Yea" votes of only a simple majority of members present and voting are necessary for a bill to be passed.

6. *Introduction to the Texas Senate.* After the House passes a bill, the bill is sent to the Senate but still carries the number assigned by the House (HB 1). Likewise, bills that have been first passed by the Senate will be sent to the House for consideration.

7. *Assignment to a committee.* The lieutenant governor assigns each bill to a Senate committee; deciding which committee considers a bill frequently determines its fate.

8. *Senate committee action.* After committee assignment, the bill may be assigned to a subcommittee, which may want to hold public hearings and have witnesses testify. The subcommittee and then the whole committee may amend, totally rewrite, pigeonhole, or report favorably or unfavorably on a bill.

9. *Senate calendar.* As described earlier, the Senate has only one calendar of bills, which lists the bills in the order they come out of committee. The Senate calendar is rarely followed.

In the usual procedure, a senator makes a motion to suspend the regular calendar order and consider a proposed bill out of sequence. The lieutenant governor must recognize the senator who will make the motion and if three-fifths of the senators agree, the bill is ready for action on the Senate floor.

10. *Senate floor.* The president of the senate (the lieutenant governor) has the power to recognize senators who wish to speak, to vote in the event of a tie, and to interpret rules and points of order. At this time, the bill's sponsor may read the bill in its entirety in the Senate chamber. The Senate then debates the bill, perhaps adding amendments and passing the bill by a majority vote.

11. *Conference committee.* If the Senate makes changes in the House-passed version of a bill, a conference committee is necessary to resolve the differences between the two houses. A separate conference committee is selected for each bill on which House and Senate versions differ. The conference committee then reports the compromised version.

12. *Final passage.* The compromised version of the bill is sent first to the chamber where it originated and then to the other chamber for final approval. The final reading of a bill in both chambers happens at this time. Both the lieutenant governor and the speaker of the house must sign the passed version of the bill before it goes to the governor.

13. *The governor.* The governor has several options concerning an act arriving on his or her desk. First, the governor may sign it into law. Second, the governor may choose not to sign, in which case it becomes law in 10 days if the legislature is in session or in 20 days if the legislature is not in session. Third, the governor may choose to veto the act, but the veto can be overridden by a two-thirds vote in each house. The governor must either accept or veto the complete act if it does not contain provisions for appropriating funds. For appropriations acts, the governor may use the line-item veto to kill any budget item.

The governor often uses the veto late in the legislative session, or within 20 days after the session has ended, without fear of the legislature's overriding it because a veto cannot be overridden in a subsequent session. If the governor signs a bill, it will become law in 90 days—sooner if it has adequate funds for implementation or the legislature has designated it as emergency legislation. If the act requires the expenditure of funds that have not already been designated for it, the comptroller of public accounts must certify that adequate revenue is available for its implementation or a four-fifths majority in each house would be required to allow deficit spending.

Applying What You Have Learned about the Texas Legislature

LO 7.5 **Apply what you have learned about the Texas Legislature.**

You have learned about the general features of the state legislature, but you may feel that it is an abstraction to discuss short legislative sessions and overworked staff, the steps in the legislative process, and whether legislators consider themselves to be delegates or trustees. So we asked state Senator José Rodríguez to give you a taste of what it is like to be a state legislator. After you have read his essay, we will ask you to link theory and actual practice in the Texas Legislature.

The son of migrant farm workers, Texas state Senator José Rodríguez was the first in his family to attend college before becoming an attorney. Today he represents Senate District 29 (SD 29), which includes El Paso, Hudspeth, Culberson, Jeff Davis, and Presidio counties and both urban and rural constituencies along more than 350 miles of the Texas–Mexico border.

POLITICS IN PRACTICE
On Being a State Legislator: A View from the Inside

by José Rodríguez
STATE SENATOR DISTRICT 29

In early 2014, constituents approached my office with a concern. The El Paso Independent School District (EPISD), which offered a groundbreaking dual-language program piloted at several campuses, wanted to expand the program district-wide.

However, there was a potential roadblock. Dual-language programs immerse students in instruction that is half in one language and half in the other. The experts who designed the EPISD program determined that the best combination for doing this is with English as a Second Language–certified teacher for the English-language component and a Bilingual Education–certified teacher for the Spanish-language portion.

Definitions of dual-language and requirements for teachers of the program are in the state education code. The Texas Education Agency had combined two parts of the code in 2012, and in so doing had come up with a new interpretation of the rules; teachers in the English-language component of the dual-language program were therefore required to be bilingually certified. This required EPISD and other school districts across the state to apply for an exception every year in order to maintain their programs.

Over the course of 2014, my office worked with stakeholders—parents, teachers, education experts, administrators, and the TEA—to come up with a bill that would clarify the rules and allow EPISD and other districts around the state, representing about 800 schools using the successful formula, to continue their work.

This is just one example of how legislation comes to my office, how much effort it takes to work something through the system, and how important it is to have the people engaged with their government. Legislation can come to us through constituents, advocates, particular interests, or our own analysis, or a combination of all these.

While there was little to no opposition to this bill, it still took me, my staff, parents, teachers, and other advocates hundreds of hours of effort to develop the bill. They discussed the issue in private and organizational meetings, took action by writing letters of support to legislators, attended committee meetings, held rallies, and spread information through newsletters and social media.

The most important thing to know about our form of government is that it takes the engagement of the people. It takes hard work by constituents, grassroots and professional advocates, staff members, and elected officials to keep our democracy functioning. It takes people like you.

During the legislative session, my office is a nonstop stream of visitors. Many are lobbyists, the professionals who represent various interests, from business to labor and everything in between. Others are single-issue advocates, and still others are day visitors from around the world. We receive tourists, school groups, and constituents from our home communities, just to name a few types of visitor.

The advocates, at least the most effective, enter armed with detailed information about legislation. It must be clear, accurate, and brief. During the 84th Texas Legislature's regular session in 2015, more than 6,500 bills were filed, with about 20 percent passing. Each of those 6,500 bills took hundreds of hours of public and private meetings, research, and, for many of them, debate in committee and on the House and Senate floors.

I start each day with a binder outlining my schedule (largely committee hearings and meetings) with the backup materials for each item. I review news clips, memos, and other relevant items. Sometimes the day begins early, and a hearing or meeting starts it off. For my staff, the day begins with preparing the materials I will need for the day, as well as their own meetings with other staff, constituents, and stakeholders.

Let's go back to the dual-language bill, which was filed in the Senate as SB 159 and in the House as HB 218. Often, bills are filed in both chambers to create options, because bills move at different speeds through each chamber based on myriad factors. Each bill must be heard in the committee, and then on the floor, of its respective chamber. If it passes the hurdles of its originating chamber, it moves to the next, where it goes through the same process—first a committee vote, and then a full floor vote. In this case, it was the House version of the bill that moved more quickly, and we were able to guide it through the Senate, where it also passed.

As a result, EPISD and other districts around the state were relieved of the uncertainty about who was able to teach their dual-language programs. And many, many Texans were engaged in the political process along the way. I personally visited with many of them in the Capitol in 2017, and I expect to see some of them there again in 2019.

Our system is not perfect, but it does demand perfect attendance. Together, we make it work.

1. How does Senator Rodriguez show the difficulty a legislator faces in dealing with detailed public policy with limited staff during a short legislative session?
2. Would the senator consider himself a delegate or a trustee? Explain.

★ Chapter Summary

LO 7.1 Describe the limits on the Texas Legislature and evaluate the concept of the "citizen legislature." Since the time the Texas Constitution was written, citizens have mistrusted institutions of government, including the state legislature. As a result, Texans have limited their state legislature to meeting only once every two years in regular session and not allowed the legislature to call itself into special session. Regular sessions are limited to only 140 days, and special sessions can last no more than 30 days. Legislative salaries are among the lowest in the nation, and legislative staffs are so restricted that legislators have become dependent on outside interests for both income and information.

LO 7.2 Analyze the selection of Texas legislators, their qualifications, and the impact of campaign financing and redistricting on elections. Texas representatives must be U.S. citizens at least 21 years old who have lived in the state

for two years; senators must be U.S. citizens at least 26 years old with five years of state residence. The Texas Legislature meets in odd-numbered years for 140 days, and has 31 senators and 150 representatives. The legal requirements to run for the legislature obscure the fact that most legislators are business or legal professionals and male. The legislature does not mirror the population of Texas as a whole. In addition, a lack of campaign funding makes it more difficult for the average citizen to be elected to the legislature.

Politically, most Texas legislators are conservative Republicans with access to major campaign contributors. Districting also has a significant impact on the kinds of people who are actually elected to the Texas Legislature. As in most states, Texas legislators have gerrymandered districts to give the majority party a significant advantage. A few states have handed the process of redistricting to a nonpartisan commission, and many Texans would favor this alternative.

LO 7.3 Analyze the powers of the legislature and its presiding officers. The state's bicameral legislature is presided over by the lieutenant governor in the Texas Senate and the speaker in the House of Representatives. The presiding officers manage floor debate and are able to use their appointive and procedural powers to control the legislative process. They appoint the members of the Legislative Budget Board, the Legislative Audit Committee, the Legislative Council, and the Sunset Advisory Commission, all of which are integral to the legislative process. They also have control over committee membership in the legislature and have decision-making powers over how bills make their way through the committee structure.

LO 7.4 Analyze legislative processes, the committee structure, and how a bill becomes a law. Any legislator may propose a piece of legislation, but the idea for much legislation originates with interest groups or the executive branch. Once introduced in the House or Senate, the bill is sent to a standing committee for initial review. Committees review proposed legislation, gather information by holding hearings, and mark up bills. Before the bill can become law, it must be scheduled for floor debate. The two houses use differing means to place legislation on the floor for a vote: the Senate uses a three-fifths rule, and the House uses the calendars. A bill must be passed by a majority vote before it is sent to the other house, where it follows similar steps through committee, scheduling, floor debate, and final vote. The presiding officers may appoint a conference committee to resolve differences between the House and Senate versions before a bill is approved and sent to the governor to be signed or vetoed.

LO 7.5 Apply what you have learned about the Texas Legislature. You explored what it is like to be a Texas legislator from the viewpoint of Senator Rodríguez. You examined what the short legislative session and limited staff means in practice as the senator deals with the details of public policy, and you evaluated the senator's role to determine if he sees himself as a delegate or a trustee.

Key Terms

Review Questions

LO 7.1 Describe the limits on the Texas Legislature and evaluate the concept of the "citizen legislature."

- What is legislative amateurism, and how does it affect the legislative process?

- Explain how low salaries, short biennial sessions, and limited staff are designed to curtail the legislature's power. Explain how such limits increase the influence of interest groups.

LO 7.2 Analyze the selection of Texas legislators, their qualifications, and the impact of campaign financing and redistricting on elections.

- What is descriptive representation, and how does the make up of Texas legislature compare with the state's population as a whole?

- What are the formal and informal qualifications for holding office in the Texas legislature?

- What are the demographic and political factors that affect who becomes a member of the legislature?

- How does the ability to attract campaign support and funding relate to who runs for the legislature?

- What are geographic single-member districts? Explain the process of gerrymandering.

LO 7.3 Analyze the powers of the legislature and its presiding officers.

- List the powers of the speaker and lieutenant governor. Explain how each of their powers is used to control the legislative process.

- How are the legislature's presiding officers selected? What are the limits on their power?

- Explain the legislative processes of passing bills and resolutions, representing constituencies, exercising bureaucratic oversight, and the power of impeachment.

- Explain the self-policing power of legislative redress and Senate confirmation powers.

- Explain the powers of the Legislative Council, the Legislative Budget Board, the Legislative Audit Committee, and the Sunset Advisory Commission.

- Explain the role of the speaker and lieutenant governor in selecting the members of these institutions

of leadership, and explain how state agencies are affected by them.

- Describe the types of legislative committees, and explain their function in the legislative process.

LO 7.4 Analyze legislative processes, the committee structure, and how a bill becomes a law.

- Describe step by step how a bill is introduced, referred to committee, marked up and reported by committee, scheduled for floor debate, debated, and voted upon in the Texas House. Then, take a bill through the same steps in the Texas Senate. Finally, explain how a compromise is reached between the House and Senate versions of a bill.

- Show how the presiding officers are able to influence the legislative process at each of the steps just described.

- Explain the role of the governor in the legislative process.

Think Critically and Get Active!

Adopt a bill of your own on a topic in which you have an interest. Or visit the website of an organization that you support or admire and choose a bill that they support. Find out which interest groups favored or opposed your bill. Why did they take the positions they took? Did your bill pass, or did it not make it out of the legislature? Where did it stop? What action did the governor take on the bill?

Start the exercise at Texas Legislature Online at **www .capitol.state.tx.us** and click on "Legislation." You will also find help at the Legislative Reference Library website at **www.lrl.state.tx.us**. Information about the governor's role and other topics can be found at **www.gov.texas.gov**.

Become a legislative intern for the Texas Legislature. Contact a member of the Texas House or Senate about internship opportunities. For a listing of Texas House members, check **www.house.state.tx.us**; for a listing of Texas Senate members, check **www.senate. state.tx.us**. To locate your representative and senator, as well as representatives and senators from nearby districts, visit **www.fyi.legis.state.tx.us**. You can also get in touch with your college or university, which may have its own legislative internship program.

Find out how interest groups rate your legislators. Interest groups rate legislators' votes on major public policy issues. Pick interest groups that share your policy views, and see how they rate Texas legislators. Vote Smart at **www.votesmart.org/interest-groups/TX** is a comprehensive site that links to such interest groups as business, environmental organizations, civil rights organizations, right-to-life groups, and gun rights groups. Interest groups provide a vital public service by keeping track of major legislative issues of which many ordinary citizens are not aware.

Texas was the first state to adopt official Twitter hashtags. Stay current with legislation and legislators by using the Texas Legislature's official hashtag, #txlege. For a list of all of the Texas legislators who are on Twitter, visit **www.lrl.state.tx.us/legeLeaders/ members/twitterDirectory.cfm**. Keep in mind that some legislators are very active on Twitter while others are not.

★ PRO **How can you use various interest group ratings of legislators' votes to help you determine how you will cast your ballot on election day?**

8 ★ The Executive

Texans reelected Republican Greg Abbott as the state's governor in 2018. In this chapter, you will evaluate the governor's powers and whether the state's executive branch is truly accountable to you and other voters.

Fort Worth Star-Telegram/MCT/Getty Images

Learning Objectives

LO 8.1 Describe the governor's office and the characteristics of the typical Texas governor.

LO 8.2 Analyze both the governor's powers of persuasion and the limits on them.

LO 8.3 Analyze the structure and characteristics of the Texas bureaucracy.

LO 8.4 Analyze the political relationships among executive agencies, the public, interest groups, and elected officials.

LO 8.5 Evaluate strategies for holding state agencies accountable.

LO 8.6 Apply what you have learned about the Texas executive branch.

Although the Texas Constitution designates the governor as chief executive, the executive branch is separated into various offices and agencies that are often beyond the governor's effective control. The division of Texas executive power is largely based on the Jacksonian democratic theory that most major officeholders should be elected. The legislature has somewhat strengthened the governor's administrative influence over several agencies, but powerful special interest groups, bureaucrats, the legislative leadership, and the public generally prefer a decentralized government and a weak chief executive. As a result, the Texas administrative structure will continue to be a hodgepodge of administratively independent entities, with no single official formally responsible for either policy initiation or implementation.

The lack of administrative authority does not mean the governor's office lacks the potential for meaningful political power. An astute, politically savvy governor can exert significant influence on both legislative and administrative policy by asserting legislative powers, managing media coverage, using party influence, and strategically appointing allies to boards, commissions, and the judiciary.

Long tenure and solid interest group support are also important factors in a governor's influence. A long-serving governor with the support of powerful interest groups can wield significant influence over the enactment and implementation of public policy in Texas. To be most effective, a governor must have appointed most members of administrative boards and commissions, convinced legislators that he or she will punish errant behavior, and won the support of powerful political and financial special interests.

The Governor's Office: Qualifications, Tenure, and Staff

LO 8.1 **Describe the governor's office and the characteristics of the typical Texas governor.**

To become governor, a candidate must meet formal or legal qualifications as well as informal requirements that are imposed by the state's political culture.

Qualifications and Elections

As is usual with elective offices, the legal requirements for becoming governor are minimal: One must be 30 years of age, an American citizen, and a resident of Texas for five consecutive years prior to running for election. Whereas the formal qualifications for governor are easily met, the informal criteria are more selective.

Ethnicity and Gender Since the Texas Revolution, all governors have been Anglos, and historically most governors have been males. The only female governor of Texas before Ann Richards (1991–1995) was Miriam A. Ferguson, who served for two nonconsecutive terms (1925–1927 and 1933–1935). She ran on the slogan "Two Governors for the Price of One" and did not really represent a deviation from male dominance in Texas politics, for it was clear that her husband, former Governor James E. Ferguson (who had been impeached in 1917 and banned from holding public office), exercised the power of the office. In reality, Governor Richards was the first truly independent woman to serve as Texas's chief executive.

Career The typical governor will usually be successful in business or law; in fact, more than one-half of the governors who have served since 1900 have been lawyers. The governor will probably have a record of elective public service in state government or some other source of name recognition.

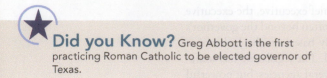

Today a Republican Texas was a solidly Democratic state following Reconstruction. This solid support began to deteriorate in the 1960s, and the state's first Republican governor in more than a hundred years, Bill Clements, was elected in 1978 and again in 1986, after having lost his 1982 reelection bid. Since 1996, Republicans have won 144 straight statewide elections, including six consecutive gubernatorial elections.

The Nomination The Republican primary has in recent years become a joust between business-oriented centrist conservative candidates and tea party or movement conservative candidates, with the more conservative candidates often winning. Once the election cycle's marquee event, featuring a battle between the party's conservative and progressive wings, the Democratic gubernatorial primary has lost much of its luster over the past two decades as conservative Texans largely migrated to the Republican Party in state elections. While there is never a shortage of talented Republicans who covet their party's nomination, the Democratic Party has in recent election cycles at times had a difficult time recruiting a top-tier gubernatorial candidate.

Well-Funded Campaigns Money is a critical factor in any serious campaign for Texas governor. Although the candidate who spends the most does not always win the office, a hefty bankroll is necessary for serious consideration. Texas is a populous and geographically vast state, with 20 separate media markets, including two among the top 10 in the nation (Dallas–Fort Worth and Houston) and two others among the top 40 (San Antonio and Austin) where advertizing is expensive. Campaign costs are rising, and the two major party candidates for governor combined now frequently spend sums of between $50 and $100 million to reach Texas voters in each election cycle.

Tenure, Removal, Succession, and Compensation

As in 47 other states, Texas governors serve a four-year term. Unlike most states, however, there is no limit on the number of terms that a governor may serve (see How Does Texas Compare). For example, former Governor Rick Perry assumed office on December 21, 2000, replacing Governor George W. Bush, who resigned following his election as the 43rd president of the United States. Perry would go on to win gubernatorial elections in 2002, 2006, and 2010 before opting not to seek reelection in 2014. He left office on January 20, 2015, after having been governor for a state record of 14 years and one month. Prior to Perry's tenure as governor, the record consecutive tenure in office was seven years and six months by Allan Shivers between 1949 and 1957 (before 1974 governors were elected for two-year terms).

The governor may be removed from office only by impeachment by the House of Representatives and conviction by the Senate. **Impeachment** is bringing formal charges against a public official; it is the legislative equivalent of indictment for improper conduct in office and requires only a simple majority vote. Conviction by the Senate removes the official from office and requires a two-thirds majority.

If the governor is impeached and convicted, dies, or resigns, the lieutenant governor becomes governor and the Texas Senate then elects one of its members to serve as the acting lieutenant governor until the next election. This process took place most recently in 2000 when Governor Bush was elected president. Following Bush's resignation, Lieutenant Governor Perry became governor and state senator Bill Ratliff was chosen by his colleagues to serve as the acting lieutenant governor.

impeachment
Bringing formal charges against a public official; the legislative equivalent of indictment for improper conduct in office.

Compensation The governor's annual salary is set by the legislature. At present, it is $153,750 and stands in marked contrast to the low salaries paid to legislators. Though the governor's salary is in the top quartile nationally, many elected and unelected state personnel earn noticeably more than the Texas governor.

In addition to the Texas Governor's Mansion, which serves as the official residence for the governor and his or her family, there is an expense account to keep the residence maintained and staffed. The governor also has a professional staff and security detail with offices in the capitol building and in the mansion. An adequate staff is important because the modern chief executive depends heavily on staff to carry out the duties of office.

> **Did you Know?** The Texas governor earns less than the governors of California, Delaware, New Jersey, New York, Pennsylvania, Tennessee, and Virginia. The head football coach at UT-Austin earns more than 30 times as much as Texas's governor.

Staff

The governor's increasing involvement in legislative affairs and the public's growing demands have intensified pressure on the chief executive's time and resources. The Texas governor, like all executives in modern government, depends on others for advice, information, and assistance when making decisions. A good staff is a key ingredient for successful service as governor.

Evaluating Appointees Among the most important concerns of the governor's staff are political appointments. Each year, the governor makes several hundred appointments to various boards, commissions, and executive agencies. The executive also fills newly created judicial offices and those vacated because of death or resignation. Staff evaluation of potential appointees is necessary because the governor may not personally know many of the individuals under consideration.

Legislative Liaisons Legislative assistants serve as liaisons between the office of the governor and the legislature. Their job is to stay in contact with key legislators, committee chairs, and the legislative leadership. These assistants are, in practice, the governor's lobbyists. They keep legislators informed and attempt to persuade them to support the governor's position on legislation. Often the success of the governor's legislative program rests on the staff's abilities and political expertise.

Budget Preparation Some administrative assistants head executive offices that compile and write budget recommendations and manage and coordinate budget activities within the governor's office.

Communications and Scheduling Staff members manage the governor's relations with the media and public, responding to requests for interviews, distributing press releases, arranging press conferences, and maintaining the governor's presence on social media. Staff members also exercise administrative control over the governor's schedule of ceremonial and official duties.

Planning The governor is the official planning officer for the state, although coordination and participation by affected state agencies are voluntary. The planning divisions also help coordinate local and regional planning between the councils of governments in an effort to bring the work of these jurisdictions into harmony with state goals. In addition, national and state funds are available through the governor's office to local units of government for comprehensive planning.

How Does Texas Compare?

Governors' Term and Term Limits

New Hampshire and Vermont elect their governors for two-year terms. While governors of the other 48 states serve for four-year terms, most states limit the number of terms they may serve. Many of them limit the governor to two consecutive terms in office but allow a former governor to seek reelection after sitting out one term. In some states, the governor may seek reelection once but may not serve more than two terms over a 12- or 16-year period. A few states impose a lifetime limit of two terms; the governor of Virginia may not serve consecutive terms but may seek the office again after sitting out one term.

Texas is one of only 14 states that do not limit the number of terms its governor may serve. Former Texas Governor Perry was in office for more than 14 years after replacing Governor Bush in 2000 and then winning three consecutive elections. Some argue an incumbent governor enjoys too many electoral advantages, such as name recognition, media coverage, fund-raising ability, and patronage, to be allowed to seek unlimited reelection. They argue that unlimited terms allow governors to gain too much power as they become too cozy with interest groups and too insulated from the needs of the general public.

Others argue term limits deprive voters of the ability to keep a governor they support in office, and that if voters believe a governor is not doing a good job they will cast him or her out at the next election. Opponents of term limits also argue that experience in office gives elected officials a deeper understanding of public policy and the needs of the general public.

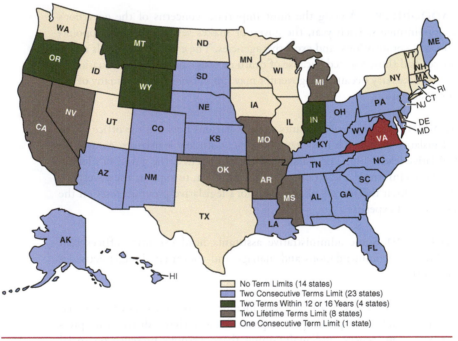

No Term Limits (14 states)
Two Consecutive Terms Limit (23 states)
Two Terms Within 12 or 16 Years (4 states)
Two Lifetime Terms Limit (8 states)
One Consecutive Term Limit (1 state)

FIGURE 8.1 Gubernatorial Term Limits: How Texas Compares

Ballotpedia: The Encyclopedia of American Politics.

FOR DEBATE

★ CTQ   Should Texas place limits on gubernatorial reelection like a majority of the other states, or should it trust voters to reelect the governor as many times as they wish?

★ CTQ   If Texas were to place some type of limit on gubernatorial reelection, what type of limit among those used by the other states do you think would be best for Texas?

The governor's staff is primarily responsible for assisting with the everyday duties of the office but can also play a critical role in attempts to persuade legislators, administrators, local governments, and political leaders to follow the governor's leadership.

The Governor's Powers of Persuasion

LO 8.2 **Analyze both the governor's powers of persuasion and the limits on them.**

The governor's ability to influence the making and executing of government policy depends on his or her bargaining skills, persuasiveness, and ability to broker effectively between competing interests—the tools of persuasion. These are **informal**, or **extralegal, powers** of the office not stated in rules, law, or the constitution but are largely derived from the **formal**, or **legal, powers** that are stated in the law or the constitution. They are as important as the legal powers, and the governor's ability to use informal power can determine his or her effectiveness. Compared to governors of other states (especially other populous, industrialized states), the governor of Texas has weak formal administrative powers. However, some Texas governors have been able to exert substantial influence on policy formulation and even on policy execution when the formal and informal powers are enhanced by a fortunate blending of other conditions, such as a charismatic personality, political expertise, prestige, a knack for public relations and political gamesmanship, good relations with the press, supporters with political and economic strength, a favorable political climate, and simple good luck.

informal (extralegal) powers
Powers that are not stated in rules, law, or a constitution but are usually derived from formal or legal powers.

formal (legal) powers
Powers that are stated in the law or the constitution.

The Governor as Chief of State

The governor, as the first citizen of Texas, serves as a symbol of Texas as surely as the bluebonnet or the Alamo. A significant part of the governor's job is related to the pomp and ceremony of the office. These ceremonial duties include greeting delegations and groups at the state capitol, appearing at major sporting events such as Super Bowl LI in Houston, visiting disaster areas such as Port Aransas, Corpus Christi, and Houston after Hurricane Harvey, riding in parades, and attending county fairs and local festivals throughout the state.

This ceremonial role is important because it can contribute indirectly to the governor's leadership effectiveness through increased popularity and prestige. The governor also broadens the image as first citizen to that of the first family of Texas whenever possible; voters identify with the governor's family, so the governor's spouse is often included in the visual enactment of the office.

International Function The governor performs ceremonial duties and represents the state at meetings with foreign officials and other governors. She or he also serves as a member of (or appoints representatives to) numerous multistate organizations and conferences that work to coordinate relations between Texas and other state governments. These conferences deal with civil defense, nuclear energy, and other important matters. It is also the governor's responsibility to ask other states to extradite fugitives from Texas law and to grant or refuse like requests from other states.

Federal–State Relations In order to facilitate the governor's job of coordinating the activities of state agencies and local governments with the national grant-in-aid programs, the Texas government has established an office in the nation's capital, the Texas Office of State–Federal Relations (OSFR). The governor appoints (and may remove) the director of this office. The director also serves as spokesperson for state agencies and local governments when their ideas and points of view differ from those held by the federal government.

The governor may request federal aid when the state has suffered a disaster, a drought, or an economic calamity. As chief of state, the governor often flies over or visits a disaster area to make a personal assessment of the damage—and also to show the victims that the governor is concerned for their welfare. Then, as a "voice of the people," the governor may make a highly publicized request for federal aid to the area.

Governor as Party Chief

Although there are varying degrees of competition from other elected officials and from political activists, governors usually maintain the de facto leadership of their political party by virtue of their position as the state's chief executive. The governor's explicit or implicit support is highly valued by legislators seeking reelection and by politicians aspiring to statewide, legislative, judicial, or local office.

National Party Leader
The Texas governor can also be a leader in national politics if so inclined. Unless the Texas governor experiences serious public relations problems, any candidate from the governor's party who seeks the nomination for president would want the support of the governor of the nation's second most populous state. During the administration of President Barack Obama (2009–2017) the Texas governor assumed an even more prominent role than usual, as the most visible and influential Republican chief executive in the country.

Positions on National Issues
National politics also affords the governor an opportunity to build a firm, clear image for the people back home. The governor can take positions on political issues that do not involve the Texas government and over which the governor has no direct control but with which people can easily identify, such as foreign policy or national defense.

Legislative Tools of Persuasion

Ironically, the most influential bargaining tools that the Texas governor has are legislative. The governor must use these tools effectively in order to be successful in office.

Message Power
As a constitutional requirement, the governor must deliver a State of the State message at the beginning of each regular legislative session. This message includes the outline for the governor's legislative program. Throughout the session, the governor may also submit messages calling for action on individual items of legislation. The receptiveness of the legislature to the various messages is influenced by the governor's popularity, the amount of favorable public opinion generated for the proposals, and the governor's political expertise.

message power
The constitutional power to deliver the State of the State message and special messages to the legislature.

The **message power** to deliver the State of the State message and special messages to the legislature derives from the state constitution, but this formal power of the governor is enhanced by the visibility of the office. Through the judicious use of the mass media (an informal power), the governor can focus public attention on a bill when it might otherwise be buried in the legislative morass. An effective governor, however, "goes to the people" only for the legislation considered most vital to the interest of the state or to the governor's political and financial supporters.

Emergency Item
The regular session of the Texas Legislature takes place every two years between January and late May/early June for a total of 140 days. The legislature can usually hold a floor debate and vote on a bill during the first 60 days of the regular session only if the governor has declared it to be an emergency item.[1] As a result, the governor often sets the legislative agenda at the start of the session when a bill will face less competition for time and attention; he or she is able call public attention to certain issues and signal which topics should be given highest priority that year.

IMAGE 8.1 The governor delivered his State of the State address to the legislature to the approval of its presiding officers. The governor's influence depends on interest group support, party loyalty, and the popularity of his agenda with the general public.

AP Images/Eric Gay

★ CTQ **What specific formal powers does the governor use to persuade the legislature to adopt his or her proposals?**

Budget Powers The governor is designated as the chief budget officer of the state. Every other year, the various agencies and institutions submit their appropriation requests to the governor's staff and to the staff of the Legislative Budget Board. Working from these estimates, the governor and staff prepare a budget that is determined by both the state's estimated income and the estimated cost of program proposals. When completed, the budget is submitted to the legislature.

Veto One of the governor's most powerful formal legislative tools is the **veto**, a power that allows the governor to stop a bill from becoming law. After a bill has passed both houses of the legislature in identical form, it is sent to the governor. If signed, the bill becomes law; if the governor vetoes the bill, he or she issues a proclamation such as the one shown in Image 8.2 and returns it to the legislature with a message stating the reasons for opposition. The legislature has the constitutional power to override the governor's veto by a two-thirds vote, but in practice vetoes are usually final.

Because legislative sessions in Texas are short, many important bills are passed and sent to the governor in the final days of the regular session. The governor need take no action on the legislation for 10 days when the legislature is in session (20 days when it is not in session), so he can often wait until the legislature has adjourned and thereby ensure that a veto will not be overridden. In fact, it is so difficult to override a veto, that since the end of World War II, out of 1,279 vetoes, only one has been overridden.[2] Thus, the veto gives the Texas governor a strong bargaining position with legislators.

veto
A power that allows the governor to stop a bill from becoming law.

IMAGE 8.2 This is an image of Governor Greg Abbott's 2015 veto of HB 3511 (discussed in Chapter 6). Governor Abbott explained his objections to the bill saying that he believed it would have weakened the state's ethics laws governing state officeholder financial disclosure by creating a "spousal loophole."

PROCLAMATION
BY THE
Governor of the State of Texas

TO ALL TO WHOM THESE PRESENTS SHALL COME:

Pursuant to Article IV, Section 14, of the Texas Constitution, I, Greg Abbott, Governor of Texas, do hereby disapprove of and veto House Bill No. 3511 as passed by the Eighty-Fourth Texas Legislature, Regular Session, because of the following objections:

Texans deserve accountability and transparency from their public officials. House Bill 3511 weakens the ethics laws governing officeholder financial disclosures. I cannot allow that.

Since the Eighty-Fourth Texas Legislature, Regular Session, by its adjournment has prevented the return of this bill, I am filing these objections in the office of the Secretary of State and giving notice thereof by this public proclamation according to the aforementioned constitutional provision.

IN TESTIMONY WHEREOF, I have signed my name officially and caused the Seal of the State to be affixed hereto at Austin, this 19th day of June, 2015.

GREG ABBOTT
Governor of Texas

ATTESTED BY:

CARLOS CASCOS
Secretary of State

★ CTQ　**Why is it so difficult for the legislature to override a veto by the Texas governor?**

No Pocket Veto   The Texas governor lacks the pocket veto that is available to many other chief executives, including the president of the United States. The pocket veto provides that if the executive chooses to ignore legislation passed at the end of a session, it dies without ever taking effect. By contrast, if the Texas governor neither signs nor vetoes a bill, it becomes law. By not signing a bill and allowing it to become law, the governor may register a symbolic protest against the bill or some of its provisions.

Line-Item Veto   The most important single piece of legislation enacted in a legislative session is the appropriations bill. If it should be vetoed in its entirety, funds for the operation of the government would be cut off, and a special session would be necessary. Thus Texas, like most other states, permits the governor a line-item veto, which allows the governor to veto provisions related to funding for specific items or projects without killing the entire bill.

If used to its fullest potential, the line-item veto is a very effective legislative tool. Money is necessary to administer laws; therefore, by vetoing an item or a category of items, the governor can in effect kill programs or whole classes of programs. Because the appropriations bill is usually passed at the end of the session, the line-item veto is virtually absolute. The governor cannot, however, reduce the appropriation for a budgetary item, as governors in some other states may.

Threat of a Veto   A veto threat is an informal power that enhances the governor's bargaining power with legislators, enabling the governor to shape the content of legislation while it is still in the legislature. By threatening a veto while a bill is still being considered by the legislature, the governor is often able to persuade legislators to reshape the bill to meet the governor's wishes.

Both the veto and the line-item veto are negative tools that simply kill bills or programs; they do not let the governor directly shape legislation. However, by threatening to use these formal powers, the governor can often persuade the legislative supporters of a bill to change its content or face the prospect of a veto. In this way, a compromise can often be negotiated. Although the veto itself is a negative, or reactive, power, the veto threat can be used positively, or proactively, to affect the content of bills during the legislative process.

The threat of a veto can also be used to consolidate lobby support for the governor's legislative proposals. Lobbyists may offer to support the governor's position on legislation if the governor will agree not to veto a particular bill that is considered vital to the interests of their employers or clients. The governor can thus bargain with both supporters and opponents of legislation in order to gain political allies.

The governor can also use this powerful informal tool of persuasion to influence bureaucrats. Bureaucrats are very active in the legislative process, often seeking increased funding for favorite programs and projects or seeking authorization to administer new programs. Because of this, the governor may be able to influence the administration of existing programs by threatening to withhold funds or veto bills actively supported by an agency. The agency's legislative liaison personnel (its lobbyists) may also be encouraged to support the governor's legislative program in exchange for support (or neutrality) with respect to agency-supported bills.

Special Sessions   The constitution gives the governor exclusive power to call the legislature into special session and to determine the legislative subjects to be considered during the session. The legislature may, however, consider any non-legislative subject, such as confirmation of appointments, resolutions, and impeachment, even if the governor does not include it in the call. Special sessions are limited to a 30-day duration, but the governor may call them as often as he or she wants. For example, after Wendy Davis successfully filibustered legislation restricting abortion access in a 2013 special session (as discussed in Chapter 3), Governor Perry within hours called a second special session in which the legislation easily passed.

Often when coalitions of legislators and lobbyists request a special session so that a "critical issue" can be brought before the legislature, other coalitions of legislators and interests oppose consideration of the issue and, therefore, oppose calling the special session. Calling a special session can create a dilemma for the governor, because groups whose priority legislation was not passed during the regular session can feel slighted if their issue is not among the topics placed on the special session agenda by the governor.

Because there is seldom any legislation that does not hurt some and help others, the governor has an opportunity to use the special session as a valuable bargaining tool. The governor may or may not call a special session on the basis of some concession or support to be delivered in the future. The supporters and opponents of legislation may also have to bargain with the governor over the inclusion or exclusion of specific policy proposals for the special session. Of course, this position may not be open to negotiation if the governor has strong feelings about the proposal and is determined to call (or not to call) a special session. If the governor does think that an issue is critical, the attention of the entire state can be focused on the proposal during the special session much more effectively than during the regular session.

Fact-Finding Task Forces Governors also appoint task forces, or "blue-ribbon commissions," consisting of influential citizens, politicians, and members of concerned special interest groups. Governors may use task forces to show urgent concern for a problem while buying time to study complex, difficult, or controversial policy decisions. Governor Abbott has appointed task forces to make recommendations to deal with difficult, long-term issues such as maternal mortality and flood control projects after Hurricane Harvey.

The Governor as Chief Executive

The Texas Constitution charges the governor, as the chief executive, with broad responsibilities. However, it systematically denies the governor the power to meet these responsibilities through direct executive action. In fact, four other important elective executive offices—lieutenant governor, comptroller of public accounts, attorney general, and commissioner of the General Land Office—are established in the same section of the constitution and are legally independent of the governor, thus undermining the governor's executive authority. Such a system, in which voters elect several independent executives, is known as a *plural executive system* and is illustrated in Figure 8.2.

Other provisions in the constitution further fragment executive power. For example, the constitution establishes the elective Railroad Commission of Texas, and although the State Board of Education can be either elected or appointed, it too is elected. Moreover, the Texas Legislature, by statute, has systematically assumed executive functions such as budgeting and auditing. It has also established an independently elected Commissioner of Agriculture, and created a multitude of boards and commissions to administer state laws that are independent of the governor's direct control. Although the members of these commissions usually are appointed by the governor, their terms are staggered, and it may be several years before the governor's appointees constitute a majority of a board or commission. Boards and commissions perform such functions as hiring and firing agency directors and establishing general agency policies.

Appointive Powers An effective governor will use the power of appointment to the maximum. The governor appoints some state executives like the secretary of state directly. When vacancies occur in elected executive and judicial positions, the governor appoints someone to fill the unexpired term until the next election.

The power to fill vacancies gives the governor some power over the courts. It is not uncommon for judges to retire or resign before the end of their term. The governor is empowered to fill these vacancies with the appointed judges, who then enjoy the advantages provided by

FIGURE 8.2 The Plural Executive System in Texas

This figure shows that Texas divides executive power as voters separately elect the governor, lieutenant governor, attorney general, comptroller of public accounts, commissioner of agriculture, and commissioner of the General Land Office.

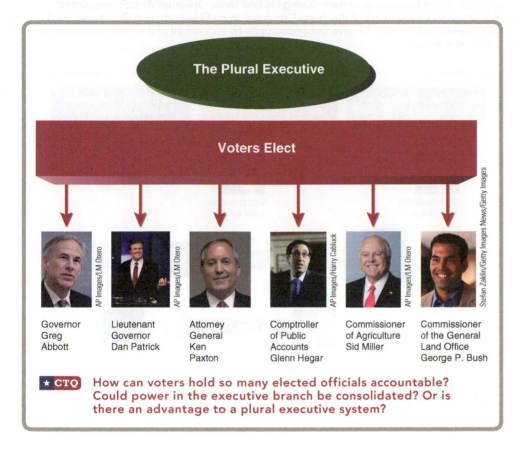

The Plural Executive

Voters Elect

| Governor Greg Abbott | Lieutenant Governor Dan Patrick | Attorney General Ken Paxton | Comptroller of Public Accounts Glenn Hegar | Commissioner of Agriculture Sid Miller | Commissioner of the General Land Office George P. Bush |

★ CTQ   **How can voters hold so many elected officials accountable? Could power in the executive branch be consolidated? Or is there an advantage to a plural executive system?**

incumbency in the next election, including enhanced name recognition and fund-raising ability.

Probably the most important appointments that the governor makes are to the independent boards and commissions. The members of these boards establish general administrative and regulatory policy for state agencies or institutions and choose the top administrators to carry out these policies.

The governor's ability to affect board policy through appointments is not immediate, however, as the boards are usually appointed for fixed six-year staggered terms that expire at two-year intervals. The governor may fill vacancies in an unexpired term, but may not remove a commissioner appointed by a previous governor. Because only one-third of these positions become vacant every two years (barring the resignation or death of a board member), a first-term governor will have appointed a majority of most boards only in the second half of his or her term. Figure 8.3 shows how these overlapping terms limit the governor's ability to control the board and commission system and most state agencies.

★ **Did you Know?** Governor Greg Abbott has the power to appoint members to well over 200 boards and commissions. Many of these are governing boards but some are advisory. Ultimately, a governor gets to appoint more than 3,000 people to various positions during the course of a four-year term.

FIGURE 8.3 Overlapping Terms at the TCEQ

This figure illustrates the effect of staggered terms on the governor's powers. Board or commission members serve six-year terms that expire at two-year intervals. The governor may fill vacancies in an unexpired term, but may not remove a commissioner appointed by a previous governor. During his first term, Governor Abbott appointed two of the three members of the Texas Commission on Environmental Quality and had to get reelected in order to have the opportunity to appoint all of the commissioners to full six-year terms.

Perry Appointees before January 2015

Abbott Appointees between January 2015 and 2019

Next Term Appointees After January 2019

Term 2011–2017 | Commissioner, Toby Baker | Term 2017–2023 | Commissioner, Toby Baker

Term 2013–2019 | Commissioner, Bryan Shaw | ? | 2019–2025

Term 2015–2021 | Chair, Jon Niermann | ?

Office of the Commissioners

★ **CTQ**   **Why does Texas make it so difficult for its chief executive to control agencies within the executive branch?**

Interest Group Concerns   Interest groups in Texas are vitally concerned with seeing that the "right kinds" of appointees are selected to serve on these boards and commissions. Industry interest groups are particularly eager to have an industry advocate (often an ex-lobbyist or industry executive) appointed to the board that oversees and sets policy for "their" agency. Appointment of a consumer advocate could disorient the close relationship that usually exists between an industry and its agency.

There can also be competing interest groups within one industry that may bargain individually with the governor for an appointee who is favorable to their particular viewpoint. Thus, an appointment to important boards often results in intense lobbying by special interest groups, which conversely gives the governor opportunities to develop support for policies and to help secure funds for future political campaigns.

senatorial courtesy
The tradition of allowing a senator to reject the governor's appointment of a political enemy from the senator's district.

The Influence of the Senate   Senators may also influence appointments from their districts as a result of **senatorial courtesy**, which is a tradition allowing a senator to reject the governor's appointment of a political enemy from the senator's district. Other senators show their courtesy to the disgruntled senator by refusing to confirm the appointment of his or her political enemy to a board or commission.

Bureaucratic Concerns Administrators want the governor to appoint sympathetic commissioners who share their goals. Making appointments that are friendly to administrator interests can strengthen a governor's influence with these administrators.

Removal Powers Although the governor possesses broad appointive power over boards and commissions, the governor's powers of removal are limited. He or she may remove members of the executive office and a few minor administrators. The governor may also remove, for cause and with the consent of two-thirds of the senate, his or her own appointments to boards and commissions. If the governor decides that an elected official is administering a law so as to violate its spirit, there is no official way to force a revision of such administrative interpretation or procedures. In general, the governor cannot issue directives or orders to state agencies or remove executive officials who do not abide by his or her wishes. Only by focusing public attention on the agency and garnering public support can the governor convince an administrator to resign.

Law Enforcement Powers The governor has little law enforcement power. Following Texas tradition, the state's law enforcement power is decentralized at both the state and local levels.

At the state level, the Texas Rangers and the Texas Highway Patrol Division are responsible for law enforcement. Both agencies are under the jurisdiction of the director of the Department of Public Safety (DPS), who is chosen by the Public Safety Commission. The five members of the Public Safety Commission are appointed by the governor for six-year staggered terms.

At the local level, police functions are under the jurisdiction of county sheriffs and constables (who are elected) and city chiefs of police (who are appointed by city officials). Criminal acts are prosecuted either by elected district or county attorneys or by appointed city attorneys. The judiciary, which tries and sentences criminals, is elective (except for municipal judges, who are appointed by city officials).

Military Powers The governor is commander-in-chief of the state militia, which consists of the Texas National Guard and the Texas State Guard. The governor appoints (and can remove) an adjutant general who exercises administrative control over both units. The Texas National Guard comprises the Texas Army National Guard (18,000 troops) and the Texas Air Guard (3,000 troops) and is funded primarily by the U.S. government. It is required to meet federal standards and may be called to active duty by the president. In the event the Texas National Guard is nationalized, command passes from the governor to the president.

The Texas State Guard was established during World War II and serves as a backup organization in the event that the National Guard is called to active duty by the president. It cannot be called into active duty by the federal government, and its approximately 2,000 members receive no pay unless mobilized by the governor.

The governor may declare a state of emergency (usually after a riot or a natural disaster) and send these units to keep the peace and protect public property. The governor may employ the militia, according to Article 4, Section 7, of the Texas Constitution "to execute the laws of the state, to suppress insurrection, and to repel invasions."

Clemency Powers The 1876 Texas Constitution granted the governor virtually unlimited power to pardon, parole, and grant reprieves to convicted criminals; these are known as **clemency powers**. Several governors were very generous with these powers, resulting in a 1936 constitutional amendment that established the Board of Pardons and Paroles. Many of the powers that had been held by the governor were transferred to the board, which grants, revokes, and determines the conditions for parole and makes clemency

clemency powers
The governor's powers to pardon, parole, and grant reprieves to convicted criminals.

recommendations to the governor. However, the governor appoints the board's members and can grant less clemency than recommended by the board but not more. Nor can the governor any longer interfere in the parole process by blocking early releases from prison. The governor can postpone executions, but only for 30 days.

The Texas Administration

LO 8.3   **Analyze the structure and characteristics of the Texas bureaucracy.**

bureaucracy
The part of the executive branch that actually administers government policies and programs.

The Texas administration or **bureaucracy** is the part of the executive branch that actually administers government policies and programs. Although nonelected employees handle day-to-day operations of the government, implement government policies, and provide services to the public, the various divisions of the executive branch are usually headed by a single elected administrator, an appointed executive, or a multimember board or commission that may be appointed, elected, or ex officio.

The most distinctive characteristic of the Texas administration, however, is that no one is really in charge of the administrative apparatus as a whole. As in many other states, the administration of laws in Texas is fragmented into several elective and numerous appointive positions. Although the principle of hierarchy exists within each department, the formal organization of the Texas bureaucracy follows the basic administrative principle of hierarchy only as far as the elected administrator or appointed board. The Texas bureaucracy can be visualized as approximately 200 separate entities, each following its own path, often oblivious to the goals and ambitions of other agencies.

Elected Executives and the Plural Executive System

The constitutional and statutory requirement that several administrators (in addition to the governor) be elected was a deliberate effort to decentralize administrative power and prevent any one official from gaining control of the government.

Lieutenant Governor
The lieutenant governor is elected for a four-year term, with no limit on the number of terms that may be served. Although technically part of the executive branch, most of the lieutenant governor's power actually comes from serving as the powerful president of the Texas Senate. In that position, the lieutenant governor is as an ex officio chair of the Legislative Budget Board and of the Legislative Council. The lieutenant governor is also a member of the Legislative Audit Committee and, if he or she desires, can exercise considerable personal influence on the Sunset Advisory Commission and the Legislative Criminal Justice Board. These legislative boards and commissions are not part of the executive branch, but they can have major influence on it as they conduct continuing reviews of administrative policies and make recommendations to the legislature.

Attorney General
The attorney general is elected for a four-year term, with no limit on the number of terms that may be served. Holding one of the four most powerful offices in Texas government, the attorney general is the lawyer for all officials, boards, and agencies in state government. The legal functions of the office include assisting in child support enforcement, antitrust actions, Medicaid fraud investigation, crime victim compensation, consumer protection, and other civil actions concerning insurance, banking, and securities. A broad spectrum of the state's business—oil and gas, law enforcement, environmental protection, highways, transportation, and charitable trusts, to name only a few—is included under the overall jurisdiction of the attorney general.

attorney general's opinion
The attorney general's interpretation of the constitution, statutory laws, or administrative rules.

The attorney general performs two major functions for the state. One is to give an **attorney general's opinion**, which is an interpretation of the constitution, statutory laws, or administrative rules. As the state's chief lawyer, the attorney general advises his or her client. In the absence of a prior judicial interpretation, the attorney general has the power to interpret law or to give an opinion as to whether or not a law or practice conflicts with other laws or the Texas or U.S. constitutions. Although these advisory opinions are technically not legally binding, they carry great weight. If state officials ignore these opinions, the attorney general will not defend them in court.

Government officials at all levels may request an opinion from the attorney general, and although they are not legally binding, government officials usually follow them. The attorney general's opinion is normally requested only after the legal staff of another agency or official has been unable to reach a decision. The requests usually concern difficult questions, and several staff attorneys general consider each question. Only agencies and officials may request these opinions, and then only for official business.

A legislator may request an attorney general's opinion during the legislative session (sometimes merely to delay, and thus help kill legislation). The vagueness of laws and, particularly, the ambiguity of the Texas Constitution require the attorney general to give numerous opinions each year.

The second major function of the attorney general is to represent the state and its government in both civil and criminal litigation. The attorney general represented the state in several suits defending the state's legislative districting system and photo ID requirements for voters while challenging the federal government on Obama-era EPA regulations and relief to undocumented immigrants. More recently, the attorney general has turned attention to other matters such as defending the state's abortion restrictions and helping challenge Houston for granting spousal benefits to same-sex spouses of city employees.

IMAGE 8.3 Attorney General Ken Paxton was first elected in 2014.

AP Images/Harry Cabluck

★ **CTQ** **Which are the attorney general's most important powers? Why?**

The attorney general also represents Texas in legal conflicts with other states such as boundary disputes with Louisiana and Oklahoma. The attorney general enforces business regulations by bringing suits against corporations for antitrust, consumer protection, or other regulatory violations.

However, the attorney general's criminal power is relatively narrow because the primary responsibility for criminal prosecution in Texas lies with the locally elected district and county attorneys. In fact, in 2015 Attorney General Ken Paxton himself was indicted in a Collin County district court on two first-degree felony charges of securities fraud and a third-degree felony charge of failing to register as a financial advisor.

Comptroller of Public Accounts
The comptroller (pronounced as controller) is elected for a four-year term, with no limit on the number of terms that may be served. The functions of the comptroller's office encompass either directly or indirectly almost all

IMAGE 8.4 Comptroller of Public Accounts Glenn Hegar is the state's chief tax collector and financial officer.

AP Images/Harry Cabluck

★ CTQ   **What is the comptroller's most important constitutional duty? Explain how Texas enforces its balanced budget requirement.**

financial activities of state government. The comptroller is the chief tax collector and the chief pre-audit accounting officer in the Texas government. The comptroller manages state deposits and investments and pays warrants on state accounts in his or her capacity as the state's chief treasurer. The comptroller also provides information on spending and debt at the state and local level, supports state economic development efforts, manages the state's college education funds, and coordinates the state's procurement system.

The comptroller's most important constitutional duty is to certify the state's approximate biennial revenue. The constitution requires a balanced budget, and the state legislature may not appropriate more funds than are anticipated as income for any two-year period. The comptroller also certifies the financial condition of the state at the close of each fiscal year. Any surplus funds can give the governor and legislature fiscal flexibility for tax cuts or increased appropriations without increasing taxes.

Commissioner of Agriculture   The commissioner of agriculture is elected for a four-year term, with no limit on the number of terms that may be served. The commissioner oversees the Texas Department of Agriculture (TDA). The TDA was created by statute in 1907 and is responsible for the administration of all laws as well as research, educational, and regulatory activities relating to agriculture. The duties of the department range from checking the accuracy of scanners at grocery stores and gasoline pumps at service stations (the next time you are filling up look for the Texas Department of Agriculture sticker on the pump) to determining labeling procedures for pesticides and promoting Texas agricultural products in national and global markets. The commissioner also administers the Texas Agricultural Finance Authority, which provides grants and low-interest loans to businesses that produce, process, market, and export Texas agricultural products.

Like the U.S. Department of Agriculture, the TDA is also charged with administering laws for both consumer and labor protection. This is a classic example of an agency with two contradictory constituencies, and at times conflicting interests, being given the function of protecting each interest from the other. A conflict of interest between these potentially incompatible groups is almost inevitable.

Commissioner of the General Land Office   The commissioner of the General Land Office is elected for a four-year term, with no limit on the number of terms that may be served. Principal duties of the commissioner are managing and collecting income from rentals and leases for state-owned lands; awarding oil, gas, and hard-mineral leases for exploration and production on state lands; and leasing mineral interests in the state's riverbeds and tidelands, including bays, inlets, and offshore areas within 10.35 miles (three marine leagues) of the Texas coast. The commissioner also enforces the Texas Open Beaches

Act to insure that the public continues to have free and unfettered access to Texas beaches, defined as the point between the water and the normal high tide line.

The land commissioner serves ex officio on several boards, as is the case with many officials, and chairs the important Veterans Land and the School Land boards, whose programs are administered by the General Land Office. (Ex officio members hold their positions because they hold some other elective or appointed office.) The Veterans Land Board was established by a grateful state after World War II. It loans money to veterans for land purchases and home purchases or improvements as well as manages four cemeteries for veterans.

The School Land Board oversees approximately 13 million acres of public land and mineral rights properties, including the Gulf Coast beaches and bays and "submerged" lands up to 10.35 miles out into the Gulf of Mexico. The lease and mineral income from these public lands varies with the production and price of oil and natural gas, but revenues from the leases, rents, and royalties from the public lands are dedicated to the Permanent School Fund. Interest and dividend income from this fund are used to assist the state's public schools.

Appointed Executives

Besides the executives that voters directly elect, several executives are appointed by the governor. In many states, the governor appoints the heads of most state agencies, but in Texas only a few agency heads answer directly to the governor. As shown in Figure 8.4, directly appointed executives include the secretary of state, the adjutant general, the health and human services commissioner, the insurance commissioner, and the education commissioner.

IMAGE 8.5 Land Commissioner George P. Bush manages Texas public lands and beaches.

Pool/Hulton Archive/Getty Images

★ CTQ **Why are lower-level executive offices considered stepping-stones to higher office? What resources could George P. Bush bring to a campaign?**

★ **Did you Know?** George P. Bush's mother, Columba Bush (née Garnica Gallo), was born and raised in the Mexican state of Guanajuato, where she met his father, former Florida governor Jeb Bush, who was teaching English there as part of a high school project.

Secretary of State
Appointed by the governor, with confirmation by the senate, the secretary of state serves at the pleasure of the governor. The secretary is keeper of the Seal of the State and also serves as chief election officer for Texas, administers Texas's election laws, assists local election officials, and receives state election results. The secretary of state's office also serves as a repository for official, business, and commercial records filed with the office, publishes government rules and regulations, and commissions public notaries. In recent years, under former Governor Perry and Governor Abbott, the secretary of state also has served as the governor's liaison for Texas border and Mexican affairs and represents Texas at international and diplomatic events as the state's chief international protocol officer.

Adjutant General
Appointed by the governor with the consent of the senate for a two-year term, the adjutant general is the state's top-ranking military officer and exercises administrative jurisdiction over the Texas National Guard and the Texas State Guard.

Health and Human Services Commissioner
The executive director of the Health and Human Services Commission is appointed by the governor with the advice

FIGURE 8.4 Appointed Executives

Although Texas governors share power with several other elected officials, they are designated as the chief executive and have the power to appoint these state executives directly. Governors also appoint numerous boards and commissions.

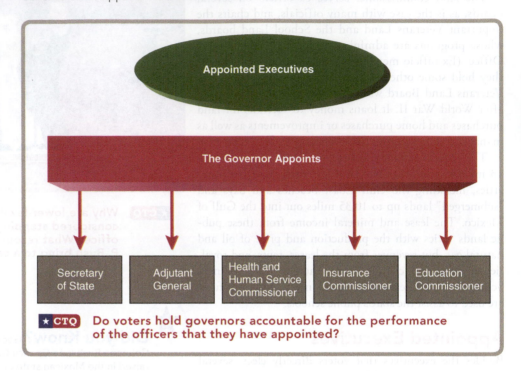

Appointed Executives

The Governor Appoints

| Secretary of State | Adjutant General | Health and Human Service Commissioner | Insurance Commissioner | Education Commissioner |

★ CTQ   **Do voters hold governors accountable for the performance of the officers that they have appointed?**

and consent of the senate. The commissioner heads the Texas Health and Human Services System, an umbrella agency or super-agency that oversees and manages several major health and welfare departments.

The director of the commission is granted extensive administrative and policy-making authority over the departments. The power within the commission clearly rests with the director, who reports directly to the governor. When the 78th Legislature created this structure in 2003, it gave the governor direct administrative control and created one of the few cabinet-style organizations in Texas government.

Insurance Commissioner The commissioner of the Texas Department of Insurance is directly appointed by the governor for a two-year fixed term, subject to senate confirmation. The department monitors and regulates the Texas insurance industry. It provides consumer information, monitors corporate solvency, prosecutes violators of insurance law, licenses agents and investigates complaints against them, develops statistics for rate determination, and regulates specific insurance lines such as property, liability, and life.

Commissioner of Education The commissioner is appointed by the governor with consent of the senate to serve as the state's principal executive officer for education. The commissioner manages the day-to-day operations of the Texas Education Agency. With a number of assistant and associate commissioners and professional staff, the commissioner carries out the regulations and policies established by the legislature and the State Board of Education concerning public school programs.

Boards and Commissions

Approximately 200 elected, appointed, or ex officio boards and commissions supervise state agencies. Their members may be salaried or only reimbursed for expenses. There are also considerable differences in their political power.

Generally speaking, the most important boards are those concerned with chartering or regulating the business, industrial, and financial powers within the state. Power is also measured by the number of people affected by the board's decisions or the size of its agency's appropriations. These are only general measures of power, however, because a relatively minor licensing board such as the Texas Real Estate Commission could be the most important agency in state government to a real estate broker whose license is about to be revoked.

Elective Boards

Elective boards include the Texas Railroad Commission and the Texas State Board of Education.

Texas Railroad Commission

One of the most important state regulatory boards is the Railroad Commission, a constitutionally authorized elective board whose three members serve for overlapping six-year terms. The governor fills vacancies on the board, and these appointees serve until the next general election, at which time they may win election to the board in their own right.

The board is politically partisan and its members must first win their party's nomination before being elected. The chair position is rotated so that each member becomes the chair during the last two years of his or her term. This forces any candidate who is challenging an incumbent commissioner to run against the chair of the commission.

The Railroad Commission was established in 1891 during the administration of Governor Jim Hogg as a populist reform to protect Texas citizens from unfair railroad practices. Its powers were soon expanded to regulate intrastate wheeled carriers, and in 1917 the oil and gas pipelines were added, followed soon after by the authority to regulate oil well drilling and production. The authority to regulate railroads and motor vehicles was gradually stripped away, and in 1994 the Texas Legislature transferred the commission's remaining motor and rail carrier responsibilities to the departments of transportation and public safety.

The commission's duties today are concerned only with the regulation of natural gas utilities, oil and gas pipelines, oil and gas drilling, and pumping activities. It is also responsible for regulation of waste disposal by the oil and gas industry and the protection of both surface and subsurface water supplies from oil- or gas-related residues. Its powers over the petroleum industry have historically made the Texas Railroad Commission one of the most powerful state regulatory bodies in the United States.

Texas State Board of Education

The State Board of Education (SBOE) is elected to serve as the policy-making body for Texas public schools. Members of the State Board of Education are elected in partisan elections to four-year overlapping terms in 15 single-member districts, and together they establish general policy regarding the content of public education, set curriculum standards, adopt instructional materials, approve charter schools, and review rules for teacher certification. The SBOE has been the center of controversy as it deals with sensitive cultural issues in determining policy for kindergarten through 12th grade public education. We will examine these controversial policies in depth in Chapter 12.

Appointed Boards

Appointed boards vary greatly in terms of importance, administrative power, and salary. The members of these boards, who are usually unsalaried, set the policies for their agencies and appoint their own chief administrators. The governor, with the consent of the senate, usually appoints board members, but because of the usual practice of appointing members to staggered terms, up to six years may lapse before a governor fills a board with his or her appointees.

Board appointees are often representatives of groups that have an economic interest in the rules and policies of the board. Appointments may be either a reward for political support or an attempt to balance competing interest groups whose economic well-being is affected by board rules and policies.

Figure 8.5 uses the example of the Department of Public Safety to show that this kind of board and commission system means that the governor does not appoint the actual administrator who manages an agency on a day-by-day basis. Such a system adds another layer of bureaucracy between the elected chief executive and agencies that should be responsible to the public.

Another example of an appointed board that has become quite powerful in recent years is the Texas Commission on Environmental Quality (TCEQ). It operates under three commissioners who are appointed by the governor for six-year overlapping terms. The TCEQ is the primary environmental regulator for the state, overseeing cleanups, permitting industrial plants, and writing rules to govern most aspects of the Texas environment including those to regulate waste disposal and enforce air-quality and drinking-water standards.

Also among the most important and influential appointed boards are the Texas Department of Transportation, the Texas Health and Human Services Commission, the Texas Board of Criminal Justice, the Texas Higher Education Coordinating Board, and the Texas Water Development Board. In fact, most state agencies are run by appointed boards and commissions. Table 8.1 provides additional examples of appointed boards and commissions.

Ex Officio Boards   Numerous boards have memberships that are completely or partly ex officio—that is, boards whose members are automatically assigned because they hold some other position. There are two basic reasons for creating such boards. One is that when travel to Austin was expensive and time-consuming, it seemed logical to establish a board whose members were already in Austin. Another reason is that subject matter expertise on the part of the ex officio members is assumed.

The Texas Bond Review Board is an example of an ex officio board. It has four ex officio members: the governor, lieutenant governor, speaker, and comptroller of public accounts. It reviews and approves all bonds and other long-term debt of state agencies and universities. It also engages in various other functions pertaining to state and local long-term debt.

A number of agency boards have some ex officio members. The Texas Appraiser Licensing and Certification Board (nine members, one ex officio) and the Texas Racing Commission (nine members, two ex officio) are examples of such boards.

Characteristics of Bureaucracy

Although bureaucracy is often thought of as being exclusive to government, it is also common to churches, colleges, corporations, and foundations. Bureaucracies develop wherever human beings organize themselves to systematically accomplish goals and in the process lose some flexibility and efficiency. This discussion concentrates on government bureaucracies, especially those in Texas government.

Size   The complexities of twenty-first-century society, together with increased demands of government at all levels have resulted in a dramatic increase in the number of people employed by public agencies. Large bureaucracies have become the target of some scorn from

FIGURE 8.5 The Board-and-Commission System

For most state agencies, the governor appoints a supervisory board that, in turn, appoints the day-to-day director of the agency. Here you see that the governor appoints the Texas Public Safety Commission that in turn appoints the Director of Public Safety who actually runs the department.

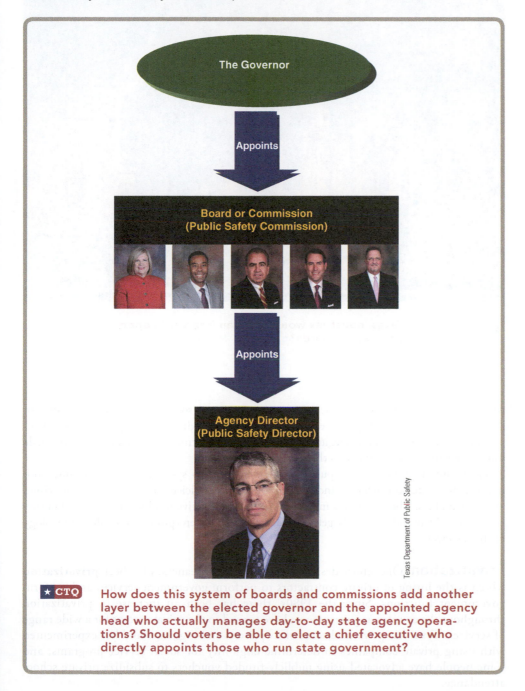

The Governor

Appoints

Board or Commission
(Public Safety Commission)

Appoints

Agency Director
(Public Safety Director)

Texas Department of Public Safety

★ CTQ   **How does this system of boards and commissions add another layer between the elected governor and the appointed agency head who actually manages day-to-day state agency operations? Should voters be able to elect a chief executive who directly appoints those who run state government?**

IMAGE 8.6 The Texas Commission on Environmental Quality, which enforces air quality standards, has resisted implementation of federal Environmental Protection Agency plans.

Tashka/iStock/Getty Images Plus/Getty Images

★ CTQ   **Which Texas industries would have an interest in opposing stricter environmental standards?**

those who have simply lost confidence in our government; some special interest groups, for their own reasons, criticize public employees as a means of discrediting specific government programs. There is, however, a legitimate concern that government agencies need to be made more efficient and accountable to the public.

From time to time, various public officials attempt to systematically streamline both national and state bureaucracies and to make them more efficient and receptive to the wishes of policy makers. These attempts may or may not have positive results, but their level of success varies widely and is based largely on the expectations, perceptions, and political ideology of the reviewer.

privatization
The hiring of private contractors to perform government services and perform government functions.

Privatization One reform designed to streamline bureaucracy has been **privatization** which is the hiring of private contractors to perform government services and perform government functions. Since the 1980s, there has been an increase in privatization throughout the country as governments have turned to the private sector for a wide range of services. Texas has privatized some of its prisons and highways and has experimented with using private companies to determine eligibility for social service programs, and some people have advocated using publicly-funded vouchers to subsidize private school attendance.

Conservative, pro-business citizens often support privatization arguing that contracting with private businesses to provide traditional public services both increases

TABLE 8.1 Examples of Appointed Boards and Commissions in Texas

This table shows selected examples of the numerous boards and commissions appointed by the governor that deal with professional licensing and regulation, public health and welfare, the environment, cultural and educational programs, and industry regulation. In fact, most state agencies are supervised by such appointed boards.

Professional Licensing and Regulation Boards
Texas Board of Nursing
Texas Board of Professional Geoscientists
Texas Real Estate Commission
Texas State Board of Acupuncture Examiners
Texas State Board of Dental Examiners
Texas State Board of Plumbing Examiners
Texas State Board of Public Accountancy
Public Health and Welfare and Environment
Cancer Prevention and Research Institute of Texas
Texas Commission on Environmental Quality
Texas Commission on Jail Standards
Texas Department of Housing and Community Affairs
Texas Indigent Defense Commission
Texas State Soil and Water Conservation Board
Texas Statewide Health Coordinating Council
Cultural and Educational
Governing Board for the Texas School for the Blind and Visually Impaired
Texas Commission on the Arts
Texas Higher Education Coordinating Board
Texas Historical Commission
Texas State Library and Archives Commission
Texas State University System Board of Regents
The University of Texas System Board of Regents
Industry Regulation
Finance Commission of Texas
Credit Union Commission
Governing Board for Manufactured Housing
Public Utility Commission of Texas
Texas Alcoholic Beverage Commission
Texas Funeral Service Commission
Texas State Securities Board

▶ What are the limits on the governor's power to appoint board members?

efficiency and reduces the size, power, and cost of government. They believe that private enterprise is inherently more effective and efficient than the public sector, and that current agencies lack the forces of the profit motive and competition that energize the private marketplace.

spoils system
A system in which elected officials hire campaign workers as public employees.

Skeptics of privatization argue that private businesses are profiteering at the public expense because they are likely to "cut corners" on services to improve their "bottom line." Opponents also contend that private businesses are not accountable to the public because their internal operations are not as well publicized as government activities.

contract spoils, or contract patronage
A practice in which politicians award contracts to their political supporters and contributors in the business community.

Opponents suspect that political contacts and campaign contributions "grease the wheels" for contractors and that a new kind of spoils system is developing. Unlike the historic **spoils system** in which elected officials hired campaign workers as public employees, today's new spoils system is based on the practice of **contract spoils, or contract patronage**, in which politicians award contracts to their political supporters and contributors in the business community. Although the contract patronage system is not new, critics believe that it has become a major political reason for support of the privatization movement. Critics have dubbed this practice "crony capitalism." See the Texas Insiders feature.

Texas Insiders

Privatization: Insider Influence, Cronyism, and Reform

Texas has begun a partial privatization of state services, contracting with private firms to do work that was formerly done by state employees. Critics have charged that the process has often become fraught with insider influence, cronyism, and conflict of interest to the detriment of competent, efficient administration of public services.

In 2005, the Texas Health and Human Services Commission (HHSC) awarded Accenture and a team of contractors a $900 million contract to operate call centers to determine eligibility for various social services including food stamps. IBM sued the HHSC over its handling of the contract, alleging excessive influence by HHSC chief information officer Gary Gumbert, who had formerly worked for an Accenture subcontractor and continued to receive a pension from the company.

Ultimately, Accenture's mismanagement of the contract resulted in a backlog of thousands of food stamp applications at its Austin call center even as regular state employees continued to do much of the work that Accenture was responsible for. After spending $522 million on the program, HHSC abandoned its contract with the company.

By 2014, the media spotlight was again focused on HHSC contracting practices. In 2012, HHSC

official Jack Stick awarded a $20 million no-bid contract for Medicaid fraud-tracking software to 21st Century Technologies (21CT), a little-known Austin company. Eyebrows were raised when it was learned that 21CT lobbyist James Frinzi had once been Jack Stick's business partner and that Stick may have also sought to arrange a job for himself at 21CT. Investigation of the original contract as well as scrutiny of a pending $90 million contract extension with 21CT in 2014 (which was cancelled) led to the resignation of several HHSC employees, and its commissioner Kyle Janek later resigned as well.

The 21CT scandal moved the legislature in 2015 to reform the state contracting process by limiting the size of no-bid contracts, preventing vendors with poor ratings from competing for contracts, forbidding state officers from doing business with companies in which they have a financial interest, and banning state employees from taking jobs with companies with which they have been doing business for at least two years after leaving state employment.

★ **SRQ**   **Can the state contracting process be reformed to assure efficient, neutral management of public services? Or is the process inevitably subject to manipulation by elites seeking political and personal gain?**

Hierarchy All bureaucracies are formally characterized as **hierarchies**, structures in which several employees report to a higher administrator who reports to higher authorities until eventually all report to the single individual with ultimate authority. Theoretically, formal authority and directives flow down through the chain of command to lower levels and information filters up through channels to the top from lower-level employees in the field. A framework of rigid rules and regulations formally assigns authority to various levels and defines the relationship between those individual bureaucrats who are of nearly equal rank.

A model hierarchy is similar to the military chain of command for the U.S. Army. The president as the commander-in-chief is at the top and outranks the secretary of defense, who outranks the secretary of the army, who outranks all the generals, who in turn outrank all the colonels, and so on, down to the new private (E-1) who is outranked by everybody. Actually, a hierarchy seldom functions according to its organizational chart. Usually, it can be influenced at all levels by legislators, the chief executive, interest groups, and other bureaucrats regardless of the formal lines of authority.

Although individual units within the Texas government are hierarchically organized, the state's overall bureaucracy is not, because final authority is not centralized in a single executive. As shown in Figure 8.6, hierarchy is evident within the Texas Commission on Environmental Quality, but there are no direct lines of authority and communication from the governor to the department.

Ironically, the governor is elected by the people to be the chief executive but has little direct authority over most administrators. However, the governor's authority to appoint the members of most boards and commissions, together with close personal ties to powerful special interest groups, makes her or him an important player in shaping the direction of independent agencies.

Neutrality Administration of the laws in a "neutral" fashion—the separation of politics and administration—has long been an aim of reformers in American government. Ideally, elected public officials should establish and define a program's priorities, goals, or services. Administrators should then administer the law efficiently and equally to all, rich or poor, black or white, powerful or weak, male or female.

The federal government took the lead in bureaucratic reform when it established a strong **civil service (or merit) system**, an employment system using competitive examinations or objective measures of qualifications for hiring and promoting employees. The spoils system—government employment and promotion based on political support—was replaced by a merit system.

Many states also adopted a merit system of public employment. However, Texas never implemented systematic statewide civil service reform; it still depends on a spoils or patronage system of public employment. Elected officials in Texas appoint major campaign supporters to top-level positions, which raises the potential for conflicts of interest and has resulted in criticism of crony capitalism practices in Austin from both the left and the right.

Texas attempted a different way to depoliticize the state bureaucracy by establishing the independent board and commission system discussed earlier, which tries to insulate the bureaucracy from the legislature and the governor, who are elected and hence political by definition. The board appoints a chief executive officer to manage the department and see to the administration of public policy. Administrative power is thus "removed from politics" and the governor is denied direct executive control over the state bureaucracy.

Local governments in Texas have attempted to accomplish similar goals by nonpartisan elections for city officials and special district boards. Most cities have also adopted the council–manager form of government in which an unelected "professional" manager supervises city departments, and in school districts a "professional" superintendent administers the public schools.

hierarchies
Structures in which several employees report to a higher administrator who reports to higher authorities until eventually all report to the single individual with ultimate authority.

civil service (or merit) system
An employment system using competitive examinations or objective measures of qualifications for hiring and promoting employees.

FIGURE 8.6 Texas Commission on Environmental Quality Organizational Structure

The organizational plan for the Texas Commission on Environmental Quality illustrates the apparent hierarchy in state agencies.

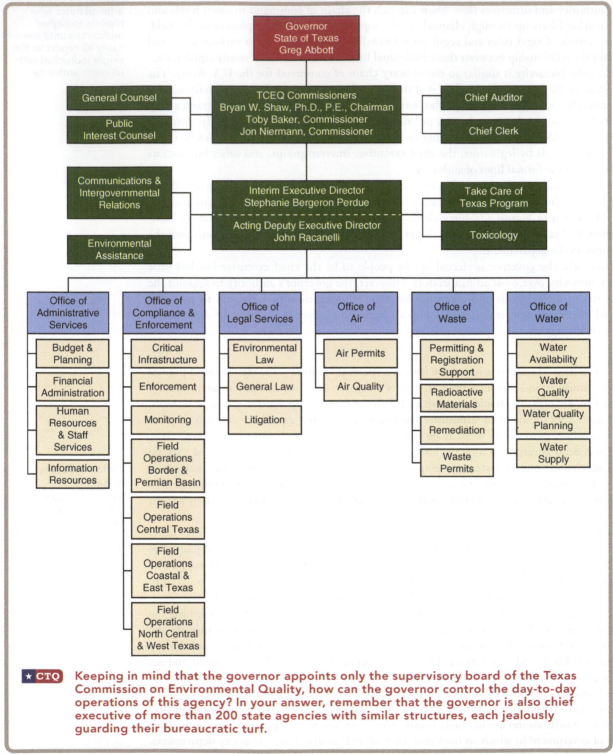

★ CTQ Keeping in mind that the governor appoints only the supervisory board of the Texas Commission on Environmental Quality, how can the governor control the day-to-day operations of this agency? In your answer, remember that the governor is also chief executive of more than 200 state agencies with similar structures, each jealously guarding their bureaucratic turf.

Texas Commission on Environmental Quality

With these safeguards, reformers believed that administrators could and would treat everyone equally and fairly, simply carrying out the policies of the elected officials. However, the theory of executive neutrality is naive, for public administration cannot be separated from politics—it is politics!

Expertise Individual bureaucrats should have an understanding of their jobs and the effects of their decisions on others. Students of administration have concluded that this can be accomplished by defining the duties of the job and the limit of its authority. Thus, individual bureaucrats, through training and experience in specific job classifications, become experts in specialized areas of administration. Ideally the result will be a more knowledgeable and efficient administration. Expertise is also a major source of bureaucratic power.

A power inherent in any professional bureaucracy stems from administrators' ability to shape public policy because of their knowledge of a given subject. Policy-making officials such as the legislature and governor are seldom as informed in policy-making areas as administrative personnel, who have often built a career in a single area of government activity. Policy-making officials, whether appointed or elected, may find themselves forced to rely on government employees for advice regarding both content and procedure. Generally seen by the public as only administrators, they are often important players in the conception, promotion, and enactment of public policy.

The Bureaucracy, Politics, and Public Policy

LO 8.4 **Analyze the political relationships among executive agencies, the public, interest groups, and elected officials.**

Each attempt to depoliticize the bureaucracy has only resulted in one kind of politics being substituted for another. Most political observers agree that the Texas bureaucracy influences public policy in its conception, development, and administration and cannot, in fact, be separated from politics. Administration is "in politics" because it operates in a political environment and must find political support from somewhere if it is to accomplish goals, gain appropriations, or even survive. The result of strong political support for an agency is increased size, jurisdiction, influence, and prestige. A less successful agency may experience reduced appropriations, static or reduced employment, narrowed administrative jurisdiction, and possibly extinction. Where, then, does a unit of the bureaucracy look for the political support so necessary for its bureaucratic well-being? It may look to clientele interest groups, the legislature, the chief executive, and the public. Political power also comes from factors within the bureaucracy, such as control of information and flexibility in the interpretation and administration of laws.

Clientele Groups

The most natural allies for an agency are its constituent or clientele interest groups—the groups that are directly affected by agency programs. The agency reciprocates by protecting its clients within the administration. Examples of close-knit alliances at the national level are defense contractors and the U.S. Department of Defense, agribusiness and the U.S. Department of Agriculture, and drug manufacturers and the U.S. Food and Drug Administration. In Texas, some of the closer alliances are highway contractors and the Texas Department of Transportation; oil and gas producers, processors, and distributors and the Texas Railroad Commission; private utility companies and the Public Utilities Commission; the banking industry and the Texas Department of Banking; and the Texas Medical Association and the Texas Medical Board.

The Agency–Clientele Alliance

The agency and its clientele groups are often allied from the agency's beginning, and this alliance continues to grow and mature as mutual convenience, power, and prosperity increase. Economic and political ties are cemented by mutual self-interest. Agencies and clients share information, have common attitudes and goals, exchange employees, and lobby the legislature together.

Mutual accommodation becomes accepted, and the clientele groups often speak of "our agency" and spend considerable time and money lobbying for it. The agency reciprocates by protecting its clients within the administration. Because neither the bureaucracy nor the special interests are single entities, there is competition between special interests and agencies for appropriations, so both seek allies in the legislative branch.

Ties do not evaporate with retirement or electoral defeat, and many former administrators and legislators work for special interests as lobbyists, consultants, and employees. State employees know from the beginning that, in time, employment may be available from deep-pocketed special interests. This creates a revolving door of employees of special interest groups who move back and forth from special interest employment to public service. This rotation of employees helps the interests influence public policy and is a practice that casts a shadow of doubt over the policy-making process. In this environment, legislators, administrators, and regulators often become promoters of the industry. At an extreme is **agency capture**, in which an agency created to regulate an industry becomes controlled by the very industry it is supposed to regulate, to the detriment of the public interest.

agency capture
An agency created to regulate an industry becoming controlled by the very industry it is supposed to regulate, to the detriment of the public interest.

The Governor

The need of administrative agencies for the governor's support depends on the extent of the governor's formal and informal powers and how successful the agency has been in finding other powerful political allies.

Even when an executive has extensive administrative powers (as the U.S. president does), most agencies have considerable independence. In Texas, where the executive branch is decentralized and the governor has few direct administrative powers, administrative autonomy is increased. Agencies still need the support of the governor, however, as the governor can influence the legislature when it considers appropriations bills and other matters important to the agency. The governor's line-item veto can also seriously affect an agency's funding.

The governor's cooperation is also essential for an agency because of the chief executive's power to appoint policy-making boards and commissions. Because an agency's interests are usually similar to those of its constituency, both want the governor to appoint board members who will advance their mutual political goals.

Public Policy and the Iron Texas Star

The explanation of how public policy is made and implemented is a complex endeavor. Teachers and writers often use models as a means of simplification to explain the process. One such model, the "Iron Texas Star," is depicted in Figure 8.7. It illustrates the relationships between the political actors in Texas government that make public policy happen. It depicts a coalition among political actors that includes interest groups, the lieutenant governor, the speaker, legislative committees, the governor, administrators, and boards and commissions.

Texas has weak legislative committees when compared with their counterparts in the U.S. Congress. This is attributable to the hands-on authority of the lieutenant governor and the speaker of the Texas House of Representatives, who select most of the members and all of the chairs of the standing committees, conference committees, and legislative boards and commissions. Their exercise of this power includes them as two points of the iron star coalition that formulates and implements public policy in Texas. The elected administrators, boards, and commissions are another point. The governor is also a point as a result of the line-item

FIGURE 8.7 The Iron Texas Star Model

This model illustrates the relationship among interest groups, the governor, state agencies, and the presiding officers of the state legislature.

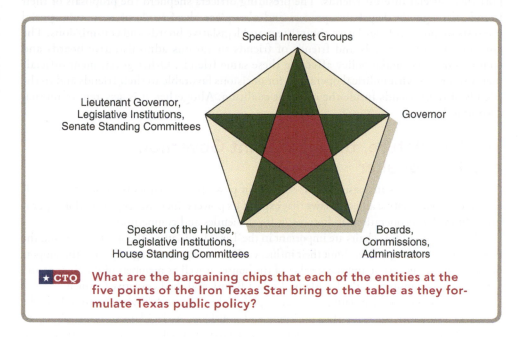

★ CTQ **What are the bargaining chips that each of the entities at the five points of the Iron Texas Star bring to the table as they formulate Texas public policy?**

veto and the power to appoint members of state policy-making boards and commissions. The virtual absence of a civil service for Texas government employees makes them more vulnerable to influence by the appointed boards. Finally, economic interest groups make up the fifth, and arguably most important, point of the star. They provide the mortar that builds and holds together this five-pointed coalition of legislators, presiding officers, the governor, administrators, and clientele interests.

How the Coalition Functions All economic interests want favorable policies that they gain by acquiring allies in the state government. Some industries, such as insurance and oil and gas, have little need for direct appropriations and basically want only to be free of government interference. This class of interests may, however, want to use the powers of government for favorable regulations and protection from consumers and competitors. Other interests, such as the Texas State Teachers Association and the highway contractors and private prison operators, literally survive on government appropriations.

The basic goal of special interests is to accumulate "friends" among political operatives in the policy-making and regulatory areas of government. It is equally critical for political operatives to acquire friends among economically powerful individuals and special interest groups. The members of the coalition also support the friends of their friends at the other points of the iron star and thereby develop a mutual support group from which all can benefit.

Legislators, administrators, the governor, and the presiding officers rely to varying degrees on the support of their interest group friends for campaign contributions, supplemental income, political advancement, financial advice and opportunity, and after-office employment and retirement income.

As time passes and members of the coalition become more interdependent, each looks to the other for support. Legislators bargain for the interest of the coalition in the legislature. Administrators issue favorable regulations and administrative policies that support their special interest friends. The presiding officers shepherd the proposals of their friends through the legislative process and also place the friends of economic special interests on powerful legislative committees and legislative boards and commissions. The governor appoints friends and friends of friends to various administrative boards and commissions that make policy affecting these same friends. Other government officials may also broker with political operatives for decisions favorable to their friends and to the friends of their friends inside the iron star coalition. Altogether, it is a system of mutual accommodation.

The Legislature, the Lieutenant Governor, and the Speaker

Bureaucratic power is increased by the support of powerful legislators because an agency is dependent on legislative allies for laws that expand its powers, increase its jurisdiction, appropriate funds for its operation, and protect it from enemies and competitors.

Although committee chairs are important in the Texas Legislature, the short session and the power of the presiding officers limit their influence. For this reason, an agency seeks the support of the lieutenant governor and the speaker of the house, as well as members of the finance and appropriations committees, the Legislative Budget Board, and the Legislative Council.

The importance of legislative support explains the intense lobbying surrounding the choice of legislators for leadership positions and continues as legislators are appointed to powerful committees. If the interest group and its agency are unable to get allies appointed or elected to positions of influence in the legislature, they are forced to try to gain support after the legislators are chosen—a more difficult endeavor.

The Control of Information

Because the bureaucracy is the branch of government that works most directly with constituent interest groups and the general public, administrative agencies gather the information used by these groups or the general public to determine what laws are needed or wanted. Information of this nature is valuable to legislators as well as to elected or appointed administrators but may be available only at the discretion of top government administrators. In other words, these administrators may dispense or interpret information in a way that benefits their agency or constituent interests during the enactment of public policy.

Administration of the Law

administrative law
The rules and regulations written by administrators to implement public policy.

Just as judges use judicial review to interpret the meaning of the law and to write case law for its implementation, bureaucrats use what might be termed "administrative review," and the rules and regulations they write to implement public policy are called **administrative law**. Administrative law defines the meaning of the law and determines its effect on both special interests and the public. A small number of laws undergo judicial review, whereas all laws undergo administrative review.

Although a law may remain on the books indefinitely, its effect is diminished with lax or selective enforcement. In this way, administrators establish public policies that not only affect the lives of the general public but can also modify the decisions of the state's elected policy makers. Although administrative decisions can be overturned by the courts and statutory law can be rewritten by legislatures, administrative review is the first, and often the last, determination of the meaning of a law and how rigidly it will be enforced.

Bureaucratic Accountability

LO 8.5 **Evaluate strategies for holding state agencies accountable.**

Throughout the history of the United States, people have tried to hold government responsible for its policies. The rise of the bureaucratic state is the most recent challenge to responsible government. The size and political power of modern bureaucracy make the problem of administrative accountability ever more difficult. Various organizational arrangements and legal restrictions have been used in attempts to make the bureaucracy accountable to the citizenry, or at least to someone the citizens can hold responsible.

Accountability to the People

The simplest approach is electing executive officers to make the bureaucracy directly accountable to the people through the democratic process—the theory of **elective accountability**. Texans sought to achieve accountability to the public by electing administrative officials, including the governor, lieutenant governor, attorney general, comptroller of public accounts, commissioner of the General Land Office, commissioner of agriculture, and members of the Railroad Commission and of the State Board of Education. Texans reasoned that the public, if given an opportunity, would keep a close watch on elected administrators and refuse to reelect those who were incompetent or dishonest. Administrators would therefore be sensitive to the wishes of the voters and would administer the law in the interest of the general public.

elective accountability
Electing executive officers to make the bureaucracy directly accountable to the people through the democratic process.

Several problems have developed with the application of this idea. The most obvious is the difficulty of determining the will of the people or even determining the public interest. Texas is a mixture of many divergent groups with many, often incompatible, interests—to please one group frequently means displeasing another.

Accountability to the Legislature

Some advocates of administrative reform argue that the bureaucracy should be accountable to the legislature because many view it as the branch of government "closest" to the people. Because it is elected to protect constituent interests and because legislators establish policies, many argue that these elected representatives should determine if public policies are being administered according to legislative intent.

This principle has been implemented in Texas by establishing legislative committees and various auditing, budgeting, and oversight boards. For example, the Texas Legislature established the Sunset Advisory Commission to make recommendations as to the alteration, termination, or continuation of many of the state's boards, commissions, and agencies. These institutions and their operations are reviewed periodically, and are automatically terminated unless specific legislative action is taken to renew them. Functions may also be expanded, diminished, or reassigned to other agencies. Even when agencies are renewed, the Sunset Commission continues to evaluate their compliance with legislative directives. The state auditor also appraises management changes recommended by the commission. It is reasoned that periodic legislative evaluation, together with agency self-evaluation, should result in better, more efficient administration.

However, the principle of accountability to the legislature is questionable. The ability of any government to separate policy formulation from its administration is difficult, and the assumption that the legislature best represents the people is arguable. Legislators' decisions can be affected by financial conflicts of interest, campaign contributions, lobbying by special interest groups, partisan considerations, primary pressures, and political ambition. Legislative accountability may serve the interests of the individual legislators and special interests but not the general public.

Finally, because the Texas Legislature is seldom in session, permanent legislative institutions such as the Legislative Budget Board and the Legislative Council are given the task of overseeing the administration. These institutions lack the visibility necessary for effective operation in the public interest.

Accountability to the Chief Executive

cabinet system
A system in which the chief executive has the power to appoint and remove top administrators.

Some reformers advocate a Texas administration patterned after the **cabinet system** of the federal government, in which the chief executive has the power to appoint and remove top administrators. This would entail a reorganization and consolidation of the executive branch into larger subject-matter departments, with the governor being given the power to appoint and remove top administrators and to control the budget. Reformers argue that a governor who had these powers would have a strong incentive to hold the appointed bureaucrats accountable for their actions as voters usually hold the governor responsible for mishaps in state agencies.

Theoretically, several benefits could result from accountability to the governor. The office is visible to the general public, so the problem of who watches the watchers would be solved. There would be no question regarding final responsibility for any corruption or incompetence in the administration. Administrative control could be simplified, resulting in coordinated planning and policy implementation. Waste and duplication could be reduced.

Consolidation and reorganization of the Texas administration is, without a doubt, necessary for an orderly, modern executive branch. If Texas reorganized public administration along the lines of the federal model, the governor would need a similar executive office. This executive staff, although largely out of the public eye, would nevertheless be accountable to the governor.

This chain of accountability—administrative agency to appointed executive to staff to governor to the people—would be weakened by the close ties usually found among administrators, constituent interest groups, and legislators. Interest groups would continue to influence administrative appointments and removals in "their agencies" just as they now influence appointments to the boards and commissions under the current system. Even under a cabinet system, the governor would have problems imposing accountability on agencies that have allies among powerful interest groups and legislators.

Bureaucratic Responsibility

To whom is the Texas administrator really accountable? The answer is to a combination of the people—the legislature, the governor, and especially the interest groups that benefit from the programs administered by the agencies.

Open Meetings and Open Records

open meetings laws
Laws requiring that meetings of government bodies at all levels of government be open to the general public, with some exceptions.

How, then, can the Texas administration be made more accountable to the public? There is no single answer. One possibility could be more transparency. A basic concept of democratic government is that policy made in the name of the public should be made in the full view of the public. Texas has made progress in this area. **Open meetings laws** require that meetings of government bodies at all levels be open to the general public except when personnel, land acquisition, or litigation matters are being discussed. The laws further prohibit unannounced sessions and splitting up to avoid a quorum, and they require that public notice be posted for both open and closed sessions. However, these laws are continuously being tested by some policy makers, who feel more comfortable operating in secret.

open records laws
Laws that require most records kept by government to be open to the public.

Openness is further encouraged by the state's **open records laws**, which require that records kept by the government be open to the public for only the expense involved in assembling and reproducing them.

Whistle-blowers and Ombudsmen Another source of transparency is **whistle-blowers**—government employees who expose bureaucratic excesses, blunders, corruption, or favoritism. These employees could be commended and protected from retribution, but too often they are instead exiled to the bureaucratic equivalent of Siberia or fired for their efforts. To its credit, Texas's whistle-blowers law prohibits governments from acting against employees who report law violations. But enforcement is difficult and time-consuming, and whistle-blowers often suffer.

An **ombudsman** is a man or woman serving as an independent official who takes, investigates, and mediates complaints about government bureaucrats or policy. The office originated in Sweden in the early nineteenth century and currently is present throughout the United States. As governor, Ann Richards established an ombudsman in her office in 1991. Today, the office of ombudsman exists in many state agencies to aid Texans with complaints or issues with the agency, including the Texas Health and Human Services Commission and the Texas Juvenile Justice Department.

The appointment of ombudsmen at every level of government would provide increased access to the bureaucracy regarding real or imagined administrative injustices. In this way, administrative error, injustice, or oversight could be rectified, allowing individual citizens to have a more positive attitude toward government.

Any lack of public accountability by Texas administrators cannot be wholly blamed on poor structural organization or the lack of consumer- or citizen-oriented agencies. No amount of reorganization and no number of consumer-focused actors can overcome the willingness of an apathetic or indifferent public to accept bureaucratic errors, inefficiency, excesses, favoritism, or corruption.

whistle-blowers
Government employees who expose bureaucratic excesses, blunders, corruption, or favoritism.

ombudsman
An independent official who takes, investigates, and mediates complaints about government bureaucrats or policy.

Applying What You Have Learned about the Texas Executive Branch

LO 8.6 **Apply what you have learned about the Texas executive branch.**

In this chapter, you have learned what the executive branch is and what it does. You explored the role of the executive branch in influencing public policy and how the state has attempted to hold the executive branch accountable. We persuaded Drew DeBerry to give you an insider's view of how the executive branch operates in practice.

Drew DeBerry is the director of budget and policy for Texas Governor Greg Abbott. Prior to joining the Abbott administration in 2015, he was the deputy commissioner of the Texas Department of Agriculture (TDA) for eight years. DeBerry also served in the administration of President George W. Bush, first as the White House liaison to the United States Department of Agriculture (USDA) and then as the USDA's deputy chief of staff.

After you have read his essay, we will ask you to identify examples of executive policy making and evaluate DeBerry's concepts of executive accountability in action.

POLITICS IN PRACTICE
The Texas Executive Branch: Does it run you, or do you run it?

by Drew DeBerry
FORMER DIRECTOR OF BUDGET AND POLICY FOR TEXAS GOVERNOR GREG ABBOTT

The executive branch brings government to life on a daily basis. In a somewhat different and more direct way than other branches of government, the executive branch operates your government day in and day out—responding to emergencies and disasters, performing essential government services throughout the day and night, working with you to establish and improve policies that affect your life, and much more.

The people of Texas have bestowed great power on the executive branch of Texas's government. And importantly, the success of this government correlates directly with a discipline of humility with which its custodians use this power each day.

A humble government executive understands one key principle—public service is a privilege. Public service also comes with numerous challenges, compounded by enormous disagreement among the people on what the principal purpose of government is.

To understand the executive branch of government through the lens with which I have the unique privilege of viewing it, we need not consume ourselves with *what* the government is supposed to do for the people—although that is an important factor dividing philosophies among your candidates for elective office. Instead, let's look at *how* it does it. The *how* is also the *what*—which is also the ultimate question of a democracy. The custodians of the executive branch are in large part left to determine *how* to accomplish the *what*—the will of the people.

Most people agree on a few general concepts behind how government should do its job. Government should be transparent and consistent. It should embody integrity and ethics. And, in a democratic form of government, it should be run *by* the people … providing services *for* the people.

Government should perform the services the people need by having a deliberative and transparent process to develop a set of rules and protocols to accomplish its purpose. These rules are often called "policies" and they ensure consistency and integrity in government.

Policies are assembled in statutes, regulations, and programmatic guidelines in a complementary way as a contract between the government and its people. This contract prevents conflicts of interest between the individuals running the government and the people the government serves by shifting as much decision making as possible to a time well before any case-specific decision is necessary.

Think about policies surrounding getting your driver's license. Without pre-developed policies, a Texas Department of Public Safety (DPS) employee could decide your driving fate based on their subjective opinion of your driving capabilities. But instead, that staff person is given a set of policies that tell them exactly what proficiencies you should demonstrate, such as your vision capabilities and what training you must have completed. Little discretion is left to the whim of the DPS employee; therefore, you can rest assured that if you meet the prescribed criteria, you will receive a license.

Ponder for a moment the impact of executive policies on your life to this point. Your parents, teachers, coaches, and community leaders have enforced policies by which you have lived every day. Curfews, budgets, class start times, speed limits, basketball practice schedules—all these things are policies developed by someone in an effort to provide some safety and reliability to your life and the lives of those around you.

Now consider the process behind those policies. Your parents likely collaborated and debated the merits of different curfews and budgets for you and your siblings. Importantly, they most likely had similar curfew and budget rules for each of you and your siblings as you matured. This way none of your siblings could claim your parents had preferences for any of you. If there were inconsistencies, the kids likely would not respect the rules and might even revolt against them. Your parents then informed you of these rules and you lived by them—until you didn't … at which time there were consequences.

This same thing happens in your government. A legislative process, involving public participation and the legislative and executive branches, develops high level policies (i.e., statutes). The executive branch, also with public comment and involvement, then implements and enforces those statutes by developing more specific policies (rules and protocols). And of course the judicial branch mediates disputes over conflicts in policies—also with the testimony of interest parties of the public. Respect for this system and the policies that it produces requires consistency and predictability—just like your parents' rules.

As the governor's director of budget and policy, I get to see all aspects of this process with a front-row seat. Since the governor has the power to veto legislation, members of the legislative branch often work with our office to craft proposed law changes in a way that might garner support from the governor.

An arguably more significant part of my job is helping to represent the head of the executive branch (the governor) to the hundreds of state agencies throughout the executive branch as these laws are implemented and enforced via rules and protocols. This is where the decisions get meaningful to the Texas citizen who will be impacted. We consider a number of things, such as the letter of the law, costs to taxpayers, and burdens on citizens. Success is measured by a consistent and efficient implementation of the will of the people—not the sustained growth of any particular program.

And inevitably we always end up back to that first question—what is the true role of government? While people like the governor, legislators, and me have our own thoughts on that question, you have to develop your own answer. And as a citizen that is in the ownership structure of your government, your opinion of the role of government is only valuable if you put it to force by either expressing it to those individuals who represent you as the stewards of government—public servants—or becoming a public servant yourself. In the end, the executive branch is entrusted to implement—transparently, consistently, and efficiently—whatever you and your fellow citizens decide is the proper role of government.

1. Describe and give examples of policy making in the executive branch. How does the author work with the legislature in budgeting and policy making?
2. How do involved citizens hold people like DeBerry and other appointed staff in the executive branch accountable for transparent, consistent, and efficient implementation of public policy? What difficulties do they encounter expressing their views in the executive decision-making process?

★ Chapter Summary

LO 8.1 Describe the governor's office and the characteristics of the typical Texas governor. Texas governors have been Anglo, predominantly male Protestants. Modern Texas governors are conservative Republicans. Elected for four-year terms, their professional backgrounds are most commonly either business or law and they have close connections to state and national moneyed interests.

LO 8.2 Analyze both the governor's powers of persuasion and the limits on them. The governor has relatively strong legislative prerogatives, among which are the veto and the line-item veto. Although shared with other legislative power bases, his or her legislative authority together with an astute use of informal powers enables the governor to exert influence on the direction and operation of the legislature and consequently affect public policy.

As chief executive, each year the governor makes hundreds of appointments to boards and commissions in the administration but without meaningful removal or direct administrative powers. Although they are elected to a legally weak office, politically savvy governors can craft a politically formidable position by weaving their legislative, executive, and party powers into a cloth held together by their supporters and lobbyists from special interests.

LO 8.3 Analyze the structure and characteristics of the Texas bureaucracy. Texas has a plural executive system in which several state executives are elected independently of the governor. Most state agencies are actually headed by multimember boards and commissions that the governor appoints but is unable to control. Board members serve fixed overlapping terms, which limits the governor's powers over the agencies. With a few exceptions, the board, rather than the governor, appoints the actual chief operating officer, and the governor has limited powers to issue orders to state agencies or to remove state officers. As a result, unlike most bureaucracies, the Texas bureaucracy is decentralized with no single hierarchy and no single officeholder in charge. Instead, the state bureaucracy is an amalgamation of hierarchies, each headed by elected or appointed officers or boards. Aside from hierarchy, the traditional model describes bureaucracies as being characterized by size, expertise, and

neutrality. Reformists have pursued the goals of a public administration that is free of bias in applying the law and neutral in politics, but efforts such as the civil service reform, and the creation of independent governing boards have simply substituted one kind of politics for another.

LO 8.4 Analyze the political relationships among executive agencies, the public, interest groups, and elected officials. Clientele interest groups form close alliances with state agencies that administer the government programs that benefit them. Elected officials such as the governor and legislative leaders depend on the political support and expertise provided by these groups. As a result, public policy often is made by a relatively closed network illustrated by the Iron Texas Star.

LO 8.5 Evaluate strategies for holding state agencies accountable. Attempts to hold agency officials accountable have taken several forms, including elective accountability, accountability to the legislature or chief executive, and the use of transparency to check agency abuses. Critics charge that none of these strategies has worked effectively.

LO 8.6 Apply what you have learned about the Texas executive branch. You took a glimpse inside the governor's office and learned how it is involved in the policy-making process. You considered whether, in practice, the public is able to hold the executive branch accountable for the transparent, consistent, and efficient implementation of public policy.

Key Terms

administrative law, *p. 228*
agency capture, *p. 226*
attorney general's opinion, *p. 212*
bureaucracy, *p. 212*
cabinet system, *p. 230*
civil service (or merit) system, *p. 223*

clemency powers, *p. 211*
contract spoils, or contract patronage, *p. 222*
elective accountability, *p. 229*
formal (legal) powers, *p. 203*
hierarchies, *p. 223*

impeachment, *p. 200*
informal (extralegal) powers, *p. 203*
message power, *p. 204*
ombudsman, *p. 231*
open meetings laws, *p. 230*
open records laws, *p. 230*

privatization, *p. 220*
senatorial courtesy, *p. 210*
spoils system, *p. 222*
veto, *p. 205*
whistle-blowers, *p. 231*

Review Questions

LO 8.1 Describe the governor's office and the characteristics of the typical Texas governor.

- Describe the politics and demographic profile of the typical Texas governor.

- Describe the Texas governor's term in office, methods for removal of the Texas governor, and the governor's ability to seek reelection.

- Explain the functions of the governor's staff. Why is a competent staff important for a successful administration?

LO 8.2 Analyze both the governor's powers of persuasion and the limits on them.

- Describe the governor's legislative tools of persuasion.

- Describe the executive tools of persuasion. What are the weaknesses in the governor's executive powers? How can the governor adapt to these limits by asserting political influence?

LO 8.3 Analyze the structure and characteristics of the Texas bureaucracy.

- Become familiar with Texas's elected executives and elected boards. To whom are they responsible?

- How does the use of appointed boards affect the governor's ability to serve as the "chief executive" of Texas?

- Define and explain the characteristics of Texas bureaucracy.

- Describe the classical model of bureaucracy, and explain how the Texas executive branch differs from other bureaucratic organizations.

- Explain how Texas's historical background and Texans' viewpoint of government influenced the current administrative structure.

LO 8.4 Analyze the political relationships among executive agencies, the public, interest groups, and elected officials.

- Discuss the importance of the Texas bureaucracy in policy formation, development, and implementation.

- Describe the Iron Texas Star model.

LO 8.5 Evaluate strategies for holding state agencies accountable.

- Discuss the various methods used to hold the bureaucracy accountable to the people.

- Which methods are used in Texas government? Which are most effective?

- How do open records and open meetings laws affect bureaucratic behavior? Why are these laws important?

Think Critically and Get Active!

Explore the organization of the governor's office at **gov.texas.gov/organization** and the appointment process at **gov.texas.gov/appointments**. Follow recent appointments at **gov.texas.gov/news/archive/appointment**. Find out how you can benefit from the activities and services of the other elected state officers: the attorney general at **www.texasattorneygeneral.gov**; the comptroller of public accounts at **https://comptroller.texas.gov/**; the commissioner of the General Land Office at **www.glo.texas.gov**; and the commissioner of the Texas Department of Agriculture at **www.texasagriculture.gov/**.

Follow the money. Investigate the interest groups and individuals that have contributed to the governor's political campaign and those of other elected executives in Texas using the database created by the National Institute on Money in State Politics at **www.followthemoney.org**.

Use state agencies to become an intelligent consumer.

- Contact the Consumer Protection Division of the Office of the Attorney General to learn about your rights and how to exercise them at **www.texasattorneygeneral.gov/cpd/consumer-protection**.

- Before you buy a new vehicle, contact the Texas Department of Motor Vehicles, which maintains "lemon law" records and processes warranty complaints at **www.txdmv.gov/motorists/consumer-protection/lemon-law**.

- Search to see if you, a friend, or a relative has unclaimed property, ranging from long forgotten bank accounts to uncashed checks to security deposits, listed in the Texas Comptroller's "Come and Get It" database at **www.ClaimItTexas.org**.

- Shop for a less expensive or more eco-friendly electricity plan at **www.powertochoose.org**.

- Get help paying for college from the Texas Higher Education Coordinating Board at **www.collegeforalltexans.com**.

- Get tips on buying insurance at **www.tdi.texas.gov/consumer/index.html**.

9

The Judiciary

Texas students at a mock trial. During their lifetimes, most Texans will see the inside of a courtroom as plaintiffs, defendants, or jurors. In this chapter, you will learn what the courts do and the kinds of cases Texas courts decide.

Bob Daemmrich/Alamy Stock Photo

Learning Objectives

LO 9.1 Describe the differences between criminal and civil cases and between original and appellate jurisdiction.

LO 9.2 Explain how the courts are organized in Texas, and identify the jurisdiction of each major court.

LO 9.3 Understand the role of grand juries and trial juries, and analyze the responsibilities of citizens in the Texas legal system.

LO 9.4 Compare and evaluate the most common methods of judicial selection in the United States and in Texas.

LO 9.5 Apply what you have learned about the Texas judiciary.

merican society has increasingly turned to the judiciary to find answers to personal, economic, social, and political problems. Courts are often asked to determine our rights, and important legal questions touch almost every aspect of our lives. For example, what level of privacy should we expect in our cars, workplaces, and homes? What treatment should people of different ethnicities, races, genders, sexual orientations, or age groups expect? In a divorce proceeding, with which parent should the children live? Should an accused person go to jail, and if so, for how long? Should a woman be allowed to terminate her pregnancy? Should a patient be allowed to refuse potentially lifesaving treatment? These are among the thousands of questions asked and answered daily by courts in the United States.

In the past few decades, Texas courts have heard important or controversial cases involving topics such as flag burning, the death penalty, school desegregation, school finance, a criminal case involving the governor, the welfare of children in a polygamist sect, and one of the largest civil cases in U.S. history, in which Texaco was found liable to Pennzoil (represented by legendary Houston attorney Joe Jamail) for $10.5 billion in 1985 (that's $24.3 billion in 2018 dollars). Court cases determine our legal rights, shape public policy, and undeniably affect our daily lives.

In this chapter, we will focus on the Texas courts, judges, and juries. The sheer size and complexity of the Texas court system will quickly become clear. We will also look at the controversies surrounding the selection of Texas judges and the politics that affect the legal process.

Legal Cases and Jurisdiction

LO 9.1 **Describe the differences between criminal and civil cases and between original and appellate jurisdiction.**

Legal cases can be classified into two broad categories, civil and criminal, based on their subject matter. Jurisdiction within the court system is determined by whether the case is being tried for the first time or if a prior court decision is being reviewed on appeal.

Civil and Criminal Cases

In the American legal system, cases are generally classified as either civil or criminal. Table 9.1 shows the most important differences between these two types of cases. A **civil case** concerns private rights and remedies and usually involves private parties or organizations (*Garcia* v. *Smith*), although the government may on occasion be a party to a civil case. A personal injury suit, a divorce case, a child custody dispute, a breach-of-contract issue, and a conflict over water rights are all examples of causes of action in civil cases.

A **criminal case** involves a violation of penal law that is prosecuted by the state. If convicted, the lawbreaker may be punished by a fine, imprisonment, or both. The action is by the state against the accused (*State of Texas* v. *Smith*). Examples of criminal actions range from murder to speeding.

One of the most important differences between civil and criminal cases is the **burden of proof** (the duty that a party has to prove its position in court). In civil cases, the standard used is a **preponderance of the evidence**, meaning that whichever party has more evidence or proof on its side should win the case, no matter how slight the advantage is. However, in a criminal case, the burden of proof falls entirely on the government or prosecution. The prosecution must prove that the defendant is guilty **beyond a reasonable doubt**, the standard used to determine the guilt or innocence of a person criminally charged. To prove a defendant guilty, the state must provide sufficient evidence of guilt so that jurors have no doubt that might cause a reasonable person to question whether the accused was guilty.

civil case
Concerns private rights and remedies and usually involves private parties or organizations (*Garcia* v. *Smith*), although the government may on occasion be a party to a civil case.

criminal case
Involves a violation of penal law that is prosecuted by the state.

burden of proof
The duty a party has to prove its position in court.

preponderance of the evidence
Whichever party has more evidence or proof on its side should win the case, no matter how slight the advantage is.

beyond a reasonable doubt
The standard used to determine the guilt or innocence of a person criminally charged. To prove a defendant guilty, the state must provide sufficient evidence of guilt so that jurors have no doubt that might cause a reasonable person to question whether the accused was guilty.

TABLE 9.1   Major Differences between Civil and Criminal Cases

Civil and criminal cases involve very different concepts of law based on different court procedures, who brings the case, and the consequences that result from court decisions in each type of case.

Civil Cases	Criminal Cases
Deal primarily with individual or property rights and involve the concept of responsibility but not guilt.	Deal with public concepts of proper behavior and morality as defined in penal law. A plea of guilty or not guilty is entered.
Plaintiff, or petitioner, who brings suit is often a private party, as is the defendant or respondent.	Case is initiated by a government prosecutor on behalf of the public.
Dispute is usually set out in a petition.	Specific charges of wrongdoing are spelled out in a grand jury indictment or a writ of information.
A somewhat more relaxed procedure is used to balance or weigh the evidence; the side with the preponderance of the evidence wins the suit.	Strict rules of procedure are used to evaluate evidence. The standard of proof is guilt beyond a reasonable doubt.
Final court remedy is relief from or compensation for the violation of legal rights.	Determination of guilt results in punishment.

▶ Why should criminal cases require a higher standard of proof than civil cases?

Sometimes an action may have both civil and criminal consequences. Suppose that in the course of an armed robbery at a cell phone store, the perpetrator shoots a sales associate. The state could prosecute the suspect for aggravated robbery and assault, which would be a criminal action. Then, the sales associate could sue the robber for compensation for medical expenses, lost earning power, and other damages, which would be a civil action.

Original and Appellate Jurisdiction

original jurisdiction
The power to try a case being heard for the first time.

appellate jurisdiction
The power vested in an appellate court to review and revise the judicial action of an inferior court.

briefs
Written arguments prepared by lawyers arguing a case in court that summarize the facts of the case, the pertinent laws, and the application of those laws to the facts supporting their positions.

Original jurisdiction is the power to try a case being heard for the first time. It involves following legal rules of procedure in hearing witnesses, viewing material evidence, and examining other evidence to determine guilt in criminal cases or responsibility in civil cases. The judge oversees procedure, but evaluating evidence is the jury's job (unless the right to a jury trial has been waived, in which case the judge weighs the evidence). The verdict or judgment is determined and the remedy set. A trial involves the determination of fact and the application of law.

Appellate jurisdiction refers to the power vested in an appellate court to review and revise the judicial action of an inferior court. Such appeals do not involve a new trial but rather a review of the law as it was applied in the original trial. Many appeals are decided by review of the record (transcript) of the case and the respective lawyers' **briefs** which are written arguments prepared by lawyers arguing a case in court that summarize the facts of the case, the pertinent laws, and the application of those laws to the facts supporting their positions. Sometimes, lawyers may appear to present oral arguments, but witnesses and material evidence are not presented because appellate proceedings are based on law and not fact. A reversal does not necessarily mean that the convicted individual is innocent, only that the legal process was improper. Consequently, that person may be tried again, and questions of **double jeopardy** (a second prosecution for the same offense after acquittal in the first trial) are not involved because the individual waives the right against double jeopardy by appealing the case.

Court Organization

LO 9.2 **Explain how the courts are organized in Texas, and identify the jurisdiction of each major court.**

Figure 9.1 shows the organizational structure of the Texas court system and the various types and levels of courts in the system. It is important to note that some courts within this rather large and complicated system have overlapping jurisdiction.

Did You Know? In 2017, 75 percent of the criminal cases filed in Texas municipal courts involved violations of state traffic laws.

Municipal Courts

The state authorizes incorporated cities and towns to establish municipal courts, and city charters or municipal ordinances provide for their status and organization. Legally, municipal courts have exclusive jurisdiction to try violations of city ordinances. They also handle minor violations of state law—class C misdemeanors for which punishment is a fine of $500 or less and does not include a jail sentence. (Justice of the peace courts have overlapping jurisdiction to handle such minor violations.) Most municipal court cases in Texas involve traffic and parking violations.

When Texas cities designate their municipal courts as *courts of record,* the records of the trial form the basis of appeal to one of the county courts. However, in many smaller cities records are not kept and defendants may demand a completely new trial in overworked county courts, where most such cases are simply dismissed. These new trials are known as *de novo* **trials** in which a higher court completely retries the case, in contrast to an appeal in which a higher court simply reviews the law as decided by a lower court.

People who favor the court-of-record concept often point to the large amount of revenue lost because trials *de novo* usually result in dismissal of minor traffic cases. Opponents of the concept argue that municipal courts are too often operated as a means of raising revenue rather than of achieving justice, and the fact that municipal courts collected $634 million in 2017 lends some support to their argument.

Judges of the municipal courts meet whatever qualifications are set by the city charter or ordinances (see Figure 9.2). Some cities require specific legal training or experience. Other charters say very little about qualifications. Most municipal court judges are appointed for two-year terms but serve at the pleasure of the governing bodies that have selected them. Furthermore, these judges' salaries are paid entirely by their respective cities and vary widely. Where statutes authorize them, some cities have established more than one municipal court or more than one judge for each court.

Justices of the Peace

The *justice of the peace* courts in Texas are authorized by the Texas Constitution, which requires that county commissioners establish at least one and not more than eight justice precincts per county; a precinct is the area from which each justice of the peace is elected for a four-year term. County commissioners determine how many justices of the peace shall be elected (determined by the population) and where their courts shall sit. Changes are made continuously, making it difficult to pin down the number of justices of the peace at any given time. The Texas Judicial Council determined that there were 802 justices of the peace in 2017.[1]

FIGURE 9.1 Court Structure of Texas

This court organizational chart arranges Texas courts from those that handle the least serious cases at the bottom to the highest appeals courts at the top. As you read the text, look for ways to simplify and professionalize the state's court structure.

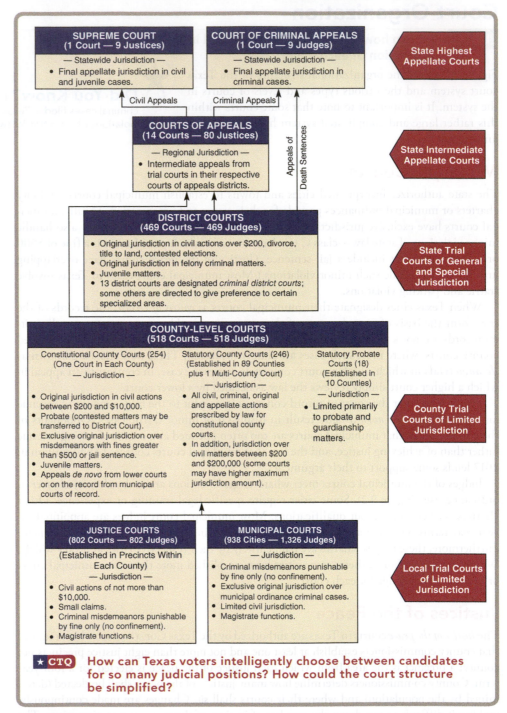

SUPREME COURT
(1 Court — 9 Justices)
— Statewide Jurisdiction —
• Final appellate jurisdiction in civil and juvenile cases.

COURT OF CRIMINAL APPEALS
(1 Court — 9 Judges)
— Statewide Jurisdiction —
• Final appellate jurisdiction in criminal cases.

State Highest Appellate Courts

Civil Appeals   Criminal Appeals

COURTS OF APPEALS
(14 Courts — 80 Justices)
— Regional Jurisdiction —
• Intermediate appeals from trial courts in their respective courts of appeals districts.

Appeals of Death Sentences

State Intermediate Appellate Courts

DISTRICT COURTS
(469 Courts — 469 Judges)
• Original jurisdiction in civil actions over $200, divorce, title to land, contested elections.
• Original jurisdiction in felony criminal matters.
• Juvenile matters.
• 13 district courts are designated *criminal district courts*; some others are directed to give preference to certain specialized areas.

State Trial Courts of General and Special Jurisdiction

COUNTY-LEVEL COURTS
(518 Courts — 518 Judges)

Constitutional County Courts (254)
(One Court in Each County)
— Jurisdiction —
• Original jurisdiction in civil actions between $200 and $10,000.
• Probate (contested matters may be transferred to District Court).
• Exclusive original jurisdiction over misdemeanors with fines greater than $500 or jail sentence.
• Juvenile matters.
• Appeals *de novo* from lower courts or on the record from municipal courts of record.

Statutory County Courts (246)
(Established in 89 Counties plus 1 Multi-County Court)
— Jurisdiction —
• All civil, criminal, original and appellate actions prescribed by law for constitutional county courts.
• In addition, jurisdiction over civil matters between $200 and $200,000 (some courts may have higher maximum jurisdiction amount).

Statutory Probate Courts (18)
(Established in 10 Counties)
— Jurisdiction —
• Limited primarily to probate and guardianship matters.

County Trial Courts of Limited Jurisdiction

JUSTICE COURTS
(802 Courts — 802 Judges)
(Established in Precincts Within Each County)
— Jurisdiction —
• Civil actions of not more than $10,000.
• Small claims.
• Criminal misdemeanors punishable by fine only (no confinement).
• Magistrate functions.

MUNICIPAL COURTS
(938 Cities — 1,326 Judges)
— Jurisdiction —
• Criminal misdemeanors punishable by fine only (no confinement).
• Exclusive original jurisdiction over municipal ordinance criminal cases.
• Limited civil jurisdiction.
• Magistrate functions.

Local Trial Courts of Limited Jurisdiction

★ CTQ **How can Texas voters intelligently choose between candidates for so many judicial positions? How could the court structure be simplified?**

Texas Judicial Council.

FIGURE 9.2 Judicial Qualifications and Selection in Texas

This figure provides the minimum qualifications to become a judge and the method by which judges are selected for the different Texas courts, from those that handle the least serious cases at the bottom to the highest appeals courts at the top.

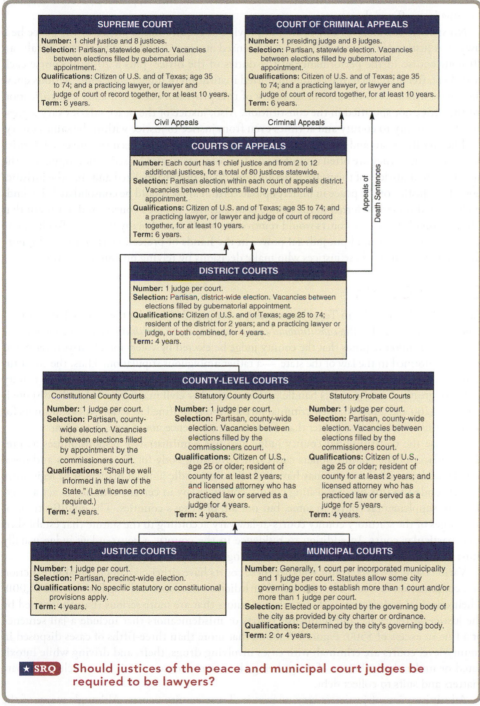

SUPREME COURT

Number: 1 chief justice and 8 justices.
Selection: Partisan, statewide election. Vacancies between elections filled by gubernatorial appointment.
Qualifications: Citizen of U.S. and of Texas; age 35 to 74; and a practicing lawyer, or lawyer and judge of court of record together, for at least 10 years.
Term: 6 years.

COURT OF CRIMINAL APPEALS

Number: 1 presiding judge and 8 judges.
Selection: Partisan, statewide election. Vacancies between elections filled by gubernatorial appointment.
Qualifications: Citizen of U.S. and of Texas; age 35 to 74; and a practicing lawyer, or lawyer and judge of court of record together, for at least 10 years.
Term: 6 years.

Civil Appeals   Criminal Appeals

COURTS OF APPEALS

Number: Each court has 1 chief justice and from 2 to 12 additional justices, for a total of 80 justices statewide.
Selection: Partisan election within each court of appeals district. Vacancies between elections filled by gubernatorial appointment.
Qualifications: Citizen of U.S. and of Texas; age 35 to 74; and a practicing lawyer, or lawyer and judge of court of record together, for at least 10 years.
Term: 6 years.

Appeals of Death Sentences

DISTRICT COURTS

Number: 1 judge per court.
Selection: Partisan, district-wide election. Vacancies between elections filled by gubernatorial appointment.
Qualifications: Citizen of U.S. and of Texas; age 25 to 74; resident of the district for 2 years; and a practicing lawyer or judge, or both combined, for 4 years.
Term: 4 years.

COUNTY-LEVEL COURTS

Constitutional County Courts

Number: 1 judge per court.
Selection: Partisan, county-wide election. Vacancies between elections filled by appointment by the commissioners court.
Qualifications: "Shall be well informed in the law of the State." (Law license not required.)
Term: 4 years.

Statutory County Courts

Number: 1 judge per court.
Selection: Partisan, county-wide election. Vacancies between elections filled by the commissioners court.
Qualifications: Citizen of U.S., age 25 or older; resident of county for at least 2 years; and licensed attorney who has practiced law or served as a judge for 4 years.
Term: 4 years.

Statutory Probate Courts

Number: 1 judge per court.
Selection: Partisan, county-wide election. Vacancies between elections filled by the commissioners court.
Qualifications: Citizen of U.S., age 25 or older; resident of county for at least 2 years; and licensed attorney who has practiced law or served as a judge for 5 years.
Term: 4 years.

JUSTICE COURTS

Number: 1 judge per court.
Selection: Partisan, precinct-wide election.
Qualifications: No specific statutory or constitutional provisions apply.
Term: 4 years.

MUNICIPAL COURTS

Number: Generally, 1 court per incorporated municipality and 1 judge per court. Statutes allow some city governing bodies to establish more than 1 court and/or more than 1 judge per court.
Selection: Elected or appointed by the governing body of the city as provided by city charter or ordinance.
Qualifications: Determined by the city's governing body.
Term: 2 or 4 years.

★ SRQ **Should justices of the peace and municipal court judges be required to be lawyers?**

Texas Judicial Council.

The functions of the justice of the peace courts are varied. Figure 9.3 shows that they mostly handle criminal cases. They have jurisdiction over criminal cases in which the fine is less than $500, but may also handle civil matters in which the dispute involves less than $10,000. They may issue warrants for search and arrest, serve *ex officio* as public notaries, conduct preliminary hearings, perform marriages, act as coroners in counties having no medical examiner, and serve as small claims courts. Most cases filed in justice courts are criminal and involve traffic violations.

No specific statutory or constitutional provisions require that a justice of the peace be a lawyer. A justice of the peace who is not a licensed attorney is required by statute to take an 80-hour course in the performance of the duties of the office, plus a 20-hour course each year thereafter at an accredited state-supported institution of higher education. Serious questions have arisen as to the constitutionality of this provision because it adds a qualification for the office not specified in the constitution. Also, justice of the peace salaries vary a great deal from county to county and at times even from justice to justice within the same county.

The qualifications and competence of justices of the peace have been controversial. Critics have argued that they are often unprofessional, incompetent, and biased. They argue that the jurisdiction of justices of the peace functions should be professionalized and that the jurisdiction of the justice of the peace in underpopulated rural areas should be consolidated. Defenders have traditionally referred to the justice courts as the "people's courts" and maintain that elimination of the justice courts would remove the local control many treasure. To eliminate them, it is argued, would put judicial power in the hands of professionals and would ignore the amateur status of these justices who make decisions by relying on common sense.

County Courts

Each of the 254 counties in Texas has a *county court* presided over by the county judge (sometimes respectively called the *constitutional county court* and the *constitutional county judge*). The Texas Constitution requires that the county judge be elected by voters for a four-year term and be "well informed in the law of the state"—a rather ambiguous stipulation. Thus, the constitution does not require that a county judge possess a law degree. Salaries are paid by the county and vary greatly. County courts handle probate and other civil matters in which the dispute is between $200 and $10,000; their criminal jurisdiction is confined to serious misdemeanors for which punishment is a fine greater than $500 or a jail sentence not to exceed one year.

Because the constitutional county judge also has administrative responsibilities as presiding officer of the commissioners court (the governing body for Texas counties and not a judicial entity at all), he or she may have little time to handle judicial matters. The legislature has responded to this by establishing county courts-at-law in certain counties to act as auxiliary or supplemental courts in some, but not all, of Texas's counties. The qualifications of the judges of the statutory county courts-at-law vary according to the statute that established each particular court. In addition to residence in the county, a court-at-law judge usually must have four years of experience as a practicing attorney or judge.

Various state laws determine whether these courts have either civil or criminal jurisdiction or a combination of both. They have civil jurisdiction in cases involving less than $200,000. Their criminal jurisdiction includes misdemeanors that are more serious than those tried by the justice of the peace and municipal courts or misdemeanors that include a jail sentence or a fine in excess of $500. Figure 9.3 shows that more than three-fifths of cases disposed in county-level courts are criminal, with cases involving drugs, theft, and driving while intoxicated or under the influence of drugs being the most common. Civil cases include probate matters and suits to collect debt.

Administration of justice is very uneven in Texas county courts. Although many of the judges are competent and run their courts in an orderly manner, others regard their courts and

FIGURE 9.3 Civil and Criminal Cases Filed in Texas Courts

This figure shows the share of civil and criminal cases filed in Texas courts in 2017. Minor cases are handled in municipal, justice of the peace, and county-level courts. District courts handle serious civil and criminal cases that are occasionally appealed to courts of appeal. The supreme court is the court of last resort in civil cases, and the court of criminal appeals is the final court of appeal for criminal cases.

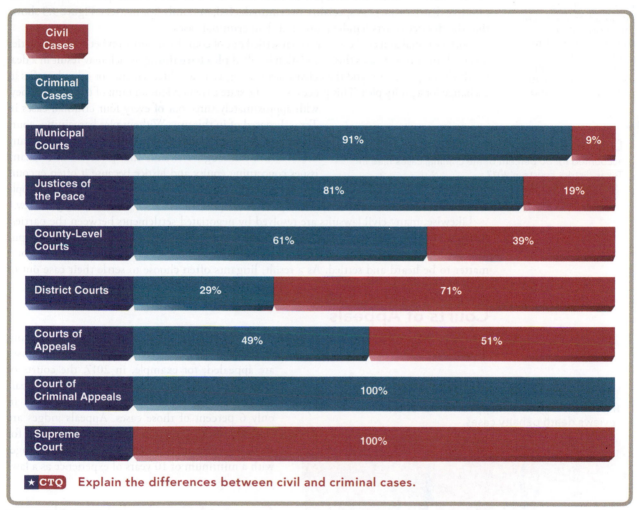

Civil Cases

Criminal Cases

Municipal Courts	91%	9%
Justices of the Peace	81%	19%
County-Level Courts	61%	39%
District Courts	29%	71%
Courts of Appeals	49%	51%
Court of Criminal Appeals	100%	
Supreme Court		100%

★ **CTQ** **Explain the differences between civil and criminal cases.**

Source: Texas Judicial Council.

official jurisdictions as personal fiefdoms, paying little attention to the finer points of law or accepted procedures. Opportunities for arbitrary action are compounded if the county judge is performing as a judicial officer as well as the chief administrative officer of the county.

District Courts

District courts are often described as the chief trial courts of the state, and as a group, these courts are called the general trial courts. Currently, there are 469 district courts in Texas, all of which function as single-judge courts. Each judge, elected for a four-year term by voters in their district, must be at least 25 years of age, a resident of the district for two years, a citizen of the United States, and a licensed practicing lawyer or judge for a combined four years.

District courts have jurisdiction in felony cases, which comprise approximately one-third of their criminal caseload. Civil cases in which the matter of controversy exceeds $200 may also be tried in district courts, and such cases constitute the greatest share of their workload. In addition, juvenile cases are usually tried in district courts. Although most district courts exercise both criminal and civil jurisdiction, there is a tendency in metropolitan areas for the multiple district courts to specialize in criminal, civil, or family law matters. Figure 9.3 shows that the district courts handle more civil than criminal cases.

Both criminal and civil cases are often settled out of court by negotiation between the parties involved. In criminal cases this negotiation is called **plea bargaining**, which may result in a deal in which the prosecutor and the defense attorney agree to a lighter sentence or other benefits in exchange for a guilty plea. This process saves the state a tremendous amount of time and money, with approximately three out of every four criminal cases in Texas disposed of in this way. Without plea bargaining, court delays would be increased by months if not years in many urban areas. Although efficient, this practice raises many issues concerning equity and justice because it often encourages innocent people to plead guilty and allows guilty people to escape with less punishment than provided for by the law.

Likewise, many civil lawsuits are resolved by negotiated settlements between the parties. At times this may be an appropriate and just recourse, but in many of the state's most populous counties, there is such a backlog of cases before the courts that it can take years for a matter to be heard and settled. As a result, litigants often choose to settle their case out of court for reasons other than justice.

plea bargaining
Negotiations between the prosecution and the defense to obtain a lighter sentence or other benefits in exchange for a guilty plea by the accused.

★ **Did You Know?** Drug offense cases accounted for 30 percent of the criminal cases filed in Texas district courts in 2017.

Courts of Appeals

Fourteen courts of appeals hear immediate appeals in both civil and criminal cases from district and county courts in their area. Actually, only a small percentage of trial court cases are appealed; for example, in 2017, the courts of appeals disposed of 10,647 cases, and the appeals courts reversed the decision of the trial court in only 6 percent of those cases. Appeals judges are elected from their districts, shown in Figure 9.4, for six-year terms and must be at least 35 years of age, with a minimum of 10 years of experience as a lawyer or judge.

Court of Criminal Appeals

Texas has a dual system of courts of last resort. The Texas Supreme Court is the highest state appellate court in civil matters, and the Texas Court of Criminal Appeals is the highest state appellate court in criminal matters. Among the other 49 states, only neighboring Oklahoma has a similar bifurcated system.

Although most criminal cases decided by the 14 courts of appeals do not advance further, some are heard by the Court of Criminal Appeals, which

IMAGE 9.1 The Texas Court of Criminal Appeals is the final court for criminal appeals in Texas and automatically reviews death penalty cases.

★ **CTQ** How representative of the ethnic/racial and gender diversity of the Texas population is the current Court of Criminal Appeals?

Texas Judicial Branch

FIGURE 9.4 Appeals Court Districts

Fourteen courts of appeals are multi-judge courts that serve the geographical areas shown on this map. These courts handle both criminal and civil appeals from district courts in their area.

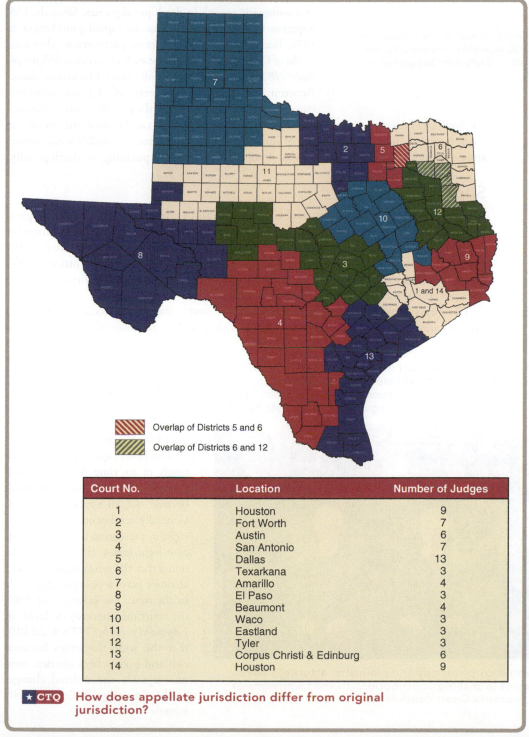

Overlap of Districts 5 and 6

Overlap of Districts 6 and 12

Court No.	Location	Number of Judges
1	Houston	9
2	Fort Worth	7
3	Austin	6
4	San Antonio	7
5	Dallas	13
6	Texarkana	3
7	Amarillo	4
8	El Paso	3
9	Beaumont	4
10	Waco	3
11	Eastland	3
12	Tyler	3
13	Corpus Christi & Edinburg	6
14	Houston	9

★ CTQ **How does appellate jurisdiction differ from original jurisdiction?**

Source: Office of Court Administration, Texas Judicial Council, Annual Statistical Report for the Texas Judiciary: Fiscal Year 2016, Austin: Texas, 2016.

consists of a presiding judge and eight other judges. Texas Court of Criminal Appeals judges are elected statewide in partisan elections for six-year overlapping terms, with three judges elected every two years. Sometimes more than three positions are on the ballot because a justice has resigned and a new judge must be elected to complete the unexpired term. Justices must be at least 35 years of age and be lawyers or judges with 10 years of experience.

Did You Know? All executions in Texas take place at the state's 169-year-old Huntsville Unit, commonly referred to as the "Walls Unit" because of its large red brick walls.

The Court of Criminal Appeals has exclusive jurisdiction over automatic appeals in death penalty cases. Since the U.S. Supreme Court restored the use of capital punishment in 1976, Texas has executed far more people than any other state.

As of October 31, 2018, the state had executed 555 people since 1982, when the death penalty was reinstated in Texas.[2] Between 2000 and 2015 an average of 21 people were executed each year. However, over the past three years the average number of executions dropped to less than 10. The decline can be attributed in part to rising concerns about the possibility of innocent people being executed and less enthusiasm among district attorneys in the state's most populous counties for pursuing the death penalty.

Supreme Court

The Texas Supreme Court is the final court of appeals in civil and juvenile cases. Original jurisdiction of the court extends to the issuance of writs and the conduct of proceedings for the involuntary retirement or removal of judges. All other cases are in appellate jurisdiction. The court also has the power to establish rules for the administration of justice—rules of civil practice and procedure for courts having civil jurisdiction. In addition, it makes rules governing the licensing of members of the state bar.

The Texas Supreme Court consists of one chief justice and eight associate justices—all elected statewide. As is the case for the Court of Criminal Appeals, three of the nine supreme court justices are elected every two years for six-year terms. A Texas Supreme Court justice must be at least 35 years of age, a citizen of the United States, a resident of Texas, and a lawyer or judge of a court of record for at least 10 years.

IMAGE 9.2 The Texas Supreme Court does not handle criminal cases, but it is the final court of appeals in civil cases. Some civil cases can have a broad impact on society, and they generate much attention from interest groups when they affect business regulation or corporate liability.

Texas Judicial Branch

Why would corporations and plaintiffs' attorneys have an interest in making contributions to the campaigns of ★ CTQ **Texas Supreme Court candidates?**

The Texas Supreme Court spends much of its time deciding which petitions for review will be granted, because not all appeals are heard. Generally, it takes only those cases it views as presenting the most significant legal issues. It should also be noted that the state's supreme court at times plays a policy-making role in the state. For example, in 1989, the court unanimously declared, in *Edgewood* v. *Kirby* (777 S.W.2d 391), that the wide disparities between rich and poor school districts were unacceptable and ordered changes in the financing of Texas's public schools.

Juries

> **LO 9.3** Understand the role of grand juries and trial juries, and analyze the responsibilities of citizens in the Texas legal system.

Juries are an important and controversial aspect of the American judicial system. Some people argue that juries are beneficial because they allow for community input and the use of common sense in the legal system. Others claim that they often do not fairly represent the community and that their reasons for their decisions are often inappropriate or suspect. What is certain is that although millions of Americans serve on juries every year, the frequency of their use is declining, and an overwhelming number of cases in our legal system are not decided by them.[3]

Grand Jury

When a person is accused of a serious crime, the matter is usually taken to a **grand jury**, which in Texas consists of 12 people who sit in pretrial proceedings to determine whether sufficient evidence exists to try an individual and therefore return an indictment. (Some states do not have grand juries, but in those that do, the size ranges from 5 to 23 members.) An alternative to a grand jury indictment is the **information**, a written accusation made by the prosecutor against a party charged with a minor crime. Filed by the prosecutor with the appropriate court, the information must be based on an investigation by the prosecutor after receiving a complaint and a sworn affidavit that a crime has been committed.

The grand jury does not determine the guilt or innocence of the accused but rather whether there is sufficient evidence to bring the accused to trial. If the evidence is determined to be sufficient, the accused is indicted. An **indictment** is a formal written accusation issued by a grand jury against a party charged with a crime when it has determined that there is sufficient evidence to bring the accused to trial; a vote of at least 9 of the 12 grand jurors is needed to indict. An indictment returned by a grand jury is sometimes referred to as a **true bill**. If an indictment is not returned, the conclusion of the grand jury is a **no bill**, which is a grand jury's refusal to return an indictment filed by the prosecutor.

At times, a grand jury may return indictments simply because the district attorney asks for them. In fact, grand juries return true bills in approximately 95 percent of the cases brought before them. This high indictment rate is attributable at least in part to the fact that the accused cannot have an attorney in the room during questioning.

Some grand juries, known as "runaway" grand juries, may consider matters independent of the district attorney's recommendation. In general, prosecutors do not like a grand jury to be so assertive and are likely to refer only routine matters to it. To bypass it, the prosecutor may refer cases to a second grand jury meeting simultaneously or postpone action for another, more favorable, grand jury.

Following a 2015 legislative reform, grand jurors are selected using the same type of broad random selection process employed to select trial jurors. This method should result in grand juries that look more like the general population in their communities. Before the recent reform, many district courts appointed members of a grand jury commission that would handpick jurors, a process derisively referred to as the "pick-a-pal" system. Under current law, a district judge is now instructed to call for between 20 and 125 prospective grand jurors to be summoned in the same way as trial jurors. From this pool of potential grand jurors, 12 are selected to become the grand jury, with four other individuals chosen as alternates.

The district attorney may determine whether or not a person indicted for a crime will be prosecuted. Some district attorneys will prosecute only if the odds are high that a conviction can be secured. This improves their "conviction rate," which can be presented to the voters when reelection time comes around. Other district attorneys may take most indicted persons

grand jury
In Texas, consists of 12 people who sit in pretrial proceedings to determine whether sufficient evidence exists to try an individual and therefore return an indictment.

information
A written accusation made by the prosecutor against a party charged with a minor crime; it is an alternative to an indictment and does not involve a grand jury.

indictment
A formal written accusation issued by a grand jury against a party charged with a crime when it has determined that there is sufficient evidence to bring the accused to trial.

true bill
An indictment returned by a grand jury.

no bill
A grand jury's refusal to return an indictment filed by the prosecutor.

to trial, even if the chances for conviction are low, but this may prove politically costly and can make the district attorney appear ineffective.

Petit (Trial) Jury

petit jury
A jury for a civil or criminal trial.

A jury for a criminal or civil trial is known as a **petit jury**. Trial by jury in criminal cases is a right guaranteed by the Texas Constitution and the Sixth Amendment of the U.S. Constitution. Even if the accused waives the right to trial by jury, expecting to be tried by the judge, the state may demand a jury trial in felony cases. Although not required by the U.S. Constitution, in Texas the parties to a civil case generally decide whether a jury trial will be held. If a jury is to be used in a civil case in district court, the party requesting it pays a nominal fee to see that a jury panel is called. After the panel is summoned, the per diem for each juror is paid from public funds, which can entail considerable expense to the public if a trial becomes lengthy. County courts, justice of the peace courts, and municipal courts have six-person juries, whereas 12 people are on juries at the district court level.

Did You Know? In Texas, jurors are selected from a list that includes individuals in a county who are registered to vote in Texas or possess a Texas driver's license or identification card.

A *venire*, or jury panel, is randomly selected from among those individuals who are registered to vote, have a Texas driver's license, or have a Texas identification card. Jurors must be literate citizens at least 18 years of age, qualified to vote, and not indicted or convicted for a theft or felony. Exemptions from jury service are now severely restricted. Persons older than 70 years of age, high school and college students, primary uncompensated caretakers for invalids, and those with legal custody of a child 12 years old or younger whose service would leave the child without adequate supervision are automatically exempt from mandatory jury service but may serve if they desire. Other excuses from jury service are at the discretion of the judge. Jurors in Texas are paid between $6 and $50 a day, although counties do not have to pay those who only attend court for one day and do not serve on a jury. At its discretion, a county may provide other compensation, including transportation reimbursement, free meals, and child-care facilities. Texas employers are not required to provide paid leave to employees serving as jurors but cannot fire employees for serving as jurors.

challenge for cause
A request to a judge that a prospective juror not be allowed to serve on the jury for a specific reason, such as bias or prior knowledge of the case.

In cases that receive a great deal of publicity, a special venire may consist of several hundred persons. Jury selection may last days or weeks, sometimes even longer than the trial itself. If either side believes that a prospective juror has a preconceived opinion about guilt or innocence, the prosecutor or defense attorneys may bring a **challenge for cause**, which is a request to a judge that a prospective juror not be allowed to serve on the jury for a specific reason, such as bias or prior knowledge of the case. Challenges for cause extend to any factor that might convince a judge

IMAGE 9.3 An attorney addresses a jury in a civil case.

Stockbyte/Getty Images

★ CTQ   **What steps are taken to eliminate bias in the jury selection process?**

that the juror could not render a fair and impartial decision. No limits are placed on the number of challenges for cause, but the judge decides whether to grant each specific challenge.

Statutes also allow challenges of jurors without cause. A challenge made to a prospective juror without being required to give a reason for removal is known as a **peremptory challenge**; no reason needs to be provided to remove a juror. The possibility exists, therefore, that nothing other than intuition can cause an attorney in a case to ask that a juror be dismissed. The only limitations to this type of challenge occur when the judge believes that prospective jurors are being eliminated solely because of their ethnicity, race, or sex. Although peremptory challenges provide lawyers with a great deal of freedom in deciding to remove jurors, each side is given only a limited number of these challenges for each case.

Many lawyers maintain that jury selection is more significant than the actual argument of a case. Some law firms hire jury and trial consulting companies to assist in the selection process. Psychological profiles of ideal jurors may be used to try to avoid jurors who might be unfavorable to a client and to identify those who might be supportive. For example, the prosecution would quite possibly want a grandparent or parent of young children on a jury dealing with child molestation, while the defense would wish to avoid such a juror. Many trial law firms and prosecutors also maintain a file on jurors from completed cases to help them select or avoid prospective jurors based on past behavior.

Although some states allow non-unanimous jury verdicts in both criminal and civil matters, juries in criminal cases in Texas must agree unanimously (this is not required in civil cases). Even if only one juror disagrees, the result is a **hung jury**, which is a jury that is unable to agree on a verdict after a suitable period of deliberation; the result is a mistrial. In this event, the prosecutor must decide whether to try the case again with a different jury or drop the matter. Because no verdict was reached with a hung jury, the accused person is not put in double jeopardy by a second trial. Usually, in the event of a second hung jury, the prosecution will drop the case.

peremptory challenge

A challenge made to a prospective juror without being required to give a reason for removal; the number of such challenges allotted to the prosecution and defense is limited.

hung jury

A jury that is unable to agree on a verdict after a suitable period of deliberation; the result is a mistrial.

Selection of Judges

LO 9.4 Compare and evaluate the most common methods of judicial selection in the United States and in Texas.

States use several methods to select judges (see How Does Texas Compare?). In fact, some states use different methods for different types of courts. One popular variant is often called the **merit plan**, or **Missouri plan**, a method of selecting judges on the basis of the merit or quality of the candidates and not on political considerations. Under this system, the governor fills court vacancies from a list of nominees submitted by a judicial commission, and these appointees later face retention elections. A relatively large number of states elect judges; in some states, the elections are partisan (candidates are officially affiliated with a political party), while in the others they are nonpartisan. Some states also provide for the appointment of judges by governors, and a few allow the legislature to make the selections. With the exception of municipal court judges, Texas elects all of its judges in partisan elections.

Reformers developed the merit plan in an attempt to make the selection of judges less political. This method supposedly bases judicial selection on the merit or quality of the candidates as opposed to political considerations. For example, under a merit plan, the governor might fill court vacancies from a list of several nominees submitted by a judicial commission chaired by a judge and composed of both lawyers and laypersons. Appointed judges would hold their posts for at least a one-year probationary period, until the next election. Their names would then be put on a retention ballot, which simply asks whether a judge should be retained. It is a "yes" or "no" vote for the candidate with no other competition. Historically, more than 90 percent of such votes result in the candidate's election (or reelection). It is important to note that scholars have overwhelmingly found that this process is no less political than other selection methods and that there is no clear evidence that this process produces different or more meritorious judges.[4]

merit plan, or **Missouri plan**

A method of selecting judges on the basis of the merit or quality of the candidates and not on political considerations. Under this system, the governor fills court vacancies from a list of nominees submitted by a judicial commission, and these appointees later face retention elections.

How Does Texas Compare?

Selecting Judges

States use different methods to choose their judges, including those who serve on their supreme court. Figure 9.5 shows that 12 states allow their governor or legislature to appoint supreme court justices. More commonly, states use elections to select their judges. There are three general types of judicial elections.

Texas (along with seven other states) holds partisan elections, whereas 14 other states use nonpartisan elections which do not include party labels on the ballot. The most popular method of selection (used in 16 states) is the merit, or Missouri, plan, which claims to be less political and combines an initial appointment with retention elections.

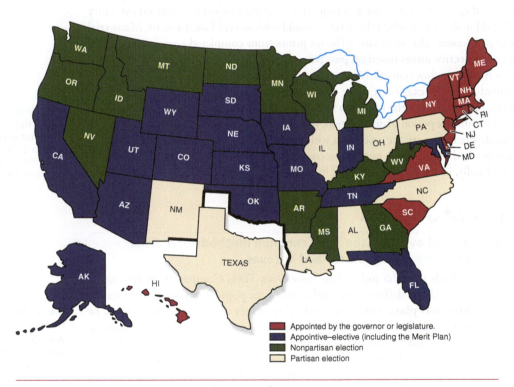

Appointed by the governor or legislature.
Appointive–elective (including the Merit Plan)
Nonpartisan election
Partisan election

FIGURE 9.5 State-by-State Selection of Supreme Court Justices

Source: Book of the States, Lexington, KY: Council of State Governments, 2017.

FOR DEBATE

 ★ CSQ What are the advantages and disadvantages of selecting judges through partisan elections? Do these advantages and disadvantages differ depending on the position, such as supreme court justice, district court judge, or justice of the peace?

The Politics of Judicial Selection in Texas

The system of judicial selection in Texas and practices related to it have been under attack. We shall examine why the courts and judges of Texas are criticized and, in doing so, gain a clearer understanding of the political nature of the court system.

Voter Knowledge Because Texas elects judges, a natural question arises: How knowledgeable are voters in these judicial elections? In other words, are voters cognizant of the candidates and their records in office? Research on the U.S. Supreme Court has repeatedly shown that the vast majority of the public knows little about its rulings and actions.[5] Therefore, if most Americans know very little about the U.S. Supreme Court—the court that receives far and away the most media attention in this country—how much do voters know about state and local courts? In a given election, Texas voters are regularly asked to cast a ballot to choose judges for the Supreme Court, the Court of Criminal Appeals, a court of appeals, district courts, county courts, and for a justice of the peace. For instance, many voters in Harris County may be presented with the task of electing more than 70 different judges in a single election. Both systematic research and abundant anecdotal evidence indicate that most voters in Texas are unaware of candidates' qualifications or experience.

Partisanship Because they know so little about individual candidates, in general elections voters rely heavily on a candidate's partisan affiliation as a cue to determine how to vote. In other words, a voter who has no knowledge of the views or backgrounds of the candidates on the ballot may cast their vote based on the party label (Republican Party, Democratic Party, and Libertarian Party) next to the candidate's name on the ballot (or simply cast a straight ticket vote for all of a party's candidates). In Texas, this is a very common approach for making selections in judicial elections.

Republican candidates have dominated recent elections for the state's highest courts, occupying all nine positions on the Supreme Court all nine spots on the Court of Criminal Appeals. Historically, Republicans also dominated among the 80 judgeships across the state's 14 courts of appeals, occupying 66 of the 80 judgeships and holding majorities in 11 of the 14 courts before the 2018 election. That changed dramatically when Democrats won three-fourths of the judgeships up for election, and with 39 appeals court judges, they now nearly equal the number of Republicans on these courts (see Table 9.2). And, whereas in 2018 Democrats constituted a majority in only three courts of appeals, in 2019 they held the majority in seven, including the influential 5th (Dallas), 1st (Houston) and 14th (Houston) courts.

It has been argued that because judges, especially at the appellate level, make significant policy decisions, it is reasonable for voters to select judges on the basis of political party affiliation. Party affiliation may provide accurate information concerning the general ideology and thus the decision-making pattern of judges. However, even if this is true, voting based solely on a judicial candidate's political party can lead to controversial results.[6]

Campaign Contributions Because voters often look for simple voting cues such as familiarity with the candidate's name or party identification, candidates often want to spend as much money as possible to make their name or candidacy well known. In recent years, spending in judicial races has increased dramatically. Candidates need to win two contests— their party's primary and the general election. In modern politics, this can be an expensive endeavor, and for more than a decade, Republican candidates have dominated the race for campaign contributions.

In addition to questions concerning fairness or the advantages of incumbency surrounding campaign finances, many critics have also asked whether justice is for sale in Texas. More directly, individuals or organizations often appear before judges to whose election campaigns

IMAGE 9.4 Like other politicians, many judges seek publicity through social media. As this screenshot makes clear, former (2005–17) Texas Supreme Court Justice Don Willett was very active on Twitter. Willett had tens of thousands of followers and was a prolific tweeter, with his tweets covering a wide range of topics from the political to the personal. In 2017 Willett was nominated by President Trump (and confirmed) to serve as a judge on the U.S. Court of Appeals for the Fifth Circuit.

★ CTQ   **How does use of social media affect a politician's rise to power? Does Twitter inform or inflame political debate?**

they have contributed money. The Texas Insiders feature puts a face on major contributors to the Texas Supreme Court candidates.

In 2009, the U.S. Supreme Court weighed in on the question of judicial bias where litigants significantly influenced the election of judges hearing their cases. In *Caperton* v. *A. T. Massey Coal Co., Inc.*, the U.S. Supreme Court held that the chairman of A. T. Massey Coal had created such a question by donating $3 million to help finance the successful election of a new justice to the Supreme Court of Appeals of West Virginia. The possible conflict of interest arose because Massey had a $50 million civil suit appeal pending before the court; it was later decided in Massey's favor by a 3–2 vote, with the new justice voting with the majority. A 5–4 U.S. Supreme Court majority reversed and remanded the case, holding "there is a serious risk of actual bias . . . when a person with a personal stake in a particular case had a significant and disproportionate influence in placing the judge on the case."[7]

TABLE 9.2 The Partisanship of Texas Judges, 2019: Supreme Court, Court of Criminal Appeals, and Courts of Appeals

Court	Appellate District (see Figure 9.4)	Total Number of Judges	Republicans	Democrats
Supreme Court		9	9	0
Court of Criminal Appeals		9	9	0
Courts of Appeals	Total	80	41	39
	First	9	4	5
	Second	7	7	0
	Third	6	2	4
	Fourth	7	1	6
	Fifth	13	5	8
	Sixth	3	3	0
	Seventh	4	4	0
	Eighth	3	0	3
	Ninth	4	2	2
	Tenth	3	3	0
	Eleventh	3	3	0
	Twelfth	3	3	0
	Thirteenth	6	0	6
	Fourteenth	9	4	5

Texas State Directory.

▶ Does the partisan balance on all of these courts accurately reflect the partisan balance among Texas voters?

Part of this debate of possible impropriety involves the battle between plaintiffs' attorneys and defense attorneys in civil cases. Texas has traditionally been a conservative, pro-business state. This perspective was usually reflected in the decisions of the judiciary, which often favored big business and professional groups (such as the medical profession). Plaintiffs' lawyers and their related interest groups have made a concerted effort in the past few decades to make the judiciary more open to consumer suits, often filed against businesses, doctors, and their insurance companies. The plaintiffs' lawyers poured millions of dollars into the campaign accounts of candidates they believed would align more favorably with their perspective. Defense and business attorneys and tort reform advocates such as Texans for Lawsuit Reform (TLR) responded with millions of dollars of their own contributions. These lawyers, from both vantage points, then often appear before the very judges to whom they have given these large sums of money.

★ Texas Insiders

Campaign Contributors in Texas Supreme Court Elections: Following the Money

Lawyers are by far the single largest group of contributors in judicial campaigns for both trial and appellate courts, including the Texas Supreme Court, as shown in Table 9.3. Contributors to candidates running for the Texas Supreme Court gave a total of $4,231,108 in 2016. As usual, Republicans won all three positions being filled that year; no candidate running as a Democrat has been elected to the Texas Supreme Court since 1994.

Thinking about the role of elites in Texas politics

The list of top contributors to Texas Supreme Court candidates is dominated by the state's preeminent corporate defense and lobbying law firms. Among the other top contributors is Texans for Lawsuit Reform (TLR), a business-sponsored group that seeks to limit the ability to bring liability suits (featured in our Texas Insiders section in Chapter 10). TLR is closely allied with the Republican Party.

Important plaintiffs' attorneys and their umbrella organization, the Texas Trial Lawyers Association, are missing from this list of top contributors. Plaintiffs' lawyers primarily represent injured workers, patients, consumers, and the insured in liability suits against corporations, insurance companies, and medical providers. These attorneys, including notables like Steve Mostyn (who unexpectedly passed away in 2017), are mostly aligned with the Democratic Party. Since these plaintiffs' attorneys have not believed that Democratic judicial candidates have had a realistic chance of winning in state-wide contests, they tend to direct their campaign contributions to other races.

 Is there a conflict of interest when law firms represent clients before a judge that their contributions helped elect? Should judges recuse themselves, or abstain, from cases that affect their largest campaign contributors? In your answer, consider whether any single contributor's share of a judge's campaign treasury could be sufficient to create a genuine conflict of interest.

TABLE 9.3 Top 10 Contributors in Texas Supreme Court Races

Contributor	Total	Percent of Total	Sector
Vinson & Elkins	$238,232	5.6%	Lawyers and lobbyists
Texans for Lawsuit Reform	$182,492	4.3%	General business
Paul Green	$154,311	3.7%	Self-funded candidate
Fulbright & Jaworski	$138,750	3.3%	Lawyers and lobbyists
Haynes & Boone	$129,000	3.1%	Lawyers and lobbyists
Michael Massengale	$116,241	2.8%	Self-funded candidate
Good Government Fund	$94,750	2.2%	Oil and gas
Bracewell & Giuliani	$85,000	2.0%	Lawyers and lobbyists
Andrews Kurth LLP	$84,000	2.0%	Lawyers and lobbyists
Jackson Walker LLP	$83,500	2.0%	Lawyers and lobbyists

National Institute on Money in State Politics and the Texas Ethics Commission.

Clearly, the current system is quite political, and many people are critical of it for a variety of reasons. This has led to repeated attempts to reform the way Texas selects its judges or change what is permissible in campaign fundraising. Proposals for change have come from many sources, including chief justices of the state supreme court and a committee formed by a lieutenant governor. However, with such divergent interests involved and no clear alternative acceptable to all groups, very little judicial reform has actually taken place.

Ethnic/Racial and Gender Diversity

A major criticism of the current partisan election system involves one of its outcomes: limited ethnic/racial and gender diversity on the bench. Figure 9.6 details the ethnic and gender profile of the state's judges. Although Anglos account for less than half (42 percent) of the state's overall population, 76 percent of the state's judges are Anglos. In contrast, only 17 percent of the state's judges are Latinos, and even fewer are African Americans or Asian Americans.

FIGURE 9.6 **Ethnicity/Race and Gender of Texas Judges**

This figure compares the ethnicity/race and gender of Texas judges with the population as a whole as of 2017.

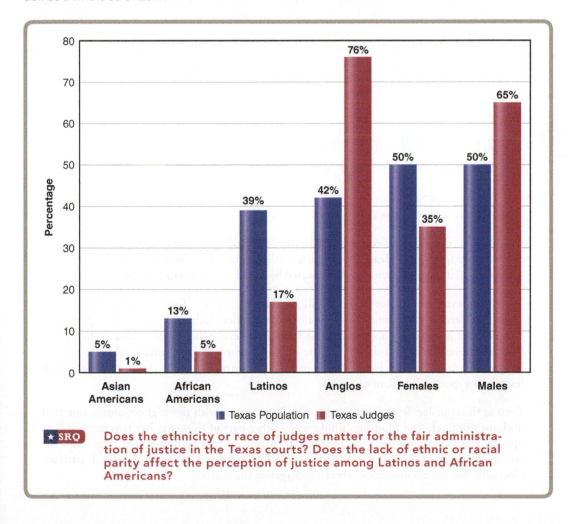

★ SRQ   Does the ethnicity or race of judges matter for the fair administration of justice in the Texas courts? Does the lack of ethnic or racial parity affect the perception of justice among Latinos and African Americans?

Women's representation in judicial posts varies considerably across the different court levels. Women are close to parity on the Texas Court of Criminal Appeals and the 14 appeals courts. However, the lower courts are more male dominated—overall, a little more than one-third (35 percent) of all Texas judges are women.

Applying What You Have Learned about Texas Courts

LO 9.5   **Apply what you have learned about the Texas judiciary.**

You have learned that Texas selects its judges using partisan elections in which parties nominate candidates who are then elected by the state's voters. You also learned that this method for selecting judges has been criticized for various reasons and that many states have turned to other strategies to select their judges. So we asked the former chief justice of the Texas Supreme Court Wallace Jefferson to explain his views of the judicial selection process based on his practical experiences inside the judiciary.

Wallace Jefferson was appointed to the Texas Supreme Court in 2001 and subsequently elected to the bench by voters in 2002. In 2004 he was named the 26th chief justice of the Texas Supreme Court. He was elected chief justice in 2006 and reelected for a six-year term in 2008. Jefferson made judicial history as the first African American justice and chief justice of the Texas Supreme Court. He is a partner at Alexander, Dubose, Jefferson & Townsend LLP.

After you have read the chief justice's essay, we will ask you to identify the major features of his proposal to reform the way Texas judges are selected and we will ask you to evaluate Chief Justice Jefferson's proposal compared to Texas's current system for selecting judges.

POLITICS IN PRACTICE
Choosing Judges: My View from the Inside

by Wallace B. Jefferson
FORMER CHIEF JUSTICE OF THE TEXAS SUPREME COURT

Historically, the states, Texas included, have rejected the federal model of executively appointed judges. When Texas was a much smaller place, this probably made sense: electing judges ensured that they were people respected by—and responsive to—the local community.

Today, however, these historical justifications make little sense. Texas now has 1,882 judges in its appellate, district, county, and justice courts. These judges sit on a dizzying array of courts. This is especially apparent at the trial court level, where judges have different but frequently overlapping jurisdictions. Some hear only criminal cases; others only cases related to specific subject matters, like family or probate cases; and some only claims worth more (or less) than a specified amount of money.

Even at the appellate level, Texas is one of only two states with *two* highest courts, one civil and one criminal. And Houston, unlike every other part of the state, has two intermediate appeals courts covering the same territory. In spite of this huge number of judges and the confusing courts system, Texas expects voters to choose good judges in contested, partisan elections. But the circumstances are stacked against the voters.

Take Harris County, for instance. A voter in the 2014 election would have voted for just nine statewide officials, her member of congress, state senator, and state representative. She also would have voted for *75 judges*.

No voter, not even the most conscientious, could be expected to make an informed choice in each of these races. For the average voter, who probably has no more than a passing familiarity with the judicial system, these choices must be flummoxing.

The result is that Texas voters choose their judges based almost exclusively on their partisan identity. Indeed, with few exceptions, that is probably all the vast majority of voters know about the judicial candidates on the ballot. Name recognition even for Supreme Court and Court of Criminal Appeals justices, who run statewide, is extremely low.

What's worse is that partisan identity is a poor proxy for judicial competence. Most judges—and nearly all trial judges, who constitute the great majority of judges in Texas—are asked infrequently, if ever, to pass upon the fraught social and constitutional issues that animate media coverage of the judiciary.

Instead, judges perform a function that is much more mundane—and much more personal. Judges probate wills and apportion divorcing spouses' assets; they preside over criminal trials; they oversee business disputes.

Most of the time, the decisions judges make matter only to the parties directly involved. Very rarely do their decisions implicate the judge's personal politics. Instead, they implicate the judge's sense of fairness, her patience, her compassion, and her intelligence. These traits are not correlated with any particular party.

Texas's current system for selecting judges thus ensures that at every election, good and bad judges alike are swept out of office based on their party membership alone. Similarly, there is evidence that judicial candidates have lost simply because they have names commonly associated with racial or ethnic minorities—or names that are just plain unusual.

To limit the pernicious effects of judicial elections, I have long advocated that Texas move towards a system that balances Texans' desire for a direct say in choosing their judges with the need to ensure that competency and integrity are valued over partisanship and name recognition.

My proposal would see the creation of a merit selection panel that recommends accomplished and distinguished lawyers for a place on the bench. Those judges recommended by the panel would be appointed by the governor, subject to nonpartisan retention elections. This recommendation is not a panacea, but it would limit both the negative effects of low information and partisan voting, and it would help ensure that Texas's judges are of the highest caliber.

1. Among the various methods states use to select their judges, which type does the former chief justice propose that Texas use? How does this system differ from the way the state currently chooses its judges?
2. What arguments does Chief Justice Jefferson use to support his proposals for a merit system? Why does he argue that party labels are unimportant in the judicial selection process?

★ Chapter Summary

LO 9.1 Describe the differences between criminal and civil cases and between original and appellate jurisdiction. Cases in the legal system can be classified in two ways. *Civil cases* deal primarily with individual or property rights. *Criminal cases* deal with violations of penal law. There are two types of jurisdiction. *Original jurisdiction* is the basic power to try a case for the first time. Courts with original jurisdiction are called *trial courts*, and they determine the facts such as guilt in criminal cases or responsibility in civil cases. Trial courts also apply the law to the facts in each case. *Appellate jurisdiction* is the ability to review the decisions of a lower court by determining if the trial judge properly applied the law.

LO 9.2 Explain how the courts are organized in Texas, and identify the jurisdiction of each major court. Among the trial courts, municipal and county courts handle minor civil or criminal cases. District courts handle all serious civil and criminal cases. Appeals from district and county courts go to one of the courts of appeal. The court of last resort for criminal cases is the Texas Court of Criminal Appeals while the Texas Supreme Court makes final decisions in most civil cases.

The organization of the Texas court system is often viewed as too big and complicated. Lines of jurisdiction sometimes overlap. Judicial salaries and the qualifications needed to serve as a judge vary widely across the different levels of the Texas judicial system. Critics have urged reorganization of the courts along more simplified lines for decades.

LO 9.3 Understand the role of grand juries and trial juries, and analyze the responsibilities of citizens in the Texas legal system. Juries are an important aspect of the American judicial system. The judicial system has two primary types of juries. A *grand jury* issues indictments that indicate whether sufficient evidence exists to bring the accused to trial in criminal cases. A *petit jury* determines guilt in a criminal case and responsibility in a civil case.

LO 9.4 Compare and evaluate the most common methods of judicial selection in the United States and in Texas. Various states use different methods for selecting judges. A few states empower the governor or legislature to appoint their judges, while others allow voters to elect their judges. In many states, the judges are elected by voters, sometimes in nonpartisan elections and sometimes in partisan elections, as in Texas. The goal of electing judges is to give voters democratic control over the judiciary. Many states attempt to combine the advantages of appointment and election by allowing the governor to appoint a judge for a short probationary period after which voters are allowed to decide whether or not to retain the judge. Regardless of the method, judicial selection is highly politicized because courts make life-altering decisions and often shape public policy.

LO 9.5 Apply what you have learned about the Texas judiciary. You explored the methods by which we presently select judges in Texas via partisan elections. You reviewed former Texas Supreme Court Chief Justice Jefferson's proposal to reform the way judges are selected. You evaluated the arguments that he presented in favor of the reform proposal.

Key Terms

appellate jurisdiction, *p. 238*
beyond a reasonable doubt, *p. 237*
briefs, *p. 238*
burden of proof, *p. 237*

challenge for cause, *p. 248*
civil case, *p. 237*
criminal case, *p. 237*
de novo trials, *p. 239*
double jeopardy, *p. 239*
grand jury, *p. 247*
hung jury, *p. 249*

indictment, *p. 247*
information, *p. 247*
merit plan, or Missouri plan, *p. 249*
no bill, *p. 247*
original jurisdiction, *p. 238*

peremptory challenge, *p. 249*
petit jury, *p. 248*
plea bargaining, *p. 244*
preponderance of the evidence, *p. 237*
true bill, *p. 247*

Review Questions

LO 9.1 Describe the differences between criminal and civil cases and between original and appellate jurisdiction.

- What are the characteristics that distinguish criminal and civil cases? What is the nature of the parties involved in both types of cases? What are the requisite standards of proof regarding evidence?

- What is the difference between original and appellate jurisdiction? What types of issues and evidence are considered in each?

LO 9.2 Explain how the courts are organized in Texas, and identify the jurisdiction of each major court.

- What types of jurisdiction do the different Texas courts have?

- What basic elements of a case determine where the case is heard?

- How do the qualifications of judges vary from court to court?

LO 9.3 Understand the role of grand juries and trial juries, and analyze the responsibilities of citizens in the Texas legal system.

- Compare and contrast grand juries and petit juries.

- How are jurors selected to serve on panels?

- What is the function of each type of jury?

LO 9.4 Compare and evaluate the most common methods of judicial selection in the United States and in Texas.

- What are some of the methods employed for selecting judges in the United States?

- How are judges chosen in Texas? How is the process of judicial selection a political one?

- What are some criticisms of the manner in which the state's judges are chosen?

Think Critically and Get Active!

Team up with groups that represent your views on the courts. Groups that advocate using the courts to protect consumers, workers, and patients include the Texas Trial Lawyers Association at **www.ttla.com** (@TTLA_). Groups that fight non-meritorious lawsuits and excessive damage claims in the Texas legal system include Texans for Lawsuit Reform (TLR) at **www .tortreform.com** (@lawsuitreform).

Find out who the municipal court judges are in your community. These are the judges who hear cases involving traffic tickets or violations of municipal ordinances. Go to **www.txcourts.gov**, click on the drop-down bar for "Judicial Data" at the top of the page, and then select the "Judicial Directory."

Learn how to join the fight against human trafficking at **www.texasattorneygeneral.gov/human-trafficking**.

Find out how various groups rate judicial candidates. For example, the Texas Bar Association rates candidates running for positions on the Supreme Court, the Court of Criminal Appeals, and the 14 courts of appeals at **www.texasbar. com/pollresults**. The Texas League of Women Voters provides valuable information about judicial candidates in their Texas Voters Guide at **www.lwvtexas.org**.

★ **PRQ** How is it possible for ordinary voters to evaluate the qualifications of judges who handle complicated legal issues? Should they take the advice of the bar association, businesses, labor organizations, or political parties? Which organizations can provide voters with reliable information about judges' qualifications, ethics, and sense of justice?

10

Law and Due Process

The quality of justice depends upon the values of the people who interpret and implement the law. In this chapter, you will evaluate the gap between the ideals and practice of justice and how it affects your basic rights and responsibilities in the real world.

Xavier Van Eegan/Alamy Stock Photo

Learning Objectives

LO 10.1 Analyze civil law and the policy issues related to it.

LO 10.2 Analyze the elements and causes of crime.

LO 10.3 Analyze the concepts of due process.

LO 10.4 Evaluate punishment and rehabilitation policies.

LO 10.5 Apply what you have learned about the due process of law.

As you have learned, there are substantial differences between criminal and civil law. Civil law deals largely with private rights and individual relationships, obligations, and responsibilities. Criminal law is concerned with public morality—concepts of right and wrong as defined by government.

Hence, criminal cases are prosecuted by public officials (usually county or district attorneys) in the name of the public. Civil suits are brought by a **plaintiff**, who is usually a private person or institution, although governments occasionally initiate civil suits when seeking to enforce antitrust laws, abate public nuisances, or pursue other noncriminal matters.

Perhaps the most important distinction between civil and criminal law is the way each deals with court findings. In criminal law the aim is punishment, but in civil law the remedy used to redress an injury is relief from ongoing injury or compensation for past damages. For example, criminal law might punish a thief, but the civil law remedy for the unlawful seizure of property might be the return of the property to its rightful owner. Regarded as civil rather than criminal, juvenile proceedings are an interesting illustration of the difference between civil and criminal law. Assigning juveniles to the custody of reform schools is not intended as punishment but as an effort to correct their delinquency. Assigning an adult to a penitentiary, however, is considered punishment.

plaintiff
The party bringing a civil suit, usually a private person or institution.

Civil Law

LO 10.1 **Analyze civil law and the policy issues related to it.**

The primary focus of civil law is defining and civilizing interpersonal relationships; it also enforces legitimate contracts between parties and assigns responsibilities for personal injuries. We will provide a sample of some civil laws, but you should remember that Texas civil law fills volumes of printed matter. Texas civil statutes are organized into 28 codes ranging from the Agriculture Code to *Vernon's Annotated Civil Statutes*. It is impossible to discuss the state's civil laws in detail—even the most competent attorneys tend to specialize in specific fields of law.

Types of Civil Law

Civil law in the states today is based in large part on centuries-old English *common law* we first discussed in Chapter 3. Common law is judge-made law; whether written or unwritten, it is based on **precedents**, previously decided cases used as a guiding principle for future cases. If the essential elements of a current case are like those of a case already decided, the judge makes the same decision as was made in the earlier case. These decisions made over the years have fallen into patterns that form the basis of common law. In contrast, *statutory law* is law that has been passed by legislative bodies and is written in codebooks. Legislatures have incorporated many common-law principles into civil statutes and thereby reduced the need to rely directly on common law.

precedents
A previously decided legal case used as a guiding principle for future cases.

Family Law The family is protected by civil law in Texas. For example, even if a man and a woman have not participated in a formal ceremony of marriage in the presence of authorized officers of religious organizations or judges, the law may nevertheless recognize the existence of a marriage. A man and a woman who live together, agree they are married, and publicly present themselves as husband and wife will have a common-law marriage, their children will be legitimate, and the marriage can be terminated through a legal divorce. However, divorce action must be taken within one year of separation, or the marriage will be treated as if it never existed.

As a *community property* state, Texas requires that a divorced couple divide property acquired during marriage, and one spouse is not usually responsible for the other's support.

Children, however, have the right to be supported by their parents even if the parents are divorced. Either parent might be given legal custody of the children, but the other parent may be responsible for part of their support.

Real Estate Law Titles to real property, like land and buildings, are registered in the office of the county clerk, and the legitimate use of any property by its owner is enforceable in the courts. The owner of a homestead will not lose it in a civil suit except to satisfy tax liens, home improvement loans, mortgage loans for initial purchase of the property, or home equity loans.

Probate Law Even in death, property rights are protected because a person may control transfer of his or her estate through a will. If a will exists at the time of death, the function of the courts (usually the county courts) is to probate the will, determining that it is the last and valid will of the deceased. If a person dies without leaving a will, civil law defines the right to inherit among various relatives; if there are no living relatives, the property passes to the state.

The right to inherit, bequeath, sell, lease, or transfer property is protected by law, but the rights of ownership do not include the privilege of misuse. The right to own a gun does not convey the right to use it as a weapon in murder; the privilege of opening an industrial plant does not include the right to pollute. The regulation of private property for public purposes is one of the oldest functions of law.

Business Regulations Texas law includes thousands of provisions regulating private property, and it establishes hundreds of courts and administrative agencies to elaborate, interpret, and enforce those regulations. State regulatory agencies include the Texas Railroad Commission, the Commissioner of Insurance, the Texas Finance Commission, the Public Utilities Commission, and occupational licensing boards. Their administrative regulations are administrative law enforced by civil rather than criminal courts, and the attorney general may also bring civil suits to enforce antitrust and consumer protection laws.

Corporate Law When corporations secure permission from the state to conduct business, the secretary of state issues them a charter, the organizing document that defines their structure, purposes, and activities. Civil law holds that when a new corporation is chartered, a new legal person is created—one who can sue and be sued. Corporations are frequently sued for breach of contracts and personal injury claims.

Contract Law When two parties enter into a valid contract, the courts will enforce the terms of the contract. However, certain kinds of contracts are not enforceable in the courts—for example, contracts with minors. Texas right-to-work laws also forbid contracts between labor and management that establish a closed shop in which management agrees to hire only labor union members or a union shop in which management agrees to require all new employees to join the union as a condition for their continued employment. Because of these restrictions, Texas is considered inhospitable to unions.

torts
A civil wrong, whether intentional or negligent, that results in the injury of another person.

Torts Cases involving a civil wrong that results in a personal injury are called **torts**. Sometimes injuries result from negligence when someone fails to act with the prudence an ordinary person would exercise. For example, victims of reckless driving or medical malpractice may bring a tort action to recover losses. Other examples of personal injury may result from intentional acts such as selling defective products or falsely defaming someone's character. Slander is spoken and libel is published defamation, but either may result in a lawsuit to recover monetary compensation for damage to one's reputation and earning potential.

Issues in Civil Law

These are only a few selected illustrations of civil law. More valuable to the average Texas citizen is an understanding of the major political issues surrounding civil suits. In fact, efforts to change civil law have been a major issue in Texas election campaigns and have occupied much of the legislature's time and energy.

Did You Know? Although Texas law effectively extends libel protections to vegetables and other foods, the Texas beef industry lost a suit against Oprah Winfrey for disparaging its product.

Tort Reform Insurance companies, corporations, medical practitioners, and others have argued that society has become overly litigious—too inclined to go to court to settle differences. They assert that "frivolous" lawsuits have overcrowded court dockets and excessive damage awards have unnecessarily driven up insurance premiums and other business costs. As a result, most Republican leaders have joined with groups representing defendants in civil actions, the Texas Civil Justice League, Texans for Lawsuit Reform, insurance companies, and a wide range of business and medical interest groups to urge **tort reform** to limit liability in civil cases.

tort reform
Efforts to limit liability in civil cases.

Because of the power of this political alliance, Texas has given judges the power to dismiss frivolous lawsuits and has capped jury awards for punitive damages intended to punish the defendant. And Texans narrowly approved a constitutional amendment to allow the legislature to limit claims for pain and suffering.

Consumer and environmentalist groups, Public Citizen, Texas Watch, Texans for Public Justice, the Texas Trial Lawyers Association, and most Democratic Party leaders generally oppose sweeping tort reform of the type Texas has enacted. They argue that isolated anecdotal instances of lawsuit abuse should not be used as a justification to restrict the fundamental right to trial by jury. They contend that only a jury hearing all evidence presented by both sides can make an appropriate judgment in cases of extreme negligence or abuse of an individual's rights.

Plaintiffs' attorneys view tort reform as a big business attack on the laws protecting consumers against defective products and deceptive trade practices; they argue that the threat of meaningful civil action is the only way to hold manufacturers and professionals responsible for their actions and to force companies to improve safety procedures. Tort reform makes lawyers reluctant to take the risk of bringing costly and time-consuming lawsuits against well-funded corporations. Under Texas's new "loser pays" system, if either party refuses an out-of-court settlement and if the jury awards damages significantly different from the settlement offer, the loser must pay all of the winner's legal expenses.

IMAGE 10.1 Texas Department of Insurance data show that medical malpractice suits have declined by two-thirds since tort reform was adopted in Texas.

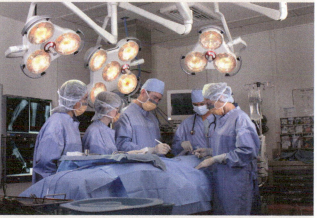

UpperCut Images/Alamy Stock Photo

★ **SRQ**   **Should statewide statutes limit malpractice claims, or should juries be allowed to evaluate them on a case-by-case basis?**

Tort reform issues are often the primary driving force in judicial campaigns. Corporations, insurance companies, health professionals, and frequently sued business groups generally contribute money to Republican judicial candidates, who are inclined to interpret the law to limit damages in civil lawsuits. Consumer groups, environmentalists, plaintiffs' lawyers, patient rights groups, and workers' organizations usually rally around Democratic judicial candidates, who tend to be friendlier to their causes. Our Texas Insiders feature puts a face on the political battle over tort reform.

★ Texas Insiders

Texans for Lawsuit Reform: Interest Groups and Justice

Dick Trabulsi, the owner of a chain of liquor stores, and Houston homebuilder Richard Weekley organized Texans for Lawsuit Reform (TLR) to support tort reform. Whether or not one agrees with TLR, there is no doubt that the group has used political means to change Texas's concept of justice.

TLR first became a fund-raising juggernaut and established itself as a major force in Texas politics with the election of former Governor George W. Bush. Funded principally by around two dozen megadonors, TLR remains one of the largest and most prominent interest groups to help bankroll Republican candidates for the Texas Legislature, the governorship, and the Texas Supreme Court.

Visualizing itself as an opponent of frivolous lawsuits, TLR argued that excessive damage awards in civil cases drive up the costs of doing business and that those costs are passed on to consumers in the form of higher prices. The group persuaded the legislature and voters to amend the Texas Constitution to restrict jury awards of punitive damages, and it successfully advocated for a "loser pays" system for legal fees.

TLR's opponents, including plaintiffs' lawyers who represent consumers, injured workers, patients, and the insured, believe that tort reform dramatically altered the rights of injured parties to sue businesses, medical providers, and insurance companies. They believe that tort reform "went far beyond limiting excessive jury awards and effectively barred the court-room door to injured Texans with legitimate claims." Mark Kincaid of the Texas Trial Lawyers Association asked, "What else is left for them to do?"

Actually, TLR continued its victories into 2016 election campaigns, boasting "Texans for Lawsuit Reform PAC (TLRPAC) endorsed candidates in 70 state races, including the Texas Railroad Commission, Texas Supreme Court, Texas House and Senate districts and numerous appellate judicial races. TLRPAC was the largest financial supporter of many of the conservative candidates in the most contested campaigns, and won 64 of 70 races – a decisive and impressive accomplishment...."

Thinking about the role of elites in Texas politics

The Texas political system tends to over-represent concentrated interests at the expense of diffused interests. Insurance companies, health care providers, manufacturers, and retailers are often sued and have a strong interest in organizing to limit legal actions that raise their cost of doing business. Meanwhile, workers, patients, and consumers have little motivation to organize to protect their right to recover damages on the off chance that they will be injured by lax workplace safety standards, medical malpractice, or defective products.

★ SRQ   **How do unorganized interests protect themselves in the political system?**

Liability Insurance Automobile insurance is one area for tort reform that the Texas legislature has not seriously considered. A no-fault insurance plan would allow an insured person to collect damages from the individual's own insurance company regardless of who is at fault in an accident. Under Texas's liability insurance plan, an expensive and time-consuming legal effort is often required to determine which of the individuals involved in an accident is to blame and thus legally responsible for damages. With no-fault insurance, insurance company costs for court trials could be substantially reduced, and the resulting savings could presumably be passed on to policy holders. Although some instances of fraud have been associated with no-fault insurance, at least a dozen states have successfully used limited no-fault insurance programs.

eminent domain
Government taking private property for public use.

Eminent Domain The Texas Constitution, like the U.S. Constitution, requires that owners must be given adequate or just compensation in cases of **eminent domain**, when government takes their private property for public use. "Just compensation" has long been interpreted to mean fair market value. Recently, however, the meaning of "public use" has become controversial. The U.S. Supreme Court interpreted public use to include private commercial development as long as it benefits the community as a whole.[1] In its ruling, the Court approved a city government seizing private residences to make way for a resort hotel, office buildings, and posh apartments.

Although this is the interpretation of "use" that was used in Texas and many other states, property rights advocates were outraged. They hoped that the Court would ban taking, or condemning, private property for the benefit of other investors. Property rights activists argued that wealthy, politically well-connected buyers have the power to profit by influencing government to displace homeowners from property to use it for their own purposes.

In response, Texas limited government's power of eminent domain. The legislature banned state and local governments from condemning private property for economic development projects except roads, parks, libraries, auditoriums, ports, and utilities. Local governments may still use eminent domain for flood control and urban renewal projects.

The Elements of Crime

LO 10.2 **Analyze the elements and causes of crime.**

Although presidential candidates often make crime a national issue, only 5 percent of crimes are actually prosecuted under federal law. Criminal justice policies are made primarily by states, not the federal government.

An act of Congress provides that federal offenses include crimes (1) committed on the high seas; (2) committed on federal property, territories, and reservations; (3) involving the crossing of state or national boundaries; (4) interfering with interstate commerce; or (5) committed against the national government or its employees while they are engaged in official duties. Otherwise, the vast majority of crimes are violations of state rather than federal law.

The Crime

A crime is an act that violates whatever a legislature defines as penal law. Many obey the law simply because it *is* law; others obey out of fear of punishment. Nevertheless, it is people's basic attitudes and values that are most important in determining whether they will respect or disobey a law. If a law reflects the values of most of society, as the law against murder does, it is usually obeyed. However, if a large element of society does not accept the values protected by law—such as alcohol prohibition in the 1920s or marijuana prohibition today—violation becomes widespread.

Felonies Serious crimes punishable by state institutions are **felonies** such as those shown in Table 10.1. Murder is the illegal, willful killing of another human being. Robbery is attempting to take something from a person by force or threat of force. It is inaccurate to say that "a house was robbed"—this implies that a masked bandit stood at the front door with a pistol drawn on the doorbell and demanded that the building deliver up all its valuables. Buildings are burglarized—unlawfully entered to commit a felony or theft.

Theft (larceny) is simply taking property from the rightful possession of another. Grand larceny—taking something valued more than $1,500—is a felony. Regardless of value, livestock rustling is a felony. It is also a felony for an adult to have sexual relations with a child less than 17 years of age.

Misdemeanors In Texas, it is a crime to disturb game hunters or for a commercial fisherman to possess a flounder less than 12 inches in length. Texting while driving is now

felonies
Serious crimes punishable by state institutions.

TABLE 10.1 Crime and Punishment under the Texas Penal Code

Offense	Examples	Terms*	Maximum Fine
Capital murder	Murder of a police officer, firefighter, prison guard, or child younger than the age of 6; murder for hire; murder committed with certain other felonies; mass murder	Execution or life sentence without parole	N/A
First-degree felony	Aggravated sexual assault, theft of money or property greater than $200,000, robbery, murder, sale of more than 4 grams of "hard" drugs such as heroin	5 to 99 years	$10,000
Second-degree felony	Theft of money or property greater than $100,000, burglary of a habitation	2 to 20 years	$10,000
Third-degree felony	Theft of money or property greater than $20,000, drive-by shootings, involuntary manslaughter	2 to 10 years	$10,000
State jail felony	Theft of money or property greater than $1,500, burglary of a building other than a habitation, sale of less than 1 gram of narcotics, auto theft, forgery	180 days to 2 years	$10,000
Class A misdemeanor	Theft of money or property greater than $500, driving while intoxicated, resisting arrest, stalking	Up to 1 year	$4,000
Class B misdemeanor	Theft of money or property greater than $50, possession of small amounts of marijuana, reckless conduct (such as pointing a gun at someone)	Up to 180 days	$2,000
Class C misdemeanor	Theft of money or property less than $50, smoking in a public elevator, disorderly conduct (such as indecent exposure)	N/A	$500

* Punishments may be reduced for murder committed in "sudden passion" or enhanced to the next level for crimes involving gang activity, the use of deadly weapons, previous convictions, or hate crimes (motivated by bias on the basis of ethnicity, religion, sexual orientation or status as a peace officer or judge).

© Cengage Learning

misdemeanors
Minor crimes punishable by a county jail sentence or fine.

outlawed. Most traffic violations are crimes, and the resulting fine is a form of punishment. Such minor crimes are called **misdemeanors** and are punishable by a sentence in county jail or a fine.

Victimless Crimes   Whether felonies or misdemeanors, some criminologists consider such crimes as prostitution, gambling, and illegal drug possession to be *victimless crimes* because their primary victims are the criminals themselves. However, the families of these criminals and society also pay a price for these activities, and they are often linked to more serious crimes.

The Criminal

What causes people to commit crimes? What leads them to adopt values different from those reflected in the laws? What are the factors in crime?

Failing to Accept Social Values Persons who become criminals vary across the broad spectrum of human personality and come from virtually any of the multitudes of social and economic classes. Yet persons who typically commit serious crimes are astonishingly similar. For one reason or another, they are unwilling to accept the values of the people who write the law. Lawbreakers are disproportionately young, poor, and members of racial or ethnic minority groups; many have acute emotional and social problems.

Most crimes are committed by people who in one way or another are on the fringes of society. In many instances, these perpetrators simply live in an environment that promotes despair, low self-esteem, and weak emotional ties to "legitimate" society. Some criminals consciously identify themselves as victims and rationalize their conduct based on their victim psychology.

Age With the decline of traditional family life and the rise of single-parent households, many young people are inadequately socialized by adults and generally lack a useful and rewarding role in society. They lack the sense of attachment that usually goes with a job or a family. The young person who has dropped out of school or who is unemployed often has difficulty functioning in legitimate society.

In some neighborhoods, street gangs provide the sole opportunity for social life and capitalistic endeavor. Membership in a gang is a powerful source of approval and a sense of belonging—often a member's only source—and thus gangs become training grounds in crime for successive generations. Lessons not learned on the streets may be picked up from the thousands of demonstrations of crime seen in the virtual world of gaming, TV, or movies.

Whether as gangs or individuals, persons younger than the age of 25 commit a disproportionate share of crime. In 2016, those young people made up just 38 percent of the Texas population but accounted for 42 percent of all arrests for theft, 51 percent for burglary, and 41 percent for arson.[2] Americans younger than age 25 accounted for 35 percent of all arrests nationwide for violent crimes (murder, non-negligent manslaughter, forcible rape, aggravated assault, and robbery) and 38 percent of property crimes (burglary, theft, motor vehicle theft, and arson).[3] Most of these make up **FBI index crimes**, which are used as a national barometer of the crime rate—murder and non-negligent manslaughter, forcible rape, robbery, aggravated assault, burglary, grand theft, and motor vehicle theft.

Many people refuse to recognize that the young are major perpetrators of crime, and others are convinced that they will "grow out of it." The truth is that disproportionate numbers of young people commit crimes and, rather than growing out of it, graduate into more serious crime; yet little is done to rehabilitate juveniles early in their criminal careers. Juvenile courts in Texas provide only limited social services for delinquents, and many have no access to vocational training, employment placement, emergency shelter, foster homes, or halfway houses. Severely limited in resources and facilities, Texas juvenile facilities not only fail to correct but also serve as breeding grounds for adult crime.

Gender Far more men than women are arrested for crimes. In 2016, men accounted for 88 percent of Texans arrested for murder, 86 percent for robbery, and 78 percent for

IMAGE 10.2 First-offense driving while intoxicated is a misdemeanor punishable in the county jail. Here a city police officer conducts a field sobriety test. Students can access alcohol-related regulations at www.tabc.state.tx.us.

Yellow Dog Productions/Getty Images

★ PRQ **How much should the law regulate individual conduct when it endangers society at large? Consider personal consumption of tobacco, narcotics, and fossil fuels in your answer. Explain the trade-offs between personal freedoms and the public good.**

FBI index crimes
Crimes used as a national barometer of the crime rate—murder and non-negligent manslaughter, forcible rape, robbery, aggravated assault, burglary, grand theft, and motor vehicle theft.

aggravated assault.[4] Perhaps traditional masculine roles, social positions, and psychological attitudes make it difficult for some of them to accept certain mores of society. Aggression, violent sports, assertiveness, protectiveness, and earning money are often regarded as essentials of a boy's training for manhood. Apparently, many young men fail to recognize the distinction between the kind of assertiveness that society approves and the kind it condemns.

Ethnicity and Race Certain members of minority groups are arrested disproportionately for crime. Although African Americans make up only 13 percent of Texas's population, in 2016 they accounted for 48 percent of Texans arrested for robbery, 37 percent of murder arrests, and 31 percent of arrests for aggravated assault. Meanwhile, 39 percent of Texans were Latinos, but they did not account for a disproportionate share of arrests—35 percent of arrests for murder, 33 percent for robbery, and 36 percent for aggravated assault.[5] Prejudice among law enforcement agencies may account for some of the disproportionate number of African Americans arrested, but it is likely that they actually commit a larger share of crime.

Income and Education Poverty is among the social injustices experienced disproportionately by ethnic and racial minorities, but it is by no means unique to them. Poor education and substantial psychological problems are also a result of poverty. The poor, regardless of racial or ethnic background, are more likely to commit violent crimes than members of the middle and upper classes.

Urban Life Crime is more likely in large metropolitan areas. More than three-fourths of all Texans live in densely populated metropolitan areas of more than 50,000 people (called *metropolitan statistical areas*). The character of urban life may contribute to crime in that larger cities are more anonymous and social sanctions seem less effective than in rural areas and small towns. Not only is there greater freedom in the city to act criminally, but there are also gangs and other organizations that openly encourage criminal activity. A majority of inmates in Texas prisons are from the Dallas-Fort Worth, Houston, and San Antonio areas.

Drug Addiction Addiction contributes to crime in a variety of ways. In 2016, some 144,013 Texans were arrested for narcotics violations,[6] and it is impossible to estimate what percentage of robberies, burglaries, and thefts are committed to finance illegal habits. Narcotics and alcohol also reduce inhibitions, and at least one-third of all crimes are committed under their influence.

Did You Know? A majority of narcotics arrests in Texas are for simple marijuana possession.[7]

Access to Weapons Access to effective weapons is a factor in violent crime. Few weapons are as efficient and readily available as firearms, which are used in more than 74 percent of all murders and a majority of all robberies in Texas.[8] These facts generate intense debate about public policy toward guns.

Gun safety advocates argue that access to guns in the home poses a health risk when people act on violent or suicidal impulses and have effective weapons at their disposal. People living in homes with guns are 2.7 times more likely to die from homicide[9] and 4.8 times more likely to die of suicide than those in homes without guns.[10] Access to firearms is also a significant factor in accidental death,[11] and guns stolen from homes are a major source of weapons for criminals.[12]

Defenders of gun owner rights argue that effective weapons are useful in self-defense, pointing out that 94 felons were killed in justifiable homicides in Texas in 2016.[13] They argue that a large majority of Americans believe that having a gun in the home makes it a safer place,[14] and that proposed gun regulations, such as background checks or limits on types of guns and ammunition, would have only a marginal effect, if any, on gun violence. Opponents of gun regulations hold that gun ownership is a constitutional right[15] that deserves protection against intrusion by government.

White-Collar Crime In contrast to street criminals, few people think of a successful businessperson or a college professor as being a criminal, yet these people may stretch the meaning and intent of federal income tax laws, keep fraudulent business accounts, and pollute the environment. But because they seldom rob, rape, murder, or commit other violent acts, they are often punished less severely. Crimes such as bribery, tax fraud, business fraud, price-fixing, and embezzlement are *white-collar crimes*, usually committed by more prosperous people who have often benefited from the very best advantages that society has to offer.

The American people have paid the costs of white-collar crime for centuries, but the recent near collapse of the economy has focused the public's attention as never before on white-collar crime. High-profile cases of fraud such as that committed by Bernie Madoff, R. Allen Sanford, and officials at Enron, and the resulting loss in confidence in the economy and stock values, cost victims many times more than all robberies, burglaries, and thefts combined.[16]

IMAGE 10.3 UT students protest a new law allowing students to carry guns on campus. The legislature also passed a separate law allowing license holders to carry handguns openly in most public places, including state-run mental institutions. Surprisingly, Texas was one of the last states to allow open carry of handguns.

AP Images/Ralph Barrera

★ SRQ **Is the public safer with more guns or fewer guns?**

The Victim

Although more affluent areas of the state and nation are sometimes victimized by perpetrators of street crime, police reports demonstrate that the greatest rates of victimization are in the poor sections of our cities. Crime is largely a neighborhood affair and is often committed against friends and families of the criminal. Acquaintance rape, or date rape, has been well publicized, and at least 42 percent of Texas killers were acquainted with their victims. In fact, 16 percent of all murder victims were killed by members of their own family. Young people and African Americans were most likely to become murder victims—37 percent were African American.[17]

Victims have the right to be informed of investigations and court proceedings against the accused and to have their victim impact statements taken into account during sentencing and parole action. The Texas Crime Victims' Compensation Fund is administered by the attorney general and financed by small fees collected from criminals when they are convicted. These meager funds are available to victims with extreme personal hardships resulting from physical injury during a crime. However, most victims are not eligible; for example, the fund does not provide compensation for the billions of dollars of property stolen each year.

Violence-centered local news coverage attracts large audiences, and national reports of school shootings and gun crime have contributed to widespread fear of becoming a victim of crime. This fear has been used to promote several agendas, with some advocates supporting harsher sentences for crimes and others supporting stricter gun control policies. Actually, Figure 10.1 shows that the crime rate has declined considerably—the crime rate has been cut in half since 1990.[18]

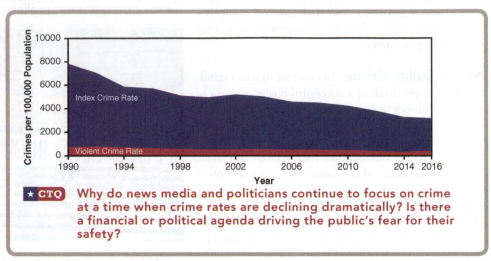

FIGURE 10.1 Texas Crime Rates since 1990

This figure shows that the total Texas index crime rate per 100,000 residents has decreased for more than two decades. The lower graph line shows that the violent crime rate (for murder, rape, robbery, and aggravated assault) has also declined.

★ CTQ **Why do news media and politicians continue to focus on crime at a time when crime rates are declining dramatically? Is there a financial or political agenda driving the public's fear for their safety?**

Based on Department of Public Safety, Crime in Texas, 2016 (Austin: Department of Public Safety 2017), p. 6.

The Due Process of Law

LO 10.3 Analyze the concepts of due process.

It is in the courts that the most general concept of justice and the broadest norms of society are enforced against specific individuals. The courts must blend two conflicting goals of society: (1) to protect society according to the state's legal concepts of right and wrong and (2) to protect the rights of the individual charged with wrongdoing.

Following proper procedures is designed to promote justice and protect the individual from the government, and together they constitute what is called **due process**. The Texas Constitution and the Fourteenth Amendment of the U.S. Constitution require that the state respect these procedural rights because due process is essential to guaranteeing fairness before the government may deprive a person of life, liberty, or property.

Figure 10.2 takes a suspect step by step from search through trial and shows the constitutional guarantees that a person should be able to expect as part of the due process of law. But these rights guaranteed to the accused are very nearly meaningless unless courts, prosecutors, and law enforcement agents are careful to protect them—in practice, due process depends on the values of those who administer and interpret the law.

due process
Proper procedures designed to promote justice and protect the individual from the government. Due process is essential to guaranteeing fairness before the government may deprive a person of life, liberty, or property.

The Search

At certain crucial points in the investigation and apprehension of suspected criminals, society has for centuries demanded various external checks and limits on law enforcement agencies to protect the innocent and the presumption of innocence. For example, the Texas Constitution and the Fourth Amendment to the U.S. Constitution prohibit "unreasonable" searches. However, warrants are not always required; warrantless searches of prisoners (to protect law enforcement personnel) and pedestrians (to protect the public safety) are permitted. Motor vehicles may be searched without warrants because it is simply impractical to require a warrant when evidence may be driven away.

FIGURE 10.2 Steps in Criminal Justice and Due Process Guarantees

This figure shows the major steps in criminal justice, from search to trial, along with the basic constitutional rights to due process that should be guaranteed at each step.

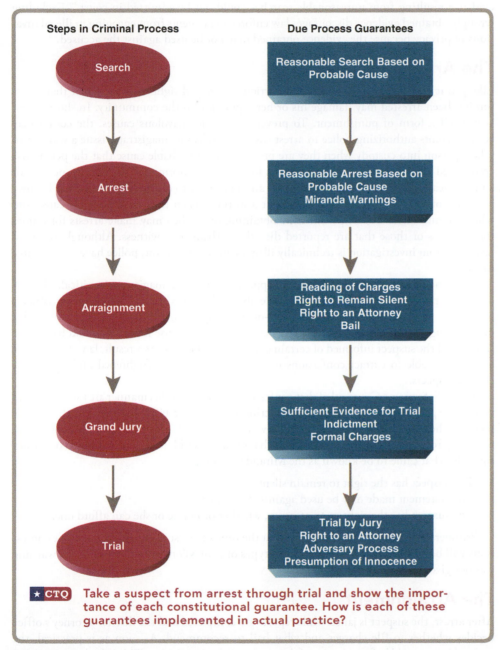

Steps in Criminal Process

- Search
- Arrest
- Arraignment
- Grand Jury
- Trial

Due Process Guarantees

- Reasonable Search Based on Probable Cause
- Reasonable Arrest Based on Probable Cause / Miranda Warnings
- Reading of Charges / Right to Remain Silent / Right to an Attorney / Bail
- Sufficient Evidence for Trial / Indictment / Formal Charges
- Trial by Jury / Right to an Attorney / Adversary Process / Presumption of Innocence

★ CTQ Take a suspect from arrest through trial and show the importance of each constitutional guarantee. How is each of these guarantees implemented in actual practice?

Probable Cause For the most part, the reasonableness of a search is determined by supposedly neutral and independent courts, which supervise the law enforcement agencies that propose to intrude on private premises in search of evidence. In Texas, justices of the peace, municipal court judges, or other magistrates appointed by district courts usually

probable cause
Sufficient information to lead a "reasonable person" to believe that evidence is probably contained on the premises and thus a warrant for the invasion of privacy is justified.

determine **probable cause**—whether the facts and circumstances are sufficient to lead a "reasonable person" to believe that evidence is probably contained on the premises and thus a warrant for the invasion of privacy is justified.

The U.S. Supreme Court ruled that states must respect an **exclusionary rule**, under which evidence resulting from unreasonable searches could not be admitted in court.[19] Excluding wrongly obtained evidence discourages law enforcement agents from engaging in illegal invasions of privacy because the evidence obtained may not be used against the accused.

exclusionary rule
Evidence resulting from unreasonable searches may not be admitted in court.

The Arrest

Like privacy, an individual's liberty is a particularly valued right. The mere fact that a person has been arrested may damage his or her reputation in the community. In short, arrest is in itself a form of punishment. To prevent arrests for frivolous causes, the courts may issue warrants authorizing police to arrest suspects. In Texas, magistrates issue a warrant to take a person into custody when they are presented with probable cause that the person has committed a crime, when a prosecutor files for a writ of information to charge a person for a misdemeanor, or when a grand jury issues an indictment to charge a person with a felony.

Police officers may make arrests without a warrant when they have probable cause and when circumstances do not permit their obtaining one. They may make arrests for crimes they witness or those that are reported directly to them by a witness. Although an arrest resulting from investigation is technically illegal without a warrant, police have considerable flexibility.

The time between a person's arrest and appearance before a magistrate is critical. Historically, this period was a time of much police abuse, during which law enforcement officers sometimes used physical violence or "third-degree" psychological tactics. Police would also delay taking a suspect before a magistrate because probable cause for arrest would have to be shown and the suspect informed of certain constitutional rights. As a result, law enforcement agents were able to extract confessions or other evidence from frightened and sometimes abused suspects.

The U.S. Supreme Court ruled that confessions obtained in this manner are unreliable and violate the guarantees against forced self-incrimination in the Fifth and Fourteenth Amendments to the U.S. Constitution. In *Miranda* v. *Arizona*,[20] the Court ruled that for a confession resulting from an interrogation to be valid, the prisoner would need to be reminded of certain rights in what came to be known as the Miranda warning:

1. The suspect has the right to remain silent.
2. Any statement made may be used against the suspect.
3. The suspect has the right to an attorney, whether or not he or she can afford one.

Prisoners are usually given this warning at the time of arrest to ensure that possible confessions will be admissible, even though some types of confessions are valid even if the warning was not given.

The Arraignment

After arrest, the suspect is jailed while reports are completed and the district attorney's office decides whether to file charges and what bail to recommend. As soon as is practical, the accused is presented before a justice of the peace or other magistrate. This initial **arraignment** is a prisoner's initial appearance before a magistrate in which the charges and basic rights are explained. Its purpose is to:

arraignment
A prisoner's initial appearance before a magistrate in which the charges and basic rights are explained.

1. Explain the charges against the accused.
2. Remind the suspect of the rights to remain silent and to be represented by counsel and to request a written acknowledgment that the Miranda warning was given and understood.

3. Set bail.
4. Inform the accused of the right to an examining trial.

The Charges The suspect is usually told the charges multiple times—upon arrest, in the arraignment, and again in subsequent proceedings. Being told the nature of charges is one of the most fundamental aspects of due process. Because the state is a government of laws, a person should never be held in custody on a whim but only for *legal* cause. In other words, there must be sufficient justification— probable cause—for being held.

> ★ **Did You Know?** Law enforcement agencies may seize and sell property from criminal suspects before they have been found guilty; critics view this as a form of policing for profit.

The Right to an Attorney The right to counsel is vital to the accused—an attorney should clearly understand the constitutional rights of the accused and be familiar with the intricacies of the law and the courts. So important is the assistance of counsel that many suspects will contact an attorney even before they first appear in front of a magistrate.

Yet this right to counsel has never been absolute. Historically, the right to counsel was interpreted to mean that the accused had a right to an attorney if he or she could afford one. In a series of cases, the courts later extended this right to a court-appointed attorney in felony and serious misdemeanor cases when the defendant could not afford one.[21] Even today, however, the right to court-appointed counsel does not necessarily guarantee equal justice for the poor.

Some Texas counties still rely on an assigned counsel system in which private lawyers are selected and paid on a case-by-case basis or in which they work by contract to defend a group of indigent cases assigned to them. Paid by the county, some attorneys find that time spent defending poor people does not significantly advance either their practice or their income. Other attorneys have developed highly successful practices based on indigent defense, and some judges have been charged with cronyism for assigning cases to lawyers who have contributed to their political campaigns.

A number of Texas counties have established a system of salaried full-time public defenders to serve as advocates for indigents in serious criminal cases. Supporters of a public defender system have argued that it is more professional and less costly than the assigned counsel system. Despite the reforms adopted in some counties, the quality of indigent representation varies tremendously from county to county and from defendant to defendant.

Setting Bail The security deposit required for the release of a suspect awaiting trial is known as **bail**. Some persons released on bail fail to appear in court, and their security deposit is forfeited. Others commit still more crimes while out on bail. However, the legal system presumes that an individual is innocent unless convicted, and bail supports this assumption by permitting the accused to resume a normal professional and social life while preparing a defense.

bail
The security deposit required for the release of a suspect awaiting trial.

Although bail may be reset or denied following indictment, the Texas Constitution guarantees the right to bail immediately after arrest, except where proof is "evident" in capital cases or when the defendant is being charged with a third felony after two previous felony convictions. The state constitution allows bail to be denied if the defendant is charged with committing a felony while released on bail or under indictment for another felony.

In practice, the right to bail exists only for those who can afford it. Private, licensed bonding companies may be willing to post bond for a fee (usually 10 to 50 percent of the bail amount set by the court), which, unlike bail, is not refunded. Many defendants cannot afford even this fee, and unless released on personal recognizance (the defendant's personal promise to appear), the prisoner will await trial in jail.

Bail was designed to free a person not yet found guilty of a crime, but some innocent people await trial in jail, unable to work, carry on their family life, or gather evidence for their own defense. In our criminal justice system, bail procedures, more than any other single practice, punish the poor for their poverty—a majority of Texas's jail inmates are simply awaiting trial and have not yet been convicted. Meanwhile, professional criminals released on bail often return to work. They may even commit more crimes to pay their attorneys' retainers and bonding fees.

Although few defendants request one, the accused has the right to an examining trial in felony cases. A magistrate reviews the facts to determine whether there is sufficient evidence to send the case to a grand jury. If the facts warrant, the charges may be dismissed or bail adjusted.

The Grand Jury and Pretrial Activity

Although a grand jury sometimes issues an indictment before the accused is arrested, a felony case is usually bound over to a grand jury for indictment after arrest and arraignment. A grand jury should not be confused with a petit jury, which is the trial jury. Grand juries do not determine a person's guilt or innocence as trial juries do; the accused may not even be asked to appear before the grand jury. Instead of hearing the defense, the grand jury primarily weighs the evidence in the hands of the prosecutor to determine whether there is sufficient evidence to convict when the case is taken to trial. If it determines the existence of such evidence, the grand jury returns a "true bill" approving an indictment, which constitutes formal charges that enable the case to go to trial; only rarely does a grand jury refuse to indict by issuing a "no bill."

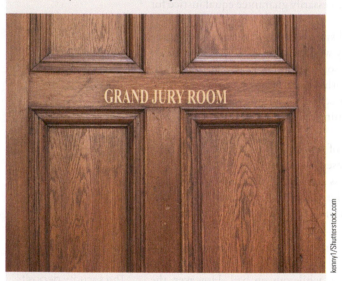

IMAGE 10.4 Grand juries operate behind closed doors to protect the identity of innocents.

kenny1/Shutterstock.com

★ SRQ   **Are grand juries effective at preventing innocents from being falsely charged?**

If the prosecutor does not have enough evidence to convict, there is no point in bringing the case to trial. Trying a case on flimsy evidence not only costs the taxpayers money but also causes the accused to suffer needless expense, lost time, and a damaged reputation. The right to a grand jury indictment is guaranteed in both the Texas and federal courts to protect the rights of innocent citizens against harassment on unjustified charges.

In practice, grand juries are usually made up of ordinary citizens who have never been trained to critically evaluate cases and so usually act as a rubber stamp for the prosecutors. Some states have abolished the grand jury in favor of writs of information, in which a judge evaluates the evidence to determine if there is sufficient evidence to go to trial. Texas guarantees the right to indictment in all felony cases but uses the writ of information to charge people with misdemeanors.

Pretrial Hearings   After the indictment, the defendant has the right to yet another hearing, sometimes called the second arraignment. A district judge (rather than a justice of the peace) presides as the formal indictment is read, and the defendant enters a plea. If the plea is guilty, a later hearing is scheduled to set punishment. Most often the defendant pleads not guilty at this point, and the case is placed on the docket scheduling the case for subsequent trial. Attorneys may present a variety of motions, such as a motion for the suppression of certain evidence or a motion for delay or a continuance. Other subjects of pretrial hearings concern possible insanity or change of venue—a change in the site of a trial.

A person cannot be held morally and criminally responsible for a crime if at the time of the offense, mental illness made it impossible for the person to recognize that it was wrong. There is considerable controversy as to the effects of mental disorder, so professional testimony may be necessary to establish legal insanity, and psychiatric opinion is frequently divided. It is rare that the courts find a defendant not guilty by reason of insanity.

A change of venue may be necessary when the news media have so publicized a case that it becomes impossible to select an unbiased jury locally or when inflamed public opinion may prevent a fair trial. A real tension exists between the rights of the free press and the rights of the accused, and in a modern society the rights of the accused can be protected only with great vigilance by the courts.

The Plea Bargain
Ideally, the trial is the final step in society's elaborate guarantees of due process. Only through the deliberations in the courtroom can our system's genuine concern for justice emerge. Yet for most people who are accused of a crime, their final day in court never comes. In fact, the system is designed to discourage and even punish those who choose to exercise their right to trial. Most cases end in *plea bargaining*—a secret bargaining session with the prosecutor.

Facing overcrowded dockets and limited staff, prosecuting attorneys usually meet with the accused and offer a deal in exchange for a plea of guilty, which eliminates the need for a trial. The usual deal is to offer to drop some of the charges, to recommend probation or a lighter sentence, or to charge the accused with a lesser crime. The prosecutor may agree to defer prosecution, delaying prosecution and later dropping charges if the defendant agrees to meet conditions like those required under probation. Such plea agreements save tax money and court time and may be useful to law enforcement, such as when certain defendants are given a lighter sentence in exchange for testifying against fellow criminals who have committed more serious crimes.

On the other hand, the guilty obviously benefit from plea bargaining because they are not punished for the full measure of their crimes. Justice is thus exchanged for a cheaper system that benefits the guilty. Defense attorneys frequently encourage their clients to accept the bargain to save them the effort of a courtroom trial, and some become as much agents for the prosecution as advocates for the defense. The innocent and those who are unwilling to trade their rights for a secret backroom bargain take the chance of being punished more severely for demanding a trial.

The Trial

Unless the defense waives the right to a trial by jury, the first major step in a trial is the selection of a jury. The right to a trial by jury is often regarded as one of the most valuable rights available in the criminal justice system.[22] In fact, every state provides for trial by jury in all but the most minor cases, and Texas goes even further, providing for the right to trial by jury in every criminal case.

Nevertheless, the right to trial by jury in a criminal case is one of the most frequently waived rights, especially in cases where the defendant is an object of community prejudice or if the alleged crime is particularly outrageous. If the right to a jury trial is waived, the presiding judge determines the verdict. Regardless of whether or not a person chooses to exercise it, the right to trial by jury remains a valuable alternative to decisions by possibly arbitrary judges.

Trial by Jury During initial questioning, known as *voir dire* questioning, attorneys may ask prospective jurors about their possible biases, their previous knowledge of the case, or any opinions they may have formed. Either the prosecution or the defense may challenge a prospective juror for reason of prejudice, and the presiding judge will evaluate that challenge. Furthermore, both the prosecution and the defense may dismiss some jurors without cause by using a limited number of peremptory challenges, also called *strikes*, depending on the kind of case involved. Considering occupations, social status, and attitudes of possible jurors, experienced attorneys and prosecutors use peremptory challenges to select a friendly jury. Some have been known to use psychologists to assist in the selection process, and lucrative consulting businesses have developed to assist attorneys in jury selection.

adversary process
The process by which two contesting parties present opposing views and evidence in open court.

The Adversary Process The trial itself is based on an **adversary process** in which two parties to a case, the prosecution and the defense, arm themselves with whatever evidence they can muster and battle in court, under the rules of law, to final judgment. Such a system cannot operate fairly unless both the defense and the prosecution have an equal opportunity to influence the verdict. Hence procedural guarantees are designed to ensure that both sides have equal access to an understanding of the laws and the evidence. So that equal knowledge of the laws is guaranteed, the legal knowledge of the prosecution is balanced by the right of the defendant to have legal counsel. Because the government has the power to seize evidence and to force witnesses to testify under oath, the defense must be given that same power.

In the adversary system, each side can challenge the material evidence and cross-examine witnesses who have been presented by the opposition. However, only evidence that is presented in court can be evaluated, and both parties to a case have an interest in concealing evidence that could benefit the opposition.

Because it is the legal responsibility of the prosecutor to prove guilt beyond a reasonable doubt, the burden of proof lies with the state. The defense has no responsibility to present evidence of the defendant's guilt, nor can the defendant be forced to take the stand to testify. On the other hand, because the responsibility of the prosecutor is to convict the guilty rather than the innocent, it is a violation of due process for the government to withhold evidence that could benefit the accused—but it happens. There is no way of knowing how many unjust verdicts have been rendered because all the evidence was not presented.

The Jury Charge In jury trials, once the evidence has been presented, the judge reads the charge to the jury—the judge's instructions about how the law applies in the case. The judge will instruct the jurors to ignore such things as hearsay testimony and other illegal evidence to which they may have been exposed during the course of the trial. (Realistically, however, it is difficult for jurors to erase from their minds the impact of illegal testimony.) The judge is supposedly neutral and cannot comment on the weight of the evidence that has been presented.

The Verdict After the judge's charge to the jury, the prosecution and defense are each allowed to summarize the case. During their summary remarks, the prosecutor will comment that the evidence points toward guilt, and the defense will conclude that the evidence is insufficient to prove guilt beyond a reasonable doubt. The jury then retires to decide the verdict—guilty or not guilty. Texas law requires that all the jurors agree on the verdict in criminal cases. The judge will declare a mistrial if the jury cannot agree, but the defendant may be tried again.

The Sentence Regardless of whether the judge or the jury determines guilt, the judge may prescribe the sentence, unless the defendant requests that the jury do so. In considering the character of the defendant, any past criminal record, and the circumstances surrounding the crime, the judge may assess a penalty between the minimum and maximum provided by law. A judge may sentence an offender to **probation**, which allows the person to serve the sentence outside a correctional institution under specific restrictions, often under the supervision of a probation officer. Similarly, a judge may use deferred adjudication to postpone final sentencing in a criminal case, and after a satisfactory probationary period, the charges are dismissed.

probation
A judge's sentence allowing an offender to serve time outside a correctional institution but under specific restrictions, often under the supervision of a probation officer.

Judges have a great deal of latitude in assessing penalties, so the fate of a defendant will depend in large part on the attitudes of the presiding judge. Different judges sometimes assess vastly different penalties for the same crime committed under similar circumstances.

If the convicted criminal is sentenced to prison, time served in jail before and during trial is usually deducted from the sentence of the guilty. For the innocent, however, the time served awaiting trial is a casualty of an imperfect system of justice that underlines the necessity for care in accusing and trying people.

Did You Know? A judge in Smith County, Texas, required that a defendant marry his girlfriend and write Bible verses as a condition for probation.

The Post-Trial Proceedings

To protect the accused from double jeopardy, a person who is acquitted (found not guilty) cannot be tried again for the same offense. However, protection from double jeopardy is much more limited than many citizens believe. In the event of a mistrial or an error in procedure in which a person is not acquitted, another trial may be held for the same offense on the theory that the defendant was never put in jeopardy by the first trial. A person found not guilty of one crime may be tried for other related offenses. For example, a person who is accused of driving 75 miles per hour through a school zone, going the wrong way on a one-way street, striking down a child in the crosswalk, and then leaving the scene of the accident has committed four crimes. Being acquitted of one of them does not free the defendant of possible charges for each of the other offenses. Likewise, such acts as bank robbery and kidnapping may violate both federal and state law, and the accused may be tried by both jurisdictions.

The Appeals Process Although the state cannot appeal a not guilty verdict, because doing so would constitute double jeopardy, prosecutors may appeal the *reversal* of a guilty verdict by a higher court, and the defendant may appeal a guilty verdict. Misdemeanor cases from justices of the peace and municipal courts may be either appealed or completely retried, *de novo*, in the county courts. Appeals from county and district courts go to one of 14 courts of appeals and finally to the Texas Court of Criminal Appeals.

Appellate procedure is designed to review the law as applied by lower courts, not to evaluate evidence to determine guilt or innocence. Its major concern is procedure. Even if overruled, the antics of defense attorneys in raising frequent objections to procedure during a trial may build a case for a later appeal. If serious procedural errors are found, the appellate courts may return the case to a lower court for retrial. Such a retrial does not constitute double jeopardy.

Having exhausted the rights of appeal in the Texas courts, a very few cases are appealed to the federal courts, which have jurisdiction in federal law. Thus, the grounds for appeal to federal courts would be the assertion that the state courts have violated the U.S. Constitution or other federal law.

IMAGE 10.5 Texas allows children to be tried as adults at age 14. Children tried as adults seem to be more likely to commit future crimes than those who are dealt with in the juvenile system, according to the U.S. Centers for Disease Control and Prevention.[23]

★ SRQ   **How should the legal rights and responsibilities of children differ from those of adults?**

The Special Case of Juveniles

As the result of a reform effort in the nineteenth century, most states began to provide special treatment for children. Texas followed their lead by replacing all adult criminal procedures in juvenile cases with special civil procedures. Under the legal fiction that juveniles were not being punished for crimes, lax procedures were used that would never have been permitted in adult criminal courts. Court proceedings were secret, the rights to counsel and to trial by jury were ignored, standards of evidence were relaxed, and frequently charges were not specific.

As a result of federal court rulings, much of due process has since been restored to juvenile proceedings—except the rights to bail, a grand jury indictment, and a public trial. Juvenile proceedings remain civil, and juvenile records may be sealed from the public with the approval of the juvenile judge, who is usually appointed by the county's judges or juvenile board to have exclusive jurisdiction in such cases. The law allows juvenile felony arrest warrants to be entered into statewide computers, and police can gather information such as juvenile fingerprints and photographs.

A majority of children arrested for lesser crimes are counseled and released on probation into the custody of their parents or placed in county facilities. Some of the more serious offenders are institutionalized at state training schools, boot camps, and halfway houses operated by the Texas Juvenile Justice Board. The most serious offenders over age 13 may be certified to stand criminal trial as adults.

Rehabilitation and Punishment

LO 10.4 Evaluate punishment and rehabilitation policies.

By providing public institutions that extract justice, society offers an alternative to private revenge and the resulting feuds that plagued the early stages of Western civilization. Until the eighteenth century, punishment meant imposing physical or financial pain. But ideas of human dignity led to the development of prisons to deny a person liberty as a more humane way of punishing. Today, although some prisoners brutalize each other, the death penalty is the only remnant of formal physical punishment left in the law.

Felony Punishment

The Texas Department of Criminal Justice (TDCJ) supervises the state's adult correctional functions for convicted felons—probation, prison, and parole.

Probation Probation allows convicts to serve their sentences outside prisons but under varying degrees of supervision—probationers may be required to report to probation officers, submit to electronic monitoring, undergo treatment for chemical dependency, or live in community residence facilities or restitution centers. Although probation functions are largely the responsibilities of local community supervision and corrections departments, TDCJ sets standards and provides funding, training, information, and technical assistance to local officers.

Prison

Prison The criminal justice department also operates correctional institutions for those offenders not granted probation. Texas has privatized some of its prisons and state jails, which now operate under contract with several prison management companies such as the Management & Training Corporation. Texas's prison population has tripled since the mid-1980s, and prison facilities, state jails, transfer facilities, and other confinement units now accommodate almost 150,000 inmates.

★ Did You Know? Only Alabama, Arizona, Arkansas, Mississippi, Louisiana, and Oklahoma have a larger percentage of their populations in prison than Texas.[24]

Parole After an initial stay in prison, **parole** allows many inmates to serve the remainder of their sentences under supervision in the community. The Board of Pardons and Paroles decides which inmates will be granted early release under parole, and the TDCJ is responsible for their supervision after release.

Inmates serving life sentences for capital crimes are not eligible for parole, and those convicted of other violent offenses must serve at least one-half of their sentences before being considered for parole. Those convicted of other offenses must serve only one-fourth of their sentences or 15 years, whichever is less. However, additional time against the sentence is allowed for making a positive effort toward rehabilitation, good behavior, and providing various services such as serving as a prison trusty assigned to assist prison staff. As a result, an inmate may become eligible for parole in fewer calendar years than the original sentence indicated.

The Board of Pardons and Paroles does not grant parole automatically when prisoners become eligible. Instead, the board examines each inmate's record for positive evidence of rehabilitation. When granted parole, the freed prisoner must abide by strict codes of conduct under the general supervision of parole officers.

Parole, as the concept has developed, should not be forgiveness but a continuation of the process of correction. Parole rehabilitation is based on the idea that the elimination of anti-social attitudes can be more effectively accomplished when the individual is not severed from society. Parole is far less expensive than incarceration—supervision of a prison inmate costs as much as 20 times that of a parolee. Seeking to cut prison costs, Texas has increased its efforts to reintegrate parolees back into society, and these efforts may gradually reduce parole revocations in future years.

parole
After an initial stay in prison, prisoners serving the remainder of their sentences under supervision in the community.

Clemency

Clemency Although it rarely does so, the Board of Pardons and Paroles may take the initiative to recommend that the governor grant executive clemency (leniency) such as a pardon, a commutation of sentence, or a reprieve. Because conviction for crime carries a legal condemnation as well as a possible sentence, a full pardon is designed to absolve a citizen from the legal consequences of his or her crime. A commutation of sentence is a reduction in punishment. A reprieve is temporary interruption of punishment. The governor may grant less, but not more, clemency than the board recommends. Without board approval, the governor may grant only one 30-day reprieve to delay execution in a capital case.

Misdemeanor Punishment

State government assumes the responsibility for convicted felons, but those convicted of the misdemeanors for which confinement is prescribed will serve their terms in jails operated by local governments, usually counties. Jails often fail to rehabilitate because jail staffs and physical facilities are designed to maintain custody rather than to rehabilitate. Many prisoners in county jails are either awaiting trial or being held for other agencies (federal or state)—these jails are designed as human warehouses.

Those who are actually serving their sentences in a county jail will be there for only a short period of time, usually less than one year. This is insufficient time to correct criminal attitudes that the prisoner may have been forming for a lifetime. Many of those who serve their sentences in local jails have been convicted of habitual vices such as gambling, prostitution, and drunkenness, which are not amenable to rehabilitation in a jail setting. Some courts, however, are now using diversionary programs that allow minor drug offenders to undergo rehabilitation as an alternative to jail sentences.

Evaluating Punishment and Rehabilitation Policies

Texas jails and penitentiaries are intended to have several functions:

1. *Justice*, including punishment (or social vengeance), is society's way of settling accounts with those who have violated its norms. The concept of justice normally requires proportionality—the punishment should fit the crime.
2. *Isolation* of criminals from the law-abiding population is designed to protect society from future crimes. Yet for most crimes, society is unwilling to prescribe the permanent imprisonment of convicted criminals.
3. **Deterrence** of criminals is society's effort at discouraging criminal behavior by threat of punishment; society uses punishment of convicted criminals as an example to discourage would-be lawbreakers.
4. **Rehabilitation** of convicted criminals is supposed to allow those who are ultimately released to take useful and noncriminal roles in society—the effort to correct criminals' antisocial attitudes and behavior.

deterrence
Discouraging criminal behavior by threat of punishment.

rehabilitation
The effort to correct criminals' antisocial attitudes and behavior.

The strongest critics of the criminal justice system argue that jails and prisons perform none of these functions in practice. Its defenders contend that the state's criminal justice policies are at least partially responsible for reducing the state's crime rate.

Punishment and Isolation   Texans have increased legal penalties for crime. Despite plea bargaining, probation, and parole practices that cut short the punishment and isolation prescribed in the law, Texas still has one of the highest rates of imprisonment in the nation.

One might expect that states like Texas with high rates of imprisonment would have a lower crime rate, yet ironically Texas continues to have a crime rate higher than 32 other states. Table 10.2 shows that Texas has put a far larger percentage of its population in prison than most other states, yet Figure 10.3 shows that it still has one of the nation's higher crime rates. Texas has executed more people than any other state, yet it still has a murder rate far exceeding that of most other states.

Deterrence   Criminologists usually argue that *severity* of punishment is less important in deterring crime than the *certainty* of punishment. Perpetrators rarely consider the severity of punishment when they commit their crimes because they expect to avoid punishment altogether. In fact, punishment is far from certain in Texas. Most crimes are never reported to police,[25] and even among those index crimes that are known to Texas law enforcement, less than 20 percent are cleared with an arrest.[26] As a result, the vast majority of criminals are never punished for the crimes they commit.

Rehabilitation   Some inmates may eventually become law-abiding citizens, but for many inmates, prisons are failures as institutions of rehabilitation—almost half of those released from prison will again be arrested for crime within three years of their release.[27]

How Does Texas Compare?

Crime and Punishment

Texas's crime rate is greater than that of 32 other states—at least 50 percent higher than states like New York, New Jersey, and Massachusetts. Figure 10.3 shows that the highest crime rates are generally in southern and western states.

Ironically, states with the highest crime rates happen to be among those with the most severe criminal penalties. Among the 50 states, only six states have a larger number of prison inmates per 100,000 population than Texas. Table 10.2 also shows that Texas has a greater proportion of its population on parole and probation than most states. Perhaps states with the highest crime rates are the ones most receptive to a "get tough" approach to crime.

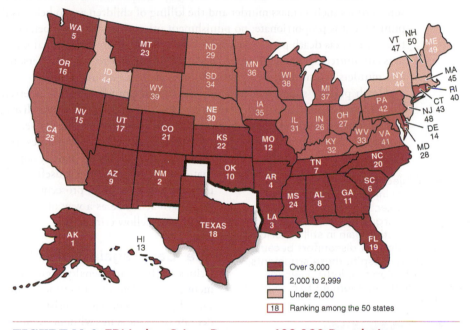

FIGURE 10.3 FBI Index Crime Rates per 100,000 Population

Source: Federal Bureau of Investigation, Uniform Crime Reports: Crime in the United States, 2010, Table 5 at http://www .fbi.gov/ about-us/cjis/ucr/crime-in-the-u.s/2010/ crime-in-the-u.s.-2010/tables/10tbl05.xls

TABLE 10.2 Persons in Prison, on Probation, and on Parole per 100,000 Population

	Federal	50 States	Texas	Texas Ranking among 50 States
Prisoners	53	397	563	7
On probation	7	1,459	1,805	10
On parole	46	303	537	5

Source: Bureau of Justice Statistics, 2016 data published April, 2018.

FOR DEBATE

★ CTQ Does Texas have a high rate of imprisonment because it has a high crime rate, or does the state's conservative political culture explain the high rate of imprisonment?

★ CTQ From this evidence, is it possible to say whether the threat of punishment deters crime? Why or why not?

recidivists
Repeat offenders who have relapsed into crime.

As many as 80 percent of all felonies may be committed by **recidivists**—repeat offenders who have relapsed into crime. A major factor in crime remains the failure of our correctional systems to correct.

Sizing Up the Death Penalty Debate

While capital punishment is still being debated across the nation, many aspects of the death penalty can be analyzed by the same standards used to evaluate other forms of punishment. To what extent does capital punishment achieve justice? Is it an effective deterrent against crime?

The Case for the Death Penalty
Proponents of the death penalty argue that some crimes such as mass murder and the killing of children are so heinous that only capital punishment is proportionate; no punishment other than the death penalty can achieve justice. The Texas death penalty statute is very specific in limiting capital punishment to murders committed against children, firefighters, or law enforcement officers, multiple murders, and murders committed during other felonies such as rape and robbery.

Death penalty supporters contend that capital punishment is a deterrent to crime and that would-be murderers and terrorists will avoid putting their own lives in jeopardy by committing these crimes. Proponents point out that inmates already serving life sentences would face no additional punishment for murdering prison guards unless they are subject to the death penalty. Death penalty supporters also argue that capital punishment is a useful tool in law enforcement; interrogators and prosecutors can use the threat of a death sentence as a way of persuading suspects to incriminate fellow criminals.

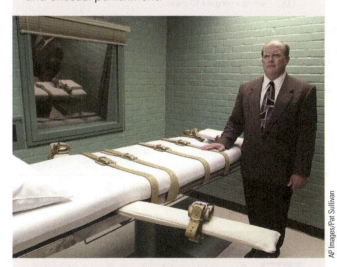

IMAGE 10.6 Lethal injection gurney. Texas was the first state to use lethal injection in executions. Today, it is an option for execution in all states with the death penalty. Critics argue that the lethal drug cocktail can cause excruciating pain in still conscious subjects, who show few signs of discomfort because of drug-induced paralysis. Despite these arguments, the U.S. Supreme Court ruled that lethal injection does not violate the Eighth Amendment ban on cruel and unusual punishment.[30]

AP Images/Pat Sullivan

★ PRQ   **What are the ethical reasons to keep the death penalty? What ethical arguments can be made to abolish it?**

The Case against the Death Penalty
Critics of the death penalty argue that capital punishment is not a deterrent to crime. Ironically, states with capital punishment have consistently had a *higher* murder rate than the states without it. For example, in 2016, the South, which had 80 percent of all executions, had the highest murder rate while the Northeast, with only 1 percent of executions, had the lowest.[28] A historic pattern of such statistics has been interpreted to mean that death penalty laws do not act as a deterrent to murder.

Opponents believe that killing can never be just, even when it is punishment for a crime. They contend that justice cannot be served when innocent people may be executed. More than a dozen inmates on Texas's death row have been exonerated, and there is a real danger that innocent persons can be and have been executed. Pointing to examples like that of Cameron Todd Willingham,[29] opponents argue that once such a prisoner has been wrongfully executed, the mistake can never be corrected.

Instead, opponents argue that every state now allows adequate alternatives to the death penalty. Life sentences without the possibility of parole serve justice and are far less expensive than the death penalty process.

Many states would appear to agree with this logic. Nineteen states have now abolished the death penalty altogether; in those states that still include capital punishment in their penal codes, prosecutors are seeking the death penalty less often. Only eight, mostly southern, states actually executed inmates during 2018, and more than one half of those executions took place in the state of Texas.[31]

Applying What You Have Learned about Law and Due Process

LO 10.5   **Apply what you have learned about the due process of law.**

You learned that in 2016 about 145,000 people were arrested in Texas for narcotics violations—most for marijuana violations. Yet the widespread use of marijuana brings into question the effectiveness of its prohibition. In fact, both liberal and conservative criminal justice reformers have advocated reducing penalties and increasing drug treatment programs for nonviolent offenders as a more humane and inexpensive approach to marijuana policy.

Some reformers have focused on the legalization of marijuana for specific medical uses as illustrated in Image 10.7. However, despite growing evidence to the contrary, the federal government still classifies marijuana as a Schedule 1 substance (the same category as heroin and LSD)—meaning that it has no currently accepted medical value and a high potential for abuse. So we asked Phillip Martin to fill you in on the practical political effort to reform Texas marijuana laws.

Phillip Martin is a former deputy director of Progress Texas, a nonprofit public relations shop promoting progressive ideals and public policies in Texas. Prior to joining Progress Texas, Martin served as the policy director for the Legislative Study Group (a progressive caucus in the Texas House). Martin also previously served as chief of staff for State Representative Garnet Coleman and presently is the executive director of the Texas House Democratic Caucus.

Once you have read Martin's article, we will ask you to think critically about the marijuana issue.

IMAGE 10.7   Many Texas veterans who suffer from post-traumatic stress disorder (PTSD) and other injuries related to their service use marijuana to provide relief. In doing so, they run the risk of being arrested and jailed, which has led groups like Texas NORML to launch a public relations campaign highlighting the plight of these veterans, Operation Trapped, to pressure lawmakers to legalize medical marijuana in Texas.

POLITICS IN PRACTICE
Marijuana Policy Reform in Texas
by Phillip Martin
FORMER DEPUTY DIRECTOR OF PROGRESS TEXAS

Marijuana policy reform can improve public safety, boost the economy, and provide much-needed health care options for struggling Texans.

Like any other major shift in public policy, improving Texas' marijuana laws requires overcoming political and regulatory changes that may take years to fulfill. Advocates must also guard against laws that look like victories, but can also set back the work they are trying to achieve.

Take, for example, Texas' first medical marijuana law. On the final day of the legislative session in 2015, Texas Governor Greg Abbott held a public bill signing for Senate Bill 339, which allowed Texas to license facilities to cultivate, manufacture, and dispense CBD-oil to assist with the treatment of child patients suffering from epilepsy. Gov. Abbott celebrated the "healing and hope for children" and families that could now access this medical marijuana.

Except, they can't. The law requires patients to get a doctor's prescription for the medicine. That's problematic, since many doctors are unwilling to prescribe marijuana so long as it is classified as a Schedule 1 drug by the federal government. States with successful medical marijuana programs allow for a doctor's recommendation, not a prescription.

Even if a patient could secure a prescription, the CBD-only marijuana by-product may not help cure the seizures. The medical marijuana that's famously cured children's seizures in Colorado and other states contains THC, the psychoactive element of the plant, which is still prohibited by Texas law.

Our marijuana advocacy coalition was conflicted on this bill. Among the 25+ organizations and 25,000 advocates that contacted legislators in support of marijuana policy reform, the legislation was both a triumph and a disappointment. It was great for Texas to finally recognize that marijuana has some medicinal value. At the same time, the law is so limited it may not help anyone—even the kids Gov. Abbott celebrated that last day of session.

And that's all before the regulatory process is completed. The bill instructed the Texas Department of Public Safety (DPS) to create regulations for what companies must do to successfully procure a state license for cultivating, manufacturing, and dispensing of the CBD-oil. Everything from what kind of security those facilities require to who can work at the dispensaries must be established by DPS—in a process that is often even more obscure than working through the Texas Legislature.

All this is to say that marijuana policy reform faces a true uphill battle in the state's political and regulatory climate. Fortunately, there is popular support for improving Texas' marijuana laws. Seventy-five percent of Texans support improving current laws, which can include:

- Replacing jail time for small possession of marijuana with a simple fine; this could help remove as many as 70,000 Texans from prison, removing criminal records for nonviolent offenders who struggle to achieve equal opportunities in employment and housing.

- Expanding medical marijuana to ensure veterans with PTSD, cancer patients, and others suffering from debilitating medical conditions have access to medicine that will help them.
- Fully understanding and studying the implications of a marijuana retail market, a process far more complicated in licensing and administration.

Each of these planks for marijuana policy reform will require the coalition and its thousands of activists to consider the full range of political challenges, and the regulatory landmines that could inhibit the growth of the new industry. Since the law passed in 2015, we have done what we can to organize in communities across the state, work with members of the press to ensure fair reporting on the subject, and educate lawmakers in the interim on our policy goals.

Fortunately, marijuana policy reform is widely supported by the public, and unlike so many issues in Texas, there are no inherent ideological barriers to our work. Republicans and Democrats alike support reform, and Republicans and Democrats alike remain skeptical.

The work in front of us is to build bridges—between myths and reality, skeptics and believers, the public and their elected officials—all year round. The Texas Legislature may only meet 140 days every other year, but if we want to be successful, our work can never stop.

1. What are arguments against the decriminalization of marijuana? Would it lead to widespread use and threaten public safety? What about the problem of traffic accidents resulting from marijuana-impaired drivers?
2. What are the disadvantages of marijuana prohibition? How much should government be empowered to limit individual personal choices?

★ Chapter Summary

LO 10.1 Analyze civil law and the policy issues related to it. Within the American legal system, cases are classified as either civil or criminal. Civil cases primarily involve the rights of private parties or organizations. Resolution is based on the concept of responsibility rather than guilt.

Some examples of the broad categories of civil law are family law, real estate law, probate, corporate law, civil regulations, labor law, and torts. Recent political issues have developed around eminent domain, liability insurance, and tort claims. The Texas legislature has undertaken tort reform in an effort to lighten overcrowded court dockets and limit allegedly frivolous suits. At the urging of business, insurance companies, and medical professionals, the legislature has restricted lawsuits and limited awards for damages.

LO 10.2 Analyze the elements and causes of crime. In an attempt to impose their values on others, the dominant elements of society have turned to government with its power to define crime and punish it. Law reflects the values of the people who make and enforce it. Criminal cases deal with public concepts of proper behavior and morality as defined by law. Punishment for a violation of these concepts ranges from a fine to imprisonment to a combination of both. More serious crimes are called felonies, and minor crimes are called misdemeanors.

The cause of crime is the failure to accept society's mores, which is related to such factors as age, gender, ethnicity, income, education, urban life, and drug addiction. Overall crime rates have, in fact, declined in recent years in Texas and in most of the nation as well.

LO 10.3 Analyze the concepts of due process. The court procedures that constitute due process aim to promote justice and protect individuals from government abuse. These procedures are generally either written into state and national constitutions and statutes or included in traditional codes of court process. They govern every step in the criminal justice process, from search and arrest to trial and final conviction. These procedures guarantee the rights against unreasonable search and arrest and against forced self-incrimination. Due process also includes the rights to an attorney, to reasonable bail, and to examining trials; the defendant has the right to be charged by a reliable process, to be able to present evidence, and to confront opposing witnesses at a trial by jury.

It is largely through due process that the courts aim to blend two conflicting goals of society: (1) to protect society according to the state's legal concepts of right and wrong and (2) to protect the rights of the individual charged with wrongdoing. Unfortunately, the goal of due process is often an ideal rather than a reality. These careful guarantees of due process are often circumvented by such practices as plea bargaining.

LO 10.4 Evaluate punishment and rehabilitation policies. Correctional institutions such as prisons and jails are intended to punish, isolate, deter, and rehabilitate. Unfortunately, they perform these functions poorly—the low rates of arrest mean that most criminals will not be punished or isolated from society, and hence they are not effectively deterred from committing crimes. Even among prisoners who have been arrested and punished, a majority of inmates return to crime after their release.

LO 10.5 Apply what you have learned about the due process of law. You explored alternatives to Texas's current marijuana policy that has resulted in the arrest of tens of thousands of Texans annually. You critically evaluated proposals presented by a prominent activist supporting reform.

Key Terms

adversary process, *p. 276*
arraignment, *p. 272*
bail, *p. 273*
deterrence, *p. 280*
due process, *p. 270*

eminent domain, *p. 264*
exclusionary rule, *p. 272*
FBI index crimes, *p. 267*
felonies, *p. 265*
misdemeanors, *p. 266*

parole, *p. 279*
plaintiff, *p. 261*
precedent, *p. 261*
probable cause, *p. 272*
probation, *p. 277*

recidivists, *p. 282*
rehabilitation, *p. 280*
tort, *p. 262*
tort reform, *p. 263*

Review Questions

LO 10.1　Analyze civil law and the policy issues related to it.

- Differentiate between civil and criminal law. Give at least six broad categories of civil law and examples of each. Explain why each example is classified as civil rather than criminal law.

- Explain Texas policies regarding eminent domain, auto liability insurance, and tort reform. What are the political interests on each side of the tort reform controversy?

LO 10.2　Analyze the elements and causes of crime.

- Define criminal law and how it develops from basic social mores. Distinguish felonies from misdemeanors, and give examples of each.

- Discuss the root causes of crime. What are the social characteristics of the typical criminal?

LO 10.3　Analyze the concepts of due process.

- Define the due process of law, and explain its origins in the state and national constitutions.

- Trace the criminal justice process step by step from search and arrest through final conviction. At each stage, show how the legal system is designed to guarantee a sense of fair play between the government and the accused.

- Identify gaps between the theory and practice of due process. Define plea bargaining and how it affects due process in practice.

LO 10.4　Evaluate punishment and rehabilitation policies.

- List the four major purposes of jails and penitentiaries, and evaluate how effectively they achieve each of them. How does the death penalty measure up against these standards?

- Discuss whether certainty or severity of punishment is more effective at preventing recidivism and deterring crime. Why?

Think Critically and Get Active!

Deal intelligently with your personal legal matters. For tips on civil legal matters, browse through **www.texaslawhelp.org** to get free legal advice, do-it-yourself, and low-cost legal strategies relating to bankruptcy, consumer complaints, divorce, identity theft, tenant rights, utility bills, and a wide range of other topics. Take control of legal issues in your life—learn about family law, tenants' rights, and how to sue in small claims court at **www.texasbar.com**. Click on "For the Public" and then on "Free Legal Resources." Learn how to deal with identity theft and how to identify registered sex offenders in your neighborhood from the Texas Department of Public Safety at **www.txdps.state.tx.us**.

Link up with the group that reflects your position on civil lawsuits. Fight frivolous lawsuits that drive up the costs of doing business and support limits on civil judgments with Texans for Lawsuit Reform at **www.tortreform.com** (@lawsuitreform). Support workers', patients', and consumers' rights to compensation for negligence from businesses, medical providers, and insurance companies with Texas Watch at **www.texaswatch.org** (@TexasWatch).

Get the facts on guns and connect with those who share your views. Start at **www.vox.com/cards/gun-violence-facts** and follow the National Rifle Association at **www.nra.org** (@nra) or the Brady Campaign to End Violence at **www.bradycampaign.org** (@Bradybuzz).

Join with those who share your views on crime and punishment. Fight the death penalty by joining Students Against the Death Penalty at **www.studentabolition.org** or the Texas Coalition to Abolish the Death Penalty at **www.tcadp.org** (@TCADPdotORG). Help The Innocence Project free the innocent at **www.ipoftexas.org** (@IPofTexas). Find a wealth of information about the death penalty at the Bureau of Justice Statistics and at the Death Penalty Information Center at **www.deathpenaltyinfo.org** (@DPInfoCtr).

Support capital punishment with Pro-Death Penalty.com at **www.prodeathpenalty.com**. Fight for a vigorous criminal justice system and victims' rights with Justice for All at **www.jfa.net**. Search for studies that show capital punishment as a deterrent to murder.

★ CSQ Develop a comparative analysis between Texas and national trends using Texas Department of Public safety statistics at www.dps.texas.gov/administration/crime_records/pages/ucr.htm and FBI data at www.fbi.gov/stats-services/crimestats. Analyze trends in the rates of prosecution, prison, probation, and capital punishment using the data-rich Bureau of Justice Statistics website at www.bjs.gov. Use at least three visuals to show these changing trends in your presentation.

★ PRQ Identify the ethical issues on both sides in the death penalty debate.

★ PRQ Evaluate the justice in civil asset forfeiture in Texas. Start at https://www.texastribune.org/2017/03/03/civil-asset-forfeiture-property-rights-law-enforcement/.

Local Government

Citizens can speak out at meetings of local policy makers. Here is what you would see at a Dallas city council meeting.
City of Dallas

Learning Objectives

LO 11.1 Describe and evaluate the organization and structure of municipal governments.

LO 11.2 Describe and evaluate the organization and structure of county governments.

LO 11.3 Describe and evaluate the organization and structure of special district governments.

LO 11.4 Evaluate the role of councils of governments as local government partners.

LO 11.5 Apply what you have learned about local government.

Local governments are responsible for a variety of services that substantially affect the public on a daily basis, including law enforcement, mass transit, sewage treatment, flood control, and emergency services. Anyone who lives in a metropolitan area is likely to be governed by two **general purpose governments**—municipal and county governments that provide a wide range of public services—in addition to numerous **special districts**, such as school districts, hospital districts, metropolitan transit authorities, and municipal utility districts.

The sheer number of local governments across Texas and the rest of the nation can challenge even the most interested members of a community who want to contact local officials about the critical needs of their own neighborhood, controversial social issues, or initiatives that can improve the community's quality of life. (See Table 11.1 for a comparison of local governments in Texas and in the United States as a whole.) To more effectively make our views known to those who are responsible for making and enforcing policies at the local level, it is vital that we learn about the inner workings of local government—that is, the various institutional features of cities, counties, and special districts. And because so many local problems affect entire regions, it is equally important to examine the role that councils of governments (COGs) play in bringing the variety of local governments together for the purposes of planning and coordinating policies.

general purpose government
A municipal or county government that provides a wide range of public services.

special districts
Local governments that provide single or closely related services that are not provided by general purpose county or municipal governments.

Did You Know? Texas has more than 5,000 local governments, most of them governed by officials who are elected by voters.

Municipalities

LO 11.1 Describe and evaluate the organization and structure of municipal governments.

How are municipalities relevant to our lives? Cities hire police officers and firefighters to protect the community. Cities enforce building and safety codes, pass anti-litter ordinances, issue garage sale permits, maintain recycling programs, launch anti-graffiti programs, impound stray animals for the safety of the community, and enforce curfews. These are just a few examples of how cities routinely affect our day-to-day lives.

TABLE 11.1 Local Governments and Public School Systems, United States and Texas, 2012

This table shows the enormous numbers of local governments in the United States and in Texas.

	Total	County	Municipal	Town or Township	Special Districts	School Districts*
United States	90,056	3,031	19,519	16,364	38,266	12,880
Texas	5,147	254	1,214	0	2,600	1,079

* Independent school districts and community college districts.

U.S. Census Bureau, 2012 Census of Governments.

▶ How is it possible for ordinary voters to keep track of the numerous elected officials that they elect to local offices? Think of ways to simplify the system of local governments to make them more accountable to the average citizen.

TABLE 11.2 Municipal Governments in Texas, 1952–2012

As general purpose governments, municipal governments provide a variety of services that are critically important to the well-being of communities.

1952	1962	1972	1982	1992	2002	2007	2012
738	866	981	1,121	1,171	1,196	1,209	1,212

U.S. Census Bureau, 2012 Census of Governments.

▶ How are city governments established?

All local governments are bound by federal and state laws as well as the U.S. and Texas constitutions. Municipalities—like counties, special districts, and school districts—are creatures of the state and have only as much power as the Texas Constitution and Texas Legislature grant them. In that sense, the state is a *unitary system of government* (see Chapter 2) with respect to local governments; they have no independent legal right to exist.

General Law and Home Rule Cities

Texas has seen a marked increase in the number of municipalities in the state since the 1950s, as shown in Table 11.2. These cities are classified as either general law or home rule cities. A **general law city** is an incorporated community with a population of 5,000 or fewer and is limited in the policy matters on which it may legislate. According to the Texas Municipal League, the vast majority of Texas cities—about 75 percent—are these smaller general law cities.

A city with a population of more than 5,000 may, by majority vote, become a **home rule city** and may retain this designation even if its population drops below this threshold. This means that it can adopt its own **city charter** (the organizing document for a municipality) and structure its local government as it sees fit, as long as charter provisions and local laws (also called ordinances) do not violate national and state constitutions and laws.

Direct Democracy at the Municipal Level Home rule permits local voters to impose their will directly on government through initiative, referendum, and recall, and most home rule cities have all three provisions. With the initiative power, local citizens, by obtaining the signatures of a designated percentage of registered voters, can force a sometimes reluctant city council to place a proposed ordinance on the ballot. If the proposal passes by a majority vote, it becomes law. Texas cities have used initiatives to resolve the following issues by popular vote:

- Should a city allow stores within the city limits to sell beer and wine?
- Should a city freeze the property tax exemption for senior citizens and people with disabilities?
- Should a city increase the minimum wage?
- Should a city impose a cap on the property tax rate?

Voters who want to repeal an existing ordinance can also petition the council to hold a referendum election to determine whether the law should remain in effect. For example, Houston voters approved referenda to remove red light cameras and to repeal a nondiscrimination ordinance. Smoking bans were put to a referendum vote in Lubbock and Baytown, but voters in both cities decided to retain the ban. A referendum election called by a city council can also permit voters to determine whether a law will go into effect. Finally, voters can, by

general law city
An incorporated community with a population of 5,000 or fewer that is limited in the subject matter on which it may legislate.

home rule city
A city with a population of more than 5,000 that can adopt its own charter and structure its local government as it sees fit, as long as charter provisions and local laws (also called ordinances) do not violate national and state constitutions and laws.

city charter
The organizing document for a municipality.

petition, force the council to hold a **recall election** that would permit voters to remove the mayor or a member of the council before the official's term expires.

The Limits of Home Rule

Although home rule cities have wider latitude than general law cities in their day-to-day operations, they are subordinate to state authority and subject to its rules governing local governments. For example, state law determines the specific dates when municipal elections can be held, how cities annex new territory, and which cities can establish metropolitan transit authorities. Local governments in Texas are subject to "sunshine" laws, such as the Public Information Act and the Open Meetings Act.

Of course, cities may not adopt policies that conflict with general state laws. This principle has resulted in conflict between state and municipal policy as several large home rule cities have adopted more progressive policies at a time when the state as a whole has become more conservative. Adoption of some liberal municipal policies has prompted the state to respond by passing state laws to preempt or supersede them. The legislature made it illegal for cities to regulate "fracking" after Denton passed an ordinance to outlaw hydraulic fracturing to extract oil and gas within its boundaries; it created a statewide regulatory framework for ride-hailing companies to preempt Austin's stricter ordinance setting standards for Lyft and Uber drivers, and it passed the "sanctuary cities" bill to override various cities' liberal policing policies toward undocumented immigrants. The state courts overturned some of Houston's antipollution ordinances and its policies providing city benefits to same-sex spouses of municipal employees.

Forms of Municipal Government

The three common forms of municipal governments are council–manager, mayor–council, and commission.

Council–Manager System

In a **council–manager form of government**, an elected city council makes laws and hires a professional administrator who is responsible for both executing council policies and managing the day-to-day operations of city government and who serves at the pleasure of the council. Figure 11.1 shows how the council–manager form is organized.

The city charter and the council assign power to the city manager. The city manager is usually responsible for selecting key personnel and for submitting a proposed budget to the council for its approval. The city council will likely seek the manager's opinion on a wide variety of matters, including what tax rate the city should adopt, whether or not the city should call a bond election, and the feasibility of proposed new ordinances. But these issues are ultimately up to the council, and the city manager is expected to implement whatever decisions the council makes.

In a council–manager form of government, the mayor may be either selected by the council from among its members or independently elected by the voters. The mayor presides over council meetings, has limited or no veto power, and has for the most part only the same legislative authority as members of the council. The mayor

recall election
An election, called by petition, that permits voters to remove an elected official before the official's term expires.

council–manager form of government
A form of government in which an elected city council makes laws and hires a professional administrator who is responsible for both executing council policies and managing the day-to-day operations of city government.

IMAGE 11.1 San Antonio Mayor Ron Nirenberg heads a council–manager city, the most common type in Texas. Despite the relatively weak institutional powers of the mayor in such a system, several of his predecessors became a force to be reckoned with during their tenure as mayors of the Alamo City.

City of San Antonio

★ **CTQ** Compare the mayor's powers in a council–manager system with those of a strong mayor. How are mayors in a council–manager system able to develop political power despite formal limits on the power of their office?

FIGURE 11.1   The Council–Manager Form of City Government

This figure shows the council–manager form of city government that is used in most Texas cities. In this form, the voters elect the city council, which then appoints a professional manager to manage the day-to-day operations of city departments.

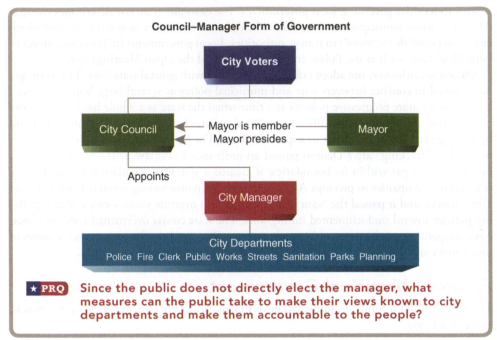

Council–Manager Form of Government

City Voters

City Council ← Mayor is member — Mayor
← Mayor presides —

Appoints

City Manager

City Departments
Police Fire Clerk Public Works Streets Sanitation Parks Planning

★ PRQ **Since the public does not directly elect the manager, what measures can the public take to make their views known to city departments and make them accountable to the people?**

Source: Cengage Learning

---

mayor–council system
A form of municipal government consisting of a mayor and a city council; this form includes both *strong mayor* and *weak mayor* variations.

strong mayor form of government
A form of municipal government in which the mayor, who is chosen in a citywide election, is both the chief executive and the leader of the city council.

also has important ceremonial powers, such as signing proclamations and issuing keys to the city to important dignitaries.

Although the office is institutionally weak, a high-profile and charismatic mayor can wield considerable political influence because access to publicity gives the mayor a platform to develop a loyal political following. Mayors of the two largest Texas cities using the council–manager system, former San Antonio mayors Henry Cisneros and Julián Castro and former Dallas mayor Ron Kirk, went on to be appointed as major federal officials.

The idea of the council–manager city structure began as part of a reform movement during the Progressive Era (1900–1920). Reformers were attempting to substitute "efficient and businesslike management" for the then prevalent system of boss rule, in which politics was the key consideration in city hall decisions. Although the council–manager system is seen as a means of separating politics from the administration of city government, critics charge that its principal shortcoming is that the voters do not directly elect the chief executive officer of the city.

Mayor–Council System

Although most Texas cities now use a council–manager system, a few, including Houston and Pasadena, still use a **mayor–council system** to govern their cities. This system, which consists of a mayor and a city council, includes both *strong mayor* and *weak mayor* variations.

In the **strong mayor form of government**, the mayor, who is chosen in a citywide election, is both the chief executive and the leader of the city council. The mayor makes appointments,

FIGURE 11.2 The Strong Mayor–Council Form of City Government

This figure shows the strong mayor form of city government such as the one used in Houston. Voters directly elect the mayor to serve as chief executive in charge of day-to-day city operations.

Strong Mayor–Council Form of Government

City Voters

City Council ← Mayor presides — Mayor

City Departments
Police Fire Clerk Public Works Streets Sanitation Parks Planning

★ **SRQ** **Does a strong mayor have too much power? How does Houston limit the potential for abuse of power in its city government?**

Source: Cengage Learning

prepares the budget, and is responsible for the management of city government. The mayor also sets the council agenda, proposes policy, and in some cities may veto council actions. Figure 11.2 shows the organizational structure of the strong mayor form.

Critics of the strong mayor system fear that the office is too powerful and may become too politicized to distribute services fairly or efficiently. This system conjures up the image of nineteenth-century urban political party machines led by mayors who appointed political cronies as department heads, hired campaign workers as city employees, and awarded contracts to supporters.

The strong mayor form of government was the target of urban reformers in the early twentieth century, but it did not completely die out. Instead, it was often restructured to include an elected city controller to separate the city's chief financial office from control by the mayor's office. Rules were also adopted to require that contracts must be awarded to the lowest and best bidder. Other reforms in strong mayor systems have included nonpartisan elections as well as ethics and campaign finance laws. In some cities, the strong mayor was stripped of the power to veto city ordinances.

The best Texas example of the strong mayor form is Houston, which has adopted most of these structural reforms. In addition, Houston's mayor now appoints professional administrative assistants who help manage city departments, but the mayor can still be held accountable for mismanagement by being voted out of office.

The **weak mayor form of government** is found in a few small cities but is very rare in Texas because of problems with accountability. It lacks unified lines of authority because the mayor and council share administrative responsibility. Some city officials are elected, others are selected by the council, and some may be appointed by the mayor. As a result, administrative power is decentralized and voters find it too difficult to know which officials to hold accountable when problems and mismanagement occur.

weak mayor form of government

A form of municipal government in which the mayor and council share administrative authority.

Commission System

commission form of government
A municipal government in which voters elect one set of officials who act as both executives and legislators. The commissioners, sitting together, are the municipal legislature, but individually each administers a city department.

Commission System The **commission form of government** is another approach to municipal government that has become almost extinct in Texas. Here, voters elect one set of officials who act as both executives and legislators. The commissioners, sitting together, are the municipal legislature, but individually each administers a city department. A manager or administrative assistant may be employed to assist the commissioners, but ultimate administrative authority still remains with the elected commissioners.

Commissioners may possess technical knowledge about city government because they supervise city departments. However, because power in the city bureaucracy is fragmented among separately elected commissioners, coordination is difficult, and the checks-and-balances system is impaired because commissioners serve both legislative and executive functions—commissioners adopt the budget for the very departments that they administer.

Municipal Election Systems

Mayors and city council members are elected for terms specified in their city charter, usually two years. Normally scheduled at a different time from the state general election, municipal elections often require that candidates receive a majority of the vote, and a runoff election may be required if no candidate receives more than 50 percent.

Nonpartisan Elections In Texas, all city elections are *nonpartisan*, meaning that political parties do not nominate candidates or officially campaign for them. Advocates of nonpartisan elections contend that municipal issues transcend traditional party divisions and that party labels are irrelevant. They argue that the two parties are overly polarized and that qualified candidates should not be excluded simply because they belong to the minority party.

Several other states use partisan elections to select city officials. Supporters of partisan elections argue that party labels provide voters with useful cues as to how a candidate will govern; in nonpartisan elections, voters often take their cues from well-financed campaigns. Parties are useful because they help winnow the field of potential candidates, unlike in Texas where dozens of candidates sometimes clutter municipal election ballots. Parties mobilize more voters and generate greater public interest than do nonpartisan campaigns. Critics of nonpartisan elections argue that they are dominated by low-visibility special interests with much to gain from city contracts and with enough money to hire campaign workers and to flood the airwaves and digital media with campaign ads.

Texas law requires that municipal elections be nonpartisan, but cities have options when it comes to adopting single-member districts or at-large election systems. As you will see, the decision to use one system or the other has enormous legal and political consequences.

at-large elections
Citywide elections in which some or all of the city council members are elected by voters of the entire municipality rather than from neighborhood districts.

pure at-large system
An election system in which candidates for city council run citywide and the top vote-getters are elected to fill the number of open seats.

at-large place system
An election system in which each candidate runs citywide for a specific seat on the council and voters cast one vote for each seat or place.

Council Election Areas Some cities do not use districts at all. Instead, they use **at-large elections**, which are citywide elections in which some or all of the city council members are elected by voters of the entire municipality rather than from neighborhood districts. At-large systems are of two types.

Some cities use a **pure at-large system**, in which all candidates for city council run citywide and the top vote-getters are elected to fill the number of open seats. Voters are allowed to cast as many votes as there are open seats (but can cast only one vote per candidate), with the winning candidates being those who receive the most votes. For example, if 20 candidates run for six seats, the six candidates getting the most votes are elected.

Some cities use an **at-large place system**—each candidate runs citywide for a specific seat on the council and voters cast one vote for each seat or place. For example, on a seven-member city council, the ballot would show perhaps several candidates running for place 1, different candidates running for place 2, and still others running for each place down through place 7. Voters would be able to cast one vote for each of the seven seats, and the candidate winning the majority of votes cast citywide would win each particular seat. Variations of either system may require a specific candidate to live in a particular district of the city, but the candidates are still elected by all of the voters in the city.

In contrast, in a system with **single-member council districts**, each council member is elected from a particular geographic district by only the voters who live in that district.

Supporters of at-large elections say that they promote the public interest because council members must take a citywide view of problems. They charge that council members elected from districts are focused on the needs of their district rather than the interests of the community as a whole. Opponents of single-member districts also claim that the election of individuals who have an outlook limited to their district makes it difficult for the council to build a consensus about the future of the city.

Critics of at-large elections maintain that the system allows a simple majority of voters to elect all council members and that, consequently, the interests of racial, ethnic, and ideological minorities in the community are not represented at city hall. Supporters of single-member districts argue that effective neighborhood representation reflects the diverse interests of the city; neighborhoods where political, cultural, racial, and ethnic minorities live have a chance to elect at least some members to the city council when a district system is used.

Although major Texas cities usually resisted single-member districts, civil rights organizations such as the Mexican American Legal Defense and Educational Fund (MALDEF), the League of United Latin American Citizens (LULAC), the American GI Forum, the National Association for the Advancement of Colored People (NAACP), Texas Rural Legal Aid, and the Southwest Voter Registration Education Project brought successful legal action, and the federal courts forced several of them to abandon at-large elections. Several cities have instituted a mixed system in which a majority of the council members are elected from single-member districts, although the mayor and some of the council members are elected at large.

Although the single-member district election system has served as the primary means of increasing minority representation on city councils, attention has also been drawn to other ways of achieving this goal. One alternative system is **cumulative voting**. Under this plan, city council members are elected in at-large elections but the number of votes a voter can cast corresponds to the number of seats on the council. If, for example, the city council has five seats, a voter can cast all five votes for a single candidate. Or a voter can cast three votes for one candidate and the remaining two votes for another candidate. In other words, voters can distribute their votes among the candidates in whatever way they choose.

More than 50 local jurisdictions in Texas have adopted cumulative voting since the 1990s, most of them school districts. In approximately 20 percent of the communities in which cumulative voting is used, the method has been adopted by both the school board and the city council. Civil rights organizations such as the MALDEF and the NAACP have backed cumulative voting in litigation, and the adoption of this election system is credited with leading to the election of minorities in two Texas independent school districts—Atlanta ISD and Amarillo ISD. The Amarillo Independent School District is the largest jurisdiction in the country to use this election system.

Term Limits
About 60 Texas cities joined the movement to impose *term limits*—that is, restrictions on the number of times that a politician can be reelected to an office or the number of years that a person may hold a particular office. Proponents of term limits believe that city hall is best governed by new blood and fresh ideas and that limiting the number of terms for mayors and council members is the best way to achieve that goal. Opponents, though, worry that cities stand to lose experienced, effective council members because of term limits.

These term limit laws are not uniform. Corpus Christi, for example, allows a person who has held a seat for four consecutive two-year terms to run again for the seat after sitting out three terms. In Austin, a council member is limited to two consecutive four-year terms, but that limit can be waived upon petition by 5 percent of the registered voters the council

single-member council districts
An electoral system in which each council member is elected from a particular geographical district by only the voters who live in that district.

cumulative voting
An election system in which city council members are elected in at-large elections but the number of votes a voter can cast corresponds to the number of seats on the council.

member represents. In Dallas, both city council members and the mayor can serve up to eight years, with the mayor limited to two four-year terms and council members limited to four two-year terms. But after meeting these limits and sitting out a single term, both the mayor and council members can seek office again.

Attempts to weaken city term limit laws have had mixed success. In 2000, voters in Austin rejected a proposition that would have repealed the city's term limits. However, in 2008, a proposal to extend the term limit to four two-year terms passed in San Antonio and a similar proposal passed in Houston in 2015.

Revenue Sources and Limitations

The local political culture determines expectations about appropriate standards of services and tolerable levels of taxation. External forces—such as a downturn in the national economy, the closing of a military base, the downsizing of industries, federal and state mandates, and natural disasters—also influence the economic climate of a community.

The sources and amount of revenue used to meet a city's budgetary obligations vary greatly among Texas municipalities according to various factors, including the following:

- The size of the city's population
- The amount and type of taxes a city is allowed and willing to levy

Texas Insiders

The Saga of Uber Ordinances

Local officials engage in intergovernmental lobbying using some of the same tactics that private interest groups employ to influence state and federal officials. For example, city officials lobby when they appeal for funding of municipal projects or try to protect the powers of municipalities. They also deploy umbrella organizations such as the Texas Municipal League to advocate for them, and they hire professional lobby outfits to represent their interests. However, large cities have lost influence with the Texas Legislature in recent years and a number of their ordinances and practices have been overturned by state law. The fate of ridesharing ordinances provides a case in point.

High-profile stories of abuse by Lyft and Uber operators have pitted new-economy businesses against traditional taxi interests. In response to such incidents and under pressure from taxi operators, Austin, Houston, Corpus Christ and other cities passed ordinances requiring drivers in ride-hailing operations undergo background checks and/or fingerprinting. In Austin, the two companies poured over $8 million into a ballot initiative to overturn the local regulations on Lyft and Uber.

After Austin voters sustained the city's regulations, Uber and Lyft turned their lobbying effort to the state capitol where the ride-sharing industry spent $2.3 million in lobbying and made $40,500 in political contributions in 2017. Despite the protestations of several mayors and city lobbyists, the legislature was receptive to the ridesharing companies' arguments in favor of less regulation; it passed HB 100 which put new, less stringent state regulations into effect, preempting or superseding city ordinances that had previously regulated the ridesharing industry.

Thinking about the role of elites in Texas politics

★ CTQ   How do interest groups affect city policy? How do cities themselves act as interest groups?

★ CSQ   Browse the website of the Texas Municipal League to find the organization's legislative agenda. Write a carefully constructed essay to explain the broad policy goals of the organization and point to specific state policies of interest to Texas cities.

- The total assessed value of taxable property within the city limits
- The needs of the residents

City revenues can also depend on how much aid money is available from the state and national governments. Our Texas Insiders feature shows that some cities, as well as some counties, use aggressive lobbying efforts to protect this intergovernmental revenue.

Sales Taxes Most Texas cities have adopted a 1 percent sales tax. Cities in the most populous counties collect an additional sales tax up to 1 percent for economic development projects. Mass transit authorities and other special districts also collect sales taxes, but total local sales taxes are capped at 2 percent.

Figure 11.3 shows that Texas cities are heavily dependent on the sales tax, which make up more than a quarter of their revenues. Although all taxes are affected by economic conditions, sales tax revenue is more sensitive to economic fluctuations than property taxes. And because budgetary problems make state and national government assistance unreliable, cities need to build into their budgets a reserve fund to compensate for these somewhat inconsistent sources of revenue.

Property Taxes Figure 11.3 shows that municipalities are also heavily dependent on ad valorem property taxes, in which the tax rate is a percentage of the assessed value of real estate. In a community with a small tax base, or total assessed value, the local government has a limited capacity to raise taxes from this source. Thus, a "poor" city must set a very high tax

FIGURE 11.3 Texas Municipal Finances: General Revenue and Expenditures

This chart shows where Texas municipalities get their revenues and how they spend them. The largest share of city revenue is the property tax, followed by sales taxes and various fees. The majority of municipal expenditures are for protective services such as police, fire, and emergency services.

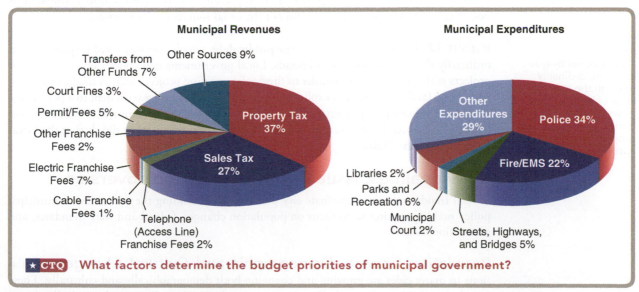

★ CTQ   What factors determine the budget priorities of municipal government?

Based on http://www.tml.org/HCW/WhereCitiesGetMoney.pdf

rate to provide adequate services. Furthermore, any drop in property values causes a decline in the city's tax base.

Texas has established a countywide appraisal authority for property taxes, and all local governments must accept its property appraisals. However, Texas state law does not require full disclosure of the sales price of real estate, making it difficult to accurately appraise property values, especially those of large commercial and industrial properties.

Limits on Property Taxes

The property tax rate of general law cities depends on the size of the city, but the maximum property tax rate of a general law city is $1.50 per $100 of the assessed value of a city's property. Home rule municipalities can set property tax rates as high as $2.50 per $100 of assessed value.

Even though no Texas city approaches these limits, property taxes have been extremely controversial, and some Texas cities have taken measures to limit their increase. For example, Corpus Christi's city charter sets a property tax cap of $0.68 per $100 valuation except for taxes to finance voter-approved bonds. Texas cities, towns, counties, and community college districts may freeze property taxes for the disabled and the elderly. Once the freeze is in place, the governing body cannot repeal it. Texas cities, as well as counties and hospital districts, may also call an election to lower property taxes by raising sales and use taxes.

rollback election
An election to limit an increase in the property tax rate to no more than 8 percent above that required for increased debt service.

Voters in non-school-district jurisdictions (cities, counties, and special districts) may petition for a **rollback election** to limit an increase in the property tax rate to no more than 8 percent above that required for increased debt service. For school districts, a rollback election is triggered automatically if a school board raises taxes more than $0.06 per $100 valuation. About half a dozen rollback elections are held annually, according to the Texas Municipal League, and more than 60 percent of such elections have resulted in tax rollbacks.

user fees
Fees paid by the individuals who receive a particular government service.

User Fees

Fees paid by the individuals who receive a particular government service are called **user fees**. Such charges are increasingly popular because voters often oppose higher taxes and generally believe that people should pay for what they actually use. Cities may charge fees for city-provided electricity, water, sewage, and garbage collection, as well as swimming pools, golf courses, and ambulance services. The Texas Municipal League has found that user fees bring in approximately 20 percent of municipal revenue. Permits, business licenses, and inspection fees round out the usual sources of city revenue.

public debt
Money owed by government, ordinarily through the issuance of bonds. Local governments issue bonds to finance major projects with voter approval.

Public Debt

Local governments use **public debt**, which is money owed by government, ordinarily through the issuance of bonds. Local governments issue bonds to finance major projects with voter approval in order to fund infrastructure projects such as roads, buildings, and public facilities. Texas law explicitly limits the amount of long-term debt to a percentage of assessed valuation of property within the boundaries of the government. This restriction is intended to keep local governments from going bankrupt, as many did during the Great Depression of the 1930s.

Municipalities: Issues, Trends, and Controversies

Several trends and issues dominate city politics; understanding the dynamics of municipal policy making requires us to focus on population changes, federal and state mandates, and annexation issues.

Population Growth, Demographic and Cultural Changes

Populations in many cities are growing and changing both demographically and culturally. These population changes present challenges to cities as they make policy in a dynamically changing environment.

How Does Texas Compare?

Population Changes in Large U.S. Cities

Texas's population grew by 35 percent between 2000 and 2017, adding more than 7 million people, more than any other state. Much of Texas's growth has been in suburban and exurban communities. Nevertheless, Table 11.3 shows that Texas still has 5 of the 15 largest cities.

The city centers continue to serve as the economic and cultural hub of most metropolitan communities across the nation. Central city governments must therefore provide several services on which the smaller surrounding communities depend. They finance most economic development activities such as building convention centers, financing airports, and funding tourism bureaus.

TABLE 11.3 The 15 Largest U.S. Cities

Rank	Place	State	2000 Census	2017 Estimate
1.	New York	New York	8,008,278	8,622,698
2.	Los Angeles	California	3,694,820	3,999,759
3.	Chicago	Illinois	2,896,016	2,716,450
4.	**Houston**	**Texas**	**1,953,631**	**2,312,717**
5.	Phoenix	Arizona	1,321,045	1,625,078
6.	Philadelphia	Pennsylvania	1,517,550	1,580,863
7.	**San Antonio**	**Texas**	**1,144,646**	**1,511,946**
8.	San Diego	California	1,223,400	1,418,516
9.	**Dallas**	**Texas**	**1,188,580**	**1,317,929**
10.	San Jose	California	894,943	1,025,350
11.	**Austin**	**Texas**	**656,562**	**950,715**
12.	Jacksonville	Florida	735,617	892,062
13.	San Francisco	California	776,733	884,363
14.	Columbus	Ohio	711,470	879,170
15.	**Fort Worth**	**Texas**	**534,694**	**874,168**

U.S. Census Bureau.

FOR DEBATE

 CTQ How can slower-growing central cities finance the costs of economic development projects that benefit the faster-growing areas that surround them?

 CTQ What challenges do changing demographics present to large urban areas?

Growing cities must expand services ranging from sewage treatment, street building, and law enforcement to urban planning and parks and recreation. Even a city with limited growth may see an internal shift in population, with one area of the city facing dramatic growth while others contend with a loss of population and businesses, vacant buildings, and urban decay. Communities with stagnant or declining populations also face the challenge of funding services from a diminished economic base. Cities with increasingly diverse, elderly, or young populations may face competing demands from the public, which will necessitate hard choices, especially if local revenue is limited.

Not only have city populations grown in size, but they have also become increasingly diverse as the burgeoning Latino population directly affects most Texas cities. Political competition among Latinos, Anglos, African Americans, and Asian Americans increases pressure on elected officials to factor ethnic, racial, and social considerations into their policy decisions.

In none of Texas's largest cities do Anglos now comprise an absolute majority of the population. African Americans account for more than one-fifth of the residents of Dallas and Houston. Latinos constitute more than one-third of the population in Austin and Fort Worth, more than 40 percent in Dallas and Houston, over 60 percent in San Antonio and 80 percent in El Paso. Houston is the home of the state's largest Asian American community and of the largest number of undocumented immigrants.

The vast majority of these diverse groups are citizens, but an estimated 1.4 million undocumented immigrants live in Texas, many of them Latinos in Texas cities. Most Texas cities had a policy of honoring federal requests to hold undocumented immigrants for deportation after they were arrested, but several did not routinely ask people about their immigration status believing that undocumented immigrants may be less willing to report crimes or cooperate with police if doing so might result in deportation and at the same time lawful city residents may resent local law enforcement demanding proof of citizenship, especially if they are being singled out for questioning because of their ethnicity.

However, these policing practices came under scrutiny by advocates of immigration enforcement and the Travis county sheriff defiantly announced she would not honor some federal detainer requests. The Texas legislature's response was to pass SB 4, the "sanctuary cities" bill, which requires law local law enforcement to cooperate with federal immigration authorities, and it allows local police to inquire about a person's immigration status during encounters such as traffic stops.

Cities must also come to grips with other cultural changes, such as the demands for LGBT rights. Because state law does not prohibit discrimination based on sexual orientation or gender identity, many major Texas cities have passed various ordinances to protect sexual minorities. Among them, Dallas, Austin, San Antonio, Fort Worth, and Plano have passed nondiscrimination ordinances that forbid businesses from denying employment or services based on sexual orientation. Houston's city council also passed a similar law, but it was repealed by voters in a 2015 referendum.

Government Mandates

mandate
A federal or state requirement that a lower level of government, like a city or county, provide a service or meet certain standards, often as a condition for receiving financial aid.

Government Mandates Texas cities—like most cities in the nation—have seen both federal and state governments cut funding even as they have increased the number of mandates imposed on local governments. A **mandate** is a federal or state requirement that a lower level of government, like a city or county, provide a service or meet certain standards, often as a condition for receiving financial aid. The federal government has imposed many such mandates as a condition for state or local governments to receive grants-in-aid. Some notable examples of federal mandates are the Americans with Disabilities Act, the National Voter Registration Act (Motor Voter Act), the Help America Vote Act, and the No Child Left Behind Act. Likewise, the state has imposed innumerable mandates on school districts, counties, and cities.

Supporters of mandates argue that they permit the federal and state governments to meet important needs in a uniform fashion. Critics charge that mandates—particularly those that are unfunded—impose a heavy financial burden on the governments that are required to fulfill the obligations they impose.

The Unfunded Mandates Interagency Work Group, including the state auditor, comptroller, director of the Legislative Budget Board, a senator (selected by the lieutenant governor), and a representative (selected by the speaker), keeps a record of unfunded mandates the legislature passes. Mandates exempt from the list include those passed by voters and those adopted to comply with the Texas Constitution, federal law, or a court order.

Annexation

The process by which cities bring unincorporated areas into their jurisdiction is **annexation**. Most major Texas municipalities have broad powers to develop plans to annex adjacent areas equal to as much as 10 percent of their existing area each year so long as they provide essential services in a timely manner.

In addition to outright annexation, municipalities have the power to establish a buffer area, or **extraterritorial jurisdiction (ETJ)**, that extends one-half mile to as much as five miles beyond the city's limits, depending on the city's population. Cities may enforce zoning and building codes and new cities may not be incorporated within their ETJs, allowing cities to plan their growth and preventing other suburban "bedroom" cities from forming to choke off their expansion. Cities have used a strategy of spoke annexation by taking in narrow "fingers" of land along highway right-of-way outward from the existing city limits, thereby placing the area between the fingers into their ETJ and reserving their right to annex them later.

Supporters of such broad annexation power argue that the "inherent power to unilaterally annex adjoining areas is one of the most important home-rule prerogatives."[1] Annexation allows Texas cities to protect their tax base to finance expensive city services and mitigate the problem of urban decay. Without broad annexation powers, cities would suffer as more prosperous residents flee central cities to low-tax suburbs, leaving core cities with hollowed-out neighborhoods and a depleted tax base from which to finance essential services such as law enforcement, cultural institutions, transportation projects, and economic development which benefit the entire metropolitan area.

In unincorporated areas around major Texas cities, some opponents of involuntary annexation have argued that it limits their opportunity for self-government and they resent taxation and regulation by central-city governments that do not share their political values; they argue that large cities have run roughshod over residents annexing property without the owners' consent, forcing them to pay higher taxes for services they oftentimes do not want. The Texas Legislature recently responded to these complaints by passing an annexation reform bill which allows residents in most areas proposed for annexation to demand an election to decide whether a city can bring them under its jurisdiction.

Different annexation-related problems have developed with regard to low income areas. Cities usually have a powerful motivation to annex outlying areas to add to their tax base, but they have been reluctant to annex outlying low-income, service-deprived areas. For example, despite the availability of state assistance, they have been slow to annex many of the **colonias,** severely impoverished unincorporated areas mostly located along the Texas–Mexico border that have a multitude of problems, including substandard housing, unsanitary drinking water, and lack of proper sewage disposal.

Counties

LO 11.2 **Describe and evaluate the organization and structure of county governments.**

County government provides a variety of services and makes public policies that have widespread and direct impact on the public. The county commissioners court draws voting precinct boundaries and voting locations in each county. In most counties, the county clerk administers state elections, issues marriage licenses, and records birth and death certificates. The County Tax Office collects county property taxes, issues license plates and stickers, and processes vehicle transfers. County Dispute Resolution Services help mediate conflicts between landlords

---

annexation
The process by which cities bring unincorporated areas into their jurisdiction.

extraterritorial jurisdiction (ETJ)
A buffer area that extends beyond a city's limits.

colonias
Severely impoverished unincorporated areas mostly located along the Texas–Mexico border that have a multitude of problems, including substandard housing, unsanitary drinking water, and lack of proper sewage disposal.

and tenants. Sheriffs enforce state laws, and district or county attorneys prosecute most criminal violations. County and district courts try most civil and criminal cases.

With 254 counties, Texas has more counties than any other state. County government is far less flexible than municipal government in its organization and functions. Texas counties do not have home rule and cannot pass ordinances unless the state legislature specifically authorizes them to do so. New statutes or constitutional amendments are often necessary to allow the county to deal with contemporary problems; many state laws apply to only one specific county's unique circumstances and do not grant flexibility to counties throughout the state. The needs of Harris County, for example, with a population of 4,092,459 in 2010, are significantly different from those of Loving County, which had only 82 inhabitants. Yet Texas law allows only modest variations to accommodate these differences.

For example, county property taxes are limited to a rate of $0.80 per $100 of assessed valuation unless voters approve additional taxes to cover long-term debt for infrastructure such as courthouses, criminal justice buildings, flood control, and county road or bridge maintenance.

Functions of Counties

county governments
General purpose local governments that also serve as administrative arms of the state.

County governments are established by the state constitution and the legislature as general purpose local governments that also serve as an administrative arm of the state, carrying out the state's laws and collecting certain state taxes. They administer county, state, and national elections but not those for municipalities, school, and other special districts. County governments act for the state in enforcing laws, securing right-of-way for highways, registering births, deaths, and marriages, housing state district courts, registering motor vehicles, recording land titles and deeds, and collecting some state taxes and fees.

County government also has optional powers specifically authorized by state law. For example, the Local Government Code authorizes counties to establish and maintain libraries, operate and maintain parks, establish recreational or cultural facilities such as auditoriums or convention centers, appoint county historicals commissions, and regulate sexually oriented businesses. County governments may also enter into agreements with other local governments to provide a service or program such as purchasing and maintaining parks, museums, and historical sites. Counties may also contract with other local governments to carry out administrative functions such as assessing and collecting taxes or managing records or to provide public services such as law enforcement and fire protection, streets and roads, public health and welfare, and waste disposal. The Health and Safety Code gives county governments the authority to maintain a county hospital.

Structure and Organization of Counties
County government consists of several independent officials elected for four-year terms in the partisan general election at the same time state officials are elected. The county governing body, the **commissioners court**, consists of the county judge, serving as the presiding officer, and four county commissioners elected from separate precincts (see Image 11.2). Despite its misleading name, commissioners court is not a judicial body; rather, it is a legislature with limited authority to approve the budget for all county operations, set the tax rate, and pass ordinances on a narrow range of policies. The commissioners court does not have direct control over the many elected department heads in county government, but it wields considerable influence through its budgetary power. The sheriff, for example, is responsible to county voters for enforcing the law and maintaining order and security in the county jail, but the quality of law enforcement depends a great deal on county commissioners' decisions. The commissioners court must provide the funds to build a jail and approve its staff, authorize expenditures for each vehicle and its gas and repairs, and authorize deputies, clerks, and their salaries.

commissioners court
The policy-making body of a county, consisting of a county judge, who serves as the presiding officer of the court, and four commissioners elected from individual precincts for four-year terms.

The **county judge** is an official elected countywide for a four-year term to preside over the commissioners court. In addition, the county judge has administrative functions that include helping prepare a budget proposal in smaller counties; supervising election-related activities such as calling elections, posting election notices, and receiving and canvassing election results; conducting hearings for beer and wine permits; performing marriage ceremonies; conducting hearings on state hospital admittance for people with mental illness; and serving as the head of civil defense and disaster relief for the county. In addition, a county judge may have judicial authority in many of the smaller counties.

Four county commissioners elected for four-year terms comprise the remaining membership of the court. Commissioners are elected in single-member districts, or precincts, as they are called in Texas. The U.S. Supreme Court has ruled that these commissioner precincts must be roughly equal in population based on the one-person, one-vote principle.[2]

IMAGE 11.2 Many bloggers report on operations inside local governments. One of the best local bloggers is Charles Kuffner, who specializes in local reporting on Houston area politics at his Off the Kuff website. This screenshot is from his coverage of the drawing of Harris County commissioner precinct lines.

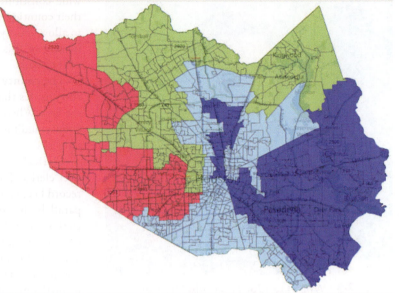

http://offthekuff.com/wp/?p=49038

★ CTQ   **Are commissioners' precincts gerrymandered?**

Commissioners were historically called "road commissioners" because they are responsible for the county roads and bridges within their precincts except in counties that have hired a road engineer. Each is given a certain amount of money and has almost total authority to determine how it will be spent on roads and bridges. Residents of rural areas often consider building and maintaining roads to be the commissioners' primary responsibility.

Law enforcement officers are the county sheriff and constables. The **sheriff** is the chief county law enforcement officer. Next to the county judge, the sheriff is usually the most powerful county officer because he or she has a relatively large budget and staff of deputies to assist in enforcing state law throughout the county. Within the corporate limits of cities, the sheriff usually refrains from patrolling to better use scarce resources and avoid jurisdictional disputes with the city police. The sheriff's department also operates the county jail and delivers and executes court orders.

Constables are county law enforcement officials who are elected to serve as the process officers of justice of the peace courts and also have general law enforcement powers. Constables are elected from the same precincts as justices of the peace. They deliver summonses and execute court orders. In some metropolitan counties, constables have added many deputies and have become important law enforcement agencies, but in others the office is so unimportant that it remains unfilled, and some county commissioners have abolished the office altogether.

Financial officers of the county include the tax assessor-collector, the treasurer, and the auditor. The responsibilities of the **tax assessor-collector** include collecting various county taxes and fees and, in some counties, registering voters. Additional responsibilities include collecting certain state taxes and fees, particularly motor vehicle registration fees (license plate fees) and the motor vehicle sales tax.

county judge
An official elected countywide for a four-year term to preside over the county commissioners court.

sheriff
The chief county law enforcement officer.

constables
County law enforcement officials who are elected to serve as the process officers of justice of the peace courts and also have general law enforcement powers.

tax assessor-collector
A county financial officer whose responsibilities include collecting various county taxes and fees and, in some counties, registering voters.

IMAGE 11.3 Sheriffs, like Sally Hernandez in Travis County, are usually the most powerful county officers after the county judges, but their department budgets must be approved by the commissioners court.

Travis County Sheriff's Office

★ **SRQ** What standards should the public use to determine if a sheriff is effectively meeting the county's law enforcement needs? How can voters hold county officials accountable when so many of them are elected to offices with divided and overlapping responsibilities?

In many counties, the **county treasurer** is responsible for receiving, depositing, and disbursing funds. However, some counties have transferred this function to the county auditor. Although the treasurer holds a constitutional office, several counties have asked the legislature to propose state-wide constitutional amendments to abolish this office in their counties. Because a general constitutional amendment to allow county voters to abolish the office is unlikely, elimination of this office is likely to proceed on a county-by-county basis.

The **county auditor** reviews all county financial records and ensures that expenditures are made in accordance with the law. Whereas other key county officials are elected, the county auditor is appointed to a two-year term by district judges.

Clerical officers in the county are the county and district clerks. The **county clerk** serves as the county's chief record keeper and election officer. In some ways, the office parallels that of the Texas secretary of state. The county clerk's duties include serving as clerk for the commissioners court; maintaining records for justices of the peace and county courts; filing mortgages, wills, and contracts; issuing marriage licenses and maintaining certain records of births and deaths; and serving on the county election board, certifying candidates running for county office, and carrying out other housekeeping functions, such as preserving the results of state, county, and special district elections. In the smallest counties, the county clerk also maintains records for district courts, but most counties elect a separate **district clerk** to serve as the chief record keeper for district courts.

The **county attorney** is a county legal officer whose responsibilities may include giving legal advice to the commissioners court and representing the county in civil litigation, whereas the **district attorney** is the officer who prosecutes most criminal cases. In a few of the largest counties, the office of county attorney has been abolished and the district attorney's office has been given the responsibility of handling civil matters in addition to the usual task of prosecuting most crime in the county.

Some counties have other executive officers, such as five or more members of the county board of school trustees, a county superintendent of schools, a county surveyor, and a county weigher. Counties may authorize such appointive officers as the county election administrator, county health officer, county medical examiner, county agricultural agent, and home demonstration agent.

county treasurer
In many counties, the official who is responsible for receiving, depositing, and disbursing funds.

county auditor
A financial officer whose duties include reviewing county financial records and ensuring that expenditures are made in accordance with the law.

Counties: Issues, Trends, and Controversies

The institutional features of Texas county government are largely a product of the nineteenth century, yet the demands of modern society are placing an increasingly heavy burden on this level of government. Reformers have frequently cited criticisms of county government and proposed measures counties can take to deal with contemporary problems.

Constitutional Rigidity

The great mass of detailed and restrictive material in the Texas Constitution creates problems of rigidity and inflexibility. Limits on county government not embedded in the constitution are scattered throughout the Local Government Code and various other statutes. The result is a collection of legal requirements, many of which apply equally to the huge metropolitan counties, such as Harris, Dallas, Tarrant, and Bexar, and to small rural counties, almost half of which have populations of fewer than 20,000. The standardization of county structure and functions often fails to account for the great variation among the counties in their individual needs and problems. At present, deviations from the uniform structure and functions must be specifically authorized by the state legislature. Some reformers argue that voters should be entrusted with restructuring their own county governments, using home rule provisions similar to those now available to many Texas cities.

Long Ballot

So many county officials are independently elected and the operations of county government are so decentralized that the voters may find it difficult to monitor the many positions involved. Reformers recommend a **short ballot**—that is, the listing of only a few independently elected offices on an election ballot. They argue that a simplified structure with a single county executive would allow voters to hold one high-profile officer accountable for the administration of county programs. They contend that a chief county executive could coordinate county programs, engage in long-range planning, and eliminate duplication among various county offices.

Defenders of the long ballot counter that the current system provides for the direct election of public officials to ensure that government remains responsive to the needs and demands of the voters, as we discussed in Chapter 3. They fear that concentrating too much power in a single chief executive invites abuse and threatens personal liberty.

Unit Road System

The *unit road system* is a system that concentrates the day-to-day responsibilities for roads in the hands of a professional engineer rather than individual county commissioners. The engineer is responsible to the commissioners court for the efficient and economical construction and maintenance of county roads. The voters may petition for an election to establish the unit road system, or commissioners may initiate the change themselves.

Supporters of this system maintain that it brings greater coordination and professionalism to road building and maintenance in rural areas. Commissioners, however, are reluctant to give up the political influence that their individual control over road building brings; some voters like the idea of directly electing the officers who build and maintain their roads.

Spoils System versus Merit System

Elected county officials hire county employees using a *spoils system*, a system that gives elected officials considerable discretion in employment and promotion decisions. This can make employee job security dependent on the continued election of and allegiance to their employer. Political loyalty rather than competence is often the main factor in the recruitment and retention of employees, and when a new official is elected, a large turnover of county employees may result.

The spoils system's defenders point out that the elected official is responsible for employees' performance and therefore should have the authority to bring in more employees than just those at the top echelon. They also argue that an elected official would be foolish to release competent employees simply because they had gained their experience under a predecessor. Finally, they argue that alternatives like the merit system provide so much job security that employees become complacent and indifferent to the public.

The spoils system's opponents propose a *merit system* that bases employment and promotion on specific qualifications and performance, as we explained in Chapter 8. Because it would

---

county clerk
The officer who serves as the county's chief record keeper and election officer.

district clerk
The record keeper for the district court in larger counties.

county attorney
A county legal officer whose responsibilities may include giving legal advice to the commissioners court and representing the county in civil litigation.

district attorney
The officer who prosecutes most criminal cases.

short ballot
The listing of only a few independently elected offices on an election ballot.

IMAGE 11.4 The nerve center of county government is the county courthouse, where courts conduct trials, the commissioners meet, taxes are collected, and vital records are kept. In Texas, county officials are elected in partisan elections on a long ballot.

RODGER MALLISON/KRT/Newscom

★ SRQ What are the advantages and disadvantages of commissioners, judges, and other major officials such as the sheriff running for office on party labels? Evaluate the use of a long ballot in terms of local government efficiency and responsiveness to public needs.

consolidation
The merging of county government with other local governments to form a single local government.

also prohibit termination of employment except for proven cause, the merit system offers job security, which should attract qualified personnel. Supporters of the merit system maintain that it encourages professionalism, increases efficiency, and allows uniform application of equal opportunity requirements.

Texas counties with a population of 200,000 or more may establish a *civil service* program for some county employees, and counties with populations of more than 500,000 may establish a civil service system for the sheriff's office. According to the Texas Association of Counties, half of the 20 counties that may establish a civil service system have done so, and all seven counties eligible to establish a civil service program in the sheriffs' department have one.

Consolidation The merging of county government with other local governments to form a single government is called **consolidation**. Some reformers point to city–county consolidation as a means of reducing the number of local governments, eliminating duplication of government services, and increasing government efficiency.

However, the consolidation of local governments faces many challenges. Consolidation requires legislative action, followed by local voter approval. Independently elected officials at the local level are likely to resist a move that would eliminate their offices and the power that goes with them. Although many cities and counties enter into partnership agreements to provide joint services, city–county consolidation bills have failed to win passage in the Texas Legislature.

Special District Governments

LO 11.3   **Describe and evaluate the organization and structure of special district governments.**

Special districts are local governments that provide single or closely related services that are not provided by general purpose county or municipal governments. We will focus on the non-school special districts in this chapter, and in Chapter 12 we will discuss special purpose governments related to education, such as school districts and community college districts.

These special districts do not always receive attention comparable with cities and counties, but they are no less important when it comes to serving the needs of the public. In a suburban area outside the city limits, for example, a special district may be established to provide water and sewer facilities for a housing development; such a special district has the authority to borrow to build the system and may assess taxes and user fees on property owners and residents.

Table 11.4 shows that the number of special districts has grown considerably. In fact, special districts are the most numerous of all local governments in Texas. Some examples are airport authorities, drainage districts, hospital authorities, municipal utility districts, library districts, navigation districts, metropolitan transit authorities, river authorities, and rural fire prevention districts; Texas even has noxious weed and mosquito control districts. According to the U.S. Census Bureau, two-thirds of the special districts in Texas provide a single service. The rest are classified as "multiple function districts," and most of those provide closely related functions like sewerage and water supply.

Multimember boards usually govern special districts. Voters elect members of some special district boards either in partisan or nonpartisan elections; city councils and county commissioners appoint others; in some cases, city council members or county commissioners themselves serve ex officio as board members.

TABLE 11.4 Special Districts in Texas, 1952–2012

Special districts have been on the rise since the mid-twentieth century. Some special districts have their own elected governing boards that have the authority to impose a property tax.

1952	1962	1972	1982	1992	2002	2007	2012
491	733	1,215	1,681	2,266	2,245	2,291	2,309

U.S. Census Bureau, 2012 Census of Governments.

▶ Does the increasing number of special districts complicate your efforts to inform yourself about government operations?

Special districts should not be confused with dependent agencies. A **dependent agency** is a classification created by the U.S. Census Bureau for governmental entities that are closely tied to general purpose governments but do not have as much independence as special district governments. An example of a dependent agency is a crime control and prevention district, a temporary agency created with voter approval. Crime control districts have become increasingly popular since the 1990s, particularly in cities located in Tarrant County. Voters have authorized more than 60 crime control districts, and most of them collect either a one-half cent or one-fourth cent sales tax. In some communities, the establishment of crime control and prevention districts has substantially increased funding for law enforcement.

dependent agency
A classification created by the U.S. Census Bureau for governmental entities that are closely tied to general purpose governments but do not have as much independence as special district governments.

Reasons for Creating Special District Governments

Having a service provided by a special district rather than a general purpose government is appealing for a variety of reasons. A city or county may have limited revenue because of a downturn in the economy, the loss of a major industry, new unfunded mandates, or fewer federal dollars. The general purpose government may have reached its state-mandated sales tax ceiling of 2 percent. Popular or political sentiment may be that city and county property taxes are already too high, and a strong anti-tax organization in the community may be eager to make that point. Little or no support may exist for increasing taxes or cutting other services to accommodate another service responsibility, so special districts may be created to avoid raising city or county taxes.

Furthermore, only a small area within a city or county may need the service. Why tax the entire jurisdiction? A district may be created for the benefit of "underserved areas," as is the case with library districts in Texas that serve rural and suburban areas. On the other hand, the demand for a service may extend beyond a single jurisdiction, calling for a special district that is multicity or multicounty in scope. For example, a river authority with the power to govern the use of water throughout the river's watershed must transcend existing political boundaries; flood control districts similarly deal with a

IMAGE 11.5 Often financed by an "economic development" sales tax, mass transit authorities are among the most visible special district governments.

Bob Thomas/Popperfoto/Getty Images

★ SRQ **Give examples of less well-known special districts and explain why their low profile makes it difficult for the public to hold them accountable through the democratic process.**

problem that crosses political boundaries. Municipal utility districts (MUDs) are often created at the insistence of developers who want to provide water and sewerage for the subdivisions they establish outside city service areas (see Image 11.6). For a host of reasons, special districts serve as alternatives to general purpose governments, and they are an attractive option as an alternative revenue source.

Special Districts: Issues, Trends, and Controversies

Although special districts provide valuable public services not provided by general purpose governments, reformers charge that they are often too small to be efficient, too low-profile to be visible to the public, and too numerous to be readily held accountable to voters.

Multiplicity of Governments and Lack of Visibility
Although special districts can be dissolved when a municipality annexes the area and provides it with services, the trend in Texas as across the rest of the nation has been toward the proliferation of special district governments, as shown in Table 11.4. The sheer number of special district governments and their small size create serious challenges for special district governments.

Special districts are sometimes called *hidden* governments because the actions of district officials and employees are less visible than if a county or city provided the services. When special district elections are held at times or places other than those for general elections, voter turnout is quite low.

Cost and Inefficiency
Because special districts are often small, they may purchase in limited quantities at higher prices than larger governments. In addition, if special districts have little or no authority to tax, they are forced to borrow money by issuing *revenue bonds*, which are paid from fees collected for the service provided, rather than *general obligation bonds*, which are paid from tax revenue. Because revenue bonds are less secure than general obligation bonds, special district residents are forced to pay higher interest rates just to service the bonded indebtedness. Special districts may also have a lower bond rating than larger, general function governments, which also increases their borrowing costs.

A study of special purpose governments in more than 300 U.S. metropolitan areas concluded that the special district approach to governing is more costly than the general purpose approach. Moreover, social welfare functions (such as hospitals, housing, and welfare) tend to receive more revenue in metropolitan areas with fewer special districts. Housekeeping functions (including fire protection, natural resources, and police protection) and development functions (including airports, water, and highways) tend to receive more revenue in areas where special districts are more prevalent.[3]

As an alternative to inefficient special districts, reformers advocate consolidation of small special districts. To deal with problems and fiscal challenges that transcend city and county boundaries, they urge general purpose governments to negotiate inter-local agreements to meet the needs of their respective communities. They argue that the need for special districts can be reduced by transferring their functions to general purpose governments.

IMAGE 11.6 In this March 6, 2016 edition of *Last Week Tonight with John Oliver,* Oliver mockingly highlighted a case in which a developer (via a contractor) hired two people to live temporarily in a trailer on a property in Montgomery County, Texas, where they were the only two people eligible to vote in an election (the notice of which is displayed in the upper left of the screen shot) that created a special district eligible to issue $500 million dollars in bonds.

★SRQ How do municipal utility districts and other special district governments serve narrow special interests in Texas?

Councils of Governments

LO 11.4 **Evaluate the role of councils of governments as local government partners.**

The multitude of local governments with different jurisdictions and missions can pose challenges when services are of a regional nature. These governments look for ways to coordinate activities and share information without compromising their respective legal responsibilities.

Councils of Governments (COGs)

Advisory bodies consisting of representatives of various local governments brought together for the purposes of regional planning and cooperation are called **councils of governments (COGs)**. COGs are not governments; instead, they are voluntary regional groupings of local governments to provide a forum to share information and coordinate public policy. Local governments are involved in the delivery of a variety of services that are the product of national, state, and local laws and policies, and many of the public needs and problems transcend governmental jurisdictions. Intergovernmental communication is essential to successful collaboration and delivery of regional services.

The Texas Association of Regional Councils consists of all COGs in the state. The association's website lists a wide range of services provided by Texas COGs, including:

councils of governments (COGs)

Advisory bodies consisting of representatives of various local governments brought together for the purposes of regional planning and cooperation.

- Planning and implementing regional homeland security strategies
- Operating law enforcement training academies
- Promoting regional municipal solid waste and environmental quality planning
- Providing cooperative purchasing options for governments
- Managing region-wide services to the elderly
- Maintaining and improving regional 9-1-1 systems
- Promoting regional economic development
- Operating specialized transit systems
- Providing management services for member governments[4]

Applying What You Have Learned about Local Government

LO 11.5 **Apply what you have learned about local government.**

You have learned that local governments face a variety of challenges and problems as they make public policy. Counties face particular problems because their structures, organizations, and powers are primarily designed to handle the needs of a rural setting even as many of them have become highly urbanized. Nowhere are these problems greater than in urban counties along the Texas border with Mexico, so we asked El Paso County Judge Veronica Escobar to provide you with a realistic view of county operations in practice.

Veronica Escobar was first elected county judge of El Paso County in 2010, was reelected in 2014, and was elected to Congress in 2018. She had previously served as an El Paso County commissioner for one term and as the communications director for the mayor of the City of El Paso. Escobar has been an advocate for modernizing county government to make it more efficient and responsive to constituents and has also been active in addressing issues of importance to U.S.–Mexico border communities.

As you read Judge Escobar's description of her role in county government, look for the practical weaknesses in the structure of county government and the special problems that Border counties face. We will ask you to reflect on the kind of reforms that might make decentralized county governments more responsive to the needs of their residents.

POLITICS IN PRACTICE
A View from Inside County Government

by Veronica Escobar

FORMER EL PASO COUNTY JUDGE

All 254 Texas county judges have duties and responsibilities that are laid out in the Texas Constitution. However, ask most of my fellow county judges in Texas to tell you about the work they do outside of what is mandated by the constitution, and you're likely to get a long list of additional obligations not outlined anywhere. That's all part of being chief executive of a county. I'd also bet that each one of us would tell you that the role of county judge and chief executive is probably one of the most challenging jobs in local government, with varying and significant responsibilities and duties to the voters and the communities we represent.

El Paso County, which I am privileged to represent, is an urban county with over 800,000 people. My colleagues and I on commissioners court deal with many of the same issues other urban counties confront. For example, while we have to address growth that occurs in the unincorporated areas, counties and commissioners courts don't have the same powers that cities and their city councils do: we can't write ordinances; we can't regulate development; and we have more limited sources of revenue. Additionally, we have mandates issued to us by the state legislature, many times with no funding to execute them and, what's more, every legislative session brings the risk of more limitations on what we can do, how we can raise revenue, and how we can govern.

At the same time, we must deal with the needs in our urban communities: transportation; delivering quality physical and mental healthcare to our citizens; administering criminal justice; remaining competitive by engaging in strategic economic development; and innumerable other pressing demands.

Because El Paso is on the Texas–Mexico border, we have challenges other urban counties don't face. For example, colonias, which are developments that lack access to water, sewer lines, and other fundamental amenities that most Americans take for granted, are found in many Border counties. They exist in large part because Texas counties have not been allowed to regulate development. So counties like mine have to do everything we can to get our families in outlying areas access to basic but necessary and costly services. While it's not easy, it's obviously a priority because no family should have to live in third-world conditions.

Additionally, as a county on the Texas–Mexico border, we have a port of entry linking us with Mexico; our community is thus key to cross-border trade and traffic and we have all the challenges and opportunities that that presents.

Within our organization, there are additional demands. One of the priorities for me as county judge has been to reform an organization based on an antiquated form of government. From the first day I took office, I've tried to make the county more accountable, transparent, and modern. During my administration, we created a position of Chief Administrator (or county manager) to centralize administrative functions; we engaged in strategic and long-term planning; and we reformed many outdated processes.

Finally, as county judge and the highest elected official in the county, I believe I have an obligation to use the bully pulpit given to me by the voters to educate the state and the nation about the Border and El Paso. I've testified before innumerable legislative committees at the state and federal level. I've been privileged to author three opinion pieces for *The New York Times* debunking myths about El Paso and the Border. While obviously this is not part of my constitutional duties, I think it's important for me as the representative of over 800,000 people to ensure my community is not mischaracterized and that the nation sees the truth about the Border—that it is a marvelous, vibrant intersection of two nations and cultures that serves as the gateway to the United States.

The challenges in county government are tremendous, and very few people know how difficult it really is, but it has been the most gratifying job I've ever had. It is a true gift to have the opportunity to improve lives, shape government, and positively impact one's community. There's no more direct or powerful way to be able to do this than in local government.

1. What are the practical limitations on the ability of county governments to solve modern problems? What sort of reforms would make county governments more effective in a modern urban setting?
2. What special problems do counties along the Texas–Mexico border face?

★ Chapter Summary

LO 11.1 Describe and evaluate the organization and structure of municipal governments. Municipalities with a population greater than 5,000 may adopt home rule, which allows them to write their own charters (comparable to a constitution) and ordinances, as long as they do not conflict with state or federal laws or constitutions. Cities that do not meet that population requirement must operate under a general law charter established by the state.

The nonpartisan election is a key feature of Texas municipal government, and the council–manager form of government and at-large elections are also characteristics of many Texas cities. Some cities with large Latino and African American populations have, under court order, replaced at-large elections with single-member districts, modified election systems, or instituted cumulative voting. Local voters may also influence their communities through initiative, referendum, and recall elections; rollback elections; term limit elections; and economic development sales tax elections. Texas's broad annexation laws allowed expansion of home rule cities, but were often criticized by voters in unincorporated areas who objected to being annexed against their will. State laws now give residents the right to vote on annexation plans and require municipal services be provided in a timely manner.

LO 11.2 Describe and evaluate the organization and structure of county governments. The structure and organization of county government are determined by the Texas Constitution and the state legislature. Texas counties range considerably in terms of population, yet they are quite similar when it comes to structural features, functions, and sources of funding. County governments have a plural executive system with many county departments being independently elected, including department heads such as law enforcement officers, financial officers, and clerical officers.

LO 11.3 Describe and evaluate the organization and structure of special district governments. Special district governments provide single or closely related services that are not provided by general purpose county or municipal governments. Special districts are the most numerous of all local governments in Texas, and they have steadily increased in number since the mid-twentieth century. The types of service they provide, how their governing boards are selected, and their sources of revenue vary.

Having a service provided by a special district rather than a general purpose government is appealing to many residents for a variety of reasons, including the lack of support among general purpose governments for increasing taxes or cutting other services to accommodate another service responsibility. Critics charge that they are often too small to be efficient, too low-profile to be visible to the public, and too numerous to be readily held accountable to voters.

LO 11.4 Evaluate the role of councils of governments as local government partners. Government is largely fragmented at the local level. Although friction between governments is common, cooperation may also result when local governments agree to share responsibility for certain services. Nevertheless, any significant changes in the structural relationship between cities, counties, and special districts will likely continue to be more incremental than sweeping. But on a routine basis, local governments can cooperate with the assistance of councils of governments (COGs), voluntary regional groupings of local governments that share information and coordinate government planning.

LO 11.5 Apply what you have learned about local government. You explored the problems of an urban county from an insider's viewpoint and looked at the special issues that counties face in the Texas–Mexico border region. You examined how a county judge views her role in county government and considered reforms of county government that might make it operate more efficiently and responsibly.

Key Terms

annexation, *p. 301*
at-large elections, *p. 294*
at-large place system, *p. 294*
city charter, *p. 290*
colonias, *p. 301*
commission form of government, *p. 294*
commissioners court, *p. 302*
consolidation, *p. 306*
constables, *p. 303*
council–manager form of government, *p. 291*

councils of governments (COGs), *p. 309*
county attorney, *p. 305*
county auditor, *p. 304*
county clerk, *p. 305*
county governments, *p. 302*
county judge, *p. 303*
county treasurer, *p. 304*
cumulative voting, *p. 295*
dependent agency, *p. 307*
district attorney, *p. 305*
district clerk, *p. 305*

extraterritorial jurisdiction (ETJ), *p. 301*
general law city, *p. 290*
general purpose government, *p. 289*
home rule city, *p. 290*
mandate, *p. 300*
mayor–council system, *p. 292*
public debt, *p. 298*
pure at-large system, *p. 294*
recall election, *p. 291*
rollback election, *p. 298*

sheriff, *p. 303*
short ballot, *p. 305*
single-member council districts, *p. 295*
special districts, *p. 289*
strong mayor form of government, *p. 292*
tax assessor-collector, *p. 303*
user fees, *p. 298*
weak mayor form of government, *p. 293*

Review Questions

LO 11.1 Describe and evaluate the organization and structure of municipal governments.

- Why do cities adopt home rule? What are some examples of limitations that are imposed on home rule cities?

- Explain the mayor's role and authority in the council–manager, weak mayor, and strong mayor forms of government.

- Compare and contrast at-large and single-member district election systems. Describe the cumulative voting alternative.

LO 11.2 Describe and evaluate the organization and structure of county governments.

- In what ways are county governments restricted by state law?

- How are members of the commissioners court elected? What are the responsibilities of the commissioners court?

- Who are the county law enforcement officers and county financial officers? What are their responsibilities?

LO 11.3 Describe and evaluate the organization and structure of special district governments.

- What is the primary purpose of special district governments? What are some examples of special district governments?

- What are some reasons for creating a special district to provide a service as opposed to giving a city or a county the responsibility for the service?

- What are some reasons for opposing the creation of special district governments?

LO 11.4 Evaluate the role of councils of governments as local government partners.

- What factors contributed to the formation of councils of governments?

- From the perspective of city councils, county commissioners courts, and special district governments, what are the primary reasons for joining councils of governments?

- What are particular examples of services provided by councils of governments?

Think Critically and Get Active!

Explore the structures of local governments in your area.

- You can find a list of Texas cities **at https://www. tml.org/links_cities** and counties at **www.county. org/about-texas-counties/county-websites/**. Search for the name of your city and county, and explore their websites to learn about the organization and structure of each government.

- Use the Texas Association of Counties information program at **www.txcip.org/tac/census/County Profiles.php** to select your home county and describe its demographic profile. Then click on "special districts" at the bottom of the page to find out how many special districts your county has and what taxes they levy. Compare these results with those of Harris County.

- Sample the 2754-page-long Texas Local Government Code at **https://statutes.capitol.texas.gov/Docs/ SDocs/LOCALGOVERNMENTCODE.pdf** to understand how much the state regulates local governments in Texas.

Learn how local governments engage in interest group activity. Visit the websites of the Texas Association of Counties at **www.county.org** (@TexasCounties) and of the Texas Municipal League at **www.tml.org** (@TML_Texas) to learn about the goals and responsibilities of these organizations.

- At the Texas Association of Counties click on the "Legislative" tab and go to the bills and issues of interest to the Association. At the TML website click on "Legislative Information" and then "Legislative Program" to learn the goals of the organization.

Drawing from this information, write a "local government priorities agenda" consisting of five major issues facing counties and cities that you think are particularly important and explain your perspective.

- Explain challenges that border communities face and the measures they are taking to deal with these challenges at the Texas Border Coalition website, **www.texasbordercoalition.org** (@tbccoalition). Read about the policy priorities of this organization. How do these priorities compare to those you placed on your "local government priorities agenda"?

Speak out at a city council meeting or a county commissioners court meeting. Sign up to speak during the time of the meeting set aside for public comments. Let city or county officials know what improvements you think could be made in your community.

Participate in a local political campaign. Candidates for local elective offices and supporters or opponents of referenda and initiatives often need volunteers to help organize campaign rallies and get-out-the-vote drives, work phone banks, and pass out campaign literature on block walks. You will find the names of city council candidates listed on the election ballot at the official websites of Texas cities. For county elections, you will find the candidates listed on the ballot by going to the official websites of county governments.

★ PRQ What kind of personal satisfaction can a political activist expect to get from being a part of a movement with shared goals that are larger than themselves?

12

Public Policy in Texas

Policy making requires public officials to determine who gets what from government and who pays the costs. Public policy involves tradeoffs between benefits and costs. Here, protestors argue that public school funding needs justify higher taxes.

Bob Daemmrich/Alamy Stock Photo

Learning Objectives

LO 12.1 Analyze and evaluate Texas tax policies.

LO 12.2 Describe the politics of state spending.

LO 12.3 Analyze Texas educational policies and the politics of education.

LO 12.4 Analyze Texas health and human service policies and the politics of income redistribution.

LO 12.5 Describe Texas transportation policies and evaluate the prospects for reform.

LO 12.6 Apply what you have learned about Texas public policy.

On May 27, 2017 the Texas Legislature finally passed and sent to the governor a $217 billion budget for fiscal years 2018 and 2019. Counting one dollar every second without resting for weekends, holidays, and coffee breaks, it would take about 6,868 years to count these appropriations! Texas has the third-largest state budget, exceeded only by those of California and New York.

State spending has steadily risen, with each successive budget larger than the preceding one, resulting in a long succession of record expenditures. However, Figure 12.1 shows that inflation and population increases have outstripped the growth in state spending.

Inflation alone explains some increases in government spending; just as it has driven up the costs of what citizens and families buy, it has also driven up the costs of what government buys. However, inflation has also driven up salaries and profits that residents use to pay their taxes.

The Texas population has grown more rapidly than that of most other states. Each new person must be served, protected, and educated. Of course, the demands of a larger population for increased state services are offset by the fact that more people are also paying taxes to support them. Adjusted for population and inflation, state spending has actually declined 11 percent over the past 10 years.

Revenues

LO 12.1 **Analyze and evaluate Texas tax policies.**

So, from where do the funds for this spending come? Surprisingly, much state revenue comes from sources other than state taxes. During the 2018–2019 fiscal years, 48 percent of Texas

---

FIGURE 12.1 **Trends in Texas State Expenditures, 2010–2019**

This figure shows the growth in state appropriations during the last decade. However, state spending has not kept pace with population growth and inflation; when they are taken into account, relative spending has declined somewhat.

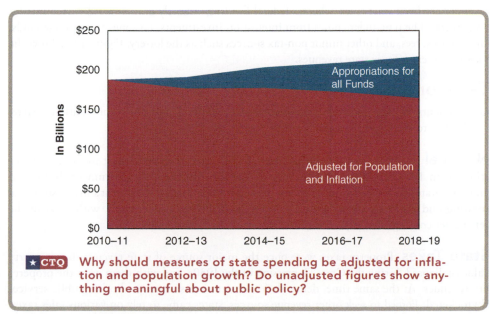

★ CTQ Why should measures of state spending be adjusted for inflation and population growth? Do unadjusted figures show anything meaningful about public policy?

Source: The Legislative Budget Board.

FIGURE 12.2 Sources of State Revenue, 2018–2019

This figure shows the multiple sources of state revenue estimated for the 2018–2019 budget cycle. Notice that the state's largest single revenue source is federal funding, and the largest state source is the general sales tax.

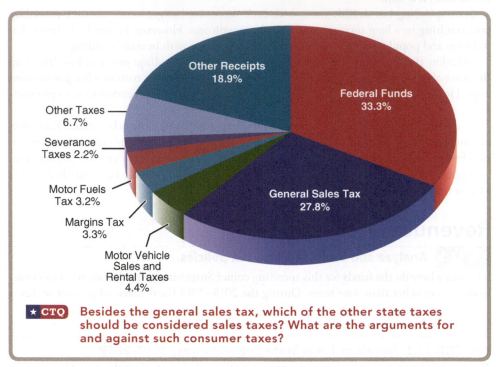

Other Receipts 18.9%
Federal Funds 33.3%
Other Taxes 6.7%
Severance Taxes 2.2%
Motor Fuels Tax 3.2%
Margins Tax 3.3%
General Sales Tax 27.8%
Motor Vehicle Sales and Rental Taxes 4.4%

★ **CTQ**   Besides the general sales tax, which of the other state taxes should be considered sales taxes? What are the arguments for and against such consumer taxes?

Source: Texas Comptroller of Public Accounts.

revenues are from state taxes, whereas federal funding—mostly grants-in-aid—accounts for 33 percent. The remainder comes from interest on investments, revenues from public lands, and licenses, fees, and other minor non-tax sources such as the lottery. Figure 12.2 shows the major sources of Texas state revenues.

Taxation

Governments rely on a variety of tax sources, and each level of government—national, state, and local—tends to specialize in certain types of taxes.

National Taxes With the ratification of the Sixteenth Amendment to the U.S. Constitution in 1913, the income tax became available to the national government. Individual and corporate income taxes immediately became the national government's major source of funding and today constitute almost 60 percent of federal tax revenues, with most of the remainder coming from payroll taxes for Social Security and Medicare.

State Taxes Property taxes were once the major source of state revenue, but property values collapsed during the Great Depression of the 1930s, and with them went the property tax revenues. At the same time, demands for economic assistance and other public services skyrocketed. Forced to seek other revenue sources, states came to rely on various sales taxes. Texas adopted a tax on cigarettes in 1931, on beer in 1933, and on distilled spirits in 1935.

Additional selective sales taxes were adopted in the 1940s and 1950s, but it became apparent that a more general and more broadly based tax would be necessary to meet revenue needs. In 1961, Texas adopted a general sales tax on most items sold. At the same time, Texas, like most states, first drastically reduced its property taxes and then abandoned them for exclusive use by local governments. As a result, states have come to depend on several types of sales taxes:

1. **General sales tax** is a broadly based tax collected on the retail price of most items.
2. **Selective sales taxes** are levied on the sale, manufacture, or use of specific items such as liquor, cigarettes, and gasoline; these are also sometimes known as excise taxes. Because these taxes are usually included in the item's purchase price, they are often **hidden taxes**.
3. **Gross receipts taxes** are taxes on the total gross revenue (sales) of certain enterprises. For example, Texas uses a broad-based margins tax (also known as the *franchise tax*) that applies to the gross sales of most corporations and limited partnerships after taking a deduction for the cost of goods or personnel. Small companies, sole proprietorships, and general partnerships are exempt.

Most state tax revenue comes from various sales tax collections. The general sales tax (6.25 percent on retail sales of most items) yields more of the state's revenues than any other tax, but Texas also has a margins tax, a motor fuels tax, and a motor vehicle sales and rental tax. **Severance taxes** on the production of raw materials such as oil and natural gas, once a major source of state revenue, have declined in importance. Texas also collects special taxes on a range of items and activities, including tobacco, alcohol, registration of motor vehicles, hotel and motel occupancy, and insurance company operations.

Local Taxes   Many services financed by state governments in other states are left to local governments in Texas. State government has also imposed many mandates (required services) on local governments, especially school districts, without funding them. As a result, state taxes have remained low, but local taxes are higher than in many states.

Property taxes are the major source of revenue for virtually all local governments—cities, counties, and special districts. **Ad valorem taxes** may be assessed on the value of real property (land and buildings) or personal property (possessions such as furniture and automobiles); most Texas local governments primarily tax real property. A central appraisal authority in each county determines property values for all taxing units in the county according to uniform state standards and procedures. The tax rate is set by local policy-making bodies—city councils, county commissioners courts, and boards of trustees for special districts.

Local governments also impose other taxes, such as sales taxes up to 2 percent applied to items taxable under the state general sales tax. Other local revenue sources include miscellaneous taxes, user fees, and federal grants-in-aid.

The Politics of Taxation

Taxes cannot be evaluated objectively. As with all public policy, the state's tax policy is designed by elected politicians who make tax decisions on the basis of which groups will be most affected by different types of taxes, and people tend to evaluate taxes according to their social and economic position. Although arguments about taxation usually focus on the "public interest," one must recognize that the millions of dollars in campaign funds, the millions of hours devoted to campaigning, the thousands of lobbyists who fill our state and national capitols—all the resources of persuasion our political system can muster—are called into play not simply to settle some abstract academic argument. Politics, especially the politics of taxation, affects the way people live in real and concrete ways. Any evaluation of taxes must be based on the way particular taxes affect various groups in society.

general sales tax
A broadly based tax collected on the retail price of most items.

selective sales taxes
Taxes levied on the sale, manufacture, or use of specific items such as liquor, cigarettes, and gasoline; these are also sometimes known as excise taxes.

hidden taxes
Taxes included in an item's purchase price.

gross receipts taxes
Taxes on the gross revenues (sales) of certain enterprises.

severance taxes
Taxes on the production of raw materials such as oil and natural gas.

ad valorem taxes
Taxes assessed on the value of real property (land and buildings) and personal property (possessions such as furniture and automobiles).

The Tax Base: Who Should Pay?

tax rates
The amount per unit of taxable item or activity.

The Tax Base: Who Should Pay? Not all taxes are equally effective in raising funds for the public till. **Tax rates** (the amount per unit on a given item or activity) may be raised or lowered, but simply raising the tax rate may not guarantee increased revenues. For example, raising sales tax rates may cause people to cut back on purchases of the taxed items.

tax base
The object or activity taxed.

Tax rates affect the **tax base** (the object or activity taxed). Excessive property taxes discourage construction and repair of buildings. High income taxes can discourage general economic activity and individual initiative, undermining the tax base. To raise necessary revenue, a tax must not discourage too much of the activity that produces the revenue.

broad-based taxes
Taxes paid by a large number of taxpayers.

Most governments tax a wide variety of items and activities because they have found that **broad-based taxes** (those paid by a large number of taxpayers), such as property taxes, general sales taxes, and income taxes, are most effective at raising revenue. High tax rates on a narrow base tend to destroy the base and thus make the tax ineffective as a source of revenue.

In the battle over taxation, one of the most intense issues is what should be taxed. The decision about *what* to tax is really a decision about *whom* to tax and how heavily. Those with influence on decision makers try to get special tax treatment for themselves and other taxpayers in their group. What seems to motivate almost every group is the principle that the best tax is the one somebody else pays. The three most common political rationalizations for taxing various social groups differently are (1) to regulate their behavior, (2) to tax them according to the benefits they receive, and (3) to tax them according to their ability to pay.

regulatory taxes
Taxes that reward approved behavior with lower taxation or punish socially undesirable action with a higher tax.

Regulatory Taxes Taxes do more than simply pay for the services of government; they often serve as a tool for social or economic control. Governments sometimes use **regulatory taxes** to reward approved behavior with lower taxation or punish socially undesirable action with a higher tax.

Most state regulatory taxes are designed to control isolated individual choices, especially those with moral overtones, and are sometimes called *sin taxes*. The most prominent example of such state regulatory taxation is the use tax to discourage the consumption of items such as alcohol or tobacco. Texas has an excise tax, or selective sales tax, on alcoholic beverages and a cigarette tax of $1.41 per pack.

★ **Did You Know?** Texas charges a $5 tax on the admission to sexually oriented businesses that is sometimes called the *pole tax* in reference to a prominent stage prop in strip clubs.

Texans continue to drink, smoke, and frequent strip clubs, so such state use taxes do not entirely prevent sin, but they place a substantial share of the tax burden on the sinner. The regulatory intent of use taxes may be a rationalization to place the tax burden on others; the most vocal advocates of alcohol and tobacco taxes are those who abstain. Proponents argue that regulatory taxes have some effect on behavior without extensive enforcement. The small annual decline in cigarette sales in Texas may be partially attributed to cost, and young people may be deterred from smoking by the high price of cigarettes.

benefits-received tax
A tax assessed according to the services received by the payers.

Benefits Received On the surface, nothing would seem fairer than taxation according to benefits received—let those who benefit from a public service pay for it. Americans have become accustomed to believing that this principle operates in the private sector of the economy and should be applied in the public sector as well.

A **benefits-received tax** is assessed according to the services received by the payers. Texas's 20-cents-per-gallon tax on gasoline is an example of a benefits-received tax. Three-fourths of the income from gasoline and diesel fuel taxes is directed into the Texas highway trust fund, which also includes the state's share of license plate fees (much of which is retained by the counties). The amount of fuel used should represent the benefits from highway building and maintenance.

Although not strictly a tax, tuition paid by students in state colleges and universities is determined on the basis of the benefits-received principle. Although much of the cost of public college education in Texas is paid out of state and local tax revenues, an increasing share of the cost of higher education is paid by student tuition and fees, on the presumption that students should pay a larger share of the cost of the service from which they so greatly benefit. Likewise, revenues from hunting and fishing permits are used for wildlife management.

The benefits-received principle seems reasonable, but few government services are truly special services that are provided only for special groups. Although the student is a major beneficiary of state-supported higher education, society also benefits from the skills that are added to the bank of human resources. Even the elderly widow who has never owned or driven a car benefits from highways when she buys fresh tomatoes from the supermarket or goes to the hospital in the event of illness. Most services of government, like highways, schools, or law enforcement, take on the character of a public or collective good because their beneficiaries cannot be accurately determined.

The benefits-received principle cannot be applied too broadly. Although private businesses efficiently provide services on a benefits-received basis, a major reason for government to provide a *public* service is to make that service available to all. Many could not afford to pay the full cost of vital public services. For example, few people could afford to attend Texas's public colleges and universities if they had to pay the full cost of higher education.

Ability to Pay Most taxes are rationalized according to some measure of taxpayers' ability to pay them. The most common **ability-to-pay taxes** are apportioned according to some measure of the taxpayers' financial capacity, such as property, sales, and income. Property taxes are rationalized on the premise that the more valuable people's property is, the wealthier they are and hence the greater is their ability to pay taxes. Sales taxes are based on the premise that the more a person buys, the greater the individual's purchasing power. Income taxes are based on the assumption that the more a person earns, the greater is that person's ability to pay.

No base is completely adequate as a measure of a person's ability to pay. During Europe's feudal era, property reflected a person's wealth. With the coming of the commercial revolution, actual wealth came to be measured mostly in terms of money rather than land. Nevertheless, the taxes on real estate remained, while more modern forms of ownership, such as stocks, bonds, and other securities, are seldom taxed.

Taxes on the earning or spending of money do not always reflect taxpayers' ability to pay. Income taxes reflect current taxable income and do not account for wealth accumulated in past years. Furthermore, exemptions allow the taxpayer to legally avoid taxes, even on current income. Sales taxes on consumption and spending are an even less equitable measure of people's ability to pay. Sales taxes measure wealth only as it is spent. Money saved or invested is not spent and, therefore, not taxed. Because it is a general rule of economic behavior that the wealthier a person is, the more the person saves or invests, sales taxes weigh disproportionately on the have-nots and have-littles, who must spend the largest portion of their income on the necessities of life.

ability-to-pay taxes
Taxes apportioned according to taxpayers' financial capacity, such as property, sales, and income.

Tax Rates: Progressive or Regressive Taxes? Most people would like to pay as little in taxes as possible, but it turns out that they pay quite a bit—almost one-third of their income. In effect, the average working American works almost one-third of the year (from the first day of January until about mid-April) to pay taxes to all levels of government—federal, state, and local.

However, these averages obscure the real effect of taxes on the individual taxpayer. The so-called loopholes in the federal income tax structure have been well publicized, but every tax—federal, state, and local—treats various taxpayers differently. What in the political world is used to justify the unequal burden of taxation?

progressive tax rates
Tax rates that increase as income increases— for example, federal income tax rates.

Progressive Tax Rates Federal income taxes illustrate **progressive tax rates** because the tax rates increase as income increases. Citizens at the very bottom of the financial totem pole have no taxable income and pay nothing, but as incomes increase, the rate increases step by step from 10 percent to 37 percent. However, the higher rates apply only to *marginal* increments in income. For example, a single person with $1,000,000 in taxable income pays 10 percent on the first $9,525, just as lower-income taxpayers do; a rate of 12 percent applies only to taxable income above $9,525 and less than $38,700; and so forth, as shown in Figure 12.3.

FIGURE 12.3 Federal Income Tax Rates for Single Individuals, 2018

This figure shows that progressive income tax rates increase in stair-step fashion as incomes increase. As you compare the seven columns of rates for various income levels, notice that, regardless of total taxable income, the tax rate on the first $9,525 is 10 percent, the 12 percent rate applies only to the income between $9,526 and $38,700, and so on. Taxpayers earning over a million dollars do not pay 37 percent on their entire income—their first $9,525 is taxed at only 10 percent. Income tax rates apply only to taxable income after deductions, exemptions, and exclusions, and various tax credits may apply. More than 40 percent of Americans pay no income taxes at all though they do pay many other types of taxes.

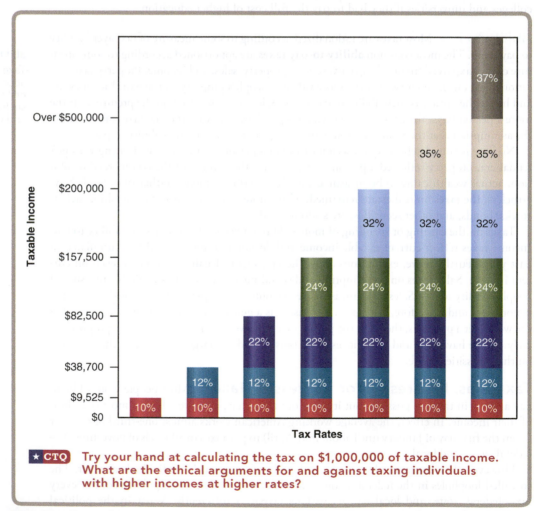

★ CTQ Try your hand at calculating the tax on $1,000,000 of taxable income. What are the ethical arguments for and against taxing individuals with higher incomes at higher rates?

Source: Internal Revenue Service.

The highest rate, 37 percent, applies *only* to the amount over $500,000 and not to an individual's entire income.

Liberals and other supporters of progressive taxation argue that persons with larger incomes can better afford to pay higher tax rates and that lower-income persons should be left with enough of their incomes to maintain the necessities of life. Lower-income persons also spend a larger share of their incomes on consumption, which is the largest driving force in the economy.

Such arguments have not convinced Texans, who adopted a state constitutional amendment that forbids a state income tax unless voters approve. Even then, it can be used only for education and property tax relief.

Regressive Tax Rates   By contrast, Texas has **regressive tax rates**, whereby the effective tax rate declines as a person's income increases. For example, the state general sales tax of 6.25 percent is proportional to the value of sales taxable items, but because of patterns of consumption, the effective rate usually declines as a person's income increases. Table 12.1 shows that if a family's income increases, so does its general sales tax payment. That fact seems reasonable— one would expect the purchases of taxable items to increase as income increases. But note that

regressive tax rates
Tax rates that effectively decline as a person's income increases.

TABLE 12.1 Texas General Sales Tax Individuals Pay in Dollars and as a Percentage of Taxable Income

Follow the income column down and notice that, as income increases, sales tax payments in dollars increase, but the rate declines as a percentage of income.

Taxable Income	Texas General Sales Tax	Percentage of Taxable Income
$10,000	$243	2.4%
25,000	399	1.6
35,000	486	1.4
45,000	562	1.2
55,000	632	1.1
65,000	697	1.1
75,000	757	1.0
85,000	813	0.96
95,000	867	0.91
110,000	940	0.85
130,000	1,036	0.79
150,000	1,126	0.75
170,000	1,211	0.71
190,000	1,292	0.68
1,000,000	2,157	0.21

Source: Internal Revenue Service.

▶ What are the arguments for this kind of regressive taxation?

as income increases, an ever smaller *percentage* of that income is used for taxable purchases. Presumably, more money is saved, invested, or spent on tax-exempt items. Thus, despite exemptions for certain essential items, the effective rate of the Texas general sales tax declines as income increases; an individual with an income of $35,000 pays an effective sales tax *rate* more than twice as high as an individual with an income of $190,000 annually. Similarly, taxpayers pay a smaller percentage of their incomes in property and excise taxes as their incomes increase.

declining marginal propensity to consume

The tendency, as income increases, for persons to save and invest more, thus spending a smaller percentage of their income on consumer items.

There is a simple explanation for the regressive quality of most consumer taxes—the **declining marginal propensity to consume**. As income increases, a person saves and invests more, thus spending a smaller percentage of that income on consumer items. Compare two smokers. One earns $20,000 per year and the other $200,000 per year. Does the typical smoker who earns $200,000 per year smoke 10 times as much as the one who earns $20,000? Of course not! Let's assume that each smoker consumes one pack of cigarettes a day; each therefore pays $514.65 a year in Texas tobacco taxes. For the low-income individual, tobacco taxes represent almost 7 days of earnings, but the other smoker earned the money to pay tobacco taxes in only 5 hours and 21 minutes.

Consumption of most items follows a similar pattern. A mansion represents a smaller share of income for the millionaire than a shack does for a poor person. Proportionately, the Rolls Royce is less of a burden to its owner than the old Ford pickup to its less affluent owner. Obviously, there are exceptions, but appetites do not increase proportionally with income. Consequently, almost any tax on consumption will not reflect ability to pay. Yet Texas's state and local taxes are based on some form of consumption—property taxes, general sales taxes, gross receipts taxes, or selective sales taxes.

tax shifting

Businesses passing taxes to consumers in the form of higher prices.

Even business taxes may be regressive for individuals because of **tax shifting**. Businesses regard their tax burden as part of their operating cost, and they pass much of that cost to customers in the form of higher prices. When property taxes increase, landlords raise rents. When business taxes are imposed, prices of consumer items usually increase as those taxes are passed on to customers as hidden taxes. Thus many business taxes become, in effect, *consumer* taxes and, like other consumer taxes, regressive relative to income.

TABLE 12.2 Texas Major State and Local Taxes as a Percentage of Household Income, Fiscal 2019

The following table shows the effective tax rates on households from those with the lowest one-fifth of incomes to the highest one-fifth. Look across each row in the table to see how major state and local taxes burden low- and middle-income taxpayers more.

	Lower Income	Lower Middle	Middle Income	Upper Middle	Upper Income
General sales tax	6.7%	3.7%	3.2%	2.8%	1.5%
Franchise (margins) tax	0.5	0.3	0.3	0.3	0.2
Gasoline tax	0.7	0.4	0.4	0.3	0.1
Motor vehicle sales tax	0.9	0.5	0.6	0.5	0.3
School property tax	7.5	3.7	2.9	2.9	2.1

Source: Texas Comptroller of Public Accounts.

▶ Why do such consumer taxes burden high-income families least? How can a business tax like the margins tax weigh most heavily on low-income families?

Taking into account all state and local taxes and tax shifting, Texas has one of the most regressive tax structures among the 50 states. Table 12.2 shows the final incidence of major state and local taxes on Texas families. Those with the lowest fifth of household incomes paid almost 7 percent of their income in general sales taxes—more than four times the percentage that upper-income households pay. Lower-income households paid an effective school property tax rate almost three times as high as upper-income households. And for low-income households, the gasoline tax represents seven times the burden that it does for upper-income households. Lower-income families even bear a disproportionate share of the state's franchise tax on business.

Some conservatives and high-income groups who support regressive taxes argue that taxes on higher-income individuals should be kept low to allow them to save and invest to stimulate the economy—this is known as **supply-side economics**. They argue that applying higher rates to higher incomes is unfair and that sales and property taxes are easier to collect, harder to evade or avoid, and generally less burdensome than progressive income taxes. Some of them advocate a national sales tax, also known as the "fair tax," to replace the progressive federal income tax.

supply-side economics
The theory that taxes on higher-income individuals should be kept low to allow them to save and invest to stimulate the economy.

★ **Did You Know?** Texans in the lowest-income households pay an effective school tax rate more than three times higher than upper-income households.

Other Revenues

Much of the state's revenue comes from federal grants-in-aid, and a smaller amount is generated from non-tax revenues such as licenses, fees, and borrowing.

Federal Grants-in-Aid Considerable federal money is provided for Texas state and local government programs. For the 2018–2019 budget period, the state will receive approximately $72 billion in federal funds, which represents 33 percent of state revenues. Much of what Texas spends for health and human services and for transportation originates as federal grants, as explained in Chapter 2.

Borrowing and Other Revenues At the beginning of each legislative session, the comptroller of public accounts reports to the legislature the total amount of revenues expected from current taxes and other sources, and the legislature can, in turn, appropriate no more than this amount unless it enacts new tax laws. The state may borrow money only if the legislature, by a very difficult to achieve four-fifths vote, declares an emergency or if voters amend the Texas Constitution to provide for the issuance of bonds for specific programs.

Constitutional amendments have authorized the state to issue some bonds. Bonds that are to be repaid from general revenues, such as those that voters have approved to finance prison construction, veterans' real estate programs, and water development, are known as **general obligation bonds**. Others are called **revenue bonds** because they are to be repaid

IMAGE 12.1 Texas Comptroller of Public Accounts Glenn Hegar is the state's chief tax collector and financial officer. His financial estimates are binding on the legislature during the appropriation process, meaning the state usually cannot spend more than the comptroller estimates it will receive in revenues.

AP Images/Eric Gay

★ CTQ **How effective are Texas's balanced budget requirements?**

How Does Texas Compare?

Tax and Spending Policies

- Consistent with Texas's conservative political culture, state and local taxes are lower than in most other states. Texans paid only 7.6 percent of personal income in all state and local taxes, compared to the 50-state average of 9.9 percent—residents of only three states paid less than Texans.

- Most states rely heavily on sales and gross receipts taxes, but few states are as dependent on them as Texas.

Texas is one of seven states without any progressive personal income taxes and one of only six states without a corporate income tax. Because Texas relies so much on consumer taxes, it has the third most regressive tax system in the nation.

- Texas ranked 44th in overall per capita spending (25 percent below the national average); Figure 12.4 shows how state per capita spending in Texas compared among the 50 states in 2016.

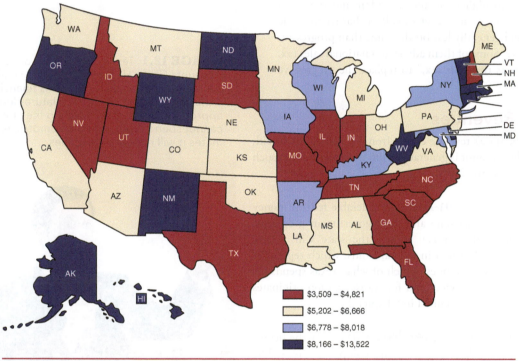

◼	$3,509 – $4,821
◻	$5,202 – $6,666
◼	$6,778 – $8,018
◼	$8,166 – $13,522

FIGURE 12.4 State Per Capita Spending among the 50 States

Sources: Kaiser Family Foundation, National Association of State Budget Officers, U.S. Census Bureau.

FOR DEBATE

★ **CTQ** Do low tax rates attract businesses and promote economic growth in Texas? What is the effect of low state tax rates on the quality of state services?

★ **SRQ** Should Texas follow the lead of many other states by adopting more progressive tax policies that are less dependent on consumer taxes? Why? Why not?

★ **CTQ** Would higher rates of state spending in Texas drive up taxes and discourage economic growth in the state? Supporters argue state expenditures for education, health, and transportation are investments; if so, how will the state realize economic gains from them?

with revenues from the service they finance, such as higher education bonds to be repaid with revenue from student tuition.

Other non-tax revenues from the lottery, various licenses, fines, and fees, dividends from investments, and the sale and leasing of public lands account for a small share of the state's income.

State Spending

LO 12.2 **Describe the politics of state spending.**

Having examined the revenue side of state policy, we now turn to the appropriations process and the politics of state spending.

The Appropriations Process

It is through the **appropriations** process that the legislature legally authorizes the state to spend money to provide its various programs and services. Appropriations bills follow the same steps as other legislation: standing committee consideration, floor action, conference committee compromise, final voting, and then approval by the governor.

During most of the process, the legislature works closely with its presiding officers and follows the recommendations of the Legislative Budget Board. The Texas governor also influences the appropriations process and may ultimately use the line-item veto to strike particular parts of the appropriations bill. Rarely does the governor veto a significant share of state spending.

The Politics of State Spending

A wide variety of political factors affect the level of state spending. Nowhere is the dynamic nature of politics so evident as in public finance; nowhere is the conflict between competing economic interests more visible than in the budgetary process. Behind the large figures that represent the state's final budget are vigorous conflict, compromise, and coalition building. Most of society's programs are evaluated not only according to their merit but also in light of the competing demands of other programs and other economic interests. Government programs and problems compete for a share of the public treasury—highways, education, urban decay, poverty, crime, the environment—in short, all the problems and challenges of a modern society.

Powerful political constituencies, interest groups, and their lobbyists join forces with state agencies to defend the programs that benefit them. This alliance between administrative agencies and interest groups brings great pressure to bear on the legislative process, especially targeting the powerful House Appropriations Committee, the Senate Finance Committee, and the presiding officers. Individual legislators trade votes among themselves, a process called "logrolling," to fund local projects that benefit their constituents.

No single decision better typifies the political character of a state than the decisions made during the appropriations process. The whole pattern of spending is, in a sense, a shorthand description of which problems the state has decided to face and which challenges it has chosen to meet. The budget shows how much of which services the state will offer and to whom. Figure 12.5 shows how Texas spent its state revenues in the 2018–2019 budget cycle. The most costly service in Texas is education. Education accounted for 37 percent of the state budget; health and human services (including Medicaid and social services) were the second most expensive, accounting for 36 percent, and transportation, primarily highways, consumed 12 percent. These three services consume more than four-fifths of the state's budget, with criminal justice and a wide variety of miscellaneous services using up the remainder.

general obligation bonds
Bonds to be repaid from general revenues, such as those that voters have approved to finance prison construction.

revenue bonds
Bonds to be repaid with revenues from the projects they finance, such as higher education bonds to be repaid with revenue from student tuition.

appropriations
The process by which a legislative body legally authorizes a government to spend specific sums of money to provide various programs and services.

FIGURE 12.5 State Appropriations by Function, 2018–2019

The largest slice of the Texas budget pie goes to education, but the portion spent for health care is rapidly increasing.

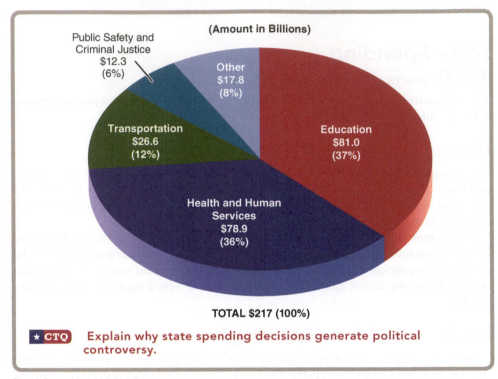

(Amount in Billions)

Public Safety and Criminal Justice
$12.3
(6%)

Other
$17.8
(8%)

Transportation
$26.6
(12%)

Education
$81.0
(37%)

Health and Human Services
$78.9
(36%)

TOTAL $217 (100%)

★ CTQ   **Explain why state spending decisions generate political controversy.**

Source: General Appropriations Act.

Both individuals and groups benefit from government services, and seeking these benefits, while denying them to others, is what motivates most political activity in the state. Political controversy develops because state services affect various groups differently and these groups evaluate state programs according to their competing self-interests and their conflicting views of the public interest (as illustrated by the Insiders feature). It is important to outline the state's most significant services and then explore some of the major political issues surrounding them.

Education

LO 12.3 **Analyze Texas educational policies and the politics of education.**

The educational system in Texas includes elementary and secondary schools (the public schools) and the college and university system (higher education).

Elementary and Secondary Schools

The concept of public schools has changed dramatically over time. Although Texans now generally agree that the state should be responsible for providing elementary and secondary schools, they intensely disagree about issues related to school governance, funding, curriculum, and school accountability.

Texas Insiders

Tapping into Texas Think Tanks and Their Influence on Public Policy: Information as Power

A successful businessman, James R. Leininger founded the conservative Texas Public Policy Foundation (TPPF), modeled after the nationally famous Heritage Foundation. TPPF continues to be funded by important powerbrokers like Charles G. Koch and has close ties to the conservative American Legislative Exchange Council (ALEC). Results of recent TPPF policy studies have been critical of "Obamacare" and supportive of states' rights, school privatization, lower taxes, and the use of fossil fuels.

In contrast, the Center for Public Policy Priorities (CPPP), allied with the National Center on Budget and Policy Priorities, Kids Count, and other liberal groups, focuses its research on poverty, health, education, and the needs of children. Although CPPP has been a vocal advocate for the needy and its studies have generated a great deal of press, CPPP has had little success in its effort to increase spending for Texas's social service and health care programs.

Thinking about the role of elites in Texas politics

Policy makers, including legislators, elected executives, and appointed administrators, are usually generalists who depend upon specialists for specific information to make decisions about the details of public policy. They have long depended on industry lobbyists, state agency bureaucrats, and their staffs to provide expert knowledge and advice in the policy-making process.

Lobbyists have long recognized that state officials' dependence on their data is perhaps their greatest source of power—political power is the ability to persuade, and little is more persuasive than facts. More recently, privately funded research organizations, known as "think tanks," have been established to harness the power of information by conducting broad-based policy research and presenting decision makers with integrated policy proposals reflecting the ideological leanings of their founders and funders. Although think tanks often bill themselves as nonprofit and nonpartisan, in some instances their work represents viewpoint-driven research in the guise of academic studies.

 How can information affect the policy-making process? Explain how information like that contained in "think tank" reports can be both accurate and biased at the same time.

History Public schools were accepted institutions in the North by the early nineteenth century, but they did not take root in the South (including Texas) until after the Civil War. Not until the Constitution of 1876 provided that alternate sections of public land grants would be set aside to finance schools did the state begin to commit itself to locally administered, optional public schools.

Meaningful state support for public education started with a compulsory attendance law, enacted in 1915, and a constitutional amendment that provided for free textbooks in 1918. In 1949, the Gilmer–Aikin Act increased state funding and established the Texas Education Agency (TEA), which carries out the state's educational program.

Recent Trends Sweeping changes in education resulted when in 1984 the Texas Legislature established statewide **school accountability** standards, using measurable standards to hold public schools responsible for their students' performance and their teachers' competence. Former President George W. Bush later took the use of high-stakes testing nationwide with his No Child Left Behind Act.

Although the standards used to measure public school performance are sometimes controversial, there has been a recent trend toward their use to bring market forces to the public

school accountability
Using measurable standards to hold public schools responsible for their students' performance and teachers' competence.

school system. Some teachers and administrators receive merit pay—bonuses for improved student achievement. To introduce the element of competition among schools, the state legislature authorized the State Board of Education to establish schools with innovative special program charters that can recruit students from across existing school district boundaries. Many conservative state legislators now also favor adding even more school choice by providing students with state-funded vouchers to help them pay for tuition at private and religious institutions.

Today, public elementary and secondary education has grown from a fledgling underfinanced local function into a major state–local partnership. The TEA administers approximately a quarter of all state expenditures, helping local school districts educate more than 5 million students. As you will see, public policy decisions affect the knowledge, attitudes, and earning potential of these students and over 300,000 teachers who teach them.

Public School Administration
As in other states, the Texas public school administration has three basic aspects:

1. Substantial local control in a joint state–local partnership
2. Emphasis on professional administration supervised by laypersons
3. Independence from the general structure of government

State Administration
The Texas Constitution and the state legislature have established the basic decision-making organizations and financial arrangements for public education in the state. The legislature approves the budget for the state's share of the cost of public education and sets statutory standards for public schools, but the elected State Board of Education (SBOE) manages the Permanent School Fund and makes decisions about the public school curriculum and selection of instructional materials. The appointed Commissioner of Education adopts rules governing the day-to-day operations of the Texas Education Agency, which regulates and services local school districts.

Independent School Districts
Texas has more than 1,200 independent school districts—more than any other state. These school districts are the basic structure for local control. Voters in independent school districts elect seven or nine members (depending on the district's population) for either three- or four-year terms. Board members may run at large or from single-member electoral districts. These trustees set the district's tax rate and determine school policies within the guidelines established by the TEA. They approve the budget, contract for instructional supplies and construction, and hire and fire personnel. Their most important decision is the hiring of a professional superintendent, who is responsible for the executive or administrative functions of the school district.

Elected state and local school boards often follow the recommendations of professional administrators such as the state education commissioner and the local school superintendents. Most educational decisions are made independently of general government. Nevertheless, one should not conclude that independence from general government, localization, or professionalism can keep education free of politics. On the contrary, elected boards, especially the State Board of Education, have become quite politically assertive in recent years. Whenever important policy decisions are made, political controversy and conflict arise.

Charter Schools
Texas law authorizes 305 open enrollment charter schools for 2019 that may operate on multiple campuses. **Charter schools** are publicly funded schools that operate independently from the district system. The TEA gives them special charters with greater flexibility in the way they operate, including considerable latitude in developing their own academic goals and curricula and in choosing their faculty and staff. Some charter

charter schools
Publicly funded schools that operate independently from the district system.

schools have been able to use this flexibility to establish successful innovative programs that compare favorably to traditional public schools, while others have been closed because of poor academic performance or financial irregularities.

The Politics of Public Education

One of the most important decisions concerning public education is what education should be. Should it promote traditional views of society, reinforce the dominant political culture, and teach acceptable attitudes? Or should it teach students to be independent thinkers, capable of evaluating ideas for themselves? Because the Texas state educational system determines the curriculum, selects textbooks, and hires and fires teachers, it must answer these fundamental questions.

Curriculum

Most of the basic curriculum is determined by the SBOE. Some school districts supplement this basic curriculum with a variety of elective and specialized courses, but it is in the basic courses—history, civics, biology, and English—that students are most likely to be exposed to issues that may fundamentally affect their attitudes.

How should a student be exposed to the theory of evolution? Should sex education courses offer discussion of artificial birth control or present abstinence as the only reliable method of birth control? In the social sciences, should the political system be pictured in terms of its ideals or as it actually operates, with all its flaws and weaknesses? How should the roles of women and minorities be presented? How should elective Bible courses be taught and by whom? Should students who are not fluent in English be gradually taught English through bilingual education, or should they immediately be immersed in the core curriculum taught in English?

Aside from social and political content, the substance of education in Texas has other important practical consequences as well. Although a large proportion of public school students in Texas will never enroll in an institution of higher learning, much educational effort and testing have been directed toward college preparatory courses that provide graduates with few, if any, usable job skills. Although almost half of high school students are enrolled in career and technology programs, much remains to be done in order to meet the need for highly skilled technical workers and to provide students with practical life skills.

The Curriculum and the Culture Wars

After adopting controversial science and literature curriculum revisions in recent years, Texas's State Board of Education caused an even louder uproar when it largely ignored the advice of professional educators and voted along party lines to establish social studies curriculum standards for the upcoming decade. Critics charged that the SBOE had hijacked the state's educational apparatus to impose a conservative, Christian fundamentalist political agenda on public school students.[1]

Critics focused on standards that require teaching the political beliefs of conservative icons like Phyllis Schlafly, Newt Gingrich, the now disbanded Moral Majority, and the National Rifle Association. Meanwhile, students will be taught that Senator Joseph McCarthy's anti-communist crusade may have been justified. Confederate President Jefferson Davis's inaugural address will be taught alongside Abraham Lincoln's speeches, and the role of slavery as a cause of the Civil War is downplayed.

Requirements that students learn the concept of "responsibility for the common good" (which one board member described as "communistic") have been removed from the curriculum. Students will learn that the United States is a "constitutional republic" rather than a "democratic society" and that the "separation of church and state" is not in the Constitution. Students will evaluate how the United Nations undermines U.S. sovereignty and learn about the devaluation of the dollar, including the abandonment of the gold standard.

The curriculum standards emphasize the biblical and Judeo-Christian influences on the Founding Fathers and the benefits of free enterprise, which is mentioned more than 80 times in the curriculum requirements.

Textbooks The SBOE selects a list of approved textbooks that the state may buy for public school courses, and like the curriculum, the textbook selection process generates intense political battles between conservative groups such as Truth in Textbooks and liberal groups such as the Texas Freedom Network. The conservatives have dominated the battle, and some publishers have withdrawn their text offerings or changed the content of their texts to satisfy the SBOE.

Legally, the SBOE can only determine the accuracy of textbooks, but it has used this power to pressure publishers to submit texts that reflect the political and religious values of its members. One publisher eliminated references to "fossil fuels formed millions of years ago" from a science text because it conflicts with some interpretations of the timeline in the Bible. Another eliminated sections that were too kind to Muslims by asserting that Osama bin Laden's actions were inconsistent with commonly accepted Islamic teachings (even though this is the official policy view of the U.S. government). An environmental science text was rejected because it favorably mentioned the Endangered Species Act and warned of the threat of global warming—one group argued that it was unpatriotic to refer to the fact that the United States represents 5 percent of the world's population but produces 25 percent of greenhouse gases. Under pressure from religious conservatives, publishers submitted health textbooks that presented an abstinence-only approach to sex education, excluding essential information about how to prevent unwanted pregnancies and sexually transmitted diseases.

Because Texas controls the second largest textbook market in the United States, the state's textbook decisions have historically determined the content of texts used in public schools in much of the nation. In the future, however, school systems in other states may have more alternatives to Texas-preferred texts. Electronic books, specialty publishing, and custom options are replacing market-dominant, fixed-content texts, and the national textbook market is becoming much more competitive.

Faculties Although the state board for educator certification establishes standards for qualification, conduct, and certification of public school teachers, actual hiring of teachers is a local matter. Most districts do not follow a publicly announced policy of hiring or dismissing teachers because of their political viewpoints, but in many districts, teachers are carefully screened for their attitudes.

Salary and working conditions are perpetual issues of dissatisfaction among teachers because they affect morale and recruitment even as increasing public demands for accountability have added reporting and other paperwork to teachers' workloads beyond the standard expectations for lesson planning, grading, and communicating with parents.

Expected income is certainly a factor when people choose their careers, and education simply does not compare favorably among the professions. Texas teachers earn even less than public school teachers in other states. The National Education Association estimated that Texas classroom teachers' average salary of $52,575 was 9 percent less than the national average.[2] The TEA reported that one-third of beginning teachers leave the profession by their fifth year.

Another issue for teachers has been the use of high-stakes testing such as the State of Texas Assessments of Academic Readiness (STAAR) test. Teachers' groups have objected to the use of these test results in retention, promotion, and

Did You Know? The average annual earnings for Texas dentists is $171,850; lawyers, $149,400; pharmacists, $123,700; and elementary school teachers, $54,780.3

salary decisions on the grounds that they do not accurately measure the full range of teachers' contributions to student knowledge and that their use causes faculty to teach the test while ignoring other valuable skills and knowledge that are not included in standardized tests. Some parent groups have joined teachers in objecting to the frequency of such tests, and many conservatives oppose any national-level testing at all.

Students Public schools have changed considerably in recent years. The number of students attending Texas public schools has been growing at a rate of approximately 2 percent per year, and that growth is expected to continue for the next decade. Texas students are increasingly from low-income backgrounds and are also becoming more ethnically diverse—52 percent Hispanic, 28 percent Anglo, 13 percent African American, and 4 percent Asian American.

This changing student population seems to present a challenge to public schools because a significant achievement gap remains between the performance of Anglo students and that of African Americans and Latinos. Scores on the standard state performance tests like STAAR indicate that the achievement gap is closing, but Anglos' passing rate is still higher than that of African Americans or Latinos.

Public School Finance In 2017, Texas schools spent $10,017 per student—20 percent less than the national average.[4] The actual distribution of these funds is governed according to extremely complex rules and mathematical formulas that occupy six chapters totaling more than 75,000 words in the Texas Education Code. Although public school accountants and financial officers must understand the nuances of these rules to maximize funding for their respective districts, you need to understand only the system's most basic features to engage intelligently in the public debate that surrounds public school finance. Three elements make up public school funding: federal (9 percent), state (41 percent), and local (50 percent).[5]

Federal funding makes up a fairly small share of the cost of public education in Texas. Most federal funding pays for ongoing aid programs for child nutrition and special-needs, military, and low-income students.

> **★ Did You Know?** In 2017, Texas spent less per public school student than 35 other states.

State funding comes from a variety of sources. The Permanent School Fund, established in 1854, invests receipts of rentals, sales, and mineral royalties from Texas's public lands. Only the interest and dividends from this permanent endowment may be spent. Earnings from the Permanent School Fund and one-fourth of the motor fuels tax make up the Available School Fund, some of which is used for instructional supplies such as textbooks; the remainder is distributed to local school districts based on average daily student attendance. Basing distribution of state funds on attendance focuses a school district's attention on truancy.

The Foundation School Program (FSP) accounts for the largest portion of state and local funding by far. State funds from general revenues, a margins tax on business (the franchise tax), and a portion of tobacco taxes are distributed to districts according to formulas based on district and student characteristics. The FSP is structured as a state–local partnership to bring some financial equality to local districts despite vast differences in local tax resources.

Local funding comes primarily from ad valorem property taxes. The county appraisal authority determines the market value of property for all local governments within the county, and local district boards then set the property tax rate stated as an amount per $100 of property value. Local school district trustees may set the property tax rate up to $1.17 per $100 valuation for maintenance and operations and an additional $0.50 per $100 for construction, capital improvements, and debt service.

Local property taxes are used to pay about 60 percent of the FSP basic operating expenses, with the state paying for the remainder. The state supplements local funds to ensure that each district has a basic allotment per student of $4,765. Although the system of basic allotments is designed to provide some financial equity among local school districts, local revenues from property taxes vary so much that the state has also been forced to establish requirements that some richer districts share their local revenue with poorer ones.

The current finance system is the result of decades of struggle and litigation,[6] including the precedent-setting case *Edgewood ISD* v. *Kirby* in which the Texas Supreme Court ruled that the state constitution requires equitably funded public schools, as we explained in Chapter 3. In 2016, the Texas Supreme Court finally upheld the current finance system despite the large gap that remains between districts in rich and poor areas.[7]

All of the legal action over equalization of school finances begs the question of whether spending more money on public schools actually enhances student achievement. For example, a number of smaller school districts spend far more per student than larger metropolitan districts, but their students do not perform noticeably better on standard tests. And despite more equalized revenues, suburban school districts like Plano and Alamo Heights continue to have far more students passing standard achievement tests than urban school districts like Dallas and Houston, which include a much larger share of minority students and those from economically disadvantaged families.

Many factors in addition to public school spending seem to determine public school students' success. Table 12.3 shows that student test scores—and the factors sometimes thought

TABLE 12.3 Selected Texas School District Profiles

This sample of school district profiles shows that some financial inequity remains among school districts but it does not entirely explain differences in student achievement. Look at the Percent Satisfying STAAR Standard column (column 6), and notice that there is little relationship with district spending per student (column 5). Now look at ethnicity (Percent Minority, column 3) and Percent Economically Disadvantaged students (column 4) to see if these factors relate to the STAAR scores (column 6).

School District (1)	Enrollment (2)	Percent Minority (3)	Percent Economically Disadvantaged (4)	Operational Spending per Student (5)	Percent Satisfying STAAR Standard (6)
Houston ISD	214,891	91.5%	76.5%	$8,522	69%
Dallas ISD	158,495	95.1	87.8	9,745	66
Plano ISD	54,322	62.6	28.7	8,791	86
Edgewood ISD	11,279	99.5	92.2	10,091	62
Huntsville ISD	6,937	60.8	58.3	8,828	64
Alamo Heights ISD	4,808	46.4	20.5	9,543	84
West Orange-Cove ISD	2,429	78.4	83.6	10,402	54
Wink-Loving ISD	439	41.7	36.2	17,061	74

Source: Texas Education Agency.

▶ Which factors most affect student achievement? What public policy changes would best improve student performance?

to affect them—vary dramatically from district to district in Texas. Besides per-student spending, ethnicity and family incomes are major variables that seem to determine public school outcomes.

School Privatization Among recent proposals for school finance changes are various voucher plans to use public funds to enable students to attend private schools. Supporters, often including conservatives and particular religious groups, argue that voucher plans offer poorer parents the choice to transfer their children out of underperforming public schools, an alternative now available only to wealthier families. They believe that increasing competition between public and private schools should stimulate improvements in public education.

Opponents, including teachers' organizations and parents in prosperous suburban schools, charge that vouchers would damage public schools by draining their financial resources and some of their best students, leaving public schools to educate students with special problems and learning disabilities. Many rural legislators fear that vouchers would threaten local public schools that have traditionally been the center of small-town community life. Opponents argue that the state should not subsidize special privileges and point to research indicating that similar students perform as well in public schools as they do in similar private schools. Despite the U.S. Supreme Court decision permitting voucher programs, some opponents contend that they compromise the separation of church and state and invite state controls over schools affiliated with religious organizations.

Short of vouchers for students to attend private schools, several programs offer school choice and foster competitiveness within the public school system. Students in failing schools may transfer to other schools within the public system, and local school districts have established successful magnet schools with attractive special programs. Meanwhile, public charter schools offer some students alternatives to traditional schools, and many reformers support making them available to even more students.

Higher Education

Like public schools, higher education is a major state service, accounting for 9 percent of state expenditure during the 2018–2019 budget period. Public institutions enroll 90 percent of all students in Texas higher education. Texas public institutions of higher education include 38 general academic institutions and universities and 79 public two-year institutions including community colleges.

Administration of Colleges and Universities

The Texas Higher Education Coordinating Board (THECB) was established to coordinate the complex system of higher education. Its 18 members are appointed by the governor, with the consent of the senate, and serve for six-year terms. The Coordinating Board appoints the commissioner of higher education to supervise its staff. Together the board and staff gather data and collaborate with public colleges and universities as they plan future needs for programs, curricula, and physical plants. Because Texas's colleges and universities were not established systematically, the Coordinating Board cannot impose a

IMAGE 12.2 A 2017 UT/Tribune poll shows 35 percent of Texans favoring and 44 percent opposing vouchers that divert money from public to private schools.

AP Images/LM Otero

★ **CTQ**   **What are the arguments for and against school vouchers?**

rational, coherent system on their existing operations. Politically powerful boards of regents complicate the Coordinating Board's efforts as they compete to impose their views on higher education, as do other groups.

Boards of regents or trustees set basic policies for their institutions, within the limits of state law and considering the guidelines established by the Coordinating Board. Governing boards provide for the selection of public university administrators, including system-wide administrators (chancellors), campus presidents, deans, and other officers. Certain boards govern institutions located on several campuses:

- The University of Texas System includes The University of Texas at Austin (with the nation's largest student population on a single campus) and other campuses at Arlington, Dallas, El Paso, the Permian Basin, the Rio Grande Valley, San Antonio, and Tyler, along with a half dozen medical and health units throughout the state.
- The Texas A&M University System has its main campus at College Station with additional campuses at Central Texas, Corpus Christi, Commerce, Kingsville, San Antonio, and Texarkana, along with Prairie View A&M University, Tarleton State University, West Texas A&M University, and Texas A&M International University.
- The Texas State University System includes Lamar University, Sam Houston State University, Sul Ross State University, and Texas State University, along with four smaller institutions.
- The University of Houston System includes its main campus in southeast Houston as well as the University of Houston-Downtown, University of Houston-Clear Lake, and University of Houston-Victoria.
- The Texas Tech University System includes the main campus at Lubbock, two medical and health units, and Angelo State University.
- The remaining boards each govern mainly single-campus institutions.

Authorized and financed partly by the state, public community colleges are also generally supervised by the Coordinating Board. However, unlike four-year institutions, which are usually designed to attract students from larger regions of the state and nation as well as international students, voters establish community colleges in one or more school districts primarily to serve area residents. They are usually governed by independently elected boards.

Historically known as junior colleges, the traditional role of two-year institutions was to serve freshmen and sophomores by offering academic courses for credits transferable to senior colleges. Although most of their students are enrolled in these transferable academic courses, two-year colleges have now responded to the demands resulting from economic diversification by adopting a **community college approach**, based on open admissions, maximizing accessibility, and incorporating technical, compensatory, and continuing education among the traditional academic course offerings. The curriculum, low cost, and geographic and financial accessibility of community colleges have resulted in increasing enrollments, especially in academic programs. Figure 12.6 shows that a majority of Texas students enroll in two-year institutions.

community college approach
Higher education policy based on open admissions, maximizing accessibility, and incorporating technical, compensatory, and continuing education among the traditional academic course offerings.

The Politics of Higher Education

It is difficult to measure objectively many of the benefits of higher education, such as personal satisfaction and contribution to society. Individual financial benefits, however, are very clear, contrary to critics' allegations that higher education is not worth increasing tuition costs. High school graduates have a median weekly income of $692 and an unemployment rate of 5.2 percent; those with an associate's degree earned $819 and had an unemployment rate of 3.6 percent; and those with a bachelor's degree had a median income of $1,156 and an unemployment rate of only 2.7 percent.[8] Those with college degrees earn substantially more and have a much lower risk of unemployment.

FIGURE 12.6 Texas Public Higher Education: Enrollments

Nine out of ten students enrolled in higher education attend public institutions in the fall of 2017. A majority of them enroll in public community colleges.

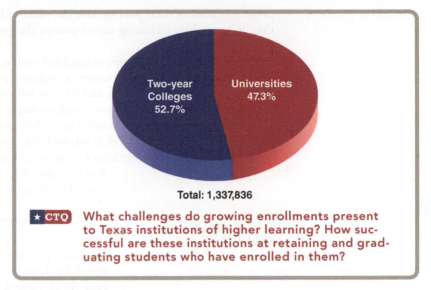

Two-year Colleges 52.7%

Universities 47.3%

Total: 1,337,836

★ CTQ **What challenges do growing enrollments present to Texas institutions of higher learning? How successful are these institutions at retaining and graduating students who have enrolled in them?**

Source: Texas Higher Education Coordinating Board.

The broader economic benefits from investments in higher education seem quite impressive as well. According to a study funded by the Bill and Melinda Gates Foundation, every $1.00 invested in higher education yields $8.00 in enhanced productivity, greater ongoing capacity, reduced social costs, and stimulus to research and development.[9]

Despite these benefits, legislative bodies and boards of regents and trustees have often been critical in their evaluations of higher education and its results. Calls for faculty and student accountability have been frequent. Yet there are no generally agreed-upon answers to the questions raised about higher education: What should its goals be? How should it measure success in achieving those goals? To whom should it be accountable? We examine some issues concerning higher education in the remainder of this section.

Faculty Issues Salaries have been a perpetual issue when Texas institutions of higher education recruit new faculty, but full-time public college and university faculty salaries have now risen slightly above the nationwide median. However, academic freedom remains an issue as college and university administrators have long sought to dilute job protection guarantees for professors. State law requires governing boards to adopt procedures for periodic reevaluation of all tenured faculty. Faculties generally fear that such policies can be a threat to academic freedom and a tool for political repression by administrators.

Financial Issues Financing higher education is a continuing issue. Like elementary and secondary schools, most colleges and universities in Texas must struggle with relatively small budgets. Meanwhile, increasing college enrollments and demands for specialized, high-cost programs are increasing at a time when social services, health care, and other services are also placing more demands on scarce state revenues. Under political pressure from conservatives to cut state taxes, Texas's legislature has been reluctant to raise revenues to cover the increasing cost of higher education and has shifted much of the cost burden to students instead.

Student Accessibility Proposals to cope with financial pressures include closing institutions with smaller enrollments, reducing duplication, restricting student services, increasing tuition, and delaying construction plans or implementation of new degree programs. Most of these policies have the effect of limiting student access to higher education, in as much as increasing costs represent the greatest obstacle to a college education for most students.

Because the Texas Legislature deregulated tuition, college and university boards have dealt with increasing costs by raising tuition, mandatory student fees, and residence costs. Between 2003 and 2016, average tuition and fees for full-time students at Texas public universities doubled to $8,669 per year. At community colleges, tuition and fees increased to $2,559 per year for full-time students.[10] Financial accessibility of higher education is a growing concern, especially because the size of Pell grants and other forms of financial aid are not keeping pace with increasing costs, and students are financing more of the increased cost of higher education by borrowing. Figure 12.7 shows the recent trends in costs of higher education for Texas students.

Did You Know? Tuition at Texas two-year public institutions is 34 percent below the national average; at four-year institutions it is 8 percent lower.

Student Diversity In addition to affordability, other cultural, structural, and historical factors have limited access to certain populations that have traditionally been underserved by Texas institutions of higher learning. Economically disadvantaged people, those who live in rural areas,

FIGURE 12.7 State Funding, Tuition, and Fees at Texas Public Colleges and Universities

These graphs show that tuition and fees have risen at both public universities and two-year institutions even as state funding has remained fairly steady. Tuition has risen most dramatically at public universities since Texas deregulated tuitions in 2003. Tuition has also risen at public two-year institutions, but not as steeply as at universities. Students are bearing a larger share of the increasing cost of higher education.

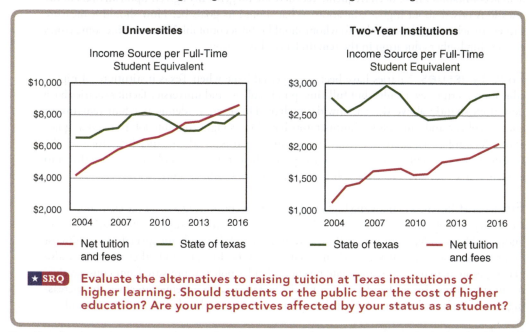

★ SRQ   **Evaluate the alternatives to raising tuition at Texas institutions of higher learning. Should students or the public bear the cost of higher education? Are your perspectives affected by your status as a student?**

Texas Higher Education Coordinating Board, 2017 Texas Public Higher Education Almanac.

women, and ethnic or racial minorities have been notably underrepresented in colleges and universities.

Institutions of higher education have struggled with underrepresented minority student recruitment and have adopted positive efforts to increase diversity and offer more access to these underserved populations. Sometimes **affirmative action** efforts are limited to positive recruitment drives among target groups, but such programs have sometimes also included ethnicity, race or gender as part of the admissions criteria.

Supporters of affirmative action argue that ethnic, racial, and economic diversity encourages lively classroom discussions from multiple perspectives, fosters cross-racial harmony, and cultivates leaders among groups that have traditionally been at a disadvantage in society. Most opponents direct their arguments against those few affirmative action programs that use race-conscious criteria to select student applicants, contending that such policies can lead to reverse discrimination against Anglos and Asian Americans as they are passed over in favor of less qualified underrepresented minority applicants.

Texas established a fairly noncontroversial form of affirmative action after the federal Fifth Circuit Court of Appeals struck down admissions criteria at The University of Texas School of Law.[11] Texas responded with a state law that broadens student admissions without using gender or ethnicity directly in admissions criteria. General academic institutions must automatically admit students from the top 10 percent of their high school graduating class regardless of test scores.

Because various school districts serve very different populations (as you have seen in Table 12.3), granting automatic admission to the top 10 percent from each graduating class ensures that public universities draw from a diverse pool of applicants. The result has been that far more female, African American, Latino, low-income, and rural students have been admitted to state universities under the "10 percent rule" than under traditional admission criteria.

Texas law was later changed to allow The University of Texas at Austin to cap the number of entering freshmen admitted under the "10 percent" rule (e.g., only the top 6 percent in each high school class will earn automatic admission in 2019), and the university administrators began to admit additional students under criteria that included ethnicity among many other factors. Although U.S. Supreme Court decisions had previously allowed race to be considered directly in college admissions policies under very limited circumstances,[12] these race-conscious admissions policies were quickly challenged in court.

After the case was bounced back and forth between various federal courts, the U.S. Supreme Court finally upheld the university's admission policies in the case *Fisher* v. *University of Texas* (2016) when it ruled that the university's admission policies met strict legal standards because they were narrowly tailored to achieve the compelling public interest of achieving an ethnically and racially diverse student population.[13] Thus, the courts have not altogether outlawed using ethnicity and race as a factor in admissions, but they have strictly limited its use.

Student Retention

Of course, admission to institutions of higher learning is hardly the only measure of success. Although students may benefit from even a short experience in college and some employers consider it in hiring, graduation or completion of occupational curriculum programs is society's respected measure of success.

Unfortunately, high costs, lack of course availability, inadequate academic preparation, and personal factors all contribute to the problem of student retention. Among full-time students at four-year public universities, 34 percent graduate within four years, and 59 percent receive degrees within six years. Community colleges face an even more difficult challenge retaining and graduating students—of those seeking a degree, 32 percent earn a postsecondary degree or certificate within six years.[14]

affirmative action
Positive efforts to recruit members of underserved populations such as ethnic minorities, women, and the economically disadvantaged. Sometimes these efforts are limited to recruitment drives among target groups, but such programs have sometimes included ethnicity or gender as part of the admissions criteria.

Texas institutions of higher education are moving toward policies incentivizing timely degree completion, limiting the number of courses that students may drop, and counseling students to enroll primarily in courses that are part of their degree programs. Powerful political forces in the business community, including the Texas Association of Business and the Texas Public Policy Foundations (see the Texas Insiders feature), are pressing the legislature to change funding formulas to reward Texas colleges and universities that have higher graduation rates.

Quality   However, even graduation rates do not fully measure the success of institutions of higher learning. Measuring the success of Texas colleges and universities must take into account their two major functions: (1) teaching—that is, imparting existing knowledge to students, and (2) research—that is, creating new knowledge.

Various rankings show that the UT and Texas A&M flagship campuses are the two most recognized public institutions of higher learning in the state. Perhaps their rankings partly reflect the resources available to these institutions. General legislative appropriations have been relatively more generous for The University of Texas (UT) at Austin and Texas A&M University, and the state constitution earmarks revenues from more than 2 million acres of public land to the Permanent University Fund for the benefit of the UT and Texas A&M systems.

Texas also established a National Research University Fund that is designed to enable emerging research universities to achieve national prominence. Texas Tech University, the University of Houston, and the University of Texas at Dallas have met the criteria to access these funds. Several other Texas universities are attempting to qualify as well, but the long-term results of their efforts cannot be fully foreseen or evaluated.

> ★ **Did You Know?** By one measure, Texas has only two public universities among the top 100 national universities: The University of Texas at Austin ranks 49th, and Texas A&M University ranks 66th. Rice, SMU, Baylor, and TCU, all private universities, are ranked 16th, 59th, 78th, and 80th, respectively.[15]

Health and Human Services

LO 12.4   **Analyze Texas health and human service policies and the politics of income redistribution.**

The second most costly category of state spending can be broadly classified as health and human services, which encompass public assistance, Medicaid for the poor, and a variety of other programs. In the 2018–2019 budget period, these programs cost $78.9 billion (36 percent of the state's total budget). However, approximately 60 percent of this funding originates as grants-in-aid from the federal government.

The Texas Health and Human Services Commission (HHSC) provides a variety of social services, including Temporary Assistance to Needy Families, Medicaid, and the Children's Health Insurance Program. The commission also provides behavioral health services, manages state hospitals, provides long-term care for people with disabilities, and licenses nursing homes as well as child care providers.

Health Programs

Health has been a concern of public authorities since Moses imposed strict hygienic codes on the Jews during their biblical exodus from Egypt. In the United States, the federal government began to provide hospital care to the Merchant Marines in 1798. Today, health care has evolved into a growing public–private partnership and, after education, is the second most expensive service that Texas provides.

Opponents of government's assuming responsibility for public health describe it as "socialized medicine." Strictly defined, **socialized medicine** is a health care system in which the government hires medical practitioners who work at government-owned facilities to directly provide health care, as in Great Britain and in U.S. veterans' and military hospitals. However, the term is often applied to health care systems in which the government provides health care insurance, such as Medicare or Medicaid, even though benefit payments are made to private health care providers.

The state has various levels of involvement in health care. In some instances, the state is the provider of direct health services for certain special populations. In other instances, the state is the payer but not the provider—acting as a public health insurer, as it does with Medicaid by paying for medical services offered by private practitioners. The state also acts as a regulator and buyer of private health insurance.

Direct Health Services
The state provides personal health services for special populations, operating infectious disease centers and psychiatric hospitals and funding local mental health community centers and chemical dependency programs. At the local level, county hospitals and clinics are legally responsible for providing medical care for uninsured indigents and have thus become the health care providers of last resort. County hospitals are usually operated by county hospital districts that have the authority to collect property taxes that partially fund their operations. Several government institutions also manage teaching hospitals that provide care to both indigent and non-indigent patients.

Instead of using county-funded hospitals and clinics, many uninsured and indigent patients obtain medical services through private hospital emergency rooms because federal and state laws require them to accept emergency patients regardless of their ability to pay. The cost of such treatment is often uncompensated and passed on to paying patients and insurance companies—a practice partially responsible for rapidly rising health insurance premiums.

State Health Insurance Programs
Texas operates two major health insurance programs for those who qualify. **Medicaid** and the **Children's Health Insurance Program (CHIP)** are insurance programs designed to provide a minimal level of care for qualified low-income individuals and families who have enrolled. Although these programs are administered by the state, they are largely funded by federal grants-in-aid.

Texas spends over one-fourth of its state budget on the Medicaid program, but about 60 percent of these Medicaid funds come from the federal government in the form of grants-in-aid. Medicaid covers a wide variety of health services that are generally provided through managed care (HMO-type) plans under contract with the state.

Medicaid should not be confused with **Medicare**, which is available to most persons older than 65 years of age regardless of income and is administered by the U.S. Department of Health and Human Services. In contrast, the Medicaid program is administered by the state and is available only to those who meet certain age and income requirements. These groups include low-income children along with their parents and caretakers, pregnant women, people age 65 and older, and those with disabilities. Income requirements for Medicaid eligibility

socialized medicine Strictly defined, socialized medicine is a health care system in which the government hires medical practitioners who work at government-owned facilities to directly provide health care, as in Great Britain and in U.S. veterans' and military hospitals. However, the term is often applied to health care systems in which the government provides health care insurance, such as Medicare or Medicaid, even though benefit payments are made to private health care providers.

IMAGE 12.3 Many uninsured and indigent patients obtain medical services through hospital emergency rooms because federal and state laws require them to accept emergency patients regardless of their ability to pay.

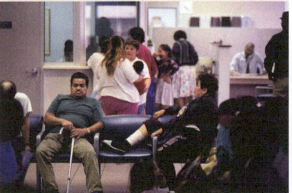

Mark Richards/Photo Edit

★ SRQ **What are the alternatives to expensive emergency room treatment for the indigent? Should government assume responsibility to pay for indigent care, or is this a matter of personal responsibility beyond the proper purview of government?**

are determined by a complex formula based on age, disability, and pregnancy status. For example, pregnant women and newborns are eligible if their income is below 198 percent of the federal poverty level (FPL); children under age 5 must reside in households with incomes below 144 percent of the FPL; for the disabled to receive benefits, their income must be below 74 percent of the FPL; parents and caretakers must have incomes below 14 percent of FPL or less than $230 per month. Of Texas's 4 million Medicaid recipients, 90 percent are elderly, disabled, or children.[16]

CHIP helps insure children of parents with incomes less than 200 percent of the poverty level who do not qualify for Medicaid. Even though about half of Texas children are insured by either CHIP or Medicaid, 623,000 Texas children remain completely uninsured.[17]

Private Health Insurance Although approximately 30 percent of Texans have some sort of public insurance coverage such as Medicare, Medicaid, or CHIP, most others rely on private insurance companies to pay for their medical expenses. Table 12.4 shows that employer-sponsored plans cover 49 percent of Texans and other private policies cover another 7 percent.

The Uninsured About one in six Texans has no health insurance coverage. Among the states, Texas has the nation's highest percentage of uninsured residents. Although Texas employers are just as likely to provide health insurance for their workers, fewer Texans have public health insurance than in other states. Texas has a large undocumented immigrant population ineligible for public insurance, and the state has resisted the health care benefits available under the Affordable Care Act, also known as "Obamacare."

Health Care Reform In 2010, Congress passed comprehensive health care reforms known as the **Affordable Care Act (ACA)**, designed to expand Medicaid coverage, to limit objectionable insurance company practices, and to make subsidized health insurance available to businesses and individuals through competitive insurance marketplaces.

The ACA provides federal funds to pay for at least 90 percent of the costs for states that expand Medicaid eligibility to all legal residents with incomes up to 138 percent of the federal poverty level. Before passage of the ACA, Medicaid was available primarily for children, the disabled, and the elderly; adults earning more than the poverty level were generally ineligible in many states, including Texas.

TABLE 12.4 How People Get Health Insurance: Percent by Insurer

This table shows how people get their primary insurance. It shows most Texans have employer-sponsored medical insurance, and despite public insurance, about one in six Texans have no health insurance at all—a larger percentage than in any other state.

	Employer	Non-Group	Medicaid	Medicare	Other Public	Uninsured
United States	49%	7%	20%	14%	2%	9%
Texas	49	7	16	11	2	17

Source: U.S. Census Bureau and Kaiser Family Foundation, "Health Insurance Coverage of the Total Population," 2016.

▶ Should health insurance be a public policy concern? Or is this a private matter beyond the proper purview of the government?

The ACA also ended some of the most unpopular insurance company practices. Health insurance companies can no longer arbitrarily drop beneficiaries when they get sick or because they have reached lifetime limits. Insurance companies must allow parents to keep their children covered under their family policies until age 26 and may not deny insurance to people with preexisting conditions.

To make it possible for insurance companies to meet these requirements, insurance companies must be able to spread risk among a larger pool of insured persons. As a result, the federal law established mandates requiring that individuals and larger businesses buy health insurance or pay a tax penalty. And to make insurance affordable, the federal government provides tax credits to subsidize premiums on a sliding scale based on income up to four times the federal poverty level. People may sign up for qualified insurance plans directly through insurance companies or through state-run or federally operated marketplaces that provide side-by-side comparisons of private insurance offerings in their state.

IMAGE 12.4 Texas Tea Party protesters attacked health care reform as being too much big government.

AP Images/Deborah Cannon

★ **CTQ** How does the ACA expand the role of the state and federal governments? Evaluate the need for the individual mandate and government regulation of the health care industry.

Health Care Politics

Passage of the ACA exposed a deep cleavage in public opinion about health care policies. The most liberal opponents argued that ACA reforms did not go far enough. Many of them believed that access to health care should be made a basic right by providing national health insurance through a publicly funded national single-payer system.

In contrast, conservative critics argued that "Obamacare" is a federal overreach and that it places government in the middle of health care decisions that are better left to the market and to private individuals. When Texas and other conservative states challenged the ACA in court, the U.S. Supreme Court upheld most of the health care reform law,[18] but it also found that states could not be required to accept funds to expand Medicaid. Despite the availability of federal funds for at least 90 percent of its cost, Texas, along with several other states, exercised its option to reject Medicaid expansion. Texas also refused to establish a state-run marketplace for the uninsured to buy health insurance, and a federally operated exchange was set up instead.

At the national level, conservatives in Congress several times failed in their efforts to repeal the ACA altogether and finally settled on a strategy of focusing on the most unpopular element of the ACA, the **individual mandate**, which requires that individuals get health insurance or pay a tax penalty to the federal government. As part of a larger tax cut, Congress repealed the tax penalty effective in 2019. Meanwhile, the Trump administration shortened the period for enrollment on the exchanges, curtailed outreach efforts, reduced certain subsidies, and provided waivers to permit less comprehensive coverage on the exchange and in state Medicaid programs.

The future of the ACA, therefore, remains uncertain. Conservatives continue to bring both legal and political challenges to the program. And, although the rate of uninsured Texans ages 18–64 dropped by nearly one-third, from 25 to 17 percent, more liberal advocates continue to argue for Medicaid expansion which would cover an additional 1.2 million persons, with some advocating the ACA be replaced with a more universal program such as "Medicare for all."

individual mandate
Requirement that individuals get health insurance or pay a tax penalty to the federal government.

Income Support Programs

Although health care services are by far the most expensive of the social services the state provides, income support programs are probably more controversial because they provide cash directly to beneficiaries. Although the amounts are relatively small, taxpayer funds are directly transferred or redistributed to recipients based on their need or lack of employment. Supporters often refer to these programs as safety net programs.

Temporary Assistance to Needy Families

Among social service programs, Temporary Assistance to Needy Families (TANF) is designed for children whose parents are incapable of providing for their children's basic needs. More than two-thirds of TANF recipients are children who are deprived of support because of the absence, unemployment, or disability of one or both parents and whose family income is less than 12 percent of the poverty level. Adult caretakers of such children are eligible for small grants, but unless they are disabled or needed at home to care for very young children, adult TANF and food stamp recipients are referred for employment counseling, assessment, and job placement.

Federal and state regulations now require recipients to cooperate in identifying an absent parent and, with few exceptions, limit TANF benefits to citizens; adult eligibility is usually limited to two years at a time, with a maximum five-year lifetime benefit. By making welfare less of an entitlement, these welfare reforms were intended to force able-bodied individuals out of dependency and into productive work. Some federal funds are now distributed as block grants to the states to allow them flexibility to develop support services, child care, job training and placement, and rehabilitation programs to help welfare recipients in finding work. These reforms have substantially reduced the number of TANF recipients in Texas.

The maximum TANF grant has been reduced and, for a family of three, it is now $290 per month. The Texas median TANF grant is less than half the national median. Today, Texas spends about 0.1 percent of its budget on this income assistance program for which a small percentage of the poor qualify.

Unemployment Insurance

Whereas TANF is designed as an income supplement for the poor and is administered by the Health and Human Services Commission, **unemployment insurance** is designed to provide a partial income replacement for those who have lost their jobs. Unlike TANF, which is a welfare program based on need, unemployment insurance is a social insurance program financed with taxes paid by employers, and eligibility is determined by previous earnings rather than need or family size.

Created in 1935 as a partnership between the states and the national government, unemployment benefits are financed from state taxes on employers, but some administrative costs are paid with federal funds. The Texas unemployment insurance program is administered by the Texas Workforce Commission (TWC) which provides benefit payments for a maximum of 26 weeks. In the past, Congress has sometimes extended the period of eligibility during periods of severe recessions when jobs were scarce.

Under Texas's rather restrictive laws, a worker must register for job placement with the TWC and is usually ineligible to receive benefits (at least for a time) if he or she voluntarily quit or was fired for cause. Because the rate at which employers are taxed is based on claims made by former employees, employers have an interest in contesting employee claims. For these reasons and others, only one-third of unemployed Texans actually receive benefits.

Handling unemployment insurance claims is only one priority for the TWC; its major functions include providing a workforce for employers, gathering employment statistics, enforcing child labor laws, and providing various special job training and rehabilitation services. Able-bodied welfare recipients are referred to the TWC for training and child care services.

unemployment insurance

The insurance program designed to provide a partial income replacement for those who have lost their jobs; it is a social insurance program financed with taxes paid by employers.

The Politics of Welfare and Income Redistribution

Social service programs are among a wide range of public policies that employ mechanisms for **income redistribution**—public taxation, spending, and regulatory policies intended to shift income from one class of recipients to another. Some redistributive programs, like regressive taxation, business subsidies, and certain government contracting policies, shift income upward from lower- and middle-income families to high-income earners; others, like unemployment compensation, TANF, Medicaid, and food stamps, primarily benefit lower-income persons. Different views about these kinds of programs drive much of the ideological conflict between liberals and conservatives in Texas.

Defining Welfare   So many public policies redistribute income among various groups that the very concept of *welfare* has no uniformly recognized definition. The broadest view is that welfare is any unearned, government-provided benefit. Governments provide direct subsidies to businesses and corporations that far exceed TANF and food stamp costs combined. Such corporate welfare includes financial bailouts, most subsidies to agribusiness, and grants to the defense industry to sell weapons to foreigners.

Programs that primarily benefit the middle class, such as federal income tax deductions for mortgage interest, are also more costly than poverty programs. Because these programs are supported by powerful special interests or large numbers of middle-class voters, they are relatively secure from serious political threat.

More often, the term *welfare* is used more narrowly to refer to controversial programs explicitly designed to assist the poor. Accordingly, old age, survivors', and disability insurance (commonly referred to as Social Security), as well as unemployment insurance, are **social insurance** programs, not public welfare programs. Eligibility for social insurance programs is based not on need alone—that is, eligibility is not based on a **means test**—but on the tax paid by beneficiaries and their employers. In this respect, they are like private insurance programs, differing primarily in that they are operated by the government and are compulsory for most employers and employees. Such programs are not aimed directly at the poor. In fact, many persons now receive public assistance for the very reason that they were ineligible to participate in adequate social insurance programs.

More myths and misunderstandings have developed about antipoverty programs than probably any other public service.

Welfare Myths   There is a mistaken impression that any poor person may be eligible for state public assistance benefits. Although more than 4 million Texans live in poverty, fewer than 4 percent of them receive monthly TANF aid, and the only able-bodied adults now receiving income assistance are parents with sole custody of young dependent children.

There is no general program of cash assistance for able-bodied adults without children, even though they may be unemployed or in need. However, the Supplemental Nutritional Assistance Program (SNAP, popularly known as food stamps) and Medicaid are available to most who fall below the federally defined poverty level, and federal Supplemental Security Income (SSI) may be available to the aged, blind, and disabled.

Resentment can be expected when shoppers waiting in grocery checkout lines to part with hard-earned cash see the customer ahead paying with federally funded food stamps. Nevertheless, contrary to popular myth, few new Cadillac drivers are legally on Texas welfare rolls because benefits furnish less than the bare essentials of life.

Nor does it seem likely, as some critics suggest, that welfare mothers have more children just to increase their monthly TANF checks. The maximum monthly TANF grant is $290 per three-person family; even when these payments are combined with food stamps and Medicaid, the average TANF child still lives in a home with resources considerably below the

income redistribution
A public policy goal intended to shift income from one class of recipients to another, regardless of whether these programs are designed to benefit lower-, middle-, or upper-income groups.

social insurance
Public insurance programs, such as Social Security and unemployment compensation, in which eligibility is based on tax premiums paid by the beneficiaries or their employers rather than need alone.

means test
A standard of benefit eligibility based on need.

poverty level. Children intensify the problems of the poor. Large family size probably results from carelessness, cultural attitudes, religious beliefs, or lack of access to birth control rather than a deliberate effort to increase welfare payments.

Several reasons explain the myths that have grown around public welfare. Because welfare benefits people according to their needs rather than according to their efforts, it seems to violate the widespread American attitude that everyone ought to be paid according to the work one does. Consequently, even the lowest wage earner often feels superior to the welfare recipient. Most Texans prefer to identify themselves with the economically secure rather than with the poor. There is also prejudice against some groups that benefit from welfare because a disproportionate number of welfare recipients are mothers of children born out of wedlock or members of ethnic and racial minority groups. Whatever the cause, these myths and prejudices remain major elements in the debate over public assistance.

Welfare Realities Public welfare faces serious substantive questions. Cheating and overpayment cost taxpayers money and dilute the limited resources that would otherwise be available for those in genuine need. It is difficult to estimate the amount of cheating. Although Texas's Lone Star Card was developed as a form of positive identification to reduce fraud, it is difficult to determine the amount of cheating that occurs during the application and qualification processes.

Probably the most serious problem for the welfare system today is that it alleviates rather than cures. Most public assistance programs are designed only to relieve the most severe pains of poverty, not to cure the disease. Welfare or other assistance programs may prevent starvation, but they offer no assurance that recipients will someday escape poverty and dependence. The vast majority of Texas welfare recipients are children, who are too young to do much about their problems. But for the able-bodied, chronic poverty is sometimes a symptom of a disease that affects both the individual and society at large.

The Causes of Poverty Those who support social service programs usually look at the problem of poverty as a systemic social problem largely beyond the control of individuals. They point to lack of job availability, poor neighborhood schools, racial or gender discrimination, and the concentration of wealth as causes of poverty. They argue that an environment of poverty disrupts family life, promotes emotional and physical disease, and denies young people role models to help them become productive members of society—the best single predictor of poverty is being born into a poor family.

Critics of antipoverty programs often view poverty as an individual rather than a social problem, arguing that the poor suffer their fate because of defects of character or problems of their own making. They point out that the long-term poor have typically dropped out of school at an early age and lack the education and skills necessary to earn a living wage. The poor may exhibit varying degrees of despair, alienation, hopelessness, emotional insecurity, or lethargy, and many have failed to form stable family relationships. The impoverished may lack a feeling that they can do much about their problem; others lack a sense of responsibility for their own fate.

Transportation

LO 12.5 **Describe Texas transportation policies and evaluate the prospects for reform.**

Road building has been a government function since ancient times and, representing 12 percent of the state budget, it remains one of the three most expensive state functions in Texas today. A relatively small share of state funding is directed to mass public transportation; the lion's share of Texas's transportation spending is for highway construction and maintenance.

Highway Programs

In Texas's early days, road construction was primarily the responsibility of the county. Most Texas counties still maintain a property tax dedicated to the construction and maintenance of roads, and in rural areas, road building remains a major function of county government. But their efforts are too small and too poorly financed to provide the expensive, coordinated statewide network of roads needed by highly mobile Texans in the modern world.

In 1916, the national government encouraged state governments to assume the major responsibility for highway construction and maintenance. The 1916 Federal Aid Road Act made available federal funds to cover one-half of the construction costs for state highways. To become eligible for those funds, a state was required to establish an agency to develop a coordinated plan for the state highway system and to administer construction and maintenance programs. Texas responded by establishing the Texas Highway Department, now known as the Texas Department of Transportation (TxDOT). The department is supervised by a five-member commission, which appoints an executive director who oversees the department and supervises the work of regional district offices.

Newer federal aid programs and increased funding for existing ones have expanded TxDOT's responsibilities. The earliest highway-building program was designed to provide only major highways along primary routes. Federal funding later became available for secondary roads, and Texas established the farm-to-market (FM) program to assume state maintenance of many county roads as the rural road network was paved, extended, and improved. Finally, beginning in 1956, Congress made funds available for 90 percent of the cost of construction of express, limited-access highways to connect major cities in the United States. Table 12.5 shows that the 80,000-mile state highway system carries about three-fourths of Texas's motor vehicle traffic.

The Politics of Transportation

Highway contractors and a variety of allied groups lobbied for the establishment of the state highway fund and for increases in highway spending, and they attempt to guard it against those who would spend any part of it for other purposes. Despite their efforts, per capita state highway funding fell far below the national average and has only recently begun to recover.

TABLE 12.5 The Texas Highway System

This table shows the share of traffic accommodated by types of roadways in the Texas highway system. These figures do not include almost a quarter-million miles of city streets and county roads, which accommodate approximately one-fourth of traffic. Maintaining this extensive, aging highway system is becoming so costly that the state has diminishing funds available to finance new highway construction.

Type of Roadway	Total Miles	Percentage of Traffic Accommodated
Interstate highways and frontage roads	10,517	26
Farm-to-market roads	40,933	10
Federal and state highways	28,474	38

Source: Texas Department of Transportation.

▶ Does Texas have alternatives to the public highway system that would accommodate the transportation needs of its growing population? How would the state pay for these alternatives?

Highway Funding

Funding for the highway program is a joint federal–state responsibility. In 2018–2019 the federal government, mostly from the federal gasoline tax, provides 39 percent of the transportation department's revenues. This large federal contribution has allowed the national government to demand such restrictions as meeting clean air standards and setting a minimum drinking age of 21 as conditions for receiving federal aid.

State monies account for about 61 percent of TxDOT funding. The state highway fund has been mostly supported by motor vehicle registration (license plate) fees and the 20-cent-per-gallon motor fuels tax. Because Texas spends more money maintaining existing highways than it does constructing new ones, the state has been forced to look to alternative revenue sources to pay for new highway construction to accommodate the population's transportation needs in one of the fastest-growing states in the nation. At the urging of the transportation industry (see Image 12.5), Texas recently amended the state constitution to direct a portion of the oil and gas severance taxes and motor vehicle sales taxes to highway construction, and the state has increasingly used tolls to fund new highways. Texas has also experimented with privatization as a way to fund new highway construction.

Highway Privatization

TxDOT planned to use comprehensive development agreements with private entities to develop a highly ambitious and controversial 50-year program to supplement existing highways. The $200 billion, 4,000-mile Trans-Texas Corridor would have included superhighways (with separate freight and commuter lanes), railways (with high-speed, commuter, and freight lines), and utility corridors (for water, electricity, natural gas, petroleum, fiber-optic telecommunications, and broadband lines). Funded by both state taxes and private investment, the project was to be operated largely by private enterprises such as toll companies.

Facing stiff opposition from property rights groups that objected to the use of eminent domain to enable such a massive state takeover of private land to benefit private investors, TxDOT abandoned the expansive Trans-Texas Corridor plan in favor of smaller, more localized projects, but it has not yet given up on the concept of highway privatization or the use of tolls to fund new highway construction. The future of highway funding remains a tough political problem for the Texas Legislature and the state's political leadership.

Mass Transit

Texans, like most Americans, remain unreceptive to mass transit as an alternative to individual motor vehicles. **Mass transit** refers to transportation systems that carry multiple passengers, such as train and bus systems; whether publicly or privately owned, mass transit systems are available to the general public and usually charge a fare. Only 4 to 6 percent of Texas residents regularly commute by urban mass transit. By contrast, mass transportation is a popular, viable alternative to personal vehicles in the northeastern United States, where one-third of all users of urban mass transit live in the New York City metropolitan area.

mass transit
Transport systems that carry multiple passengers, such as train and bus systems; whether publicly or privately owned, mass transit systems are available to the general public and usually charge a fare.

IMAGE 12.5 In 2014, Texas voters overwhelmingly approved Proposition 1 to direct approximately $1 billion (the amount varies depending on the amount of oil and gas tax revenue) annually to the State Highway Fund. Proponents of the constitutional amendment, which included the transportation industry, were able to win voters over by promising them (via campaign ads like the one captured in this screenshot) that they would be able to enjoy "better and safer roads" without having to pay more tolls or taxes, or see the state take on even more debt.

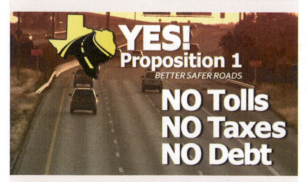

★ CTQ **Why are many Texans opposed to the construction of additional toll roads as a partial solution to the growing gridlock and poor road quality that Texans experience across the state, especially in its most populated metro regions?**

Automotive transportation is close to the hearts of Texans, and no other mode of transportation seems as convenient because no other is as individualized. Buses and trains cannot take individuals exactly where they want to go exactly when they want to go there. Automobiles have become a way of life, and their manufacture, maintenance, and fueling have become dominant elements of the economy.

TxDOT spends less than 1 percent of its budget on mass transit. Instead, most of the effort in mass transportation is sponsored by local metropolitan governments. As we mentioned in Chapter 11, municipalities may impose a city sales tax for economic development projects, and many of them have used such a tax to subsidize mass transit authorities (MTAs). Most MTAs have focused their resources on bus transportation, but several larger metro areas have in recent years made significant investments in light rail. Houston, Dallas, Fort Worth, and Austin have substantial rail projects in various stages of implementation, and plans are being developed for a privately funded high-speed rail line between Houston and the Dallas–Fort Worth Metroplex.

Proponents of mass transit point to the enormous social and personal costs of automotive transportation. Texas's annual highway death toll is over 3,000, and thousands more are injured. The motor vehicle is also the single most important contributor to atmospheric pollution, a major factor in climate change, and a significant source of refuse that finds its way into junkyards and landfills. As the least efficient mode of transportation currently available, dependence on the individual motor vehicle is in direct conflict with the need to conserve energy and reduce our dependence on fossil fuels.

Urban mass transit was widely used before the end of World War II, and supporters of mass transit argue that adequate public funding could once again make railroads and buses rapid and comfortable alternatives to automotive transportation. When gasoline prices increase, more Texans seem to be receptive to the use of mass transit where it is available.

Critics argue that making mass transit a viable alternative to motor vehicle transportation would require a massive investment of public funds. And, given Texans' love affair with the automobile and their strong cultural individualism, they are skeptical that the public will respond to a costly investment in mass transit with increased ridership without a catastrophic energy or environmental crisis. In Texas's conservative political environment, it is doubtful that Texas will readily increase public funding for local mass transit authorities.

Applying What You Have Learned about Public Policy Issues

LO 12.6 **Apply what you have learned about Texas public policy.**

In this chapter, you learned that in the process of making public policy, government makes decisions that determine who gets what, who pays, and how much. It is the process of applying general political philosophy and ideology in the real-world practice of government. So we asked Eva DeLuna Castro to cue you into her group's philosophy of government and how it works to influence the state's tax and spending policy.

Eva DeLuna Castro has since 1998 been a state budget analyst for the Austin-based Center for Public Policy Priorities (CPPP), one of Texas's most visible and influential independent progressive public policy organizations, where she also is the Program Director of the Invest in Texas Team. Prior to joining the CPPP, she served as an analyst for the Texas Comptroller of Public Accounts and as a legislative staffer in the Texas House.

After you have read her essay, we will ask you to identify the author's political viewpoint. And we will invite you to reflect on Texas's budget priorities and to contrast the author's views with those who favor a low-tax, limited-government approach to government.

POLITICS IN PRACTICE
The Practical Politics of Texas's Budget
by Eva DeLuna Castro
STATE BUDGET ANALYST, CENTER FOR PUBLIC POLICY PRIORITIES

More than 30 years ago, the Benedictine Sisters of Boerne founded the Center for Public Policy Priorities to expand access to health care, primarily by advocating before the state legislature. By the time the Center spun off in 1999 as a self-sustaining, independent organization, we were a persistent and credible presence at the Capitol, educating legislators and stakeholders and advocating for smart policies. Having added child well-being, nutrition, tax and budget policy, and economic opportunity to our areas of expertise, we envision and work towards a Texas where everyone is healthy, well-educated, and financially secure.

Of all the policy issues that find us at the Capitol in committee hearings or one-on-one meetings with legislators and their staff, tax policy in particular may have taken us farther afield than our Benedictine founders ever imagined. Even today, our advocacy on how state and local revenue should be generated, as well as how it should be used, sets us apart from many other public interest groups at the Capitol. But anyone who understands that the legislature's "power of the purse" stems from the responsibility of the House and Senate to craft the state budget, as well as from legislators' ability to shape state and local taxes, can see how important it is to understand both sides of the balance sheet. The state budget process determines how much will be spent on our schools, colleges, roads, health care, and other public services, as well as who will pay, making the Tax Code as much a "moral document" as public budgets are often said to be.

Much of CPPP's tax policy advocacy in its early years focused on making Texas taxes more fair, especially for middle- and lower-income families—the "who pays" question. More recently, the "how much" debate has dominated legislative sessions. Strident calls for new tax cuts are ignoring what past rounds of tax cuts and recession-driven budget slashing have already created in many Texas communities—overcrowded elementary and secondary school classrooms, rising public college tuition and fees, and congested or poorly maintained roads and highways. Given that Texas was already taking an extremely conservative approach to investing in its human and physical infrastructure, we must ask: at what point will taxes be so low that our economic competitiveness is seriously damaged? Even the conservative speaker of the Texas House has said, "at some point you can't cut your way to prosperity."

CPPP has had some success in enlisting other advocacy groups in the fight against tax cuts through Texas Forward, a revenue coalition created in 2010. Texas Forward's member organizations represent a broad spectrum of interests, but all believe that meeting the needs of Texans and moving our state forward to greater prosperity and opportunity will require more than just state budget cuts and cost-shifting to local governments. CPPP and other Texas Forward members have their work cut out for them in the foreseeable future, as tax cut proposals show few signs of losing support. Tax cut fever remains strong even with the school finance system perennially in the courts, a booming population and rapidly changing economy demanding more from our higher education, highways, and water/wastewater systems, and responsibilities such as border security and public safety added to the part of the state budget that is supported almost entirely by general tax revenue.

It's often said, and rightly so, that the politics of public budgeting boils down to a struggle and compromise over how to allocate scarce resources. In Texas, whose residents take pride in living in the best state in the wealthiest nation in the world, we should keep in mind that any scarcity is the direct result of tax policy choices our elected officials have made. Tax cuts increase the struggle over those public dollars and make it less likely that Texas will have the more highly skilled and healthy workforce, transportation systems, and other human and physical infrastructure that could truly improve our economic competitiveness in the decades to come. More than 25 years have passed since a majority of legislators cast the tough votes to raise state taxes significantly. CPPP will be there the next time it happens, advocating for changes that better prepare Texas for changing demographics, technology, and economic competition.

1. Would you describe the author's ideology as progressive or conservative? What arguments does the author make to defend her policy views? What is the counterargument in favor of lower taxes and less government?
2. How would state policy be different if the author's views were implemented in practice?

★ Chapter Summary

LO 12.1 Analyze and evaluate Texas tax policies. About half of state revenues are raised through taxes, which are low compared to other states. A substantial portion (more than one-third) comes from federal grants-in-aid, and miscellaneous sources account for the rest. State borrowing is limited.

Tax policy may be rationalized as serving some regulatory purpose or reflecting benefits received or ability to pay. Both narrow- and broad-based taxes are used in Texas.

The largest single state tax is the general sales tax, which is regressive relative to income because it falls most heavily on middle- and lower-income people. Most state taxes, including selective sales taxes and gross receipts taxes, are also consumer taxes and regressive relative to income. Even business taxes are shifted onto consumers. Local ad valorem and sales taxes also burden those least able to pay. Among taxes that Texans pay, only the federal income tax is somewhat progressive.

Individuals and groups evaluate tax policies and virtually all public policies according to who benefits and who pays the cost. The process of allocating costs and benefits is the very essence of politics.

LO 12.2 Describe the politics of state spending. The Legislative Budget Board dominates the process of proposing Texas's state budget because the state legislature frequently follows its recommendations during the appropriations process. The governor's most effective tool in spending decisions is the item veto. The spending process is political. Perhaps no other type of decision evokes more consistent and passionate political efforts from interest groups, think tanks, and administrative agencies.

State spending as a percentage of personal income remains fairly steady and consistently lower than in most other states. Education, health and human services, and transportation are the major services that state government offers, together constituting more than four-fifths of the total cost of Texas's state government. These services have a significant effect on the way Texans live and even on the way they think. It is nearly impossible to evaluate them objectively because they affect different groups so differently.

LO 12.3 Analyze Texas educational policies and the politics of education. The public educational system of Texas is generally decentralized and independent of the normal course of partisan politics. Its administrators and curricula are conservative, as is much of Texas politics. Public schools are financed by local school property taxes and a variety of state funds, using funding formulas developed as a result of several lawsuits brought under state constitutional provisions guaranteeing a suitable and efficient school system. Today's efforts to privatize Texas public schools are less focused on vouchers and more directed at increasing the number of public charter schools.

A majority of students in higher education attend public community colleges, which, together with state universities, face numerous challenges. Major political issues relate to funding, curriculum, student accessibility, quality, and diversity. Critics are beginning to challenge the nature and the very purpose of higher education.

LO 12.4 Analyze Texas health and human service policies and the politics of income redistribution. Health care services are both publicly and privately financed in Texas, as in the rest of the nation, and they are plagued by a similar problem—the rising costs of providing better services to more people. A smaller proportion of residents are insured to cover these costs in Texas than in any other state, and national health care reform is unlikely to dramatically expand either public or private health insurance in Texas.

Income support for the poor (such as Temporary Aid to Needy Families) is not a major state priority, and it is not designed to eliminate the root causes of poverty. However, the underlying goal of many social programs is income redistribution, and the politics of redistribution remains a central issue at all levels of government.

LO 12.5 Describe Texas transportation policies and evaluate the prospects for reform. Financed largely by

motor fuels taxes and federal funds, the cost of maintaining the extensive highway system is growing faster than revenues. Construction of new highways to relieve traffic congestion has become problematic as the state seeks alternative funding sources such as the use of tolls. Facing budget limits, it is unlikely that TxDOT will substantially increase funding for local mass transit authorities.

LO 12.6 Apply what you have learned about Texas public policy. You explored a critique of Texas public policy presented by a budget analyst for one of the state's more liberal policy groups, and you evaluated her arguments for higher taxes and a more active role for state government. You considered how state policies would be different if the group's views were implemented in practice.

Key Terms

ability-to-pay taxes, *p. 319*
ad valorem taxes, *p. 317*
affirmative action, *p. 337*
Affordable Care Act (ACA), *p. 340*
appropriations, *p. 325*
benefits-received tax, *p. 318*
broad-based taxes, *p. 318*
charter schools, *p. 328*
children's health insurance program (CHIP), *p. 339*

community college approach, *p. 334*
declining marginal propensity to consume, *p. 322*
general obligation bonds, *p. 323*
general sales tax, *p. 317*
gross receipts taxes, *p. 317*
hidden taxes, *p. 317*
income redistribution, *p. 343*
individual mandate, *p. 341*

mass transit, *p. 346*
means test, *p. 343*
Medicaid, *p. 339*
Medicare, *p. 339*
progressive tax rates, *p. 320*
regressive tax rates, *p. 321*
regulatory taxes, *p. 318*
revenue bonds, *p. 323*
school accountability, *p. 327*
selective sales (excise) tax, *p. 317*

severance taxes, *p. 317*
social insurance, *p. 343*
socialized medicine, *p. 339*
supply-side economics, *p. 323*
tax base, *p. 318*
tax rate, *p. 318*
tax shifting, *p. 322*
unemployment insurance, *p. 342*

Review Questions

LO 12.1 Analyze and evaluate Texas tax policies.

- Describe the major types of taxes imposed by state and local governments. How does Texas compare with other states?

- What are the advantages and disadvantages of regulatory taxes? Of taxes based on the benefits-received principle? Of taxes based on the ability-to-pay principle?

- Define progressive and regressive tax rates. What are the arguments for and against each type? Which social groups benefit from each type?

LO 12.2 Describe the politics of state spending.

- Describe the appropriations process from budgeting through legislative action and the item veto.

- Describe the state's budget priorities. How does spending on Texas public services compare with other states?

LO 12.3 Analyze Texas educational policies and the politics of education.

- Describe the functions of state and local institutions in governing Texas public elementary and secondary schools. What are the major issues that these institutions face?

- What are the major political issues that higher education faces in Texas?

LO 12.4 Analyze Texas health and human service policies and the politics of income redistribution.

- Explain why health care is the state's second-largest expenditure. How will national health care reform affect Texas? Why are social service programs controversial?

- Describe the perspectives on income redistribution.

LO 12.5 Describe Texas transportation policies and evaluate the prospects for reform.

- Describe the state's role in providing transportation. What major political controversies have developed in planning for future transportation development?

- What is the future of highway privatization in Texas? What are the political prospects for mass transit?

Think Critically and Get Active!

Compare conservative and liberal views on public policy. Check out the conservative view on taxes and other policies at the Texas Public Policy Foundation at **www.texaspolicy.com** (@TPPF). Connect with the Texas Taxpayers and Research Association representing the conservative and business perspective on taxation at **www.ttara.org** (@txtaxpayers). Investigate the Private Enterprise Research Center at **http://perc.tamu.edu/perc/index.htm** and learn about its research on health care, welfare, and taxes. See the American Legislative Council (ALEC) at **www.alec.org** (@ALEC_states), which plays a major role in drafting and lobbying in favor of conservative legislation in state legislatures throughout the country.

Tune into the liberal and labor position on taxes by browsing the Citizens for Tax Justice site at **www.ctj.org** (@taxjustice). Select "State Tax Issues" and go to "Texas." See a liberal take on the taxes and public policy in Texas by consulting with the Center for Public Policy Priorities at **www.forabettertexas.org** (@CPPP_TX). Probe budget and fiscal policies in the 50 states with the Center on Budget and Policy Priorities at **www.cbpp.org/topics/state-budget-and-tax** (@CenterOnBudget) and with the Pew Charitable Trusts at **www.pewtrusts.org/en/research-and-analysis/blogs/stateline**. (@pewtrusts & @pewresearch). Get the facts on health care in Texas and the rest of the nation at the Kaiser Family Foundation website at **www.kff.org/statedata** (@KaiserFamFound).

Look into the causes of rising tuition costs in the 10-article series featured in the *Washington Post*'s Wonkblog, which can all be accessed at **www.washingtonpost.com/news/wonk/wp/tag/the-tuition-is-too-damn-high**.

Take a stand on the Texas environment. Browse the different stances of groups in Texas on environmental issues, including Environment Texas at **www.environmenttexas.org** (@EnvironmentTex), the Texas Water Conservation Association at **www.twca.org** (@TexasWCA), the Coastal Conservation Association of Texas at **www.ccatexas.org** (@CCA_Texas), the Lone Star Chapter of the Sierra Club at **www.sierraclub.org/texas** (@TexasSierraClub), and the contrasting views of the Texas Oil and Gas Association at **www.txoga.org** (@TXOGA) and the Texas Farm Bureau at **www.texasfarmbureau.org** (@TexasFarmBureau).

Evaluate affirmative action in higher education. Gather information about ethnic/racial and gender group enrollment from the *2017 Texas Public Higher Education Almanac: A Profile of State and Institutional Performance and Characteristics*, p. 13, at **www.thecb.state.tx.us**.

★ **CSQ** Use websites in this section to develop a table describing how conservatives and liberals differ on the five major policy areas of taxing, spending, education, health care, and the environment.

★ **PRQ** Should Texas universities take gender, ethnicity, and race into account in establishing their admissions criteria? Is it ethical for minorities who score lower on admissions tests to be given special consideration in an effort to educate underserved populations? Does affirmative action actually promote cross-cultural harmony and bring diverse perspectives into the classroom?

Notes

PROLOGUE

1. See David Montejano, *Anglos and Mexicans in the Making of Texas, 1836–1986* (Austin: University of Texas, 1987).
2. The information in this and subsequent sections depends heavily on Seymour V. Connor, *Texas: A History* (New York: Thomas Y. Crowell, 1971); Rupert N. Richardson, *Texas: The Lone Star State*, 3rd ed. (Englewood Cliffs, NJ: Prentice Hall, 1970); T R. Fehrenbach, *Lone Star: A History of Texas and the Texans* (Boston: De Capo Press, 2000).
3. The Annexation of Texas, Joint Resolution of Congress, March 1, 1845, *U.S. Statutes at Large, Vol. 5.*
4. See *A Declaration of the Causes Which Impel the State of Texas to Secede from the Federal Union*, www.avalon.law.yale.edu/19th_ century/csa_texsec.asp.
5. T R. Fehrenbach, *Lone Star: A History of Texas and the Texans* (Boston: De Capo Press, 2000).
6. 777 S.W.2d 391 (Tex. 1989).

CHAPTER 1
Texas Political Culture and Diversity

1. The Texas Politics Project at the University of Texas at Austin, *Polling Data Archive*, www.texaspolitics.utexas.edu/polling-data-archive.
2. Richard Fry, "Millennials Surpass Gen Xers as the Largest Generation in U.S. Labor Force," *Pew Research Center*, May 11, 2015, www.pewresearch.org/fact-tank/2015/05/11/millennials-surpass-gen-xers-as-the-largest-generation-in-u-s-labor-force.
3. University of Texas at Austin/Texas Tribune Poll, June 2017.
4. D. W. Meinig, *Imperial Texas: An Interpretive Essay in Cultural Geography* (Austin: University of Texas Press, 1969).
5. Jorge Bustamante, "A Conceptual and Operative Vision of the Population. Problems on the Border," in *Demographic Dynamics on the U.S.–Mexico Border*, eds. John R. Weeks and Roberto Ham Chande (El Paso, TX: Texas Western Press, 1992).
6. Elizabeth York Enstam, "Women and the Law," *Handbook of Texas Online*, published by the Texas State Historical Association at www.tshaonline.org.
7. Ibid.
8. Women of the West Museum, "Western Women's Suffrage—Texas," published by the Autry Museum of the American West at www.theautry.org.
9. Ibid.
10. Ibid.
11. Enstam, "Women and the Law."
12. Christopher Long, "Ku Klux Klan," *Handbook of Texas Online*, published by the Texas State Historical Association at www.tshaonline.org.

13. Ibid.
14. Seymour V. Connor, *Texas: A History* (New York: Thomas Y. Crowell, 1971).
15. *Sweatt* v. *Painter*, 339 U.S. 629 (1950); *Plessy* v. *Ferguson*, 163 U.S. 537 (1892).
16. George B. Green, "Mansfield School Desegregation Incident," *Handbook of Texas Online*, published by the Texas State Historical Association at www.tshaonline.org.
17. Frank R. Kemerer, "*United States* v. *Texas*" (1970), *Handbook of Texas Online*, published by the Texas State Historical Association at www.tshaonline.org.
18. Alicia A. Garza, "Raymondville Peonage Cases," *Handbook of Texas Online*, published by the Texas State Historical Association at www.tshaonline.org.
19. V. Carl Allsup, "Felix Longoria Affair," *Handbook of Texas Online*, published by the Texas State Historical Association at www.tshaonline.org.
20. See Robert E. Hall, "Pickets, Politics and Power: The Farm Worker Strike in Starr County," *Texas Bar Journal* 70, no. 5 (2007).
21. V. Carl Allsup, "*Delgado* v. *Bastrop ISD*," *Handbook of Texas Online*, published by the Texas State Historical Association at www.tshaonline.org.
22. V. Carl Allsup, "*Hernandez* v. *State of Texas*," 347 U.S. 475 (1954), *Handbook of Texas Online*, published by the Texas State Historical Association at www.tshaonline.org.
23. *Defense of Marriage Act*, enacted September 21, 1996.

CHAPTER 2

Texas in the Federal System

1. James Madison, *Federalist 10*, November 23, 1787.
2. *The Constitution of the United States*, Article I, Section 8.
3. *McCulloch* v. *Maryland*, 17 U.S. 316 (1819).
4. Ibid.
5. Edward S. Corwin, "The Passing of Dual Federalism," *Virginia Law Review* 36, no. 1 (1950): 4.
6. Ibid.
7. Ibid.
8. *Annals of Congress, The Debates and Proceedings in the Congress of the United States*, "History of Congress," 42 vols. (Washington, DC: Gales & Seaton), pp. 1834–1856.
9. See *New York* v. *Miln*, 36 US 11 Pet. 102 (1837).
10. Corwin, "The Passing of Dual Federalism," 2.
11. Ibid., 19.
12. Ibid.
13. *Racial/Ethnic Minority Attorneys: Attorney Statistical Profile (2017–18)* (Austin, TX: Department of Research and Analysis, State Bar of Texas, 2018).
14. "Terral Smith Says That 40 Years Ago, U.S. Placed Texas Under Voting Rights Act for Failing to Print Ballots in Spanish," *Austin American-Statesman/PolitiFact Texas*, November 16, 2012.
15. John Kinkaid, "From Cooperative to Coercive Federalism," *Annals of the American Academy of Political and Social Sciences* 509 (1990): 139–152.
16. *Governor's Initiatives* (Austin, TX: Office of the Governor Rick Perry, June 2010), p. 3.
17. Texas Military Preparedness Commission Report: 2015–2016 (2017 Update). Austin, Texas: Texas Military Preparedness Commission (2017).
18. Ibid.

19. Texas Veterans Commission, "Hazlewood Act," at https://www.tvc.texas.gov/education/hazlewood-act/.

20. *The Coverage Gap: Uninsured Poor Adults in States That Do Not Expand Medicaid* (Menlo Park, CA: Kaiser Family Foundation, 2018).

21. Ibid.

22. *Current Status of State Medicaid Expansion Decisions* (Menlo Park, CA: Kaiser Family Foundation, 2018), https://kaiserfamilyfoundation.files.wordpress.com/2018/07/current-status-of-the-medicaid-expansion-decisions-healthreform.png.

23. "Health Law Is Dividing Republican Governors," *New York Times*, November 21, 2013.

24. Stan Dorn, Megan McGrath, and John Holahan, *What Is the Result of States Not Expanding Medicaid?* (Washington, DC: Robert Wood Johnson Foundation and Urban Institute, 2014).

25. *Gaming in Neighboring States* (Austin, TX: Let Texans Decide, 2013), www.lettexansdecide.com/facts/gaming-in-neighboring-states.

CHAPTER 3
The Texas Constitution in Perspective

1. *San Antonio Independent School District* v. *Rodriguez*, 411 U.S. 1 (1973).

2. *Edgewood* v. *Kirby*, 777 S.W. 2d 391 (Tex. 1989).

3. *2017 Book of the States* (Lexington, KY: Council of State Governments, 2017).

4. *Commissioner of Education, et al.* v. *Texas Taxpayer and Student Fairness Coalition*, No. 14-0776 at www.txcourts.gov/media/1371141/140776.pdf.

5. *Mike Morath, et al.* v. *Texas Taxpayer and Student Fairness Coalition, et al.* (2016), http://www.txcourts.gov/media/1371141/140776.pdf.

CHAPTER 4
Voting and Elections

1. Raymond E. Wolfinger and Steven Rosenstone, *Who Votes?* (New Haven, CT: Yale University Press, 1980). Also see Sydney Verba and Norman H. Nie, *Participation in America* (New York: Harper & Row, 1972).

2. Note that some Republican-controlled legislatures have tried to repeal election-day registration and were successful in Montana and Maine, although voters in the latter overturned the decision in a referendum. Efforts to repeal it still are under way in Wisconsin. In Democrat-controlled Connecticut, conversely, there are moves to institute election-day registration.

3. Mark P. Jones, Renée Cross, and Jim Granato, "The Texas ID Law and the 2016 Election," University of Houston Hobby School of Public Affairs at http://www.uh.edu/class/hobby/voterid2016/voterid2016.pdf.

4. The VAP is an imperfect measure of the voting-eligible population (VEP) because it includes some people who cannot vote (noncitizens and felons) and excludes others who can (eligible citizens living overseas). Because the number of noncitizens and felons is large, far exceeding the number of overseas eligibles, the VAP exaggerates the actual VEP. In 2018, for example, the difference was approximately 20 million people. The VAP measure therefore understates participation rates. Unfortunately, reliable measures of VEP over long stretches of time are not readily available, particularly at the state level,

which is why VAP is used here. For more information on measuring turnout, see the United States Elections Project at www.electproject.org.

5. When the VEP is used (see footnote 4), the estimated turnout in 2016 was 58.3 percent, almost 4 points greater than that estimated with the VAP.

6. See Paul R. Abramson and John H. Aldrich, "The Decline of Electoral Participation in American," *American Political Science Review* 76 (June 1982), pp. 502–521.

7. Some scholars attribute part of the decline in turnout to the increasing tendency toward divided government at the national level, in which the president is from one political party and the majority in Congress is from the other. The argument is that divided government makes it more difficult for voters to assign responsibility for policy decisions and that, as a result, voters cannot easily reward or punish specific elected officials at the polls. See Mark N. Franklin and Wolfgang P. Hirczy De Mino, "Separated Powers, Divided Government, and Turnout in U.S. Presidential Elections," *American Journal of Political Science Review* 42 (January 1998), pp. 316–326.

8. Included here are countries that were ranked the most free (1.0 or 1.5) by Freedom House in 2018 and had a population greater than 3 million.

9. See Glenn Mitchell II and Christopher Wlezien, "The Impact of Legal Constraints on Voter Registration, Turnout, and the Composition of the American Electorate," *Political Behavior* 17 (June 1995), pp. 179–202.

10. In Louisiana, state legislative and local elections are not held at the same time as federal elections, so the motivation for voting is low. Louisiana's "blanket primary" ballot lists all candidates from all parties. If no one receives a majority of the votes in a given race, the top two vote recipients compete in a runoff primary, irrespective of political party affiliation, and the winner of the primary is elected.

11. The grandfather clause gave white citizens who were disenfranchised by poll tax or literacy requirements the right to vote if they had been eligible to vote before the passage of the restricting legislation. These laws were found unconstitutional by the U.S. Supreme Court in *Guinn* v. *United States*, 238 U.S. 347 (1915).

12. Education data from U.S Census Bureau, www.census.gov/prod/2011pubs/acsbr10-01.pdf and www.census.gov/hhes/www/poverty/data/threshld/thresh10.xls. Poverty data is based on the size and composition of the family. For a family of four (two adults and two children), the threshold in 2016 was an annual income of $24,250 or less.

13. Daniel J. Elazar, *American Federalism: A View from the States*, 3rd ed. (New York: Harper & Row, 1984).

14. David C. Saffel, *State Politics* (Reading, MA: Addison-Wesley, 1984), p. 8.

15. *Grovey* v. *Townsend*, 295 U.S. 45 (1935).

16. *Smith* v. *Allwright*, 321 U.S. 649 (1944).

17. The La Raza Unida Party challenged this limitation. The Justice Department and federal courts sustained the challenge but only as it applied to La Raza Unida, which was permitted to conduct a primary in 1978. Otherwise, the law stands as written.

18. The necessity of notarizing the pages increases the difficulty. The application of technical aspects of the law and adverse interpretations are but a part of the harassment that minor parties and independents have traditionally encountered in their quest for a place on the ballot. For example, in 1976, the secretary of state interpreted the law as requiring that each signature must be notarized. The next year, the legislature specified that a notary need sign only each part of the petition. See Richard H. Kraemer, Ernest Crain, and William Earl Maxwell, *Understanding Texas Politics* (St. Paul, MN: West, 1975), pp. 155–157.

19. County officials help administer general elections on behalf of the state.

20. The nonpartisan nature relates only to the fact that the party label does not appear on the ballot and certification by the party is not necessary. Special elections are, in fact, often partisan because regular party supporters work for "their" candidates.

21. Signers must be registered voters and cannot have participated in the selection of a nominee for that office in another party's primary.

22. Optional at first, the Australian ballot was made mandatory in 1903.

23. For an excellent description of early voting and a preliminary assessment of its effects, see Robert M. Stein and Patricia A. Garcia-Monet, "Voting Early But Not Often," *Social Science Quarterly* 78 (December 1997), pp. 657–671. For a more recent assessment, see Barry C. Burden, David T. Canon, Kenneth R. Mayer, and Donald P. Moynihan, "Election Laws, Mobilization, and Turnout: The Unanticipated Consequences of Election Reform," *American Journal of Political Science* 58 (January 2014), pp. 95–109.

24. Most of the research has focused on presidential elections. See Robert S. Erikson and Christopher Wlezien, *The Timeline of Presidential Elections: How Campaigns Do (and Don't) Matter* (Chicago: University of Chicago Press, 2012).

25. For an analysis of how membership in various demographic groups influences voting behavior, see Robert S. Erikson, Thomas B. Lancaster, and David W. Romero, "Group Components of the Presidential Vote, 1952–1984," *Journal of Politics* 50 (May 1988), pp. 337–346. For an analysis of how identification with various social groups influences voting behavior, see Christopher Wlezien and Arthur H. Miller, "Social Groups and Political Judgments," *Social Science Quarterly* 78 (December 1997), pp. 625–640.

26. Quoted in Dave McNeely, "Campaign Strategists Preparing Spin Systems," *Austin American-Statesman*, October 21, 1993, p. A11.

27. For a comprehensive treatment of money in election campaigns, see Anthony Corrado, Thomas El Mann, Daniel R. Ortiz, and Trevor Potter, *The New Campaign Finance Sourcebook* (Washington, DC: Brookings Institution Press, 2005).

28. Nancy Sims of Pierpont Communications, with offices in Austin and Houston, graciously provided this information.

29. *Buckley* v. *Valeo*, 424 U.S. 1 (1976).

30. *Federal Elections Commission* v. *National Conservative Political Action Committee*, 470 U.S. 480 (1985).

CHAPTER 5

Political Parties

1. There is even more incentive in other countries, many of which use proportional representation, in which parties gain seats in proportion to their share of the vote. The principle that single-member districts and plurality elections encourage two parties is known as "Duverger's Law," so named after the French sociologist Maurice Duverger, who identified the pattern back in the 1960s. Note that it is not really a law but a tendency, as there are plenty of examples that contradict what Duverger would have predicted based on the electoral system.

2. Marjorie Randon Hershey, *Party Politics in America*, 14th ed. (New York: Longman, 2011), p. 289.

3. For an overview of the literature, see Barbara Sinclair, *Party Wars: Polarization and the Politics of National Policy-Making* (Norman: University of Oklahoma Press, 2006).

4. Norman J. Ornstein, Andrew Kohut, and Larry McCarthy, *The People, the Press, and Politics: The Times Mirror Study of the American Electorate* (Washington, DC: Times Mirror Center for the People and the Press, 1988).

5. Hershey, *Party Politics in America*, pp. 71–74.
6. For a general analysis of partisan sorting, see Matthew Levendusky's *The Partisan Sort: How Liberals Became Democrats and Conservatives Became Republicans* (Chicago: University of Chicago Press, 2009).
7. Angus Campbell, Philip E. Converse, Warrant E. Miller, and Donald E. Stokes, *The American Voter* (New York: Wiley, 1960).
8. For more on the role of race in the development of partisan identification in the United States, see Edward Carmines and James Stimson, *Issue Evolution: Race and the Transformation of American Politics* (Princeton: Princeton University Press, 1989).
9. Rob Griffin, William H. Frey, and Ruy Teixeira, "The Demographic Evolution of the American Electorate, 1980–2060," Center for American Progress, February 24, 2015.
10. V. O. Key, *Political Parties and Pressure Groups*, 3rd ed. (New York: Crowell, 1952).

CHAPTER 6
Interest Groups

1. "The Future is Texas," *Economist*, December 19, 2002, p.29.
2. TCEQ Interoffice Memo to Susan Jablonski, Director, Radioactive Materials Division from TCEQ RML Team, regarding groundwater intrusion into proposed LLRW facility, August 14, 2007, www.texasnuclearsafety.org/downloads/TCEQ_interoffice_memo_81407.pdf.
3. Brandi Grissom, "Ex-Lawmaker's Lobbying Looks Bad, Group Says," *El Paso Times*, May 21, 2009.
4. R.G. Ratcliffe and Lise Olsen, "Dozens of Lawmakers Fail to Meet Ethics Rules," *Houston Chronicle*, August 12, 2007.

CHAPTER 7
The Legislature

1. Jeffrey R. Lax and Justin H. Phillips, "The Democratic Deficit," Unpublished paper, Midwestern Political Science Association meeting, 2010.
2. National Council of State Legislatures, "Staff Legislative Table," 2015.
3. Brandi Grissom, "Campaign Accounts Help Legislators Pay Staff," *The Texas Tribune*, April 18, 2013, at www.texastribune.org/2013/04/18/campaign-funds-prop-lawmakers-capitol-operations.
4. The public can access much of the House Research Organization data by visiting its website, www.hro.house.state.tx.us; the Senate Research Center can be found at www.senate.state.tx.us/SRC/Index.htm.
5. National Institute on Money in State Politics, "Election Overview, Texas, 2016," https://www.followthemoney.org/tools/election-overview/?s=TX&y=2016.
6. Ibid.
7. Robert Bernstein, "Texas Becomes Nation's Newest 'Majority-Minority' State, Census Bureau Announces," *US Census Bureau News* 11 (August 2005).
8. U.S. Census Bureau, *State and County QuickFacts*, www.quickfacts.census.gov/qfd/states/48000.html.
9. Ibid.
10. Ryan Murphy et al., "The Makeup of the Lege, from Education to Employment," *The Texas Tribune*, January 11, 2013, at www.texastribune.org.

11. Alexa Ura and Jolie McCulloch, "Once again, the Texas Legislatures Is mostly white, male, middle-aged," at https://www.texastribune.org/2017/01/09/texas-legislature-mostly-white-male-middle-aged/.

12. National Conference of State Legislators, "Personal Financial Disclosure for Legislators: Income Requirements," updated January 2016, at www.ncsl.org/research/ethics/financial-disclosure-legislators-income.aspx#TX.

13. Ibid.

14. *Reynolds* v. *Sims*, 377 U.S. 533 (1964).

15. University of Texas/Texas Tribune Poll, February 2012, www.texaspolitics.laits.utexas.edu/11_5_0.html.

16. Ibid.

17. *Shaw* v. *Reno*, 509 US 630 (1993); *Miller* v. *Johnson*, 515 US 900 (1995).

18. *Miller* v. *Johnson*, 515 US 900 (1995).

19. Chris Tomlinson and Paul J. Weber, "Texas Redistricting Maps 2012: Candidates Study New Setup," *The Huffington Post*, February 29, 2012, at www.huffingtonpost.com/2012/02/29/texas-redistricting-maps-2012_n_1310569.html.

20. The U.S. Supreme Court did later rule that one Texas house district (HD 90 in Tarrant County) constituted an illegal racial gerrymander; see *Abbott v. Perez*, 585 U.S.__(2018).

21. www.tlc.state.tx.us.

22. www.lbb.state.tx.us.

23. www.sunset.texas.gov.

24. CBS Channel 42, *Keye TV Investigates: One Lawmaker, Many Votes?*, May 14, 2007, at www.youtube.com/watch?v=eG6X-xtVask; see also Wilson, Nanci, *One Lawmaker, Many Votes?*, May 14, 2007, at www.keyetv.com/topstories/local_story_134224129.html.

CHAPTER 8

The Texas Executive Branch

1. The one exception is in the case of bills where at least four-fifths of the chamber supports a motion to suspend the constitutional rule prohibiting the consideration of a bill during the first 60 days of a regular session.

2. In 1979, Governor Bill Clements' veto of a bill that would have empowered the Comal County Commissioners Court to adopt its own hunting and fishing regulations (e.g., setting the length of turkey season within the county) was overridden by 90–42 and 25–6 super-majorities in the House and Senate, respectively.

CHAPTER 9

The Judiciary

1. Office of Court Administration, Texas Judicial Council, *Annual Statistical Report for the Texas Judiciary: Fiscal Year 2017* (Austin: 2018).

2. Death Penalty Information Center, *Execution Database* (Washington, DC: 2018), at www.deathpenaltyinfo.org/views-executions.

3. G. Alan Tarr, *Judicial Process & Judicial Policymaking*, 6th ed. (Boston: Wadsworth Publishing, 2012).

4. Henry Glick and Craig Emmert, "Selection Systems and Judicial Characteristics: The Recruitment of State Supreme Court Judges," *Judicature* 70 (1986): 228–35; Roy Schotland, "New Challenges to States' Judicial Selection," *Georgetown Law Journal* 95 (2007): 1077–1105.

5. James L. Gibson and Gregory A. Caldeira, "Knowing the Supreme Court? A Reconsideration of Public Ignorance of the High Court," *Journal of Politics* 71, no. 2 (2009): 429–41.

6. Kiah Collier, "Embattled Judge Pratt Resigns, Suspends Campaign," *Houston Chronicle*, March 28, 2014; Kiah Collier, "Little Recourse in Pratt Case Stirs Reform Calls," *Houston Chronicle*, May 5, 2014.

7. *Caperton* v. *A. T. Massey Coal Co., Inc.*, 556 U.S. (2009).

CHAPTER 10
Law and Due Process

1. *Kelo* v. *City of New London Connecticut*, 545 U.S. 469 (2005).

2. Calculated from data provided in Texas Department of Public Safety, *Texas Crime Report for 2016* (Austin: Department of Public Safety, 2017), pp. 74–79; and Census 2010 Summary File 1 (machine-readable data file), prepared by the U.S. Census Bureau, August 11, 2011, for *Texas Profile* prepared by the Texas State Demographic Center, at http://txsdc.utsa.edu, p. 2.

3. Calculated using data from the Federal Bureau of Investigation, *Crime in the United States, 2016* (Washington, DC: Uniform Crime Reports, 2017), Table 20.

4. *Texas Crime Report for 2016*, pp. 16–20.

5. *Texas Crime Report for 2016*, pp. 13–20; *Texas Profile*, p. 2.

6. *Texas Crime Report for 2016*, p. 31.

7. *Texas Crime Report for 2016*, p. 32.

8. *Texas Crime Report for 2016*, pp. 11, 18.

9. Arthur Kellerman et al., "Gun Ownership as a Factor for Homicide in the Home," *New England Journal of Medicine* 329, no. 15 (October 27, 1993): 1084–91.

10. Arthur Kellerman et al., "Suicide in the Home in Relation to Gun Ownership," *New England Journal of Medicine* 327, no. 7 (August 13. 1992): 467–72.

11. Centers for Disease Control, searchable database at www.webappa.cdc.gov/cgi-bin/broker.exe.

12. Bureau of Justice Statistics, "Firearms Stolen During Household Burglaries and Other Property Crimes," 2005–2010, at www.bjs.gov/content/pub/press/fshbopc0510pr.cfm.

13. *Texas Crime Report for 2016*, p. 12.

14. Pew Research Center, "Despite Lower Crime Rates, Support for Gun Rights Increases," at www.pewresearch.org/fact-tank/2015/04/17/despite-lower-crime-rates-support-for-gun-rights-increases/.

15. *District of Columbia* v. *Heller*, 554 U.S. 570 (2008); *McDonald* v. *Chicago*, 561 U.S. 742 (2010).

16. Calculated from data in *Texas Crime Report for 2016*, p. 8.

17. *Texas Crime Report for 2016*, p. 13.

18. Calculated from data in *Texas Crime Report for 2016*, p. 6.

19. *Mapp* v. *Ohio*, 367 U.S. 643 (1961).

20. 384 U.S. 436 (1966).

21. *Powell* v. *Alabama*, 287 U.S. 45 (1932); *Gideon* v. *Wainwright*, 372 U.S. 335 (1963); *Argersinger* v. *Hamlin*, 407 U.S. 25 (1972).

22. The U.S. Supreme Court held in the case of *Duncan* v. *Louisiana*, 391 U.S. 145 (1968) that trial by jury is an essential part of due process when state criminal proceedings involve more than petty offenses.

23. Centers for Disease Control, "Effects on Violence of Laws Facilitating the Transfer of Youth from the Juvenile to the Adult Justice System," *Morbidity and Mortality Weekly Report* 56, no. RR-9 (November 30, 2007), at www.cdc.gov/mmwr/pdf/rr/rr5609.pdf.

24. Bureau of Justice Statistics, *Prisoners in 2016*, Table 7, p. 9, at https://www.bjs.gov/content/pub/pdf/p16.pdf.

25. Bureau of Justice Statistics, *Criminal Victimization, 2016*, revised November 2017, Table 6, p. 8, at www.bjs.gov/content/pub/pdf/cv16.pdf.

26. *Texas Crime Report for 2016*, p. 8.

27. Legislative Budget Board, *Statewide Criminal Justice Recidivism and Revocation Rates*, January 2017, p. 2.

28. Death Penalty Information Center, at www.deathpenaltyinfo.org/.

29. Watch PBS Frontline, "Death by Fire" at www.pbs.org/wgbh/pages/frontline/death-by-fire/.

30. *Baze et al.* v. *Rees et al.*, 553 U.S. 35 (2008).

31. Death Penalty Information Center, www.deathpenaltyinfo.org.

CHAPTER 11
Local Government

1. *2015 Handbook for Mayors and Councilmembers* (Austin: Texas Municipal League), p.12 at www.tml.org/pub_handbooks.

2. *Avery* v. *Midland County*, 390 U.S. (1968).

3. Kathryn A. Foster, *The Political Economy of Special Purpose Government* (Washington, DC: Georgetown University Press, 1997), pp. 221–224.

4. www.txregionalcouncil.org.

CHAPTER 12
Public Policy in Texas

1. The Texas Essential Knowledge and Skills (TEKS) curriculum standards are available on the TEA website at http://tea.texas.gov/index2.aspx?id=6148.

2. National Education Association, *NEA Rankings and Estimates*, March 2017, at http://www.nea.org/assets/docs/2017_Rankings_and_Estimates_Report-FINAL-SECURED.pdf.

3. U.S. Department of Labor, Bureau of Labor Statistics, *May 2016 State Occupational Employment and Wage Estimates*, Texas table at www.bls.gov/oes/current/oes_tx.htm#23-0000.

4. National Education Association, *NEA Rankings and Estimates*, March 2017, at http://www.nea.org/assets/docs/2017_Rankings_and_Estimates_Report-FINAL-SECURED.pdf.

5. Ibid.

6. The Texas Association of School Boards provides a brief compendium of recent court challenges to the school finance system at www.tasb.org/Legislative/Issue-Based-Resources/School-Finance.aspx.

7. *Morath, et al.* v. *The Texas Taxpayer and Student Fairness Coalition, et al.,* March 13, 2016 at www.txcourts.gov/media/1371141/140776.pdf.

8. Bureau of Labor Statistics, Earnings and Unemployment Rate by Educational Attainment, October 24, 2017, at www.bls.gov/emp/ep_chart_001.htm.

9. The Perryman Group, *A Tale of Two States—And One Million Jobs*, March 2007, published by the Texas Higher Education Coordinating Board at www.thecb.state.tx.us/reports/pdf/1345.pdf.

10. Texas Higher Education Coordinating Board, *2017 Texas Public Higher Education Almanac: A Profile of State and Institutional Performance and Characteristics.*

11. *Hopwood* v. *Texas*, 85 F.3d 720 (5th Cir., 1996).

12. *Grutter* v. *Bollinger*, 539 U.S. 306 (2003); *Gratz* v. *Bollinger*, 539 U.S. 234 (2003).

13. *Fisher* v. *University of Texas at Austin*, Docket No. 14–981, decided June 23, 2016 at www.supremecourt.gov/opinions/15pdf/14-981_4g15.pdf.

14. Texas Higher Education Coordinating Board, *2017 Texas Public Higher Education Almanac: A Profile of State and Institutional Performance and Characteristics.*

15. *U.S. News & World Report*, "National University Rankings," at https://www.usnews .com/best-colleges/rankings/national-universities. These imperfect rankings are based on reputation, selectivity in admissions, and financial resources.

16. Texas Health and Human Services Commission at hhs.texas.gov/services/health/medicaid-chip/about-medicaid-chip.

17. Texas Medical Association, "The Uninsured in Texas," at www.texmed.org/uninsured_in_texas/.

18. *National Federation of Independent Business* v. *Sebelius, Secretary of Health and Human Services*, 567 U.S. 519 (2012).

Glossary

ability-to-pay taxes Taxes apportioned according to taxpayers' financial capacity, such as property, sales, and income.

access The ability to "get in the door" to sit down and talk to public officials. Campaign contributions are often used to gain access.

ad hoc committees A committee designed to address one specific task in the legislative process. Its function is temporary, and the committee is disbanded when the function is complete.

ad valorem taxes Taxes assessed on the value of real property (land and buildings) and personal property (possessions such as furniture and automobiles).

administrative law The rules and regulations written by administrators to implement public policy.

adversary process The process by which two contesting parties present opposing views and evidence in open court.

affirmative action Positive efforts to recruit members of underserved populations such as ethnic minorities, women, and the economically disadvantaged. Sometimes these efforts are limited to recruitment drives among target groups, but such programs have sometimes included ethnicity or gender as part of the admissions criteria.

Affordable Care Act (ACA) The comprehensive federal health care reforms designed to expand Medicaid coverage, to limit objectionable insurance company practices, and to make subsidized health insurance available to businesses and individuals through competitive insurance marketplaces.

agency capture An agency created to regulate an industry becoming controlled by the very industry it is supposed to regulate, to the detriment of the public interest.

annexation The process by which cities bring unincorporated areas into their jurisdiction.

appellate jurisdiction The power vested in an appellate court to review and revise the judicial action of an inferior court.

appropriations The process by which a legislative body legally authorizes a government to spend specific sums of money to provide various programs and services.

arraignment A prisoner's initial appearance before a magistrate in which the charges and basic rights are explained.

astroturf lobbying Special interest groups orchestrating demonstrations to give the impression of widespread and spontaneous public support.

at-large elections Citywide elections in which some or all of the city council members are elected by voters of the entire municipality rather than from neighborhood districts.

at-large place system An election system in which each candidate runs citywide for a specific seat on the council and voters cast one vote for each seat or place.

attorney general's opinion The attorney general's interpretation of the constitution, statutory laws, or administrative rules.

Australian ballot A ballot printed by the government (as opposed to the political parties) that allows people to vote in secret.

bail The security deposit required for the release of a suspect awaiting trial.

benefits-received tax A tax assessed according to the services received by the payers.

beyond a reasonable doubt The standard used to determine the guilt or innocence of a person criminally charged. To prove a defendant guilty, the state must provide sufficient evidence of guilt so that jurors have no doubt that might cause a reasonable person to question whether the accused was guilty.

bicameral Consisting of two houses or chambers, such as a senate and a house of representatives.

bicultural Encompassing two cultures.

biennial regular sessions In Texas, regular legislative sessions are scheduled by the Constitution. They are held once every two years and are consequently referred to as biennial regular sessions.

block grants Federal grants to state or local governments for more general purposes and with fewer restrictions than categorical grants.

blocking bill The first bill placed on the senate calendar in each session, which is usually a bill that will never be considered by the full senate.

briefs Written arguments prepared by lawyers arguing a case in court that summarize the facts of the case, the pertinent laws, and the application of those laws to the facts supporting their positions.

broad-based taxes Taxes paid by a large number of taxpayers.

budgetary power The power to recommend to the legislature how much it should appropriate for various executive agencies.

burden of proof The duty a party has to prove its position in court.

bureaucracy The part of the executive branch that actually administers government policies and programs.

bureaucratic oversight The legislature monitoring state agencies to see that these agencies are carrying out public policies as intended.

cabinet system A system in which the chief executive has the power to appoint and remove top administrators.

categorical grants Federal aid to state or local governments for specific purposes, granted under restrictive conditions and often requiring matching funds from the receiving government.

challenge for cause A request to a judge that a prospective juror not be allowed to serve on the jury for a specific reason, such as bias or prior knowledge of the case.

charter schools Publicly funded schools that operate independently from the district system.

checks and balances The concept that each branch of government is assigned power to limit abuses by the others.

Children's Health Insurance Program (CHIP) The program that provides health insurance for qualified low-income children who have been enrolled by their parents; although administered by the state, this program is largely funded by federal grants-in-aid.

chubbing Slowing the legislative process by debating earlier bills for the maximum allotted time, asking the bill's sponsor trivial questions, and proposing so many amendments and raising so many points of order that the house does not get around to the bill to which they ultimately object.

city charter The organizing document for a municipality.

civil case Concerns private rights and remedies and usually involves private parties or organizations (*Garcia* v. *Smith*), although the government may on occasion be a party to a civil case.

civil service (or merit) system An employment system using competitive examinations or objective measures of qualifications for hiring and promoting employees.

clemency powers The governor's powers to pardon, parole, and grant reprieves to convicted criminals.

clientele groups The groups most affected by a government agency's regulations and programs; frequently these interest groups form close alliances with the agency based on mutual support and accommodation.

closed primary A type of primary in which a voter is required to specify a party preference when registering to vote.

coercive federalism A relationship between the national government and states in which the former directs the states on policies they must undertake.

colonias Severely impoverished unincorporated areas mostly located along the Texas–Mexico border that have a multitude of problems, including substandard hous-ing, unsanitary drinking water, and lack of proper sewage disposal.

commerce clause An enumerated power in Article I, Section 8 of the U.S. Constitution that gives Congress the power to regulate commerce between the states.

commission form of government A municipal government in which voters elect one set of officials who act as both executives and legislators. The commissioners, sitting together, are the municipal legislature, but individually each administers a city department.

commissioners court The policy-making body of a county, consisting of a county judge, who serves as the presiding officer of the court, and four commissioners elected from individual precincts for four-year terms.

committee of the whole The entire 31-member senate acting as a committee.

common law Law developed from judicial rulings and customs over time.

community college approach Higher education policy based on open admissions, maximizing accessibility, and incorporating technical, compensatory, and continuing education among the traditional academic course offerings.

community property Property acquired during marriage and owned equally by both spouses.

concurrent powers Those powers shared by the national government and the states.

concurrent resolution A resolution requiring the House and the Senate to agree by simple majority and usually requiring approval by the governor.

confederal system A system of government in which member states or regional governments have all authority, and any central government has only the power that state governments choose to delegate to it.

conference committee A temporary committee that meets to resolve differences between Senate and House versions of a bill; a separate conference committee is appointed for each bill with differences between the House and Senate versions.

conference committee report A compromise between the House and Senate versions of a bill reached by a conference committee and then delivered to each house.

conflict of interest A situation in which public officers stand to benefit personally from their official decisions.

conservative A political ideology marked by the belief in a limited role for government in taxation, economic regulation, and providing social services; conservatives support traditional values and lifestyles, and are cautious in response to social change.

consolidation The merging of county government with other local governments to form a single local government.

constables County law enforcement officials who are elected to serve as the process officers of justice of the peace courts and also have general law enforcement powers.

consulting fees Fees charged by legislators who may contract with business clients to consult on matters pending in the legislature, thereby helping their clients to benefit from legislation being considered.

contract spoils, or contract patronage A practice in which politicians award contracts to their political supporters and contributors in the business community.

cooperative federalism A relationship where "the National Government and the States are mutually complementary parts of a *single* government mechanism all of whose powers are intended to realize the current purposes of government according to their applicability to the problem in hand."

cooptation Development of such a close alliance between state regulatory agencies and their clientele group that the regulated have, in effect, become the regulators; the interest group has captured such complete control of their regulatory agency that they are essentially self-regulated.

council–manager form of government A form of government in which an elected city council makes laws and hires a professional administrator who is responsible for both executing council policies and managing the day-to-day operations of city government.

councils of governments (COGs) Advisory bodies consisting of representatives of various local governments brought together for the purposes of regional planning and cooperation.

county attorney A county legal officer whose responsibilities include giving legal advice to the commissioners court, representing the county in civil litigation.

county auditor A financial officer whose duties include reviewing county financial records and ensuring that expenditures are made in accordance with the law.

county clerk The officer who serves as the county's chief record keeper and election officer.

county governments General purpose local governments that also serve as administrative arms of the state.

county judge An official elected countywide for a four-year term to preside over the county commissioners court.

county treasurer In many counties, the official who is responsible for receiving, depositing, and disbursing funds.

cracking A gerrymandering technique of dividing up a minority party's voters into so many geographical districts that their voting power in any one district is negligible.

Creole A descendant of European Spanish immigrants to the Americas.

criminal case Involves a violation of penal law that is prosecuted by the state.

crossover voting When members of one political party vote in the other party's primary to influence the selection of the nominee.

cumulative voting An election system in which city council members are elected in at-large elections but the number of votes a voter can cast corresponds to the number of seats on the council.

de novo trials Trials in which a higher court completely retries the case, in contrast to an appeal in which a higher court simply reviews the law as decided by a lower court.

deadwood Inoperable constitutional provisions that have been either voided by a conflicting U.S. constitutional or statutory law or made irrelevant by changing circumstances and contexts.

dealignment When increasing numbers of voters choose not to identify with either of the two parties and consider themselves to be independents.

decentralization Exercise of power at the state and local levels of government in addition to the national level.

declining marginal propensity to consume The tendency, as income increases, for persons to save and invest more, thus spending a smaller percentage of their income on consumer items.

delegate type representatives Legislators who interpret their role as being elected to represent a majority of voters' interests in their districts.

delegated powers Those powers that the Constitution gives to the national government. These include those enumerated powers found in Article I, Section 8 of the U.S. Constitution as well as a few other powers that have evolved over time.

Demographics Population characteristics, such as age, gender, ethnicity, employment, and income, that social scientists use to describe groups in society.

dependent agency A classification created by the U.S. Census Bureau for governmental entities that are closely tied to general purpose governments but do not have as much independence as special district governments.

descriptive representation The idea that elected bodies should accurately represent not only constituents' political views but also the ethnic and social characteristics that affect their political perspectives.

deterrence Discouraging criminal behavior by threat of punishment.

devolution The attempt to enhance the power of state or local governments, especially by replacing relatively restrictive categorical grants-in-aid with more flexible block grants.

direct primary A method of selecting party nominees in which party members participate directly in the selection of a candidate to represent them in the general election.

directive power The power to issue binding orders to state agencies.

discretion Wide latitude to make decisions within the broad requirements set out in the law.

district attorney The officer who prosecutes most criminal cases.

district clerk The record keeper for the district court in larger counties.

double jeopardy A second prosecution for the same offense after acquittal in the first trial.

dual federalism The understanding that the federal government and state governments are both sovereign within their sphere of influence.

due process Proper procedures designed to promote justice and protect the individual from the government. Due process is essential to guaranteeing fairness before the government may deprive a person of life, liberty, or property.

early voting The practice of voting before election day at traditional voting locations, such as schools, and other locations, such as grocery and convenience stores.

elective accountability Electing executive officers to make the bureaucracy directly accountable to the people through the democratic process.

electronic voting Voting on a touch screen.

elitist theory The view that the state is ruled by a small number of participants who exercise power to further their own self-interest.

eminent domain Government taking private property for public use.

evangelical or **fundamentalist Christians** A bloc of conservative Christians who are concerned with such issues as family, religion, abortion, gay rights, and community morals, and often support the Republican Party.

ex officio Holding a position automatically because one also holds some other office.

exclusionary rule Evidence resulting from unreasonable searches may not be admitted in court.

expressed powers Those powers that are clearly listed in Article I, Section 8 of the U.S. Constitution.

extraterritorial jurisdiction (ETJ) A buffer area that extends beyond a city's limits.

FBI index crimes Crimes used as a national barometer of the crime rate—murder and non-negligent manslaughter, forcible rape, robbery, aggravated assault, burglary, grand theft, and motor vehicle theft.

federal system A system of government in which governmental power is divided and shared between a national or central government and state or regional governments.

felonies Serious crimes punishable by state institutions.

filibuster A prolonged debate by a senator to delay passage of a bill.

floor action Action by the entire House or the entire Senate to debate, amend, and vote on legislation.

floor leaders The legislators who are responsible for getting legislation passed or defeated.

formal (legal) powers Powers that are stated in the law or the Constitution.

general law city An incorporated community with a population of 5,000 or fewer that is limited in the subject matter on which it may legislate.

general obligation bonds Bonds to be repaid from general revenues, such as those that voters have approved to finance prison construction.

general purpose government A municipal or county government that provides a wide range of public services.

general sales tax A broadly based tax collected on the retail price of most items.

gerrymandering The practice of drawing district lines in such a way as to give candidates from a certain party, ethnic group, or faction an advantage.

grand jury In Texas, 12 people who sit in pretrial proceedings to determine whether sufficient evidence exists to try an individual and therefore return an indictment.

gross receipts taxes Taxes on the gross revenues (sales) of certain enterprises.

hidden taxes Taxes included in an item's purchase price.

hierarchies Structures in which several employees report to a higher administrator who reports to higher authorities until eventually all report to the single individual with ultimate authority.

home rule city A city with a population of more than 5,000 that can adopt its own charter and structure its local government as it sees fit, as long as charter provisions and local laws (also called ordinances) do not violate national and state constitutions and laws.

homesteads Owner-occupied properties protected from forced sale under most circumstances.

hung jury A jury that is unable to agree on a verdict after a suitable period of deliberation; the result is a mistrial.

impeachment Bringing formal charges against a public official; the legislative equivalent of indictment for improper conduct in office.

implementation Administrative agencies carrying out broad public policies, enforcing state laws, providing public services, and managing day-to-day government activities.

implied powers Those delegated powers that are assumed to exist in order for the federal government to perform the functions that are expressly delegated. These powers are granted by the necessary and proper clause in Article I, Section 8 of the U.S. Constitution.

income redistribution A public policy goal intended to shift income from one class of recipients to another, regardless of whether these programs are designed to benefit lower-, middle-, or upper-income groups.

incumbent Currently elected officials.

independent expenditures Money individuals and organizations spend to promote a candidate without working or communicating directly with the candidate's campaign organization.

indictment A formal written accusation issued by a grand jury against a party charged with a crime when it has determined that there is sufficient evidence to bring the accused to trial.

indirect appointive powers Texas governor's authority to appoint supervisory boards but not the operational directors for most state agencies.

individual mandate Requirement that individuals get health insurance or pay a tax penalty to the federal government.

informal (extralegal) powers Powers that are not stated in rules, law, or a constitution but are usually derived from formal or legal powers.

information A written accusation made by the prosecutor against a party charged with a minor crime; it is an alternative to an indictment and does not involve a grand jury.

inherent powers Those delegated powers that come with an office or position—generally, the executive branch. Although the U.S. Constitution does not clearly specify powers granted to the executive branch, over time, inherent powers have evolved as part of the powers needed to perform the functions of the executive branch.

initiative A process that empowers citizens to place a proposal on the ballot for voter approval. If the measure passes, it becomes law (permitted in some Texas cities but not at the state level).

interest group A voluntary organization that strives to influence public policy; sometimes known as a pressure group.

interim committee A committee that meets between legislative sessions.

iron triangles Long-standing alliances among interest groups, legislators, and bureaucrats held together by mutual self-interest that act as subsystems in the legislative and administrative decision-making process.

issue networks Dynamic alliances among a wide range of individuals and groups activated by broad public policy questions.

Jim Crow laws State and local laws that mandated racial segregation in almost every aspect of life.

joint committee A committee that includes both senators and representatives.

joint resolution A resolution, such as one dealing with constitutional amendments, that requires approval of both houses but not the governor.

Ku Klux Klan (KKK) A white supremacist organization.

late-train contributions Campaign funds given to the winning candidate after the election up to 30 days before the legislature comes into session. Such contributions are designed to curry favor with winning candidates.

legislative redress The power of the legislature to monitor and police itself.

legitimacy General public acceptance of government's "right to govern."

liberal A political ideology marked by the advocacy of using government to improve the welfare of individuals, government regulation of the economy, support for civil rights, and tolerance for social change.

line-item veto The power to strike out sections of a bill without vetoing the entire bill.

lobbying Directly contacting public officials to advocate for a public policy.

long ballot A ballot that results from the independent election of a large number of executive and judicial officers; in contrast, giving the chief executive the power to appoint most of them results in a short ballot.

malapportionment The drawing of district lines so that one district's population is substantially larger or smaller than another's.

mandate A federal or state requirement that a lower level of government, like a city or county, provide a service or meet certain standards, often as a condition for receiving financial aid.

maquiladoras Mexican factories where U.S. corporations employ inexpensive Mexican labor for assembly and piecework.

mark up To rewrite or change a bill by adding or deleting provisions before it is considered for passage.

mass transit Transport systems that carry multiple passengers, such as train and bus systems; whether publicly or privately owned, mass transit systems are available to the general public and usually charge a fare.

mayor–council system A form of municipal government consisting of a mayor and a city council; this form includes both *strong mayor* and *weak mayor* variations.

means test A standard of benefit eligibility based on need.

Medicaid The program to provide medical care for qualified low-income individuals who have enrolled; although administered by the state, this program is largely funded by federal grants-in-aid.

Medicare The federal program to provide medical insurance for most persons older than 65 years of age.

merit plan, or **Missouri plan** A method of selecting judges on the basis of the merit or quality of the candidates and not on political considerations. Under this system, the governor fills court vacancies from a list of nominees submitted by a judicial commission, and these appointees later face retention elections.

message power The constitutional power to deliver the State of the State message and special messages to the legislature.

Mestizo A person of both Spanish and Native American lineage.

Metroplex The greater Dallas–Fort Worth metropolitan area.

misdemeanors Minor crimes punishable by a county jail sentence or fine.

necessary and proper clause The last clause in Article I, Section 8 of the U.S. Constitution; also known as the elastic clause, which was given a very expansive meaning early in the nation's history.

negative campaigning A strategy used in election campaigns in which candidates attack their opponents' issue positions or character.

no bill A grand jury's refusal to return an indictment filed by the prosecutor.

North American Free Trade Agreement (NAFTA) A treaty that has helped remove trade barriers among Canada, Mexico, and the United States and is an economic stimulus for the Texas Border because it is a conduit for much of the commerce with Mexico.

office block ballot A type of ballot used in a general election in which the names of the parties' candidates are listed randomly under each office.

ombudsman An independent official who takes, investigates, and mediates complaints about government bureaucrats or policy.

open meetings laws Laws requiring that meetings of government bodies at all levels of government be open to the general public, with some exceptions.

open primary A type of party primary in which a voter can choose on election day in which primary to participate.

open records laws Laws that require most records kept by government to be open to the public.

original jurisdiction The power to try a case being heard for the first time.

packing Gerrymandering technique in which members of a party are concentrated into one district, thereby ensuring that the group will influence only one district's election rather than several.

pairing Placing two current officeholders and parts of their political bases in the same elective district through redistricting.

parole After an initial stay in prison, prisoners serving the remainder of their sentences under supervision in the community.

participation paradox The fact that citizens vote even though a single vote rarely decides an election.

partisan elections General elections in which political parties nominate candidates whose party labels appear on the ballot.

partisan identification A person's attachment to one political party or the other.

party column ballot A type of ballot used in a general election in which all of the candidates from each party are listed in parallel columns under the party label.

party platform The formal issue positions of a political party; specific elements are often referred to as "planks" in the party's platform.

party realignment The long-term transition from a system in which one party is consistently dominant to one in which another party is consistently dominant.

per diem The amount paid each day that a legislator is working, both in regular and special sessions, and when committees meet during the interim between sessions.

peremptory challenge A challenge made to a prospective juror without being required to give a reason for removal; the number of such challenges allotted to the prosecution and defense is limited.

petit jury A jury for a civil or criminal trial.

pigeonhole To set a bill aside and not take any action on it throughout the entire legislative session; many bills are pigeonholed.

plaintiff The party bringing a civil suit, usually a private person or institution.

plea bargaining Negotiations between the prosecution and the defense to obtain a lighter sentence or other benefits in exchange for a guilty plea by the accused.

plural executive An executive branch in which power is divided among several independently elected officials, thereby weakening the governor's power to act as the chief executive.

pluralist theory The view that, in a free society, public policy should be made by a multitude of competing interest groups, ensuring that policies will not benefit a single elite at the expense of the many.

plurality vote An election rule in which the candidate with the most votes wins even if that candidate get less than 50 percent.

pocket veto The power to kill legislation by simply ignoring it after the end of the legislative session; this power is not available to Texas's governor.

point of order A formal objection that rules of procedure are not being followed on the house floor.

political action committees (PACs) Organizations that raise and then contribute money to political candidates.

political culture The dominant political values and beliefs of a people.

political movement A mass alliance of like-minded groups and individuals seeking broad changes in the direction of government policies.

popular recall A special election to remove an official before the end of his or her term, initiated by citizen petition (permitted in some Texas cities but not at the state level).

position issues Issues on which the public is divided.

pragmatism The philosophy that ideas should be judged on the basis of their practical results rather than the purity of their principles.

precedents A previously decided legal case used as a guiding principle for future cases.

precinct convention A gathering of party members who voted in the party's primary for the purpose of electing delegates to the county or district convention.

preclearance Any administrative or legislative change to the rules governing elections in covered states must be submitted for preapproval to either the U.S. Department of Justice or the U.S. District Court for the District of Columbia.

preponderance of the evidence Whichever party has more evidence or proof on its side should win the case, no matter how slight the advantage is.

presidential preference primary A primary election that allows voters to express their preference among the candidates seeking to become their party's presidential nominee.

privatization The hiring of private contractors to perform government services and perform government functions.

probable cause Sufficient information to lead a "reasonable person" to believe that evidence is probably contained on the premises and thus a warrant for the invasion of privacy is justified.

probation A judge's sentence allowing an offender to serve time outside a correctional institution but under specific restrictions, often under the supervision of a probation officer.

progressive tax rates Tax rates that increase as income increases—for example, federal income tax rates.

proposal of constitutional amendments In Texas, the proposal of a constitutional amendment must be supported by two-thirds of the total membership of each house of the legislature—at least 21 senators and 100 representatives.

public debt Money owed by government, ordinarily through the issuance of bonds. Local governments issue bonds to finance major projects with voter approval.

pure at-large system An election system in which candidates for city council run citywide and the top vote-getters are elected to fill the number of open seats.

quorum To take official action, both houses require two-thirds of the total membership to be present.

ranchero culture A quasi-feudal system whereby a property's owner, or patrón, gives workers protection and employment in return for their loyalty and service.

ratification of constitutional amendments To actually put a constitutional amendment into effect requires approval by a majority of those persons voting on the amendment in either a regular or a special election.

reapportionment The redistricting, or redrawing of district lines, after every census to reflect the population changes over the previous decade.

recall election An election, called by petition, that permits voters to remove an elected official before the official's term expires.

recidivists Repeat offenders who have relapsed into crime.

recorded votes On final bill passage, votes and the names of those casting them are recorded in each house's journal.

reduction veto The power to reduce amounts in an appropriations bill without striking them out altogether; this power is not available to Texas's governor.

referendums An election that permits voters to determine if an ordinance or statute will go into effect (permitted in some Texas cities but not at the state level).

regressive tax rates Tax rates that effectively decline as a person's income increases.

regulatory taxes Taxes that reward approved behavior with lower taxation or punish socially undesirable action with a higher tax.

rehabilitation The effort to correct criminals' antisocial attitudes and behavior.

removal power The authority to fire appointed officials.

reserved powers Those powers that belong to the states. The legitimacy of these powers comes from the Tenth Amendment.

resolution A formal expression of legislative sentiment, such as recognizing people, memorializing events, or making decisions that do not involve passing statutes.

retainer fees Fees charged by lawyer-legislators for services to clients, including those who have business with state agencies or may have lawsuits against state agencies.

revenue bonds Bonds to be repaid with revenues from the projects they finance, such as higher education bonds to be repaid with revenue from student tuition.

revolving door The interchange of employees between government agencies and the private businesses with which they have dealings.

rollback election An election to limit an increase in the property tax rate to no more than 8 percent above that required for increased debt service.

runoff primary A second primary election that pits the two top vote-getters from the first primary against each other when the winner of the first primary did not receive a majority.

school accountability Using measurable standards to hold public schools responsible for their students' performance and teachers' competence.

select committees A temporary committee that is created for one specific purpose and usually serves in an advisory capacity.

selective sales taxes Taxes levied on the sale, manufacture, or use of specific items such as liquor, cigarettes, and gasoline; these are also sometimes known as excise taxes.

senatorial courtesy The tradition of allowing a senator to reject the governor's appointment of a political enemy from the senator's district.

separate but equal doctrine Doctrine that resulted from the Supreme Court ruling in *Plessy* v. *Ferguson* that legalized segregation.

separation of powers The principle behind the concept of a government in which power is distributed among three different branches—legislative, executive, and judicial.

severance taxes Taxes on the production of raw materials such as oil and natural gas.

sheriff The chief county law enforcement officer.

short ballot The listing of only a few independently elected offices on an election ballot.

simple resolution A resolution passed by a single house of the legislature affecting only that house and needing no action by the governor.

single-member council districts An electoral system in which each council member is elected from a particular geographical district by only the voters who live in that district.

single-member district A district that elects one senator or one representative; districts should be equal in population.

social insurance Public insurance programs, such as Social Security and unemployment compensation, in which eligibility is based on tax premiums paid by the beneficiaries or their employers rather than need alone.

socialized medicine Strictly defined, socialized medicine is a health care system in which the government hires medical practitioners who work at government-owned facilities to directly provide health care, as in Great Britain and in U.S. veterans' and military hospitals. However, the term is often applied to health care systems in which the government provides health care insurance, such as Medicare or Medicaid, even though benefit payments are made to private health care providers.

soft money Money spent by political parties on behalf of political candidates, especially for the purposes of increasing voter registration and turnout.

special districts Local governments that provide single or closely related services that are not provided by general purpose county or municipal governments.

special sessions Legislative sessions called by the Texas governor, who also sets their agenda.

split ticket voting A voter selecting candidates from one party for some offices and candidates from the other party for other offices.

spoils system A system in which elected officials hire campaign workers as public employees.

standing committees Permanent committees that function throughout the legislative session. There are two types: substantive and procedural.

statutory law Law passed by legislatures and written into books of code.

straight ticket voting Selecting all of the candidates of one particular party.

strong mayor form of government A form of municipal government in which the mayor, who is chosen in a citywide election, is both the chief executive and the leader of the city council.

subcommittees Subdivisions of standing committees that consider specialized areas and categories of proposed legislation.

suffrage The legal right to vote.

supply-side economics The theory that taxes on higher-income individuals should be kept low to allow them to save and invest to stimulate the economy.

supremacy clause The clause that states that the U.S. Constitution, as well as laws and treaties created in accordance with the U.S. Constitution, supersedes or preempts state and local laws.

suspension of the rule Setting aside the rule that puts bills in chronological order so that other bills can be considered.

swing voters Voters who are not bound by party identification and who support candidates of different parties in different election years.

tax assessor-collector A county financial officer whose responsibilities include collecting various county taxes and fees and, in some counties, registering voters.

tax base The object or activity taxed.

tax rates The amount per unit of taxable item or activity.

tax shifting Businesses passing taxes to consumers in the form of higher prices.

tea party A faction or group of very conservative Republicans generally resistant to any compromise of its principles.

Tenth Amendment Section of the U.S. Constitution that reserves powers to the states. It reads as follows: "The powers not delegated to the United States by the Constitution, nor prohibited by it to the States, are reserved to the States respectively, or to the people."

term limits Legally mandated restrictions on the number of times that a politician can be reelected to an office or the number of years that a person may hold a particular office.

The Valley An area along the Texas side of the Rio Grande known for its production of citrus fruits.

tipping A phenomenon that occurs when a group grows large enough to change the political balance in the electorate.

tort reform Efforts to limit liability in civil cases.

torts A civil wrong, whether intentional or negligent, that results in the injury of another person.

true bill An indictment returned by a grand jury.

trustee type representatives Legislators who interpret their role as being elected to use their judgment in making decisions in the best interest of the state as a whole.

two-party system A political system characterized by two dominant parties competing for political offices. In such systems, minor or third parties have little chance of winning.

umbrella organizations Associations formed by smaller interests joining together to promote common policy goals by making campaign contributions and hiring lobbyists to represent their interests.

unemployment insurance The insurance program designed to provide a partial income replacement for those who have lost their jobs; it is a social insurance program financed with taxes paid by employers.

unfunded mandates Obligations the federal government imposes on state governments while providing little to no funds to pay for the mandated activities.

unitary system A system of government in which constitutional authority rests with a national or central government; all regional or local governments are subordinate to the central government.

user fees Fees paid by the individuals who receive a particular government service.

valence issues Issues on which virtually all of the public agrees, such as peace and prosperity.

veto A power that allows the governor to stop a bill from becoming law.

voice vote An oral vote that is not put in the official record.

voter turnout The proportion of eligible Americans who actually vote.

voting-age population (VAP) The total number of persons in the United States who are 18 years of age or older.

weak mayor form of government A form of municipal government in which the mayor and council share administrative authority.

whistle-blowers Government employees who expose bureaucratic excesses, blunders, corruption, or favoritism.

white primary The practice of excluding African Americans from primary elections in the Texas Democratic Party.

writ of habeas corpus A court order to present a person and show the legal cause for confining the individual; it may result in a prisoner's release from unlawful detention.

Index

Note: Page numbers followed by *f*, *t* & *p* represents figures, tables and photographs, respectively

A

A. T. Massey Coal Company, 252
Abbott, Greg, 39, 42, 43, 45, 51–52, 65*p*, 85*p*, 104, 125*p*, 126, 147, 161, 198*p*, 206, 209*p*, 210*f*, 215, 231, 284
Abbott's veto of HB 3511, 206*p*
Ability-to-pay taxes, 319
Abortion, 15
ACA. *s* Affordable Care Act (ACA)
Accenture, 222
Access, 149
Access to weapons, criminals, 268–269
Adams, Norman, 146*p*
Ad hoc committees, 186
Adjutant general, 215
Administration
of colleges/universities, 333–334
of public schools, 328–329
Administration, Texas, 212–225
appointed executives, 215–216
attorney general, 212–213
boards and commissions, 217–218
bureaucracy in, 218–225. *See also* Bureaucracy *entries*
commissioner of agriculture, 214
commissioner of General Land Office, 214–215
comptroller of public accounts, 213–214
governor, 226
lieutenant governor, 212
Administrative law, 228
Ad valorem taxes, 317
Adversary process, 276
Affirmative action, 337

Affordable Care Act (ACA), 39, 42–45, 43*p*, 50, 155, 340–341
AFL–CIO, 19, 118, 140*t*
African American (s)
and Democrats, 118
equal rights, 15–17
income, 24*f*
in legislature, 174*f*
judges, 255*f*
liberals, 3
population, 22, 22*f*
students, 331
voter turnout, 88
African American Texans, 15–17, 88
Age
of criminals, 267
of Texas executive branch, 199
Agency-clientele alliance, 226
Agriculture, lobbyists and, 154
Alvarado, Carol, 157
Amending/revising, Texas Constitution, 70–73
American Civil Liberties Union of Texas, 140*t*
American GI Forum, 118, 295
American Legislative Exchange Council (ALEC), 327
American Recovery and Reinvestment Act, 154–155
Americans with Disabilities Act, 300
Anglo (s)
income, 24*f*
in legislature, 174*f*
judges, 255*f*
population, 22, 22*f*
students, 331
Annexation, 301
Appeals courts, 244–246
Appeals process, 277
Appellate jurisdiction, 238–239
Appointed boards, 217–218, 221*t*
Appointed executives, 215–216

adjutant general, 215
commissioner of education, 216
health and human services commissioner, 215–216
insurance commissioner, 216
secretary of state, 215
Appointees, evaluating, 201
Appointive powers, of governor, bureaucracy and, 208–211
Appointment process, lobbyist and, 146
Appropriation process, 325
Appropriations Committee, 185
Arraignment, 272–274
Arrests, due process and, 272
Astroturf lobbying, 150
At-large city elections, 294
Asian American (s)
income, 24*f*
in legislature, 174*f*
judges, 255*f*
population, 21–22, 22*f*
Associated General Contractors of TX, 106*t*
At-large place system, 294–295
AT&T, 106*t*, 151, 161
Attorney, right to, 273
Attorney general, 212–213
Australian ballot, 99
Available school fund, 331

B

Bail, setting, 273–274
Ballot(s)
construction, 97–100
counting and recounting, 100–101
getting on, 97–99
long, 305
politics of, 97
secret, 99–100
short, 305